See the Difference with LearningCurve!

 LearningCurve
macmillan learning

learningcurveworks.com

LearningCurve is a winning solution for everyone: students come to class better prepared and instructors have more flexibility to go beyond the basic facts and concepts in class. LearningCurve's game-like quizzes are book-specific and link back to the textbook in LaunchPad so that students can brush up on the reading when they get stumped by a question. The reporting features help instructors track overall class trends and spot topics that are giving students trouble so that they can adjust lectures and class activities.

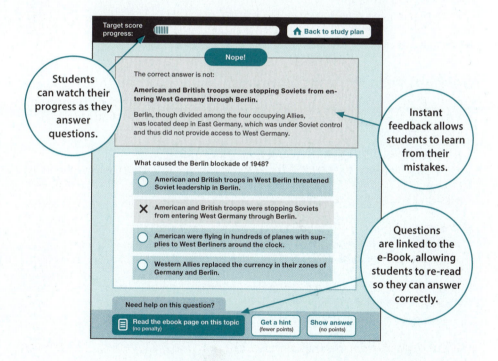

Students can watch their progress as they answer questions.

Instant feedback allows students to learn from their mistakes.

Questions are linked to the e-Book, allowing students to re-read so they can answer correctly.

LearningCurve is easy to assign, easy to customize, and easy to complete. See the difference LearningCurve makes in teaching and learning history.

CONTEMPORARY EUROPE

Elevation

Feet	Meters
Over 13,120	Over 4,001
6,561–13,120	2,001–4,000
1,641–6,560	501–2,000
661–1,640	201–500
0–660	0–200
Below sea level	Below sea level

✳ National capital
• Major city

ATLANTIC OCEAN

Norwegian Sea

NORWAY

SWEDEN

FINLAND

Gulf of Bothnia

Bergen
Oslo
Stockholm
Göteborg
Helsinki
Tallinn
St. Petersburg

RUSSIA

Baltic Sea

NORTHERN IRELAND
SCOTLAND
Edinburgh
Glasgow
Belfast
IRELAND
Dublin
Cork
UNITED KINGDOM
ENGLAND
Liverpool
Birmingham
WALES
London

DENMARK
Aarhus
Copenhagen

Riga
LATVIA
Jelgava
Kaunas
LITHUANIA
Vilnius
Kaliningrad

ESTONIA
Pärnu

MOSCOW

Volga R.

RUSSIAN FEDERATION

KAZAKHSTAN

Ural R.

North Sea

NETHERLANDS
Amsterdam
Rotterdam
Antwerp
BELGIUM
Brussels
LUXEMBOURG
Luxembourg

GERMANY
Berlin
Frankfurt
Munich
Rhine R.
Elbe R.
Danube R.

POLAND
Warsaw
Gdańsk
Kraków
Vistula R.
Oder R.

BELARUS
Minsk
Brest
Gomel

Kiev
UKRAINE
Kharkiv
Dnieper R.

Moscow

English Channel

Paris
FRANCE
Lyons
Marseilles
Loire R.
Seine R.
Rhône R.

Bay of Biscay

SPAIN
Madrid
Barcelona
Seville
Oporto
PORTUGAL
Lisbon
Ebro R.

ANDORRA
Andorra la Vella
PYRENEES

Balearic Is.

Corsica
MONACO
Sardinia

CZECH REP.
Prague
Brno
SLOVAKIA
Bratislava
AUSTRIA
Vienna
Graz
LIECHTENSTEIN
Vaduz
SWITZERLAND
Bern
Innsbruck
Milan
ALPS
SLOVENIA
Ljubljana
SAN MARINO
San Marino

HUNGARY
Budapest
Miskolc

CARPATHIAN MTS.

ROMANIA
Cluj
Timişoara
Bucharest
Danube R.

MOLDOVA
Chişinău
Tiraspol
Odessa

Sea of Azov

Black Sea

CROATIA
Zagreb
Split
BOSNIA AND HERZEGOVINA
Sarajevo
SERBIA
Belgrade
MONTENEGRO
Podgorica
Tiranë
ALBANIA
KOSOVO
Pristina
MACEDONIA
Skopje

BULGARIA
Sofia
Plovdiv

Istanbul
İzmir

TURKEY
Ankara

GEORGIA
Tbilisi
CAUCASUS MTS.
ARMENIA
Yerevan
AZERBAIJAN
Baku

Caspian Sea

IRAN

IRAQ
Baghdad
Tigris R.
Euphrates R.

SYRIA
Damascus
LEBANON
Beirut
Nicosia
CYPRUS
ISRAEL
JORDAN
Amman
WEST BANK
SAUDI ARABIA

ITALY
APENNINES
Rome
Naples
Palermo
Sicily
MALTA
Valletta

Tyrrhenian Sea

Adriatic Sea

Ionian Sea

GREECE
Salonica
Athens

Aegean Sea

Crete

Mediterranean Sea

TUNISIA
Tunis
Tripoli

ALGERIA
Algiers

MOROCCO
Rabat

N
E
W
S

300 miles
300 kilometers
0 150
150

20°W 10°W 0° 10°E 20°E 30°E 40°E 50°E 60°E
30°N 40°N 50°N 60°N

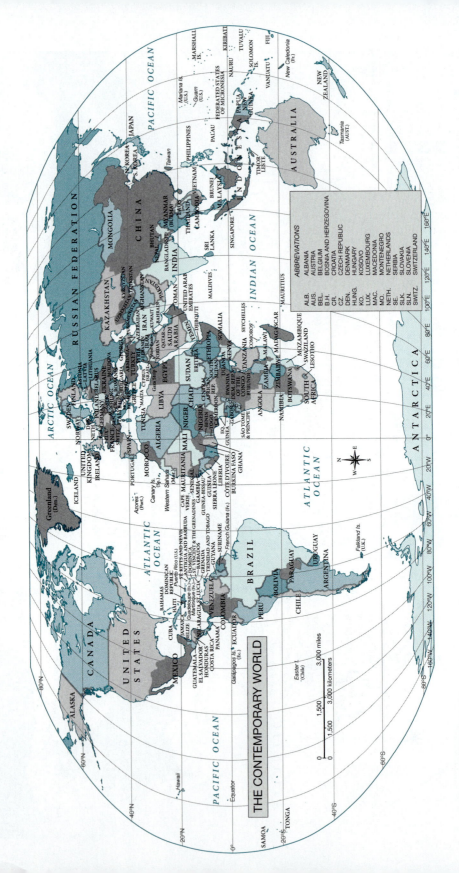

THE CONTEMPORARY WORLD

VALUE EDITION

A History of Western Society

Twelfth Edition

VOLUME 2
From the Age of Exploration to the Present

John P. McKay
University of Illinois at Urbana-Champaign

Bennett D. Hill
Late of *Georgetown University*

John Buckler
Late of *University of Illinois at Urbana-Champaign*

Clare Haru Crowston
University of Illinois at Urbana-Champaign

Merry E. Wiesner-Hanks
University of Wisconsin–Milwaukee

Joe Perry
Georgia State University

bedford/st.martin's
Macmillan Learning

Boston | New York

FOR BEDFORD/ST. MARTIN'S

Vice President, Editorial, Macmillan Learning Humanities: Edwin Hill
Publisher for History: Michael Rosenberg
Director of Development for History: Jane Knetzger
Acquiring Editor for History: Laura Arcari
Senior Developmental Editor: Leah R. Strauss
Senior Production Editor: Christina M. Horn
Senior Media Producer: Michelle Camisa
Senior Production Supervisor: Jennifer Wetzel
History Marketing Manager: Melissa Famiglietti
Media Editor: Jennifer Jovin
Associate Editor: Tess Fletcher
Editorial Assistant: Melanie McFadyen
Copy Editor: Jennifer Brett Greenstein
Indexer: Leoni Z. McVey
Cartography: Mapping Specialists, Ltd.
Photo Editor: Robin Fadool
Photo Researcher: Bruce Carson
Permissions Editor: Eve Lehmann
Senior Art Director: Anna Palchik
Text Design: Boynton Hue Studio
Cover Design: William Boardman
Volume 2 Cover Art: Black Man with a Mandolin, ca. 1930 (oil on canvas) (see also 287577), André
    Derain (1880–1954)/Musée de l'Orangerie, Paris, France/Bridgeman Images/© 2016 Artists Rights
    Society (ARS), New York/ADAGP, Paris
Composition: Jouve
Printing and Binding: RR Donnelley and Sons

Manufactured in the United States of America.

1 0 9 8 7
f e d c

For information, write: Bedford/St. Martin's, 75 Arlington Street, Boston, MA 02116
    (617-399-4000)

ISBN 978-1-319-03104-6 (Combined Edition)   ISBN 978-1-319-03106-0 (Volume 2)
ISBN 978-1-319-03105-3 (Volume 1)   ISBN 978-1-319-05954-5 (Loose-leaf Edition,
ISBN 978-1-319-05955-2 (Loose-leaf Edition,   Volume 2)
    Volume 1)

ACKNOWLEDGMENTS

Preface
Why This Book This Way

WE ARE PLEASED TO PUBLISH THE VALUE EDITION of *A History of Western Society*. The Value Edition provides our signature approach to history in a two-color, trade-sized format at a low price. Featuring the full narrative of the parent text and select images, maps, and pedagogical tools, the Value Edition continues to incorporate the latest and best scholarship in the field in an accessible, student-friendly manner. *A History of Western Society* grew out of the initial three authors' desire to infuse new life into the study of Western Civilization. The three current authors, Clare Haru Crowston, Merry E. Wiesner-Hanks, and Joe Perry, who first used the book as students or teachers and took over full responsibilities with the eleventh edition, continue to incorporate the latest and best scholarship in the field. All three of us regularly teach introductory history courses and thus bring insights into the text from the classroom, as well as from new secondary works and our own research in archives and libraries. In this new twelfth edition we aim to enhance the distinctive attention to daily life that sparks students' interest while also providing a number of innovative tools—both print and digital—designed to help students think historically and master the material.

Helping Instructors Teach with Digital Resources

We know that many students today are on a budget and that instructors want greater flexibility and more digital options in their choice of course materials. Accordingly, *A History of Western Society* is offered in Macmillan's premier learning platform, **LaunchPad**, an intuitive, interactive e-Book and course space. Free when packaged with the print text or available at a low price when used stand-alone, LaunchPad grants students and teachers access to a wealth of online tools and resources built specifically for our text to enhance reading comprehension and promote in-depth study.

Developed with extensive feedback from history instructors and students, **LaunchPad for *A History of Western Society*** includes the complete narrative of the print book; the companion reader, *Sources for Western Society*; and **LearningCurve**, an adaptive learning tool that is designed to get students to read before they come to class. With **new source-based questions in the test bank and in the LearningCurve**, instructors now have more ways to test students on their understanding of sources and narrative in the book.

This edition also includes **Guided Reading Exercises** that prompt students to be active readers of the chapter narrative and auto-graded **primary source quizzes** to test comprehension of written and visual sources. These features, plus **additional primary source documents, video tools for making video assignments, map activities, flashcards, and customizable test banks**, make LaunchPad a great asset for any instructor who wants to enliven the history of Western Civilization for students.

These new directions have not changed the central mission of the book, which is to introduce students to the broad sweep of Western Civilization in a fresh yet balanced manner. Every edition has incorporated new research to keep the book up-to-date and respond to the changing needs of readers and instructors, and we have continued to do this in the twelfth edition. As we have made these changes, large and small, we have sought to give students and teachers an integrated perspective so that they can pursue—on their own or in the classroom—the historical questions that they find particularly exciting and significant. To learn more about the benefits of LearningCurve and LaunchPad, see the "Versions and Supplements" section on page xv.

The Story of *A History of Western Society*: Bringing the Past to Life for Students

At the point when *A History of Western Society* was first conceptualized, social history was dramatically changing the ways we understood the past, and the original authors decided to create a book that would re-create the lives of ordinary people in appealing human terms, while also giving major economic, political, cultural, and intellectual developments the attention they unquestionably deserve. The current authors remain committed to advancing this vision for today's classroom, with a broader definition of social history that brings the original idea into the twenty-first century.

History as a discipline never stands still, and over the last several decades cultural history has joined social history as a source of dynamism. Because of its emphasis on the ways people made sense of their lives, *A History of Western Society* has always included a large amount of cultural history, ranging from foundational works of philosophy and literature to popular songs and stories. This focus on cultural history has been enhanced in recent editions in a way that highlights the interplay between men's and women's lived experiences and the ways men and women reflect on these experiences to create meaning. The joint social and cultural perspective requires—fortunately, in our opinion—the inclusion of objects as well as texts as important sources for studying history, which has allowed us to incorporate the growing emphasis on material culture in the work of many historians. We know that engaging students' interest in the past is often a challenge, but we also know that the text's hallmark approach—the emphasis on daily life and individual experience in its social and cultural dimensions—connects with students and makes the past vivid and accessible.

"Life" Chapters Connect the Past to the Present

Although social and cultural history can be found in every chapter, they are particularly emphasized in the acclaimed "Life" chapters that spark student interest by making the past palpable and approachable in human terms. The five chapters are Chapter 4: Life in the Hellenistic World, 336–30 B.C.E.; Chapter 10: Life in Villages and Cities of the High Middle Ages, 1000–1300; Chapter 18: Life in the Era of Expansion, 1650–1800; Chapter 22: Life in the Emerging Urban Society, 1840–1914; and Chapter 30: Life in an Age of Globalization, 1990 to the Present. Because we know that a key challenge of teaching history—and Western Civilization in particular—is encouraging students to appreciate the relevance of the past to our lives today.

Primary Sources and Historical Thinking

In response to the growing emphasis on historical thinking skills in the teaching of history at all levels, as well as to requests from our colleagues and current adopters, we have significantly expanded the book's primary source program to offer a wide variety of sources, both written and visual, presented in several ways. Those using LaunchPad will have access to *A History of Western Society*'s distinctive primary sources features. **"Thinking Like a Historian"** (one in each chapter) groups at least five sources around a central question, with additional questions to guide students' analysis of the evidence and suggestions for essays that will allow them to put these sources together with what they have learned in class. Topics include "Land Ownership and Social Conflict in the Late Republic" (Chapter 5); "The Rights of Which Men?" (Chapter 19); and "The Conservative Reaction to Immigration and Islamist Terrorism" (Chapter 30). Also available in LaunchPad, **"Evaluating the Evidence"** (three in each chapter) features an individual source, with headnotes and questions that help students understand the source and connect it to the information in the rest of the chapter. Selected for their interest and carefully integrated into their historical context, these sources provide students with firsthand encounters with people of the past along with the means and tools for building historical skills, including chronological reasoning, explaining causation, evaluating context, and assessing perspective. The suggestions for essays based on the primary sources encourage students to further expand their skills as they use their knowledge to develop historical arguments and write historical analyses.

In addition, in the print book we have quoted extensively from a wide range of primary sources in the narrative, demonstrating that such quotations are the "stuff" of history. We believe that our extensive use of **primary source extracts** as an integral part of the narrative as well as in extended form in the primary source boxes in LaunchPad will give students ample practice in thinking critically and historically.

Finally, **the companion reader, *Sources for Western Society*, Third Edition,** continues to provide a rich selection of documents to complement each chapter of the text. It is **FREE** when packaged with the textbook and is also available in LaunchPad.

Distinctive Essay Features Punctuate Larger Developments

In addition to the expanded primary source program, we are pleased to offer LaunchPad users two unique boxed essay features in each chapter — **"Individuals in Society"** and **"Living in the Past"** — that personalize larger developments and make them tangible.

To give students a chance to see the past through ordinary people's lives, each chapter includes one of the popular **"Individuals in Society" biographical essays**, which offer brief studies of individuals or groups, informing students about the societies in which they lived. We have found that readers empathize with these human beings as they themselves seek to define their own identities. The spotlighting of individuals, both famous and obscure, perpetuates the book's continued attention to cultural and intellectual developments, highlights human agency, and reflects changing interests within the historical profession as well as the development of "microhistory." Features include essays on Aristophanes, the ancient Athenian playwright who mercilessly satirized the demagogues and thinkers of his day; Anna Jansz of Rotterdam, an Anabaptist martyr; Hürrem, a concubine who became a powerful figure in the Ottoman Empire during the sixteenth century; Rebecca Protten, a former slave and leader in the Moravian missionary movement; Samuel Crompton, the inventor of the spinning mule during the Industrial Revolution who struggled to control and profit from his invention; and Edward Snowden, a former CIA operative who leaked classified documents about American surveillance programs to the world press and was considered by some a hero and by others a traitor.

To introduce students to the study of material culture, **"Living in the Past"** essays use social and cultural history to show how life in the past was both similar to and different from our lives today. These features are richly illustrated with images and artifacts and include a short essay and questions for analysis. We use these essays to explore the deeper ramifications of aspects of their own lives that students might otherwise take for granted, such as consumer goods, factories, and even currency. Students connect to the people of the past through a diverse range of topics such as "Farming in the Hellenistic World," "Roman Table Manners," "Child's Play," "Coffeehouse Culture," "The Immigrant Experience," "Nineteenth-Century Women's Fashion," and "The Supermarket Revolution."

Because we know that a key challenge of teaching history — and Western Civilization in particular — is encouraging students to appreciate the relevance of the past to our lives today, the five "Life" chapters each include a feature called **"The Past Living Now"** that examines an aspect of life today with origins in the period covered in that chapter. Featuring engaging topics such as the development of the modern university (Chapter 10) and the dawn of commercialized sports (Chapter 18), these essays were conceived with student interest in mind.

New Coverage and Updates to the Narrative

This edition is enhanced by the incorporation of a wealth of new scholarship and subject areas that immerse students in the dynamic and ongoing work of history. Chapters 1–6 incorporate the exciting cross-disciplinary scholarship that has emerged over the last several decades on the Paleolithic and Neolithic eras, river valley civilizations, and the ancient Mediterranean. For example, archaeologists working at Göbekli Tepe in present-day Turkey have unearthed rings of massive, multi-ton, elaborately carved limestone pillars built around 9000 B.C.E. by groups of foragers, which has led to a rethinking of the links among culture, religion, and the initial development of agriculture. Similarly, new research on the peoples of Mesopotamia, based on cuneiform writing along with other sources, has led scholars to revise the view that Mesopotamians were fatalistic and to emphasize instead that they generally anticipated being well treated by the gods if they behaved morally. Throughout these chapters, material on cross-cultural connections, the impact of technologies, and changing social relationships has been added. In Chapter 14, we have updated and expanded the coverage of the conquest of the Aztec and Inca Empires and the impact of the conquest on indigenous peoples, including new material on the economic exploitation of indigenous people, religious conversion, and European debates about indigenous people.

In Chapter 16, there are several significant revisions. First, there is more coverage of global/colonial issues and of the interaction between intellectual ideas and social change. Second, with regard to the Scientific Revolution, there is a new section called "Why Europe?" that asks why the Scientific Revolution happened in Europe, as well as an expanded discussion of the relationship between religion and science. Third, a new section called "The Social Life of the Enlightenment" draws attention to recent scholarship linking the ideas of the Enlightenment to the social changes of the eighteenth century; this section includes coverage of the impact of contact with non-Europeans, debates on race, and women's role in the Enlightenment. Chapter 20 pays increased attention to the global context of industrialization, including two new sections: "Why Britain?" explains why the Industrial Revolution originated in Britain and not elsewhere in the world, such as China or India; and "The Global Picture" discusses the global spread of industrialization. A new section on living standards for the working class addresses the impact of industrialization on working people.

Other additions include a streamlined discussion of the role of women in classical Athens (Chapter 3); updated coverage of medicine in the Hellenistic period (Chapter 4); new material on the Vikings of western Europe (Chapter 8); expanded treatment of the growth of Russia's land empire to complement attention to western European acquisition of overseas empires and new material on Peter the Great's campaigns against the Ottomans (Chapter 15); increased coverage of communities and identities of the Atlantic world with material on the way colonial contacts help create national European identities as well as "African" and "Indian" identities (Chapter 17); updated coverage of the history of the family, popular culture, and medicine, including material on the use of colonial plants as medicines (Chapter 18); new material on the Congress of Vienna (Chapter 21) and expanded coverage of political ideologies of liberalism, republicanism, and nationalism (Chapters 21 and 23); new material on women's roles in the European colonies and on women and imperialism (Chapter 24); expanded coverage of the First World War in the Middle East, the collapse of the Ottoman Empire, and the postwar mandate system (Chapter 25); new discussion of Jewish resistance to the Holocaust and extended coverage of anti-Semitism and eugenics in Nazi Germany (Chapter 27); new material on violence and decolonization in the Algerian War of Independence (Chapter 28); and up-to-date coverage of contemporary events in the final chapter, including the refugee crisis, the euro crisis and Greek debt relief, Russian expansionism, issues surrounding terrorism and anti-Muslim sentiment in Europe, and the potential fragmentation of the European Union (Chapter 30).

Helping Students Understand the Narrative

We know firsthand and take seriously the challenges students face in understanding, retaining, and mastering so much material that is often unfamiliar. With the goal of making this the most student-centered edition yet, we continued to enhance the book's pedagogy on many fronts. To focus students' reading, each chapter has **focus questions** keyed to the main chapter headings. These questions are repeated again in the **"Chapter Review" section** at the end of each chapter that provides helpful guidance for reviewing key topics, as well as the **chapter chronologies**, which review major developments discussed in each chapter.

To help students understand the bigger picture and prepare for exams, each chapter includes **"Looking Back, Looking Ahead" conclusions** that provide an insightful synthesis of the chapter's main developments, while connecting to events that students will encounter in the chapters to come. In this way students are introduced to history as an ongoing process of interrelated events. These conclusions are followed by **"Make Connections" questions** that prompt students to assess larger developments across chapters, thus allowing them to develop skills in evaluating change and continuity, making comparisons, and analyzing context and causation. To promote clarity and comprehension, boldface **key terms** in the text are defined in the Glossary and listed in the Chapter Review. **Phonetic spellings** are located directly after terms that readers are likely to find hard to pronounce.

The high-quality art and map program has been thoroughly revised and features more than a hundred **contemporaneous illustrations**. As in earlier editions, all illustrations have been carefully selected to complement the text, and all include captions that inform students while encouraging them to read the text more deeply. High-quality **full-size maps** illustrate major developments in the narrative. Finally, all of the full-color images and maps included in the parent text appear in LaunchPad.

In addition, whenever an instructor assigns the **LaunchPad e-Book** (which is free when bundled with the print book), students get full access to **LearningCurve**, an online adaptive learning tool that promotes mastery of the book's content and diagnoses students' trouble spots. With this adaptive quizzing, students accumulate points toward a target score as they go, giving the interaction a game-like feel. Feedback for incorrect responses explains why the answer is incorrect and directs students back to the text to review before they attempt to answer the question again. The end result is a better understanding of the key elements of the text. Instructors who actively assign LearningCurve report their students come to class prepared for discussion and their students enjoy using it. In addition, LearningCurve's reporting feature allows instructors to quickly diagnose which concepts students in their classes are struggling with so they can adjust lectures and activities accordingly. The LaunchPad e-Book with LearningCurve is thus an invaluable asset for instructors who need to support students in all settings, from traditional lectures to hybrid, online, and newer "flipped" classrooms. To learn more about the benefits of LearningCurve and LaunchPad, see the "Versions and Supplements" section on page xv.

Acknowledgments

It is a pleasure to thank the instructors who reviewed the eleventh edition in preparation for the twelfth edition:

Robert Blackey, California State University, San Bernardino
Kevin Caldwell, Blue Ridge Community College
Amy Colon, SUNY Sullivan
Maia Conrad, Thomas Nelson Community College
Scott Gavorsky, Great Basin College
George Kaloudis, Rivier College
Roy Koepp, University of Nebraska at Kearney

Jesse Lynch, Shasta College
Michael McKeown, Daytona State College
Jennifer Morris, Mount St. Joseph University
Stephen Santelli, Northern Virginia Community College
Calvin Tesler, Lehigh University
Doris Tishkoff, Quinnipiac University

It is also a pleasure to thank the many editors who have assisted us over the years, first at Houghton Mifflin and now at Bedford/St. Martin's. At Bedford/St. Martin's, these include senior development editor Leah Strauss, senior production editor Christina Horn, associate editor Tess Fletcher and editorial assistant Melanie McFadyen, director of development Jane Knetzger, acquiring editor for history Laura Arcari, and publisher for history Michael Rosenberg. Other key contributors were photo researcher Bruce Carson, text permissions editor Eve Lehmann, text designer Cia Boynton, copy editor Jennifer Brett Greenstein, proofreaders Linda McLatchie and Angela Morrison, indexer Leoni McVey, and cover designer Billy Boardman.

Many of our colleagues at the University of Illinois, the University of Wisconsin–Milwaukee, and Georgia State University continue to provide information and stimulation, often without even knowing it. We thank them for it. We also thank the many students over the years with whom we have used earlier editions of this book. Their reactions and opinions helped shape the revisions to this edition, and we hope it remains worthy of the ultimate praise that they bestowed on it: that it's "not boring like most textbooks." Merry Wiesner-Hanks would, as always, also like to thank her husband, Neil, without whom work on this project would not be possible. Clare Haru Crowston thanks her husband, Ali, and her children, Lili, Reza, and Kian, who are a joyous reminder of the vitality of life that we try to showcase in this book. Joe Perry thanks his colleagues and students at Georgia State for their intellectual stimulation and is grateful to Joyce de Vries for her unstinting support and encouragement.

Each of us has benefited from the criticism of our coauthors, although each of us assumes responsibility for what he or she has written. Merry Wiesner-Hanks intensively reworked John Buckler's Chapters 1–6 and revised Chapters 7–13; Clare Crowston wrote and revised Chapters 14–19 and took responsibility for John McKay's Chapter 20; and Joe Perry took responsibility for John McKay's Chapters 21–24 and wrote and revised Chapters 25–30.

We'd especially like to thank the founding authors, John P. McKay, Bennett D. Hill, and John Buckler, for their enduring contributions and for their faith in each of us to carry on their legacy.

CLARE HARU CROWSTON
MERRY E. WIESNER-HANKS
JOE PERRY

Versions and Supplements

Adopters of *A History of Western Society* and their students have access to abundant print and digital resources and tools, including documents, assessment and presentation materials, the acclaimed Bedford Series in History and Culture volumes, and much more. The LaunchPad course space provides access to the narrative with all assignment and assessment opportunities at the ready. See below for more information, visit macmillanlearning.com, or contact your local Bedford/St. Martin's sales representative.

Get the Right Version for Your Class

To accommodate different course lengths and course budgets, *A History of Western Society* is available in several different formats, including a Concise Edition (narrative with select features, maps, and images), a Value Edition (narrative only in two colors with select maps and images), loose-leaf versions, and low-priced PDF e-Books. And for the best value of all, package a new print book with LaunchPad at no additional charge to get the best each format offers—a print version for easy portability and reading with a LaunchPad interactive e-Book and course space with LearningCurve and loads of additional assignment and assessment options.

- **Combined Edition** (Chapters 1–30): available in paperback, Concise Edition, Value Edition, loose-leaf, e-Book formats, and in LaunchPad
- **Volume 1, From Antiquity to the Enlightenment** (Chapters 1–16): available in paperback, Concise Edition, Value Edition, loose-leaf, e-Book formats, and in LaunchPad
- **Volume 2, From the Age of Exploration to the Present** (Chapters 14–30): available in paperback, Concise Edition, Value Edition, loose-leaf, e-Book formats, and in LaunchPad
- **Volume A, From Antiquity to 1500** (Chapters 1–12): available in paperback, e-Book formats, and in LaunchPad
- **Volume B, From the Later Middle Ages to 1815** (Chapters 11–19): available in paperback, e-Book formats, and in LaunchPad
- **Volume C, From the Revolutionary Era to the Present** (Chapters 19–30): available in paperback, e-Book formats, and in LaunchPad
- **Since 1300** (Chapters 11–30): available in paperback, e-Book formats, and in LaunchPad

As noted below, any of these volumes can be packaged with additional titles for a discount. To get ISBNs for discount packages, visit macmillanlearning.com or contact your Bedford/St. Martin's representative.

Assign LaunchPad — an Assessment-Ready Interactive e-Book and Course Space

Available for discount purchase on its own or for packaging with new books at no additional charge, LaunchPad is a breakthrough solution for today's courses. Intuitive and easy to use for students and instructors alike, LaunchPad is ready to use as is and can be edited, customized with your own material, and assigned quickly. LaunchPad for *A History of Western Society* provides Bedford/St. Martin's high-quality content all in one place, including the full interactive e-Book and companion reader, *Sources for Western Society,* plus LearningCurve formative quizzing; guided reading activities designed to help students read actively for key concepts; autograded quizzes for primary sources; and chapter summative quizzes. Through a wealth of formative and summative assessment, including the adaptive learning program of LearningCurve (see the full description ahead), students gain confidence and get into their reading before class. These features, plus additional primary source documents, video tools for making video assignments, map activities, flashcards, and customizable test banks, make LaunchPad an invaluable asset for any instructor.

LaunchPad easily integrates with course management systems, and with fast ways to build assignments, rearrange chapters, and add new pages, sections, or links, it lets teachers build the courses they want to teach and hold students accountable. For more information, visit **launchpadworks.com**, or to arrange a demo, contact us at **history@macmillan.com**.

 ## Assign LearningCurve So Your Students Come to Class Prepared

Students using LaunchPad receive access to LearningCurve for *A History of Western Society.* Assigning LearningCurve in place of reading quizzes is easy for instructors, and the reporting features help instructors track overall class trends and spot topics that are giving students trouble so they can adjust their lectures and class activities. This online learning tool is popular with students because it was designed to help them rehearse content at their own pace in a nonthreatening, game-like environment. The feedback for wrong answers provides instructional coaching and sends students back to the book for review. Students answer as many questions as necessary to reach a target score, with repeated chances to revisit material they haven't mastered. When LearningCurve is assigned, students come to class better prepared.

Take Advantage of Instructor Resources

Bedford/St. Martin's has developed a rich array of teaching resources for this book and for this course. They range from lecture and presentation materials and assessment tools to course management options. Most can be found in LaunchPad or can be downloaded or ordered at **macmillanlearning.com**.

Bedford Coursepack for Blackboard, Canvas, Brightspace by D2L, or Moodle. We can help you integrate our rich content into your course management system. Registered instructors can download coursepacks that include our popular free resources and book-specific content for *A History of Western Society.*

Instructor's Manual. The *Instructor's Manual* offers both experienced and first-time instructors tools for presenting textbook material in engaging ways. It includes content learning objectives, annotated chapter outlines, and strategies for teaching with the textbook, plus suggestions on how to get the most out of LearningCurve and a survival guide for first-time teaching assistants.

Guide to Changing Editions. Designed to facilitate an instructor's transition from the previous edition of *A History of Western Society* to this new edition, this guide presents an overview of major changes as well as of changes in each chapter.

Online Test Bank. The test bank includes a mix of fresh, carefully crafted multiple-choice, matching, short-answer, and essay questions for each chapter. Many of the multiple-choice questions feature a map, an image, or a primary source excerpt as the prompt. All questions appear in easy-to-use test bank software that allows instructors to add, edit, re-sequence, and print questions and answers. Instructors can also export questions into a variety of course management systems.

The Bedford Lecture Kit: **Lecture Outlines, Maps, and Images.** Look good and save time with *The Bedford Lecture Kit*. These presentation materials include fully customizable multimedia presentations built around chapter outlines that are embedded with maps, figures, and images from the textbook and are supplemented by more detailed instructor notes on key points and concepts.

Print, Digital, and Custom Options for More Choice and Value

For information on free packages and discounts up to 50%, visit macmillanlearning .com or contact your local Bedford/St. Martin's sales representative.

Sources for Western Society, **Third Edition.** This primary source collection — available in Volume 1, Volume 2, and Since 1300 versions — provides a revised and expanded selection of sources to accompany *A History of Western Society*, Twelfth Edition. Each chapter features five or six written and visual sources by well-known figures and ordinary individuals alike. With over fifty new selections — including a dozen new visual sources — and enhanced pedagogy throughout, this book gives students the tools to engage critically with canonical and lesser-known sources and prominent and ordinary voices. Each chapter includes a "Sources in Conversation" feature that presents differing views on key topics. This companion reader is an exceptional value for students and offers plenty of assignment options for instructors. Available free when packaged with the print text and included in the LaunchPad e-Book. Also available on its own as a downloadable PDF e-Book.

NEW *Bedford Custom Tutorials for History.* Designed to customize textbooks with resources relevant to individual courses, this collection of brief units, each sixteen pages long and loaded with examples, guides students through basic skills such as using historical evidence effectively, working with primary sources, taking effective notes, avoiding plagiarism and citing sources, and more. Up to two tutorials can be added to a Bedford/St. Martin's history survey title at no additional charge, freeing you to spend your class time focusing on content and interpretation. For more information, visit macmillanlearning.com/historytutorials.

The Bedford Series in History and Culture. More than one hundred titles in this highly praised series combine first-rate scholarship, historical narrative, and important primary documents for undergraduate courses. Each book is brief, inexpensive, and focused on a specific topic or period. Revisions of several bestselling titles, such as *The Prince by Niccolò Machiavelli with Related Documents,* edited by William J. Connell; *The Enlightenment: A Brief History with Documents,* by Margaret C. Jacob; *Candide by Voltaire with Related Documents,* edited by Daniel Gordon; and *The French Revolution and Human Rights: A Brief History with Documents,* by Lynn Hunt, are now available. For a complete list of titles, visit **macmillanlearning.com**. Package discounts are available.

Rand McNally Atlas of Western Civilization. This collection of over fifty full-color maps highlights social, political, and cross-cultural change and interaction from classical Greece and Rome to the postindustrial Western world. Each map is thoroughly indexed for fast reference. Free when packaged.

Trade Books. Titles published by sister companies Hill and Wang; Farrar, Straus and Giroux; Henry Holt and Company; St. Martin's Press; Picador; and Palgrave Macmillan are available at a 50% discount when packaged with Bedford/St. Martin's textbooks. For more information, visit **macmillanlearning.com/tradeup**.

A Pocket Guide to Writing in History. This portable and affordable reference tool by Mary Lynn Rampolla provides reading, writing, and research advice useful to students in all history courses. Concise yet comprehensive advice on approaching typical history assignments, developing critical reading skills, writing effective history papers, conduct-ing research, using and documenting sources, and avoiding plagiarism — enhanced with practical tips and examples throughout — has made this slim reference a bestseller. Package discounts are available.

A Student's Guide to History. This complete guide to success in any history course provides the practical help students need to be successful. In addition to introducing students to the nature of the discipline, author Jules Benjamin teaches a wide range of skills from preparing for exams to approaching common writing assignments, and explains the research and documentation process with plentiful examples. Package discounts are available.

The Social Dimension of Western Civilization. Combining current scholarship with classic pieces, this reader's forty-eight secondary sources, compiled by Richard M. Golden, hook students with the fascinating and often surprising details of how everyday Western people worked, ate, played, celebrated, worshipped, married, procreated, fought, per-secuted, and died. Package discounts are available.

The West in the Wider World: Sources and Perspectives. Edited by Richard Lim and David Kammerling Smith, the first college reader to focus on the central historical question "How did the West become the West?" offers a wealth of written and visual source materials that reveal the influence of non-European regions on the origins and development of Western Civilization. Package discounts are available.

Brief Contents

Contents

CHAPTER 14

European Exploration and Conquest 1450–1650   410

CHAPTER 22

Life in the Emerging Urban Society 1840–1914   688

CHAPTER 23

The Age of Nationalism 1850–1914   722

CHAPTER 26

The Age of Anxiety 1880–1940   832

Maps, Figures, and Tables

at Jerusalem, which became the symbol of Hebrew unity. This unity did not last long, however, as at Solomon's death his kingdom broke into two separate states, Israel and Judah.

In their migration, the Hebrews had come in contact with many peoples, such as the Mesopotamians and the Egyptians, who had many gods. The Hebrews came to believe in a single god, Yahweh, who had created all things and who took a strong personal interest in the individual. According to the Bible, Yahweh made a covenant with the Hebrews: if they worshipped Yahweh as their only god, he would consider them his chosen people and protect them from their enemies. This covenant was to prove a constant force in the Hebrews' religion, Judaism, a word taken from the kingdom of Judah.

Worship was embodied in a series of rules of behavior, the Ten Commandments, which Yahweh gave to Moses. These required certain kinds of religious observances and forbade the Hebrews to steal, lie, murder, or commit adultery, thus creating a system of ethical absolutes. From the Ten Commandments a complex system of rules of conduct was created and later written down as Hebrew law, beginning with the Torah — the first five books of the Hebrew Bible. Hebrew Scripture, a group of books written over many centuries, also contained history, hymns of praise, prophecy, traditions, advice, and other sorts of writings. Jews today revere these texts, as do many Christians, and Muslims respect them, all of which gives them particular importance.

The Greeks

The people of ancient Greece built on the traditions and ideas of earlier societies to develop a culture that fundamentally shaped Western civilization. Drawing on their day-to-day experiences as well as logic and empirical observation, the Greeks developed ways of understanding and explaining the world around them, which grew into modern philosophy and science. They also created new political forms, including the small independent city-state known as the *polis*. Scholars label the period dating from around 1100 B.C.E. to 323 B.C.E., in which the polis predominated, the Hellenic period. Two poleis were especially powerful: Sparta, which created a military state in which men remained in the army most of their lives, and Athens, which created a democracy in which male citizens had a direct voice.

Athens created a brilliant culture, with magnificent art and architecture whose grace and beauty still speak to people. In their comedies and tragedies, Athenians Aeschylus, Sophocles, and Euripides were the first playwrights to treat eternal problems of the human condition. Athens also experimented with the political system we call democracy. Greek democracy meant the rule of citizens, not "the people" as a whole, and citizenship was generally limited to free adult men whose parents were citizens. Women were citizens for religious and reproductive purposes, but their citizenship did not give them the right to participate in government. Slaves, resident foreigners, and free men who were not children of a citizen were not citizens and had no political voice. Thus ancient Greek democracy did not reflect the modern concept that all people are created equal, but it did permit male citizens to share in determining the diplomatic and military policies of the polis.

Classical Greece of the fifth and fourth centuries B.C.E. also witnessed an incredible flowering of philosophical ideas. Some Greeks began to question their old beliefs and myths, and sought rational rather than supernatural explanations for natural phenomena. They began an intellectual revolution with the idea that nature was predictable, creating what we now call philosophy and science. These ideas also emerged in medicine: Hippocrates, the most prominent physician and teacher of medicine of his time, sought natural explanations for diseases and natural means to treat them.

The Sophists, a group of thinkers in fifth-century-B.C.E. Athens, applied philosophical speculation to politics and language, questioning the beliefs and laws of the polis to understand their origin. They believed that excellence in both politics and language could be taught, and they provided lessons for the young men of Athens who wished to learn how to persuade others in the often-tumultuous Athenian democracy.

Socrates (ca. 470–399 B.C.E.), whose ideas are known only through the works of others, also applied philosophy to politics and to people. Because he posed questions rather than giving answers, it is difficult to say exactly what Socrates thought about many things, although he does seem to have felt that through knowledge people could approach the supreme good and thus find happiness. Most of what we know about Socrates comes from his student Plato (427–347 B.C.E.), who wrote dialogues in which Socrates asks questions and who also founded the Academy, a school dedicated to philosophy. Plato developed the theory that there are two worlds: the impermanent, changing world that we know through our senses, and the eternal, unchanging realm of "forms" that constitute the essence of true reality. According to Plato, true knowledge and the possibility of living a virtuous life come from contemplating ideal forms. Plato's student Aristotle (384–322 B.C.E.) also thought that true knowledge was possible, but he believed that such knowledge came from observation of the world, analysis of natural phenomena, and logical reasoning, not contemplation. He investigated the nature of government, ideas of matter and motion, outer space, ethics, and language and literature, among other subjects. Aristotle's ideas later profoundly shaped both Muslim and Western philosophy and theology.

Echoing the broader culture, Plato and Aristotle viewed philosophy as an exchange between men in which women had no part. The ideal for Athenian citizen women was a secluded life, although how far this ideal was actually a reality is impossible to know. Women in citizen families probably spent most of their time at home, leaving the house only to attend religious festivals and perhaps occasionally plays.

Greek political and intellectual advances took place against a background of constant warfare. The long and bitter struggle between the cities of Athens and Sparta called the Peloponnesian War (431–404 B.C.E.) ended in Athens's defeat. Shortly afterward, Sparta, Athens, and Thebes contested for hegemony in Greece, but no single state was strong enough to dominate the others. Taking advantage of the situation, Philip II (r. 359–336 B.C.E.) of Macedonia, a small kingdom encompassing part of modern Greece and other parts of the Balkans, defeated a combined Theban-Athenian army in 338 B.C.E. Unable to resolve their domestic quarrels, the Greeks lost their freedom to the Macedonian invader.

Philip was assassinated just two years after he had conquered Greece, and his throne was inherited by his son, Alexander. In twelve years, Alexander conquered an empire stretching from Macedonia across the Middle East into Asia as far as India. He established cities and military colonies in strategic spots as he advanced eastward, but he died at the age of thirty-two while planning his next campaign.

The wars of conquest eventually created serious political problems for the Romans, which surfaced toward the end of the second century B.C.E. Overseas warfare required huge armies for long periods of time. A few army officers gained fabulous wealth, but most soldiers did not and returned home to find their farms in ruins. Those with cash to invest bought up small farms, creating vast estates called *latifundia*. Landless veterans migrated to Rome seeking work. Unable to compete with the tens of thousands of slaves in Rome, they formed a huge unemployed urban population. Rome divided into political factions, each of which named a supreme military commander, who led Roman troops against external enemies but also against each other. Civil war erupted.

Out of the violence and disorder emerged Julius Caesar (100–44 B.C.E.), a victorious general, shrewd politician, and highly popular figure. He took practical steps to end the civil war, such as expanding citizenship and sending large numbers of the urban poor to found colonies and spread Roman culture in Gaul, Spain, and North Africa. Fearful that Caesar's popularity and ambition would turn Rome into a monarchy, a group of aristocratic conspirators assassinated him in 44 B.C.E. Civil war was renewed. In 31 B.C.E. Caesar's grandnephew and adopted son Octavian defeated his rivals and became master of Rome. For his success, the Senate in 27 B.C.E. gave Octavian the name Augustus, meaning "revered one." Although the Senate did not mean this to be a decisive break, that date is generally used to mark the end of the Roman Republic and the start of the Roman Empire.

Augustus rebuilt effective government. Although he claimed that he was restoring the republic, he actually transformed the government into one in which all power was held by a single ruler, gradually taking over many of the offices that traditionally had been held by separate people. Without specifically saying so, Augustus created the office of emperor. The English word *emperor* is derived from the Latin word *imperator*, an origin that reflects the fact that Augustus's command of the army was the main source of his power.

Augustus ended domestic turmoil and secured the provinces. He founded new colonies, mainly in the western Mediterranean basin, which promoted the spread of Greco-Roman culture and the Latin language to the West. Magistrates exercised authority in their regions as representatives of Rome. Augustus broke some of the barriers between Italy and the provinces by extending citizenship to many of the provincials who had supported him. Later emperors added more territory, and a system of Roman roads and sea-lanes united the empire, with trade connections extending to India and China. For two hundred years the Mediterranean world experienced what later historians called the *pax Romana*—a period of prosperity, order, and relative peace. The city of Rome grew to a huge size, and the emperor provided grain and bread at low prices to prevent social unrest. Emperors and other wealthy citizens also entertained the city's residents with gladiatorial contests, chariot racing, and other forms of popular entertainment.

In the third century C.E. this prosperity and stability gave way to a period of domestic upheaval and foreign invasion. Rival generals backed by their troops contested the imperial throne in civil wars. Groups the Romans labeled "barbarians," such as the Visigoths, Ostrogoths, Gauls, and others, migrated into and invaded the Roman Empire from the north and east. Civil war and invasions devastated towns and farms, causing severe economic depression. The emperors Diocletian (r. 284–305 C.E.) and Constantine (r. 306–337 C.E.) tried to halt the general disintegration by reorganizing the empire, expanding the state bureaucracy, building more defensive works, and imposing heavier taxes. For administrative purposes, Diocletian divided the empire into a western half and an eastern half, and Constantine established the new capital city of Constantinople in the East. Their attempts to solve the empire's problems failed, however. The emperors ruling from Constantinople could not provide enough military assistance to repel invaders in the western half of the Roman Empire. In 476 a Germanic chieftain, Odoacer, deposed the Roman emperor in the West and did not take on the title of emperor, calling himself instead the king of Italy. This date thus marks the official end of the Roman Empire in the West, although the Roman Empire in the East, later called the Byzantine Empire, would last for nearly another thousand years.

After the Western Roman Empire's decline, the rich legacy of Greco-Roman culture was absorbed by the medieval world. The Latin language remained the basic medium of communication among educated people in central and western Europe for the next thousand years; for almost two thousand years, Latin literature formed the core of all Western education. Roman roads, buildings, and aqueducts remained in use. Rome left its mark on the legal and political systems of most European countries. Rome had preserved the best of ancient culture for later times.

The Spread of Christianity

The ancient world also left behind a powerful religious legacy, Christianity. Christianity derives from the teachings of a Jewish man, Jesus of Nazareth (ca. 3 B.C.E.–29 C.E.). According to the accounts of his life written down and preserved by his followers, Jesus preached of a heavenly kingdom of eternal happiness in a life after death and of the importance of devotion to God and love of others. His teachings were based on Hebrew Scripture and reflected a conception of God and morality that came from Jewish tradition, but he deviated from traditional Jewish teachings in insisting that he taught in his own name, not simply in the name of Yahweh. He came to establish a spiritual kingdom, he said, not an earthly one, and he urged his followers and listeners to concentrate on the world to come, not on material goods or earthly relationships. Some Jews believed that Jesus was the long-awaited savior who would bring prosperity and happiness, while others thought he was religiously dangerous. The Roman official of Judaea, Pontius Pilate, feared that the popular agitation surrounding Jesus could lead to revolt against Rome. He arrested Jesus, met with him, and sentenced him to death by crucifixion — the usual method for common criminals. Jesus's followers maintained that he rose from the dead three days later.

Those followers might have remained a small Jewish sect but for the preaching of a Hellenized Jew, Paul of Tarsus (ca. 5–67 C.E.). Paul traveled widely and wrote letters of advice, many of which were copied and circulated, transforming Jesus's ideas into more specific moral teachings. Paul urged that Jews and non-Jews be accepted on an equal basis, and the earliest converts included men and women from all social classes. People were attracted to Christian teachings for a variety of reasons: it offered a message of divine forgiveness and eternal life, taught that every individual has a role to play in building the kingdom of God, and fostered a deep sense of community and identity in the often highly mobile Roman world.

Some Roman officials and emperors opposed Christianity and attempted to stamp it out, but most did not, and by the second century Christianity began to establish simple houses in small villages, but a slow increase in population led to new areas being cultivated, and some serfs were able to buy their freedom.

Relative security and the increasing food supply allowed for the growth and development of towns in the High Middle Ages. Towns gained legal and political rights, merchant and craft guilds grew more powerful, and towns became centers of production as well as trading centers. In medieval social thinking, three classes existed: the clergy, who prayed; the nobility, who fought; and the peasantry, who tilled the land. The merchant class, engaging in manufacturing and trade, seeking freedom from the jurisdiction of feudal lords, and pursuing wealth with a fiercely competitive spirit, fit none of the standard categories. Townspeople represented a radical force for change. Trade brought in new ideas as well as merchandise, and towns developed into intellectual and cultural centers.

The growth of towns and cities went hand in hand with a revival of regional and international trade. For example, Italian merchants traveled to the regional fairs of France and Flanders to exchange silk from China and slaves from the Crimea for English woolens, French wines, and Flemish textiles. Merchants adopted new business techniques and a new attitude toward making money. They were eager to invest surplus capital to make more money. These developments added up to what scholars have termed a commercial revolution, a major turning point in the economic and social life of the West. The development of towns and commerce was to lay the foundations for Europe's transformation, centuries later, from a rural agricultural society into an urban industrial society—a change with global implications.

The High Middle Ages also saw the birth of the modern centralized state. The concept of the state had been one of Rome's great legacies to Western civilization, but for almost five hundred years after the disintegration of the Roman Empire in the West, political authority was weak. Charlemagne had far less control of what went on in his kingdom than Roman emperors had, and after the Carolingian Empire broke apart, political authority was completely decentralized, with power spread among many feudal lords. Beginning in the last half of the tenth century, however, feudal rulers started to develop new institutions of law and government that enabled them to assert their power over lesser lords and the general population. Centralized states slowly crystallized, first in France and England, and then in Spain and northern Europe. In Italy and Germany, however, strong independent local authorities predominated.

Medieval rulers required more officials, larger armies, and more money with which to pay for them. They developed financial bureaucracies, of which the most effective were those in England. They also sought to transform a hodgepodge of oral and written customs and rules into a uniform system of laws acceptable and applicable to all their peoples. In France, local laws and procedures were maintained, but the king also established a royal court that published laws and heard appeals. In England, the king's court regularized procedures, and the idea of a common law that applied to the whole country developed. Fiscal and legal measures enacted by King John led to opposition from the high nobles of England, who in 1215 forced him to sign the Magna Carta, agreeing to observe the law. English kings following John recognized this common law, a law that their judges applied throughout the country. Exercise of common law often involved juries of local people to answer questions of fact. The common law and jury systems of the Middle Ages have become integral features of Anglo-American jurisprudence. In the fourteenth century kings also summoned meetings of the leading classes in their kingdoms, and thus were born representative assemblies, most notably the English Parliament.

In their work of consolidation and centralization, kings increasingly used the knowledge of university-trained officials. Universities first emerged in western Europe in the twelfth century. Medieval universities were educational institutions for men that produced trained officials for the new bureaucratic states. The universities at Bologna in Italy and Montpellier in France, for example, were centers for the study of Roman law. Paris became the leading university for the study of philosophy and theology. Medieval Scholastics (philosophers and theologians) sought to harmonize Greek philosophy, especially the works of Aristotle, with Christian teaching. They wanted to use reason to deepen the understanding of what was believed on faith. At the University of Paris, Thomas Aquinas (1225–1274) wrote an important synthesis of Christian revelation and Aristotelian philosophy in his *Summa Theologica*. Medieval universities developed the basic structures familiar to modern students: colleges, universities, examinations, and degrees. Colleges and universities are another major legacy of the Middle Ages to the modern world.

At the same time that states developed, energetic popes built their power within the Western Christian Church and asserted their superiority over kings and emperors. A papal call to retake the holy city of Jerusalem led to nearly two centuries of warfare between Christians and Muslims. Christian warriors, clergy, and settlers moved out from western and central Europe in all directions, so that through conquest and colonization border regions were gradually incorporated into a more uniform European culture.

Most people in medieval Europe were Christian, and the village or city church was the center of community life, where people attended services, honored the saints, and experienced the sacraments. The village priest blessed the fields before the spring planting and the fall harvesting. In everyday life people engaged in rituals heavy with religious symbolism, and every life transition was marked by a ceremony with religious elements. Guilds of merchants sought the protection of patron saints and held elaborate public celebrations on the saints' feast days. Indeed, the veneration of saints — men and women whose lives contemporaries perceived as outstanding in holiness — and an increasingly sophisticated sacramental system became central features of popular religion. University lectures and meetings of parliaments began with prayers. Kings relied on the services of bishops and abbots in the work of the government. Gothic cathedrals, where people saw beautiful stained-glass windows and listened to complex music, manifested medieval people's deep Christian faith and their pride in their own cities.

The high level of energy and creativity that characterized the twelfth and thirteenth centuries could not be sustained indefinitely. In the fourteenth century every conceivable disaster struck western Europe. The climate turned colder and wetter, leading to poor harvests and widespread famine. People weakened by hunger were more susceptible to disease, and in the middle of the fourteenth century the bubonic plague (or Black Death) swept across the continent, taking a terrible toll on population. England and France became deadlocked in a long and bitter struggle known as the Hundred Years' War (1337–1453). War devastated the countryside, especially in France, leading to widespread discontent and peasant revolts. Workers in cities also revolted against and focus on service to the poor. Some asserted that basic teachings of the church were not truly Christian and that changes were needed in theology as well as in institutional structures and practices. The Christian humanists of the late fifteenth and early sixteenth centuries urged reform, primarily through educational and social change. Throughout the centuries, men and women believed that the early Christian Church represented a golden age akin to the golden age of the classical past celebrated by Renaissance humanists.

Thus sixteenth-century cries for reformation were hardly new. What was new, however, was the breadth with which they were accepted and their ultimate impact. In 1500 there was one Christian Church in western Europe to which all Christians at least nominally belonged. Fifty years later there were many, a situation that continues today. Thus, along with the Renaissance, the Reformation is often seen as a key element in the creation of the "modern" world.

In 1517 Martin Luther (1483–1546), a priest and professor of theology at a small German university, launched an attack on clerical abuses. The Catholic Church in the early sixteenth century had serious problems, and many individuals and groups had long called for reform. This background of discontent helps explain why Martin Luther's ideas found such a ready audience. Luther and other Protestants developed a new understanding of Christian doctrine that emphasized faith, the power of God's grace, and the centrality of the Bible. Protestant ideas were attractive to educated people and urban residents, and they spread rapidly through preaching, hymns, and the printing press. By 1530 many parts of the Holy Roman Empire and Scandinavia had broken with the Catholic Church.

Some reformers developed more radical ideas about infant baptism, ownership of property, and the separation between church and state. Both Protestants and Catholics regarded these as dangerous, and radicals were banished or executed. The German Peasants' War, in which Luther's ideas were linked to calls for social and economic reform, was similarly put down harshly. The Protestant reformers did not break with medieval ideas about the proper gender hierarchy, though they did elevate the status of marriage by denying the value of clerical celibacy and viewed orderly households as the key building blocks of society.

The progress of the Reformation was shaped by the political situation in the Holy Roman Empire. The Habsburg emperor, Charles V, ruled almost half of Europe along with Spain's overseas colonies. Within the empire his authority was limited, however, and local princes, nobles, and cities actually held the most power. This decentralization allowed the Reformation to spread. Charles remained firmly Catholic, and in the 1530s religious wars began in Germany. These were brought to an end with the Peace of Augsburg in 1555, which allowed rulers to choose whether their territory would be Catholic or Lutheran.

In England, the political issue of the royal succession triggered that country's break with Rome, and a Protestant Church was established. Protestant ideas also spread into France and eastern Europe. In all these areas, a second generation of reformers built on Lutheran and Zwinglian ideas to develop their own theology and plans for institutional change. The most important of the second-generation reformers was John Calvin, whose ideas would come to shape Christianity over a much wider area than did Luther's. The Roman Catholic Church responded slowly to the Protestant challenge, but by the 1530s the papacy was leading a movement for reform within the church instead of blocking it. Catholic doctrine was reaffirmed at the Council of Trent, and reform measures, such as the opening of seminaries for priests and a ban on holding multiple church offices, were introduced. New religious orders such as the Jesuits and the Ursulines spread Catholic ideas through teaching, and in the case of the Jesuits through missionary work.

Religious differences led to riots, civil wars, and international conflicts in the later sixteenth century. In France and the Netherlands, Calvinist Protestants and Catholics used violence against each other, and religious differences became mixed with political and economic grievances. Long civil wars resulted; one in the Netherlands became an international conflict. War ended in France with the Edict of Nantes in which Protestants were given some civil rights, and in the Netherlands with a division of the country into a Protestant north and a Catholic south. The era of religious wars was also the time of the most extensive witch persecutions in European history, as both Protestants and Catholics tried to rid their cities and states of people they regarded as linked to the Devil.

The Renaissance and the Reformation are often seen as two of the key elements in the creation of the "modern" world. The radical changes brought by the Reformation contained many aspects of continuity, however. Sixteenth-century reformers looked back to the early Christian Church for their inspiration, and many of their reforming ideas had been advocated for centuries. Most Protestant reformers worked with political leaders to make religious changes, just as early church officials had worked with Emperor Constantine and his successors as Christianity became the official religion of the Roman Empire in the fourth century. The spread of Christianity and the spread of Protestantism were accomplished not only by preaching, persuasion, and teaching, but also by force and violence. The Catholic Reformation was carried out by activist popes, a church council, and new religious orders, as earlier reforms of the church had been.

Just as they linked with earlier developments, the events of the Reformation were also closely connected with what is often seen as the third element in the "modern" world, discussed in the first chapter of this book: European Exploration and Conquest. Only a week after Martin Luther stood in front of Emperor Charles V at the Diet of Worms declaring his independence in matters of religion, Ferdinand Magellan, a Portuguese sea captain with Spanish ships, was killed in a group of islands off the coast of Southeast Asia. Charles V had provided the backing for Magellan's voyage, the first to circumnavigate the globe. Magellan viewed the spread of Christianity as one of the purposes of his trip, and later in the sixteenth century institutions created as part of the Catholic Reformation, including the Jesuit order and the Inquisition, would operate in European colonies overseas as well as in Europe itself. The islands where Magellan was killed were later named the Philippines, in honor of Charles's son Philip, who sent an ill-fated expedition, the Spanish Armada, against Protestant England. Philip's opponent Queen Elizabeth was similarly honored when English explorers named a huge chunk of territory in North America "Virginia" as a tribute to their "Virgin Queen." The desire for wealth and power was an important motivation in the European voyages and colonial ventures, but so was religious zeal.

A History of Western Society

VALUE EDITION

14

European Exploration and Conquest

1450–1650

IN 1450 EUROPEANS WERE RELATIVELY MARGINAL PLAYERS in a centuries-old trading system that linked Africa, Asia, and Europe. The Indian Ocean was the locus of a vibrant cosmopolitan Afroeurasian trade world in which Arab, Persian, Turkish, Indian, African, Chinese, and European merchants and adventurers competed for trade in spices, silks, and other goods. Elites everywhere prized Chinese porcelains and silks, while wealthy members of the Celestial Kingdom, as China called itself, wanted gold, ivory, and rhinoceros horn from Africa, and exotic goods and peacocks from India. African people wanted textiles from India and cowrie shells from the Maldives in the Indian Ocean. Europeans craved Asian silks and spices, but they had few desirable goods to offer their trading partners.

By 1550 the European search for better access to Asian trade goods had led to a new overseas empire in the Indian Ocean and the accidental discovery of the Western Hemisphere. South and North America were soon drawn into a global network of trade centers and political empires, which Europeans came to dominate. The era of globalization had begun, creating new political systems and forms of economic exchange as well as cultural assimilation, conversion, and resistance. Europeans sought to impose their values on the peoples they encountered while struggling to comprehend these peoples' societies. The Age of Discovery (1450–1650), as the time of these encounters is known, laid the foundations for the modern world.

World Contacts Before Columbus

Focus Question	What was the Afroeurasian trading world prior to the era of European exploration?

In the fifteenth century a type of world economy, known as the Afroeurasian trade world, linked the products and people of Asia, Africa, and Europe. Before Christopher Columbus began his voyages to the New World in 1492, the West was not the dominant player in world trade. Nevertheless, wealthy Europeans were eager consumers of luxury goods from the East, which they received through Venetian and Genoese middlemen.

The Trade World of the Indian Ocean

The Indian Ocean was the center of the Afroeurasian trade world, serving as a crossroads for exchange among China, India, the Middle East, Africa, and Europe (Map 14.1). From the seventh through the fourteenth centuries, the volume of this trade steadily increased, declining only during the catastrophic years of the Black Death.

Merchants congregated in a series of cosmopolitan port cities strung around the Indian Ocean. Most of these cities had some form of autonomous self-government. Mutual self-interest largely limited violence and prevented attempts to monopolize trade. The most developed area of this commercial web was the South China Sea. In the fifteenth century the port of Malacca became a great commercial entrepôt (AHN-truh-poh), a trading post to which goods were shipped for storage while awaiting redistribution. To Malacca came Chinese porcelains, silks, and camphor (used in the manufacture of many medications); pepper, cloves, nutmeg, and raw materials such as sandalwood from the Moluccas; sugar from the Philippines; and Indian textiles, copper weapons, incense, dyes, and opium.

The Mongol emperors opened the doors of China to the West, encouraging Europeans like the Venetian trader and explorer Marco Polo to do business there. Marco Polo's tales of his travels from 1271 to 1295 and his encounter with the Great Khan fueled Western fantasies about the exotic Orient. Polo vividly recounted the splendors of the khan's court and the city of Hangzhou, which he described as "the finest and noblest in the world" in which "the number and wealth of the merchants, and the amount of goods that passed through their hands, was so enormous that no man could form a just estimate thereof."[1] After the Mongols fell to the Ming Dynasty in 1368, China entered a period of economic expansion, population growth, and urbanization. By the end of the dynasty in 1644, the Chinese population had tripled to between 150 million and 200 million people. The city of Nanjing had 1 million inhabitants, making it the largest city in the world, while the new capital, Beijing, had more than 600,000 inhabitants, more than any European city. Historians agree that China had the most advanced economy in the world until at least the start of the eighteenth century.

China also took the lead in exploration, sending Admiral Zheng He's fleet along the trade web as far west as Egypt. From 1405 to 1433 each of his seven expeditions

The Port of Calicut in India   The port of Calicut, located on the west coast of India, was a center of the Indian Ocean spice trade during the Middle Ages. Vasco da Gama arrived in Calicut in 1498 and obtained permission to trade there, leading to hostilities between the Portuguese and the Arab traders who had previously dominated the port. (From *Civitates Orbis Terrarum*, ca. 1572/Private Collection/The Stapleton Collection/Bridgeman Images)

Legends about Africa played an important role in Europeans' imagination of the outside world. They long cherished the belief in a powerful Christian nation in Africa ruled by a mythical king, Prester John, who was believed to be a descendant of one of the three kings who visited Jesus after his birth.

The Ottoman and Persian Empires

The Middle East served as an intermediary for trade between Asia, Africa, and Europe and was also an important supplier of goods for foreign exchange, especially silk and cotton. Two great rival Muslim empires, the Persian Safavids (sah-FAH-vidz) and the Turkish Ottomans, dominated the region. Persian merchants could be found in trading communities as far away as the Indian Ocean. Persia was also a major producer and exporter of silk.

The Persians' Shi'ite Muslim faith clashed with the Ottomans' adherence to Sunnism. Economically, the two competed for control over western trade routes to the East. Under Sultan Mohammed II (r. 1451–1481), the Ottomans captured Europe's largest city, Constantinople, in May 1453. Renamed Istanbul, the city became the capital of the Ottoman Empire. By the mid-sixteenth century the Ottomans controlled the sea trade in the eastern Mediterranean, Syria, Palestine, Egypt, and the rest of North Africa, and their power extended into Europe as far west as Vienna.

Ottoman expansion frightened Europeans. The Ottoman armies seemed invincible and the empire's desire for expansion limitless. In France in the sixteenth century, only forty books were published on the American discoveries compared to eighty on Turkey and the Turks.[4] The strength of the Ottomans helps explain some of the missionary fervor Christians brought to new territories. It also raised economic concerns. With trade routes to the East dominated by the Ottomans, Europeans wished to find new trade routes free of Ottoman control.

Genoese and Venetian Middlemen

Compared to the riches and vibrancy of the East, Europe constituted a minor outpost of the world trading system. European craftsmen produced few products to rival the fine wares and coveted spices of Asia. In the late Middle Ages, the Italian city-states of Venice and Genoa controlled the European luxury trade with the East.

In 1304 Venice established formal relations with the sultan of Mamluk Egypt, opening operations in Cairo, a gateway to Asian trade. Venetian merchants specialized in goods like spices, silks, and carpets, which they obtained from middlemen in the eastern Mediterranean and Asia Minor. A little went a long way. Venetians purchased no more than five hundred tons of spices a year around 1400, with a profit of about 40 percent. The most important spice was pepper, grown in India and Indonesia, which constituted 60 percent of the spices they purchased in 1400.[5]

The Venetians exchanged Eastern luxury goods for European products they could trade abroad, including Spanish and English wool, German metal goods, Flemish textiles, and silk cloth made in their own manufactures with imported raw materials. Eastern demand for such items, however, was low, leading Venetians to fund their purchases through shipping and trade in firearms and slaves. At least half of what they traded with the East took the form of precious metal, much of it acquired in Egypt and North Africa. When the Portuguese arrived in Asia in the late fifteenth century, they found Venetian coins everywhere.

Venice's ancient rival was Genoa. In the wake of the Crusades, Genoa dominated the northern route to Asia through the Black Sea. Expansion in the thirteenth and fourteenth centuries took the Genoese as far as Persia and the Far East. In 1291 they sponsored an expedition into the Atlantic in search of India. The ships were lost, and their exact destination and motivations remain unknown. This voyage reveals the long roots of Genoese interest in Atlantic exploration.

In the fifteenth century, with Venice claiming victory in the spice trade, the Genoese shifted focus from trade to finance and from the Black Sea to the western Mediterranean. Located on the northwestern coast of Italy, Genoa had always been active in the western Mediterranean, trading with North African ports, southern France, Spain, and even England and Flanders through the Strait of Gibraltar. When Spanish and Portuguese voyages began to explore the western Atlantic, Genoese merchants, navigators, and financiers provided their skills and capital to the Iberian monarchs. The Genoese, for example, ran many of the sugar plantations established on the Atlantic islands colonized by the Portuguese. Genoese merchants would eventually help finance Spanish colonization of the New World.

A major element of Italian trade was slavery. Merchants purchased slaves, many of whom were fellow Christians, in the Balkans. The men were sold to Egypt for the

The small number of Europeans who could read provided a rapt audience for tales of fantastic places and unknown peoples. Cosmography, natural history, and geography aroused enormous interest among educated people in the fifteenth and sixteenth centuries. One of the most popular books of the time was the fourteenth-century text *The Travels of Sir John Mandeville*, which purported to be a firsthand account of the author's travels in the Middle East, India, and China. Although we now know the stories were fictional, these fantastic tales of cannibals, one-eyed giants, men with the heads of dogs, and other marvels convinced audiences through their vividly and persuasively described details. Christopher Columbus took a copy of Mandeville and the equally popular and more reliable *The Travels of Marco Polo* on his voyage in 1492.

Technology and the Rise of Exploration

The Iberian powers actively sought technological improvements in shipbuilding, weaponry, and navigation in order to undertake successful voyages of exploration and trade. Medieval European seagoing vessels consisted of single-masted sailing ships or narrow, open galleys propelled by oars, which were common in Mediterranean trade. Though adequate for short journeys that hugged the shoreline, such vessels were incapable of long-distance journeys or high-volume trade. To sail to the Indian Ocean or cross the Atlantic, larger and sturdier craft were necessary. In the course of the fifteenth century, the Portuguese developed the **caravel**, a three-mast sailing ship. Its multiple sails and sternpost rudder made the caravel a more maneuverable vessel that required fewer crewmen to operate. It could carry more cargo than a galley, which meant it could sail farther without stopping for supplies and return with a larger cache of profitable goods. When fitted with cannon, it could dominate larger vessels and bombard port cities.[10]

Great strides in cartography and navigational aids were also made during this period. Around 1410 Arab scholars reintroduced Europeans to **Ptolemy's *Geography***. Written in the second century C.E. by a Hellenized Egyptian, the work synthesized the geographical knowledge of the classical world. Ptolemy's work provided significant improvements over medieval cartography, clearly depicting the world as round and introducing the idea of latitude and longitude to plot position accurately. It also contained crucial errors. Unaware of the Americas, Ptolemy showed the world as much smaller than it is, so that Asia appeared not very distant from Europe to the west. Both the assets and the flaws of Ptolemy's work shaped the geographical knowledge that explorers like Christopher Columbus brought to their voyages.

Originating in China, the compass was brought to the West in the late Middle Ages; by using the compass to determine their direction and estimating their speed of travel over a set length of time, mariners could determine the course of a ship's voyage, a system of navigation known as "dead reckoning." In the late fifteenth century Portuguese scholars devised a new technique of "celestial reckoning," which involved using the astrolabe, an instrument invented by the ancient Greeks to determine the position of the stars and other celestial bodies. Commissioned by Portuguese king John II, a group of astronomers in the 1480s showed that mariners could determine their latitude at sea by using a specially designed astrolabe to determine the altitude of the polestar or the sun, and consulting tables of these bodies' movements. This was a crucial step forward in maritime navigational techniques.

Much of the new technology that Europeans used on their voyages was borrowed from the East. Gunpowder, the compass, and the sternpost rudder were Chinese inventions. The triangular lateen sail, which allowed caravels to tack against the wind, was a product of the Indian Ocean trade world. Advances in navigational techniques and cartography, including the maritime astrolabe, drew on a rich Iberian tradition of Jewish and Arab mathematics and astronomy. Sometimes assistance to Europeans came from humans rather than instruments. The famed explorer Vasco da Gama employed a local Indian pilot to guide his expedition from the East African coast to India. In exploring new territories, European sailors thus called on techniques and knowledge developed over centuries in China, the Muslim world, and the Indian Ocean.

The Portuguese Overseas Empire

For centuries Portugal was a small, poor nation on the margins of European life whose principal activities were fishing and subsistence farming. It would have been hard for a European to predict Portugal's phenomenal success overseas after 1450. Yet Portugal had a long history of seafaring and navigation. Blocked from access to western Europe by Spain, the Portuguese turned to the Atlantic and North Africa, whose waters they knew better than other Europeans did. Nature favored the Portuguese: winds blowing along their coast offered passage to Africa, its Atlantic islands, and, ultimately, Brazil. Once they had mastered the secret to sailing against the wind to return to Europe (by sailing further west to catch winds from the southwest), they were ideally poised to lead Atlantic exploration.

In the early phases of Portuguese exploration, Prince Henry (1394–1460), a younger son of the king, played a leading role. A nineteenth-century scholar dubbed Henry "the Navigator" because of his support for the study of geography and navigation and for the annual expeditions he sponsored down the western coast of Africa. Although he never personally participated in voyages of exploration, Henry's involvement ensured that Portugal did not abandon the effort despite early disappointments.

The objectives of Portuguese exploration included military glory; the conversion of Muslims; and a quest to find gold, slaves, and an overseas route to the spice markets of India. Portugal's conquest of Ceuta, an Arab city in northern Morocco, in 1415 marked the beginning of European overseas expansion. In the 1420s, under Henry's direction, the Portuguese began to settle the Atlantic islands of Madeira (ca. 1420) and the Azores (1427). In 1443 they founded their first African commercial settlement at Arguin in North Africa. By the time of Henry's death in 1460, his support for exploration was vindicated—from the Portuguese point of view—by thriving sugar plantations on the Atlantic islands, the first arrival of enslaved Africans in Portugal (see page 434), and new access to African gold.

The Portuguese next established fortified trading posts, called factories, on the gold-rich Guinea coast and penetrated into the African continent all the way to Timbuktu (Map 14.2). By 1500 Portugal controlled the flow of African gold to Europe. In contrast to the Spanish conquest of the Americas (see pages 424–427), the Portuguese did not establish large settlements in West Africa or seek to control the political or cultural lives of those with whom they traded. Instead, they sought easier and faster profits by inserting themselves into pre-existing trading systems. For the first century of their relations,

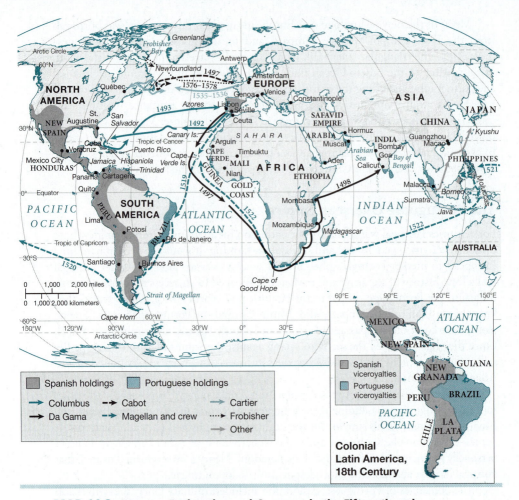

MAP 14.2 Overseas Exploration and Conquest in the Fifteenth and Sixteenth Centuries

The voyages of discovery marked a dramatic new phase in the centuries-old migrations of European peoples. This world map depicts the voyages of the most significant European explorers of this period, while the inset map shows Spanish and Portuguese colonies of the eighteenth century.

African rulers were equal partners with the Portuguese, benefiting from their experienced armies and European vulnerability to tropical diseases.

The Portuguese then pushed farther south down the west coast of Africa. In 1487 Bartholomew Diaz rounded the Cape of Good Hope at the southern tip of Africa, but storms and a threatened mutiny forced him to turn back. A decade later Vasco da Gama succeeded in rounding the Cape while commanding a fleet of four ships in search of a sea route to India. With the help of an Indian guide, da Gama reached the port of Calicut in India. He returned to Lisbon loaded with spices and samples of Indian cloth, having proved the possibility of lucrative trade with the East via the Cape route. Thereafter, a Portuguese convoy set out for passage around the Cape every March.

Lisbon became the entrance port for Asian goods into Europe, but this was not accomplished without a fight. Muslim-controlled port city-states had long controlled the rich trade of the Indian Ocean, and they did not surrender their dominance willingly. From 1500 to 1515 the Portuguese used a combination of bombardment and diplomatic treaties to establish trading forts at Goa, Malacca, Calicut, and Hormuz, thereby laying the foundation for a Portuguese trading empire in the sixteenth and seventeenth centuries. The acquisition of port cities and their trade routes brought riches to Portugal, but, as in Africa, the Portuguese had limited impact on the lives and religious faith of peoples beyond their coastal holdings. Moreover, despite their advances in shipbuilding, weaponry, and navigation, the Portuguese were never able to enforce a total monopoly on trading in the Indian Ocean.

Inspired by the Portuguese, the Spanish had also begun the quest for empire. Theirs was to be a second, entirely different, mode of colonization, leading to the conquest of existing empires, large-scale settlement, and the assimilation of a subjugated indigenous population.

Spain's Voyages to the Americas

We now know that Christopher Columbus was not the first to explore the Atlantic. Ninth-century Vikings established short-lived settlements in Newfoundland, and it is probable that others made the voyage, either on purpose or accidentally, carried by westward currents off the coast of Africa. In the late fifteenth century the achievements of Portugal's decades of exploration made the moment right for Christopher Columbus's attempt to find a westward route across the Atlantic to Asia.

A native of the port city of Genoa, Christopher Columbus was early on drawn to the life of the sea. He became an experienced seaman and navigator and worked as a mapmaker in Lisbon. He was familiar with *portolans*—written descriptions of the courses along which ships sailed—and the use of the compass for dead reckoning. (He carried an astrolabe on his first voyage, but did not use it for navigation.) As he asserted in his journal: "I have spent twenty-three years at sea and have not left it for any length of time worth mentioning, and I have seen every thing from east to west [meaning he had been to England] and I have been to Guinea [North and West Africa]."[11]

Columbus was also a deeply religious man. He had witnessed the Spanish conquest of Granada and shared fully in the religious and nationalistic fervor surrounding that event. Like the Spanish rulers and most Europeans of his age, Columbus understood Christianity as a missionary religion that should be carried to all places of the earth. He viewed himself as a divine agent: "God made me the messenger of the new heaven and the new earth of which he spoke in the Apocalypse of St. John . . . and he showed me the post where to find it."[12]

Rejected for funding by the Portuguese in 1483 and by Ferdinand and Isabella in 1486, Columbus's project to find a westward passage to the Indies finally won the backing of the Spanish monarchy in 1492. Buoyed by the success of the reconquista and eager to earn profits from trade, the Spanish crown named Columbus viceroy over any territory he might discover and promised him one-tenth of the material rewards of the journey.

Columbus and his small fleet left Spain on August 3, 1492. Inspired by the stories of Mandeville and Marco Polo, Columbus dreamed of reaching the court of the Mongol emperor, the Great Khan (not realizing that the Ming Dynasty had overthrown the Mongols in 1368). Based on Ptolemy's *Geography* and other texts, he expected to pass the islands of Japan and then land on the east coast of China.

After a brief stop in the Canary Islands, he landed in the Bahamas, which he christened San Salvador, on October 12, 1492. In a letter he wrote to Ferdinand and Isabella on his return to Spain, Columbus described the natives as handsome, peaceful, and primitive people whose body painting reminded him of that of the Canary Islands natives. Believing he was somewhere off the east coast of Japan, in what he considered the Indies, he called them "Indians," a name later applied to all inhabitants of the Americas. Columbus concluded that they would make good slaves and could easily be converted to Christianity.

Scholars have identified the inhabitants of the islands as the Taino people, speakers of the Arawak language, who inhabited Hispaniola (modern-day Haiti and Dominican Republic) and other islands in the Caribbean. From San Salvador, Columbus sailed southwest, landing on Cuba on October 28. Deciding that he must be on the mainland near the coastal city of Quinsay (now Hangzhou), he sent a small embassy inland with letters from Ferdinand and Isabella and instructions to locate the grand city. Although they found no large settlement or any evidence of a great kingdom, the sight of Taino people wearing gold ornaments on Hispaniola suggested that gold was available in the region. In January, confident that its source would soon be found, he headed back to Spain to report on his discovery. News of his voyage spread rapidly across Europe.[13]

On his second voyage, Columbus forcibly subjugated the island of Hispaniola and enslaved its indigenous peoples. On this and subsequent voyages, Columbus brought with him settlers for the new Spanish territories, along with agricultural seed and livestock. Columbus himself, however, had limited skills in governing. Revolt soon broke out against him and his brother on Hispaniola. A royal expedition sent to investigate returned the brothers to Spain in chains, and a royal governor assumed control of the colony.

Columbus was very much a man of his times. To the end of his life in 1506, he believed that he had found small islands off the coast of Asia. He never realized the scope of his achievement: he had found a vast continent unknown to Europeans, except for a fleeting Viking presence centuries earlier. He could not know that the scale of his discoveries would revolutionize world power and set in motion a new era of trade, empire, and human migration.

Spain "Discovers" the Pacific

The Florentine navigator Amerigo Vespucci (veh-SPOO-chee) (1454–1512) realized what Columbus had not. Writing about his discoveries on the coast of modern-day Venezuela, Vespucci stated: "Those new regions which we found and explored with the fleet . . . we may rightly call a New World." This letter, titled *Mundus Novus* (The New World), was the first document to describe America as a continent separate from Asia. In recognition of Amerigo's bold claim, the continent was named for him.

To settle competing claims to the Atlantic discoveries, Spain and Portugal turned to Pope Alexander VI. The resulting **Treaty of Tordesillas** (tor-duh-SEE-yuhs) in 1494 gave Spain everything to the west of an imaginary line drawn down the Atlantic, and Portugal everything to the east. This arbitrary division worked in Portugal's favor when in 1500 an expedition led by Pedro Álvares Cabral, en route to India, landed on the coast of Brazil, which Cabral claimed as Portuguese territory.

The search for profits determined the direction of Spanish exploration. Because its profits from Hispaniola and other Caribbean islands were insignificant compared to the enormous riches that the Portuguese were reaping in Asia, Spain renewed the search for a western passage to Asia. In 1519 Charles V of Spain sent the Portuguese mariner Ferdinand Magellan (1480–1521) to find a sea route to the spices of the Moluccas off the southeast coast of Asia. Magellan sailed southwest across the Atlantic to Brazil, and after a long search along the coast he located the treacherous straits that now bear his name (see Map 14.2). The new ocean he sailed into after a rough passage through the straits seemed so calm that Magellan dubbed it the Pacific, from the Latin word for peaceful. His fleet sailed north up the west coast of South America and then headed west into the immense expanse of the Pacific toward the Malay Archipelago. (Some of these islands were conquered later, in the 1560s, and named the "Philippines" for Philip II of Spain.)

Magellan's first impressions of the Pacific were utterly mistaken. Terrible storms, disease, starvation, and violence devastated the expedition. Magellan had set out with a fleet of five ships and around 270 men. Sailors on two of the ships attempted mutiny on the South American coast; one ship was lost, and another ship deserted and returned to Spain before even traversing the straits. The trip across the Pacific took ninety-eight days, and the men survived on rats and sawdust. Magellan himself died in a skirmish in the Malay Archipelago. Only one ship, with eighteen men aboard, returned to Spain from the east by way of the Indian Ocean, the Cape of Good Hope, and the Atlantic in 1522. The voyage — the first to circumnavigate the globe — had taken close to three years.

Despite the losses, this voyage revolutionized Europeans' understanding of the world by demonstrating the vastness of the Pacific. The earth was clearly much larger than Ptolemy's map had shown. Although the voyage made a small profit in spices, it also demonstrated that the westward passage to the Indies was too long and dangerous for commercial purposes. Spain soon abandoned the attempt to oust Portugal from the Eastern spice trade and concentrated on exploiting her New World territories.

Early Exploration by Northern European Powers

Spain's northern European rivals also set sail across the Atlantic during the early days of exploration in search of a northwest passage to the Indies. In 1497 John Cabot, a Genoese merchant living in London, undertook a voyage to Brazil, but landed on Newfoundland instead. The next year he returned and reconnoitered the New England coast. These forays proved futile, and the English established no permanent colonies in the territories they explored. News of the riches of Mexico and Peru later inspired the English to renew their efforts, this time in the extreme north. Between 1576 and 1578 Martin Frobisher made three voyages in and around the

The Mexica Capital of Tenochtitlan This woodcut map was published in 1524 along with Cortés's letters describing the conquest of the Mexica. As it shows, Tenochtitlan occupied an island and was laid out in concentric circles. The administrative and religious buildings were at the heart of the city, which was surrounded by residential quarters. Cortés himself marveled at the city in his letters: "The city is as large as Seville or Cordoba. . . . There are bridges, very large, strong, and well constructed, so that, over many, ten horsemen can ride abreast. . . . The city has many squares where markets are held. . . . There is one square . . . where there are daily more than sixty thousand souls, buying and selling. In the service and manners of its people, their fashion of living was almost the same as in Spain, with just as much harmony and order." (Newberry Library, Chicago, Illinois, USA/Bridgeman Images)

in population and complexity. The Incas' strength lay largely in their bureaucratic efficiency. They divided their empire into four major regions containing eighty provinces and twice as many districts. Officials at each level used an extensive network of roads to transmit information and orders back and forth through the empire. While the Aztecs used a system of glyphs for writing, the Incas had devised a complex system of colored and knotted cords, called *khipus*, for administrative bookkeeping. The empire also benefited from the use of llamas as pack animals (by contrast, no beasts of burden existed in Mesoamerica).

By the time of the Spanish invasion, however, the Inca Empire had been weakened by a civil war over succession and an epidemic of disease, possibly smallpox, which may have spread through trade with groups in contact with Europeans. Francisco Pizarro (ca. 1475–1541), a conquistador of modest Spanish origins, landed on the northern coast of Peru on May 13, 1532, the very day the Inca leader Atahualpa (ah-tuh-WAHL-puh) won control of the empire after five years of fighting. As Pizarro advanced across the steep Andes toward Cuzco, the capital of the Inca Empire, Atahualpa was also heading there for his coronation.

Like Moctezuma in Mexico, Atahualpa was aware of the Spaniards' movements. He sent envoys to invite the Spanish to meet him in the provincial town of Cajamarca. His plan was to lure the Spanish into a trap, seize their horses and ablest men for his army, and execute the rest. With an army of some forty thousand men stationed nearby, Atahualpa felt he had little to fear. Instead, the Spaniards ambushed and captured him, collected an enormous ransom in gold, and then executed him in 1533 on trumped-up charges. The Spanish then marched on to Cuzco, profiting once again from internal conflicts to form alliances with local peoples. When Cuzco fell in 1533, the Spanish plundered immense riches in gold and silver.

How was it possible for several hundred Spanish conquistadors to defeat powerful empires commanding large armies, vast wealth, and millions of inhabitants? Historians seeking answers to this question have emphasized a combination of factors: the boldness and audacity of conquistadors like Cortés and Pizarro; the military superiority provided by Spanish firepower and horses; divisions within the Aztec and Inca Empires, which produced many native allies for the Spanish; and, of course, the devastating impact of contagious diseases among the indigenous population. Ironically, the well-organized, urban-based Aztec and Inca Empires were more vulnerable to wholesale takeover than more decentralized and fragmented groups like the Maya in the Yucatán peninsula, whose independence was not wholly crushed until the end of the seventeenth century.

Portuguese Brazil

Unlike Mesoamerica or the Andes, the territory of Brazil contained no urban empires, but instead roughly 2.5 million nomadic and settled people divided into small tribes and many different language groups. In 1500 the Portuguese crown named Pedro Álvares Cabral commander of a fleet headed for the spice trade of the Indies. En route the fleet sailed far to the west, accidentally landing on the coast of Brazil, which Cabral claimed for Portugal under the terms of the Treaty of Tordesillas (see page 423). The Portuguese soon undertook a profitable trade with local people in brazilwood, a valued source of red dye.

In the 1520s Portuguese settlers brought sugarcane production to Brazil. They initially used enslaved indigenous laborers on sugar plantations, but the rapid decline in the indigenous population soon led to the use of forcibly transported Africans (see page 436). In Brazil the Portuguese thus created a new form of colonization in the Americas: large plantations worked by enslaved people. This model would spread throughout the Caribbean along with sugar production in the seventeenth century.

Colonial Empires of England and France

For almost a century after the fall of the Aztec capital of Tenochtitlan, the Spanish and Portuguese dominated European overseas trade and colonization. In the early seventeenth century, however, northern European powers profited from Spanish weakness was centered on cities and towns. In each city, the municipal council, or *cabildo*, exercised local authority. Women were denied participation in public life, a familiar pattern from both Spain and precolonial indigenous society.

Portugal adopted similar patterns of rule, with India House in Lisbon functioning much like the Spanish House of Trade and royal representatives overseeing Portuguese possessions in West Africa and Asia. To secure the vast expanse of Brazil, in the 1530s the Portuguese implemented the system of captaincies, hereditary grants of land given to nobles and loyal officials who bore the costs of settling and administering their territories. Over time, the Crown secured greater power over the captaincies, appointing royal governors to act as administrators. The captaincy of Bahia was the site of the capital, Salvador, home to the governor general and other royal officials.

Throughout the Americas, the Catholic Church played an integral role in Iberian rule. Churches and cathedrals were consecrated, often on precolonial sacred sites, and bishoprics were established. The papacy allowed Portuguese and Spanish officials greater control over the church than was the case at home, allowing them to appoint clerics and collect tithes. This control allowed colonial powers to use the church as an instrument to indoctrinate indigenous people in European ways of life (see page 432).

By the end of the seventeenth century the French crown had followed the Iberian example and imposed direct rule over its North American colonies. The king appointed military governors to rule alongside intendants, royal officials possessed of broad administrative and financial authority within their intendancies. In the mid-eighteenth century reform-minded Spanish king Charles III (r. 1759–1788) adopted the intendant system for the Spanish colonies.

England's colonies followed a distinctive path. Drawing on English traditions of representative government (see Chapter 15), its colonists established their own proudly autonomous assemblies to regulate local affairs. Wealthy merchants and landowners dominated the assemblies, yet common men had more say in politics than was the case in England. Up to the mid-eighteenth century, the Crown found little reason to dispute colonial liberties in the north, but it did acquire greater control over the wealthy plantation colonies of the Caribbean and tobacco-rich Virginia.

The Era of Global Contact

Focus Question	How was the era of global contact shaped by new forms of exploitation, commercial exchange, and forced migration?

The New and Old Worlds were brought into contact and forever changed by the European voyages of discovery and their aftermath. For the first time, a truly global economy emerged in the sixteenth and seventeenth centuries, and it forged new links among far-flung peoples, cultures, and societies. The ancient civilizations of Europe, Africa, the Americas, and Asia confronted each other in new and rapidly evolving ways. Those confrontations led to conquest, forced migration, devastating population losses, and brutal exploitation. The exchange of goods and people between Europe and the New World brought highly destructive diseases to the Americas, but it also gave both the New and Old Worlds new crops that eventually altered consumption patterns across the globe.

Indigenous Population Loss and Economic Exploitation

From the time of Christopher Columbus in Hispaniola, the Spanish made use of the encomienda system to profit from the peoples and territories they subjugated in the Americas. This system was a legacy of the methods used to reward military leaders in the time of the reconquista, when victorious officers received feudal privileges over conquered areas in return for their service. First in the Caribbean and then on the mainland, conquistadors granted their followers the right to employ groups of indigenous people as laborers and to demand tribute payments from them in exchange for providing food, shelter, and instruction in the Christian faith. Commonly, an individual conquistador was assigned a tribal chieftain along with all of the people belonging to his kin group. This system was first used in Hispaniola to work goldfields and then in Mexico for agricultural labor and, when silver was discovered in the 1540s, for silver mining.

A 1512 Spanish law authorizing the use of encomiendas called for indigenous people to be treated fairly, but in practice the system led to terrible abuses, including overwork, beatings, and sexual violence. Spanish missionaries publicized these abuses, leading to debates in Spain about the nature and proper treatment of indigenous people (see pages 440–441). King Charles I responded to such complaints in 1542 with the New Laws, which set limits on the authority of encomienda holders, including their ability to transmit their privileges to heirs.

The New Laws provoked a revolt in Peru and were little enforced throughout Spanish territories. Nonetheless, the Crown gradually gained control over encomiendas in central areas of the empire and required indigenous people to pay tributes in cash, rather than in labor. To respond to a growing shortage of indigenous workers, royal officials established a new government-run system of forced labor, called *repartimiento* in New Spain and *mita* in Peru. Administrators assigned a certain percentage of the inhabitants of native communities to labor for a set period each year in public works, mining, agriculture, and other tasks. Laborers received modest wages in exchange, which they could use to fulfill tribute obligations. In the seventeenth century, as land became a more important source of wealth than labor, elite settlers purchased *haciendas*, enormous tracts of farmland worked by dependent indigenous laborers and slaves.

Spanish systems for exploiting the labor of indigenous peoples were both a cause of and a response to the disastrous decline in their numbers that began soon after the arrival of Europeans. Some indigenous people died as a direct result of the violence of conquest and the disruption of agriculture and trade caused by warfare. The most important cause of death, however, was infectious disease, a tragic consequence of the Europeans' arrival (see page 433).

Indigenous people's ability to survive infectious disease was reduced by overwork and exhaustion. Moreover, labor obligations diverted local people from tending to their own crops and thus contributed to malnutrition, reduced fertility rates, and starvation. Women were separated from their babies, producing high infant mortality rates. Malnutrition and hunger in turn lowered resistance to disease.

The pattern of devastating disease and population loss established in the Spanish colonies was repeated everywhere Europeans settled. Overall, population declined by as much as 90 percent or more across the Americas after European contact, but with important regional variations. In general, densely populated urban centers were worse hit than rural areas, and tropical, low-lying regions suffered more than cooler, higher-altitude ones. Some scholars have claimed that losses may have been overreported, since many indigenous people fled their communities—or listed themselves as mixed race (and thus immune from forced labor)—to escape Spanish exploitation. By the mid-seventeenth century the worst losses had occurred and a slight recovery began.

Colonial administrators responded to native population decline by forcibly combining dwindling indigenous communities into new settlements and imposing the rigors of the encomienda and the repartimiento. By the end of the sixteenth century the search for fresh sources of labor had given birth to the new tragedy of the Atlantic slave trade (see page 436).

Life in the Colonies

Many factors helped shape life in European colonies, including geographical location, pre-existing indigenous cultures, patterns of European settlement, and the policies and cultural values of the European nations that claimed them as empire. Throughout the New World, colonial settlements were hedged by immense borderlands where European power was weak and Europeans and non-Europeans interacted on a more equal basis.

Women played a crucial role in the emergence of colonial societies. The first explorers formed unions with native women, through coercion or choice, and relied on them as translators and guides and to form alliances with indigenous powers. As settlement developed, the character of each colony was influenced by the presence or absence of European women. Where women and children accompanied men, as in the British colonies and the Spanish mainland colonies, new settlements took on European languages, religion, and ways of life that have endured, with input from local cultures, to this day. Where European women did not accompany men, as on the west coast of Africa and most European outposts in Asia, local populations largely retained their own cultures, to which male Europeans acclimatized themselves. The scarcity of women in all colonies, at least initially, opened up opportunities for those who did arrive, leading one cynic to comment that even "a whore, if handsome, makes a wife for some rich planter."[15]

It was not just the availability of Englishwomen that prevented Englishmen from forming unions with indigenous women. English cultural attitudes drew strict boundaries between "civilized" and "savage," and even settlements of Christianized native peoples were segregated from the English. This was in strong contrast with the situation in New France, where royal officials initially encouraged French traders to form ties with indigenous people, including marrying local women. Assimilation of the native population was seen as one solution to the low levels of immigration from France.

The vast majority of women who crossed the Atlantic were captive Africans, constituting four-fifths of the female newcomers before 1800.[16] Wherever slavery existed, masters profited from their power to engage in sexual relations with enslaved women. One important difference among European colonies was in the status of children born from such unions. In some colonies, mostly those dominated by the Portuguese, Spanish, or French, substantial populations of free people of color descended from the freed children of such unions. In English colonies, masters were less likely to free children they fathered with female slaves.

A Mixed-Race Procession
The Incas used drinking vessels, known as *keros*, for the ritual consumption of maize beer at feasts. This kero from the early colonial period depicts a multiracial procession: an Inca dignitary is preceded by a Spanish trumpet player and an African drummer. This is believed to be one of the earliest visual representations of an African in the Americas.
(British Museum, London, UK/Werner Forman/Universal Images Group/Getty Images)

The mixing of indigenous peoples with Europeans and Africans created whole new populations and ethnicities and complex forms of identity (see Chapter 17). In Spanish America the word *mestizo*—*métis* in French—described people of mixed Native American and European descent. The blanket terms "mulatto" and "people of color" were used for those of mixed African and European origin. With its immense slave-based plantation agriculture system, large indigenous population, and relatively low Portuguese immigration, Brazil developed a particularly complex racial and ethnic mosaic.

The Columbian Exchange

The travel of people and goods between the Old and New Worlds led to an exchange of animals, plants, and diseases, a complex process known as the **Columbian exchange**. As we have seen, the introduction of new diseases to the Americas had devastating consequences. But other results of the exchange brought benefits not only to the Europeans but also to indigenous peoples.

European immigrants to the Americas wanted a familiar diet, so they searched for climatic zones favorable to familiar crops. Everywhere they settled, the Spanish and Portuguese brought and raised wheat with labor provided by the encomienda system. Grapes and olives brought over from Spain did well in parts of Peru and Chile. Europeans also introduced domestic livestock and horses, which allowed for faster travel and easier transport of heavy loads. In turn, Europeans returned home with many food crops that became central elements of their diet, such as potatoes, maize (corn), and tomatoes.

While the exchange of foods was a great benefit to both cultures, the introduction of European pathogens to the New World had a disastrous impact on the native population. In Europe, infectious diseases like smallpox, measles, and influenza—originally

passed on from domestic animals living among the population—killed many people each year. Given the size of the population and the frequency of outbreaks, in most of Europe these diseases were experienced in childhood, and survivors carried immunity or resistance. Over centuries of dealing with these diseases, the European population had had time to adapt. Prior to contact with Europeans, indigenous peoples of the New World suffered from insect-borne diseases and some infectious ones, but their lack of domestic livestock spared them the host of highly infectious diseases known in the Old World. The arrival of Europeans spread these microbes among a completely unprepared population, and they fell victim in vast numbers (see pages 431–432). The wave of catastrophic epidemic disease that swept the Western Hemisphere after 1492 can be seen as an extension of the swath of devastation wreaked by the Black Death in the fourteenth century, first on Asia and then on Europe. The world after Columbus was thus unified by disease as well as by trade and colonization.

Sugar and Slavery

Two crucial and interrelated elements of the Columbian exchange were the transatlantic trade in sugar and slaves. Throughout the Middle Ages slavery was deeply entrenched in the Mediterranean, but it was not based on race; many slaves were European in origin. How, then, did black African slavery enter the European picture and take root in the Americas? In 1453 the Ottoman capture of Constantinople halted the flow of slaves from the eastern Mediterranean to western Europe. Additionally, the successes of the Iberian reconquista drastically diminished the supply of Muslim captives. Cut off from its traditional sources of slaves, Mediterranean Europe turned to sub-Saharan Africa, which had a long history of internal slave trading.

As Portuguese explorers began their voyages along the western coast of Africa, one of the first commodities they sought was slaves. In 1444 the first ship returned to Lisbon with a cargo of enslaved Africans. While the first slaves were simply seized by small raiding parties, Portuguese merchants soon found that it was easier to trade with local leaders, who were accustomed to dealing in slaves captured through warfare with neighboring powers. In 1483 the Portuguese established an alliance with the kingdom of Kongo. The royal family eventually converted to Christianity, and Portuguese merchants intermarried with Kongolese women, creating a permanent Afro-Portuguese community. From 1490 to 1530 Portuguese traders brought hundreds of enslaved Africans to Lisbon each year (Map 14.3), where they eventually constituted 10 percent of the city's population.

In this stage of European expansion, the history of slavery became intertwined with the history of sugar. Originally sugar was an expensive luxury, but population increases and monetary expansion in the fifteenth century led to increasing demand. Native to the South Pacific, sugar was taken in ancient times to India, where farmers learned to preserve cane juice as granules that could be stored and shipped. From

< **MAP 14.3 Seaborne Trading Empires in the Sixteenth and Seventeenth Centuries**
By the mid-seventeenth century trade linked all parts of the world except for Australia. Notice that trade in slaves was not confined to the Atlantic but involved almost all parts of the world.

there, sugar crops traveled to China and the Mediterranean, where islands like Crete and Sicily had the warm and wet climate needed for growing sugarcane. When Genoese and other Italians colonized the Canary Islands and the Portuguese settled on the Madeira Islands, sugar plantations came to the Atlantic.

Sugar was a particularly difficult crop to produce for profit. Seed-stems were planted by hand, thousands to the acre. When mature, the cane had to be harvested and processed rapidly to avoid spoiling. Moreover, sugar has a virtually constant growing season, meaning that there was no fallow period when workers could recuperate from the arduous labor. The invention of roller mills to crush the cane more efficiently meant that yields could be significantly augmented, but only if a sufficient labor force was found to supply the mills. Europeans solved the labor problem by forcing first native islanders and then enslaved Africans to provide the backbreaking work.

The transatlantic slave trade began in 1518 when the Spanish emperor Charles V authorized traders to bring enslaved Africans to the Americas. The Portuguese brought the first slaves to Brazil around 1550; by 1600 four thousand were being imported annually. After its founding in 1621, the Dutch West India Company, with the full support of the United Provinces, transported thousands of Africans to Brazil and the Caribbean, mostly to work on sugar plantations. In the mid-seventeenth century the English got involved. From 1660 to 1698 the Royal African Company held a monopoly over the slave trade from the English crown.

Before 1700, when slavers decided it was better business to improve conditions, some 20 percent of slaves died on the voyage.[17] The most common cause of death was from dysentery induced by poor-quality food and water, crowding, and lack of sanitation. Men were often kept in irons during the passage, while women and girls were considered fair game for sailors. To increase profits, slave traders packed several hundred captives on each ship. One slaver explained that he removed his boots before entering the slave hold because he had to crawl over the slaves' packed bodies.[18] On sugar plantations, death rates from the brutal pace of labor were extremely high, leading to a constant stream of new shipments of slaves from Africa.

In total, scholars estimate that European traders embarked over 12 million enslaved Africans across the Atlantic from 1500 to 1875 (of whom roughly 10.7 million disembarked), with the peak of the trade occurring in the eighteenth century.[19] By comparison, only 2 to 2.5 million Europeans migrated to the New World during the same period. Slaves worked in an infinite variety of occupations: as miners, soldiers, sailors, servants, and artisans and in the production of sugar, cotton, rum, indigo, tobacco, wheat, and corn.

Spanish Silver and Its Economic Effects

The sixteenth century has often been called Spain's golden century, but silver mined in the Americas was the true source of Spain's wealth. In 1545, at an altitude of fifteen thousand feet, the Spanish discovered an extraordinary source of silver at Potosí (poh-toh-SEE) (in present-day Bolivia) in territory conquered from the Inca Empire. The frigid place where nothing grew had been unsettled. A half century later 160,000 people lived there, making it about as populous as the city of London. By 1550 Potosí yielded perhaps 60 percent of all the silver mined in the world. From Potosí and the mines at Zacatecas (za-kuh-TAY-kuhs) and Guanajuato (gwah-nah-HWAH-toh) in Mexico, huge quantities of precious metals poured forth. To protect this treasure from French and English pirates, armed convoys transported it to Spain each year. Between 1503 and 1650, 35 million pounds of silver and over 600,000 pounds of gold entered Seville's port. Spanish predominance, however, proved temporary.

In the sixteenth century Spain experienced a steady population increase, creating a sharp rise in the demand for food and goods. Spanish colonies in the Americas also demanded consumer goods, such as cloth and luxury goods. Since Spain had expelled some of its best farmers and businessmen—the Muslims and Jews—in the fifteenth century, the Spanish economy was suffering and could not meet the new demands. The excess of demand over supply led to widespread inflation. The result was a rise in production costs and a further decline in Spain's productive capacity.

Did the flood of silver bullion from America cause the inflation? Prices rose most steeply before 1565, but bullion imports reached their peak between 1580 and 1620. Thus silver did not cause the initial inflation. It did, however, greatly exacerbate the situation, and, along with the ensuing rise in population, the influx of silver significantly contributed to the upward spiral of prices. Inflation severely strained government budgets. Several times between 1557 and 1647, Spain's King Philip II and his successors wrote off the state debt, thereby undermining confidence in the government and leaving the economy in shambles. After 1600, when the population declined, prices gradually stabilized.

As Philip II paid his armies and foreign debts with silver bullion, Spanish inflation was transmitted to the rest of Europe. Between 1560 and 1600 much

Philip II, ca. 1533 This portrait of Philip II as a young man and crown prince of Spain is by the celebrated artist Titian, court painter to Philip's father, Charles V. After taking the throne, Philip became another great patron of the artist. (Palazzo Pitti, Florence, Italy/Bridgeman Images)

of Europe experienced large price increases. Prices doubled and in some cases quadrupled. Spain suffered most severely, but all European countries were affected. Because money bought less, people who lived on fixed incomes, such as nobles, were badly hurt. Those who owed fixed sums of money, such as the middle class, prospered because in a time of rising prices, debts lessened in value each year. Food costs rose most sharply, and the poor fared worst of all.

In many ways, though, it was not Spain but China that controlled the world trade in silver. The Chinese demanded silver for their products and for the payment of imperial taxes. China was thus the main buyer of world silver, absorbing half the world's production. The silver market drove world trade, with New Spain and Japan being mainstays on the supply side and China dominating the demand side. The world trade in silver is one of the best examples of the new global economy that emerged in this period.

The Birth of the Global Economy

With the Europeans' discovery of the Americas and their exploration of the Pacific, the entire world was linked for the first time in history by seaborne trade. The opening of that trade brought into being three successive commercial empires: the Portuguese, the Spanish, and the Dutch.

The Portuguese were the first worldwide traders. In the sixteenth century they controlled the sea route to India (see Map 14.3). From their fortified bases at Goa on the Arabian Sea and at Malacca on the Malay Peninsula, ships carried goods to the Portuguese settlement at Macao, founded in 1557, in the South China Sea. From Macao Portuguese ships loaded with Chinese silks and porcelains sailed to the Japanese port of Nagasaki and to the Philippine port of Manila, where Chinese goods were exchanged for Spanish silver from New Spain. Throughout Asia the Portuguese traded in slaves—sub-Saharan Africans, Chinese, and Japanese. The Portuguese exported horses from Mesopotamia and copper from Arabia to India; from India they exported hawks and peacocks for the Chinese and Japanese markets. Back to Portugal they brought Asian spices that had been purchased with textiles produced in India and with gold and ivory from East Africa. They also shipped back sugar from their colony in Brazil, produced by enslaved Africans whom they had transported across the Atlantic.

Coming to empire a few decades later than the Portuguese, the Spanish were determined to claim their place in world trade. The Spanish Empire in the New World was basically a land empire, but across the Pacific the Spaniards built a seaborne empire centered at Manila in the Philippines. The city of Manila served as the transpacific bridge between Spanish America and China. In Manila, Spanish traders used silver from American mines to purchase Chinese silk for European markets. The European demand for silk was so huge that in 1597, for example, 12 million pesos of silver, almost the total value of the transatlantic trade, moved from Acapulco in New Spain to Manila (see Map 14.3).

In the final years of the sixteenth century the Dutch challenged the Spanish and Portuguese Empires. During this period the Protestant Dutch were engaged in a long war of independence from their Spanish Catholic overlords. The joining of the Portuguese crown to Spain in 1580 meant that the Dutch had both strategic and commercial reasons to attack Portugal's commercial empire. In 1599 a Dutch fleet returned to Amsterdam carrying 600,000 pounds of pepper and 250,000 pounds of cloves and nutmeg. Those who had invested in the expedition received a 100 percent profit. The voyage led to the establishment in 1602 of the Dutch East India Company, founded with the stated intention of capturing the Asian spice trade from the Portuguese.

In return for assisting Indonesian princes in local squabbles and disputes with the Portuguese, the Dutch won broad commercial concessions. Through agreements, seizures, and outright military aggression, they gained control of the western access to the Indonesian archipelago in the first half of the seventeenth century. Gradually, they acquired political domination over the archipelago itself. The Dutch were willing to use force more ruthlessly than the Portuguese and had superior organizational efficiency. These factors allowed them to expel the Portuguese from Ceylon and other East Indian islands in 1660 and henceforth control the immensely lucrative production and trade of spices. The company also established the colony of Cape Town on the southern tip of Africa as a provisioning point for its Asian fleets.

Not content with challenging the Portuguese in the Indian Ocean, the Dutch also aspired to a role in the Americas. Founded in 1621, during their war with Spain, the Dutch West India Company aggressively sought to open trade with North and South America and capture Spanish territories there. The company captured or destroyed hundreds of Spanish ships, seized the Spanish silver fleet in 1628, and captured portions of Brazil and the Caribbean. The Dutch also successfully interceded in the transatlantic slave trade, establishing a large number of trading stations on the west coast of Africa. Ironically, the nation that was known throughout Europe as a bastion of tolerance and freedom came to be one of the principal operators of the slave trade starting in the 1640s.

Changing Attitudes and Beliefs

Focus Question	How did new encounters shape cultural attitudes and beliefs in Europe and the rest of the world?

The age of overseas expansion heightened Europeans' contacts with the rest of the world. Religion was one of the most important arenas of cultural contact, as European missionaries aimed to spread Christianity in both the New World and East Asia, with mixed results. While Christianity was embraced in parts of the New World, it was met largely with suspicion in China and Japan. However, the East-West contacts did lead to exchanges of influential cultural and scientific ideas.

These contacts also gave birth to new ideas about the inherent superiority or inferiority of different races, sparking vociferous debate about the status of Africans and indigenous peoples of the Americas. The essays of Michel de Montaigne epitomized a new spirit of skepticism and cultural relativism, while the plays of William Shakespeare reflected the efforts of one great writer to come to terms with the cultural complexity of his day.

Religious Conversion

Converting indigenous people to Christianity was one of the most important justifications for European expansion. Jesuit missionaries were active in Japan and China in the sixteenth and seventeenth centuries, until authorities banned their teachings. The first missionaries to the New World accompanied Columbus on his second voyage, and more than 2,500 Franciscans, Dominicans, Jesuits, and other friars crossed the Atlantic in the following century. Later French explorers were also accompanied by missionaries who preached to the Native American tribes with whom the French traded.

Catholic friars were among the first Europeans to seek an understanding of native cultures and languages as part of their effort to render Christianity comprehensible to indigenous people. In Mexico they not only learned the Nahuatl language, but also taught it to non-Nahuatl-speaking groups to create a shared language for Christian teaching. They were also the most vociferous opponents of abuses committed by Spanish settlers.

Religion had been a central element of pre-Columbian societies, and many — if not all — indigenous people were receptive to the new religion that accompanied the victorious Iberians. It is estimated that missionaries had baptized between 4 and 9 million indigenous people in New Spain by the mid-1530s.[20] In addition to spreading Christianity, missionaries taught indigenous peoples European methods of agriculture and instilled loyalty to colonial masters.

Despite the success of initial conversion efforts, authorities became suspicious about the thoroughness of native peoples' conversion and their lingering belief in the old gods. They could not prevent the melding together of Catholic teachings with elements of pagan beliefs and practices. For example, a sixteenth-century apparition of the Virgin Mary in Mexico City, known as the Virgin of Guadalupe, which became a central icon of New World Catholicism, seems to have been based on veneration of the Aztec Mother Earth goddess, Tonantzin.

European Debates About Indigenous Peoples

Iberian exploitation of the native population of the Americas began from the moment of Columbus's arrival in 1492. Denunciations of this abuse by Catholic missionaries, however, quickly followed, inspiring vociferous debates both in Europe and in the colonies about the nature of indigenous peoples and how they should be treated. Bartolomé de Las Casas (1474–1566), a Dominican friar and former encomienda holder, was one of the earliest and most outspoken critics of the brutal treatment inflicted on indigenous peoples. He wrote:

> To these quiet Lambs . . . came the Spaniards like most c(r)uel Tygres, Wolves and Lions, enrag'd with a sharp and tedious hunger; for these forty years past, minding nothing else but the slaughter of these unfortunate wretches, whom with divers kinds of torments neither seen nor heard of before, they have so cruelly and inhumanely butchered, that of three millions of people which Hispaniola itself did contain, there are left remaining alive scarce three hundred persons.[21]

Spanish Atrocities in the New World   The illustrations provided by Theodor de Bry to accompany Bartolomé de Las Casas's *Short Account of the Destruction of the Indies* depict atrocities committed by the Spanish in their conquest and settlement of the Americas. De Bry, a converted Protestant, thereby contributed to the "Black Legend" of Spanish colonization. (Engraving by Theodor de Bry, from a work by Bartolomé de Las Casas, 1598/Photo 12/UIG via Getty Images)

Mounting criticism in Spain led King Charles I to assemble a group of churchmen and lawyers to debate the issue in 1550 in the city of Valladolid. One side, led by Juan Ginés de Sepúlveda, argued that conquest and forcible conversion were both necessary and justified to save indigenous people from the horrors of human sacrifice, cannibalism, and idolatry. He described them as barbarians who belonged to a category of inferior beings identified by the ancient Greek philosopher Aristotle as naturally destined for slavery. Against these arguments, Las Casas and his supporters depicted indigenous people as rational and innocent children, who deserved protection and tutelage from more advanced civilizations. Both sides claimed victory in the debate, but it had little effect on the situation in the Americas.

Eagerly reading denunciations of Spanish abuses by critics like Las Casas, northern Europeans derived the **"Black Legend"** of Spanish colonialism, the notion that the Spanish were uniquely brutal and cruel in their conquest and settlement of the Americas. However, the legend also helped northern European powers, like France and England, overlook their own record of colonial violence and exploitation.

New Ideas About Race

At the beginning of the transatlantic slave trade, most Europeans would have thought of Africans, if they thought of them at all, as savages in their social customs, religious practices, language, and methods of war. They grouped Africans into the despised categories of pagan heathens and Muslim infidels.

As Europeans turned to Africa for new sources of slaves, they drew on beliefs about Africans' supposed primitiveness and barbarity to defend slavery and even argue, like Sepúlveda with regard to indigenous Americans, that enslavement benefited Africans by bringing them the light of Christianity. In 1444 an observer defended the enslavement of the first Africans by Portuguese explorers as necessary for their salvation "because they lived like beasts, without any of the customs of rational creatures, since they did not even know what were bread and wine, nor garments of cloth, nor life in the shelter of a house; and worse still was their ignorance, which deprived them of knowledge of good, and permitted them only a life of brutish idleness."[22]

Over time, the institution of slavery fostered unprecedented ideas about racial inequality. Africans gradually became seen as utterly distinct from and wholly inferior to Europeans. From rather vague assumptions about Africans' non-Christian religious beliefs and general lack of civilization, Europeans developed increasingly rigid ideas of racial superiority and inferiority to safeguard the growing profits gained from plantation slavery. Black skin became equated with slavery itself as Europeans at home and in the colonies convinced themselves that blacks were destined by God to serve them as slaves in perpetuity.

Support for this belief went back to the Greek philosopher Aristotle's argument that some people are naturally destined for slavery and to biblical associations between darkness and sin. A more explicit justification was found in the story of Noah's curse upon the descendants of his disobedient son Ham to be the "servant[s] of servants." Biblical genealogies listing Ham's sons as those who peopled North Africa and Cush (which includes parts of modern Egypt and Sudan) were read to mean that all inhabitants of those regions bore Noah's curse. From the sixteenth century onward, many defenders of slavery cited this story as justification for their actions.

After 1700 the emergence of new methods of observing and describing nature led to the use of science to define race. Although the term originally referred to a nation or an ethnic group, henceforth "race" would be used to describe supposedly biologically distinct groups of people, whose physical differences produced differences in culture, character, and intelligence. Biblical justifications for inequality thereby gave way to supposedly scientific ones (see pages 508–509).

Michel de Montaigne and Cultural Curiosity

Racism was not the only possible reaction to the new worlds emerging in the sixteenth century. Decades of religious fanaticism, bringing civil anarchy and war, led some Catholics and Protestants to doubt that any one faith contained absolute truth. Added to these doubts was the discovery of peoples in the New World who had radically different ways of life. These shocks helped produce ideas of skepticism and cultural relativism. Skepticism is a school of thought founded on doubt that total certainty or definitive knowledge is ever attainable. The skeptic is cautious and critical and suspends judgment. Cultural relativism suggests that one culture is not necessarily superior to another, just different. Both notions found expression in the work of Frenchman Michel de Montaigne (duh mahn-TAYN) (1533–1592).

Montaigne developed a new literary genre, the essay — from the French *essayer*, meaning "to test or try" — to express his ideas. Published in 1580, Montaigne's *Essays* consisted of short reflections drawing on his extensive reading in ancient texts, his experience as a government official, and his own moral judgment. Intending his works to be accessible to ordinary people, Montaigne wrote in French rather than Latin and in an engaging conversational style. His essays were quickly translated into other European languages and became some of the most widely read texts of the early modern period.

Montaigne's essay "Of Cannibals" reveals the impact of overseas discoveries on one thoughtful European. In contrast to the prevailing views of his day, he rejected the notion that one culture is superior to another. Speaking of native Brazilians, he wrote:

> I find that there is nothing barbarous and savage in this nation [Brazil], . . . except, that everyone gives the title of barbarism to everything that is not according to his usage; as, indeed, we have no other criterion of truth and reason, than the example and pattern of the opinions and customs of the place wherein we live. . . . They are savages in the same way that we say fruits are wild, which nature produces of herself and by her ordinary course; whereas, in truth, we ought rather to call those wild whose natures we have changed by our artifice and diverted from the common order.[23]

In his own time, few would have agreed with Montaigne's challenge to ideas of European superiority or his even more radical questioning of the superiority of humans over animals. Nevertheless, his popular essays contributed to a basic shift in attitudes. "Wonder," he said, "is the foundation of all philosophy, research is the means of all learning, and ignorance is the end."[24] Montaigne thus inaugurated an era of doubt.

William Shakespeare and His Influence

In addition to the essay as a literary genre, the period fostered remarkable creativity in other branches of literature. England — especially in the latter part of Queen Elizabeth I's reign and in the first years of her successor, James I (r. 1603–1625) — witnessed remarkable literary expression. The undisputed master of the period was the dramatist William Shakespeare, whose genius lay in the originality of his characterizations, the diversity of his plots, his understanding of human psychology, and his unsurpassed gift for language. Born in 1564 to a successful glove manufacturer in Stratford-upon-Avon, Shakespeare grew into a Renaissance man with a deep appreciation of classical culture, individualism, and humanism. Although he wrote sparkling comedies and stirring historical plays, his greatest masterpieces were his later tragedies, including *Hamlet, Othello*, and *Macbeth*, which explore an enormous range of human problems and are open to an almost infinite variety of interpretations.

Like Montaigne's essays, Shakespeare's work reveals the impact of the new discoveries and contacts of his day. The title character of *Othello* is described as a "Moor of Venice." In Shakespeare's day, the term "Moor" referred to Muslims of North African origin, including those who had migrated to the Iberian Peninsula. It could also be applied, though, to natives of the Iberian Peninsula who converted to Islam or to non-Muslim Berbers in North Africa. To complicate things even more, references in the play to Othello as "black" in skin color have led many to believe that Shakespeare intended him to be a sub-Saharan African. This confusion in the play aptly reflects the uncertainty in Shakespeare's own time about racial and religious classifications. In contrast to the prevailing view of Moors as inferior, Shakespeare presents Othello as a complex human figure, whose only crime is to have "loved [his wife] not wisely, but too well."

Shakespeare's last play, *The Tempest*, also highlights the issue of race and race relations. The plot involves the stranding on an island of sorcerer Prospero and his daughter Miranda. There Prospero finds and raises Caliban, a native of the island, whom he instructs in his own language and religion. After Caliban's attempted rape of Miranda, Prospero enslaves him, earning the hatred of his erstwhile pupil. Modern scholars often note the echoes between this play and the realities of imperial conquest and settlement in Shakespeare's day. It is no accident, they argue, that the poet portrayed Caliban as a monstrous dark-skinned island native who was best suited for slavery. Shakespeare himself borrows words from Montaigne's essay "Of Cannibals," suggesting that he may have intended to criticize, rather than endorse, racial intolerance. Shakespeare's work shows us one of the finest minds of the age grasping to come to terms with the racial and religious complexities around him.

NOTES

1. Marco Polo, *The Book of Ser Marco Polo, the Venetian: Concerning the Kingdoms and Marvels of the East*, vol. 2, trans. and ed. Colonel Sir Henry Yule (London: John Murray, 1903), pp. 185–186.
2. Thomas Benjamin, *The Atlantic World: Europeans, Africans, Indians and Their Shared History, 1400–1900* (Cambridge: Cambridge University Press, 2009), p. 56.
3. Quoted in J. Devisse, "Africa in Inter-Continental Relations," in *General History of Africa*, vol. 4, *Africa from the Twelfth to the Sixteenth Century*, ed. D. T. Niane (Berkeley, Calif.: Heinemann Educational Books, 1984), p. 664.
4. Geoffrey Atkinson, *Les nouveaux horizons de la Renaissance française* (Paris: Droz, 1935), pp. 10–12.
5. G. V. Scammell, *The World Encompassed: The First European Maritime Empires, c. 800–1650* (Berkeley: University of California Press, 1981), p. 101.
6. Quoted in C. M. Cipolla, *Guns, Sails, and Empires: Technological Innovation and the Early Phases of European Expansion, 1400–1700* (New York: Minerva Press, 1965), p. 132.
7. Quoted in F. H. Littell, *The Macmillan Atlas: History of Christianity* (New York: Macmillan, 1976), p. 75.
8. Pablo E. Pérez-Mallaína, *Spain's Men of the Sea: Daily Life on the Indies Fleet in the Sixteenth Century* (Baltimore: Johns Hopkins University Press, 1998), p. 133.
9. Ibid., p. 19.
10. John Law, "On the Methods of Long Distance Control: Vessels, Navigation, and the Portuguese Route to India," in *Power, Action and Belief: A New Sociology of Knowledge?* ed. John Law, Sociological Review Monograph 32 (London: Routledge & Kegan Paul, 1986), pp. 234–263.

11. Quoted in F. Maddison, "Tradition and Innovation: Columbus' First Voyage and Portuguese Navigation in the Fifteenth Century," in *Circa 1492: Art in the Age of Exploration*, ed. J. A. Levenson (Washington, D.C.: National Gallery of Art, 1991), p. 69.

12. Quoted in R. L. Kagan, "The Spain of Ferdinand and Isabella," in *Circa 1492: Art in the Age of Exploration*, ed. J. A. Levenson (Washington, D.C.: National Gallery of Art, 1991), p. 60.

13. Peter Hulme, *Colonial Encounters: Europe and the Native Caribbean, 1492–1797* (London: Methuen, 1986), pp. 22–31.

14. Benjamin, *The Atlantic World*, p. 141.

15. Cited in Geoffrey Vaughn Scammell, *The First Imperial Age: European Overseas Expansion, c. 1400–1715* (London: Routledge, 2002), p. 62.

16. Ibid., p. 432.

17. Herbert S. Klein, "Profits and the Causes of Mortality," in *The Atlantic Slave Trade*, ed. David Northrup (Lexington, Mass.: D. C. Heath and Co., 1994), p. 116.

18. Malcolm Cowley and Daniel P. Mannix, "The Middle Passage," in *The Atlantic Slave Trade*, ed. David Northrup (Lexington, Mass.: D. C. Heath and Co., 1994), p. 101.

19. Voyages: The Trans-Atlantic Slave Trade Database, http://www.slavevoyages.org/tast/assessment/estimates.

20. David Carrasco, *The Oxford Encyclopedia of Mesoamerican Cultures* (Oxford: Oxford University Press, 2001), p. 208.

21. Quoted in C. Gibson, ed., *The Black Legend: Anti-Spanish Attitudes in the Old World and the New* (New York: Knopf, 1971), pp. 74–75.

22. Quoted in James H. Sweet, "The Iberian Roots of American Racist Thought," *The William and Mary Quarterly* 54 (1997): 155.

23. C. Cotton, trans., *The Essays of Michel de Montaigne* (New York: A. L. Burt, 1893), pp. 207, 210.

24. Ibid., p. 523.

LOOKING BACK LOOKING AHEAD

In 1517 Martin Luther issued his "Ninety-five Theses," launching the Protestant Reformation; just five years later, Ferdinand Magellan's expedition sailed around the globe, shattering European notions of terrestrial geography. Within a few short years, old medieval certainties about Heaven and earth began to collapse. In the ensuing decades, Europeans struggled to come to terms with religious difference at home and the multitudes of new peoples and places they encountered abroad. While some Europeans were fascinated and inspired by this new diversity, too often the result was violence. Europeans endured decades of civil war between Protestants and Catholics, and indigenous peoples suffered massive population losses as a result of European warfare, disease, and exploitation. Tragically, both Catholic and Protestant religious leaders condoned the African slave trade that brought suffering and death to millions of people.

Even as the voyages of discovery coincided with the fragmentation of European culture, they also played a role in longer-term processes of state centralization and consolidation. The new monarchies of the Renaissance produced stronger and wealthier governments capable of financing the huge expenses of exploration and colonization. Competition to gain overseas colonies became an integral part of European politics. Spain's investment in conquest proved spectacularly profitable and yet, as we will see in Chapter 15, the ultimate result was a weakening of its power. Over time the Netherlands, England, and France also reaped tremendous profits from colonial trade, which helped them build modernized, centralized states. The path from medieval Christendom to modern nation-states led through religious warfare and global encounter.

MAKE CONNECTIONS

Think about the larger developments and continuities within and across chapters.

1. Michel de Montaigne argued that people's assessments of what was "barbaric" merely drew on their own habits and customs; based on the earlier sections of this chapter, how widespread was this openness to cultural difference? Was he alone or did others share this view?

2. To what extent did the European voyages of expansion and conquest inaugurate an era of global history? Is it correct to date the beginning of "globalization" from the late fifteenth century? Why or why not?

Chapter Review

IDENTIFY KEY TERMS

Identify and explain the significance of each item below.

conquistador (p. 417)

caravel (p. 418)

Ptolemy's *Geography* (p. 418)

Treaty of Tordesillas (p. 423)

Aztec Empire (p. 425)

Inca Empire (p. 425)

viceroyalties (p. 429)

encomienda system (p. 431)

Columbian exchange (p. 433)

"Black Legend" (p. 441)

REVIEW THE MAIN IDEAS

Answer the focus questions from each section of the chapter.

1. What was the Afroeurasian trading world prior to the era of European exploration? (p. 411)

2. How and why did Europeans undertake ambitious voyages of expansion? (p. 416)

3. How did European powers acquire colonies in the Americas, and how were they governed? (p. 424)

4. How was the era of global contact shaped by new forms of exploitation, commercial exchange, and forced migration? (p. 430)

5. How did new encounters shape cultural attitudes and beliefs in Europe and the rest of the world? (p. 439)

CHRONOLOGY	
1271–1295	Marco Polo travels to China
1443	Portuguese establish first African trading post at Arguin
1492	Columbus lands in the Americas
1511	Portuguese capture Malacca from Muslims
1518	Spanish king authorizes slave trade to New World colonies
1519–1522	Magellan's expedition circumnavigates the world
1521	Cortés conquers the Mexica Empire
1533	Pizarro conquers the Inca Empire
1602	Dutch East India Company established

Peasants Working the Land   Working the land was harsh toil for seventeenth-century peasants, but strong family and community bonds gave life meaning and made survival possible. The rich and colorful clothing of the peasants shown here reflects an idealized vision of the peasants' material circumstances. (*The Month of March*, by the Studio of Pieter de Witte [ca. 1548–1628], [oil on canvas], undated/© Sotheby's/akg-images)

like a king ruled his domains. Religious and secular law commanded a man's wife, children, servants, and apprentices to defer to his will. Fathers did not possess the power of life and death, like Roman patriarchs, but they were entitled to use physical violence, imprisonment, and other forceful measures to impose their authority. These powers were balanced by expectations that a good father would provide and care for his dependents.

In the seventeenth century most Europeans lived in the countryside. The hub of the rural world was the small peasant village centered on a church and a manor. Life was in many ways circumscribed by the village, although we should not underestimate the mobility induced by war, food shortage, and the desire to seek one's fortune or embark on religious pilgrimage.

In western Europe, a small number of peasants in each village owned enough land to feed themselves and had the livestock and plows necessary to work their land. These independent farmers were leaders of the peasant village. They employed the landless poor, rented out livestock and tools, and served as agents for the noble lord. Below them were small landowners and tenant farmers who did not have enough land to be self-sufficient. These families sold their best produce on the market to earn cash for taxes, rent, and food. At the bottom were villagers who worked as dependent laborers and servants. In eastern Europe, the vast majority of peasants toiled as serfs for noble landowners and did not own land in their own right (see page 465).

Rich or poor, east or west, bread was the primary element of the diet. The richest ate a white loaf, leaving brown bread to those who could not afford better. Peasants paid stiff fees to the local miller for grinding grain into flour and sometimes to the lord for the right to bake bread in his oven. Bread was most often accompanied by a soup made of roots, herbs, beans, and perhaps a small piece of salt pork. An important annual festival in many villages was the killing of the family pig. The whole family gathered to help, sharing a rare abundance of meat with neighbors and carefully salting the extra and putting down the lard. In some areas, menstruating women were careful to stay away from the kitchen because of superstitious fears that they would cause the lard to spoil.

Famine and Economic Crisis

European rural society lived on the edge of subsistence. Because of the crude technology and low crop yield, peasants were constantly threatened by scarcity and famine. In the seventeenth century a period of colder and wetter climate throughout Europe, dubbed the "little ice age" by historians, meant a shorter farming season with lower yields. A bad harvest created food shortages; a series of bad harvests could lead to famine. Recurrent famines significantly reduced the population of early modern Europe. Most people did not die of outright starvation but perished through the spread of diseases like smallpox and typhoid, which were facilitated by malnutrition and exhaustion. Outbreaks of bubonic plague continued in Europe until the 1720s.

The Estates of Normandy, a provincial assembly, reported on the dire conditions in northern France during an outbreak of plague:

> Of the 450 sick persons whom the inhabitants were unable to relieve, 200 were turned out, and these we saw die one by one as they lay on the roadside. A large number still remain, and to each of them it is only possible to dole out the least scrap of bread. We only give bread to those who would otherwise die. The staple dish here consists of mice, which the inhabitants hunt, so desperate are they from hunger. They devour roots which the animals cannot eat; one can, in fact, not put into words the things one sees. . . . We certify to having ourselves seen herds, not of cattle, but of men and women, wandering about the fields between Rheims and Rhétel, turning up the earth like pigs to find a few roots; and as they can only find rotten ones, and not half enough of them, they become so weak that they have not strength left to seek food.[1]

Industry also suffered. The output of woolen textiles, one of the most important European manufactures, declined sharply in the first half of the seventeenth century. Food prices were high, wages stagnated, and unemployment soared. This economic crisis was not universal: it struck various regions at different times and to different degrees. In the middle decades of the century, for example, Spain, France, Germany, and England all experienced great economic difficulties, but these years were the "golden age" of the Netherlands.

The urban poor and peasants were the hardest hit. When the price of bread rose beyond their capacity to pay, they frequently expressed their anger by rioting. In towns they invaded bakers' shops to seize bread and resell it at a "just price." In rural areas they attacked convoys taking grain to the cities. Women often led these actions, since their role as mothers gave them some impunity in authorities' eyes. Historians have used the term "moral economy" for this vision of a world in which community needs predominate over competition and profit.

The Thirty Years' War

Harsh economic conditions in the seventeenth century were greatly exacerbated by the decades-long conflict known as the Thirty Years' War (1618–1648). The Holy Roman Empire was a confederation of hundreds of principalities, independent cities, duchies, and other polities loosely united under an elected emperor. The uneasy truce between Catholics and Protestants created by the Peace of Augsburg in 1555 deteriorated as the faiths of various areas shifted. Lutheran princes felt compelled to form the Protestant Union (1608), and Catholics retaliated with the Catholic League (1609). Each alliance was determined that the other should make no religious or territorial advance. Dynastic interests were also involved; the Spanish Habsburgs strongly supported the goals of their Austrian relatives: the unity of the empire and the preservation of Catholicism within it.

The war is traditionally divided into four phases. The first, or Bohemian, phase (1618–1625) was characterized by civil war in Bohemia between the Catholic League and the Protestant Union. In 1620 Catholic forces defeated Protestants at the Battle of the White Mountain. The second, or Danish, phase of the war (1625–1629)—so called because of the leadership of the Protestant king Christian IV of Denmark (r. 1588–1648)—witnessed additional Catholic victories. The Catholic imperial army led by Albert of Wallenstein swept through Silesia, north to the Baltic, and east into Pomerania, scoring smashing victories. Under Charles I, England briefly and unsuccessfully intervened in this phase of the conflict by entering alliances against France and Spain. Habsburg power peaked in 1629. The emperor issued the Edict of Restitution, whereby all Catholic properties lost to Protestantism since 1552 were restored, and only Catholics and Lutherans were allowed to practice their faiths.

The third, or Swedish, phase of the war (1630–1635) began with the arrival in Germany of the Swedish king Gustavus Adolphus (r. 1594–1632) and his army. The ablest administrator of his day and a devout Lutheran, he intervened to support the empire's Protestants. The French chief minister, Cardinal Richelieu, subsidized the Swedes, hoping to weaken Habsburg power in Europe. Gustavus Adolphus won two important battles but was fatally wounded in combat. The final, or French, phase of the war (1635–1648) was prompted by Richelieu's concern that the Habsburgs would rebound after the death of Gustavus Adolphus. Richelieu declared war on

Spain and sent military as well as financial assistance. Finally, in October 1648 peace was achieved.

The 1648 **Peace of Westphalia** that ended the Thirty Years' War marked a turning point in European history. For the most part, conflicts fought over religious faith receded. The treaties recognized the independent authority of more than three hundred German princes (Map 15.1), reconfirming the emperor's severely limited authority. The Augsburg agreement of 1555 became permanent, adding Calvinism to Catholicism and Lutheranism as legally permissible creeds. The north German states remained Protestant, the south German states Catholic.

The Thirty Years' War was the most destructive event for the central European economy and society prior to the world wars of the twentieth century. Perhaps one-third of urban residents and two-fifths of the rural population died, leaving entire areas depopulated. Trade in southern German cities, such as Augsburg, was virtually destroyed. Agricultural areas suffered catastrophically. Many small farmers lost their land, allowing nobles to enlarge their estates and consolidate their control.[2]

Achievements in State-Building

In the context of warfare, economic crisis, and demographic decline, seventeenth-century monarchs took urgent measures to restore order and rebuild their states. Traditionally, historians have distinguished between the absolutist governments of France, Spain, central Europe, and Russia and the constitutionalist governments of England and the Dutch Republic. Whereas absolutist monarchs gathered all power under their personal control, English and Dutch rulers were obliged to respect laws passed by representative institutions. More recently, historians have emphasized commonalities among these powers. Despite their political differences, all these states shared common projects of protecting and expanding their frontiers, raising new taxes, consolidating central control, and competing for the new colonies opening up in the New and Old Worlds. In so doing, they followed a broad pattern of state-building and consolidation of power found across Eurasia in this period.

Rulers encountered formidable obstacles in achieving these goals. Without paved roads, telephones, or other modern technology, it took weeks to convey orders from the central government to the provinces and even longer to distant colonies. Rulers also suffered from lack of reliable information about their realms, making it impossible to police and tax the population effectively. Local power structures presented another serious obstacle. Nobles, the church, provincial and national assemblies, town councils, guilds, and other bodies held legal privileges, which could not easily be rescinded. Many kingdoms were composed of groups of people of different ethnicities who spoke a language different from that of the ruling dynasty, which further diminished their willingness to obey.

Nonetheless, over the course of the seventeenth century both absolutist and constitutional governments achieved new levels of power and national unity. They did so by transforming emergency measures of wartime into permanent structures of government and by subduing privileged groups through the use of force and through economic and social incentives. Increased state authority may be seen in four areas in

Legend:
- Austrian Habsburg lands
- Spanish Habsburg lands
- Other German states
- Swedish lands by 1648
- Ottoman Empire and tributary states
- Boundary of the Holy Roman Empire

particular: greater taxation, growth in armed forces, larger and more efficient bureau-cracies, and territorial expansion both within Europe and overseas.

Over time, centralized power added up to something close to sovereignty. A state may be termed sovereign when it possesses a monopoly over the instruments of justice and the use of force within clearly defined boundaries. In a sovereign state, no system of courts, such as church tribunals, competes with state courts in the dispensation of justice; and private armies, such as those of feudal lords, present no threat to central authority. While seventeenth-century states did not acquire total sovereignty, they made important strides toward that goal.

Warfare and the Growth of Army Size

The driving force of seventeenth-century state-building was warfare. In medieval times, feudal lords had raised armies only for particular wars or campaigns; now monarchs began to recruit their own forces and maintain permanent standing armies. Instead of serving their own interests, army officers were required to be loyal and obedient to state officials. New techniques for training and deploying soldiers meant a rise in the professional standards of the army.

Along with professionalization came an explosive growth in army size. The French took the lead, with the army growing from roughly 125,000 men in the Thirty Years' War to 340,000 at the end of the seventeenth century.[3] Changes in the style of armies encouraged this growth. Mustering a royal army took longer than simply hiring a mer-cenary band, giving enemies time to form coalitions. For example, the large coalitions Louis XIV confronted (see pages 461–463) required him to fight on multiple fronts with huge armies. In turn, the relative size and wealth of France among European nations allowed Louis to field enormous armies and thereby to pursue the ambitious foreign policies that caused his alarmed neighbors to form coalitions against him.

Noble values of glory and honor outshone concerns for safety or material benefit. Because they personally led their men in battle, noble officers experienced high death rates on the battlefield. Nobles also fell into debt because they had to purchase their positions in the army and the units they commanded, which meant that they were obliged to assume many of the costs involved in creating and maintaining their units. It was not until the 1760s that the French government assumed the full cost of equip-ping troops.

Other European powers were quick to follow the French example. The rise of absolutism in central and eastern Europe was thus accompanied by a vast expansion in the size of armies. Great Britain followed a similar, albeit distinctive pattern. Instead of building a land army, the island nation focused on naval forces and eventually built the largest navy in the world.

< MAP 15.1 Europe After the Thirty Years' War

This map shows the political division of Europe after the Treaty of Westphalia (1648) ended the war. France emerged as the strongest power in Europe at the end of the Thirty Years' War. Based on this map, what challenges did the French state still face in dominating Europe after 1648? How does the map represent Swedish gains and Spanish losses in the Treaty of Westphalia?

Popular Political Action

As governments continuously raised taxes to meet the costs of war, neighborhood riots over the cost of bread turned into armed uprisings. Popular revolts were extremely common in England, France, Spain, Portugal, and Italy during the Thirty Years' War. In 1640 Philip IV of Spain faced revolt in Catalonia, the economic center of his realm. At the same time he struggled to put down uprisings in Portugal and in the northern provinces of the Netherlands. In 1647 the city of Palermo, in Spanish-occupied Sicily, exploded in protest over food shortages caused by a series of bad harvests. Fearing public unrest, the city government subsidized the price of bread, attracting even more starving peasants from the countryside. When Madrid ordered an end to subsidies, municipal leaders decided to lighten the loaf rather than raise prices. Not fooled by this change, local women led a bread riot, shouting "Long live the king and down with the taxes and the bad government!" Insurgency spread to the rest of the island and eventually to Naples on the mainland. Apart from affordable food, rebels demanded the suppression of extraordinary taxes and participation in municipal government. Some dreamed of a republic that would abolish noble tax exemptions. Despite initial successes, the revolt lacked unity and strong leadership and could not withstand the forces of the state.

In France urban uprisings became a frequent aspect of the social and political landscape. Beginning in 1630 and continuing intermittently through the early 1700s, major insurrections occurred at Dijon, Bordeaux (bor-DOH), Montpellier, Lyons, and Amiens. All were characterized by deep popular anger and violence directed at outside officials sent to collect taxes. These officials were sometimes seized, beaten, and hacked to death. For example, in 1673 Louis XIV's imposition of new taxes on legal transactions, tobacco, and pewter ware provoked an uprising in Bordeaux.

Municipal and royal authorities often struggled to overcome popular revolt. They feared that stern repressive measures, such as sending in troops to fire on crowds, would create martyrs and further inflame the situation, while full-scale occupation of a city would be very expensive and detract from military efforts elsewhere. The limitations of royal authority gave some leverage to rebels. To quell riots, royal edicts were sometimes suspended, prisoners released, and discussions initiated.

By the beginning of the eighteenth century this leverage had largely disappeared. Municipal governments were better integrated into the national structure, and local authorities had prompt military support from the central government. People who publicly opposed royal policies and taxes received swift and severe punishment.

Absolutism in France and Spain

Focus Question	What factors led to the rise of the French absolutist state under Louis XIV, and why did absolutist Spain experience decline in the same period?

In the Middle Ages jurists held that as a consequence of monarchs' coronation and anointment with sacred oil, they ruled "by the grace of God." Law was given by God; kings "found" the law and acknowledged that they must respect and obey it. Kings in absolutist states amplified these claims, asserting that they were responsible to God alone. They claimed exclusive power to make and enforce laws, denying any other institution or group the authority to check their power. In France the founder of the Bourbon monarchy, Henry IV, established foundations upon which his successors Louis XIII and Louis XIV built a stronger, more centralized French state. Louis XIV is often seen as the epitome of an "absolute" monarch, with his endless wars, increased taxes and economic regulation, and glorious palace at Versailles. In truth, his success relied on collaboration with nobles, and thus his example illustrates both the achievements and the compromises of absolutist rule.

As French power rose in the seventeenth century, the glory of Spain faded. Once the fabulous revenue from American silver declined, Spain's economic stagnation could no longer be disguised, and the country faltered under weak leadership.

The Foundations of French Absolutism

At the beginning of the seventeenth century France's position appeared extremely weak. Struggling to recover from decades of religious civil war, France posed little threat to Spain's predominance in Europe. Yet by the end of the century the countries' positions were reversed.

Henry IV (r. 1589–1610) inaugurated a remarkable recovery by defusing religious tensions and rebuilding France's economy. He issued the Edict of Nantes, allowing Huguenots (French Protestants) the right to worship in 150 traditionally Protestant towns throughout France. He built new roads and canals to repair the ravages of years of civil war and raised revenue by selling royal offices instead of charging high taxes. Despite his efforts at peace, Henry was murdered in 1610 by a Catholic zealot.

Cardinal Richelieu (1585–1642) became first minister of the French crown on behalf of Henry's young son, Louis XIII (r. 1610–1643). Richelieu's domestic policies were designed to strengthen royal control. He acted to repress Protestantism, which he viewed as a divisive force in the realm. He also extended the use of intendants, commissioners for each of France's thirty-two districts who were appointed directly by the monarch, to whom they were solely responsible. These officials recruited men for the army, supervised tax collection, presided over the administration of local law, checked up on the local nobility, and regulated economic activities in their districts. As the intendants' power increased under Richelieu, so did the power of the centralized French state.

Richelieu's main foreign policy goal was to destroy the Habsburgs' grip on territories that surrounded France. Consequently, Richelieu supported Habsburg enemies, including Protestants during the Thirty Years' War (see page 452). For the French cardinal, interests of state outweighed religious considerations.

Cardinal Jules Mazarin (1602–1661) succeeded Richelieu as chief minister for the next child-king, the four-year-old Louis XIV, who inherited the throne from his father in 1643. Along with the regent, Queen Mother Anne of Austria, Mazarin continued Richelieu's centralizing policies. His struggle to increase royal revenues to meet the costs of war led to the uprisings of 1648–1653 known as the **Fronde**. In Paris, magistrates of the Parlement of Paris, the nation's most important law court, were outraged by the Crown's autocratic measures. These so-called robe nobles (named for the robes they wore in court) encouraged violent protest by the common people. As rebellion spread outside Paris and to the sword nobles (the traditional warrior nobility), civil order broke down completely, and young Louis XIV had to flee Paris for his safety.

Much of the rebellion died away, however, when Louis XIV was declared king in his own right in 1651, ending the regency of his mother Anne of Austria. (French law prohibited a woman from inheriting the throne, so periods when a queen mother acted as regent for a child-king were always vulnerable moments.) The French people were desperate for peace and stability after the disorders of the Fronde and were willing to accept a strong monarch who could reimpose order. Louis pledged to do just that when he assumed personal rule of his realm at Mazarin's death in 1661.

Louis XIV and Absolutism

In the reign of Louis XIV (r. 1643–1715), the longest in European history, the French monarchy reached the peak of absolutist development. Louis believed in the doctrine of the divine right of kings: God had established kings as his rulers on earth, and they were answerable ultimately to him alone. To symbolize his central role in the divine order, when he was fifteen years old Louis danced at a court ballet dressed as the sun, thereby acquiring the title "Sun King." In addition to parading his power before the

court, Louis worked very hard at the business of governing. He ruled his realm through several councils of state and insisted on taking a personal role in many of their decisions. He selected councilors from the recently ennobled or the upper middle class and offered this explanation: "[T]he public should know, from the rank of those whom I chose to serve me, that I had no intention of sharing power with them."[4] Despite increasing financial problems, Louis never called a meeting of the Estates General, thereby depriving nobles of united expression

Hyacinthe Rigaud, Portrait of Louis XIV, 1701. This was one of Louis XIV's favorite portraits of himself. He liked it so much that he had many copies of the portrait made; his successors had their own portraits painted in the same posture with the same clothing and accoutrements. (Musée du Louvre, Paris, France/Bridgeman Images) or action. Nor did Louis have a first minister. In this way he avoided the inordinate power of a Richelieu.

Although personally tolerant, Louis hated division within the realm and insisted that religious unity was essential to his royal dignity and to the security of the state. He thus pursued the policy of Protestant repression launched by Richelieu. In 1685 Louis revoked the Edict of Nantes. The new law ordered the Catholic baptism of Huguenots (French Calvinists), the destruction of Huguenot churches, the closing of schools, and the exile of Huguenot pastors who refused to renounce their faith. Around two hundred thousand Protestants, including some of the king's most highly skilled artisans, fled into exile.

Despite his claims to absolute authority, multiple constraints existed on Louis's power. As a representative of divine power, he was obliged to rule in a manner consistent with virtue and benevolence. He had to uphold the laws issued by his royal predecessors. Moreover, he also relied on the collaboration of nobles, who maintained tremendous prestige and authority in their ancestral lands. Without their cooperation, it would have been impossible to extend his power throughout France or wage his many foreign wars. Louis's efforts to elicit noble cooperation can be witnessed in the court life he created at his spectacular palace at Versailles.

Life at Versailles

Through most of the seventeenth century the French court had no fixed home, following the monarch to his numerous palaces and country residences. In 1682 Louis moved his court and government to the newly renovated palace at Versailles, a former hunting lodge. The palace quickly became the center of political, social, and cultural life. The king required all great nobles to spend at least part of the year in attendance on him there, so he could keep an eye on their activities. Since he controlled the distribution of state power and wealth, nobles had no choice but to obey and compete with each other for his favor at Versailles.

The glorious palace, with its sumptuous interiors and extensive formal gardens, was a mirror to the world of French glory, soon copied by would-be absolutist monarchs across Europe. The reality of daily life in the palace was less glamorous. Versailles served as government offices for royal bureaucrats, as living quarters for the royal family and nobles, and as a place of work for hundreds of domestic servants. It was also open to the public at certain hours of the day. As a result, it was crowded with three thousand to ten thousand people every day. Even high nobles had to put up with cramped living space, and many visitors complained of the noise, smell, and crowds.

Louis further revolutionized court life by establishing an elaborate set of etiquette rituals to mark every moment of his day, from waking up and dressing in the morning to removing his clothing and retiring at night. Courtiers vied for the honor of participating in these ceremonies, with the highest in rank claiming the privilege of handing the king his shirt. Endless squabbles broke out over what type of chair one could sit on at court and the order in which great nobles entered and were seated in the chapel for Mass.

These rituals may seem absurd, but they were far from trivial. The king controlled immense resources and privileges; access to him meant favored treatment for government offices, military and religious posts, state pensions, honorary titles, and a host of other benefits. Courtiers sought these rewards for themselves and their family members and followers. A system of patronage—in which a higher-ranked individual protected a lower-ranked one in return for loyalty and services—flowed from the court to the provinces. Through this mechanism Louis gained cooperation from powerful nobles.

Although they could not hold public offices or posts, women played a central role in the patronage system. At court the king's wife, mistresses, and other female relatives recommended individuals for honors, advocated policy decisions, and brokered alliances between factions. Noblewomen played a similar role, bringing their family connections to marriage to form powerful social networks. Onlookers sometimes resented the influence of powerful women at court. The duke of Saint-Simon said of Madame de Maintenon, Louis XIV's mistress and secret second wife, "Many people have been ruined by her, without having been able to discover the author of the ruin, search as they might."

Louis XIV was also an enthusiastic patron of the arts, commissioning many sculptures and paintings for Versailles as well as performances of dance and music. Scholars characterize the art and literature of the age of Louis XIV as French classicism. By this they mean that the artists and writers of the late seventeenth century imitated the subject matter and style of classical antiquity, that their work resembled that of Renaissance Italy, and that French art possessed the classical qualities of discipline, balance, and restraint. Louis XIV also loved the stage, and in the plays of Molière and Racine his court witnessed the finest achievements in the history of French theater. In this period aristocratic ladies wrote many genres of literature and held salons in their Parisian mansions where they engaged in witty and cultured discussions of poetry, art, theater, and the latest worldly events. Their refined conversational style led Molière and other observers to mock them as "*précieuses*" (PREH-see-ooz; literally "precious"), or affected and pretentious. Despite this mockery, the précieuses represented an important cultural force ruled by elite women.

With Versailles as the center of European politics, French culture grew in international prestige. French became the language of polite society and international diplomacy, gradually replacing Latin as the language of scholarship and learning. Royal courts across Europe spoke French, and the great aristocrats of Russia, Sweden, Germany, and elsewhere were often more fluent in French than in the tongues of their homelands. France inspired a cosmopolitan European culture in the late seventeenth century that looked to Versailles as its center.

The French Economic Policy of Mercantilism

France's ability to build armies and fight wars depended on a strong economy. Fortunately for Louis, his controller general, Jean-Baptiste Colbert (1619–1683), proved to be a financial genius. Colbert's central principle was that the wealth and the economy of France should serve the state. To this end, from 1665 to his death in 1683, Colbert rigorously applied mercantilist policies to France.

Mercantilism is a collection of governmental policies for the regulation of economic activities by and for the state. It derives from the idea that a nation's international power is based on its wealth, specifically its supply of gold and silver. To accumulate wealth, a country always had to sell more goods abroad than it bought. To decrease

French purchases of goods from outside the country, Colbert insisted that French industry should produce everything needed by the French people.

To increase exports, Colbert supported old industries and created new ones, focusing especially on textiles, which were the most important sector of manufacturing. Colbert enacted new production regulations, created guilds to boost quality standards, and encouraged foreign craftsmen to immigrate to France. To encourage the purchase of French goods, he abolished many domestic tariffs and raised tariffs on foreign products. In 1664 Colbert founded the Company of the East Indies with (unfulfilled) hopes of competing with the Dutch for Asian trade.

Colbert also hoped to make Canada — rich in untapped minerals and some of the best agricultural land in the world — part of a vast French empire. He sent four thousand colonists to Quebec, whose capital had been founded in 1608 under Henry IV. Subsequently, the Jesuit Jacques Marquette and the merchant Louis Joliet sailed down the Mississippi River, which they named Colbert in honor of their sponsor (the name soon reverted to the original Native American one). Marquette and Joliet claimed possession of the land on both sides of the river as far south as present-day Arkansas. In 1684 French explorers continued down the Mississippi to its mouth and claimed vast territories for Louis XIV. The area was called, naturally, "Louisiana."

During Colbert's tenure as controller general, Louis was able to pursue his goals without massive tax increases and without creating a stream of new offices. The constant pressure of warfare after Colbert's death, however, undid many of his economic achievements.

Louis XIV's Wars

Louis XIV wrote that "the character of a conqueror is regarded as the noblest and highest of titles." In pursuit of the title of conqueror, he kept France at war for thirty-three of the fifty-four years of his personal rule. François le Tellier, marquis de Louvois, Louis's secretary of state for war, equaled Colbert's achievements in the economic realm. Louvois created a professional army in which the French state, rather than private nobles, employed the soldiers. Uniforms and weapons were standardized, and a rational system of training and promotion was devised. Many historians believe that the new loyalty, professionalism, and growth of the French army represented the peak of Louis's success in reforming government. As in so many other matters, his model was followed across Europe.

Louis's goal was to expand France to what he considered its natural borders. His armies managed to extend French borders to include important commercial centers in the Spanish Netherlands and Flanders as well as the entire province of Franche-Comté between 1667 and 1678. In 1681 Louis seized the city of Strasbourg, and three years later he sent his armies into the province of Lorraine. At that moment the king seemed invincible. In fact, Louis had reached the limit of his expansion. The wars of the 1680s and 1690s brought no additional territories but placed unbearable strains on French resources. Colbert's successors resorted to desperate measures to finance these wars, including devaluation of the currency and new taxes.

Louis's last war was endured by a French people suffering high taxes, crop failure, and widespread malnutrition and death. In 1700 the childless Spanish king Charles II (r. 1665–1700) died, opening a struggle for control of Spain and its colonies. His will

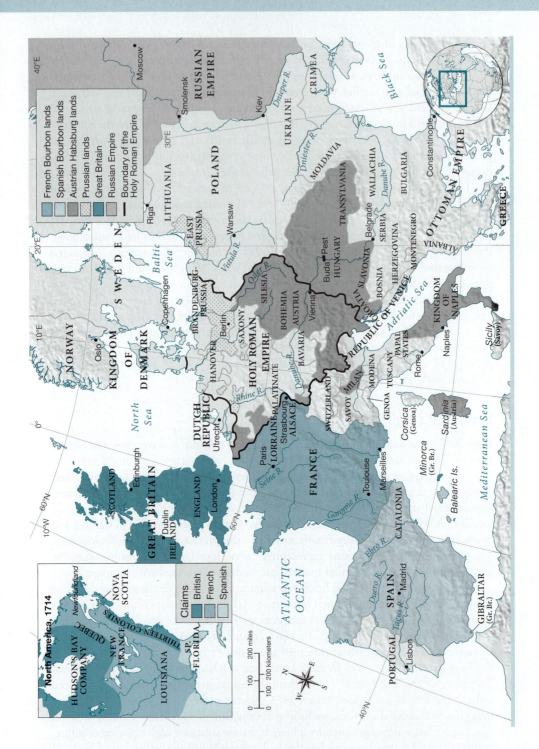

Legend:
French Bourbon lands
Spanish Bourbon lands
Austrian Habsburg lands
Prussian lands
Great Britain
Russian Empire
Boundary of the Holy Roman Empire

North America, 1714

Claims
British
French
Spanish

bequeathed the Spanish crown and its empire to Philip of Anjou, Louis XIV's grandson (Louis's wife, Maria-Theresa, was Charles's sister). The will violated a prior treaty by which the European powers had agreed to divide the Spanish possessions between the king of France and the Holy Roman emperor, both brothers-in-law of Charles II. Claiming that he was following both Spanish and French interests, Louis broke with the treaty and accepted the will, thereby triggering the War of the Spanish Succession (1701–1713).

In 1701 the English, Dutch, Austrians, and Prussians formed the Grand Alliance against Louis XIV. War dragged on until 1713. The **Peace of Utrecht**, which ended the war, allowed Louis's grandson Philip to remain king of Spain on the understanding that the French and Spanish crowns would never be united. France surrendered Nova Scotia, Newfoundland, and the Hudson Bay territory to England, which also acquired Gibraltar, Minorca, and control of the African slave trade from Spain (Map 15.2).

The Peace of Utrecht represented the balance-of-power principle in operation, setting limits on the extent to which any one power — in this case, France — could expand. It also marked the end of French expansion. Thirty-five years of war had given France the rights to all of Alsace and some commercial centers in the north. But at what price? In 1714 an exhausted France hovered on the brink of bankruptcy. It is no wonder that when Louis XIV died on September 1, 1715, many subjects felt as much relief as they did sorrow.

The Decline of Absolutist Spain in the Seventeenth Century

At the beginning of the seventeenth century France's position appeared extremely weak. Struggling to recover from decades of religious civil war that had destroyed its infra-structure and economy, France could not dare to compete with Spain's empire or its mighty military. Yet by the end of the century their positions were reversed, and France had surpassed all expectations to attain European dominance.

By the early seventeenth century the seeds of Spanish disaster were sprouting. Between 1610 and 1650 Spanish trade with the colonies in the New World fell 60 per-cent due to competition from local industries in the colonies and from Dutch and English traders. At the same time, the native Indian and African slaves who toiled in the South American silver mines suffered frightful epidemics of disease. Ultimately, the mines that filled the empire's treasury started to run dry, and the quantity of metal produced steadily declined after 1620.

In Madrid, however, royal expenditures constantly exceeded income. To meet mountainous state debt, the Crown repeatedly devalued the coinage and declared bank-ruptcy, which resulted in the collapse of national credit. Meanwhile, manufacturing and

< MAP 15.2 Europe After the Peace of Utrecht, 1715
The series of treaties commonly called the Peace of Utrecht ended the War of the Spanish Succession and redrew the map of Europe. A French Bourbon king succeeded to the Spanish throne. France surrendered the Spanish Netherlands (later Belgium), then in French hands, to Austria, and recognized the Hohenzollern rulers of Prussia. Spain ceded Gibraltar to Great Britain, for which it has been a strategic naval station ever since. Spain also granted Britain the *asiento*, the contract for supplying African slaves to the Americas.

commerce shrank. In contrast to the other countries of western Europe, Spain had a tiny middle class. The elite condemned moneymaking as vulgar and undignified. Thousands entered economically unproductive professions: there were said to be nine thousand monasteries in the province of Castile alone. To make matters worse, the Crown expelled some three hundred thousand *Moriscos*, or former Muslims, in 1609, significantly reducing the pool of skilled workers and merchants. Those working in the textile industry were forced out of business by steep inflation that pushed their production costs to the point where they could not compete in colonial and international markets.[5]

Spanish aristocrats, attempting to maintain an extravagant lifestyle they could no longer afford, increased the rents on their estates. High rents and heavy taxes in turn drove the peasants from the land, leading to a decline in agricultural productivity. In cities wages and production stagnated. Spain also ignored new scientific methods that might have improved agricultural or manufacturing techniques because they came from the heretical nations of Holland and England.

The Spanish crown had no solutions to these dire problems. Philip III (r. 1598–1621), a melancholy and deeply pious man, handed the running of the government over to the duke of Lerma, who used it to advance his personal and familial wealth. Philip IV (r. 1621–1665) left the management of his several kingdoms to Gaspar de Guzmán, Count-Duke of Olivares. Olivares was an able administrator who has often been compared to Richelieu. He did not lack energy and ideas, and he succeeded in devising new sources of revenue. But he clung to the grandiose belief that the solution to Spain's difficulties rested in a return to the imperial tradition of the sixteenth century. Unfortunately, the imperial tradition demanded the revival of war with the Dutch at the expiration of a twelve-year truce in 1622 and a long war with France over Mantua (1628–1659). Spain thus became embroiled in the Thirty Years' War. These conflicts, on top of an empty treasury, brought disaster.

Spain's situation worsened with internal conflicts and fresh military defeats through the remainder of the seventeenth century. In 1640 Spain faced serious revolts in Catalonia and Portugal. In 1643 the French inflicted a crushing defeat on a Spanish army at Rocroi in what is now Belgium. By the Treaty of the Pyrenees of 1659, which ended the French-Spanish conflict, Spain was compelled to surrender extensive territories to France. In 1688 the Spanish crown reluctantly recognized the independence of Portugal, almost a century after the two crowns were joined. The era of Spanish dominance in Europe had ended.

Absolutism in Austria and Prussia

Focus Question	What were the social conditions of eastern Europe, and how did the rulers of Austria and Prussia transform their nations into powerful absolutist monarchies?

The rulers of eastern Europe also labored to build strong absolutist states in the seventeenth century. But they built on social and economic foundations far different from those in western Europe, namely serfdom and the strong nobility who benefited from it. The endless wars of the seventeenth century allowed monarchs to increase their power by building large armies, increasing taxation, and suppressing representative institutions. In exchange for their growing political authority, monarchs allowed nobles to remain as unchallenged masters of their peasants, a deal that appeased both king and nobility, but left serfs at the mercy of the lords. The most successful states were Austria and Prussia, which witnessed the rise of absolutism between 1620 and 1740.

The Return of Serfdom in the East

While economic and social hardship was common across Europe, important differences existed between east and west. In the west the demographic losses of the Black Death allowed peasants to escape from serfdom as they acquired enough land to feed themselves. In eastern Europe seventeenth-century peasants had largely lost their ability to own land independently. Eastern lords dealt with the labor shortages caused by the Black Death by restricting the right of their peasants to move to take advantage of better opportunities elsewhere. In Prussian territories by 1500 the law required that runaway peasants be hunted down and returned to their lords. Moreover, lords steadily took more and more of their peasants' land and arbitrarily imposed heavier labor obligations. By the early 1500s lords in many eastern territories could command their peasants to work for them without pay for as many as six days a week.

The gradual erosion of the peasantry's economic position was bound up with manipulation of the legal system. The local lord was also the local prosecutor, judge, and jailer. There were no independent royal officials to provide justice or uphold the common law. The power of the lord reached far into serfs' everyday lives. Not only was their freedom of movement restricted, but they also required permission to marry or could be forced to marry. Lords could reallocate the lands worked by their serfs at will or sell serfs apart from their families. These conditions applied even on lands owned by the church.

Between 1500 and 1650 the consolidation of serfdom in eastern Europe was accompanied by the growth of commercial agriculture, particularly in Poland and eastern Germany. As economic expansion and population growth resumed after 1500, eastern lords increased the production of their estates by squeezing sizable surpluses out of the impoverished peasants. They then sold these surpluses to foreign merchants, who exported them to the growing cities of wealthier western Europe. The Netherlands and England benefited the most from inexpensive grain from the east.

It was not only the peasants who suffered in eastern Europe. With the approval of kings, landlords systematically undermined the medieval privileges of the towns and the power of the urban classes. Instead of selling products to local merchants, landlords sold directly to foreigners, bypassing local towns. Eastern towns also lost their medieval right of refuge and were compelled to return runaways to their lords. The population of the towns and the urban middle classes declined greatly. This development both reflected and promoted the supremacy of noble landlords in most of eastern Europe in the sixteenth century.

The Austrian Habsburgs

Like all the people of central Europe, the Habsburgs emerged from the Thirty Years' War impoverished and exhausted. Their efforts to destroy Protestantism in the German lands and to turn the weak Holy Roman Empire into a real state had failed. Although the Habsburgs remained the hereditary emperors, real power lay in the hands of a bewildering variety of separate political jurisdictions. Defeat in central Europe encouraged the Habsburgs to turn away from a quest for imperial dominance and to focus inward and eastward in an attempt to unify their diverse holdings. If they could not impose Catholicism in the empire, at least they could do so in their own domains.

Habsburg victory over Bohemia during the Thirty Years' War was an important step in this direction. Ferdinand II (r. 1619–1637) drastically reduced the power of the Bohemian Estates, the largely Protestant representative assembly. He also confiscated the landholdings of Protestant nobles and gave them to loyal Catholic nobles and to the foreign aristocratic mercenaries who led his armies. After 1650 a large portion of the Bohemian nobility was of recent origin and owed its success to the Habsburgs.

With the support of this new nobility, the Habsburgs established direct rule over Bohemia. Under their rule the condition of the enserfed peasantry worsened substantially: three days per week of unpaid labor became the norm. Protestantism was also stamped out. These changes were significant advances in creating absolutist rule in Bohemia.

Ferdinand III (r. 1637–1657) continued to build state power. He centralized the government in the empire's German-speaking provinces, which formed the core Habsburg holdings. For the first time, a permanent standing army was ready to put down any internal opposition. The Habsburg monarchy then turned east toward the plains of Hungary, which had been divided between the Ottomans and the Habsburgs in the early sixteenth century. Between 1683 and 1699 the Habsburgs pushed the Ottomans from most of Hungary and Transylvania. The recovery of all the former kingdom of Hungary was completed in 1718.

The Hungarian nobility, despite its reduced strength, effectively thwarted the full development of Habsburg absolutism. Throughout the seventeenth century Hungarian nobles rose in revolt against attempts to impose absolute rule. They never triumphed decisively, but neither were they crushed the way the nobility in Bohemia had been in 1620. In 1703, with the Habsburgs bogged down in the War of the Spanish Succession, the Hungarians rose in one last patriotic rebellion under Prince Francis Rákóczy. The prince and his forces were eventually defeated, but the Habsburgs agreed to restore many of the traditional privileges of the aristocracy in return for Hungarian acceptance of hereditary Habsburg rule. Thus Hungary, unlike Austria and Bohemia, was never fully integrated into a centralized, absolute Habsburg state.

Despite checks on their ambitions in Hungary, the Habsburgs made significant achievements in state-building elsewhere by forging consensus with the church and the nobility. A sense of common identity and loyalty to the monarchy grew among elites in Habsburg lands, even to a certain extent in Hungary. German became the language of the state, and zealous Catholicism helped fuse a collective identity.

Vienna became the political and cultural center of the empire. By 1700 it was a thriving city with a population of one hundred thousand and its own version of Versailles, the royal palace of Schönbrunn.

Prussia in the Seventeenth Century

In the fifteenth and sixteenth centuries the Hohenzollern family had ruled parts of eastern Germany as the imperial electors of Brandenburg and the dukes of Prussia. The title of "elector" gave its holder the privilege of being one of only seven princes or archbishops entitled to elect the Holy Roman emperor, but the electors had little real power. When he came to power in 1640, the twenty-year-old Frederick William, later known as the "Great Elector," was determined to unify his three provinces and enlarge his holdings. These provinces were Brandenburg; Prussia, inherited in 1618; and scattered territories along the Rhine inherited in 1614 (Map 15.3). Each was inhabited by German-speakers, but each had its own estates. Although the estates had not met regularly during the chaotic Thirty Years' War, taxes could not be levied without their consent. The estates of Brandenburg and Prussia were dominated by the nobility and the landowning classes, known as the **Junkers**.

Frederick William profited from ongoing European war and the threat of invasion from Russia when he argued for the need for a permanent standing army. In 1660 he persuaded Junkers in the estates to accept taxation without consent in order to fund an army. They agreed to do so in exchange for reconfirmation of their own privileges, including authority over the serfs. Having won over the Junkers, the king crushed potential opposition to his power from the towns. One by one, Prussian cities were eliminated from the estates and subjected to new taxes on goods and services.

MAP 15.3 The Growth of Austria and Brandenburg-Prussia to 1748
Austria expanded to the southwest into Hungary and Transylvania at the expense of the Ottoman Empire. It was unable to hold the rich German province of Silesia, however, which was conquered by Brandenburg-Prussia.

Despite stereotypes, however, the Ottoman Empire was in many ways more tolerant than its Western counterparts, providing protection and security to other religions while steadfastly maintaining the Muslim faith. The Ottoman state combined the Byzantine heritage of the territory it had conquered with Persian and Arab traditions. Flexibility and openness to other ideas and practices were sources of strength for the empire.

Mongol Rule in Russia and the Rise of Moscow

In the thirteenth century the Mongols had conquered Kievan Rus, the medieval Slavic state centered first at Novgorod and then at Kiev, a city on the Dnieper River; this state included most of present-day Ukraine, Belarus, and part of northwest Russia. For two hundred years, the Mongols forced the Slavic princes to submit to their rule and to render tribute and slaves. The princes of the Grand Duchy of Moscow, a principality within Kievan Rus, became particularly adept at serving the Mongols. They loyally put down uprisings and collected the khan's taxes. Eventually the Muscovite princes were able to destroy the other princes who were their rivals for power. Ivan III (r. 1462–1505), known as Ivan the Great, successfully expanded the principality of Moscow eastward toward the Baltic Sea and westward to the Ural Mountains and the Siberian frontier.

By 1480 Ivan III was strong enough to refuse to pay tribute to the Mongols and declare the autonomy of Moscow. To legitimize their new position, Ivan and his successors borrowed elements of Mongol rule. They forced weaker Slavic principalities to render tribute previously paid to Mongols and borrowed Mongol institutions such as the tax system, postal routes, and census. Loyalty from the highest-ranking nobles, or **boyars**, helped the Muscovite princes consolidate their power.

Another source of legitimacy for Moscow was its claim to the political and religious legacy of the Byzantine Empire. After the fall of Constantinople to the Turks in 1453, the princes of Moscow saw themselves as the heirs of both the Byzantine caesars (or emperors) and the empire's Orthodox Christianity. The title "tsar," first taken by Ivan IV in 1547, is in fact a contraction of *caesar*. The tsars considered themselves rightful and holy rulers, an idea promoted by Orthodox churchmen who spoke of "holy Russia" as the "Third Rome." The marriage of Ivan III to the daughter of the last Byzantine emperor further enhanced Moscow's assertion of imperial authority.

Building the Russian Empire

Developments in Russia took a chaotic turn with the reign of Ivan IV (r. 1533–1584), the famous "Ivan the Terrible," who rose to the throne at age three. His mother died, possibly poisoned, when he was eight, leaving Ivan to suffer insults and neglect from the boyars at court. At age sixteen Ivan pushed aside his advisers, and in an awe-inspiring ceremony, with gold coins pouring down on his head, he majestically crowned himself tsar.

After the sudden death of his wife, however, Ivan began a campaign of persecution against those he suspected of opposing him. He executed members of leading boyar families, along with their families, friends, servants, and peasants. To replace them, Ivan created a new service nobility, whose loyalty was guaranteed by their dependence on the state for land and titles.

As landlords demanded more from the serfs who survived the persecutions, growing numbers of peasants fled toward wild, recently conquered territories to the east and south. There they joined free groups and warrior bands known as **Cossacks**. Ivan responded by tying peasants ever more firmly to the land and to noble landholders. Simultaneously, he ordered that urban dwellers be bound to their towns and jobs so that he could tax them more heavily. The urban classes had no security in their property, and even the wealthiest merchants were dependent agents of the tsar. These restrictions checked the growth of the Russian middle classes and stood in sharp contrast to economic and social developments in western Europe.

Ivan combined domestic oppression with external aggression. His reign was successful in defeating the remnants of Mongol power, adding vast new territories to the realm, and laying the foundations for the huge, multiethnic Russian empire. In the 1550s, strengthened by an alliance with Cossack bands, Ivan conquered the Muslim khanates of Kazan and Astrakhan and brought the fertile steppe region around the Volga River under Russian control. In the 1580s Cossacks fighting for the Russian state crossed the Ural Mountains and began the long conquest of Siberia. Because of the size of the new territories and their distance from Moscow, the Russian state did not initially seek to impose the Orthodox religion and maintained local elites in positions of honor and leadership, buying their loyalty with grants of land. In relying on cooperation from local elites and ruthlessly exploiting the common people, the Russians followed the pattern of the Spanish and other early modern European imperial states.

Following Ivan's death, Russia entered a chaotic period known as the "Time of Troubles" (1598–1613). While Ivan's relatives struggled for power, Cossacks and peasants rebelled against nobles and officials. This social explosion from below brought the nobles together. They crushed the Cossack rebellion and brought Ivan's sixteen-year-old grandnephew, Michael Romanov, to the throne (r. 1613–1645). The Romanov dynasty would endure as one of the most successful European absolutist dynasties until the Russian Revolution of 1917.

Like their Western counterparts, the Romanov tsars made several important achievements in state-building during the second half of the seventeenth century. After a long war, Russia gained land in Ukraine from Poland in 1667 and completed the conquest of Siberia by the end of the century. Territorial expansion was accompanied by growth of the bureaucracy and the army. The tsars employed foreign experts to reform the Russian army, and enlisted Cossack warriors to fight Siberian campaigns. The great profits from Siberia's natural resources, especially furs, funded the Romanovs' bid for Great Power status. Russian imperialist expansion to the east paralleled the Western powers' exploration and conquest of the Atlantic world in the same period.

The growth of state power did nothing to improve the lot of the common people. In 1649 a new law code extended serfdom to all peasants in the realm, giving lords unrestricted rights over their serfs and establishing penalties for harboring runaways. The new code also removed the privileges that non-Russian elites had enjoyed within the empire and required conversion to Russian Orthodoxy. Henceforth, Moscow maintained strict control of trade and administration throughout the empire.

The peace imposed by harsh Russian rule was disrupted in 1670 by a rebellion led by the Cossack Stenka Razin, who attracted a great army of urban poor and peasants. He and his followers killed landlords and government officials and proclaimed freedom from oppression, but their rebellion was defeated in 1671. The ease with which Moscow crushed the rebellion testifies to the success of the Russian state in unifying and consolidating its empire.

The Reforms of Peter the Great

Heir to Romanov efforts at state-building, Peter the Great (r. 1682–1725) embarked on a tremendous campaign to accelerate and complete these processes. A giant for his time at six feet seven inches, and possessing enormous energy and willpower, Peter built on the service obligations of Ivan the Terrible and his successors and continued their tradition of territorial expansion. In particular, he was determined to gain access to the sea for his virtually landlocked state.

Peter realized a first step toward this goal by conquering the Ottoman fort of Azov in 1696 and quickly built Russia's first navy base. In 1697 the tsar led a group of 250 Russian officials and young nobles on an eighteen-month tour of western European capitals. Peter was fascinated by foreign technology and he hoped to forge an anti-Ottoman alliance to strengthen his claims on the Black Sea. Traveling unofficially to avoid lengthy diplomatic ceremonies, Peter met with foreign kings, master shipbuilders, gunners, and other specialists. He failed to secure a military alliance, but he did learn his lessons from the growing power of the Dutch and the English. He also engaged more than a hundred foreign experts to return with him to Russia to help build the navy and improve Russian infrastructure.

Peter the Great Cutting a Boyar's Beard As part of his westernization program, Peter the Great obliged Russian men to shave their long beards, a shock to traditional Orthodox notions of masculinity. Like many of his reforms, these were aimed primarily at the noble boyars; many peasants continued to wear beards in the countryside. (Universal History Archive/Getty Images)

Having failed to gain support for an anti-Ottoman alliance and suffering a reversal of fortune at Azov, Peter switched tactics and entered into a secret agreement with Denmark and Poland to wage a sudden war of aggression against Sweden with the goal of securing access to the Baltic Sea. Peter and his allies believed that their combined forces could win easy victories because Sweden was in the hands of a new and inexperienced king.

Eighteen-year-old Charles XII of Sweden (1697–1718) surprised Peter. He defeated Denmark quickly in 1700, then turned on Russia. In a blinding snowstorm, his well-trained professional army attacked and routed unsuspecting Russians besieging the Swedish fortress of Narva on the Baltic coast. It was, for the Russians, a grim beginning to the long and brutal Great Northern War, which lasted from 1700 to 1721.

Peter responded to this defeat with new measures to increase state power, strengthen his military forces, and gain victory. He required all nobles to serve in the army or in the civil administration — for life. Since a more modern army and government required skilled experts, Peter created new schools and universities and required every young nobleman to spend five years in education away from home. Peter established an interlocking military-civilian bureaucracy with fourteen ranks, and he decreed that all had to start at the bottom and work toward the top. The system allowed some people of non-noble origins to rise to high positions, a rarity in Europe at the time. These measures gradually combined to make the army and government more powerful and efficient.

Peter also greatly increased the service requirements of commoners. In the wake of the Narva disaster, he established a regular standing army of more than two hundred thousand peasant-soldiers, drafted for life and commanded by noble officers. He added an additional hundred thousand men in special regiments of Cossacks and foreign mercenaries. To fund the army, taxes on peasants increased threefold during Peter's reign. Serfs were also arbitrarily assigned to work in the growing number of factories and mines that supplied the military. Under Peter, Russia's techniques for governing its territories — including the policing of borders and individual identity documents — were far ahead of those of most other imperial powers.

In 1709 Peter's new war machine was able to crush the small army of Sweden in Ukraine at Poltava, one of the most significant battles in Russian history. Russia's victory against Sweden was conclusive in 1721, and Estonia and present-day Latvia came under Russian rule for the first time. The cost was high: warfare consumed 80 to 85 percent of all revenues. But Russia became the dominant power in the Baltic and very much a great European power.

After his victory at Poltava, Peter channeled enormous resources into building a new Western-style capital on the Baltic to rival the great cities of Europe. Originally a desolate and swampy Swedish outpost, the magnificent city of St. Petersburg was designed to reflect modern urban planning, with wide, straight avenues, buildings set in a uniform line, and large parks. Each summer, twenty-five thousand to forty thousand peasants were sent to provide construction labor in St. Petersburg without pay.

There were other important consequences of Peter's reign. For Peter, modernization meant westernization, and he encouraged the spread of Western culture along with technology and urban planning. Peter required nobles to shave their heavy beards and

RUSSIA

Caspian Sea

PERSIA

Isfahan

ARABIA

Campaign to India

1551

Mecca

Land disputed with Persia

CAUCASUS MTS.

Volga R.

GEORGIA

ARMENIA

Tigris R.

MESOPOTAMIA

Baghdad

Euphrates R.

Red Sea

Campaigns to Oman, Malindi

1551, 1584

CIRCASSIA

Don R.

KHANATE OF THE CRIMEA

1569

Azov

KURDISTAN

SYRIA

Aleppo

Damascus

SYRIAN DESERT

Adana

PALESTINE

Jerusalem

GRAND DUCHY OF MOSCOW

Dnieper R.

YEDISAN

Black Sea

Constantinople

ANATOLIA

Angora

KARAMAN

Cyprus

Cairo

Nile R.

Aswan

POLAND

MOLDAVIA

Bursa

Smyrna

EGYPT

Alexandria

Danube R.

WALLACHIA

Bucharest

Sofia

BULGARIA

Gallipoli

KINGDOM OF HUNGARY

TRANSYLVANIA

Pest

1529

Buda

1532

OTTOMAN HUNGARY

Mohács

SERBIA 1526

BOSNIA

RUMELIA

GREECE

Lepanto 1571

Crete

Mediterranean Sea

BOHEMIA

AUSTRIA

Vienna

1529

MONTENEGRO

RAGUSA

1537

LIBYAN DESERT

HOLY ROMAN EMPIRE

A L P S

Venice

NAPLES

1543

1565

Rome

Corsica

Sardinia

Sicily

Malta

Tripoli

SAHARA

FRANCE

Tunis

1543–1544

ALGERIA

TUNISIA

N E S W

200 miles

0 100 200

0 100 200 kilometers

Ottoman state, ca. 1300

Ottoman Empire under Suleiman, 1566

Tributary states of the Sultan, 1566

Major Ottoman campaign, 1530–1584

Habsburg Empire, ca. 1550

wear Western clothing, previously banned in Russia. He also ordered them to attend parties where young men and women would mix together and freely choose their own spouses. From these efforts a new elite class of Western-oriented Russians began to emerge.

Peter's reforms were unpopular with many Russians. For nobles, one of Peter's most detested reforms was the imposition of unigeniture—inheritance of land by one son alone—cutting daughters and other sons from family property. For peasants, the reign of the tsar saw a significant increase in the bonds of serfdom, and the gulf between the enserfed peasantry and the educated nobility increased. Despite the unpopularity of Peter's reforms, his modernizing and westernizing of Russia paved the way for it to move somewhat closer to the European mainstream in its thought and institutions during the Enlightenment, especially under Catherine the Great.

The Ottoman Empire

Most Christian Europeans perceived the Ottomans as the antithesis of their own values and traditions and viewed the empire as driven by an insatiable lust for warfare and conquest. In their view the fall of Constantinople was a historic catastrophe and the taking of the Balkans a form of despotic imprisonment. To Ottoman eyes, the world looked very different. The siege of Constantinople liberated a glorious city from its long decline under the Byzantines. Rather than being a despoiled captive, the Balkans were a haven for refugees fleeing the growing intolerance of Western Christian powers. The Ottoman Empire provided a safe haven for Jews, Muslims, and even some Christians from the Inquisition and religious war.

The Ottomans came out of Central Asia as conquering warriors, settled in Anatolia (present-day Turkey), and, at their peak in the mid-sixteenth century, ruled one of the most powerful empires in the world (see Chapter 14). Their possessions stretched from western Persia across North Africa and into the heart of central Europe (Map 15.4).

The Ottoman Empire was built on a unique model of state and society. Agricultural land was the personal hereditary property of the **sultan**, and peasants paid taxes to use the land. There was therefore an almost complete absence of private landed property and no hereditary nobility. The Ottomans also employed a distinctive form of government administration. The top ranks of the bureaucracy were staffed by the sultan's slave corps. Because Muslim law prohibited enslaving other Muslims, the sultan's agents purchased slaves along the borders of the empire. Within the realm, the sultan levied a "tax" of one thousand to three thousand male children on the conquered Christian populations in the Balkans every year. These young slaves were raised in Turkey as Muslims and were trained to fight and to administer. Unlike enslaved Africans in European colonies, who faced a dire fate, the most talented Ottoman slaves rose to

< MAP 15.4 **The Ottoman Empire at Its Height, 1566**

The Ottomans, like their great rivals the Habsburgs, rose to rule a vast dynastic empire encompassing many different peoples and ethnic groups. The army and the bureaucracy served to unite the disparate territories into a single state under an absolutist ruler.

Religious issues also embittered relations between the king and the House of Commons. In the early seventeenth century many English people felt dissatisfied with the Church of England established by Henry VIII (r. 1509–1547). Calvinist **Puritans** wanted to take the Reformation further by "purifying" the Anglican Church of Roman Catholic elements — elaborate vestments and ceremonials, bishops, and even the giving and wearing of wedding rings.

James I responded to such ideas by declaring, "No bishop, no king." For James, bishops were among the chief supporters of the throne. His son and successor, Charles I, further antagonized religious sentiments by marrying a French princess and supporting the heavy-handed policies of the archbishop of Canterbury William Laud (1573–1645). Laud provoked outrage by imposing two new elements on church organization in Scotland: a new prayer book, modeled on the Anglican *Book of Common Prayer*, and bishoprics.

Charles avoided addressing grievances against him by refusing to call Parliament into session from 1629 to 1640. Instead, he financed his government through extraordinary stopgap levies considered illegal by most English people. However, when Scottish Calvinists revolted against his religious policies, Charles was forced to summon Parliament to obtain funds for an army to put down the revolt. Accordingly, this Parliament, called the "Long Parliament" because it sat from 1640 to 1660, enacted legislation that limited the power of the monarch, and made government without Parliament impossible.

In 1641 the Parliament passed the Triennial Act, which compelled the king to summon Parliament every three years. The Commons impeached Archbishop Laud and then threatened to abolish bishops. King Charles, fearful of a Scottish invasion — the original reason for summoning Parliament — reluctantly accepted these measures.

The next act in the conflict was precipitated by the outbreak of rebellion in Ireland, where English governors and landlords had long exploited the people. In 1641 the Catholic gentry of Ireland led an uprising in response to a feared invasion by anti-Catholic forces of the British Long Parliament.

Without an army, Charles I could neither come to terms with the Scots nor respond to the Irish rebellion. After a failed attempt to arrest parliamentary leaders, Charles left London for the north of England, where he began to raise an army. In response, Parliament formed its own army, the New Model Army, composed of the militia of the city of London and country squires with business connections. During the spring of 1642 both sides prepared for war. In July a linen weaver became the first casualty of the civil war during a skirmish between royal and parliamentary forces in Manchester.

The English civil war (1642–1649) pitted the power of the king against that of the Parliament. After three years of fighting, Parliament's New Model Army defeated the king's armies at the Battles of Naseby and Langport in the summer of 1645. Charles, though, refused to concede defeat. Both sides jockeyed for position, waiting for a decisive event. This arrived in the form of the army under the leadership of Oliver Cromwell, a member of the House of Commons and a devout Puritan. In 1647 Cromwell's forces captured the king and dismissed anti-Cromwell members of the Parliament. In 1649 the remaining representatives, known as the "Rump Parliament," put Charles on trial for high treason. Charles was found guilty and beheaded on January 30, 1649, an act that sent shock waves around Europe.

The Puritan Protectorate

With the execution of Charles, kingship was abolished. The question remained of how the country would be governed. One answer was provided by philosopher Thomas Hobbes (1588–1679). Hobbes held a pessimistic view of human nature and believed that, left to themselves, humans would compete violently for power and wealth. The only solution, as he outlined in his 1651 treatise *Leviathan*, was a social contract in which all members of society placed themselves under the absolute rule of the sovereign, who

Puritan Occupations   These twelve engravings depict typical Puritan occupations and show that the Puritans came primarily from the artisan and lower middle classes. The governing classes and peasants made up a much smaller percentage of the Puritans and generally adhered to the traditions of the Church of England. (Private Collection/© Look and Learn/Peter Jackson Collection/Bridgeman Images)

would maintain peace and order. Hobbes imagined society as a human body in which the monarch served as head and individual subjects together made up the body. Just as the body cannot sever its own head, so Hobbes believed that society could not, having accepted the contract, rise up against its king.

Hobbes's longing for a benevolent absolute monarch was not widely shared in England. Instead, Oliver Cromwell and his supporters enshrined a commonwealth, or republican government, known as the **Protectorate**. Theoretically, legislative power rested in the surviving members of Parliament, and executive power was lodged in a council of state. In fact, the army controlled the government, and Oliver Cromwell controlled the army, ruling what was essentially a military dictatorship.

The army prepared a constitution, the Instrument of Government (1653), that invested executive power in a lord protector (Cromwell) and a council of state. It provided for triennial parliaments and gave Parliament the sole power to raise taxes. But after repeated disputes, Cromwell dismissed Parliament in 1655, and the instrument was never formally endorsed. Cromwell continued the standing army and proclaimed quasi-martial law. He divided England into twelve military districts, each governed by a major general. Reflecting Puritan ideas of morality, Cromwell's state forbade sports, closed the theaters, and rigorously censored the press.

On the issue of religion, Cromwell favored some degree of toleration, and the Instrument of Government gave all Christians except Roman Catholics the right to practice their faith. Cromwell had long associated Catholicism in Ireland with sedition and heresy, and led an army there to reconquer the country in August 1649. One month later, his forces crushed a rebellion at Drogheda and massacred the garrison. After Cromwell's departure for England, atrocities worsened. The English banned Catholicism in Ireland, executed priests, and confiscated land from Catholics for English and Scottish settlers. These brutal acts left a legacy of Irish hatred for England.

Cromwell adopted mercantilist policies similar to those of absolutist France. He enforced a Navigation Act (1651) requiring that English goods be transported on English ships. The act was a great boost to the development of an English merchant marine and brought about a short but successful war with the commercially threatened Dutch. While mercantilist legislation ultimately benefited English commerce, for ordinary people the turmoil of foreign war only added to the harsh conditions of life induced by years of civil war. Cromwell also welcomed the immigration of Jews because of their skills in business, and they began to return to England after four centuries of absence.

The Protectorate collapsed when Cromwell died in 1658 and his ineffectual son succeeded him. Fed up with military rule, the English longed for a return to civilian government and, with it, common law and social stability. By 1660 they were ready to restore the monarchy.

The Restoration of the English Monarchy

The Restoration of 1660 brought to the throne Charles II (r. 1660–1685), eldest son of Charles I, who had been living on the continent. Both houses of Parliament were also restored, together with the established Anglican Church. The Restoration failed to resolve two serious problems, however. What was to be the attitude of the state toward

Puritans, Catholics, and dissenters from the established church? And what was to be the relationship between the king and Parliament?

To answer the first question, Parliament enacted the **Test Act** of 1673 against those outside the Church of England, denying them the right to vote, hold public office, preach, teach, attend the universities, or even assemble for meetings. But these restrictions could not be enforced. When the Quaker William Penn held a meeting of his Friends and was arrested, the jury refused to convict him.

In politics, Charles II's initial determination to work well with Parliament did not last long. Finding that Parliament did not grant him an adequate income, in 1670 Charles entered into a secret agreement with his cousin Louis XIV. The French king would give Charles £200,000 annually, and in return Charles would relax the laws against Catholics, gradually re-Catholicize England, and convert to Catholicism himself. When the details of this treaty leaked out, a great wave of anti-Catholic sentiment swept England.

When Charles died and his Catholic brother James became king, the worst English anti-Catholic fears were realized. In violation of the Test Act, James II (r. 1685–1688) appointed Roman Catholics to positions in the army, the universities, and local government. When these actions were challenged in the courts, the judges, whom James had appointed, decided in favor of the king. James and his supporters opened new Catholic churches and schools and issued tracts promoting Catholicism. Attempting to broaden his base of support with Protestant dissenters and nonconformists, James granted religious freedom to all.

James's opponents, a powerful coalition of eminent persons in Parliament and the Church of England, bitterly resisted James's ambitions. They offered the English throne to James's heir, his Protestant daughter Mary, and her Dutch husband, Prince William of Orange. In December 1688 James II, his queen, and their infant son fled to France and became pensioners of Louis XIV. Early in 1689 William and Mary were crowned king and queen of England.

Constitutional Monarchy

The English call the events of 1688 and 1689 the "Glorious Revolution" because they believe it replaced one king with another with barely any bloodshed. In truth, William's arrival sparked revolutionary riots and violence across the British Isles and in North American cities such as Boston and New York. Uprisings by supporters of James, known as Jacobites, occurred in 1689 in Scotland. In Ireland, the two sides waged outright war from 1689 to 1691. William's victory at the Battle of the Boyne (1690) and the subsequent Treaty of Limerick (1691) sealed his accession to power.

In England, the revolution represented the final destruction of the idea of divine-right monarchy. The men who brought about the revolution framed their intentions in the Bill of Rights, which was formulated in direct response to Stuart absolutism. Law was to be made in Parliament; once made, it could not be suspended by the Crown. Parliament had to be called at least once every three years. The independence of the judiciary was established, and there was to be no standing army in peacetime. Protestants could possess arms, but the Catholic minority could not. A Catholic could not inherit the throne. Additional legislation granted freedom of worship to Protestant dissenters, but not to Catholics. William and Mary accepted these principles when they took the throne, and the House of Parliament passed the Bill of Rights in December 1689.

The Glorious Revolution and the concept of representative government found its best defense in political philosopher John Locke's *Two Treatises of Government* (1690). Locke (1632–1704) maintained that a government that oversteps its proper function — protecting the natural rights of life, liberty, and property — becomes a tyranny. By "natural" rights Locke meant rights basic to all men because all have the ability to reason. Under a tyrannical government, the people have the natural right to rebellion. On the basis of this link, he justified limiting the vote to property owners. Locke's idea that there are natural or universal rights equally valid for all peoples and societies was especially popular in colonial America. American colonists also appreciated his arguments that Native Americans had no property rights since they did not cultivate the land and, by extension, no political rights because they possessed no property.

Although the events of 1688 and 1689 brought England closer to Locke's ideal, they did not constitute a democratic revolution. The revolution placed sovereignty in Parliament, and Parliament represented the upper classes. The age of aristocratic government lasted at least until 1832 and in many ways until 1928, when women received full voting rights.

The Dutch Republic in the Seventeenth Century

In the late sixteenth century the seven northern provinces of the Netherlands fought for and won their independence from Spain. The independence of the Republic of the United Provinces of the Netherlands was recognized in 1648 in the treaty that ended the Thirty Years' War. In this period, often called the "golden age" of the Netherlands, Dutch ideas and attitudes played a profound role in shaping a new and modern worldview. At the same time, the United Provinces developed its own distinctive model of a constitutional state.

Rejecting the rule of a monarch, the Dutch established a republic, a state in which power rested in the hands of the people and was exercised through elected representatives. Other examples of republics in early modern Europe included the Swiss Confederation and several autonomous city-states of Italy and the Holy Roman Empire. Among the Dutch, an oligarchy of wealthy businessmen called regents handled domestic affairs in each province's Estates (assemblies). The provincial Estates held virtually all the power. A federal assembly, or States General, handled foreign affairs and war, but it did not possess sovereign authority. All issues had to be referred back to the local Estates for approval, and each of the seven provinces could veto any proposed legislation. Holland, the province with the largest navy and the most wealth, usually dominated the republic and the States General.

In each province, the Estates appointed an executive officer, known as the **stadholder**, who carried out ceremonial functions and was responsible for military defense. Although in theory the stadholder was freely chosen by the Estates and was answerable to them, in practice the strong and influential House of Orange usually held the office of stadholder in several of the seven provinces of the republic. This meant that tensions always lingered between supporters of the House of Orange and those of the staunchly republican Estates, who suspected that the princes of Orange harbored monarchical ambitions. When one of them, William III, took the English throne in 1688 with his wife, Mary, the republic simply continued without stadholders for several decades.

The political success of the Dutch rested on their phenomenal commercial prosperity. The Dutch originally came to dominate European shipping by putting profits from their original industry—herring fishing—into shipbuilding. They boasted the lowest shipping rates and largest merchant marine in Europe, allowing them to undersell foreign competitors (see Chapter 14). In the seventeenth century global trade and commerce brought the Dutch the highest standard of living in Europe, perhaps in the world. Salaries were high, and all classes of society ate well. A scholar has described the Netherlands as "an island of plenty in a sea of want." Consequently, the Netherlands experienced very few of the food riots that characterized the rest of Europe.[10]

The moral and ethical bases of Dutch commercial wealth were thrift, frugality, and religious toleration. Although there is scattered evidence of anti-Semitism, Jews enjoyed a level of acceptance and assimilation in business and general culture unique in early modern Europe. In the Dutch Republic, toleration paid off: it attracted a great deal of foreign capital and investment. After Louis XIV revoked the Edict of Nantes, many Huguenots fled France for the Dutch Republic. They brought with them a high level of artisanal skill and business experience as well as a loathing for state repression that would inspire the political views of the Enlightenment (see page 500).

Baroque Art and Music

Throughout European history, the cultural tastes of one age have often seemed unsatisfactory to the next. So it was with the baroque. The term *baroque* may have come from the Portuguese word for an "odd-shaped, imperfect pearl" and was commonly used by late-eighteenth-century art critics as an expression of scorn for what they considered an overblown, unbalanced style. Specialists now agree that the baroque style marked one of the high points in the history of European culture.

Rome and the revitalized Catholic Church of the late sixteenth century spurred the early development of the baroque. The papacy and the Jesuits encouraged the growth of an intensely emotional, exuberant art. These patrons wanted artists to go beyond the Renaissance focus on pleasing a small, wealthy cultural elite. They wanted artists to appeal to the senses and thereby touch the souls and kindle the faith of ordinary churchgoers while proclaiming the power and confidence of the reformed Catholic Church. In addition to this underlying religious emotionalism, the baroque drew its sense of drama, motion, and ceaseless striving from the Catholic Reformation. The interior of the famous Jesuit Church of Jesus in Rome—the Gesù—combined all these characteristics in its lavish, wildly active decorations and frescoes.

Taking definite shape in Italy after 1600, the baroque style in the visual arts developed with exceptional vigor in Catholic countries—in Spain and Latin America, Austria, southern Germany, and Poland. Yet baroque art was more than just "Catholic art" in the seventeenth century and the first half of the eighteenth. True, neither Protestant England nor the Netherlands ever came fully under the spell of the baroque, but neither did Catholic France. And Protestants accounted for some of the finest examples of baroque style, especially in music. The baroque style spread partly because its tension and bombast spoke to an agitated age that was experiencing great violence and controversy in politics and religion.

In painting, the baroque reached maturity early with Peter Paul Rubens (1577–1640), the most outstanding and most representative of baroque painters. Studying in his native Flanders and in Italy, where he was influenced by masters of the High Renaissance such as Michelangelo, Rubens developed his own rich, sensuous, colorful style, which was characterized by animated figures, melodramatic contrasts, and monumental size. Rubens excelled in glorifying monarchs such as Queen Mother Marie de' Medici of France. He was also a devout Catholic; nearly half of his pictures treat Christian subjects. Yet one of Rubens's trademarks was the fleshy, sensual nudes who populate his canvases as Roman goddesses, water nymphs, and remarkably voluptuous saints and angels.

In music, the baroque style reached its culmination almost a century later in the dynamic, soaring lines of the endlessly inventive Johann Sebastian Bach (1685–1750). Organist and choirmaster of several Lutheran churches across Germany, Bach was equally at home writing secular concertos and sublime religious cantatas. Bach's organ music combined the baroque spirit of invention, tension, and emotion in an unforgettable striving toward the infinite. Unlike Rubens, Bach was not fully appreciated in his lifetime, but since the early nineteenth century his reputation has grown steadily.

NOTES

1. Quoted in Cecile Hugon, *Social France in the XVII Century* (London: McMilland, 1911), p. 189.
2. H. Kamen, "The Economic and Social Consequences of the Thirty Years' War," *Past and Present* 39 (1968): 44–61.
3. John A. Lynn, "Recalculating French Army Growth," in *The Military Revolution Debate: Readings on the Military Transformation of Early Modern Europe*, ed. Clifford J. Rogers (Boulder, Colo.: Westview Press, 1995), p. 125.
4. Quoted in John A. Lynn, *Giant of the Grand Siècle: The French Army, 1610–1715* (Cambridge: Cambridge University Press, 1997), p. 74.
5. J. H. Elliott, *Imperial Spain, 1469–1716* (New York: Mentor Books, 1963), pp. 306–308.
6. German History Documents, http://germanhistorydocs.ghi-dc.org/docpage.cfm?docpage_id=3733.
7. H. Rosenberg, *Bureaucracy, Aristocracy, and Autocracy: The Prussian Experience, 1660–1815* (Boston: Beacon Press, 1966), p. 43.
8. Cited in Giles MacDonogh, *Frederick the Great: A Life in Deed and Letters* (New York: St. Martin's, 2001), p. 23.
9. Rosenberg, *Bureaucracy, Aristocracy, and Autocracy*, p. 40.
10. S. Schama, *The Embarrassment of Riches: An Interpretation of Dutch Culture in the Golden Age* (New York: Alfred A. Knopf, 1987), pp. 165–170; quotation is on p. 167.

LOOKING BACK LOOKING AHEAD

The seventeenth century represented a difficult passage between two centuries of dynamism and growth. On one side lay the sixteenth century of religious enthusiasm and strife, overseas expansion, rising population, and vigorous commerce. On the other side stretched the eighteenth-century era of renewed population growth, economic development, and cultural flourishing. The first half of the seventeenth century was marked by the spread of religious and dynastic warfare across Europe, resulting in the death and dislocation of many millions. This catastrophe was compounded by recurrent episodes of crop failure, famine, and epidemic disease, all of which contributed to a stagnant economy and population loss. In the middle decades of the seventeenth century, the very survival of the European monarchies established in the Renaissance appeared in doubt.

With the re-establishment of order in the second half of the century, maintaining political and social stability was of paramount importance to European rulers and elites. In western and eastern Europe, a host of monarchs proclaimed their God-given and "absolute" authority to rule in the name of peace, unity, and good order. Rulers' ability to impose such claims in reality depended a great deal on compromise with local elites, who acquiesced to state power in exchange for privileges and payoffs. In this way, absolutism and constitutionalism did not always differ as much as they claimed. Both systems relied on political compromises forged from decades of strife.

The eighteenth century was to see this status quo thrown into question by new Enlightenment aspirations for human society, which themselves derived from the inquisitive and self-confident spirit of the Scientific Revolution. By the end of the century, demands for real popular sovereignty would challenge the foundations of the political order so painfully achieved in the seventeenth century.

MAKE CONNECTIONS

Think about the larger developments and continuities within and across chapters.

1. This chapter has argued that, despite their political differences, rulers in absolutist and constitutionalist nations faced similar obstacles in the mid-seventeenth century and achieved many of the same goals. What evidence for this argument do you find in the chapter? Do you think that absolutist and constitutionalist rulers were, on the whole, more similar or more different?

2. Proponents of absolutism in western Europe believed that their form of monarchical rule was fundamentally different from and superior to what they saw as the "despotism" of Russia and the Ottoman Empire. What was the basis of this belief, and how accurate do you think it was?

Chapter Review

IDENTIFY KEY TERMS

Identify and explain the significance of each item below.

Peace of Westphalia (p. 453)

Fronde (p. 457)

mercantilism (p. 460)

Peace of Utrecht (p. 462)

Junkers (p. 467)

boyars (p. 470)

Cossacks (p. 471)

sultan (p. 475)

janissary corps (p. 476)

millet system (p. 476)

constitutionalism (p. 477)

republicanism (p. 477)

Puritans (p. 478)

Protectorate (p. 480)

Test Act (p. 481)

stadholder (p. 482)

REVIEW THE MAIN IDEAS

Answer the focus questions from each section of the chapter.

1. What were the common crises and achievements of seventeenth-century European states? (p. 449)

2. What factors led to the rise of the French absolutist state under Louis XIV, and why did absolutist Spain experience decline in the same period? (p. 456)

3. What were the social conditions of eastern Europe, and how did the rulers of Austria and Prussia transform their nations into powerful absolutist monarchies? (p. 464)

4. What were the distinctive features of Russian and Ottoman absolutism? (p. 469)

5. Why and how did the constitutional state triumph in the Dutch Republic and England? (p. 477)

CHRONOLOGY	
ca. 1500–1650	Consolidation of serfdom in eastern Europe
1533–1584	Reign of Ivan the Terrible in Russia
1589–1610	Reign of Henry IV in France
1598–1613	Time of Troubles in Russia
1620–1740	Growth of absolutism in Austria and Prussia
1642–1649	English civil war, which ends with execution of Charles I
1643–1715	Reign of Louis XIV in France
1653–1658	Military rule in England under Oliver Cromwell (the Protectorate)
1660	Restoration of English monarchy under Charles II
1665–1683	Jean-Baptiste Colbert applies mercantilism to France
1670	Charles II agrees to re-Catholicize England in secret agreement with Louis XIV
1670–1671	Cossack revolt led by Stenka Razin
ca. 1680–1750	Construction of absolutist palaces
1682	Louis XIV moves court to Versailles
1682–1725	Reign of Peter the Great in Russia
1683–1718	Habsburgs push the Ottoman Turks from Hungary
1685	Edict of Nantes revoked in France
1688–1689	Glorious Revolution in England
1701–1713	War of the Spanish Succession

16

Toward a New Worldview

1540–1789

THE INTELLECTUAL DEVELOPMENTS OF THE SIXTEENTH AND SEVENTEENTH CENTURIES created the modern worldview that the West continues to hold—and debate—to this day. In this period, fundamentally new ways of understanding the natural world emerged. Those leading the changes saw themselves as philosophers and referred to their field of study as "natural philosophy." Whereas medieval scholars looked to authoritative texts like the Bible or the classics, early modern natural philosophers performed experiments and relied on increasingly complex mathematical calculations. The resulting conception of the universe and its laws remained in force until Albert Einstein's discoveries at the beginning of the twentieth century. Along with new discoveries in botany, zoology, chemistry, and other domains, these developments constituted a fundamental shift in the basic framework for understanding the natural world and the methods for examining it known collectively as the "Scientific Revolution."

In the eighteenth century philosophers extended the use of reason from the study of nature to human society. They sought to bring the light of reason to bear on the darkness of prejudice, outmoded traditions, and ignorance. Self-proclaimed members of an "Enlightenment" movement, they wished to bring the same progress to human affairs as their predecessors had brought to the understanding of the natural world. While the Scientific Revolution ushered in modern science, the Enlightenment created concepts of human rights, equality, progress, universalism, and tolerance that still guide Western societies today. At the same time, some people used their new understanding of nature and reason to proclaim their own superiority, thus rationalizing attitudes now regarded as racist and sexist. Transformations in science and philosophy were enabled and encouraged by European overseas expansion, which challenged traditional ways of thinking by introducing an enormous variety of new peoples, plants, and animals.

The Scientific Revolution

Focus Question	What revolutionary discoveries were made in the sixteenth and seventeenth centuries, and why did they occur in Europe?

Until the middle of the sixteenth century, Europeans relied on an understanding of motion and matter drawn from the ancient Greek philosopher Aristotle and adapted to Christian theology. The rise of the university, along with the intellectual vitality of the Renaissance and technological advancements, inspired European scholars to seek better explanations. From the sun-centered universe proposed by the Polish astronomer Nicolaus Copernicus to the great synthesis of physics and astronomy accomplished by the English scientist Isaac Newton, a revolutionary new understanding of the universe had emerged by the end of the seventeenth century. Collectively known as the "Scientific Revolution," the work of these scientists constituted highly significant milestones in the creation of modern science.

Hailed today as pioneers of a modern worldview, the major figures of the Scientific Revolution were for the most part devout Christians who saw their work as heralding the glory of creation and who combined older traditions of magic, astrology, and alchemy with their pathbreaking experimentation. Their discoveries took place in a broader context of international trade, imperial expansion, and cultural exchange. Alongside developments in modern science and natural philosophy, the growth of natural history in this period is now recognized by historians as a major achievement of the Scientific Revolution.

Why Europe?

In 1500 scientific activity flourished in many parts of the world. With the expansion of Islam into the lands of the Byzantine Empire in the seventh and eighth centuries, Muslim scholars inherited ancient Greek learning, which itself was built on centuries of borrowing from older civilizations in Egypt, Babylonia, and India. The interaction of peoples and cultures across the vast Muslim world, facilitated by religious tolerance and the common scholarly language of Arabic, was highly favorable to advances in learning.

In a great period of cultural and intellectual flourishing from 1000 to 1500, Muslim scholars thrived in cultural centers such as Baghdad and Córdoba, the capital of Islamic Spain. They established the world's first universities in Constantinople, Fez (Morocco), and Cairo. In this fertile atmosphere, scholars surpassed the texts they had inherited in areas such as mathematics, physics, astronomy, and medicine. Arab and Persian mathematicians, for example, invented algebra, the concept of the algorithm, and decimal point notation, while Arab astronomers improved on measurements recorded in ancient works.

China was also a vital center of scientific activity, which reached a peak in the mid-fourteenth century. Among its many achievements, papermaking, gunpowder, and the use of the compass in navigation were the most influential for the West. In Mesoamerica, civilizations such as the Maya and the Aztecs devised complex calendar systems based on astronomical observations and developed mathematics and writing.

Given the multiple world sites of learning and scholarship, it was by no means inevitable that Europe would take the lead in scientific thought or that "modern science" as we know it would emerge. In world history, periods of advancement produced by intense cultural interaction, such as those that occurred after the spread of Islam, are often followed by stagnation and decline during times of conflict and loss of authority. This is what happened in western Europe after the fall of the Western Roman Empire in the fifth century and in the Maya civilization after the collapse of its cultural and political centers around 900. The Muslim world successfully resisted a similar threat after the Mongol invasions.

The re-establishment of stronger monarchies and the growth of trade in the High Middle Ages contributed to a renewal of learning in western Europe. As Europeans began to encroach on Islamic lands in Iberia, Sicily, and the eastern Mediterranean, they became aware of the rich heritage of ancient Greek learning in these regions and the ways scholars had improved upon received knowledge. In the twelfth century many Greek texts — including works of Aristotle, Ptolemy, Galen, and Euclid previously unknown in the West — were translated into Latin, along with the commentaries of Arab scholars. A number of European cities created universities in which Aristotle's works dominated the curriculum.

As Europe recovered from the ravages of the Black Death in the late fourteenth and fifteenth centuries, the intellectual and cultural movement known as the Renaissance provided a crucial foundation for the Scientific Revolution (see Chapter 12). Scholars called humanists, working in the bustling mercantile city-states of Italy, emphasized the value of acquiring knowledge for the practical purposes of life. The quest to restore the glories of the ancient past led to the rediscovery of other classical texts such as Ptolemy's *Geography*, which was translated into Latin around 1410. An encyclopedic treatise on botany by Theophrastus was rediscovered in the 1450s moldering on the shelves of the Vatican library. The fall of Constantinople to the Ottomans in 1453 resulted in a great influx of little-known Greek works, as Christian scholars fled to Italy with their precious texts.

In this period, western European universities established new professorships of mathematics, astronomy, and natural philosophy. The prestige of the new fields was low, especially mathematics, which was reserved for practical problems such as accounting, surveying, and computing planetary tables, but not used as a tool to understand the functioning of the physical world itself. Nevertheless, these professorships eventually enabled the union of mathematics with natural philosophy that was to be a hallmark of the Scientific Revolution.

European overseas expansion in the fifteenth and sixteenth centuries provided another catalyst for new thought about the natural world. In particular, the navigational problems of long oceanic voyages in the age of expansion stimulated scientific research and invention. To help solve these problems, inventors developed many new scientific instruments, such as the telescope, barometer, thermometer, pendulum clock, microscope, and air pump. Better instruments, which permitted more accurate observations, often led to important new knowledge. Another crucial technology in this period was printing, which provided a faster and less expensive way to circulate knowledge.

Political and social conflicts were widespread in Eurasia in the sixteenth and early seventeenth centuries, but they had different results. The three large empires of the

Muslim world—the Ottomans, Safavid Persians, and Mughals—that arose in the wake of the Mongol Empire sought to restore order and assert legitimacy in part by imposing Islamic orthodoxy. Their failure to adopt the printing press can be seen as part of a wider reaction against earlier traditions of innovation. Similarly, in China, under the Qing Dynasty, political newcomers legitimized their authority through stricter adherence to traditional ways. In contrast, western Europe remained politically fragmented into smaller competitive nations, divisions that were augmented by the religious fracturing of the Protestant Reformation. These conditions made it impossible for authorities to impose one orthodox set of ideas and thus allowed individuals to question dominant patterns of thinking.

Scientific Thought to 1500

The term *science* as we use it today came into use only in the nineteenth century. For medieval scholars, philosophy was the path to true knowledge about the world, and its proofs consisted of the authority of ancients (as interpreted by Christian theologians) and their techniques of logical argumentation. Questions about the physical nature of the universe and how it functioned belonged to a minor branch of philosophy, called **natural philosophy**. Natural philosophy was based primarily on the ideas of Aristotle, the great Greek philosopher of the fourth century B.C.E. Medieval theologians such as Thomas Aquinas brought Aristotelian philosophy into harmony with Christian doctrines. According to the Christianized view of Aristotle, a motionless earth stood at the center of the universe and was encompassed by ten separate concentric crystal spheres in which were embedded the moon, the sun, planets, and stars. Beyond the spheres was Heaven, with the throne of God and the souls of the saved. Angels kept the spheres moving in perfect circles.

Aristotle's views also dominated thinking about physics and motion on earth. Aristotle had distinguished between the world of the celestial spheres and that of the earth—the sublunar world. The spheres consisted of a perfect, incorruptible "quintessence," or fifth essence. The sublunar world, however, was made up of four imperfect, changeable elements: air, fire, water, and earth. Aristotle and his followers also believed that a uniform force moved an object at a constant speed and that the object would stop as soon as that force was removed.

Aristotle's cosmology made intellectual sense, but it could not account for the observed motions of the stars and planets and, in particular, provided no explanation for the apparent backward motion of the planets (which we now know occurs as planets closer to the sun periodically overtake the earth on their faster orbits). The great second-century scholar Ptolemy, a Hellenized Egyptian, offered a theory for this phenomenon. According to Ptolemy, the planets moved in small circles, called epicycles, each of which moved in turn along a larger circle, or deferent. Ptolemaic astronomy was less elegant than Aristotle's neat nested circles and required complex calculations, but it provided a surprisingly accurate model for predicting planetary motion.

The work of Ptolemy also provided the basic foundation of knowledge about the earth. Rediscovered around 1410, his *Geography* presented crucial advances on medieval cartography by representing a round earth divided into 360 degrees with the major latitude marks. Ptolemy's work reintroduced the idea of using coordinates of

The Aristotelian Universe as Imagined in the Sixteenth Century
A round earth is at the center, surrounded by spheres of water, air, and fire. Beyond this small nucleus, the moon, the sun, and the five planets were embedded in their own rotating crystal spheres, with the stars sharing the surface of one enormous sphere. Beyond, the heavens were composed of unchanging ether. (From *Cosmographia*, by Peter Apian, 1630/Universal History Archive/UIG/Bridgeman Images)

latitude and longitude to plot points on the earth's surface, a major advantage for long-distance navigation. However, Ptolemy's map reflected the limits of ancient knowledge, showing only the continents of Europe, Africa, and Asia, with land covering three-quarters of the world. Lacking awareness of the Pacific Ocean and the Americas, Ptolemy vastly underestimated the distance west from Europe to Asia.

These two frameworks reveal the strengths and limitations of European knowledge on the eve of the Scientific Revolution. Overcoming the authority of the ancients to develop a new understanding of the natural world, derived from precise techniques of observation and experimentation, was a monumental achievement. Europeans were not the first to use experimental methods—of which there was a long tradition in the Muslim world and elsewhere—but they were the first to separate scientific knowledge decisively from philosophical and religious beliefs and to accord mathematics a fundamental role in understanding the natural world.

The Copernican Hypothesis

The first great departure from the medieval system was the work of the Polish cleric Nicolaus Copernicus (1473–1543). Copernicus studied astronomy, medicine, and church law at the famed universities of Bologna, Padua, and Ferrara before taking up a church position in East Prussia. Copernicus came to believe that Ptolemy's cumbersome rules detracted from the majesty of a perfect creator. He preferred an idea espoused by some ancient Greek and Arab scholars: that the sun, rather than the earth, was at the center of the universe. Without questioning the Aristotelian belief in crystal spheres or the idea that circular motion was divine, Copernicus theorized that the stars and planets, including the earth, revolved around a fixed sun. Copernicus worked on his hypothesis from 1506 to 1530, but, fearing the ridicule of other scholars, he did not publish his *On the Revolutions of the Heavenly Spheres* until 1543, the year of his death.

The **Copernican hypothesis** had enormous scientific and religious implications, many of which the conservative Copernicus did not anticipate. First, it put the stars at rest, their apparent nightly movement simply a result of the earth's rotation. Thus it destroyed the main reason for believing in crystal spheres capable of moving the stars around the earth. Second, Copernicus's theory suggested a universe of staggering size. If in the course of a year the earth moved around the sun and yet the stars appeared to remain in the same place, then the universe was unthinkably large. Third, by using mathematics, instead of philosophy, to justify his theories, Copernicus challenged the traditional hierarchy of the disciplines. Finally, by characterizing the earth as just another planet, Copernicus destroyed the basic idea of Aristotelian physics — that the earthly sphere was quite different from the heavenly one. Where then were Heaven and the throne of God?

Religious leaders varied in their response to Copernicus's theories. A few Protestant scholars became avid Copernicans, while others accepted some elements of his criticism of Ptolemy, but firmly rejected the notion that the earth moved, a doctrine that contradicted the literal reading of some passages of the Bible. Among Catholics, Copernicus's ideas drew little attention prior to 1600. Because the Catholic Church had never held to literal interpretations of the Bible, it did not officially declare the Copernican hypothesis false until 1616.

Other events were almost as influential in creating doubts about traditional astronomy. In 1572 a new star appeared and shone very brightly for almost two years. The new star, which was actually a distant exploding star, made an enormous impression on people. It seemed to contradict the idea that the heavenly spheres were unchanging and therefore perfect. In 1577 a new comet suddenly moved through the sky, cutting a straight path across the supposedly impenetrable crystal spheres. It was time, as a sixteenth-century scientific writer put it, for "the radical renovation of astronomy."[1]

Brahe, Kepler, and Galileo: Proving Copernicus Right

One astronomer who agreed with the Copernican hypothesis was the Danish astronomer Tycho Brahe (TEE-koh BRAH-hee) (1546–1601). Brahe established himself as Europe's leading astronomer with his detailed observations of the new star that appeared in 1572. Impressed by his work, the king of Denmark provided funds for Brahe to build the most sophisticated observatory of his day.

Upon the king's death, Brahe acquired a new patron in the Holy Roman emperor Rudolph II and built a new observatory in Prague. For twenty years Brahe observed the stars and planets with the naked eye in order to create new and improved tables of planetary motions, dubbed the *Rudolphine Tables* in honor of his patron. His limited understanding of mathematics and his sudden death in 1601, however, prevented him from making much sense out of his mass of data. Part Ptolemaic, part Copernican, he believed that all the planets except the earth revolved around the sun and that the entire group of sun and planets revolved in turn around the earth-moon system.

Brahe's assistant, Johannes Kepler (1571–1630), carefully re-examined his predecessor's notations and came to believe that they could not be explained by Ptolemy's astronomy. Abandoning the notion of epicycles and deferents—which even Copernicus had retained in part—Kepler developed three revolutionary laws of planetary motion. First, largely through observations of the planet Mars, he demonstrated that the orbits of the planets around the sun are elliptical rather than circular. Second, he demonstrated that the planets do not move at a uniform speed in their orbits. When a planet is close to the sun it moves more rapidly, and it slows as it moves farther away from the sun. Finally, Kepler's third law stated that the time a planet takes to make its complete orbit is precisely related to its distance from the sun.

Kepler's contribution was monumental. Whereas Copernicus had used mathematics to describe planetary movement, Kepler proved mathematically the precise relations of a sun-centered (solar) system. He thus united for the first time the theoretical cosmology of natural philosophy with mathematics. His work demolished the old system of Aristotle and Ptolemy, and with his third law he came close to formulating the idea of universal gravitation (see the next section). In 1627 he also completed Brahe's *Rudolphine Tables*, which were used by astronomers for many years.

While Kepler was unraveling planetary motion, a young Florentine named Galileo Galilei (1564–1642) was challenging Aristotelian ideas about motion on earth. Like Kepler and so many early scientists, Galileo was a poor nobleman first marked for a religious career. Instead, his fascination with mathematics led to a professorship in which he examined motion and mechanics in a new way. Galileo focused on deficiencies in Aristotle's theories of motion. He measured the movement of a rolling ball across a surface, repeating the action again and again to verify his results. In his famous acceleration experiment, he showed that a uniform force—in this case, gravity—produced a uniform acceleration. Through another experiment, he formulated the **law of inertia**. He found that rest was not the natural state of objects. Rather, an object continues in motion forever unless stopped by some external force. His discoveries proved Aristotelian physics wrong.

On hearing details about the invention of the telescope in Holland, Galileo made one for himself and trained it on the heavens. He quickly discovered the first four moons of Jupiter, which clearly suggested that Jupiter could not possibly be embedded in an impenetrable crystal sphere as Aristotle and Ptolemy maintained. This discovery provided new evidence for the Copernican theory, in which Galileo already believed. Galileo then pointed his telescope at the moon. He wrote in 1610 in *The Sidereal Messenger*: "By the aid of a telescope anyone may behold [the Milky Way] in a manner which so distinctly appeals to the senses that all the disputes which have tormented philosophers through so many ages are exploded by the irrefutable evidence of our eyes, and we are freed from wordy disputes upon the subject."[2]

Reading these famous lines, one feels a crucial corner in Western civilization being turned. No longer should one rely on established authority. A new method of learning and investigating was being developed, one that proved useful in any field of inquiry. A historian investigating documents of the past, for example, is not so different from a Galileo studying stars and rolling balls.

Newton's Synthesis

By about 1640 the work of Brahe, Kepler, and Galileo had been largely accepted by the scientific community despite opposition from religious leaders. The old Aristotelian astronomy and physics were in ruins, and several fundamental breakthroughs had been made. But the new findings failed to explain what forces controlled the movement of the planets and objects on earth. That challenge was taken up by English scientist Isaac Newton (1642–1727), a genius who spectacularly united the experimental and theoretical-mathematical sides of modern science.

Newton was born into the lower English gentry, and he enrolled at Cambridge University in 1661. He arrived at some of his most basic ideas about physics in 1666 at age twenty-four, but was unable to prove them mathematically. In 1684, after years of studying optics, Newton returned to physics for eighteen intensive months. The result was his towering accomplishment, a single explanatory system that could integrate the astronomy of Copernicus, as corrected by Kepler's laws, with the physics of Galileo and his predecessors. Newton did this through a set of mathematical laws that explain motion and mechanics. These laws were published in 1687 in Newton's *Mathematical Principles of Natural Philosophy* (also known as the *Principia*). Because of their complexity, it took scientists and engineers two hundred years to work out all their implications.

The key feature of the Newtonian synthesis was the **law of universal gravitation**. According to this law, every body in the universe attracts every other body in the universe in a precise mathematical relationship, whereby the force of attraction is proportional to the quantity of matter of the objects and inversely proportional to the square of the distance between them. The whole universe—from Kepler's elliptical orbits to Galileo's rolling balls—was unified in one majestic system. Newton's synthesis of mathematics with physics and astronomy prevailed until the twentieth century and established him as one of the most important figures in the history of science. Yet, near the end of his life, this acclaimed figure declared: "I do not know what I may appear to the world; but to myself I seem to have been only like a boy, playing on the seashore, and diverting myself, in now and then finding a smoother pebble or a prettier shell than ordinary, whilst the great ocean of truth lay all undiscovered before me."[3]

Natural History and Empire

At the same time that they made advances in astronomy and physics, Europeans embarked on the pursuit of knowledge about unknown geographical regions and the useful and valuable resources they contained. Because they were the first to acquire a large overseas empire, the Spanish pioneered these efforts. Following the conquest of the Aztec and Inca Empires (see Chapter 14), they sought to learn about and profit from their New World holdings. The Spanish crown sponsored many scientific expeditions to gather information and specimens, out of which emerged new discoveries that reshaped the fields of botany, zoology, cartography, and metallurgy, among others. These accomplishments have attracted less attention from historians in part because the strict policy of secrecy imposed on scientific discoveries by the Spanish crown limits the number of available documents about them.

Plants were a particular source of interest because they offered tremendous profits in the form of spices, medicines, dyes, and cash crops. King Philip II of Spain sent his personal physician, Francisco Hernández, to New Spain for seven years in the 1560s. Hernández filled fifteen volumes with illustrations of three thousand plants previously unknown in Europe. He extensively interviewed local healers about the plants' medicinal properties, thereby benefiting from centuries of Mesoamerican botanical knowledge. In the seventeenth century, for example, the Spanish obtained a monopoly on the world's supply of cinchona bark, which comes from a tree native to the high altitudes of the Andes and was the first effective treatment for malaria.

Other countries followed the Spanish example as their global empires expanded, relying on both official expeditions and the private initiative of merchants, missionaries, and settlers. Royal botanical gardens served as living laboratories for cultivating valuable foreign plants. Over time, the stream of new information about plant and animal species overwhelmed existing intellectual frameworks. Carl Linnaeus (1707–1778) of Sweden sent his students on exploratory voyages around the world and, based on their observations and the specimens they collected, devised a formal system of naming and classifying living organisms still used today (with substantial revisions).

New encyclopedias of natural history popularized this knowledge with realistic drawings and descriptions emphasizing the usefulness of animals and plants. Audiences at home eagerly read the accounts of naturalists who braved the heat, insects, and diseases of tropical jungles to bring home exotic animal, vegetable, and mineral specimens (along with indigenous human subjects). They heard much less about the many local guides, translators, and practitioners of medicine and science who made these expeditions possible and who contributed rich knowledge about the natural world.

Magic and Alchemy

Recent historical research on the Scientific Revolution has focused on the contribution of ideas and practices that no longer belong to the realm of science, such as astrology and alchemy. For most of human history, interest in astronomy was inspired by the belief that the movement of heavenly bodies influenced events on earth. Many of the most celebrated astronomers also worked as astrologers. Used as a diagnostic tool in medicine, astrology formed a regular part of the curriculum of medical schools.

Centuries-old practices of magic and alchemy also remained important traditions for natural philosophers. Early modern practitioners of magic strove to understand and control hidden connections they perceived among different elements of the natural world, such as that between a magnet and iron. The idea that objects possessed hidden or "occult" qualities that allowed them to affect other objects was a particularly important legacy of the magical tradition. Belief in occult qualities—or numerology or cosmic harmony—was not antithetical to belief in God. On the contrary, adherents believed that only a divine creator could infuse the universe with such meaningful mystery.

Johannes Kepler exemplifies the interaction among these different strands of interest in the natural world. His duties as court mathematician included casting horoscopes for the royal family, and he guided his own life by astrological principles.

He also wrote at length on cosmic harmonies and explained elliptical motion through ideas about the beautiful music created by the combined motion of the planets. Kepler's fictional account of travel to the moon, written partly to illustrate the idea of a non-earth-centered universe, caused controversy and may have contributed to the arrest and trial of his mother as a witch in 1620. Kepler also suffered because of his unorthodox brand of Lutheranism, which led to his condemnation by both Lutherans and Catholics.

Another example of the interweaving of ideas and beliefs is Sir Isaac Newton, who was both intensely religious and fascinated by alchemy, whose practitioners believed (among other things) that base metals could be turned into gold. Critics complained that his idea of universal gravitation was merely a restatement of old magical ideas about the innate sympathies between bodies; Newton himself believed that the attraction of gravity resulted from God's actions in the universe.

Important Changes in Scientific Thinking and Practice

Focus Question	**What intellectual and social changes occurred as a result of the Scientific Revolution?**

The Scientific Revolution was not accomplished by a handful of brilliant individuals working alone. Advancements occurred in many fields—medicine, chemistry, and botany, among others—as scholars developed new methods to seek answers to long-standing problems. They did so in collaboration with skilled craftsmen who invented new instruments and helped conduct experiments. These results circulated in an intellectual community from which women were usually excluded.

The Methods of Science: Bacon and Descartes

One of the keys to the achievement of a new worldview in the seventeenth century was the development of better ways of obtaining knowledge. Two important thinkers, Francis Bacon (1561–1626) and René Descartes (day-KAHRT) (1596–1650), were influential in describing and advocating for improved scientific methods based, respectively, on experimentation and mathematical reasoning.

The English politician and writer Francis Bacon was the greatest early propagandist for the experimental method. Rejecting the Aristotelian and medieval method of using speculative reasoning to build general theories, Bacon argued that new knowledge had to be pursued through empirical research. The researcher who wants to learn more about leaves or rocks, for example, should not speculate about the subject but rather collect a multitude of specimens and then compare and analyze them to derive general principles. Bacon formalized the empirical method, which had already been used by Brahe and Galileo, into the general theory of inductive reasoning known as empiricism. Bacon's work, and his prestige as lord chancellor under James I, led to the widespread adoption of what was called "experimental philosophy" in England after his death. In 1660 followers of Bacon created the Royal Society (still in existence), which met weekly to conduct experiments and discuss the latest findings of scholars across Europe.

On the continent, more speculative methods retained support. In 1619, as a twenty-three-year-old soldier serving in the Thirty Years' War, the French philosopher René Descartes experienced a life-changing intellectual vision. Descartes saw that there was a perfect correspondence between geometry and algebra and that geometrical spatial figures could be expressed as algebraic equations and vice versa. A major step forward in the history of mathematics, Descartes's discovery of analytic geometry provided scientists with an important new tool.

Descartes used mathematics to elaborate a highly influential vision of the workings of the cosmos. Accepting Galileo's claim that all elements of the universe are composed of the same matter, Descartes began to investigate the basic nature of matter. Drawing on ancient Greek atomist philosophies, Descartes developed the idea that matter was made up of identical "corpuscles" (tiny particles) that collided together in an endless series of motions, akin to the workings of a machine. All occurrences in nature could be analyzed as matter in motion and, according to Descartes, the total "quantity of motion" in the universe was constant. Descartes's mechanistic view of the universe depended on the idea that a vacuum was impossible, which meant that every action had an equal reaction, continuing in an eternal chain reaction.

Although Descartes's hypothesis about the vacuum was proved wrong, his notion of a mechanistic universe intelligible through the physics of motion proved inspirational. Decades later, Newton rejected Descartes's idea of a full universe and several of his other ideas, but retained the notion of a mechanistic universe as a key element of his own system.

Descartes's greatest achievement was to develop his initial vision into a whole philosophy of knowledge and science. The Aristotelian cosmos was appealing in part because it corresponded with the evidence of the human senses. When experiments proved that sensory impressions could be wrong, Descartes decided it was necessary to doubt them and everything that could reasonably be doubted, and to then, as in geometry, use deductive reasoning from self-evident truths, which he called "first principles," to ascertain scientific laws. Descartes's reasoning ultimately reduced all substances to "matter" and "mind" — that is, to the physical and the spiritual. The devout Descartes believed that God had endowed man with reason for a purpose and that rational speculation could provide a path to the truths of creation. His view of the world as consisting of two fundamental entities is known as **Cartesian dualism**. Descartes's thought was highly influential in France and the Netherlands, but less so in England, where experimental philosophy won the day.

Both Bacon's inductive experimentalism and Descartes's deductive mathematical reasoning had flaws. Bacon's inability to appreciate the importance of mathematics and his obsession with practical results clearly showed the limitations of antitheoretical empiricism. Likewise, some of Descartes's positions demonstrated the inadequacy of rigid, dogmatic rationalism. For example, he believed that it was possible to deduce the whole science of medicine from first principles. Although insufficient on their own, Bacon's and Descartes's extreme approaches are combined in the modern scientific method, which began to crystallize in the late seventeenth century.

Medicine, the Body, and Chemistry

The Scientific Revolution, which began with the study of the cosmos, soon transformed the understanding of the microcosm of the human body. For many centuries the ancient Greek physician Galen's explanation of the body carried the same authority as Aristotle's account of the universe. According to Galen, the body contained four humors: blood, phlegm, black bile, and yellow bile. Illness was believed to result from an imbalance of humors, which is why doctors frequently prescribed bloodletting to expel excess blood.

Swiss physician and alchemist Paracelsus (1493–1541) was an early proponent of the experimental method in medicine and pioneered the use of chemicals and drugs to address what he saw as chemical, rather than humoral, imbalances. Another experimentalist, Flemish physician Andreas Vesalius (1516–1564), studied anatomy by dissecting human bodies, often those of executed criminals. In 1543, the same year Copernicus published *On the Revolutions*, Vesalius issued his masterpiece, *On the Structure of the Human Body*. Its two hundred precise drawings revolutionized the understanding of human anatomy, disproving Galen, just as Copernicus and his successors had disproved Aristotle and Ptolemy. The experimental approach also led English royal physician William Harvey (1578–1657) to discover the circulation of blood through the veins and arteries in 1628. Harvey was the first to explain that the heart worked like a pump and to explain the function of its muscles and valves.

Frontispiece to *De Humani Corporis Fabrica* (*On the Structure of the Human Body*) The frontispiece to Vesalius's pioneering work, published in 1543, shows him dissecting a corpse. This was a revolutionary new hands-on approach for physicians, who usually worked from a theoretical, rather than a practical, understanding of the body. Based on direct observation, Vesalius replaced ancient ideas drawn from Greek philosophy with a much more accurate account of the structure and function of the body. (© SSPL/Science Museum/The Image Works)

Robert Boyle (1627–1691) was a key figure in the victory of experimental methods in England and helped create the Royal Society in 1660. Boyle's scientific work led to the development of modern chemistry. Following Paracelsus's lead, he undertook experiments to discover the basic elements of nature, which he believed was composed of infinitely small atoms. Boyle was the first to create a vacuum, thus disproving Descartes's belief that a vacuum could not exist in nature, and he discovered Boyle's law (1662), which states that the pressure of a gas varies inversely with volume.

Science and Religion

It is sometimes assumed that the relationship between science and religion is fundamentally hostile and that the pursuit of knowledge based on reason and proof is incompatible with faith. Yet during the Scientific Revolution most practitioners were devoutly religious and saw their work as contributing to the celebration of God's glory rather than undermining it. However, the concept of heliocentrism, which displaced the earth from the center of the universe, threatened the understanding of the place of mankind in creation as stated in Genesis. All religions derived from the Old Testament—Catholic, Protestant, Jewish, and Muslim—thus faced difficulties accepting the Copernican system. The leaders of the Catholic Church were initially less hostile than Protestant and Jewish religious leaders, but in the first decades of the sixteenth century the Catholic attitude changed. In 1616 the Holy Office placed the works of Copernicus and his supporters, including Kepler, on a list of books Catholics were forbidden to read.

Out of caution, Galileo Galilei silenced his views on heliocentrism for several years, until 1623 saw the ascension of Pope Urban VIII, a man sympathetic to the new science. However, Galileo's 1632 *Dialogue on the Two Chief Systems of the World* went too far. Published in Italian and widely read, it openly lampooned the Aristotelian view and defended Copernicus. In 1633 Galileo was tried for heresy by the papal Inquisition. Imprisoned and threatened with torture, the aging Galileo recanted, "renouncing and cursing" his Copernican errors.

Thereafter, the Catholic Church became more hostile to science, a change that helped account for the decline of science in Italy (but not in Catholic France) after 1640. At the same time, some Protestant countries, including the Netherlands, Denmark, and England, became quite "pro-science." This was especially true in countries without a strong religious authority capable of imposing religious orthodoxy on scientific questions.

Science and Society

The rise of modern science had many consequences. First, it created a new social group—the international scientific community. Members of this community were linked together by common interests and values as well as by scholarly journals and associations. The personal success of scientists and scholars depended on making new discoveries, and science became competitive. Second, as governments intervened to support and sometimes direct research, the new scientific community became closely tied to the state and its agendas. National academies of science were created under state sponsorship in London in 1660, Paris in 1666, Berlin in 1700, and later across Europe.

It was long believed that the Scientific Revolution had little relationship to practical concerns and the life of the masses until the late-eighteenth-century Industrial Revolution (see Chapter 20). More recently, historians have emphasized the importance of skilled craftsmen in the rise of science, particularly in the development of the experimental method. Many artisans developed a strong interest in emerging scientific ideas, and, in turn, the practice of science in the seventeenth century often relied on artisans' expertise in making instruments and conducting precise experiments.

Some things did not change in the Scientific Revolution. For example, scholars willing to challenge received ideas about the natural universe did not question the seemingly natural inequalities between the sexes. Instead, the emergence of professional science may have worsened them in some ways. When Renaissance courts served as centers of learning, talented noblewomen could find niches in study and research. But the rise of a scientific community raised new barriers for women because the universities and academies that furnished professional credentials refused them entry.

There were, however, a number of noteworthy exceptions. In Italy, universities and academies did offer posts to women. Across Europe, women worked as makers of wax anatomical models and as botanical and zoological illustrators, like Maria Sibylla Merian. They were also very much involved in informal scientific communities, attending salons (see page 510), participating in scientific experiments, and writing learned treatises. Some female intellectuals became full-fledged members of the philosophical dialogue. In England, Margaret Cavendish, Anne Conway, and Mary Astell all contributed to debates about Descartes's mind-body dualism, among other issues. Descartes himself conducted an intellectual correspondence with the princess Elizabeth of Bohemia, of whom he stated: "I attach more weight to her judgment than to those messieurs the Doctors, who take for a rule of truth the opinions of Aristotle rather than the evidence of reason."[4]

The Rise and Spread of Enlightenment Thought

Focus Question	**How did the Enlightenment emerge, and what were major currents of Enlightenment thought?**

The political, intellectual, and religious developments of the early modern period that gave rise to the Scientific Revolution further contributed to a series of debates about key issues in eighteenth-century Europe and the wider world that came to be known as the **Enlightenment**. The conflicts of the Reformation that led to the devastating violence of the Thirty Years' War brought old religious certainties into question; the strong states that emerged to quell the disorder soon inspired questions about political sovereignty and its limits. Increased movement of peoples, goods, and ideas within and among the continents of Asia, Africa, Europe, and America offered examples of surprisingly different ways of life and values. Finally, the tremendous achievements of the Scientific Revolution inspired intellectuals to believe that answers to all the questions being asked could be found through observation and the use of reason.

Intellectual turmoil in the late seventeenth century thus gave rise to the new worldview of the eighteenth-century Enlightenment. This worldview, which has played a large role in shaping the modern mind, grew out of a rich mix of diverse and often conflicting ideas that were debated in international networks. Despite the diversity, three central concepts stand at the core of Enlightenment thinking. The first and foremost idea was that the methods of natural science could and should be used to examine and understand all aspects of life. This was what intellectuals meant by *reason*, a favorite word of Enlightenment thinkers. Nothing was to be accepted on faith; everything was to be submitted to **rationalism**, a secular, critical way of thinking. A second important Enlightenment concept was that the scientific method was capable of discovering the laws of human society as well as those of nature. These tenets led to the third key idea, that of progress. Enlightenment thinkers believed that, armed with the proper method of discovering the laws of human existence, human beings could create better societies and better people.

The Early Enlightenment

Loosely united by certain key ideas, the European Enlightenment (ca. 1690–1789) was a broad intellectual and cultural movement that gained strength gradually and did not reach its maturity until about 1750. Its origins in the late seventeenth century lie in a combination of developments, including political opposition to absolutist rule; religious conflicts between Protestants and Catholics and within Protestantism; European contacts with other cultures; and the attempt to apply principles and practices from the Scientific Revolution to human society. The generation that came of age between the publication of Newton's *Principia* in 1687 and the death of Louis XIV in 1715 thus tied the knot between the Scientific Revolution and a new outlook on life. Whereas medieval and Reformation thinkers had been concerned primarily with abstract concepts of sin and salvation, and Renaissance humanists had drawn their inspiration from the classical past, Enlightenment thinkers believed that their era had gone far beyond antiquity and that intellectual progress was within their reach.

A key crucible for Enlightenment thought was the Dutch Republic, with its proud commitment to religious tolerance and republican rule. When Louis XIV demanded that all Protestants convert to Catholicism, around two hundred thousand French Protestants, or Huguenots, fled the country, many destined for the Dutch Republic. From this haven of tolerance, Huguenots and their supporters began to publish tracts denouncing religious intolerance and suggesting that only a despotic monarch, not a legitimate ruler, would deny religious freedom. Their challenge to authority thus combined religious and political issues.

These dual concerns drove the career of one important early Enlightenment writer, Pierre Bayle (1647–1706), a Huguenot who took refuge in the Dutch Republic. Bayle critically examined the religious beliefs and persecutions of the past in his *Historical and Critical Dictionary* (1697). Demonstrating that human beliefs had been extremely varied and very often mistaken, he concluded that nothing can ever be known beyond all doubt, a view known as skepticism. His influential *Dictionary* was found in more private libraries of eighteenth-century France than any other book.

The Dutch Jewish philosopher Baruch Spinoza (1632–1677) was another key figure in the transition from the Scientific Revolution to the Enlightenment. Deeply inspired by advances in science—in particular by debates about Descartes's thought—Spinoza sought to apply natural philosophy to thinking about human society. He borrowed Descartes's emphasis on rationalism and his methods of deductive reasoning, but rejected the French thinker's mind-body dualism. Instead, Spinoza came to espouse monism, the idea that mind and body were united in one substance and that God and nature were merely two names for the same thing. He envisioned a deterministic universe in which good and evil were merely relative values and human actions were shaped by outside circumstances, not free will. Spinoza was excommunicated by the relatively large Jewish community of Amsterdam for his controversial religious ideas, but he was heralded by his Enlightenment successors as a model of personal virtue and courageous intellectual autonomy.

The German philosopher and mathematician Gottfried Wilhelm von Leibniz (1646–1716), who had developed calculus independently of Isaac Newton, refuted both Cartesian dualism and Spinoza's monism. Instead, he adopted the idea of an infinite number of substances, or "monads," from which all matter is composed. His *Theodicy* (1710) declared that ours must be "the best of all possible worlds" because it was created by an omnipotent and benevolent God. Leibniz's optimism was later ridiculed by the French philosopher Voltaire in *Candide or Optimism* (1759).

Out of this period of intellectual turmoil came John Locke's *Essay Concerning Human Understanding* (1690). In this work Locke (1632–1704), a physician and member of the Royal Society, brilliantly set forth a new theory about how human beings learn and form their ideas. Whereas Descartes based his deductive logic on the conviction that certain first principles, or innate ideas, are imbued in humans by God, Locke insisted that all ideas are derived from experience. The human mind at birth is like a blank tablet, or tabula rasa, on which understanding and beliefs are inscribed by experience. Human development is therefore determined by external forces, like education and social institutions, not innate characteristics. Locke's essay contributed to the theory of **sensationalism**, the idea that all human ideas and thoughts are produced as a result of sensory impressions.

Along with Newton's *Principia*, the *Essay Concerning Human Understanding* was one of the great intellectual inspirations of the Enlightenment. Locke's equally important contribution to political theory, *Two Treatises of Government* (1690), insisted on the sovereignty of the Parliament against the authority of the Crown (see Chapter 15).

The Influence of the Philosophes

Divergences among the early thinkers of the Enlightenment show that, while they shared many of the same premises and questions, the answers they found differed widely. The spread of this spirit of inquiry owed a great deal to the work of the **philosophes** (fee-luh-ZAWFZ), a group of intellectuals in France who proudly proclaimed that they, at long last, were bringing the light of reason to their ignorant fellow humans.

Philosophes' Dinner Party   This engraving depicts one of the famous dinners hosted by Voltaire at Ferney, the estate on the French-Swiss border where he spent the last twenty years of his life. A visit to the great philosophe (pictured in the center with arm raised) became a cherished pilgrimage for Enlightenment writers. (Engraving by Jean Huber [1721–1786]/Album/Art Resource, NY)

Philosophe is the French word for "philosopher," and in the mid-eighteenth century France became a hub of Enlightenment thought. There were at least three reasons for this. First, French was the international language of the educated classes, and France was the wealthiest and most populous country in Europe. Second, the rising unpopularity of King Louis XV and his mistresses generated growing discontent and calls for reform among the educated elite. Third, the French philosophes made it their goal to reach a larger audience of elites, many of whom were joined together in a concept inherited from the Renaissance known as the Republic of Letters—an imaginary transnational realm of the critical thinkers and writers.

To appeal to the public and get around the censors, the philosophes wrote novels and plays, histories and philosophies, and dictionaries and encyclopedias, all filled with satire and double meanings to spread their message. One of the greatest philosophes, the baron de Montesquieu (mahn-tuhs-KYOO) (1689–1755), pioneered this approach in *The Persian Letters*, an extremely influential social satire published in 1721 and considered the first major work of the French Enlightenment. It consisted of amusing letters supposedly written by two Persian travelers who as outsiders saw European customs in unique ways, thereby allowing Montesquieu a vantage point for criticizing existing practices and beliefs.

Disturbed by the growth in absolutism under Louis XIV and inspired by the example of the physical sciences, he set out to apply the critical method to the problem

Within this broad international conversation, scholars have identified numerous regional and national particularities. Outside of France, many strains of Enlightenment—Protestant, Catholic, and Jewish—sought to reconcile reason with faith, rather than emphasizing the errors of religious fanaticism and intolerance. Some scholars point to a distinctive "Catholic Enlightenment" that aimed to renew and reform the church from within, looking to divine grace rather than human will as the source of progress.

The Scottish Enlightenment, which was centered in Edinburgh, was marked by an emphasis on common sense and scientific reasoning. After the Act of Union with England in 1707, Scotland was freed from political crisis to experience a vigorous period of intellectual growth. Advances in philosophy were also stimulated by the creation of the first public educational system in Europe.

A central figure in Edinburgh was David Hume (1711–1776), whose emphasis on civic morality and religious skepticism had a powerful impact at home and abroad. Hume strove to apply Newton's experimental methods to what he called the "science of man." Building on Locke's writings on learning, Hume argued that the human mind is really nothing but a bundle of impressions. These impressions originate only in sensory experiences and our habits of mentally joining these experiences together. Therefore, reason cannot tell us anything about questions that cannot be verified by sensory experience (in the form of controlled experiments or mathematics), such as the origin of the universe or the existence of God. Hume further argued, in opposition to Descartes, that reason alone could not supply moral principles and that they derived instead from emotions and desires, such as feelings of approval or shame. Hume's rationalistic inquiry thus ended up undermining the Enlightenment's faith in the power of reason by emphasizing the superiority of the senses and the passions over reason in driving human thought and behavior.

Hume's emphasis on human experience, rather than abstract principle, had a formative influence on another major figure of the Scottish Enlightenment, Adam Smith (1723–1790). Smith argued that social interaction produced feelings of mutual sympathy that led people to behave in ethical ways, despite inherent tendencies toward self-interest. By observing others and witnessing their feelings, individuals imaginatively experienced such feelings and learned to act in ways that would elicit positive sentiments and avoid negative ones. Smith believed that the thriving commercial life of the eighteenth century was likely to produce civic virtue through the values of competition, fair play, and individual autonomy. In *An Inquiry into the Nature and Causes of the Wealth of Nations* (1776), Smith attacked the laws and regulations created by mercantilist governments that, he argued, prevented commerce from reaching its full capacity (see Chapter 17).

Inspired by philosophers of moral sentiments, like Hume and Smith, as well as by physiological studies of the role of the nervous system in human perception, the celebration of sensibility became an important element of eighteenth-century culture. *Sensibility* referred to an acute sensitivity of the nerves and brains to outside stimuli, which produced strong emotional and physical reactions. Novels, plays, and other literary genres depicted moral and aesthetic sensibility as a particular characteristic of women and the upper classes. The proper relationship between reason and the emotions (or between *Sense and Sensibility*, as Jane Austen put it in the title of her 1811 novel) became a key question.

After 1760 Enlightenment ideas were hotly debated in the German-speaking states, often in dialogue with Christian theology. Immanuel Kant (1724–1804), a professor in East Prussia, was the greatest German philosopher of his day. Kant posed the question of the age when he published a pamphlet in 1784 titled *What Is Enlightenment?* He answered, "*Sapere Aude* [dare to know]! 'Have the courage to use your own understanding' is therefore the motto of enlightenment." He argued that if intellectuals were granted the freedom to exercise their reason publicly in print, enlightenment would almost surely follow. Kant was no revolutionary; he also insisted that in their private lives, individuals must obey all laws, no matter how unreasonable, and should be punished for "impertinent" criticism. Like other Enlightenment figures in central and east-central Europe, Kant thus tried to reconcile absolute monarchical authority and religious faith with a critical public sphere.

Northern Europeans often regarded the Italian states as culturally backward, yet important developments in Enlightenment thought took place in the Italian peninsula. After achieving independence from Habsburg rule (1734), the kingdom of Naples entered a period of intellectual flourishing as reformers struggled to lift the heavy weight of church and noble power. In northern Italy a central figure was Cesare Beccaria (1738–1794), a nobleman educated at Jesuit schools and the University of Pavia. His *On Crimes and Punishments* (1764) was a passionate plea for reform of the penal system that decried the use of torture, arbitrary imprisonment, and capital punishment, and advocated the prevention of crime over the reliance on punishment. The text was quickly translated into French and English and made an impact throughout Europe and its colonies.

The Social Life of the Enlightenment

Focus Question	How did Enlightenment thinkers address issues of racial and social difference, and how did new institutions and social practices diffuse Enlightenment thought?

The Scientific Revolution and the political and religious conflicts of the late seventeenth century were not the only developments that influenced European thinkers. Europeans' increased interactions with non-European peoples and cultures also helped produce the Enlightenment spirit.

Global Contacts

In the wake of the great discoveries of the fifteenth and sixteenth centuries, the rapidly growing travel literature taught Europeans that the peoples of China, India, Africa, and the Americas had very different beliefs and customs. Europeans shaved their faces and let their hair grow. Ottomans shaved their heads and let their beards grow. In Europe a man bowed before a woman to show respect. In Siam a man turned his back on a woman when he met her because it was disrespectful to look directly at her. Countless similar examples discussed in travel accounts helped change the perspective of educated Europeans. They began to look at truth and morality in relative, rather than absolute, terms. If anything was possible, who could say what was right or wrong?

The powerful and advanced nations of Asia were obvious sources of comparison with the West. Seventeenth-century Jesuit missionaries served as a conduit for transmission of knowledge to the West about Chinese history and culture. The philosopher and mathematician Leibniz corresponded with Jesuits stationed in China, coming to believe that Chinese ethics and political philosophy were superior but that Europeans had equaled China in science and technology; some scholars believe his concept of monads was influenced by Confucian teaching on the inherent harmony between the cosmic order and human society.[8]

During the eighteenth-century Enlightenment, opinion on China was divided. Voltaire and some other philosophes revered China—without ever visiting or seriously studying it—as an ancient culture replete with wisdom and learning, ruled by benevolent absolutist monarchs. They enthusiastically embraced Confucianism as a natural religion in which universal moral truths were uncovered by reason. By contrast, Montesquieu and Diderot criticized China as a despotic land ruled by fear.

Attitudes toward Islam and the Muslim world were similarly mixed. As the Ottoman military threat receded at the end of the seventeenth century, some Enlightenment thinkers assessed Islam favorably. Some deists praised Islam as superior to Christianity and Judaism in its rationality, compassion, and tolerance. Others, including Spinoza, saw Islamic culture as superstitious and favorable to despotism. In most cases, writing about Islam and Muslim cultures served primarily as a means to reflect on Western values and practices. Thus Montesquieu's *Persian Letters* used the Persian harem as a symbol of despotic rule that he feared his own country was adopting. Voltaire's play about the life of the Prophet portrayed Muhammad as the epitome of the religious fanaticism the philosophes opposed.

One writer with considerable personal experience in a Muslim country was Lady Mary Wortley Montagu, wife of the English ambassador to the Ottoman Empire. Her letters challenged prevailing ideas by depicting Turkish people as sympathetic and civilized. Montagu also disputed the notion that women were oppressed in Ottoman society.

Apart from debates about Asian and Muslim lands, the "discovery" of the New World and subsequent explorations in the Pacific Ocean also destabilized existing norms and values in Europe. One popular idea, among Rousseau and others, was that indigenous peoples of the Americas were living examples of "natural man," who embodied the essential goodness of humanity uncorrupted by decadent society. Other popular candidates for utopian natural men were the Pacific Island societies explored by Captain James Cook and others from the 1770s on.

Enlightenment Debates About Race

As scientists developed taxonomies of plant and animal species in response to discoveries in the Americas, they also began to classify humans into hierarchically ordered "races" and to speculate on the origins of such races. In *The System of Nature* (1735),

Swedish botanist Carl von Linné argued that nature was organized into a God-given hierarchy. The comte de Buffon (komt duh buh-FOHN) argued that humans originated with one species that then developed into distinct races due largely to climatic conditions.

Enlightenment thinkers such as David Hume and Immanuel Kant helped popularize these ideas. In *Of Natural Characters* (1748), Hume wrote:

> I am apt to suspect the negroes and in general all other species of men (for there are four or five different kinds) to be naturally inferior to the whites. There never was a civilized nation of any other complexion than white, nor even any individual eminent amongst them, no arts, no sciences. . . . Such a uniform and constant difference could not happen, in so many countries and ages if nature had not made an original distinction between these breeds of men.[9]

Kant taught and wrote as much about "anthropology" and "geography" as he did about standard philosophical themes such as logic, metaphysics, and moral philosophy. He elaborated his views about race in *On the Different Races of Man* (1775), claiming that there were four human races, each of which had derived from an original race. According to Kant, the closest descendants of the original race were the white inhabitants of northern Germany. (Scientists now know the human race originated in Africa.)

Using the word *race* to designate biologically distinct groups of humans, akin to distinct animal species, was new. Previously, Europeans had grouped other peoples into "nations" based on their historical, political, and cultural affiliations, rather than on supposedly innate physical differences. Unsurprisingly, when European thinkers drew up a hierarchical classification of human species, their own "race" was placed at the top. Europeans had long believed they were culturally superior to "barbaric" peoples in Africa and, since 1492, the New World. Now emerging ideas about racial difference taught them they were biologically superior as well. In turn, scientific racism helped legitimate and justify the tremendous growth of slavery that occurred during the eighteenth century. If one "race" of humans was fundamentally different and inferior, its members could be seen as particularly fit for enslavement and liable to benefit from tutelage by the superior race.

Racist ideas did not go unchallenged. The abbé Raynal's *History of the Two Indies* (1770) fiercely attacked slavery and the abuses of European colonization. *Encyclopedia* editor Denis Diderot adopted Montesquieu's technique of criticizing European attitudes through the voice of outsiders in his dialogue between Tahitian villagers and their European visitors. Scottish philosopher James Beattie (1735–1803) responded directly to claims of white superiority by pointing out that Europeans had started out as savage as nonwhites supposedly were and that many non-European peoples in the Americas, Asia, and Africa had achieved high levels of civilization. Former slaves, like Olaudah Equiano (see Chapter 17) and Ottobah Cugoana, published eloquent memoirs testifying to the horrors of slavery and the innate equality of all humans. These challenges to racism, however, were in the minority. Many other Enlightenment voices supporting racial inequality—Thomas Jefferson among them—may be found.

Women and the Enlightenment

Dating back to the Renaissance *querelle des dames*, the debate over women's proper role in society and the nature of gender differences continued to fascinate Enlightenment thinkers. Some philosophes championed greater rights and expanded education for women, claiming that the position and treatment of women were the best indicators of a society's level of civilization and decency.[10] In *Persian Letters*, Montesquieu used the oppression of women in the harem, described in letters from the wives of Usbek—one of the Persian voyagers—as a potent symbol of the political tyranny he identified with the Persian Empire. At the end of the book, the rebellion of the harem against the cruel eunuchs Usbek left in charge serves to make Montesquieu's point that despotism must ultimately fail.

In the 1780s the marquis de Condorcet, a celebrated mathematician and contributor to the *Encyclopedia*, went so far as to urge that women should share equal rights with men. This was an extremely rare position. Most philosophes accepted that women were inferior to men intellectually as well as physically. They sought moderate reform at best, particularly in the arena of female education, and had no desire to upend men's traditional dominance over women.

From the first years of the Enlightenment, women writers made crucial contributions both to debates about women's rights and to the broader Enlightenment discussion. In 1694 Mary Astell published *A Serious Proposal to the Ladies*, which encouraged women to aspire to the life of the mind and proposed the creation of a women's college. Astell also harshly criticized the institution of marriage. Echoing arguments made against the absolute authority of kings during the Glorious Revolution (see Chapter 15), she argued that husbands should not exercise absolute control over their wives in marriage. Yet Astell, like most female authors of the period, was careful to acknowledge women's God-given duties to be good wives and mothers.

The explosion of printed literature over the eighteenth century (see the next section) brought significant numbers of women writers into print, but they remained a small proportion of published authors. In the second half of the eighteenth century, women produced some 15 percent of published novels, the genre in which they enjoyed the greatest success. They represented a much tinier proportion of nonfiction authors.[11]

If they remained marginal in the world of publishing, women played a much more active role in the informal dimensions of the Enlightenment: conversation, letter writing, travel, and patronage. A key element of their informal participation was as salon hostesses, or *salonnières* (sah-lahn-ee-EHRZ). **Salons** were weekly meetings held in wealthy households, which brought together writers, aristocrats, financiers, and noteworthy foreigners for meals and witty discussions of the latest trends in literature, science, and philosophy. One prominent salonnière was Madame du Deffand, whose weekly Parisian salon included such guests as Montesquieu, d'Alembert, and Benjamin Franklin, then serving as the first U.S. ambassador to France. Invitations to salons were highly coveted; introductions to the rich and powerful could make the career of an ambitious writer, and, in turn, the social elite found amusement and cultural prestige in their ties to up-and-coming artists and men of letters.

Elite women also exercised great influence on artistic taste. Soft pastels, ornate interiors, sentimental portraits, and starry-eyed lovers protected by hovering cupids were all hallmarks of the style they favored. This style, known as **rococo** (ruh-KOH-koh), was popular throughout Europe in the period from 1720 to 1780. It was particularly associated with the mistress of Louis XV, Madame de Pompadour, who used her position to commission paintings, furniture, and other luxury objects in the rococo style.

Women's prominent role as society hostesses and patrons of the arts and letters outraged some Enlightenment thinkers. According to Jean-Jacques Rousseau, women and men were radically different by nature and should play diametrically opposed roles in life. Destined by nature to assume the active role in sexual relations, men were naturally suited for the rough-and-tumble of politics and public life. Women's role was to attract male sexual desire in order to marry and create families and then to care for their homes and children in private. For Rousseau, wealthy Parisian women's love for attending social gatherings and pulling the strings of power was unnatural and had a corrupting effect on both politics and society. Some women eagerly accepted Rousseau's idealized view of their domestic role, but others—such as the English writer Mary Wollstonecraft—vigorously rejected his notion of women's limitations.

Rousseau's emphasis on the natural laws governing women echoed a wider shift in ideas about gender during this period, as doctors, scientists, and philosophers increasingly agreed that women's essential characteristics were determined by their sexual organs and reproductive functions. This turn to nature, rather than tradition or scripture, as a means to understand human society had parallels in contemporary views on racial difference. Just as writers like Rousseau used women's "natural" passivity to argue for their subordinate role in society, so Kant and others used ideas about non-Europeans' "natural" inferiority to defend slavery and colonial domination. The new powers of science and reason were thus marshaled to imbue traditional stereotypes with the force of natural law. Scholars continue to debate the apparent paradox between Enlightenment thinkers' ideals of equality, progress, and reason and their acceptance of racial and gender inequality.

Urban Culture and Life in the Public Sphere

Enlightenment ideas did not float on thin air. A series of new institutions and practices encouraged the spread of enlightened ideas. From about 1700 to 1789, the production and consumption of books grew significantly and the types of books people read changed dramatically. For example, the proportion of religious and devotional books published in Paris declined after 1750; history and law held constant; the arts and sciences surged.

Reading more books on many more subjects, the educated public approached reading in a new way. The old style of reading in Europe had been centered on a core of sacred texts read aloud by the father to his assembled family. Now reading involved a broader field of books that constantly changed. Reading became individual and silent, and texts could be questioned.

For those who could not afford to purchase books, lending libraries offered access to the new ideas of the Enlightenment. Coffeehouses, which first appeared in the late seventeenth century, became meccas of philosophical discussion. In addition to these institutions, book clubs, debating societies, Masonic lodges (groups of Freemasons, a secret society that accepted craftsmen and shopkeepers as well as middle-class men and nobles), salons, and newspapers all played roles in the creation of a new **public sphere** that celebrated open debate informed by critical reason. The public sphere was an idealized space where members of society came together as individuals to discuss issues relevant to the society, economics, and politics of the day.

What of the common people? Did they participate in the Enlightenment? Enlightenment philosophes did not direct their message to peasants or urban laborers. They believed that the masses had no time or talent for philosophical speculation and that elevating them would be a long and potentially dangerous process. Deluded by superstitions and driven by violent passions, the people, they thought, were like children in need of firm parental guidance. D'Alembert characteristically made a sharp distinction between "the truly enlightened public" and "the blind and noisy multitude."[12]

Despite these prejudices, the ideas of the philosophes did find an audience among some members of the common people. At a time of rising literacy, book prices were dropping and many philosophical ideas were popularized in cheap pamphlets and through public reading. Although they were barred from salons and academies, ordinary people were not immune to the new ideas in circulation.

Enlightened Absolutism

Focus Question	**What impact did new ways of thinking have on political developments and monarchical absolutism?**

How did the Enlightenment influence political developments? To this important question there is no easy answer. Most Enlightenment thinkers outside of England and the Netherlands, especially in central and eastern Europe, believed that political change could best come from above—from the ruler—rather than from below. Royal absolutism was a fact of life, and the monarchs of Europe's leading states clearly had no intention of giving up their great power. Therefore, the philosophes and their sympathizers realistically concluded that a benevolent absolutism offered the best opportunities for improving society.

Many government officials were interested in philosophical ideas. They were among the best-educated members of society, and their daily involvement in complex affairs of state made them naturally attracted to ideas for improving human society. Encouraged and instructed by these officials, some absolutist rulers tried to reform their governments in accordance with Enlightenment ideals—what historians have called the **enlightened absolutism** of the later eighteenth century. In both Catholic and Protestant lands, rulers typically fused Enlightenment principles with religion, drawing support for their innovations from reform-minded religious thinkers. The most influential of the new-style monarchs were in Prussia, Russia, and Austria, and their example illustrates both the achievements and the great limitations of enlightened absolutism. France experienced its own brand of enlightened absolutism in the contentious decades prior to the French Revolution (see Chapter 19).

Frederick the Great of Prussia

Frederick II (r. 1740–1786), commonly known as Frederick the Great, built masterfully on the work of his father, Frederick William I (see Chapter 15). Although in his youth he embraced culture and literature rather than the militarism championed by his father, by the time he came to the throne Frederick was determined to use the splendid army he had inherited.

Therefore, when the young empress Maria Theresa of Austria inherited the Habsburg dominions upon the death of her father, Charles VI, Frederick pounced. He invaded her rich province of Silesia (sigh-LEE-zhuh), defying solemn Prussian promises to respect the Pragmatic Sanction, a diplomatic agreement that had guaranteed Maria Theresa's succession. In 1742, as other greedy powers vied for her lands in the European War of the Austrian Succession (1740–1748), Maria Theresa was forced to cede almost all of Silesia to Prussia. In one stroke Prussia had doubled its population to 6 million people. Now Prussia unquestionably stood as a European Great Power.

Though successful in 1742, Frederick had to fight against great odds to save Prussia from total destruction after the ongoing competition between Britain and France for colonial empire brought another great conflict in 1756. Maria Theresa, seeking to regain Silesia, formed an alliance with the leaders of France and Russia. The aim of the alliance during the resulting Seven Years' War (1756–1763) was to conquer Prussia and divide up its territory. Despite invasions from all sides, Frederick fought on with stoic courage. In the end he was miraculously saved: Peter III came to the Russian throne in 1762 and called off the attack against Frederick, whom he greatly admired.

The terrible struggle of the Seven Years' War tempered Frederick's interest in territorial expansion and brought him to consider how more humane policies for his subjects might also strengthen the state. Thus Frederick went beyond a superficial commitment to Enlightenment culture for himself and his circle. He tolerantly allowed his subjects to believe as they wished in religious and philosophical matters. He promoted the advancement of knowledge, improving his country's schools and permitting scholars to publish their findings. Moreover, Frederick tried to improve the lives of his subjects more directly. As he wrote to his friend Voltaire, "I must enlighten my people, cultivate their manners and morals, and make them as happy as human beings can be, or as happy as the means at my disposal permit."

The legal system and the bureaucracy were Frederick's primary tools. Prussia's laws were simplified, torture was abolished, and judges decided cases quickly and impartially. Prussian officials became famous for their hard work and honesty. After the Seven Years' War ended in 1763, Frederick's government energetically promoted the reconstruction of agriculture and industry. Frederick himself set a good example. He worked hard and lived modestly, claiming that he was "only the first servant of the state." Thus Frederick justified monarchy in terms of practical results and said nothing of the divine right of kings.

Frederick's dedication to high-minded government went only so far, however. While he condemned serfdom in the abstract, he accepted it in practice and did not free the serfs on his own estates. He accepted and extended the privileges of the nobility, who remained the backbone of the army and the entire Prussian state.

In reforming Prussia's bureaucracy, Frederick drew on the principles of **cameralism**, the German science of public administration that emerged in the decades following the Thirty Years' War. Influential throughout the German lands, cameralism held that monarchy was the best of all forms of government, that all elements of society should be placed at the service of the state, and that, in turn, the state should make use of its resources and authority to improve society. Predating the Enlightenment, cameralist interest in the public good was usually inspired by the needs of war. Cameralism shared with the Enlightenment an emphasis on rationality, progress, and utilitarianism.

Catherine the Great of Russia

Catherine the Great of Russia (r. 1762–1796) was one of the most remarkable rulers of her age, and the French philosophes adored her. Catherine was a German princess from Anhalt-Zerbst, an insignificant principality sandwiched between Prussia and Saxony. Her father commanded a regiment of the Prussian army, but her mother was related to the Romanovs of Russia, and that proved to be Catherine's opening to power.

Catherine's Romanov connection made her a suitable bride at the age of fifteen for the heir to the Russian throne. It was a mismatch from the beginning, but her

Catherine the Great and Denis Diderot   Self-proclaimed adherent of Enlightenment ideals, Russian empress Catherine the Great enthusiastically corresponded with philosophes like Voltaire and Denis Diderot. When Diderot put his library on sale to raise much-needed funds, Catherine sent him the money but allowed him to keep his books. Historians have long debated the "enlightened despotism" represented by Catherine and other absolutist rulers. (Catherine: Based on a work by Alexander Roslin [1718–1793], [oil on canvas]/Museum of Art, Serpukhov, Russia/ Bridgeman Images; Diderot: By Louis Michel van Loo [1707–1771]/Musée du Louvre, Paris, France/Fine Art Images/ Heritage Images/Getty Images)

Memoirs made her ambitions clear: "I did not care about Peter, but I did care about the crown." When her husband, Peter III, came to power during the Seven Years' War, his decision to withdraw Russian troops from the coalition against Prussia alienated the army. Catherine profited from his unpopularity to form a conspiracy to depose her husband. In 1762 Catherine's lover Gregory Orlov and his three brothers, all army officers, murdered Peter, and the German princess became empress of Russia.

Catherine had drunk deeply at the Enlightenment well. Never questioning that absolute monarchy was the best form of government, she set out to rule in an enlightened manner. She had three main goals. First, she worked hard to continue Peter the Great's effort to bring the culture of western Europe to Russia (see Chapter 15). To do so, she imported Western architects, musicians, and intellectuals. She bought masterpieces of Western art and patronized the philosophes. An enthusiastic letter writer, she corresponded extensively with Voltaire and praised him as the "champion of the human race." When the French government banned the *Encyclopedia*, she offered to publish it in St. Petersburg, and she sent money to Diderot when he needed it. With these actions, Catherine won good press in the West for herself and for her country. Moreover, this intellectual ruler, who wrote plays and loved good talk, set the tone for the entire Russian nobility. Peter the Great westernized Russian armies, but it was Catherine who westernized the imagination of the Russian nobility.

Catherine's second goal was domestic reform, and she began her reign with sincere and ambitious projects. In 1767 she appointed a legislative commission to prepare a new law code. This project was never completed, but Catherine did restrict the practice of torture and allowed limited religious toleration. She also tried to improve education and strengthen local government. The philosophes applauded these measures and hoped more would follow.

Such was not the case. In 1773 a common Cossack soldier named Emelian Pugachev sparked a gigantic uprising of serfs, very much as Stenka Razin had done a century earlier (see Chapter 15). Proclaiming himself the true tsar, Pugachev issued orders abolishing serfdom, taxes, and army service. Thousands joined his cause, slaughtering landlords and officials over a vast area of southwestern Russia. Pugachev's untrained forces eventually proved no match for Catherine's noble-led army. Betrayed by his own company, Pugachev was captured and savagely executed.

Pugachev's rebellion put an end to any intentions Catherine had about reforming the system. The peasants were clearly dangerous, and her empire rested on the support of the nobility. After 1775 Catherine gave the nobles absolute control of their serfs, and she extended serfdom into new areas, such as Ukraine. In 1785 she freed nobles forever from taxes and state service. Under Catherine the Russian nobility attained its most exalted position, and serfdom entered its most oppressive phase.

Catherine's third goal was territorial expansion, and in this respect she was extremely successful. Her armies subjugated the last descendants of the Mongols and the Crimean Tartars, and began the conquest of the Caucasus (KAW-kuh-suhs). Her greatest coup by far was the partition of Poland (Map 16.1). When, between 1768 and 1772, Catherine's armies scored unprecedented victories against the Ottomans and thereby threatened to disturb the balance of power between Russia and Austria in eastern Europe, Frederick of Prussia obligingly came forward with a deal. He proposed that Turkey be let off easily and that Prussia, Austria, and Russia each compensate itself

MAP 16.1 The Partition of Poland, 1772–1795
In 1772 war between Russia and Austria threatened over Russian gains from the Ottoman Empire. To satisfy desires for expansion without fighting, Prussia's Frederick the Great proposed that parts of Poland be divided among Austria, Prussia, and Russia. In 1793 and 1795 the three powers partitioned the remainder, and the republic of Poland ceased to exist.

by taking a gigantic slice of the weakly ruled Polish territory. Catherine jumped at the chance. The first partition of Poland took place in 1772. Subsequent partitions in 1793 and 1795 gave away the rest of Polish territory, and the ancient republic of Poland vanished from the map.

The Austrian Habsburgs

Another female monarch, Maria Theresa (r. 1740–1780) of Austria, set out to reform her nation, although traditional power politics was a more important motivation for her than were Enlightenment teachings. A devoutly Catholic mother and wife who inherited power from her father, Charles VI, Maria Theresa was a remarkable but old-fashioned absolutist. Her more radical son, Joseph II (r. 1780–1790), drew on Enlightenment ideals, earning the title of "revolutionary emperor."

Emerging from the long War of the Austrian Succession in 1748 with the serious loss of Silesia, Maria Theresa was determined to introduce reforms that would make the state stronger and more efficient. First, she initiated church reform, with measures aimed at limiting the papacy's influence, eliminating many religious holidays, and reducing the number of monasteries. Second, a whole series of administrative renovations strengthened the central bureaucracy, smoothed out some provincial differences, and revamped the tax system, taxing even the lands of nobles, previously exempt from taxation. Third, the government sought to improve the lot of the agricultural population, cautiously reducing the power of lords over their hereditary serfs and their partially free peasant tenants.

Coregent with his mother from 1765 onward and a strong supporter of change from above, Joseph II moved forward rapidly when he came to the throne in 1780. Most notably, Joseph abolished serfdom in 1781, and in 1789 he decreed that peasants could pay landlords in cash rather than through labor on their land. This measure was violently rejected not only by the nobility but also by the peasants it was intended to help, because they lacked the necessary cash. When a disillusioned Joseph died prematurely at forty-nine, the entire Habsburg empire was in turmoil. His brother Leopold II (r. 1790–1792) canceled Joseph's radical edicts in order to re-establish order. Peasants once again were required to do forced labor for their lords.

Despite differences in their policies, Joseph II and the other absolutists of the later eighteenth century combined old-fashioned state-building with the culture and critical thinking of the Enlightenment. In doing so, they succeeded in expanding the role of the state in the life of society. They perfected bureaucratic machines that were to prove surprisingly adaptive and enduring. Their failure to implement policies we would recognize as humane and enlightened—such as abolishing serfdom—may reveal inherent limitations in Enlightenment thinking about equality and social justice, rather than deficiencies in their execution of Enlightenment programs. The fact that leading philosophes supported rather than criticized eastern rulers' policies exposes the blind spots of the era.

Jewish Life and the Limits of Enlightened Absolutism

Perhaps the best example of the limitations of enlightened absolutism are the debates surrounding the emancipation of the Jews. Europe's small Jewish populations lived under highly discriminatory laws. For the most part, Jews were confined to tiny, overcrowded ghettos, were excluded by law from most professions, and could be ordered out of a kingdom at a moment's notice. Still, a very few did manage to succeed and to obtain the right of permanent settlement, usually by performing some special service for the state. Many rulers relied on Jewish bankers for loans to raise armies and run their kingdoms. Jewish merchants prospered in international trade because they could rely on contacts with colleagues in Jewish communities scattered across Europe.

In the eighteenth century an Enlightenment movement known as the **Haskalah** emerged from within the European Jewish community, led by the Prussian philosopher Moses Mendelssohn (1729–1786). Christian and Jewish Enlightenment philosophers, including Mendelssohn, began to advocate for freedom and civil rights for European Jews. In an era of reason and progress, they argued, restrictions on religious grounds could not stand. The Haskalah accompanied a period of controversial social change within Jewish communities, in which rabbinic controls loosened and heightened interaction with Christians took place.

Arguments for tolerance won some ground. The British Parliament passed a law allowing naturalization of Jews in 1753, but later repealed the law due to public outrage. The most progressive reforms took place under Austrian emperor Joseph II. Among his liberal edicts of the 1780s were measures intended to integrate Jews more fully into society, including eligibility for military service, admission to higher education and artisanal trades, and removal of requirements for special clothing or emblems. Welcomed by many Jews, these reforms raised fears among traditionalists of assimilation into the general population.

Many monarchs rejected all ideas of emancipation. Although he permitted freedom of religion to his Christian subjects, Frederick the Great of Prussia firmly opposed any general emancipation for the Jews, as he did for the serfs. Catherine the Great, who acquired most of Poland's large Jewish population when she annexed part of that country in the late eighteenth century, similarly refused. In 1791 she established the Pale of Settlement, a territory including parts of modern-day Poland, Latvia, Lithuania, Ukraine, and Belarus, in which most Jews were required to live. Jewish habitation was restricted to the Pale until the Russian Revolution in 1917.

The first European state to remove all restrictions on the Jews was France under the French Revolution. Over the next hundred years, Jews gradually won full legal and civil rights throughout the rest of western Europe. Emancipation in eastern Europe took even longer and aroused more conflict and violence.

NOTES

1. Quoted in H. Butterfield, *The Origins of Modern Science* (New York: Macmillan, 1951), p. 47.
2. Ibid., p. 120.
3. Quoted in John Freely, *Aladdin's Lamp: How Greek Science Came to Europe Through the Islamic World* (New York: Knopf, 2009), p. 225.
4. Jacqueline Broad, *Women Philosophers of the Seventeenth Century* (Cambridge: Cambridge University Press, 2003), p. 17.
5. L. Schiebinger, *The Mind Has No Sex? Women in the Origins of Modern Science* (Cambridge, Mass.: Harvard University Press, 1989), p. 64.
6. Quoted in G. L. Mosse et al., eds., *Europe in Review* (Chicago: Rand McNally, 1964), p. 156.
7. Quoted in P. Gay, "The Unity of the Enlightenment," *History* 3 (1960): 25.
8. D. E. Mungello, *The Great Encounter of China and the West, 1500–1800*, 2d ed. (Lanham, Md.: Rowman & Littlefield, 2005), p. 98.
9. Quoted in Emmanuel Chukwudi Eze, ed., *Race and the Enlightenment: A Reader* (Oxford: Blackwell, 1997), p. 33.
10. See E. Fox-Genovese, "Women in the Enlightenment," in *Becoming Visible: Women in European History*, 2d ed., ed. R. Bridenthal, C. Koonz, and S. Stuard (Boston: Houghton Mifflin, 1987), esp. pp. 252–259, 263–265.
11. Aurora Wolfgang, *Gender and Voice in the French Novel, 1730–1782* (Aldershot, U.K.: Ashgate, 2004), p. 8.
12. Jean Le Rond d'Alembert, *Eloges lus dans les séances publiques de l'Académie française* (Paris, 1779), p. ix, quoted in Mona Ozouf, "'Public Opinion' at the End of the Old Regime," *The Journal of Modern History* 60, Supplement: Rethinking French Politics in 1788 (September 1988): S9.

LOOKING BACK LOOKING AHEAD

Hailed as the origin of modern thought, the Scientific Revolution must also be seen as a product of its past. Medieval universities gave rise to important new scholarship, and the ambition and wealth of Renaissance patrons nurtured intellectual curiosity. Religious faith also influenced the Scientific Revolution, inspiring thinkers to understand the glory of God's creation, while bringing censure and personal tragedy to others. Natural philosophers following Copernicus pioneered new methods of observing and explaining nature while drawing on centuries-old traditions of mysticism, astrology, alchemy, and magic.

The Enlightenment ideas of the eighteenth century were a similar blend of past and present; they could serve as much to bolster absolutist monarchical regimes as to inspire revolutionaries to fight for individual rights and liberties. Although the Enlightenment fostered critical thinking about everything from science to religion, the majority of Europeans, including many prominent thinkers, remained devout Christians.

The achievements of the Scientific Revolution and the Enlightenment are undeniable. Key Western values of rationalism, human rights, and open-mindedness were born from these movements. With their new notions of progress and social improvement, Europeans would embark on important revolutions in industry and politics in the centuries that followed. Nonetheless, others have seen a darker side. For these critics, the mastery over nature permitted by the Scientific Revolution now threatens to overwhelm the earth's fragile equilibrium, and the Enlightenment belief in the universal application of reason can lead to arrogance and intolerance of other people's spiritual, cultural, and political values. Such vivid debates about the legacy of these intellectual and scientific developments testify to their continuing importance in today's world.

MAKE CONNECTIONS

Think about the larger developments and continuities within and across chapters.

1. How did the era of European exploration and discovery (Chapter 14) affect the ideas of scientists and philosophers discussed in this chapter? In what ways did contact with new peoples and places stimulate new forms of thought among Europeans?

2. What was the relationship between the Scientific Revolution and the Enlightenment? How did new ways of understanding the natural world influence thinking about human society?

3. Compare the policies and actions of seventeenth-century absolutist rulers (Chapter 15) with their "enlightened" descendants described in this chapter. How accurate is the term *enlightened absolutism*?

Chapter Review

IDENTIFY KEY TERMS

Identify and explain the significance of each item below.

natural philosophy (p. 490)

Copernican hypothesis (p. 492)

law of inertia (p. 493)

law of universal gravitation (p. 494)

empiricism (p. 496)

Cartesian dualism (p. 497)

Enlightenment (p. 500)

rationalism (p. 501)

sensationalism (p. 502)

philosophes (p. 502)

deism (p. 504)

salon (p. 510)

rococo (p. 510)

public sphere (p. 511)

enlightened absolutism (p. 512)

cameralism (p. 513)

Haskalah (p. 517)

REVIEW THE MAIN IDEAS

Answer the focus questions from each section of the chapter.

1. What revolutionary discoveries were made in the sixteenth and seventeenth centuries, and why did they occur in Europe? (p. 488)

2. What intellectual and social changes occurred as a result of the Scientific Revolution? (p. 496)

3. How did the Enlightenment emerge, and what were major currents of Enlightenment thought? (p. 500)

4. How did Enlightenment thinkers address issues of racial and social difference, and how did new institutions and social practices diffuse Enlightenment thought? (p. 507)

5. What impact did new ways of thinking have on political developments and monarchical absolutism? (p. 512)

CHRONOLOGY	
ca. 1540–1700	Scientific Revolution
ca. 1690–1789	Enlightenment
ca. 1700–1800	Growth of book publishing
1720–1780	Rococo style in art and decoration
1740–1748	War of the Austrian Succession
1740–1780	Reign of the empress Maria Theresa of Austria
1740–1786	Reign of Frederick the Great of Prussia
ca. 1740–1789	Salons led by Parisian elites
1751–1772	Philosophes publish *Encyclopedia: The Rational Dictionary of the Sciences, the Arts, and the Crafts*
1756–1763	Seven Years' War
1762–1796	Reign of Catherine the Great of Russia
1780–1790	Reign of Joseph II of Austria
1791	Establishment of the Pale of Settlement

17

The Expansion of Europe

1650–1800

ABSOLUTISM AND ARISTOCRACY, a combination of raw power and elegant refinement, were a world apart from the common people. For most people in the eighteenth century, life remained a struggle with poverty and uncertainty, with the landlord and the tax collector. In 1700 peasants on the land and artisans in their shops lived little better than had their ancestors in the Middle Ages, primarily because European societies still could not produce very much as measured by modern standards. Despite the hard work of ordinary men, women, and children, there was seldom enough good food, warm clothing, and decent housing. The idea of progress, of substantial improvement in the lives of great numbers of people, was still the dream of only a small elite in fashionable salons.

Yet the economic basis of European life was beginning to change. In the course of the eighteenth century, the European economy emerged from the long crisis of the seventeenth century, responded to challenges, and began to expand once again. Population resumed its growth, while colonial empires extended and developed. Some areas were more fortunate than others. The rising Atlantic powers—the Dutch Republic, France, and above all England—and their colonies led the way. The expansion of agriculture, industry, trade, and population marked the beginning of a surge comparable to that of the eleventh- and twelfth-century springtime of European civilization. But this time, broadly based expansion was not cut short by plague and famine. This time the response to new challenges led toward one of the most influential developments in human history, the Industrial Revolution, considered in Chapter 20.

Working the Land

Focus Question	What important developments led to increased agricultural production, and how did these changes affect peasants?

At the end of the seventeenth century the economy of Europe was agrarian. With the exception of the Dutch Republic and England, at least 80 percent of the people of western Europe drew their livelihoods from agriculture. In eastern Europe the percentage was considerably higher. Men and women were tied to the land, plowing fields and sowing seed, reaping harvests and storing grain. Yet even in a rich agricultural region such as the Po Valley in northern Italy, every bushel of wheat seed sown yielded on average only five or six bushels of grain at harvest. By modern standards, output was distressingly low.

In most regions of Europe, climatic conditions produced poor or disastrous harvests every eight or nine years. In famine years the number of deaths soared far above normal. A third of a village's population might disappear in a year or two. But new developments in agricultural technology and methods gradually brought an end to the ravages of hunger in western Europe.

The Legacy of the Open-Field System

Why, in the late seventeenth century, did many areas of Europe produce barely enough food to survive? The answer lies in patterns of farming inherited from the Middle Ages, which sustained fairly large numbers of people, but did not produce material abundance. From the Middle Ages up to the seventeenth century, much of Europe was farmed through the open-field system. The land to be cultivated was divided into several large fields, which were in turn cut up into long, narrow strips. The fields were open, and the strips were not enclosed into small plots by fences or hedges. The whole peasant village followed the same pattern of plowing, sowing, and harvesting in accordance with long-standing traditions.

The ever-present problem was soil exhaustion. Wheat planted year after year in a field will deplete nitrogen in the soil. Since the supply of manure for fertilizer was limited, the only way for the land to recover was to lie fallow for a period of time. Clover and other annual grasses that sprang up in unplanted fields restored nutrients to the soil and also provided food for livestock. In the early Middle Ages a year of fallow was alternated with a year of cropping; then three-year rotations were introduced. On each strip of land, a year of wheat or rye was followed by a year of oats or beans and only then by a year of fallow. Peasants staggered the rotation of crops, so some wheat, legumes, and pastureland were always available. The three-year system was an important achievement because cash crops could be grown two years out of three, rather than only one year in two.

Traditional village rights reinforced communal patterns of farming. In addition to rotating field crops in a uniform way, villages maintained open meadows for hay and natural pasture. After the harvest villagers also pastured their animals on the wheat or rye stubble. In many places such pasturing followed a brief period, also established by tradition, for the gleaning of grain. In this process, poor women would go through the fields picking up the few single grains that had fallen to the ground in the course of the harvest. Many villages were surrounded by woodlands, also held in common, which provided essential firewood, building materials, and nutritional roots and berries.

The state and landlords continued to levy heavy taxes and high rents, thereby stripping peasants of much of their meager earnings. The level of exploitation varied. Generally speaking, the peasants of eastern Europe were worst off. As we saw in Chapter 15, they were serfs bound to their lords in hereditary service. In much of eastern Europe, working several days per week on the lord's land was not uncommon. Well into the nineteenth century, individual Russian serfs and serf families were regularly bought and sold.

Social conditions were better in western Europe, where peasants were generally free from serfdom. In France, western Germany, England, and the Low Countries (modern-day Belgium and the Netherlands), peasants could own land and could pass it on to their children. In years with normal harvests, most people had enough food to fill their bellies. Yet life in the village was hard, and poverty was the reality for most people.

New Methods of Agriculture

The seventeenth century saw important gains in productivity in some regions that would slowly extend to the rest of Europe. By 1700 less than half of the population of Britain and the Dutch Republic worked in agriculture, producing enough to feed the remainder of the population. Many elements combined in this production growth, but the key was new ways of rotating crops that allowed farmers to forgo the unproductive fallow period altogether and maintain their land in continuous cultivation. The secret to eliminating the fallow lay in deliberately alternating grain with crops that restored nutrients to the soil, such as peas and beans, root crops like turnips and potatoes, and clover and other grasses.

Clover was one of the most important crops, because it restores nitrogen directly to the soil through its roots. Other crops produced additional benefits. Potatoes and many types of beans came to Europe as part of the sixteenth-century Columbian exchange between the New and the Old Worlds (see Chapter 14). Originally perceived by Europeans as fit only for animal feed, potatoes eventually made their way to the human table, where they provided a nutritious supplement to the peasant's meager diet. With more fodder, hay, and root vegetables for the winter months, peasants and larger farmers could build up their herds of cattle and sheep. More animals meant more manure to fertilize and restore the soil. More animals also meant more meat and dairy products as well as more power to pull plows in the fields and bring carts to market.

Over time, crop rotation spread to other parts of Europe, and farmers developed increasingly specialized patterns of crop rotation to suit different kinds of soils. For example, in the late eighteenth century farmers in French Flanders near Lille alternated a number of grain, root, and hay crops in a given field on a ten-year schedule. Ongoing experimentation, fueled by developments in the Scientific Revolution (see Chapter 16), led to more methodical farming.

Advocates of the new crop rotations, who included an emerging group of experimental scientists, some government officials, and a few big landowners, believed that new methods were scarcely possible within the traditional framework of open fields and common rights. A farmer who wanted to experiment with new methods would have to get all the landholders in the village to agree to the plan. Advocates of improvement argued that innovating agriculturalists needed to enclose and consolidate their scattered holdings into compact, fenced-in fields in order to farm more effectively. In doing so, the innovators also needed to enclose the village's natural pastureland, or common, into individual shares. According to proponents of this movement, known as **enclosure**, the upheaval of village life was the necessary price of technical progress.

That price seemed too high to many rural people who had small, inadequate holdings or very little land at all. Traditional rights were precious to these poor peasants, who used commonly held pastureland to graze livestock, and marshlands or forest outside the village as a source for foraged goods that could make the difference between survival and famine in harsh times. Thus, when the small landholders and the village poor could effectively oppose the enclosure of the open fields and the common lands, they did so. In many countries they found allies among the larger, predominantly noble landowners who were also wary of enclosure because it required large investments in purchasing and fencing land and thus posed risks for them as well.

The old system of unenclosed open fields and the new system of continuous rotation coexisted in Europe for a long time. Open fields could still be found in much of France and Germany as late as the nineteenth century because peasants there had successfully opposed eighteenth-century efforts to introduce the new techniques. Through the end of the eighteenth century, the new system of enclosure was extensively adopted only in the Low Countries and England.

The Leadership of the Low Countries and England

The seventeenth-century Dutch Republic, already the most advanced country in Europe in many areas of human endeavor (see Chapter 15), pioneered advancements in agriculture. By the middle of the seventeenth century intensive farming was well established, and the innovations of enclosed fields, continuous rotation, heavy manuring, and a wide variety of crops were all present. Agriculture was highly specialized and commercialized, especially in the province of Holland.

One reason for early Dutch leadership in farming was that the area was one of the most densely populated in Europe. In order to feed themselves and provide employment, the Dutch were forced at an early date to seek maximum yields from their land and to increase the cultivated area through the steady draining of marshes and swamps. The pressure of population was connected with the second cause: the growth of towns and cities. Stimulated by commerce and overseas trade, Amsterdam grew from thirty thousand to two hundred thousand inhabitants in its golden seventeenth century. The growing urban population provided Dutch peasants with markets for all they could produce and allowed each region to specialize in what it did best. Thus the Dutch could develop their potential, and the Low Countries became, as one historian wrote, "the Mecca of foreign agricultural experts who came . . . to see Flemish agriculture with their own eyes, to write about it and to propagate its methods in their home lands."[1]

The English were among their best students. In the mid-seventeenth century English farmers borrowed the system of continuous crop rotation from the Dutch.

They also drew on Dutch expertise in drainage and water control. Large parts of seventeenth-century Holland had once been sea and sea marsh, and the efforts of centuries had made the Dutch the world's leaders in drainage. In the first half of the seventeenth century, Dutch experts made a great contribution to draining the extensive marshes, or fens, of wet and rainy England. The most famous of these Dutch engineers, Cornelius Vermuyden, directed one large drainage project in Yorkshire and another in Cambridgeshire. In the Cambridge fens, Vermuyden and his Dutch workers eventually reclaimed forty thousand acres, which were then farmed intensively in the Dutch manner. Swampy wilderness was converted into thousands of acres of some of the best land in England.

Based on the seventeenth-century achievements, English agriculture continued to progress during the eighteenth century, growing enough food to satisfy a rapidly growing population. Jethro Tull (1674–1741), part crank and part genius, was an important English innovator. A true son of the early Enlightenment, Tull adopted a critical attitude toward accepted ideas about farming and tried to develop better methods through empirical research. He was especially enthusiastic about using horses, rather than slower-moving oxen, for plowing. He also advocated sowing seed with drilling equipment rather than scattering it by hand. Drilling distributed seed in an even manner and at the proper depth. There were also improvements in livestock, inspired in part by the earlier successes of English country gentlemen in breeding ever-faster horses for the races and fox hunts that were their passions. Selective breeding of ordinary livestock was a marked improvement over the haphazard breeding of the past.

One of the most important—and bitterly contested—aspects of English agricultural development was the enclosure of open fields and commons. More than half the

The Seed Drill   The seed drill had a metal plow in front (depicted behind the horse's back feet) to dig channels in the earth and a container behind it that distributed seed evenly into the channels. The drill allowed farmers to plant seeds at consistent depths and in straight lines, a much more efficient system than the old method of simply scattering seed across the field. (Prisma/UIG via Getty Images)

farmland in England was enclosed through private initiatives prior to 1700; Parliament completed this work in the eighteenth century. From the 1760s to 1815 a series of acts of Parliament enclosed most of the remaining common land. Arthur Young, another agricultural experimentalist, celebrated large-scale enclosure as a necessary means to achieve progress. Many of his contemporaries, as well as the historians that followed him, echoed that conviction. More recent research, however, has shown that regions that maintained open-field farming were still able to adopt crop rotation and other innovations, suggesting that enclosures were not a prerequisite for increased production.

Many critics of Arthur Young's day emphasized the social upheaval caused by enclosure. By eliminating common rights and greatly reducing the access of poor men and women to the land, the eighteenth-century enclosure movement marked the completion of two major historical developments in England—the rise of capitalist market-oriented estate agriculture and the emergence of a landless rural proletariat. By the early nineteenth century a tiny minority of wealthy English and Scottish landowners held most of the land and pursued profits aggressively, leasing their holdings through agents at competitive prices to middle-size farmers, who relied on landless laborers for their workforce. These landless laborers worked very long hours, usually following a dawn-to-dusk schedule six days a week all year long. Not only was the small landholder deprived of his land, but improvements in technology meant that fewer laborers were needed to work the large farms, and unemployment spread throughout the countryside. As one observer commented:

> It is no uncommon thing for four or five wealthy graziers to engross a large inclosed lordship, which was before in the hands of twenty or thirty farmers, and as many smaller tenants or proprietors. All these are thereby thrown out of their livings, and many other families, who were chiefly employed and supported by them, such as blacksmiths, carpenters, wheelwrights and other artificers and tradesmen, besides their own labourers and servants.[2]

In no other European country had this **proletarianization**—this transformation of large numbers of small peasant farmers into landless rural wage earners—gone so far. England's village poor found the cost of change heavy and unjust.

The Beginning of the Population Explosion

Focus Question	Why did the European population rise dramatically in the eighteenth century?

Another factor that affected the existing order of life and drove economic changes in the eighteenth century was the beginning of the population explosion. Explosive growth continued in Europe until the twentieth century, by which time it was affecting non-Western areas of the globe. In this section we examine the background and causes of the population growth; the following section considers how the challenge of more mouths to feed and more hands to employ affected the European economy.

Long-Standing Obstacles to Population Growth

Until 1700 the total population of Europe grew slowly much of the time, and it followed an irregular cyclical pattern (Figure 17.1). This cyclical pattern had a great influence on many aspects of social and economic life. The terrible ravages of the Black Death of 1348–1350 caused a sharp drop in population and food prices after 1350 and also created a labor shortage throughout Europe. Some economic historians calculate that for common people in western Europe who managed to steer clear of warfare and of power struggles within the ruling class, the later Middle Ages was an era of exceptional well-being.

By the mid-sixteenth century much of Europe had returned to its pre-plague population levels. In this buoyant period, farmers brought new land into cultivation and urban settlements grew significantly. But this well-being eroded in the course of the sixteenth century. Population growth outstripped the growth of production after about 1500. There was less food, housing, fuel, and other resources per person, and prices rose more rapidly than wages, a development intensified by the inflow of precious metals from the Americas (see Chapter 14). The century-long period of general, if uneven, inflation that followed, known as the European price revolution, substantially lowered living standards. Population figures stagnated or declined across much of Europe, and widespread poverty was an undeniable reality.

During the seventeenth century births and deaths, fertility and mortality, returned to a crude but effective balance. The population grew modestly in normal years at a rate of perhaps 0.5 to 1 percent, or enough to double the population in 70 to 140 years. This is, of course, a generalization encompassing many different patterns. In areas such as Russia and colonial New England, where there was a great deal of frontier to be settled, the annual rate of natural increase, not counting immigration, might well have exceeded 1 percent. In a country such as France, where the land had long been densely settled, the rate of increase might have been less than 0.5 percent.

Although population growth of even 1 percent per year seems fairly modest, it will produce a very large increase over a long period: in three hundred years it will result in sixteen times as many people. Yet such significant increases did not occur in agrarian Europe. In certain abnormal years and tragic periods — the Black Death was only the most extreme example — many more people died than were born, and total population fell sharply, even catastrophically. A number of years of modest growth would then be necessary to make up for those who had died in an abnormal year. Such savage increases in deaths occurred periodically in the seventeenth century on a local

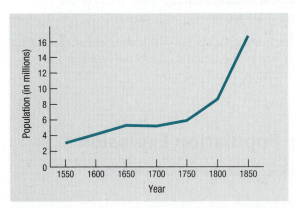

FIGURE 17.1 The Growth of Population in England, 1550–1850

England is a good example of both the uneven increase of European population before 1700 and the third great surge of growth that began in the eighteenth century.

(Source: Data from E. A. Wrigley et al., *English Population History from Family Reconstitution, 1580–1837* [Cambridge: Cambridge University Press, 1997], p. 614.)

and regional scale, and these demographic crises combined to check the growth of population until after 1700.

The grim reapers of demographic crisis were famine, epidemic disease, and war. Episodes of famine were inevitable in all eras of premodern Europe, given low crop yields and unpredictable climatic conditions. In the seventeenth century much of Europe experienced unusually cold and wet weather, which produced even more severe harvest failures and food shortages than usual. Contagious diseases, like typhus, smallpox, syphilis, and the ever-recurring bubonic plague, also continued to ravage Europe's population on a periodic basis. War was another scourge, and its indirect effects were even more harmful than the purposeful killing during military campaigns. Soldiers and camp followers passed all manner of contagious diseases throughout the countryside. Armies requisitioned scarce food supplies and disrupted the agricultural cycle while battles destroyed precious crops, livestock, and farmlands. The Thirty Years' War (1618–1648) witnessed all possible combinations of distress (see Chapter 15). The number of inhabitants in the German states alone declined by more than two-thirds in some large areas and by at least one-third almost everywhere else.

The New Pattern of the Eighteenth Century

In the eighteenth century the traditional demographic pattern of Europe was transformed. Growth took place unevenly, with Russia growing very quickly after 1700 and France much more slowly. Nonetheless, the explosion of population was a major phenomenon in all European countries. Europeans grew in numbers steadily from 1720 to 1789, with especially dramatic increases after about 1750 (Figure 17.2). Between 1700 and 1835 the population of Europe doubled in size.

What caused this population growth? In some areas, especially England, women had more babies than before because new opportunities for employment in rural industry (see page 535) allowed them to marry at an earlier age. But the basic cause of European population increase as a whole was a decline in mortality—fewer deaths.

One of the primary reasons behind this decline was the still-unexplained disappearance of the bubonic plague. Following the Black Death in the fourteenth century, plague had remained part of the European experience, striking again and again with savage force, particularly in towns. In 1720 a ship from Syria and the Levant brought the disease to Marseilles. As a contemporary account described it, "The Porters employ'd in unloading the Vessel, were immediately seiz'd with violent Pains in the Head . . . soon after they broke out in Blotches and Buboes, and died in three Days."[3] Plague quickly spread within and beyond Marseilles, killing up to one hundred thousand. By 1722 the epidemic had passed, and that was the last time plague fell on western and central Europe. Exactly why plague disappeared is unknown. Stricter measures of quarantine in Mediterranean ports and along the Austrian border with the Ottoman Empire helped by carefully isolating human carriers of plague. Chance and plain good luck were probably just as important.

Advances in medical knowledge did not contribute much to reducing the death rate in the eighteenth century. The most important advance in preventive medicine in this period was inoculation against smallpox, a disease that killed approximately four hundred thousand people each year in Europe. Widely practiced in the Ottoman Empire, inoculation was popularized in England in the 1720s by the wife of the former English

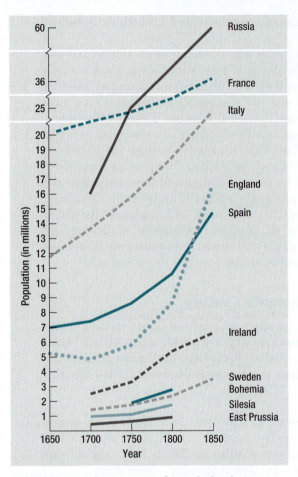

FIGURE 17.2 The Increase of Population in Europe, 1650–1850

Population grew across Europe in the eighteenth century, though the most dramatic increases occurred after 1750. Russia experienced the largest increase and emerged as Europe's most populous state, as natural increase was complemented by growth from territorial expansion.

(Source: Data from Massimo Livi Bacci, *The Population of Europe* [Wiley-Blackwell, 2000], p. 8.)

ambassador, but did not spread to the rest of the continent for decades. Improvements in the water supply and sewage, which were frequently promoted by strong absolutist monarchies, did contribute to somewhat better public health and helped reduce such diseases as typhoid and typhus in urban areas of western Europe. Improvements in water supply and the drainage of swamps also reduced Europe's large insect population. Flies and mosquitoes played a major role in spreading diseases, especially those striking children and young adults. Thus early public health measures contributed to the decline in mortality that began with the disappearance of plague and continued into the early nineteenth century.

Human beings also became more successful in their efforts to safeguard the supply of food. The eighteenth century was a time of considerable canal and road building in western Europe. These advances in transportation, which were also among the more positive aspects of strong absolutist states, lessened the impact of local crop failure and famine. Emergency supplies could be brought in, and localized starvation became less frequent. Wars became less destructive than in the seventeenth century and spread fewer epidemics.

None of the population growth would have been possible if not for the advances in agricultural production in the seventeenth and eighteenth centuries, which increased the food supply and contributed nutritious new foods, particularly the potato from South America. In short, population grew in the eighteenth century primarily because years of higher-than-average death rates were less catastrophic. Famines, epidemics, and wars continued to occur and to affect population growth, but their severity moderated.

Population growth intensified the imbalance between the number of people and the economic opportunities available to them. Deprived of land by the enclosure movement, the rural poor were forced to look for new ways to make a living.

The Plague at Marseilles   The bishop of Marseilles blesses victims of the plague that overwhelmed Marseilles in 1720. Some one hundred thousand people died in the outbreak, which was the last great episode of plague in western Europe. (By Nicolas-André Monsiau [1754–1837], [oil on canvas]/Photo: Christian Jean/Musée du Louvre, Paris, France/© RMN–Grand Palais/Art Resource, NY)

The Growth of Rural Industry

| Focus Question | How and why did rural industry intensify in the eighteenth century? |

The growth of population increased the number of rural workers with little or no land, and this in turn contributed to the development of industry in rural areas. The poor in the countryside increasingly needed to supplement their agricultural earnings with other types of work, and urban capitalists were eager to employ them, often at lower wages than urban workers received. **Cottage industry**, which consisted of manufacturing with hand tools in peasant cottages and work sheds, grew markedly in the eighteenth century and became a crucial feature of the European economy.

To be sure, peasant communities had always made clothing, processed food, and constructed housing for their own use. But medieval peasants did not produce manufactured goods on a large scale for sale in a market. By the eighteenth century, however, the pressures of rural poverty led many poor villagers to seek additional work, and far-reaching changes for daily rural life were set in motion.

The Putting-Out System

Cottage industry was often organized through the **putting-out system**. The two main participants in the putting-out system were the merchant capitalist and the rural worker. In this system, the merchant loaned, or "put out," raw materials to cottage workers, who processed the raw materials in their own homes and returned the finished products to the merchant. There were endless variations on this basic relationship. Sometimes rural workers bought their own raw materials and produced goods that they sold to the merchant. Sometimes whole families were involved in domestic industry; at other times the tasks were closely associated with one gender or age group. Sometimes several workers toiled together to perform a complicated process in a workshop outside the home. The relative importance of earnings from the land and from industry varied greatly for handicraft workers, although industrial wages usually became more important for a given family with time.

As industries grew in scale and complexity, production was often broken into many stages. For example, a merchant would provide raw wool to one group of workers for spinning into thread. He would then pass the thread to another group of workers to be bleached, to another for dyeing, and to another for weaving into cloth. The merchant paid outworkers by the piece and proceeded to sell the finished product to regional, national, or international markets.

The putting-out system grew because it had competitive advantages. Underemployed labor was abundant, and poor peasants and landless laborers would work for low wages. Since production in the countryside was unregulated, workers and merchants could change procedures and experiment as they saw fit. Because workers did not need to meet rigid guild standards, cottage industry became capable of producing many kinds of goods. Textiles; all manner of knives, forks, and housewares; buttons and gloves; and clocks could be produced quite satisfactorily in the countryside. Although luxury goods for the rich, such as exquisite tapestries and fine porcelain, demanded special training, close supervision, and centralized workshops, the limited skills of rural industry were sufficient for everyday articles.

Rural manufacturing did not spread across Europe at an even rate. It developed most successfully in England, particularly for the spinning and weaving of woolen cloth. By 1500 half of England's textiles were being produced in the countryside. By 1700 English industry was generally more rural than urban and heavily reliant on the putting-out system. Most continental countries, with the exception of Flanders and the Dutch Republic, developed rural industry more slowly. The latter part of the eighteenth century witnessed a remarkable expansion of rural industry in certain densely populated regions of continental Europe (Map 17.1).

< MAP 17.1 Industry and Population in Eighteenth-Century Europe
The growth of cottage manufacturing in rural areas helped country people increase their income and contributed to population growth. The putting-out system began in England, and much of the work was in the textile industry. Cottage industry was also strong in the Low Countries — modern-day Belgium and the Netherlands.

The Lives of Rural Textile Workers

Until the nineteenth century the industry that employed the most people in Europe was textiles. The making of linen, woolen, and eventually cotton cloth was the typical activity of cottage workers engaged in the putting-out system. A look inside the cottage of the English weaver illustrates a way of life as well as an economic system. The rural worker lived in a small cottage with tiny windows and little space. The cottage was often a single room that served as workshop, kitchen, and bedroom. There were only a few pieces of furniture, of which the weaver's loom was by far the largest and most important. That loom changed somewhat in the early eighteenth century when John Kay's invention of the flying shuttle enabled the weaver to throw the shuttle back and forth between the threads with one hand. Aside from that improvement, however, the loom was as it had been for much of history and as it would remain until the arrival of mechanized looms in the first decades of the nineteenth century.

Handloom weaving was a family enterprise. All members of the family helped in the work, so that "every person from seven to eighty (who retained their sight and who could move their hands) could earn their bread," as one eighteenth-century English observer put it.[4] Operating the loom was usually considered a man's job, reserved for the male head of the family. Women and children worked at auxiliary tasks; they prepared the warp (vertical) threads and mounted them on the loom, wound threads on bobbins for the weft (horizontal) threads, and sometimes operated the warp frame while the father passed the shuttle.

The work of four or five spinners was needed to keep one weaver steadily employed. Since the weaver's family usually could not produce enough thread, merchants hired the wives and daughters of agricultural workers, who took on spinning work in their spare time. In England, many widows and single women also became "spinsters," so many in fact that the word became a synonym for an unmarried woman. In parts of Germany, spinning employed whole families and was not reserved for women.

Relations between workers and employers were often marked by sharp conflict. There were constant disputes over the weights of materials and the quality of finished work. Merchants accused workers of stealing raw materials, and weavers complained that merchants delivered underweight bales. Suspicion abounded.

Conditions were particularly hard for female workers. While men could earn decent wages through long hours of arduous labor, women's wages were usually much lower because they were not considered the family's primary wage earner. In England's Yorkshire wool industry, a male wool comber earned a good wage of 12 shillings or more a week, while a female spinner could hope for only 3½ shillings.[5] A single or widowed spinner faced a desperate struggle with poverty. Any period of illness or unemployment could spell disaster for her and any children she might have. In 1788 one English writer condemned the low wages of spinners in Norwich: "The suffering of thousands of wretched individuals, willing to work, but starving from their ill requited labour; of whole families of honest industrious children offering their little hands to the wheel, and asking bread of the helpless mother, unable through this well regulated manufacture to give it to them."[6]

From the merchant capitalist's point of view, the problem was not low wages but maintaining control over the labor force. Cottage workers were scattered across the countryside and their work depended on the agricultural calendar. In spring and late summer planting and haymaking occupied all hands in the rural village, leading to shortages in the supply of thread. Merchants bitterly resented their lack of control over rural labor because their own livelihood depended on their ability to meet orders on time. They accused workers—especially female spinners—of laziness, drunkenness, and immorality. If workers failed to produce enough thread, they reasoned, it must be because their wages were too high and they had little incentive to work.

Merchants thus insisted on maintaining the lowest possible wages to force the "idle" poor into productive labor. They also lobbied for, and obtained, new police powers over workers. Imprisonment and public whipping became common punishments for pilfering small amounts of yarn or cloth. For poor workers, their right to hold on to the bits and pieces left over in the production process was akin to the traditional peasant right of gleaning in common lands. With progress came the loss of traditional safeguards for the poor.

The Industrious Revolution

One scholar has used the term **industrious revolution** to summarize the social and economic changes taking place in northwestern Europe in the late seventeenth and early eighteenth centuries.[7] This occurred as households reduced leisure time, stepped up the pace of work, and, most important, redirected the labor of women and children away from the production of goods for household consumption and toward wage work. In the countryside the spread of cottage industry can be seen as one manifestation of the industrious revolution, while in the cities there was a rise in female employment outside the home (see page 537). By working harder and increasing the number of wageworkers, rural and urban households could purchase more goods, even in a time of stagnant or falling wages.

The effect of these changes is still debated. While some scholars lament the encroachment of longer work hours and stricter discipline on traditional family life, others insist that poor families made decisions based on their own self-interests. With more finished goods becoming available at lower prices, households sought cash income to participate in an emerging consumer economy.

The role of women and girls in this new economy is particularly controversial. When women entered the labor market, they almost always worked at menial, tedious jobs for very low wages. Yet when women earned their own wages, they also seem to have exercised more independence in marriage choices and household decision making. Most of their scant earnings went for household necessities, items of food and clothing they could no longer produce now that they worked full-time, but sometimes a few shillings were left for a ribbon or a new pair of stockings. Women's use of their surplus income thus helped spur the rapid growth of the textile industries in which they labored so hard.

These new sources and patterns of labor established important foundations for the Industrial Revolution of the late eighteenth and nineteenth centuries (see Chapter 20). They created households in which all members worked for wages rather than in a family business and in which consumption relied on market-produced rather than homemade goods. It was not until the mid-nineteenth century, with rising industrial wages, that a new model emerged in which the male "breadwinner" was expected to earn enough to support the whole family and women and children were relegated back to the domestic sphere. With women estimated to compose more than 40 percent of the global workforce, today's world is experiencing a second industrious revolution in a similar climate of stagnant wages and increased demand for consumer goods.[8]

The Debate over Urban Guilds

Focus Question	What were guilds, and why did they become controversial in the eighteenth century?

One consequence of the growth of rural industry was an undermining of the traditional **guild system** that protected urban artisans. Guilds continued to dominate production in towns and cities, providing their masters with economic privileges as well as a proud social identity, but they increasingly struggled against competition from rural workers. Meanwhile, those excluded from guild membership—women, day laborers, Jews, and foreigners—worked on the margins of the urban economy.

In the second half of the eighteenth century, critics like Adam Smith attacked the guilds as outmoded institutions that obstructed technical progress and innovation. Until recently, most historians repeated that view. An ongoing reassessment of guilds now emphasizes their ability to adapt to changing economic circumstances.

Urban Guilds

Originating around 1200 during the economic boom of the Middle Ages, the guild system reached its peak in most of Europe in the seventeenth and eighteenth centuries. During this period, urban guilds increased dramatically in cities and towns across Europe. In Louis XIV's France, for example, finance minister Jean-Baptiste Colbert revived the urban guilds and used them to encourage high-quality production and to collect taxes (see Chapter 15). The number of guilds in the city of Paris grew from 60 in 1672 to 129 in 1691.

Guild masters occupied the summit of the world of work. Each guild possessed a detailed set of privileges, including exclusive rights to produce and sell certain goods, access to restricted markets in raw materials, and the rights to train apprentices, hire workers, and open shops. Any individual who violated these monopolies could be prosecuted. Guilds also served social and religious functions, providing a locus of sociability and group identity to the middling classes of European cities.

To ensure there was enough work to go around, guilds restricted their membership to men who were Christians, had several years of work experience, paid membership fees, and successfully completed a masterpiece. Masters' sons enjoyed automatic access to their fathers' guilds, while outsiders—including Jews and Protestants in Catholic countries—were barred from entering. Most urban men and women worked in non-guild trades as domestic servants, manual laborers, and vendors of food, used clothing, and other goods.

The guilds' ability to enforce their barriers varied a great deal across Europe. In England, national regulations superseded guild rules, sapping their importance. In

France, the Crown developed an ambiguous attitude toward guilds, relying on them for taxes and enforcement of quality standards, yet allowing non-guild production to flourish in the countryside in the 1760s, and even in some urban neighborhoods. The German guilds were perhaps the most powerful in Europe, and the most conservative. Journeymen in German cities, with their masters' support, violently protested the encroachment of non-guild workers.

While most were hostile to women, a small number of guilds did accept women. Most involved needlework and textile production, occupations that were considered appropriate for women. In 1675 seamstresses gained a new all-female guild in Paris, and soon seamstresses joined tailors' guilds in parts of France, England, and the Dutch Republic. By the mid-eighteenth century male masters began to hire more female workers, often in defiance of their own guild statutes.

Adam Smith and Economic Liberalism

At the same time that cottage industry began to infringe on the livelihoods of urban artisans, new Enlightenment ideals called into question the very existence of the guild system. Eighteenth-century critics derided guilds as outmoded and exclusionary institutions that obstructed technical innovation and progress. One of the best-known critics of government regulation of trade and industry was Adam Smith (1723–1790), a leading figure of the Scottish Enlightenment (see Chapter 16). Smith developed the general idea of freedom of enterprise and established the basis for modern economics in his groundbreaking work *Inquiry into the Nature and Causes of the Wealth of Nations* (1776). Smith criticized guilds for their stifling restrictions, a critique he extended to all state monopolies and privileged companies. Far preferable, in his view, was free competition, which would protect consumers from price gouging and give all citizens an equal right to do what they did best. Smith advocated a more highly developed "division of labor," which entailed separating craft production into individual tasks to increase workers' speed and efficiency.

In keeping with his fear of political oppression and with the "system of natural liberty" that he championed, Smith argued that government should limit itself to "only three duties": it should provide a defense against foreign invasion, maintain civil order with courts and police protection, and sponsor certain indispensable public works and institutions that could never adequately profit private investors. He believed that the pursuit of self-interest in a competitive market would be sufficient to improve the living conditions of citizens, a view that quickly emerged as the classic argument for **economic liberalism**.

However, Smith did not advocate unbridled capitalism. Unlike many disgruntled merchant capitalists, he applauded the modest rise in real wages of British workers in the eighteenth century, stating: "No society can surely be flourishing and happy, of which the far greater part of the members are poor and miserable." Smith also acknowledged that employers were "always and everywhere in a sort of tacit, but constant and uniform combination, not to raise the wages of labor above their actual rate" and sometimes entered "into particular combinations to sink the wages even below this rate." While he celebrated the rise in productivity allowed by the division of labor, he also acknowledged its demoralizing effects on workers and called for government intervention to raise workers' living standards.[9]

Many educated people in France, including government officials, shared Smith's ideas. In 1774, the reform-minded economics minister Anne-Robert-Jacques Turgot issued a law in the name of Louis XV, ordering the grain trade to be freed from state regulation. Two years later, another edict abolished all French guilds. The law stated:

> We wish to abolish these arbitrary institutions, which do not allow the poor man to earn his living; which reject a sex whose weakness has given it more needs and fewer resources . . . ; which destroy emulation and industry and nullify the talents of those whose circumstances have excluded them from membership of a guild; which deprive the state and the arts of all the knowledge brought to them by foreigners; which retard the progress of these arts . . . ; [and which] burden industry with an oppressive tax, which bears heavily on the people.[10]

Vociferous popular protest against these measures led to Turgot's disgrace shortly afterward and the cancellation of his reforms, but the legislators of the French Revolution (see Chapter 19) returned to a liberal economic agenda in 1789. The National Assembly definitively abolished guilds in 1791. Other European countries followed suit more slowly, with guilds surviving in central Europe and Italy into the second half of the nineteenth century. By the middle of the nineteenth century economic liberalism was championed by most European governments and elites.

Some artisans welcomed the deregulation espoused by Smith and Turgot, but many continued to uphold the ideals of the guilds. In the late eighteenth and early nineteenth centuries, skilled artisans across Europe espoused the values of high-quality hand craftsmanship and limited competition in contrast to the proletarianization and loss of skills they endured in mechanized production. Recent scholarship has challenged wholly negative views of the guilds, emphasizing the flexibility and adaptability of the guild system and the role it played in fostering confidence in quality standards.

The Atlantic World and Global Trade

Focus Question | **How did colonial markets boost Europe's economic and social development, and what conflicts and adversity did world trade entail?**

In addition to agricultural improvement, population pressure, and growing cottage industry, the expansion of Europe in the eighteenth century was characterized by the increase of world trade. Adam Smith himself declared that "the discovery of America and that of a passage to the East Indies by the Cape of Good Hope, are the two greatest and most important events recorded in the history of mankind."[11] In the eighteenth century Spain and Portugal revitalized their empires and began drawing more wealth from renewed colonial development. Yet once again the countries of northwestern Europe — the Dutch Republic, France, and above all Great Britain — benefited most.

The Atlantic economy that these countries developed from 1650 to 1790 would prove crucial in the building of a global economy. Great Britain, which was formed in 1707 by the union of England and Scotland into a single kingdom, gradually became the leading maritime power. Thus the British played the critical role in building a fairly unified Atlantic economy that provided remarkable opportunities for them and their colonists. They also competed ruthlessly with France and the Netherlands for trade and territory in the Americas and Asia.

Mercantilism and Colonial Competition

Britain's commercial leadership in the eighteenth century had its origins in the mercantilism of the seventeenth century (see Chapter 15). Eventually eliciting criticism from Enlightenment thinker Adam Smith and other proponents of free trade in the late eighteenth century, European mercantilism was a system of economic regulations aimed at increasing the power of the state. As practiced by a leading figure such as Colbert under Louis XIV, mercantilism aimed particularly at creating a favorable balance of foreign trade in order to increase a country's stock of gold. A country's gold holdings served as an all-important treasure chest that could be opened periodically to pay for war in a violent age.

In England, the desire to increase both military power and private wealth resulted in the mercantile system of the **Navigation Acts**. Oliver Cromwell established the first of these laws in 1651, and the restored monarchy of Charles II extended them in 1660 and 1663. The acts required that most goods imported from Europe into England and Scotland (Great Britain after 1707) be carried on British-owned ships with British

Colonel James Tod of the East India Company Traveling by Elephant Through Rajasthan, India   By the end of the eighteenth century agents of the British East India Company exercised growing military and political authority in India, in addition to monopolizing Britain's lucrative economic trade with the subcontinent. (Victoria and Albert Museum, London, UK/ Bridgeman Images)

crews or on ships of the country producing the articles. Moreover, these laws gave British merchants and shipowners a virtual monopoly on trade with British colonies. The colonists were required to ship their products on British (or American) ships and to buy almost all European goods from Britain. It was believed that these economic regulations would eliminate foreign competition, thereby helping British merchants and workers as well as colonial plantation owners and farmers. It was hoped, too, that the emerging British Empire would develop a shipping industry with a large number of experienced seamen who could serve during wartime in the Royal Navy.

The Navigation Acts were a form of economic warfare. Their initial target was the Dutch, who were far ahead of the English in shipping and foreign trade in the mid-seventeenth century (see Chapter 15). In conjunction with three Anglo-Dutch wars between 1652 and 1674, the Navigation Acts seriously damaged Dutch shipping and commerce. The British seized the thriving Dutch colony of New Amsterdam in 1664 and renamed it New York. By the late seventeenth century the Dutch Republic was falling behind England in shipping, trade, and colonies.

Thereafter France stood clearly as England's most serious rival in the competition for overseas empire. Rich in natural resources, with a population three or four times that of England, and allied with Spain, continental Europe's leading military power was already building a powerful fleet and a worldwide system of rigidly monopolized colonial trade. Thus from 1701 to 1763 Britain and France were locked in a series of wars to decide, in part, which nation would become the leading maritime power and claim the profits of Europe's overseas expansion (Map 17.2).

The first round was the War of the Spanish Succession (see Chapter 15), which started in 1701 when Louis XIV accepted the Spanish crown willed to his grandson. Besides upsetting the continental balance of power, a union of France and Spain threatened to encircle and destroy the British colonies in North America (see Map 17.2). Defeated by a great coalition of states after twelve years of fighting, Louis XIV was forced in the Peace of Utrecht (YOO-trehkt) in 1713 to cede his North American holdings in Newfoundland, Nova Scotia, and the Hudson Bay territory to Britain. Spain was compelled to give Britain control of its West African slave trade — the so-called *asiento* (ah-SYEHN-toh) — and to let Britain send one ship of merchandise into the Spanish colonies annually.

Conflict continued among the European powers over both domestic and colonial affairs. The War of the Austrian Succession (1740–1748), which started when Frederick the Great of Prussia seized Silesia from Austria's Maria Theresa (see Chapter 16), gradually became a world war that included Anglo-French conflicts in India and North America. The war ended with no change in the territorial situation in North America. This inconclusive standoff helped set the stage for the Seven Years' War (1756–1763; see Chapter 19). In central Europe, France aided Austria's Maria Theresa in her quest to win back Silesia from the Prussians, who had formed an alliance with England. In

---

MAP 17.2 The Atlantic Economy in 1701   >

The growth of trade encouraged both economic development and military conflict in the Atlantic basin. Four continents were linked together by the exchange of goods and peoples.

Territorial claims
- Great Britain
- France
- Portugal
- Spain
- Netherlands

- Trade from Europe
- Trade from Africa
- Trade from Americas
- Trade from Asia
- *Sugar* Trade good

PACIFIC OCEAN

Silver (to the Philippines)

Silks, spices, porcelain

ARCTIC OCEAN

ASIA

NORTH AMERICA

Hudson Bay

NEW SPAIN

LOUISIANA

RUPERT'S LAND

EUROPE

MEXICO

Mississippi R.

NEW FRANCE

QUEBEC

GREAT BRITAIN

DUTCH REPUBLIC

Veracruz

THIRTEEN COLONIES

NEWFOUNDLAND

Acapulco

FLORIDA

ACADIA

Tobacco

Furs

Colonial products

FRANCE

Manufactured goods

SPAIN

Havana

CUBA

Silver

PORTUGAL

JAMAICA

Sugar

SAINT DOMINGUE (Fr.)

Hispaniola

Canary Is. (Spain)

Porto Bello

SANTO DOMINGO

Guadeloupe (Fr.)

NORTH ATLANTIC OCEAN

Gold

AFRICA

Martinique (Fr.)

Silver

NEW GRANADA

Barbados (Gr. Br.)

Cape Verde Is. (Port.)

Cape Verde

Amazon R.

DUTCH GUIANA

Lima

PERU

FRENCH GUIANA

Sugar

Gold Coast

Slave Coast

Silver

SOUTH AMERICA

Slaves

PACIFIC OCEAN

BRAZIL

ANGOLA

Buenos Aires

SOUTH ATLANTIC OCEAN

North America, French and British settlers engaged in territorial skirmishes that eventually resulted in all-out war that drew in Native American allies on both sides of the conflict (see Map 19.1, page 590). By 1763 Prussia had held off the Austrians, and British victory on all colonial fronts was ratified in the **Treaty of Paris**. British naval power, built in large part on the rapid growth of the British shipping industry after the passage of the Navigation Acts, had triumphed decisively: Britain had realized its goal of monopolizing a vast trading and colonial empire.

The Atlantic Economy

As the volume of transatlantic trade increased, the regions bordering the ocean were increasingly drawn into an integrated economic system. Commercial exchange in the Atlantic has often been referred to as the "triangle trade," designating a three-way transport of goods: European commodities, like guns and textiles, to Africa; enslaved Africans to the colonies; and colonial goods, such as cotton, tobacco, and sugar, back to Europe (see Map 17.2).

Over the course of the eighteenth century, the economies of European nations bordering the Atlantic Ocean, especially England, relied more and more on colonial exports. In England, sales to the mainland colonies of North America and the West Indian sugar islands—with an important assist from West Africa and Latin America—soared from £500,000 to £4 million (Figure 17.3). Exports to England's colonies in Ireland and India also rose substantially from 1700 to 1800. By 1800 sales to European countries—England's traditional trading partners—represented only one-third of exports, down from two-thirds a century earlier. England also benefited from importing colonial products. Colonial monopolies allowed the English to obtain a steady supply of such goods at beneficial prices and to re-export them to other nations at high profits. Moreover, many colonial goods, like sugar and tobacco, required processing before consumption and thus contributed new manufacturing jobs in England. In the eighteenth century, stimulated by trade and empire building, England's capital city, London, grew into the West's largest and richest city. Thus the mercantilist system achieved remarkable success for England, and

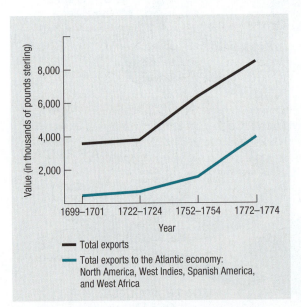

FIGURE 17.3 Exports of English Manufactured Goods, 1700–1774
While trade between England and Europe stagnated after 1700, English exports to Africa and the Americas boomed and greatly stimulated English economic development.
(Source: Data from R. Davis, "English Foreign Trade, 1700–1774," *Economic History Review*, 2d ser., 15 [1962]: 302–303.)

by the 1770s the country stood on the threshold of the epoch-making changes that would become known as the Industrial Revolution (see Chapter 20).

Although they lost many possessions to the English in the Seven Years' War, the French still profited enormously from colonial trade. The colonies of Saint-Domingue (modern-day Haiti), Martinique, and Guadeloupe remained in French hands and provided immense fortunes in plantation agriculture and slave trading during the second half of the eighteenth century. By 1789 the population of Saint-Domingue included five hundred thousand slaves whose labor had allowed the colony to become the world's leading producer of coffee and sugar and the most profitable plantation colony in the New World.[12] The wealth generated from colonial trade fostered the confidence of the merchant classes in Paris, Bordeaux, and other large cities, and merchants soon joined other elite groups clamoring for political reforms.

The third major player in the Atlantic economy, Spain, also saw its colonial fortunes improve during the eighteenth century. Not only did it gain Louisiana from France in 1763, but its influence expanded westward all the way to northern California through the efforts of Spanish missionaries and ranchers. Its mercantilist goals were boosted by a recovery in silver production, which had dropped significantly in the seventeenth century.

Silver mining also stimulated food production for the mining camps, and wealthy Spanish landowners developed a system of **debt peonage** to keep indigenous workers on their estates. Under this system, which was similar to serfdom, a planter or rancher would keep workers in perpetual debt bondage by advancing them food, shelter, and a little money.

Although the "triangle trade" model highlights some of the most important flows of commerce across the Atlantic, it significantly oversimplifies the picture. For example, a brisk intercolonial trade also existed, with the Caribbean slave colonies importing food in the form of fish, flour, and livestock from the northern colonies and rice from the south, in exchange for sugar and slaves (see Map 17.2). Many colonial traders violated imperial monopolies to trade with the most profitable partners, regardless of nationality. Moreover, the Atlantic economy was inextricably linked to trade with the Indian and Pacific Oceans (see pages 548–549).

The Atlantic Slave Trade

At the core of the Atlantic world were the misery and profit of the **Atlantic slave trade**. The forced migration of millions of Africans—cruel, unjust, and tragic—was a key element in the Atlantic system and western European economic expansion throughout the eighteenth century. The brutal practice intensified dramatically after 1700 and especially after 1750 with the growth of trade and demand for slave-produced goods like sugar and cotton. According to the most authoritative source, European traders purchased and shipped 6.5 million enslaved Africans across the Atlantic between 1701 and 1800—more than half of the estimated total of 12.5 million Africans transported between 1450 and 1900, of whom 15 percent died in procurement and transit.[13] By the peak decade of the 1780s, shipments averaged about eighty thousand individuals per year in an attempt to satisfy the constantly rising demand for labor power—and also for slave owners' profits—in the Americas.

Numerous poor or middling whites worked as clerks, shopkeepers, craftsmen, and, in North America, farmers and laborers. With the exception of British North America, white Europeans made up a minority of the population; they were out-numbered in Spanish America by indigenous peoples and in the Caribbean by the growing numbers of enslaved people of African descent. Since European migrants were disproportionately male, much of the population of the Atlantic world descended from unions — forced or through choice — of European men and indig-enous or African women (see the painting on page 547). Colonial attempts to iden-tify and control racial categories greatly influenced developing Enlightenment thought on racial difference (see Chapter 16).

Mixed-race populations sometimes rose to the colonial elite. The Spanish conquis-tadors often consolidated their power through marriage to the daughters of local rulers, and their descendants were among the most powerful inhabitants of Spanish America. In the Spanish and French Caribbean, as in Brazil, many masters acknowledged and freed their mixed-race children, leading to sizable populations of free people of color. Advantaged by their fathers, some became wealthy land and slave owners in their own right. In the second half of the eighteenth century, the prosperity of some free people of color brought a backlash from the white population of Saint-Domingue in the form of new race laws prohibiting nonwhites from marrying whites and forcing them to adopt distinctive attire.

British colonies followed a distinctive pattern. There, whole families, rather than individual men, migrated, resulting in a rapid increase in the white population. This development was favored by British colonial law, which forbade marriage between English men and women and Africans or Native Americans. In the British colonies of the Caribbean and the southern mainland, masters tended to leave their mixed-race progeny in slavery rather than freeing them, maintaining a stark discrepancy between free whites and enslaved people of color.[16] The identities inspired by the Atlantic world were equally complex. In some ways, the colonial encounter helped create new and more fixed forms of identity. Inhabitants of distinct regions of European nations came to see themselves as "Spanish" or "English" when they crossed the Atlantic; similarly, their colonial governments imposed the identity of "Indian" and "African" on peoples with vastly different linguistic, cultural, and political origins. The result was the crea-tion of new Creole communities that melded cultural and social elements of various groups of origin with the new European cultures.

The status of mixed-race people, known as mestizos in Spanish America and métis in New France, was ambiguous. Spanish administrators applied purity of blood (*limpieza de sangre*) laws — originally used to exclude Jews and Muslims dur-ing the reconquista — to indigenous and African peoples. Some mixed-race people sought to enter Creole society and obtain its many official and unofficial privileges by passing as white. Over time, where they existed in any number, mestizos and free people of color established their own communities and social hierarchies based on wealth, family connections, occupation, and skin color.

Converting indigenous people to Christianity was a key ambition for all European powers in the New World. Galvanized by the Protestant Reformation and the perceived need to protect and spread Catholicism, Catholic powers actively sponsored missionary efforts. Jesuits, Franciscans, Dominicans, and other religious orders established missions throughout Spanish, Portuguese, and French colonies (see Chapter 14). In Central and

***Castas* Painting** In the second half of the eighteenth century, fascination with the emerging mixed-race population of Spanish America gave rise to the genre of *castas* paintings, sets of sixteen families, each depicting a specific racial mixture. Here the painter has identified the mother as "Indian" and the father as a *chino,* a term referring to the offspring of a union between an Indian and an African. (*A Half-Breed and His Lobo Indian Wife and Their Child,* Mexican [oil on canvas]/Museo de America, Madrid, Spain/Index/Bridgeman Images)

South America, large-scale conversion forged enduring Catholic cultures in Portuguese and Spanish colonies. Conversion efforts in North America were less effective because indigenous settlements were more scattered and native people were less integrated into colonial communities. On the whole, Protestants were less active as missionaries in this period, although some dissenters, like Moravians, Quakers, and Methodists, did seek converts among indigenous and enslaved people.

The practice of slavery reveals important limitations on efforts to spread Christianity. Slave owners often refused to baptize their slaves, fearing that enslaved people would use their Christian status to claim additional rights. In some areas, particularly among the mostly African-born slaves of the Caribbean, elements of African religious belief and practice endured, often incorporated with Christian traditions.

Restricted from owning land and holding many occupations in Europe, Jews were eager participants in the new Atlantic economy and established a network of mercantile communities along its trade routes. As in the Old World, Jews in European colonies faced discrimination; for example, restrictions existed on the number of slaves they could own in Barbados in the early eighteenth century.[18] Jews were considered to be white Europeans and thus ineligible to be slaves, but they did not enjoy equal status with Christians. The status of Jews adds one more element to the complexity of Atlantic identities.

The Atlantic Enlightenment

Enlightenment ideas thrived in the colonies, although with as much diversity and disagreement as in Europe (see Chapter 16). The colonies of British North America were deeply influenced by the Scottish Enlightenment, with its emphasis on pragmatic approaches to the problems of life. Following the Scottish model, leaders in the colonies adopted a moderate, "commonsense" version of the Enlightenment that emphasized self-improvement and ethical conduct. In most cases, this version of the Enlightenment was perfectly compatible with religion and was chiefly spread through the growing colleges and universities of the colonies, which remained church-based institutions.

Some thinkers went even further in their admiration for Enlightenment ideas. Benjamin Franklin's writings and political career provide an outstanding example of the combination of the pragmatism and economic interests of the Scottish Enlightenment with the constitutional theories of John Locke, Jean-Jacques Rousseau, and the baron de Montesquieu. Franklin was privately a lifelong deist, meaning that he believed in God but not in organized religion. Nonetheless, he continued to attend church and respect religious proprieties, a cautious pattern followed by fellow deist Thomas Jefferson and other leading thinkers of the American Enlightenment.

Northern Enlightenment thinkers often depicted Spain and its American colonies as the epitome of the superstition and barbarity they contested. The Catholic Church strictly controlled the publication of books on the Iberian Peninsula and in Spanish America. Nonetheless, the Bourbon dynasty that took power in Spain in the early eighteenth century followed its own course of enlightened absolutism, just like its counterparts in the rest of Europe (see Chapter 16). Under King Carlos III (r. 1759–1788) and his son Carlos IV (r. 1788–1808), Spanish administrators attempted to strengthen colonial rule by posting a standing army in the colonies and increasing royal monopolies and taxes to pay for it. They also ordered officials to gather more accurate information about the colonies as a basis for improving the government. Enlightened administrators debated the status of indigenous peoples and whether it would be better for these peoples (and for the prosperity of Spanish America) if they maintained their distinct legal status or were integrated into Spanish society.

Educated Creoles were well aware of the new currents of thought, and the universities, newspapers, and salons of Spanish America produced their own reform ideas. The establishment of a mining school in Mexico City in 1792, the first in the Spanish colonies, illuminates the practical achievements of reformers. As in other European colonies, one effect of Enlightenment thought was to encourage Creoles to criticize the policies of the mother country and aspire toward greater autonomy.

Trade and Empire in Asia and the Pacific

As the Atlantic economy took shape, Europeans continued to vie for dominance in the Asian trade. Between 1500 and 1600 the Portuguese had become major players in the Indian Ocean trading world, eliminating Venice as Europe's chief supplier of spices and other Asian luxury goods. The Portuguese dominated but did not fundamentally alter the age-old pattern of Indian Ocean trade, which involved merchants from many areas as more or less autonomous players. This situation changed radically with the intervention of the Dutch and then the English (see Chapter 14).

Formed in 1602, the Dutch East India Company had taken control of the Portuguese spice trade in the Indian Ocean, with the port of Batavia (Jakarta) in Java as its center of operations. Within a few decades it had expelled the Portuguese from Ceylon and other East Indian islands. Unlike the Portuguese, the Dutch transformed the Indian Ocean trading world. Whereas East Indian states and peoples maintained independence under the Portuguese, who treated them as autonomous business partners, the Dutch established outright control and reduced them to dependents.

After these successes, the Dutch hold in Asia faltered in the eighteenth century due to the company's failure to diversify to meet changing consumption patterns. Spices continued to compose much of its shipping, despite their declining importance in the European diet, probably due to changing fashions in food and luxury consumption. Fierce competition from its main rival, the English East India Company (established 1600), also severely undercut Dutch trade.

Britain initially struggled for a foothold in Asia. With the Dutch monopolizing the Indian Ocean, the British turned to India, the source of lucrative trade in silks, textiles, and pepper. Throughout the seventeenth century the English East India Company relied on trade concessions from the powerful Mughal emperor, who granted only piecemeal access to the subcontinent. Finally, in 1716 the Mughals conceded empire-wide trading privileges. As Mughal power waned, British East India Company agents increasingly intervened in local affairs and made alliances or waged war against Indian princes.

Britain's great rival for influence in India was France. During the War of the Austrian Succession, British and French forces in India supported opposing rulers in local power struggles. In 1757 East India Company forces under Robert Clive conquered the rich northeastern province of Bengal at the Battle of Plassey. French-English rivalry was finally resolved by the Treaty of Paris, which granted all of France's possessions in India to the British with the exception of Pondicherry, an Indian Ocean port city. With the elimination of their rival, British ascendancy in India accelerated. In 1765 the Mughal shah granted the East India Company *diwani*, the right to civil administration and tax collection, in Bengal and neighboring provinces. By the early nineteenth century the company had overcome vigorous Indian resistance to gain economic and political dominance of much of the subcontinent; direct administration by the British government replaced East India Company rule after a large-scale rebellion in 1857.

The late eighteenth century also witnessed the beginning of British settlement of the continent of Australia. The continent was first sighted by Europeans in the early seventeenth century, and thereafter parts of the coast were charted by European ships. Captain James Cook claimed the east coast of Australia for England in 1770, naming it New South Wales. The first colony was established there in the late 1780s, relying on the labor of convicted prisoners forcibly transported from Britain. Settlement of the western portion of the continent followed in the 1790s. The first colonies struggled for survival and, after an initial period of friendly relations, soon aroused the hostility and resistance of aboriginal peoples. Cook himself was killed by islanders in Hawaii in 1779, having charted much of the Pacific Ocean for the first time.

The rising economic and political power of Europeans in this period drew on the connections they established between the Asian and Atlantic trade worlds. An outstanding example is the trade in cowrie shells. These seashells, originating in the Maldive Islands in the Indian Ocean, were used as a form of currency in West Africa. European traders obtained them in Asia, packing them alongside porcelains, spices, and silks for the journey home. The cowries were then brought from European ports to the West African coast to be traded for slaves. Indian textiles were also prized in Africa and played a similar role in exchange. Thus the trade of the Atlantic was inseparable from Asian commerce, and Europeans were increasingly found dominating commerce in both worlds.

NOTES

1. B. H. Slicher van Bath, *The Agrarian History of Western Europe, A.D. 500–1850* (New York: St. Martin's Press, 1963), p. 240.

2. Quoted in Paul Mantoux, *The Industrial Revolution in the Eighteenth Century: An Outline of the Beginnings of the Modern Factory System* (1961; Abingdon, U.K.: Routledge, 2005), p. 175.

3. Thomas Salmon, *Modern History: Or the Present State of All Nations* (London, 1730), p. 406.

4. Quoted in I. Pinchbeck, *Women Workers and the Industrial Revolution, 1750–1850* (1930; Abingdon, U.K.: Frank Cass, 1977), p. 113.

5. Richard J. Soderlund, "'Intended as a Terror to the Idle and Profligate': Embezzlement and the Origins of Policing in the Yorkshire Worsted Industry, c. 1750–1777," *Journal of Social History* 31 (Spring 1998): 658.

6. Quoted in Maxine Berg, *The Age of Manufactures, 1700–1820: Industry, Innovation, and Work in Britain* (London: Routledge, 1994), p. 124.

7. Jan de Vries, *The Industrious Revolution: Consumer Behavior and the Household Economy, 1650 to the Present* (Cambridge: Cambridge University Press, 2008).

8. Jan de Vries, "The Industrial Revolution and the Industrious Revolution," *The Journal of Economic History* 54, no. 2 (June 1994): 249–270; discusses the industrious revolution of the second half of the twentieth century.

9. R. Heilbroner, *The Essential Adam Smith* (New York: W. W. Norton, 1986), p. 196.

10. S. Pollard and C. Holmes, eds., *Documents of European Economic History*, vol. 1, *The Process of Industrialization, 1750–1870* (New York: St. Martin's Press, 1968), p. 53.

11. Ibid., p. 281.

12. Laurent Dubois and John D. Garrigus, *Slave Revolution in the Caribbean, 1789–1904* (New York: Palgrave, 2006), p. 8.

13. Figures obtained from Voyages: The Trans-Atlantic Slave Trade Database, http://www.slavevoyages.org /assessment/estimates (accessed January 17, 2016).

14. Quoted in Thomas Benjamin, *The Atlantic World: Europeans, Africans, Indians and Their Shared History, 1400–1900* (Cambridge: Cambridge University Press, 2009), p. 211.

15. Pierre Marie François Paget, *Travels Round the World in the Years 1767, 1768, 1769, 1770, 1771*, vol. 1 (London, 1793), p. 262.

16. Orlando Patterson, *Slavery and Social Death* (Cambridge, Mass.: Harvard University Press, 1982), p. 255.

17. Tamar Herzog, "Identities and Processes of Identification in the Atlantic World," in *The Oxford Handbook of the Atlantic World, 1450–1850*, ed. Nicholas Canny and Philip Morgan (Oxford: Oxford University Press, 2011), pp. 480–491.

18. Erik R. Seeman, "Jews in the Early Modern Atlantic: Crossing Boundaries, Keeping Faith," in *The Atlantic in Global History, 1500–2000*, ed. Jorge Cañizares-Esguerra and Erik R. Seeman (Upper Saddle River, N.J.: Pearson Prentice Hall, 2007), p. 43.

LOOKING BACK LOOKING AHEAD

By the turn of the eighteenth century, western Europe had begun to shake off the effects of a century of famine, disease, warfare, economic depression, and demographic stagnation. The eighteenth century witnessed a breakthrough in agricultural production that, along with improved infrastructure and the retreat of epidemic disease, contributed to a substantial increase in population. One crucial catalyst for agricultural innovation was the Scientific Revolution, which provided new tools of empirical observation and experimentation. The Enlightenment as well, with its emphasis on progress and public welfare, convinced government officials, scientists, and informed landowners to seek better solutions to old problems. By the end of the century, industry and trade had also attracted enlightened commentators who advocated free markets and less government control. Modern ideas of political economy thus constitute one more legacy of the Enlightenment, but—like the Enlightenment itself—they drew criticism from nineteenth- and twentieth-century thinkers.

As the era of European exploration and conquest gave way to colonial empire building, the eighteenth century witnessed increased consolidation of global markets and bitter competition among Europeans for the spoils of empire. From its slow inception in the mid-fifteenth century, the African slave trade reached brutal heights in the second half of the eighteenth century. The eighteenth-century Atlantic world thus tied the shores of Europe, the Americas, and Africa in a web of commercial and human exchange that also had strong ties with the Pacific and the Indian Oceans.

The new dynamics of the eighteenth century prepared the way for world-shaking changes. Population growth and rural industry began to undermine long-standing traditions of daily life in western Europe. The transformed families of the industrious revolution developed not only new habits of work, but also a new sense of confidence in their abilities. By the 1770s England was approaching an economic transformation fully as significant as the great political upheaval destined to develop shortly in neighboring France. In the same period, the first wave of resistance to European domination rose up in the colonies. The great revolutions of the late eighteenth century would change the world forever.

MAKE CONNECTIONS

Think about the larger developments and continuities within and across chapters.

1. How did agriculture, industry, and population affect each other in the eighteenth century? How and why did developments in one area affect the other areas?

2. Compare the economic and social situation of western Europe in the mid-eighteenth century with that of the seventeenth century (Chapter 15). What were the achievements of the eighteenth century, and what factors allowed for such progress to be made?

3. The eighteenth century was the period of the European Enlightenment, which celebrated tolerance and human liberty (Chapter 16). Paradoxically, it was also the era of a tremendous increase in slavery, which brought suffering and death to millions. How can you explain this paradox?

Chapter Review

IDENTIFY KEY TERMS

Identify and explain the significance of each item below.

enclosure (p. 525)

proletarianization (p. 527)

cottage industry (p. 531)

putting-out system (p. 533)

industrious revolution (p. 535)

guild system (p. 536)

economic liberalism (p. 537)

Navigation Acts (p. 539)

Treaty of Paris (p. 542)

debt peonage (p. 543)

Atlantic slave trade (p. 543)

REVIEW THE MAIN IDEAS

Answer the focus questions from each section of the chapter.

1. What important developments led to increased agricultural production, and how did these changes affect peasants? (p. 523)
2. Why did the European population rise dramatically in the eighteenth century? (p. 527)
3. How and why did rural industry intensify in the eighteenth century? (p. 531)
4. What were guilds, and why did they become controversial in the eighteenth century? (p. 536)
5. How did colonial markets boost Europe's economic and social development, and what conflicts and adversity did world trade entail? (p. 538)

CHRONOLOGY	
1600–1850	Growth in agriculture, pioneered by the Dutch Republic and England
1651–1663	British Navigation Acts
1652–1674	Anglo-Dutch wars
1700–1790	Height of Atlantic slave trade; expansion of rural industry in Europe
1701–1763	British and French mercantilist wars of empire
1720–1722	Last outbreak of bubonic plague in Europe
1720–1789	Growth of European population
1756–1763	Seven Years' War
1760–1815	Height of parliamentary enclosure in England
1763	Treaty of Paris; France cedes its possessions in India and North America
1770	James Cook claims the east coast of Australia for England
1776	Adam Smith publishes *An Inquiry into the Nature and Causes of the Wealth of Nations*
1805	British takeover of India complete
1807	British slave trade abolished

18

Life in the Era of Expansion

1650–1800

THE DISCUSSION OF AGRICULTURE AND INDUSTRY in the last chapter showed the common people at work, straining to make ends meet within the larger context of population growth, gradual economic expansion, and ferocious competition at home and overseas. This chapter shows us how that world of work was embedded in a rich complex of family organization, community practices, everyday experiences, and collective attitudes. As with the economy, traditional habits and practices of daily life changed considerably over the eighteenth century. Change was particularly dramatic in the growing cities of northwestern Europe, where traditional social controls were undermined by the anonymity and increased social interaction of the urban setting.

Historians have studied many aspects of popular life, including marriage patterns and family size, childhood and education, nutrition, health care, and religious worship. Uncovering the life of the common people is a formidable challenge because they left few written records and regional variations abounded. Yet imaginative research has resulted in major findings and much greater knowledge. It is now possible to follow the common people into their homes, workshops, churches, and taverns and to ask, "What were the everyday experiences and attitudes of ordinary people, and how did they change over the eighteenth century?"

Marriage and the Family

Focus Question	What changes occurred in marriage and the family in the course of the eighteenth century?

The basic unit of social organization is the family. Within the structure of the family, human beings love, mate, and reproduce. The family bears primary responsibility to teach the child, imparting values and customs that condition an individual's behavior for a lifetime. The family is also an institution woven into the web of history. It evolves and changes, assuming different forms in different times and places. The eighteenth century was an important moment of change in family life, as patterns of marriage shifted and individuals adapted and conformed to the new and changing realities of the family unit.

Late Marriage and Nuclear Families

Because census data before the modern period are rare, historians have turned to parish registers of births, deaths, and marriages to uncover details of European family life before the nineteenth century. These registers reveal that the three-generation extended family was a rarity in western and central Europe. When young European couples married, they normally established their own households and lived apart from their parents, much like the nuclear families (a family group consisting of parents and their children with no other relatives) common in the United States today. If a three-generation household came into existence, it was usually because a widowed parent moved into the home of a married child.

Most people did not marry young in the seventeenth and eighteenth centuries. The average person married surprisingly late, many years after reaching adulthood and many more after beginning to work. Studies of western Europe in the seventeenth and eighteenth centuries show that both men and women married for the first time at an average age of twenty-five to twenty-seven. Furthermore, 10 to 20 percent of men and women in western Europe never married at all. Matters were different in eastern Europe, where the multigeneration household was the norm, marriage occurred around age twenty, and permanent celibacy was much less common.

Why did young people in western Europe delay marriage? The main reason was that couples normally did not marry until they could start an independent household and support themselves and their future children. Peasants often needed to wait until their father's death to inherit land and marry. In the towns, men and women worked to accumulate enough savings to start a small business and establish their own home. As one father stated in an advice book written for his son: "Money is the sinew of love, as well as war; you can do nothing happily in wedlock without it; the other [virtue and beauty] are court-cards, but they are not of the trump-suit and are foiled by every sneaking misadventure."[1]

Laws and tradition also discouraged early marriage. In some areas couples needed permission from the local lord or landowner in order to marry. Poor couples had particular difficulty securing the approval of local officials, who believed that freedom to marry for the lower classes would result in more landless paupers, more abandoned children, and more money for welfare. Village elders often agreed.

The custom of late marriage combined with the nuclear-family household distinguished western European society from other areas of the world. Historians have argued that this late-marriage pattern was responsible for at least part of the economic advantage western Europeans acquired relative to other world regions. Late marriage joined a mature man and a mature woman—two adults who had already accumulated social and economic capital and could transmit self-reliance and skills to the next generation. The relative closeness in age between husband and wife favored a greater degree of gender equality than existed in areas where older men married much younger women.

Work Away from Home

Many young people worked within their families until they could start their own households. Boys plowed and wove; girls spun and tended the cows. Many others left home to work elsewhere. Around age fifteen, an apprentice from a rural village would typically move to a city or town to learn a trade, earning little and working hard. If he was lucky and had connections, he might eventually be admitted to a guild and establish his economic independence. Many poor families could not afford apprenticeships for their sons. Without craft skills, these youths drifted from one tough job to another: hired hand for a small farmer, wage laborer on a new road, carrier of water or domestic servant in a nearby town.

Many adolescent girls also left their families to work. The range of opportunities open to them was more limited, however. Apprenticeship was sometimes available with mistresses in traditionally female occupations like seamstress, linen draper, or midwife. With the growth in production of finished goods for the emerging consumer economy during the eighteenth century (see Chapter 17), demand rose for skilled female labor and, with it, a wider range of jobs became available for women. Nevertheless, women still continued to earn much lower wages for their work than men.

Service in another family's household was by far the most common job for girls, and even middle-class families often sent their daughters into service. The legions of young servant girls worked hard but had little independence. Constantly under the eye of her mistress, the servant girl had many tasks—cleaning, shopping, cooking, and child care. Often the work was endless, for there were few laws to limit exploitation. Court records are full of servant girls' complaints of physical mistreatment by their mistresses. There were many like the fifteen-year-old English girl in the early eighteenth century who told the judge that her mistress had not only called her "very opprobrious names, as Bitch, Whore and the like," but also "beat her without provocation and beyond measure."[2]

Male apprentices told similar tales of abuse and they shared the legal status of "servants" with housemaids, but they were far less vulnerable to the sexual exploitation that threatened young girls. In theory, domestic service offered a girl protection and security in a new family. But in practice, she was often the easy prey of a lecherous master or his sons or friends. If the girl became pregnant, she could be fired and thrown out in disgrace. Many families could not or would not accept such a girl back into the home. Forced to make their own way, these girls had no choice but to turn to a harsh life of prostitution (see page 558) and petty thievery. "What are we?"

Young Serving Girl
Increased migration to urban areas in the eighteenth century contributed to a loosening of traditional morals and soaring illegitimacy rates. Young women who worked as servants or shopgirls could not be supervised as closely as those who lived at home. The themes of seduction, fallen virtue, and familial conflict were popular in eighteenth-century art. (*The Beautiful Kitchen Maid*, by François Boucher [1703–1770], [oil on canvas]/Musée Cognacq-Jay, Paris, France/ Bridgeman Images)

exclaimed a bitter Parisian prostitute. "Most of us are unfortunate women, without origins, without education, servants and maids for the most part."[3] Adult women who remained in service, at least in large towns and cities, could gain more autonomy and distressed their employers by changing jobs frequently.

Premarital Sex and Community Controls

Ten years between puberty and marriage was a long time for sexually mature young people to wait. Many unmarried couples satisfied their sexual desires with fondling and petting. Others went further and engaged in premarital intercourse. Those who did so risked pregnancy and the stigma of illegitimate birth. Birth control was not unknown in Europe before the nineteenth century, but it was primitive and unreliable. Condoms, made from sheep intestines, became available in the mid-seventeenth century, replacing uncomfortable earlier versions made from cloth. They were expensive and mainly used by aristocratic libertines and prostitutes. The most common method of contraception was coitus interruptus—withdrawal by the male before ejaculation.

The French, who were early leaders in contraception, were using this method extensively by the end of the eighteenth century.

Despite the lack of reliable contraception, premarital sex did not result in a large proportion of illegitimate births in most parts of Europe until 1750. English parish registers seldom listed more than one illegitimate child out of every twenty children baptized. Some French parishes in the seventeenth century had extraordinarily low rates of illegitimacy, with less than 1 percent of babies born out of wedlock. Illegitimate babies were apparently a rarity, at least as far as the official records are concerned.

Where collective control over sexual behavior among youths failed, community pressure to marry often prevailed. A comparison of marriage and birth dates of seven representative parishes in seventeenth-century England shows that around 20 percent of children must have been conceived before the couple was married, but only 2 percent were born out of wedlock.[4] Figures for the French village of Auffay in Normandy in the eighteenth century were remarkably similar. No doubt many of these French and English couples were already engaged, or at least in a committed relationship, before they entered into intimate relations, and pregnancy simply set the marriage date once and for all.

The combination of low rates of illegitimate birth with large numbers of pregnant brides reflects the powerful **community controls** of the traditional village, particularly the open-field village, with its pattern of cooperation and common action. An unwed mother with an illegitimate child was inevitably viewed as a grave threat to the economic, social, and moral stability of the community. Irate parents, anxious village elders, indignant priests, and stern landlords all combined to pressure young people who wavered about marriage in the face of unexpected pregnancies. In the countryside these controls meant that premarital sex was not entered into lightly and that it was generally limited to those contemplating marriage.

The concerns of the village and the family weighed heavily on couples' lives after marriage as well. Whereas uninvolved individuals today try to stay out of the domestic disputes of their neighbors, the people in peasant communities gave such affairs loud and unfavorable publicity either at the time or during the carnival season (see page 568). Relying on degrading public rituals, known as **charivari**, the young men of the village would typically gang up on their victim and force him or her to sit astride a donkey facing backward and holding up the donkey's tail. They would parade the overly brutal spouse-beater or the adulterous couple around the village, loudly proclaiming the offenders' misdeeds. The donkey ride and other colorful humiliations ranging from rotten vegetables splattered on the doorstep to obscene and insulting midnight serenades were common punishments throughout much of Europe. They epitomized the community's effort to police personal behavior and maintain moral standards.

New Patterns of Marriage and Illegitimacy

In the second half of the eighteenth century, long-standing patterns of marriage and illegitimacy shifted dramatically. One important change was an increased ability for young people to make decisions about marriage for themselves, rather than following the interests of their families. This change occurred because social and economic transformations made it harder for families and communities to supervise their behavior. More youths in the countryside worked for their own wages, rather than on a family farm, and their economic autonomy translated into increased freedom of action. Moreover, many youths joined the flood of migrants to the cities, either with their families or in search of work on their own. Urban life provided young people with more social contacts and less social control.

A less positive outcome of loosening social control was an **illegitimacy explosion**, concentrated in England, France, Germany, and Scandinavia. In Frankfurt, Germany, for example, births out of wedlock rose steadily from about 2 percent of all births in the early eighteenth century to a peak of about 25 percent around 1850. In Bordeaux, France, 36 percent of all babies were being born out of wedlock by 1840. Small towns and villages experienced less startling climbs, but between 1750 and 1850 increases from an initial range of 1 to 3 percent to a range of 10 to 20 percent were commonplace. Given the meager economic opportunities open to single mothers, their circumstances were desperate.

Why did the number of illegitimate births skyrocket? One reason was a rise in sexual activity among young people. The loosened social controls that gave young people more choice in marriage also provided them with more opportunities to yield to sexual desire. As in previous generations, many of the young couples who engaged in sexual activity intended to marry. In one medium-size French city in 1787–1788, the great majority of unwed mothers stated that sexual intimacy had followed promises of marriage. Their sisters in rural Normandy frequently reported that they had been "seduced in anticipation of marriage."[5]

The problem for young women who became pregnant was that fewer men followed through on their promises. The second half of the eighteenth century witnessed sharply rising prices for food, homes, and other necessities of life. Many soldiers, day laborers, and male servants were no doubt sincere in their proposals, but their lives were insecure, and they hesitated to take on the burden of a wife and child.

The romantic yet practical dreams and aspirations of young people were thus frustrated by low wages, inequality, and changing economic and social conditions. Old patterns of marriage and family were breaking down. Only in the late nineteenth century would more stable patterns reappear.

Sex on the Margins of Society

Not all sex acts took place between men and women hopeful of marriage. Prostitution offered both single and married men an outlet for sexual desire. After a long period of relative tolerance, prostitutes encountered increasingly harsh and repressive laws in the sixteenth and early seventeenth centuries as officials across Europe closed licensed brothels and declared prostitution illegal.

Despite this repression, prostitution continued to flourish in the eighteenth century. Most prostitutes were working women who turned to the sex trade when confronted with paltry wages and unemployment. Such women did not become social pariahs, but retained ties with the communities of laboring poor to which they belonged. If caught by the police, however, they were liable to imprisonment or banishment. Venereal disease was also a constant threat. Prostitutes were subjected to humiliating police examinations for disease, although medical treatments were at best rudimentary. Farther up the social scale were courtesans whose wealthy protectors provided apartments, servants, fashionable clothing, and cash allowances. After a brilliant but brief career, an aging courtesan faced with the loss of her wealthy client could descend once more to streetwalking.

Relations between individuals of the same sex attracted even more condemnation than did prostitution, since they defied the Bible's limitation of sex to the purposes of procreation. Male same-sex relations, described as "sodomy" or "buggery," were prohibited by law in most European states, under pain of death. Such laws, however, were enforced unevenly, most strictly in Spain and far less so in the Scandinavian countries and Russia.[6]

Protected by their status, nobles and royals sometimes openly indulged their same-sex desires, which were accepted as long as they married and produced legitimate heirs. It was common knowledge that King James I, sponsor of the first translation of the Bible into English, had male lovers, but these relationships were tolerated because they did not prevent him from having seven children with his wife, Anne of Denmark. The duchess of Orléans, sister-in-law of French king Louis XIV, complained in her letters about her husband's male lovers, one of whom was appointed tutor to the couple's son. She also repeated rumors about the homosexual inclinations of King William of England, hero of the Glorious Revolution (see Chapter 15).

In the late seventeenth century homosexual subcultures began to emerge in Paris, Amsterdam, and London, with their own slang, meeting places, and styles of dress. Unlike the relations described above, which involved men who took both wives and male lovers, these groups included men exclusively oriented toward other men. In London, they called themselves "mollies," a term originally applied to prostitutes, and some began to wear women's clothing and adopt effeminate behavior. A new self-identity began to form among homosexual men: a belief that their same-sex desire made them fundamentally different from other men. As a character in one late-eighteenth-century fiction declared, he was in "a category of men different from the other, a class Nature has created in order to diminish or minimize propagation."[7]

Same-sex relations existed among women as well, but they attracted less anxiety and condemnation than those among men. Some women were prosecuted for "unnatural" relations; others attempted to escape the narrow confines imposed on them by dressing as men. Cross-dressing women occasionally snuck into the armed forces, such as Ulrika Elenora Stålhammar, who served as a man in the Swedish army for thirteen years and married a woman. After confessing her transgressions, she was sentenced to a lenient one-month imprisonment.[8] The beginnings of a distinctive lesbian subculture appeared in London and other large cities at the end of the eighteenth century.

Across the early modern period, traditional tolerance for sexual activities outside of heterosexual marriage—be they sex with prostitutes or same-sex relations among male courtiers—faded. This process accelerated in the eighteenth century as Enlightenment critics attacked court immorality and preached virtue and morality for middle-class men, who were expected to prove their worthiness to claim the reins of political power.

Children and Education

Focus Question	What was life like for children, and how did attitudes toward childhood evolve?

On the whole, western European women married late, but then began bearing children rapidly. If a woman married before she was thirty, and if both she and her husband lived to fifty, she would most likely give birth to six or more children. Infant mortality varied across Europe, but was very high by modern standards, and many women died in childbirth due to limited medical knowledge and technology.

For those children who did survive, Enlightenment ideals that emerged in the latter half of the century stressed the importance of parental nurturing. The new worldview also led to an increase in elementary schools throughout Europe. Despite the efforts of enlightened absolutists and religious institutions, however, formal education reached only a minority of ordinary children.

Child Care and Nursing

Newborns entered a dangerous world. They were vulnerable to infectious diseases, and many babies died of dehydration brought about by bad bouts of ordinary diarrhea. Of those who survived infancy, many more died in childhood. Even in a rich family, little could be done for an ailing child. Childbirth was also dangerous. Women who bore six children faced a cumulative risk of dying in childbirth of 5 to 10 percent, a thousand times as great as the risk in Europe today.[9] They died from blood loss and shock during delivery and from infections caused by unsanitary conditions. The joy of pregnancy was thus shadowed by fear of loss of the mother or her child.

In the countryside, women of the lower classes generally breast-fed their infants for two years or more. Although not a foolproof means of birth control, breast-feeding decreases the likelihood of pregnancy by delaying the resumption of ovulation. By nursing their babies, women limited their fertility and spaced their children two or three years apart. Nursing also saved lives: breast-fed infants received precious immunity-producing substances and were more likely to survive than those who were fed other food.

Areas where babies were not breast-fed—typically in northern France, Scandinavia, and central and eastern Europe—experienced the highest infant mortality rates. In these areas, many people believed that breast-feeding was bad for a woman's health or appearance. Across Europe, women of the aristocracy and upper middle class seldom nursed their own children because they found breast-feeding undignified and it interfered with their social responsibilities. The alternatives to breast-feeding consisted of feeding babies cow's or goat's milk or paying lactating women to provide their milk.

Wealthy women hired live-in wet nurses to suckle their babies (which usually meant sending the nurse's own infant away to be nursed by someone else). Working women in the cities also relied on wet nurses because they needed to earn a living. Unable to afford live-in wet nurses, they often turned to the cheaper services of women in the countryside. Rural **wet-nursing** was a widespread business in the eighteenth century, conducted within the framework of the putting-out system. The traffic was in babies rather than in yarn or cloth, and two or three years often passed before the wet-nurse worker in the countryside finished her task.

Wet-nursing was particularly common in northern France. Toward the end of the century, roughly twenty thousand babies were born in Paris each year. Almost half were placed with rural wet nurses through a government-supervised distribution network; 20 to 25 percent were placed in the homes of Parisian nurses personally selected by their parents; and another 20 to 25 percent were abandoned to foundling hospitals, which would send them to wet nurses in the countryside. The remainder (perhaps 10 percent) were nursed at home by their mothers or live-in nurses.[10]

Reliance on wet nurses raised levels of infant mortality because of the dangers of travel, the lack of supervision of conditions in wet nurses' homes, and the need to share milk between a wet nurse's own baby and the one or more babies she was hired to feed. A study of mortality rates in mid-eighteenth-century France shows that 25 percent of babies died before their first birthday, and another 30 percent before age ten.[11] In England, where more mothers nursed, only some 30 percent of children did not reach their tenth birthday.

Within each country and across Europe, tremendous regional variation existed. Mortality rates were higher in overcrowded and dirty cities; in low-lying, marshy regions; and during summer months when rural women were busy in agricultural work and had less time to tend to infants. The corollary of high infant mortality was high fertility. Women who did not breast-feed their babies or whose children died in infancy became pregnant more quickly and bore more children. Thus, on balance, the number of children who survived to adulthood tended to be the same across Europe, with higher births balancing the greater loss of life in areas that relied on wet-nursing.

In the second half of the eighteenth century, critics mounted a harsh attack against wet-nursing. Enlightenment thinkers proclaimed that wet-nursing was robbing European society of reaching its full potential. They were convinced, incorrectly, that the population was declining (in fact it was rising, but they lacked accurate population data) and blamed this decline on women's failure to nurture their children properly. Some also railed against practices of contraception and masturbation, which they believed were robbing their nations of potential children. Despite these complaints, many women continued to rely on wet nurses for convenience or from necessity.

Foundlings and Infanticide

The young woman who could not provide for an unwanted child had few choices, especially if she had no prospect of marriage. Abortions were illegal, dangerous, and apparently rare. In desperation, some women, particularly in the countryside, hid unwanted pregnancies, delivered in secret, and smothered their newborn infants. The punishment for infanticide was death. Yet across Europe, convictions for infanticide dropped in the second half of the eighteenth century, testimony, perhaps, to growing social awareness of the crushing pressures caused by unwanted pregnancies.

Another sign of this awareness was the spread of homes for abandoned children in cities across Europe. Homes for abandoned children first took hold in Italy, Spain, and Portugal in the sixteenth century, spreading to France in 1670 and the rest of Europe thereafter. In eighteenth-century England the government acted on a petition calling for a foundling hospital "to prevent the frequent murders of poor, miserable infants at birth" and "to suppress the inhuman custom of exposing newborn children to perish in the streets."

By the end of the eighteenth century, European foundling hospitals were admitting annually about one hundred thousand abandoned children, nearly all of them infants. One-third of all babies born in Paris in the 1770s were immediately abandoned to foundling homes. There appears to have been no differentiation by sex in the numbers of children sent to foundling hospitals. Many of the children were the offspring of single women, the result of the illegitimacy explosion of the second half of the eighteenth century. But fully one-third of all the foundlings were abandoned by married couples too poor to feed another child.[12]

At their best, foundling homes were a good example of Christian charity and social concern in an age of great poverty and inequality. They provided the rudiments of an education and sought to place the children in apprenticeship or domestic service once they reached an appropriate age. Philosopher Jean-Jacques Rousseau defended his decision to place his five illegitimate children in a foundling home—despite their mother's opposition—on the grounds of "poverty and misfortune." He also claimed that the hospital would shield them from the stigma of illegitimacy and provide a home that was "better, or at least more secure, than what [he] would have been able to provide."[13]

Yet the foundling home was no panacea. Even in the best of these homes, 50 percent of the babies normally died within a year. In the worst, fully 90 percent did not survive, falling victim to infectious disease, malnutrition, and neglect.[14] None of Rousseau's children are known to have survived.

Attitudes Toward Children

What were the typical circumstances of children's lives? Some scholars have claimed that high mortality rates prevented parents from forming emotional attachments to young children. With a reasonable expectation that a child might die, some scholars believe, parents maintained an attitude of indifference, if not downright negligence. Most historians now believe, however, that seventeenth- and eighteenth-century parents did love their children, suffered anxiously when they fell ill, and experienced extreme anguish when they died.

Parents were well aware of the dangers of infancy and childhood. The great eighteenth-century English historian Edward Gibbon (1737–1794) wrote, with some exaggeration, that "the death of a new born child before that of its parents may seem unnatural but it is a strictly probable event, since of any given number the greater part are extinguished before the ninth year, before they possess the faculties of the mind and the body." Gibbon's father named all his boys Edward after himself, hoping that at least one of them would survive to carry his name. His prudence was not misplaced. Edward the future historian and eldest survived. Five brothers and sisters who followed him all died in infancy.

Emotional prudence could lead to emotional distance. The French essayist Michel de Montaigne, who lost five of his six daughters in infancy, wrote, "I cannot abide that passion for caressing new-born children, which have neither mental activities nor recognisable bodily shape by which to make themselves loveable and I have

The First Step of Childhood   This tender snapshot of a baby's first steps toward an adoring mother exemplifies new attitudes toward children and raising them ushered in by the Enlightenment. Authors like Jean-Jacques Rousseau encouraged elite mothers like the one pictured here to take a more personal interest in raising their children, instead of leaving them in the hands of indifferent wet nurses and nannies. Many women responded eagerly to this call, and the period saw a more sentimentalized view of childhood and family life. (By François Gerard [1770–1837]/Fogg Art Museum, Harvard Art Museums, Cambridge, Massachusetts, USA/Erich Lessing/Art Resource, NY)

never willingly suffered them to be fed in my presence."[15] In contrast to this harsh picture, however, historians have drawn ample evidence from diaries, letters, and family portraits that parents of all social classes did cherish their children. This was equally true of mothers and fathers and of attitudes toward sons and daughters. The English poet Ben Jonson wrote movingly in "On My First Son" of the death of his six-year-old son Benjamin, which occurred during a London plague outbreak in 1603:

> Farewell, thou child of my right hand, and joy;
> My sin was too much hope of thee, loved boy.
> Seven years thou wert lent to me, and I thee pay,
> Exacted by thy fate, on the just day.

In a society characterized by much violence and brutality, discipline of children was often severe. The axiom "Spare the rod and spoil the child" seems to have been coined in the mid-seventeenth century. Susannah Wesley (1669–1742), mother of John Wesley, the founder of Methodism (see page 575), agreed. According to her, the first task of a parent toward her children was "to conquer the will, and bring them to an obedient temper." She reported that her babies were "taught to fear the rod, and to cry softly; by which means they escaped the abundance of correction they might otherwise have had, and that most odious noise of the crying of children was rarely heard in the house."[16] They were beaten for lying, stealing, disobeying, and quarreling, and forbidden from playing with other neighbor children. Susannah's methods of disciplining her children were probably extreme even in her own day, but they do reflect a broad consensus that children were born with an innately sinful will that parents must overcome.

The Enlightenment produced an enthusiastic new discourse about childhood and child rearing. Starting around 1760 critics called for greater tenderness toward children and proposed imaginative new teaching methods. In addition to supporting foundling homes and urging women to nurse their babies, these new voices ridiculed the practice of swaddling babies and using whaleboned corsets to mold children's bones. Rejecting the custom of dressing children in miniature versions of adult clothing, critics called for comfortable clothing to allow freedom of movement. Rather than emphasizing original sin, these enlightened voices celebrated the child as an innocent product of nature. Since they viewed nature as inherently positive, Enlightenment educators advocated safeguarding and developing children's innate qualities rather than thwarting and suppressing them. Accordingly, they believed the best hopes for a new society, untrammeled by the prejudices of the past, lay in a radical reform of child-rearing techniques.

One of the century's most influential works on child rearing was Jean-Jacques Rousseau's *Emile, or On Education* (1762), inspired in part, Rousseau claimed, by remorse for the abandonment of his own children. In *Emile*, Rousseau argued that boys' education should include plenty of fresh air and exercise and that boys should be taught practical craft skills in addition to book learning. Reacting to what he perceived as the vanity and frivolity of upper-class Parisian women, Rousseau insisted that girls' education focus on their future domestic responsibilities. For Rousseau, women's "nature" destined them solely for a life of marriage and child rearing. The sentimental ideas of Rousseau and other reformers were enthusiastically adopted by elite women, some of whom began to nurse their own children.

The Spread of Elementary Schools

The availability of education outside the home gradually increased over the early modern period. The wealthy led the way in the sixteenth century with special colleges, often run by Jesuits in Catholic areas. Schools charged specifically with educating children of the common people began to appear in the second half of the seventeenth century. They taught six- to twelve-year-old children basic literacy, religion, and perhaps some arithmetic for the boys and needlework for the girls. The number of such schools expanded in the eighteenth century, although they were never sufficient to educate the majority of the population.

Religion played an important role in the spread of education. From the middle of the seventeenth century, Presbyterian Scotland was convinced that the path to salvation lay in careful study of the Scriptures, and it established an effective network of parish schools for rich and poor alike. The Church of England and the dissenting congregations—Puritans, Presbyterians, Quakers, and so on—established "charity schools" to instruct poor children. The first proponents of universal education, in Prussia, were inspired by the Protestant idea that every believer should be able to read the Bible and by the new idea of raising a population capable of effectively serving the state. As early as 1717 Prussia made attendance at elementary schools compulsory for boys and girls in areas where schools existed.[17] More Protestant German states, such as Saxony and Württemberg (VUHR-tuhm-burg), followed suit in the eighteenth century.

Catholic states pursued their own programs of popular education. In the 1660s France began setting up charity schools to teach poor children their catechism and prayers as well as reading and writing. These were run by parish priests or by new educational teaching orders. One of the most famous orders was Jean-Baptiste de la Salle's Brothers of the Christian Schools. Founded in 1684, the schools had thirty-five thousand students across France by the 1780s. Enthusiasm for popular education was even greater in the Habsburg empire. Inspired by the expansion of schools in rival Protestant German states, Maria Theresa issued her own compulsory education edict in 1774, imposing five hours of school, five days a week, for all children aged six to twelve.[18] Across Europe some elementary education was becoming a reality, and schools became increasingly significant in the life of the child.

Popular Culture and Consumerism

Focus Question	How did increasing literacy and new patterns of consumption affect people's lives?

Because of the new efforts in education, basic literacy expanded among the popular classes, whose reading habits centered primarily on religious material, but who also began to incorporate more practical and entertaining literature. In addition to reading, people of all classes enjoyed a range of leisure activities including storytelling, fairs, festivals, and sports.

One of the most important developments in European society in the eighteenth century was the emergence of a fledgling consumer culture. Much of the expansion took place among the upper and upper-middle classes, but a boom in cheap reproductions of luxury items also opened doors for people of modest means. From food to ribbons and from coal stoves to umbrellas, the material worlds of city dwellers grew richer and more diverse. This "consumer revolution," as it has been called, created new expectations for comfort, hygiene, and self-expression, thus dramatically changing European daily life in the eighteenth century.

Popular Literature

The surge in childhood education in the eighteenth century led to a remarkable growth in literacy between 1600 and 1800. Whereas in 1600 only one male in six was barely literate in France and Scotland, and one in four in England, by 1800 almost nine out

MAP 18.1 **Literacy in France, ca. 1789**
Literacy rates increased but still varied widely between and within states in eighteenth-century Europe.

Percentage of bridegrooms able to sign their names to marriage register
- 80–100
- 50–79
- 20–49
- 0–19
- Unknown

of ten Scottish males, two out of three French males (Map 18.1), and more than half of English males were literate. In all three countries, most of the gains occurred in the eighteenth century. Women were also increasingly literate, although they lagged behind men.

The growth in literacy promoted growth in reading, and historians have carefully examined what the common people read. While the Bible remained the overwhelming favorite, especially in Protestant countries, short pamphlets known as chapbooks were the staple of popular literature. Printed on the cheapest paper, many chapbooks featured Bible stories, prayers, and the lives of saints and exemplary Christians. This pious literature gave believers moral teachings and a faith that helped them endure their daily struggles.

Entertaining, often humorous stories formed a second element of popular literature. Fairy tales, medieval romances, true crime stories, and fantastic adventures were some of the delights that filled the peddler's pack as he approached a village. These tales presented a world of danger and magic, of supernatural powers, fairy godmothers, and evil trolls, that provided a temporary flight from harsh everyday reality. They also contained nuggets of ancient folk wisdom, counseling prudence in a world full of danger and injustice, where wolves dress like grandmothers and eat Little Red Riding Hoods.

Finally, some popular literature was highly practical, dealing with rural crafts, household repairs, useful plants, and similar matters. Much lore was stored in almanacs, where calendars listing secular, religious, and astrological events were mixed with agricultural schedules, arcane facts, and jokes. The almanac was highly appreciated even by many in the comfortable classes. In this way, elites shared some elements of a common culture with the masses.

While it is safe to say that the vast majority of ordinary people—particularly peasants in isolated villages—did not read the great works of the Enlightenment, they were not immune from the new ideas. Urban working people were exposed to Enlightenment thought through the news and gossip that spread across city streets, workshops, markets, and taverns. They also had access to cheap pamphlets that helped translate Enlightenment critiques into ordinary language. Servants, who usually came from rural areas and traveled home periodically, were well situated to transmit ideas from educated employers to the village.

Certainly some ordinary people did assimilate Enlightenment ideals. Thomas Paine, author of some of the most influential texts of the American Revolution, was an English corset-maker's son who left school at age twelve and carried on his father's trade before emigrating to the colonies. His 1776 pamphlet *Common Sense* attacked the weight of custom and the evils of government against the natural society of men. This text, which sold 120,000 copies in its first months of publication, is vivid proof of working people's reception of Enlightenment ideas. Paine's stirring mastery of such ideas was perhaps unique, but his access to them was certainly not.

Leisure and Recreation

Despite the spread of literacy, the culture of the village remained largely oral rather than written. In the cold, dark winter months, peasant families gathered around the fireplace to sing, tell stories, do craftwork, and keep warm. In some parts of Europe, women would gather together in someone's cottage to chat, sew, spin, and laugh. Sometimes a few young men would be invited so that the daughters (and mothers) could size up potential suitors in a supervised atmosphere. A favorite recreation of men was drinking and talking with buddies in public places, and it was a sorry village that had no tavern. In addition to old favorites such as beer and wine, the common people turned with gusto to cheap and potent hard liquor, which fell in price because of improved techniques for distilling grain in the eighteenth century.

Towns and cities offered a wider range of amusements, including pleasure gardens, theaters, and lending libraries. Urban fairs featured prepared foods, acrobats, and conjuring acts. Leisure activities were another form of consumption marked by growing commercialization. For example, commercial, profit-making spectator sports emerged in this period, including horse races, boxing matches, and bullfights. Modern sports heroes, such as brain-bashing heavyweight champions and haughty bullfighting matadors, made their appearance on the historical scene.

Blood sports, such as bullbaiting and cockfighting, also remained popular with the masses. In bullbaiting, the bull, usually staked on a chain in the courtyard of an inn, was attacked by ferocious dogs for the amusement of the innkeeper's clients. Eventually the maimed and tortured animal was slaughtered by a butcher and sold as meat. In cockfighting, two roosters, carefully trained by their owners and armed with razor-sharp steel spurs, slashed and clawed each other in a small ring until the victor won—and the loser died. An added attraction of cockfighting was that the screaming spectators could bet on the lightning-fast combat.

Popular recreation merged with religious celebration in a variety of festivals and processions throughout the year. The most striking display of these religiously inspired events was **carnival**, a time of reveling and excess in Catholic Europe, especially in Mediterranean countries. Carnival preceded Lent—the forty days of fasting and penitence before Easter—and for a few exceptional days in February or March, a wild release of drinking, masquerading, and dancing reigned. Moreover, a combination of plays, processions, and raucous spectacles turned the established order upside down. Peasants dressed as nobles and men as women, and rich masters waited on their servants at the table. This annual holiday gave people a much-appreciated chance to release their pent-up frustrations and aggressions before life returned to the usual pattern of hierarchy and hard work.

The rowdy pastimes of the populace attracted criticism from clerical and lay elites in the second half of the eighteenth century. In 1772 the Spanish crown banned dragons and giants from the Corpus Christi parade, and the vibrant carnival of Venice was outlawed under Napoleon's rule in 1797. In the same period English newspapers publicly denounced boxing, gambling, blood sports, and other uncouth activities; one described bullbaiting in 1791 as "a disgrace to a civilized people."[19] However, historians have tended to overstate claims for a "culture war" between elites and the populace in the eighteenth century. Certainly, many wealthy and educated Europeans continued to enjoy the folktales of the chapbooks and they shared the love of gambling, theater, and sport. Moreover, both peasants and patricians—even most enlightened thinkers—shared a deep religiosity. In turn, as we have seen, common people were by no means cut off from the new currents of thought. Thus cultural elements continued to be shared across social divides.

New Foods and Appetites

At the beginning of the eighteenth century, ordinary men and women depended on grain as fully as they had in the past. Bread was quite literally the staff of life. Peasants in the Beauvais region of France ate two pounds of bread a day, washing it down with water, wine, or beer. Their dark bread was made from roughly ground wheat and rye—the standard flour of the common people. Even peasants normally needed to buy some grain for food, and, in full accord with landless laborers and urban workers, they believed in the moral economy and the **just price**. That is, they believed that prices should be "fair," protecting both consumers and producers, and that just prices should be imposed by government decree if necessary. When prices rose above this level, they often took action in the form of bread riots (see Chapter 15).

The rural poor also ate a quantity of vegetables. Peas and beans were probably the most common. Grown as field crops in much of Europe since the Middle Ages, they were eaten fresh in late spring and summer. Dried, they became the basic ingredients in the soups and stews of the long winter months. In most regions other vegetables appeared on the tables of the poor in season, primarily cabbages, carrots, and wild greens. Fruit was mostly limited to the summer months. Too precious to drink, milk was used to make cheese and butter, which peasants sold in the market to earn cash for taxes and land rents.

The common people of Europe ate less meat in 1700 than in 1500 because their general standard of living had declined and meat was more expensive. Moreover, harsh laws in most European countries reserved the right to hunt and eat game, such as rabbits, deer, and partridges, to nobles and large landowners. Few laws were more bitterly resented—or more frequently broken—by ordinary people than those governing hunting.

The diet of small traders and artisans—the people of the towns and cities—was less monotonous than that of the peasantry. Bustling markets provided a substantial variety of meats, vegetables, and fruits, although bread and beans still formed the bulk of such families' diets. Not surprisingly, the diet of the rich was quite different from that of the poor. The upper classes were rapacious carnivores, and a truly elegant dinner consisted of an abundance of rich meat and fish dishes laced with piquant sauces and complemented with sweets, cheeses, and wine in great quantities. During such dinners, it was common to spend five or more hours at table, eating and drinking and enjoying the witty banter of polite society.

Patterns of food consumption changed markedly as the century progressed. Because of a growth of market gardening, a greater variety of vegetables appeared in towns and cities. This was particularly the case in the Low Countries and England, which pioneered new methods of farming. Introduced into Europe from the Americas—along with corn, squash, tomatoes, and many other useful plants— the humble potato provided an excellent new food source. Containing a good supply of carbohydrates, calories, and vitamins A and C, the potato offset the lack of vitamins in the poor person's winter and early-spring diet, and it provided a much higher caloric yield than grain for a given piece of land. After initial resistance, the potato became an important dietary supplement in much of Europe by the end of the century.

The most remarkable dietary change in the eighteenth century was in the consumption of commodities imported from abroad. Originally expensive and rare luxury items, goods like tea, sugar, coffee, chocolate, and tobacco became staples for people of all social classes. With the exception of tea—which originated in China—most of the new consumables were produced in European colonies in the Americas. In many cases, the labor of enslaved peoples enabled the expansion in production and drop in prices that allowed such items to spread to the masses.

Why were colonial products so popular? Part of the motivation for consuming these products was a desire to emulate the luxurious lifestyles of the elite. Having seen pictures of or read about the fine lady's habit of "teatime" or the gentleman's appreciation for a pipe, common Europeans sought to experience these pleasures for themselves. Moreover, the quickened pace of work in the eighteenth century created new needs for stimulants among working people. Whereas the gentry took tea as a leisurely and genteel ritual, the lower classes drank tea or coffee at work to fight monotony and fatigue. With the widespread adoption of these products (which turned out to be mildly to extremely addictive), working people in Europe became increasingly dependent on faraway colonial economies and enslaved labor. Their understanding of daily necessities and how to procure those necessities shifted definitively, linking them to global trade networks they could not comprehend or control.

Toward a Consumer Society

Along with foodstuffs, all manner of other goods increased in variety and number in the eighteenth century. This proliferation led to a growth in consumption and new attitudes toward consumer goods so wide-ranging that some historians have referred to an eighteenth-century **consumer revolution**.[20] The result of this revolution was the birth of a new type of society in which people derived their self-identity as much from their consuming practices as from their working lives and place in the production process. As people gained the opportunity to pick and choose among a wide variety of consumer goods, new notions of individuality and self-expression developed. A shopgirl could stand out from her peers by her choice of a striped jacket, a colored parasol, or simply a new ribbon for her hair. The full emergence of a consumer society did not take place until much later, but its roots lie in the eighteenth century.

Increased demand for consumer goods was not merely an innate response to increased supply. Eighteenth-century merchants cleverly pioneered new techniques to incite demand: they initiated marketing campaigns, opened fancy boutiques with

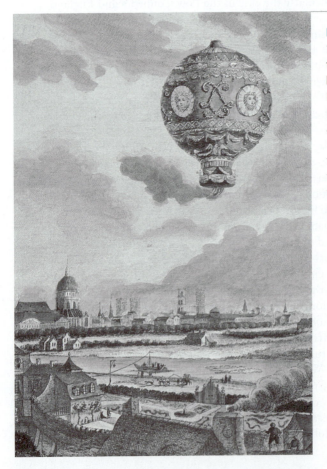

First Hot-Air Balloon Flight, 1783 This engraving depicts the world's first free hot-air balloon flight as seen from the Parisian residence of Benjamin Franklin, who was then serving as American ambassador to France. The balloon, invented by the Montgolfier brothers, traveled over five miles in a twenty-minute flight to great public acclaim. (Bibliothèque Nationale, Paris, France/Bridgeman Images)

large windows, and advertised the patronage of royal princes and princesses. By diversifying their product lines and greatly accelerating the turnover of styles, they seized the reins of fashion from the courtiers who had earlier controlled it. Instead of setting new styles, duchesses and marquises now bowed to the dictates of fashion merchants. Fashion also extended beyond court circles to touch many more items and social groups.

Clothing was one of the chief indicators of the growth of consumerism. Shrewd entrepreneurs made fashionable clothing seem more desirable, while legions of women entering the textile and needle trades made it ever cheaper. As a result, eighteenth-century western Europe witnessed a dramatic rise in the consumption of clothing, particularly in large cities. One historian has documented an enormous growth in the size and value of Parisians' wardrobes from 1700 to 1789, as well as a new level of diversity in garments and accessories, colors, and fabrics.[21] Colonial economies again played an important role in lowering the cost of materials, such as cotton cloth and vegetable dyes, largely due to the unpaid toil of enslaved Africans. Cheaper copies of elite styles made it possible for working people to aspire to follow fashion for the first time.

Elite onlookers were sometimes shocked by the sight of lower-class people in stylish outfits. In 1784 Mrs. Fanny Cradock described encountering her milkman during an evening stroll "dressed in a fashionable suit, with an embroidered waistcoat, silk knee-breeches and lace cuffs."[22] The spread of fashion challenged the traditional social order of Europe by blurring the boundaries between social groups and making it harder to distinguish between noble and commoner on the bustling city streets.

Mrs. Cradock's milkman notwithstanding, women took the lead in the spread of fashion. Parisian women significantly out-consumed men, acquiring larger and more expensive wardrobes than those of their husbands, brothers, and fathers. This was true across the social spectrum; in ribbons, shoes, gloves, and lace, European working women reaped in the consumer revolution what they had sown in the industrious revolution (see Chapter 17). There were also new gender distinctions in dress. Previously, noblemen had vied with noblewomen in the magnificence of their apparel; by the end of the eighteenth century men had renounced brilliant colors and voluptuous fabrics to don early versions of the plain dark suit that remains standard male formal wear in the West. This was one more aspect of the increasingly rigid boundaries drawn between appropriate male and female behavior.

Changes in outward appearances were reflected in inner spaces, as new attitudes about privacy, individualism, and intimate life also emerged. Historians have used notaries' probate inventories to peer into ordinary people's homes. In 1700 the cramped home of a modest family consisted of a few rooms, each of which had multiple functions. The same room was used for sleeping, receiving friends, and working. In the eighteenth century rents rose sharply, making it impossible to gain more space, but families began attributing specific functions to specific rooms. They also began to erect inner barriers within the home to provide small niches in which individuals could seek privacy.

New levels of comfort and convenience accompanied this trend toward more individualized ways of life. In 1700 a meal might be served in a common dish, with each person dipping his or her spoon into the pot. By the end of the eighteenth century even humble households contained a much greater variety of cutlery and dishes, making it possible for each person to eat from his or her own plate. More books and prints, which also proliferated at lower prices, decorated the shelves and walls. Improvements in glassmaking provided more transparent glass, which allowed daylight to penetrate into gloomy rooms. Cold and smoky hearths were increasingly replaced by more efficient and cleaner coal stoves, which also eliminated the backache of cooking over an open fire. Rooms were warmer, better lit, more comfortable, and more personalized, and the spread of street lighting made it safer to travel in cities at night.

Standards of bodily and public hygiene also improved. Public bathhouses, popular across Europe in the Middle Ages, had gradually closed in the early modern period due to concerns over sexual promiscuity and infectious disease. Many Europeans came to fear that immersing the body in hot water would allow harmful elements to enter the skin. Carefully watched by his physician, Louis XIII of France took his first bath at age seven, while James I of England refused to wash more than his hands. Personal cleanliness consisted of wearing fresh linen and using perfume to mask odors, both expensive practices that bespoke wealth and social status. From the mid-eighteenth century on, enlightened doctors revised their views and began to urge more frequent bathing. Spa towns, like Bath, England, became popular sites for the wealthy to see each other and be seen. Officials also took measures to improve the cleaning of city streets in which trash, human soil, and animal carcasses were often left to rot.

The scope of the new consumer economy should not be exaggerated. These developments were concentrated in large cities in northwestern Europe and North America. Even in these centers the elite benefited the most from new modes of life. This was not yet the society of mass consumption that emerged toward the end of the nineteenth century with the full expansion of the Industrial Revolution. The eighteenth century did, however, lay the foundations for one of the most distinctive features of modern Western life: societies based on the consumption of goods and services obtained through the market in which individuals form their identities and self-worth through the goods they consume.

Religious Authority and Beliefs

Focus Question	What were the patterns of popular religion, and how did they interact with the worldview of the educated public and their Enlightenment ideals?

Though the critical spirit of the Enlightenment made great inroads in the eighteenth century, the majority of ordinary men and women, especially those in rural areas, retained strong religious faith. The church promised salvation, and it gave comfort in the face of sorrow and death. Religion also remained strong because it was embedded in local traditions and everyday social experience.

Yet the popular religion of village Europe was also enmeshed in a larger world of church hierarchies and state power. These powerful outside forces sought to regulate religious life at the local level. Their efforts created tensions that helped set the scene for vigorous religious revivals in Protestant Germany and England as well as in Catholic France.

Church Hierarchy

In the eighteenth century religious faith not only endured, but grew more fervent in many parts of Europe. The local parish church remained the focal point of religious devotion and community cohesion. Congregants gossiped and swapped stories after services, and neighbors came together in church for baptisms, marriages, funerals, and special events. Priests and parsons kept the community records of births, deaths, and marriages; distributed charity; looked after orphans; and provided primary education to the common people. Thus the parish church was woven into the very fabric of community life.

While the parish church remained central to the community, it was also subject to greater control from the state. In Protestant areas, princes and monarchs headed the official church, and they regulated their "territorial churches" strictly, selecting personnel and imposing detailed rules. Clergy of the official church dominated education, and followers of other faiths suffered religious and civil discrimination. By the eighteenth century the radical ideas of the Reformation had resulted in another version of church bureaucracy.

Catholic monarchs in this period also took greater control of religious matters in their kingdoms, weakening papal authority. In both Spain and Portugal, the Catholic Church was closely associated with the state, a legacy of the long internal reconquista and sixteenth-century imperial conquests overseas. In the eighteenth century the Spanish crown took firm control of ecclesiastical appointments. Papal proclamations could not even be read in Spanish churches without prior approval from the government. In Portugal, religious enthusiasm led to a burst of new churches and monasteries in the early eighteenth century.

France went even further in establishing a national Catholic Church, known as the Gallican Church. Louis XIV's expulsion of Protestants in 1685 was accompanied by an insistence on the king's prerogative to choose and control bishops and issue laws regarding church affairs. Catholicism gained new ground in the Holy Roman Empire with the conversion of a number of Protestant princes and successful missionary work by Catholic orders among the populace. While it could not eradicate Protestantism altogether, the Habsburg monarchy successfully consolidated Catholicism as a pillar of its political control.

The Jesuit order played a key role in fostering the Catholic faith, providing extraordinary teachers, missionaries, and agents of the papacy. In many Catholic countries they exercised tremendous political influence, holding high government positions and educating the nobility in their colleges. By playing politics so effectively, however, the Jesuits elicited a broad coalition of enemies. Bitter controversies led Louis XV to order the Jesuits out of France in 1763 and to confiscate their property. France and Spain then pressured Rome to dissolve the Jesuits completely. In 1773 a reluctant pope caved in, although the order was revived after the French Revolution.

The Jesuit order was not the only Christian group to come under attack in the middle of the eighteenth century. The dominance of the larger Catholic Church and established Protestant churches was also challenged, both by enlightened reformers from above and by the faithful from below. Influenced by Enlightenment ideals, some Catholic rulers believed that the clergy in monasteries and convents should make a more practical contribution to social and religious life. Austria, a leader in controlling the church (see Chapter 16) and promoting primary education, showed how far the process could go. Maria Theresa began by sharply restricting entry into what she termed "unproductive" orders. In his Edict on Idle Institutions, her successor, Joseph II, abolished contemplative orders, henceforth permitting only orders that were engaged in teaching, nursing, or other practical work. The state expropriated the dissolved monasteries and convents and used their wealth to create more parishes throughout Austria. This edict had a disproportionate effect on women because most of their orders were cloistered from the outside world and thus were not seen as "useful." Joseph II also issued edicts of religious tolerance, including for Jews, making Austria one of the first European states to lift centuries-old restrictions on its Jewish population.

Protestant Revival

Official efforts to reform state churches in the eighteenth century were confronted by a wave of religious enthusiasm from below. By the late seventeenth century the vast transformations of the Protestant Reformation were complete and had been widely adopted in most Protestant churches. Medieval practices of idolatry, saint worship, and pageantry were abolished; stained-glass windows were smashed and murals whitewashed. Yet many official Protestant churches had settled into a smug complacency. This, along with the growth of state power and bureaucracy in local parishes, threatened to eclipse one of the Reformation's main goals — to bring all believers closer to God.

In the Reformation heartland, one concerned German minister wrote that the Lutheran Church "had become paralyzed in forms of dead doctrinal conformity" and badly needed a return to its original inspiration.[23] His voice was one of many that prepared and then guided a Protestant revival that succeeded because it answered the intense but increasingly unsatisfied needs of common people.

The Protestant revival began in Germany in the late seventeenth century. It was known as **Pietism** (PIGH-uh-tih-zum), and three aspects helped explain its powerful appeal. First, Pietism called for a warm, emotional religion that everyone could experience. Enthusiasm — in prayer, in worship, in preaching, in life itself — was the key concept. "Just as a drunkard becomes full of wine, so must the congregation become filled with spirit," declared one exuberant writer.[24]

Second, Pietism reasserted the earlier radical stress on the priesthood of all believers, thereby reducing the gulf between official clergy and Lutheran laity. Bible reading and study were enthusiastically extended to all classes, and this provided a powerful spur for popular literacy as well as individual religious development. Pietists were largely responsible for the educational reforms implemented by Prussia in the early eighteenth century (see page 565). Third and finally, Pietists believed in the practical power of Christian rebirth in everyday affairs. Reborn Christians were expected to lead good, moral lives and to come from all social classes.

Pietism soon spread through the German-speaking lands and to Scandinavia. It also had a major impact on John Wesley (1703–1791), who served as the catalyst for popular religious revival in England. Wesley came from a long line of ministers, and when he went to Oxford University to prepare for the clergy, he mapped a fanatically earnest "scheme of religion." After becoming a teaching fellow at Oxford, Wesley organized a Holy Club for similarly minded students, who were soon known contemptuously as **Methodists** because they were so methodical in their devotion. Yet like the young Martin Luther, Wesley remained intensely troubled about his own salvation even after his ordination as an Anglican priest in 1728.

Wesley's anxieties related to grave problems of the faith in England. The government shamelessly used the Church of England to provide favorites with high-paying jobs. Both church and state officials failed to respond to the spiritual needs of the people, and services and sermons had settled into an uninspiring routine. The separation of religion from local customs and social life was symbolized by church doors that were customarily locked on weekdays. Moreover, Enlightenment skepticism was making inroads among the educated classes, and deism—a belief in God but not in organized religion—was becoming popular. Some bishops and church leaders seemed to believe that doctrines such as the virgin birth were little more than elegant superstitions.

Hogarth's Satirical View of the Church   William Hogarth (1697–1764) was one of the foremost satirical artists of his day. This image mocks a London Methodist meeting, where the congregation swoons in enthusiasm over the preacher's sermon. The woman in the foreground giving birth to rabbits is an allusion to a hoax perpetrated in 1726 by a servant named Mary Tofts; the gullibility of those who believed Tofts is likened to that of the Methodist congregation. (From *Hogarth Restored: The Whole Works of the Celebrated William Hogarth,* 1812/Private Collection/The Stapleton Collection/Bridgeman Images)

Wesley's inner search in the 1730s was deeply affected by his encounter with Moravian Pietists, whom he first met on a ship as he traveled across the Atlantic to take up a position in Savannah, Georgia. The small Moravian community in Georgia impressed him as a productive, peaceful, and pious world, reflecting the values of the first apostles. After returning to London, following a disastrous failed engagement and the disappointment of his hopes to convert Native Americans, he sought spiritual counseling from a Pietist minister from Germany. Their conversations prepared Wesley for a mystical, emotional "conversion" in 1738. He described this critical turning point in his *Journal*:

> In the evening I went to a [Christian] society in Aldersgate Street where one was reading Luther's preface to the Epistle to the Romans. About a quarter before nine, while he was describing the change which God works in the heart through faith in Christ, I felt my heart strangely warmed. I felt I did trust in Christ, Christ alone for salvation; and an assurance was given me that he had taken away my sins, even mine, and saved me from the law of sin and death.[25]

Wesley's emotional experience resolved his intellectual doubts about the possibility of his own salvation. Moreover, he was convinced that any person, no matter how poor or uneducated, might have a similarly heartfelt conversion and gain the same blessed assurance. He took the good news to the people, traveling some 225,000 miles by horseback and preaching more than forty thousand sermons between 1750 and 1790. Since existing churches were often overcrowded and the church-state establishment was hostile, Wesley preached in open fields. People came in large numbers. Of critical importance was Wesley's rejection of Calvinist predestination — the doctrine of salvation granted to only a select few. Instead, he preached that all men and women who earnestly sought salvation might be saved. It was a message of hope and joy, of free will and universal salvation.

Wesley's ministry used lay preachers to reach new converts, formed Methodist cells, and eventually resulted in a new denomination. And just as Wesley had been inspired by the Pietist revival in Germany, so evangelicals in the Church of England and the old dissenting groups now followed Wesley's example of preaching to all people, giving impetus to an even broader awakening among the lower classes. Thus in Protestant countries religion continued to be a vital force in the lives of the people.

Catholic Piety

Religion also flourished in Catholic Europe around 1700, but there were important differences from Protestant practice. First, the visual contrast was striking; baroque art still lavished rich and emotionally exhilarating figures and images on Catholic churches, whereas most Protestant churches had removed their art during the Reformation. Moreover, people in Catholic Europe on the whole participated more actively in formal worship than did Protestants. More than 95 percent of the population probably attended church for Easter communion, the climax of the religious year.

The tremendous popular strength of religion in Catholic countries can in part be explained by the church's integral role in community life and popular culture. Thus, although Catholics reluctantly confessed their sins to priests, they enthusiastically came together in religious festivals to celebrate the passage of the liturgical year. In addition to the great processional days — such as Palm Sunday, the joyful re-enactment of Jesus's triumphal entry into Jerusalem — each parish had its own saints' days, processions, and pilgrimages. Led by its priest, a congregation might march around the village or across the countryside to a local shrine. Millions of Catholic men and women also joined religious associations, known as confraternities, where they participated in prayer and religious services and collected funds for poor relief and members' funerals. The Reformation had largely eliminated such activities in Protestant areas.

Catholicism had its own version of the Pietist revivals that shook Protestant Europe. **Jansenism** has been described by one historian as the "illegitimate off-spring of the Protestant Reformation and the Catholic Counter-Reformation."[26] It originated with Cornelius Jansen (1585–1638), bishop of Ypres in the Spanish Netherlands, who called for a return to the austere early Christianity of Saint Augustine. In contrast to the worldly Jesuits, Jansen emphasized the heavy weight of original sin and accepted the doctrine of predestination. Although outlawed by papal and royal edicts as Calvinist heresy, Jansenism attracted Catholic followers eager for religious renewal, particularly among the French. Many members of France's urban elite, especially judicial nobles and some parish priests, became known for their Jansenist piety and spiritual devotion. Such stern religious values encouraged the judiciary's increasing opposition to the French monarchy in the second half of the eighteenth century.

Among the urban poor, a different strain of Jansenism took hold. Prayer meetings brought men and women together in ecstatic worship, and some participants fell into convulsions and spoke in tongues. The police of Paris posted spies to report on such gatherings and conducted mass raids and arrests.

Marginal Beliefs and Practices

In the countryside, many peasants continued to hold religious beliefs that were marginal to the Christian faith altogether, often of obscure or even pagan origin. On the Feast of Saint Anthony, for example, priests were expected to bless salt and bread for farm animals to protect them from disease. Catholics believed that saints' relics could bring fortune or attract lovers, and there were healing springs for many ailments. In 1796 the Lutheran villagers of Beutelsbach in southern Germany incurred the ire of local officials when they buried a live bull at a crossroads to ward off an epidemic of hoof-and-mouth disease.[27] The ordinary person combined strong Christian faith with a wealth of time-honored superstitions.

Inspired initially by the fervor of the Reformation era, then by the critical rationalism of the Enlightenment, religious and secular authorities sought increasingly to "purify" popular spirituality. Thus one parish priest in France lashed out at his parishioners, claiming that they were "more superstitious than devout . . . and sometimes appear as baptized idolators."[28] French priests particularly denounced the "various remnants of paganism" found in popular bonfire ceremonies during Lent, in which young men, "yelling and screaming like madmen," tried to jump over the bonfires in order to help the crops grow and to protect themselves from illness. One priest saw rational Christians regressing into pagan animals — "the triumph of Hell and the shame of Christianity."[29]

The severity of the attack on popular belief varied widely by country and region. Where authorities pursued purification vigorously, as in Austria under Joseph II, pious peasants saw only an incomprehensible attack on age-old faith and drew back in anger. It was in this era of rationalism and disdain for superstition that the persecution of witches slowly came to an end across Europe. Common people in the countryside continued to fear the Devil and his helpers, but the elite increasingly dismissed such fears and refused to prosecute suspected witches. The last witch was executed in England in 1682, the same year France prohibited witchcraft trials. By the late eighteenth century the witchcraft hunts had ended across Europe.

Medical Practice

Focus Question	How did the practice of medicine evolve in the eighteenth century?

Although significant breakthroughs in medical science would not come until the middle and late nineteenth century, the Enlightenment's inherent optimism and its focus on improving human life through understanding of the laws of nature produced a great deal of research and experimentation in the eighteenth century. Medical practitioners greatly increased in number, although their techniques did not differ much from those of previous generations. Care of the sick in this era was the domain of several competing groups: traditional healers, apothecaries (pharmacists), physicians, surgeons, and midwives. From the Middle Ages through the seventeenth century, both men and women were medical practitioners. However, since women were generally denied admission to medical colleges and lacked the diplomas necessary to practice, the range of medical activities open to them was restricted. In the eighteenth century women's traditional roles as midwives and healers eroded even further.

Faith Healing and General Practice

In the course of the eighteenth century, traditional healers remained active, drawing on centuries of folk knowledge about the curative properties of roots, herbs, and other plants. Faith healing also remained popular, especially in the countryside. Faith healers and their patients believed that evil spirits caused illness by lodging in people and that the proper treatment was to exorcise, or drive out, the offending devil. Religious and secular officials did their best to stamp out such practices, but with little success.

In the larger towns and cities, apothecaries sold a vast number of herbs, drugs, and patent medicines for every conceivable "temperament and distemper." By the eighteenth century many of these medicines were derived from imported plants. The Asian spices prized since medieval times often had medicinal uses; from the sixteenth century onward, the Portuguese and then the Dutch dominated the Indian Ocean trade in these spices (see Chapter 14). As Europeans expanded to the New World, they brought a keen interest in potentially effective and highly profitable medicinal plants. Botanists accompanied European administrators and explorers to the Americas, where they profited from the healing traditions of indigenous peoples and, in the plantation societies of the Caribbean, enslaved Africans. They returned to Europe with a host of medicinal plants such as ipecacuanha, sarsaparilla, opium, and cinchona, the first effective treatment for fever. Over the course of the seventeenth century, imports of medicinal plants boomed. By the late eighteenth century, England was importing annually £100,000 worth of drugs, compared to only £1,000 or £2,000 in 1600.[30]

Like all varieties of medical practitioners, apothecaries advertised their wares, their high-class customers, and their miraculous cures in newspapers and commercial circulars. Medicine, like food and fashionable clothing, thus joined the era's new and loosely regulated commercial culture.

Physicians, who were invariably men, were apprenticed in their teens to practicing physicians for several years of on-the-job training. This training was then rounded out with hospital work or some university courses. Seen as gentlemen who did not labor with their hands, many physicians diagnosed and treated patients by correspondence or through oral dialogue, without conducting a physical examination. Because their training was expensive, physicians came mainly from prosperous families and usually concentrated on urban patients from similar social backgrounds. Nevertheless, even poor people spent hard-won resources to seek treatment for their loved ones.

Physicians in the eighteenth century were increasingly willing to experiment with new methods, but time-honored practices lay heavily on them. They laid great stress on purging, and bloodletting was still considered a medical cure-all. It was the way "bad blood," the cause of illness, was removed and the balance of humors necessary for good health was restored.

Improvements in Surgery

Long considered to be craftsmen comparable to butchers and barbers, surgeons began studying anatomy seriously and improved their art in the eighteenth century. With endless opportunities to practice, army surgeons on gory battlefields led the way. They learned that a soldier with an extensive wound, such as a shattered leg or arm, could perhaps be saved if the surgeon could obtain a flat surface above the wound that could be cauterized with fire. Thus, if a soldier had a broken limb and the bone stuck out, the surgeon amputated so that the remaining stump could be cauterized and the likelihood of death reduced.

The eighteenth-century surgeon (and patient) labored in the face of incredible difficulties. Almost all operations were performed without painkillers, for the anesthesia of the day was hard to control and too dangerous for general use. Many patients died from the agony and shock of such operations. Surgery was also performed in utterly unsanitary conditions, for there was no knowledge of bacteriology and the nature of infection. The simplest wound treated by a surgeon could fester and lead to death.

Midwifery

Midwives continued to deliver the overwhelming majority of babies throughout the eighteenth century. Trained initially by another woman practitioner—and regulated by a guild in many cities—the midwife primarily assisted in labor and delivering babies. She also treated female problems, such as irregular menstrual cycles, breast-feeding difficulties, infertility, and venereal disease, and ministered to small children.

The midwife orchestrated labor and birth in a woman's world, where friends and relatives assisted the pregnant woman in the familiar surroundings of her own home. The male surgeon (and the husband) rarely entered this female world, because most births, then as now, were normal and spontaneous. After the invention of forceps became publicized in 1734, surgeon-physicians used their monopoly over this and other instruments to seek lucrative new business. Attacking midwives as ignorant and dangerous, they sought to undermine faith in midwives and persuaded growing numbers of wealthy women of the superiority of their services. As one male expert proclaimed:

> A midwife is usually a creature of the lowest class of human beings, and of course utterly destitute of education, who from indigence, and that she is incapable of everything else, has been compelled to follow, as the last and sole resources a profession which people fondly imagine no very difficult one, never dreaming that the least glimpse of previous instruction is required for that purpose. . . . Midwives are universally ignorant. For where or how should she come by any thing deserving the name of knowledge.[31]

Research suggests that women practitioners successfully defended much but not all of their practice in the eighteenth century. One enterprising French midwife, Madame du Coudray, wrote a widely used textbook, *Manual on the Art of Childbirth* (1757), in order to address complaints about incompetent midwives. She then secured royal financing for her campaign to teach birthing techniques. Du Coudray traveled all over France using a life-size model of the female torso and fetus to help teach illiterate women. Despite criticism, it appears that midwives generally lost no more babies than did male doctors, who were still summoned to treat non-elite women only when life-threatening situations required surgery.

Women also continued to perform almost all nursing. Female religious orders ran many hospitals, and at-home nursing was almost exclusively the province of women. Thus, although they were excluded from the growing ranks of formally trained and authorized practitioners, women continued to perform the bulk of informal medical care. Nursing as a secular profession did not emerge until the nineteenth century.

The Conquest of Smallpox

Experimentation and the intensified search for solutions to human problems led to some real advances in medicine after 1750. The eighteenth century's greatest medical triumph was the eradication of smallpox. With the progressive decline of bubonic plague, smallpox became the most terrible of the infectious diseases, and it is estimated that 60 million Europeans died of it in the eighteenth century.

The first step in the conquest of this killer in Europe came in the early eighteenth century. An English aristocrat whose beauty had been marred by the pox, Lady Mary Wortley Montagu, learned about the long-established practice of smallpox inoculation

The Wonderful Effects of the New Inoculation! The talented caricaturist James Gillray satirized widespread anxieties about the smallpox vaccination in this lively image. The discoveries of Edward Jenner a few years prior to Gillray's caricature had led to the adoption of a safer vaccine derived from cowpox. The artist mocks this breakthrough by showing cows bursting from the boils supposedly brought on by the vaccine. (Private Collection/Bridgeman Images)

in the Muslim lands of western Asia while her husband was serving as British ambassador to the Ottoman Empire. She had her own son successfully inoculated with the pus from a smallpox victim and was instrumental in spreading the practice in England after her return in 1722. But inoculation was risky and was widely condemned because about one person in fifty died from it. In addition, people who had been inoculated were infectious and often spread the disease.

While the practice of inoculation with the smallpox virus was refined over the century, the crucial breakthrough was made by Edward Jenner (1749–1823), a talented country doctor. His starting point was the countryside belief that dairymaids who had contracted cowpox did not get smallpox. Cowpox produces sores that resemble those of smallpox, but the disease is mild and is not contagious.

For eighteen years Jenner practiced a kind of Baconian science, carefully collecting data. Finally, in 1796 he performed his first vaccination on a young boy using matter taken from a milkmaid with cowpox. After performing more successful vaccinations, Jenner published his findings in 1798. The new method of treatment spread rapidly, and smallpox soon declined to the point of disappearance in Europe and then throughout the world.

NOTES

1. Archibald Campbell, Marquis of Argyll, *Instructions to a Son, Containing Rules of Conduct in Publick and Private Life* (Glasgow: E. Foulis, 1743), p. 33.
2. Quoted in J. M. Beattie, "The Criminality of Women in Eighteenth-Century England," *Journal of Social History* 8 (Summer 1975): 86.
3. Quoted in R. Cobb, *The Police and the People: French Popular Protest, 1789–1820* (Oxford: Clarendon Press, 1970), p. 238.
4. Peter Laslett, *Family Life and Illicit Love: Essays in Historical Sociology* (Cambridge: Cambridge University Press, 1977).
5. G. Gullickson, *Spinners and Weavers of Auffay: Rural Industry and the Sexual Division of Labor in a French Village, 1750–1850* (Cambridge: Cambridge University Press, 1986), p. 186.
6. Louis Crompton, *Homosexuality and Civilization* (Cambridge, Mass.: Belknap Press, 2003), p. 321.
7. D. S. Neff, "Bitches, Mollies, and Tommies: Byron, Masculinity and the History of Sexualities," *Journal of the History of Sexuality* 11, no. 3 (July 2002): 404.
8. George E. Haggerty, ed., *Encyclopedia of Gay Histories and Cultures* (New York: Garland Publishing, 2000), pp. 1311–1312.
9. Pier Paolo Viazzo, "Mortality, Fertility, and Family," in *Family Life in Early Modern Times, 1500–1789*, ed. David I. Kertzer and Marzio Barbagli (New Haven, Conn.: Yale University Press, 2001), p. 180.
10. George Sussman, *Selling Mother's Milk: The Wet-Nursing Business in France, 1715–1914* (Urbana: University of Illinois Press, 1982), p. 22.
11. Yves Blayo, "La Mortalité en France de 1740 à 1820," *Population*, special issue 30 (1975): 135.
12. Viazzo, "Mortality, Fertility, and Family," pp. 176–178.
13. Quoted in Matthew Gerber, *Bastards: Politics, Family, and Law in Early Modern France* (Oxford: Oxford University Press, 2012), p. 125.
14. Alysa Levene, "The Estimation of Mortality at the London Foundling Hospital, 1741–99," *Population Studies* 59, no. 1 (2005): 87–97.
15. Quoted in Robert Woods, "Did Montaigne Love His Children? Demography and the Hypothesis of Parental Indifference," *Journal of Interdisciplinary History* 33, no. 3 (2003): 421.
16. Quoted in Gay Ochiltree and Don Edgar, *The Changing Face of Childhood* (Melbourne: Institute of Family Studies, 1981), p. 11.
17. James Van Horn Melton, *Absolutism and the Eighteenth-Century Origins of Compulsory Schooling in Prussia and Austria* (Cambridge: Cambridge University Press, 2003), p. 46.
18. James Van Horn Melton, "The Theresian School Reform of 1774," in *Early Modern Europe*, ed. James B. Collins and Karen L. Taylor (Oxford: Blackwell, 2006).
19. Jeremy Black, *The English Press in the Eighteenth Century* (Philadelphia: University of Pennsylvania Press, 1987), p. 262.
20. Neil McKendrik, John Brewer, and J. H. Plumb, *The Birth of a Consumer Society: The Commercialization of Eighteenth-Century England* (Bloomington: Indiana University Press, 1982).
21. Daniel Roche, *The Culture of Clothing: Dress and Fashion in the Ancien Regime*, trans. Jean Birrell (Cambridge: Cambridge University Press, 1996).
22. Quoted in Cissie Fairchilds, "The Production and Marketing of Populuxe Goods in Eighteenth-Century Paris," in *Consumption and the World of Goods*, ed. John Brewer and Roy Porter (London: Routledge, 1993), p. 228.
23. Quoted in K. Pinson, *Pietism as a Factor in the Rise of German Nationalism* (New York: Columbia University Press, 1934), p. 13.
24. Ibid., pp. 43–44.
25. Quoted in S. Andrews, *Methodism and Society* (London: Longmans, Green, 1970), p. 327.
26. Dale Van Kley, "The Rejuvenation and Rejection of Jansenism in History and Historiography," *French Historical Studies* 29 (Fall 2006): 649–684.
27. David Sabean, *The Power in the Blood: Popular Culture and Village Discourse in Early Modern Germany* (Cambridge: Cambridge University Press, 1984), p. 174.
28. Quoted in I. Woloch, *Eighteenth-Century Europe: Tradition and Progress, 1715–1789* (New York: W. W. Norton, 1982), p. 292.
29. Quoted in T. Tackett, *Priest and Parish in Eighteenth-Century France* (Princeton, N.J.: Princeton University Press, 1977), p. 214.

30. Patrick Wallis, "Exotic Drugs and English Medicine: England's Drug Trade, c. 1550–c. 1800," *Social History of Medicine* 2, no. 1 (2012): 26.

31. Louis Lapeyre, *An Enquiry into the Merits of These Two Important Questions: I. Whether Women with Child Ought to Prefer the Assistance of Their Own Sex to That of Men-Midwives? II. Whether the Assistance of Men-Midwives Is Contrary to Decency?* (London: S. Bladon, 1772), p. 29.

LOOKING BACK LOOKING AHEAD

The fundamental patterns of life in early modern Europe remained very much the same up to the eighteenth century. The vast majority of people lived in the countryside and followed age-old rhythms of seasonal labor in the fields and farmyard. Community ties were close in small villages, where the struggle to prevail over harsh conditions called on all hands to work together and to pray together. The daily life of a peasant in 1700 would have been familiar to his ancestors in the fifteenth century. Indeed, the three orders of society enshrined in the medieval social hierarchy—clergy, nobility, peasantry—were binding legal categories in France up to 1789.

And yet, the economic changes inaugurated in the late seventeenth century—intensive agriculture, cottage industry, the industrious revolution, and colonial expansion—contributed to the profound social and cultural transformation of daily life in eighteenth-century Europe. Men and women of the laboring classes, especially in the cities, experienced change in many facets of their daily lives: in loosened community controls over sex and marriage, rising literacy rates, new goods and new forms of self-expression, and a wave of religious piety that challenged traditional orthodoxies. Lay and secular elites attacked some forms of popular life, but considerable overlap continued between popular and elite culture.

Economic, social, and cultural change would culminate in the late eighteenth century with the outbreak of revolution in the Americas and Europe. Initially led by the elite, political upheavals relied on the enthusiastic participation of the poor and their desire for greater inclusion in the life of the nation. Such movements also encountered resistance from the common people when revolutionaries trampled on their religious faith. For many observers, contemporaries and historians alike, the transformations of the eighteenth century constituted a fulcrum between the old world of hierarchy and tradition and the modern world with its claims to equality and freedom.

MAKE CONNECTIONS

Think about the larger developments and continuities within and across chapters.

1. How did the expansion of agriculture and trade (Chapter 17) contribute to changes in daily life in the eighteenth century?

2. What were the main areas of improvement in the lives of the common people in the eighteenth century, and what aspects of life remained unchanged or even deteriorated?

3. How did Enlightenment thought (Chapter 16) affect education, child care, medicine, and religion in the eighteenth century?

Chapter Review

IDENTIFY KEY TERMS

Identify and explain the significance of each item below.

community controls (p. 557)

charivari (p. 557)

illegitimacy explosion (p. 558)

wet-nursing (p. 560)

blood sports (p. 567)

carnival (p. 568)

just price (p. 568)

consumer revolution (p. 570)

Pietism (p. 574)

Methodists (p. 575)

Jansenism (p. 577)

REVIEW THE MAIN IDEAS

Answer the focus questions from each section of the chapter.

1. What changes occurred in marriage and the family in the course of the eighteenth century? (p. 554)

2. What was life like for children, and how did attitudes toward childhood evolve? (p. 560)

3. How did increasing literacy and new patterns of consumption affect people's lives? (p. 565)

4. What were the patterns of popular religion, and how did they interact with the worldview of the educated public and their Enlightenment ideals? (p. 572)

5. How did the practice of medicine evolve in the eighteenth century? (p. 578)

CHRONOLOGY	
1684	Jean-Baptiste de la Salle founds Brothers of the Christian Schools
1717	Elementary school attendance mandatory in Prussia
1750–1790	John Wesley preaches revival in England
1750–1850	Illegitimacy explosion
1757	Madame du Coudray publishes *Manual on the Art of Childbirth*
1762	Jean-Jacques Rousseau advocates more attentive child care in *Emile*
1763	Louis XV orders Jesuits out of France
1774	Elementary school attendance mandatory in Austria
1776	Thomas Paine publishes *Common Sense*
1796	Edward Jenner performs first smallpox vaccination

19

Revolutions in Politics

1775–1815

A GREAT WAVE OF REVOLUTION rocked both sides of the Atlantic Ocean in the last decades of the eighteenth century. As trade goods, individuals, and ideas circulated in ever-greater numbers across the Atlantic Ocean, debates and events in one locale soon influenced those in another. As changing social realities challenged the old order of life and Enlightenment ideals of freedom and equality flourished, reformers in many places demanded fundamental changes in politics and government. At the same time, wars fought for dominance of the Atlantic economy left European states weakened by crushing debts, making them vulnerable to calls for reform.

The revolutionary era began in North America in 1775, and the United States of America won freedom from Britain in 1783. Then in 1789, France, the most populous country in western Europe and a center of culture and intellectual life, became the leading revolutionary nation. It established first a constitutional monarchy, then a radical republic, and finally a new empire under Napoleon that would last until 1815. During this period of constant domestic turmoil, French armies brought revolution to much of Europe. Inspired both by the ideals of the Revolution on the continent and by their own experiences and desires, the slaves of Saint-Domingue rose up in 1791. Their rebellion would eventually lead to the creation of the new independent nation of Haiti in 1804. In Europe and its colonies abroad, the age of modern politics was born.

Background to Revolution

Focus Question	What were the factors leading to the revolutions of the late eighteenth century?

The origins of the late-eighteenth-century revolutions in British North America, France, and Haiti were complex. No one cause lay behind them, nor was revolution inevitable or certain of success. However, a set of shared factors helped set the stage for revolt. Among them were fundamental social and economic changes and political crises that eroded state authority. Another significant cause of revolutionary fervor was the impact of political ideas derived from the Enlightenment. Even though most Enlightenment writers were cautious about political reform, their confidence in reason and progress helped inspire a new generation to fight for greater freedom from repressive governments. Perhaps most important, financial crises generated by the expenses of imperial warfare brought European states to their knees and allowed abstract discussions of reform to become pressing realities.

Social Change

Eighteenth-century European society was legally divided into groups with special privileges, such as the nobility and the clergy, and groups with special burdens, such as the peasantry. Nobles were the largest landowners, possessing one-quarter of the agricultural land of France, while constituting less than 2 percent of the population. They enjoyed exemption from direct taxation as well as exclusive rights to hunt game, bear swords, and use gold thread in their clothing. In most countries, various middle-class groups — professionals, merchants, and guild masters — enjoyed privileges that allowed them to monopolize all sorts of economic activity. Poor peasants and urban laborers, who constituted the vast majority of the population, bore the brunt of taxation and were excluded from the world of privilege.

Traditional prerogatives persisted in societies undergoing dramatic and destabilizing change. Europe's population rose rapidly after 1750, and its cities and towns swelled in size. Inflation kept pace with population growth, making it ever more difficult to find affordable food and living space. One way the poor kept up, and even managed to participate in the new consumer revolution (see Chapter 18), was by working harder and for longer hours. More women and children entered the paid labor force, challenging the traditional hierarchies and customs of village life.

Economic growth created new inequalities between rich and poor. While the poor struggled with rising prices, investors grew rich from the spread of rural manufacture and overseas trade, including the trade in enslaved Africans and in the products of slave labor. Old distinctions between landed aristocracy and city merchants began to fade as enterprising nobles put money into trade and rising middle-class bureaucrats and merchants purchased landed estates and noble titles. Marriages between proud nobles and wealthy, educated commoners (called the *bourgeoisie* [boor-ZHWAH-zee] in France) served both groups' interests, and a mixed-caste elite began to take shape. In the context of these changes, ancient privileges seemed to pose an intolerable burden to many observers.

Another social change involved the racial regimes established in European colonies to legitimize and protect slavery. By the late eighteenth century European law accepted that only Africans and people of African descent were subject to slavery. Even free people of color — a term for nonslaves of African or mixed African-European descent — were subject to special laws restricting the property they could own, whom they could marry, and what clothes they could wear. Racial privilege conferred a new dimension of entitlement on European settlers in the colonies, and they used extremely brutal methods to enforce it. The contradiction between slavery and the Enlightenment ideals of liberty and equality was all too evident to the enslaved and the free people of color.

Growing Demands for Liberty and Equality

In addition to destabilizing social changes, the ideals of liberty and equality helped fuel revolutions in the Atlantic world. What did these concepts mean to eighteenth-century politicians and other people, and why were they so radical and revolutionary in their day?

The call for liberty was first of all a call for individual human rights. Before the revolutionary period, even the most enlightened monarchs believed they needed to regulate what people wrote and believed. Opposing this long-standing practice, supporters of the cause of individual liberty (who became known as "liberals" in the early nineteenth century) demanded freedom to worship according to the dictates of their consciences, an end to censorship, and freedom from arbitrary laws and from judges who simply obeyed orders from the government. The Declaration of the Rights of Man and of the Citizen, issued at the beginning of the French Revolution, proclaimed that "liberty consists in being able to do anything that does not harm another person." In the context of the monarchical and absolutist forms of government then dominating Europe, this was a truly radical idea.

The call for liberty was also a call for a new kind of government. Reformers believed that the people had sovereignty — that is, that the people alone had the authority to make laws limiting an individual's freedom of action. In practice, this system of government meant choosing legislators who represented the people and were accountable to them. Monarchs might retain their thrones, but their rule should be constrained by the will of the people.

Equality was a more ambiguous idea. Eighteenth-century liberals argued that, in theory, all citizens should have identical rights and liberties and that the nobility had no right to special privileges based on birth. However, they accepted a number of distinctions. First, most eighteenth-century liberals were men of their times, and they generally believed that equality between men and women was neither practical nor desirable. Women played an important political role in the revolutionary movements at several points, but the men who wrote constitutions for the new republics limited formal political rights — the right to vote, to run for office, and to participate in government — to men. Second, few questioned the superiority of people of European descent over those of indigenous or African origin. Even those who believed that the slave trade was unjust and should be abolished usually felt that emancipation was so dangerous that it needed to be an extremely gradual process.

Third, liberals never believed that everyone should be equal economically. Although Thomas Jefferson wrote in an early draft of the American Declaration of Independence that everyone was equal in "the pursuit of property," liberals certainly did not expect equal success in that pursuit. (Jefferson later changed "property" to the more noble-sounding "happiness.") Great differences in fortune between rich and poor were perfectly acceptable. The essential point was that every free white male should have a legally equal chance at economic gain. However limited they appear to modern eyes, these demands for liberty and equality were revolutionary, given that a privileged elite had long existed with little opposition.

The two most important Enlightenment references for late-eighteenth-century liberals were John Locke and the baron de Montesquieu (see Chapter 16). Locke maintained that England's long political tradition rested on "the rights of Englishmen" and on representative government through Parliament. He argued that if a government oversteps its proper function of protecting the natural rights of life, liberty, and private property, it becomes a tyranny. Montesquieu was also inspired by English constitutional history and the Glorious Revolution of 1688–1689, which placed sovereignty in Parliament (see Chapter 15). He, too, believed that powerful "intermediary groups"—such as the judicial nobility of which he was a proud member—offered the best defense of liberty against despotism.

The belief that representative institutions could defend their liberty and interests appealed powerfully to the educated middle classes. Yet liberal ideas about individual rights and political freedom also appealed to members of the hereditary nobility, at least in western Europe and as formulated by Montesquieu. Representative government did not mean democracy, which liberal thinkers tended to equate with mob rule. Rather, they envisioned voting for representatives as being restricted to men who owned property—those with "a stake in society." The blurring of practical distinctions between landed aristocrats and wealthy commoners meant that there was no clear-cut opposition between nobles and non-nobles on political issues.

Revolutions thus began with aspirations for equality and liberty among the social elite. Soon, however, dissenting voices emerged as some revolutionaries became frustrated with the limitations of liberal notions of equality and liberty and clamored for a fuller realization of these concepts. Depending on location, their demands included universal male suffrage, political rights for women and free people of color, the emancipation of slaves, and government regulations to reduce economic inequality. The age of revolution was thus marked by bitter conflicts over how far reform should go and to whom it should apply.

The Seven Years' War

The roots of revolutionary ideas could be found in Enlightenment texts, but it was by no means inevitable that their ideas would result in revolution. Many members of the educated elite were satisfied with the status quo or too intimidated to challenge it. Instead, events—political, economic, and military—created crises that opened the door for the development of radical thought and action. One of the most important was the global conflict known as the Seven Years' War (1756–1763).

The war's battlefields stretched from central Europe to India to North America (where the conflict was known as the French and Indian War), pitting a new alliance of England and Prussia against the French, Austrians, and, later, Spanish. Its origins were in conflicts left unresolved at the end of the War of the Austrian Succession in 1748 (see Chapter 16), during which Prussia seized the Austrian territory of Silesia. In central Europe, Austria's Maria Theresa vowed to win back Silesia and to crush Prussia, thereby re-establishing the Habsburgs' traditional leadership in German affairs. By the end of the Seven Years' War, Maria Theresa had almost succeeded, but Prussia survived with its boundaries intact.

Unresolved tensions also lingered in North America, particularly regarding the border between the French and British colonies. The encroachment of English settlers into territory claimed by the French in the Ohio Valley resulted in skirmishes that soon became war. Although the inhabitants of New France were greatly outnumbered—Canada counted 55,000 inhabitants, compared to 1.2 million in the thirteen English colonies—French forces achieved major victories until 1758. Both sides relied on the participation of Native American tribes with whom they had long-standing trading contacts and actively sought new indigenous allies during the conflict. The tide of the conflict turned when the British diverted resources from the war in Europe, using superior sea power to destroy France's fleet and choke its commerce around the world. In 1759 the British laid siege to Quebec for four long months, finally defeating the French in a battle that sealed the nation's fate in North America.

British victory on all colonial fronts was ratified in the 1763 Treaty of Paris. Canada and all French territory east of the Mississippi River passed to Britain, and France ceded Louisiana to Spain as compensation for Spain's loss of Florida to Britain. France also gave up most of its holdings in India, opening the way to British dominance on the subcontinent (Map 19.1).

By 1763 Britain had realized its goal of monopolizing a vast trading and colonial empire, but at a tremendous cost in war debt. France emerged from the conflict humiliated and broke, but with its profitable Caribbean colonies intact. In the aftermath of war, both British and French governments had to raise taxes to repay loans, raising a storm of protest and demands for fundamental reform. Since the Caribbean colony of Saint-Domingue remained French, political turmoil in the mother country would directly affect its population. The seeds of revolutionary conflict in the Atlantic world were thus sown.

The American Revolutionary Era, 1775–1789

Focus Question	Why and how did American colonists forge a new, independent nation?

Increased taxes and government control were a crucial factor behind colonial protests in the New World, where the era of liberal political revolution began. After revolting against their home country, the thirteen mainland colonies of British North America

Europe, 1763
- Allies: Austria, France, Russia, Saxony, Spain, Sweden
- Allies: Great Britain, Portugal, Prussia

The Seven Years' War, 1756–1763
- Main areas of conflict

North America, 1763
Territorial claims
- British, 1755
- Additional British, 1763
- French, 1763
- Spanish, 1763
- Russian, 1763
- French fishing rights

India, 1767
- British claims, 1767

succeeded in establishing a new unified government. Participants in the revolution believed they were demanding only the traditional rights of English men and women. But those traditional rights were liberal rights, and in the American context they had strong democratic and popular overtones. Thus the American Revolution was fought in the name of ideals that were still quite radical for their time. In founding a government based on liberal principles, the Americans set an example that would have a forceful impact on France and its colonies. Yet the revolution did not resolve the question of social and political equality, which eluded the enslaved, women, free blacks, and indigenous people.

The Origins of the Revolution

The high cost of the Seven Years' War doubled the British national debt. Anticipating further expenses to defend the half a billion acres in new territory granted by the Treaty of Paris, the government in London imposed bold new administrative measures. Breaking with a tradition of loose colonial oversight, the British announced that they would maintain a large army in North America and tax the colonies directly. In 1765 Parliament passed the Stamp Act, which levied taxes on a long list of commercial and legal documents, diplomas, newspapers, almanacs, and playing cards. A stamp glued to each article indicated that the tax had been paid.

These measures seemed perfectly reasonable to the British, for a much heavier stamp tax already existed in Britain, and proceeds from the tax were to fund the defense of the colonies. Nonetheless, the colonists vigorously protested the Stamp Act by rioting and by boycotting British goods. Thus Parliament reluctantly repealed it.

Another area of contention was settlement of the new territory acquired by the Treaty of Paris. At the end of the Seven Years' War, land-squeezed settlers quickly moved west across the Appalachian Mountains into the Ohio Valley, sparking conflict with the Ottawa and other tribes already present in the region as well as remaining French settlers. To prevent costly wars in distant territory, the British government in 1763 issued a royal proclamation prohibiting colonists to settle west of the Appalachian Mountains. The so-called Proclamation Line did little to stem land speculation and the flow of migrants, but it did exacerbate suspicion and tensions between Britain and its colony. These disputes raised important political questions. To what extent could the British government reassert its power while limiting the authority of elected colonial bodies? Who had the right to make laws for Americans? The British government replied that Americans were represented in Parliament, albeit indirectly (like most British people), and that Parliament ruled throughout the empire. Many Americans felt otherwise. In

< **MAP 19.1** The Seven Years' War in Europe, North America, and India, 1755–1763

As a result of the war, France lost its vast territories in North America and India. In an effort to avoid costly conflicts with Native Americans living in the newly conquered territory, the British government in 1763 prohibited colonists from settling west of the Appalachian Mountains. One of the few remaining French colonies in the Americas, Saint-Domingue (on the island of Hispaniola) was the most profitable plantation colony in the New World.

Framing the Constitution

The liberal program of the American Revolution was consolidated by the federal Constitution, the Bill of Rights, and the creation of a national republic. Assembling in Philadelphia in the summer of 1787, the delegates to the Constitutional Convention were determined to end the period of economic depression, social uncertainty, and leadership under a weak central government that had followed independence. The delegates thus decided to grant the federal, or central, government important powers: regulation of domestic and foreign trade, the right to tax, and the means to enforce its laws.

Strong rule would be placed squarely in the context of representative self-government. Senators and congressmen would be the lawmaking delegates of the voters, and the president of the republic would be an elected official. The central government would operate in Montesquieu's framework of checks and balances, under which authority was distributed across three different branches — the executive, legislative, and judicial branches — that would prevent one interest from gaining too much power. The power of the federal government would in turn be checked by that of the individual states.

When the results of the Constitutional Convention were presented to the states for ratification, a great public debate began. The opponents of the proposed Constitution — the Antifederalists — charged that the framers of the new document had taken too much power from the individual states and made the federal government too strong. Moreover, many Antifederalists feared for the individual freedoms for which they had fought. To overcome these objections, the Federalists promised to spell out these basic freedoms as soon as the new Constitution was adopted. The result was the first ten amendments to the Constitution, which the first Congress passed shortly after it met in New York in March 1789. These amendments, ratified in 1791, formed an effective Bill of Rights to safeguard the individual. Most of them — trial by jury, due process of law, the right to assemble, freedom from unreasonable search — had their origins in English law and the English Bill of Rights of 1689. Other rights — the freedoms of speech, the press, and religion — reflected natural-law theory and the strong value colonists had placed on independence from the start.

Limitations of Liberty and Equality

The American Constitution and the Bill of Rights exemplified the strengths and the limits of what came to be called classical liberalism. Liberty meant individual freedoms and political safeguards. Liberty also meant representative government, but it did not mean democracy, with its principle of one person, one vote. Equality meant equality before the law, not equality of political participation or wealth. It did not mean equal rights for slaves, indigenous peoples, or women.

A vigorous abolitionist movement during the 1780s led to the passage of emancipation laws in all northern states, but slavery remained prevalent in the South, and discord between pro- and antislavery delegates roiled the Constitutional Convention of 1787. The result was a compromise stipulating that an enslaved person would count as three-fifths of a person in tallying population numbers for taxation and proportional representation in the House of Representatives. This solution levied higher taxes on the South, but also guaranteed slaveholding states greater representation in Congress, which they used to oppose emancipation. Congress did ban slavery in federal territory in 1789, then the export of slaves from any state, and finally, in 1808, the import of slaves to any state.

The new republic also failed to protect the Native American tribes whose lands fell within or alongside the territory ceded by Britain at the Treaty of Paris. The 1787 Constitution promised protection to Native Americans and guaranteed that their land would not be taken without consent. Nonetheless, the federal government forced tribes to concede their land for meager returns; state governments and the rapidly expanding population paid even less heed to the Constitution and often simply seized Native American land for new settlements.

Although lacking the voting rights enjoyed by so many of their husbands and fathers in the relatively democratic colonial assemblies, women played a vital role in the American Revolution. As household provisioners, women were essential participants in boycotts of British goods, like tea, which squeezed profits from British merchants and fostered the revolutionary spirit. After the outbreak of war, women raised funds for the Continental Army and took care of homesteads, workshops, and other businesses when their men went off to fight. Yet despite Abigail Adams's plea to her husband, John Adams, that the framers of the Declaration of Independence should "remember the ladies," women did not receive the right to vote in the new Constitution, an omission confirmed by a clause added in 1844.

Revolution in France, 1789–1791

Focus Question	How did the events of 1789 result in a constitutional monarchy in France, and what were the consequences?

No country felt the consequences of the American Revolution more deeply than France. Hundreds of French officers served in America and were inspired by the experience. The most famous of these, the young and impressionable marquis de Lafayette, left home as a great aristocrat determined to fight France's traditional foe, England. He returned with a love of liberty and firm republican convictions. French intellectuals engaged in passionate analysis of the federal Constitution as well as the constitutions of the various states of the new United States. The American Revolution undeniably fueled dissatisfaction with the old monarchical order in France. Yet the French Revolution did not mirror the American example. It was more radical and more complex, more influential and more controversial, more loved and more hated. For Europeans and most of the rest of the world, it was the great revolution of the eighteenth century, the revolution that opened the modern era in politics.

Breakdown of the Old Order

As did the American Revolution, the French Revolution had its immediate origins in the government's financial difficulties. The efforts of the ministers of King Louis XV (r. 1715–1774) to raise taxes to meet the expenses of the War of the Austrian Succession in favor of replacing absolutism with a constitutional monarchy in which laws and taxes would require the consent of the Estates General in regular meetings. There was also the strong feeling that individual liberties would have to be guaranteed by law and that economic regulations should be loosened.

On May 5, 1789, the twelve hundred delegates of the three estates gathered in Versailles for the opening session of the Estates General. Despite widespread hopes for serious reform, the Estates General quickly deadlocked over the issue of voting procedures. Controversy had begun during the electoral process itself, when the government confirmed that, following precedent, each estate should meet and vote separately. During the lead-up to the Estates General, critics had demanded a single assembly dominated by the third estate. In his famous pamphlet *What Is the Third Estate?* the abbé Emmanuel Joseph Sieyès (himself a member of the first estate) argued that the nobility was a tiny, overprivileged minority and that the third estate constituted the true strength of the French nation. The government granted the third estate as many delegates as the clergy and the nobility combined, but then nullified the reform by granting one vote per estate instead of one vote per person. This meant that the two privileged estates could always outvote the third.

In angry response, in June 1789 delegates of the third estate refused to meet until the king ordered the clergy and nobility to sit with them in a single body. On June 17 the third estate, which had been joined by a few parish priests, voted to call itself the **National Assembly**. On June 20, excluded from their hall because of "repairs," the delegates moved to a large indoor tennis court where they swore the famous Tennis Court Oath, pledging not to disband until they had been recognized as a national assembly and had written a new constitution.

The king's response was disastrously ambivalent. On June 23 he made a conciliatory speech urging reforms, and four days later he ordered the three estates to meet together. At the same time, Louis apparently followed the advice of relatives and court nobles who urged him to dissolve the Assembly by force. The king called an army of eighteen thousand troops toward the capital to bring the delegates under control, and on July 11 he dismissed his finance minister and other more liberal ministers. It appeared that the monarchy was prepared to use violence to restore its control.

Popular Uprising and the Rights of Man

While delegates at Versailles were pressing for political rights, economic hardship gripped the common people. Conditions were already tough, due to the government's disastrous financial situation. A poor grain harvest in 1788 caused the price of bread to soar, and inflation spread quickly through the economy. As a result, demand for manufactured goods collapsed, and many artisans and small traders lost work. In Paris perhaps 150,000 of the city's 600,000 people were unemployed by July 1789.

Against this background of poverty and political crisis, the people of Paris entered decisively onto the revolutionary stage. They believed that, to survive, they should have steady work and enough bread at fair prices. They also feared that the dismissal of the king's liberal finance minister would put them at the mercy of aristocratic landowners and grain speculators. At the beginning of July, knowledge spread of the massing of troops near Paris. On July 14, 1789, several hundred people stormed the

Bastille (ba-STEEL), a royal prison, to obtain weapons for the city's defense. Faced with popular violence, Louis soon announced the reinstatement of his finance minister and the withdrawal of troops from Paris. The National Assembly was now free to continue its work.

Just as the laboring poor of Paris had decisively intervened in the Revolution, the struggling French peasantry also took matters into their own hands. Peasants bore the brunt of state taxation, church tithes, and noble privileges. Since most did not own enough land to be self-sufficient, they were hard-hit by the rising price of bread. In the summer of 1789, throughout France peasants began to rise in insurrection against their lords, ransacking manor houses and burning feudal documents that recorded their obligations. In some areas peasants reoccupied common lands enclosed by landowners and seized forests. Fear of marauders and vagabonds hired by vengeful landlords—called the **Great Fear** by contemporaries—seized the rural poor and fanned the flames of rebellion.

Faced with chaos, the National Assembly responded to the swell of popular uprising with a surprise maneuver on the night of August 4, 1789. By a decree of the Assembly, all the old noble privileges—peasant serfdom where it still existed, exclusive hunting rights, fees for having legal cases judged in the lord's court, the right to make peasants work on the roads, and a host of other dues—were abolished along with the tithes paid to the church. From this point on, French peasants would seek mainly to protect and consolidate this victory.

On August 27, 1789, the Assembly further issued the Declaration of the Rights of Man and of the Citizen. This clarion call of the liberal revolutionary ideal guaranteed equality before the law, representative government for a sovereign people, and individual freedom. This revolutionary credo, only two pages long, was disseminated throughout France and the rest of Europe and around the world.

The National Assembly's declaration had little practical effect for the poor and hungry people of France. The economic crisis worsened after the fall of the Bastille, as aristocrats fled the country and the luxury market collapsed. Foreign markets also shrank, and unemployment among the urban working classes grew. In addition, women—the traditional managers of food and resources in poor homes—could no longer look to the church, which had been stripped of its tithes, for aid.

On October 5 some seven thousand women marched the twelve miles from Paris to Versailles to demand action. This great crowd, "armed with scythes, sticks and pikes," invaded the National Assembly. Interrupting a delegate's speech, an old woman defiantly shouted into the debate, "Who's that talking down there? Make the chatterbox shut up. That's not the point: the point is that we want bread."[2] Hers was the genuine voice of the people, essential to any understanding of the French Revolution. The women invaded the royal apartments, killed some of the royal bodyguards, and searched for the queen, Marie Antoinette, who was widely despised for her frivolous and supposedly immoral behavior. It seems likely that only the intervention of Lafayette and the National Guard saved the royal family. But the only way to calm the disorder was for the king to live closer to his people in Paris, as the crowd demanded.

Liberal elites brought the Revolution into being and continued to lead politics. Yet the people of France were now roused and would henceforth play a crucial role in the unfolding of events.

As Robespierre's closest supporters followed their leader to the guillotine, the respectable middle-class lawyers and professionals who had led the liberal Revolution of 1789 reasserted their authority. This period of **Thermidorian reaction**, as it was called, hearkened back to the ideals of the early Revolution; the new leaders of government proclaimed an end to the revolutionary expediency of the Terror and the return of representative government, the rule of law, and liberal economic policies. In 1795 the National Convention abolished many economic controls, let prices rise sharply, and severely restricted the local political organizations through which the sans-culottes exerted their strength.

In the same year, members of the National Convention wrote a new constitution to guarantee their economic position and political supremacy. As in previous elections, the mass of the population could vote only for electors who would in turn elect the legislators, but the new constitution greatly reduced the number of men eligible to become electors by instating a substantial property requirement. It also inaugurated a bicameral legislative system for the first time in the Revolution, with a Council of 500 serving as the lower house that initiated legislation and a Council of Elders (composed of about 250 members aged forty years or older) acting as the upper house that approved new laws. To prevent a new Robespierre from monopolizing power, the new Assembly granted executive power to a five-man body, called the Directory.

The Directory continued to support French military expansion abroad. War was no longer so much a crusade as a response to economic problems. Large, victorious

The Execution of Robespierre   After overseeing the Terror, during which thousands of men and women accused of being enemies of the Revolution faced speedy trial and execution, it was Maximilien Robespierre's turn to face the guillotine on 9 Thermidor Year II (July 28, 1794). (Musée de la Ville de Paris, Musée Carnavalet, Paris, France/Bridgeman Images)

French armies reduced unemployment at home. However, the French people quickly grew weary of the corruption and ineffectiveness that characterized the Directory. The trauma of years of military and political violence had alienated the public, and the Directory's heavy-handed and opportunistic policies did not reverse the situation. This general dissatisfaction revealed itself clearly in the national elections of 1797, which returned a large number of conservative and even monarchist deputies who favored peace at almost any price. Two years later Napoleon Bonaparte ended the Directory in a coup d'état (koo day-TAH) and substituted a strong dictatorship for a weak one.

The Napoleonic Era, 1799–1815

Focus Question	How did Napoleon Bonaparte assume control of France and much of Europe, and what factors led to his downfall?

For almost fifteen years, from 1799 to 1814, France was in the hands of a keen-minded military dictator of exceptional ability. One of history's most fascinating leaders, Napoleon Bonaparte (1769–1821) realized that he needed to put an end to civil strife in France in order to create unity and consolidate his rule. And he did. But Napoleon saw himself as a man of destiny, and the glory of war and the dream of universal empire proved irresistible. For years he spiraled from victory to victory, but in the end he was destroyed by a mighty coalition united in fear of his restless ambition.

Napoleon's Rule of France

Born in Corsica into an impoverished noble family in 1769, Napoleon left home and became a lieutenant in the French artillery in 1785. Converted to the revolutionary cause and rising rapidly in the republican army, Napoleon was placed in command of French forces in Italy and won brilliant victories there in 1796 and 1797. His next campaign, in Egypt, was a failure, but Napoleon returned to France before the fiasco was generally known, and his reputation remained intact. French aggression in Egypt and elsewhere provoked the British to organize a new alliance in 1798, the Second Coalition, that also included Austria and Russia.

Napoleon soon learned that some prominent members of the legislature were plotting against the Directory. The plotters' dissatisfaction stemmed not so much from the Directory's ruling dictatorially as from the fact that it was a weak dictatorship. Ten years of upheaval and uncertainty had made firm rule much more appealing than liberty and popular politics to these disillusioned revolutionaries. The abbé Sieyès personified this evolution in thinking. In 1789 he had written that the nobility was grossly overprivileged and that the entire people should rule the French nation. Now Sieyès's motto was "Confidence from below, authority from above."

The flamboyant thirty-year-old Napoleon, nationally revered for his heroism, was an ideal figure of authority. On November 9, 1799, Napoleon and his conspirators ousted the Directors, and the following day soldiers disbanded the legislature at bayonet point. Napoleon was named first consul of the republic, and a new constitution consolidating his position was overwhelmingly approved by a nationwide vote in of Catholics, monarchists, and patriots rebelled against Napoleon's attempts to make Spain a French satellite. French armies occupied Madrid, but the foes of Napoleon fled to the hills and waged uncompromising guerrilla warfare. Spain was a clear warning: resistance to French imperialism was growing.

Yet Napoleon pushed on. In 1810, when the Grand Empire was at its height, Britain still remained at war with France, helping the guerrillas in Spain and Portugal. The Continental System was a failure. Instead of harming Britain, the system provoked the British to set up a counter-blockade, which created hard times in France. Perhaps looking for a scapegoat, Napoleon turned on Alexander I of Russia, who in 1811 openly repudiated Napoleon's war of prohibitions against British goods.

Napoleon's invasion of Russia began in June 1812 with a force that eventually numbered 600,000, probably the largest force yet assembled in a single army. Only one-third of this army was French, however; nationals of all the satellites and allies were drafted into the operation. Originally planning to winter in the Russian city of Smolensk, Napoleon recklessly pressed on toward Moscow. The great Battle of Borodino that followed was a draw. Alexander ordered the evacuation of Moscow, which the Russians then burned in part, and he refused to negotiate. Finally, after five weeks in the scorched and abandoned city, Napoleon ordered a retreat, one of the greatest military disasters in history. The Russian army, the Russian winter, and starvation cut Napoleon's army to pieces. When the frozen remnants staggered into Poland and Prussia in December, 370,000 men had died and another 200,000 had been taken prisoner.[6]

Leaving his troops to their fate, Napoleon raced to Paris to raise yet another army. Possibly he might still have saved his throne if he had been willing to accept a France reduced to its historical size—the proposal offered by Austria's foreign minister, Prince Klemens von Metternich. But Napoleon refused. Austria and Prussia deserted Napoleon and joined Russia and Great Britain in the Treaty of Chaumont in March 1814, by which the four powers formed the Quadruple Alliance to defeat the French emperor.

All across Europe patriots called for a "war of liberation" against Napoleon's oppression. Less than a month later, on April 4, 1814, a defeated Napoleon abdicated his throne. After this unconditional abdication, the victorious allies granted Napoleon the island of Elba off the coast of Italy as his own tiny state. Napoleon was allowed to keep his imperial title, and France was required to pay him a yearly income of 2 million francs.

The allies also agreed to the restoration of the Bourbon dynasty under Louis XVIII (r. 1814–1824) and promised to treat France with leniency in a peace settlement. The new monarch sought support among the people by issuing the Constitutional Charter, which accepted many of France's revolutionary changes and guaranteed civil liberties.

Yet Louis XVIII lacked the magnetism of Napoleon. Hearing of political unrest in France and diplomatic tensions in Vienna, Napoleon staged a daring escape from Elba in February 1815 and marched on Paris with a small band of followers. French officers and soldiers who had fought so long for their emperor responded to the call. Louis XVIII fled, and once more Napoleon took command. But Napoleon's gamble was a desperate long shot, for the allies were united against him. At the end of a frantic period known as the Hundred Days, they crushed his forces at Waterloo on June 18, 1815, and imprisoned him on the rocky island of St. Helena, off the western coast of

Africa. Louis XVIII returned to the throne, and the allies dealt more harshly with the French. As for Napoleon, he took revenge by writing his memoirs, nurturing the myth that he had been Europe's revolutionary liberator, a romantic hero whose lofty work had been undone by oppressive reactionaries.

The Haitian Revolution, 1791–1804

Focus Question	How did slave revolt on colonial Saint-Domingue lead to the creation of the independent nation of Haiti in 1804?

The events that led to the creation of the independent nation of Haiti constitute the third, and perhaps most extraordinary, chapter of the revolutionary era in the late eighteenth century. Prior to 1789 Saint-Domingue, the French colony that was to become Haiti, reaped huge profits through a ruthless system of slave-based plantation agriculture. News of revolution in France lit a powder keg of contradictory aspirations among white planters, free people of color, and slaves. While revolutionary authorities debated how far to extend the rights of man on Saint-Domingue, first free people of color and then enslaved people took matters into their own hands, rising up to claim their freedom. They succeeded, despite invasion by the British and Spanish and Napoleon Bonaparte's bid to reimpose French control. In 1804 Haiti became the only nation in history to claim its freedom through slave revolt.

Revolutionary Aspirations in Saint-Domingue

On the eve of the French Revolution, Saint-Domingue — the most profitable of all Caribbean colonies — was even more rife with social tensions than France itself. The colony, which occupied the western third of the island of Hispaniola, was inhabited by a variety of social groups who resented and mistrusted one another. The European population included French colonial officials, wealthy plantation owners and merchants, and poor artisans and clerks. Individuals of French or European descent born in the colonies were called "Creoles," and over time they had developed their own interests, at times distinct from those of metropolitan France. Vastly outnumbering the white population were the colony's five hundred thousand enslaved people alongside a sizable population of some forty thousand free people of African and mixed African and European descent. Members of this last group referred to themselves as free people of color.

Legal and economic conditions on Saint-Domingue vastly favored the white population. Most of the island's enslaved population performed grueling toil in the island's sugar plantations. The highly outnumbered planters used extremely brutal methods, such as beating, maiming, and executing slaves, to maintain their control. The 1685 Code Noir (Black Code) that set the parameters of slavery was intended to provide minimal standards of humane treatment, but its tenets were rarely enforced. Masters calculated that they could earn more by working slaves ruthlessly and purchasing new ones when they died, than by providing the food, rest, and medical care needed to allow the enslaved population to reproduce naturally. This meant a constant inflow of newly enslaved people from Africa was necessary to work the plantations.

Despite their brutality, slaveholders on Saint-Domingue freed a surprising number of their slaves, mostly their own mixed-race children, thereby producing one of the largest populations of free people of color in any slaveholding colony. The Code Noir had originally granted free people of color the same legal status as whites: they could own property, live where they wished, and pursue any education or career they desired. From the 1760s on, however, the rising prosperity and visibility of this group provoked resentment from the white population. In response, colonial administrators began rescinding the rights of free people of color, and by the time of the French Revolution myriad aspects of their lives were subject to discriminatory laws.

The political and intellectual turmoil of the 1780s, with its growing rhetoric of liberty, equality, and fraternity, raised new challenges and possibilities for each of Saint-Domingue's social groups. For enslaved people, who constituted approximately 90 percent of the population, news of abolitionist movements in France led to hopes that the mother country might grant them freedom. Free people of color looked to reforms in Paris as a means of gaining political enfranchisement and reasserting equal status with whites. The Creole elite, not surprisingly, saw matters very differently. Infuriated by talk of abolition and determined to protect their way of life, they looked to revolutionary ideals of representative government for the chance to gain control of their own affairs, as had the American colonists before them.

The National Assembly frustrated the hopes of all these groups. Cowed by colonial representatives who claimed that support for free people of color would result in slave insurrection and independence, the Assembly refused to extend French constitutional safeguards to the colonies. After dealing this blow to the aspirations of slaves and free people of color, the Assembly also reaffirmed French monopolies over colonial trade, thereby angering Creole planters as well. Like the American settlers before them, the colonists chafed under the rule of the mother country.

In July 1790 Vincent Ogé (aw-ZHAY) (ca. 1750–1791), a free man of color, returned to Saint-Domingue from Paris determined to win rights for his people. He raised an army of several hundred and sent letters to the new Provincial Assembly of Saint-Domingue demanding political rights for all free citizens. But Ogé's demands were refused, so he and his followers turned to armed insurrection. After initial victories, his army was defeated, and Ogé was tortured and executed by colonial officials. Revolutionary leaders in Paris were more sympathetic to Ogé's cause. In May 1791, responding to what it perceived as partly justified grievances, the National Assembly granted political rights to free people of color born to two free parents who possessed sufficient property. When news of this legislation arrived in Saint-Domingue, the white elite was furious, and the colonial governor refused to enact it. Violence now erupted between groups of whites and free people of color in parts of the colony.

The Outbreak of Revolt

Just as the sans-culottes helped push forward more radical reforms in France, the second stage of revolution in Saint-Domingue also resulted from decisive action from below. In August 1791 slaves, who had witnessed the confrontation between whites and free people of color for over a year, took events into their own hands. Groups of slaves held a series of nighttime meetings to plan a mass insurrection. In doing so, they drew on

Slave Revolt on Saint-Domingue   This illustration, from the proslavery perspective, emphasizes the violence and destructiveness of the slave rebellion in Saint-Domingue. Many white settlers fled to the United States and other Caribbean islands with as much of their property, including slaves, as they could take with them. (The Library Company of Philadelphia)

their own considerable military experience; the majority of slaves had been born in Africa, and many had served in the civil wars of the kingdom of Kongo and other conflicts before being taken into slavery.[7] They also drew on a long tradition of slave resistance prior to 1791, which had ranged from work slowdowns, to running away, to taking part in African-derived religious rituals and dances known as *vodou* (or voodoo). According to some sources, the August 1791 pact to take up arms was sealed by such a voodoo ritual.[8]

Revolts began on a few plantations on the night of August 22. Within a few days the uprising had swept much of the northern plain, creating a slave army estimated at around 2,000 individuals. By August 27 it was described by one observer as "10,000 strong, divided into 3 armies, of whom 700 or 800 are on horseback, and tolerably well-armed."[9] During the next month enslaved combatants attacked and destroyed hundreds of sugar and coffee plantations.

On April 4, 1792, as war loomed with the European states, the National Assembly issued a decree extending full citizenship rights to free people of color, including the right to vote. As in France, voting rights and the ability to hold public office applied to men only. The Assembly hoped this measure would win the loyalty of free people of color and their aid in defeating the slave rebellion.

Warfare in Europe soon spread to Saint-Domingue (Map 19.3). Since the beginning of the slave insurrection, the Spanish colony of Santo Domingo, on the eastern side of the island of Hispaniola, had supported rebel slaves. In early 1793 the Spanish began

NOTES

1. Quoted in G. Wright, *France in Modern Times*, 4th ed. (New York: W. W. Norton, 1987), p. 34.
2. G. Pernoud and S. Flaisser, eds., *The French Revolution* (Greenwich, Conn.: Fawcett, 1960), p. 61.
3. Quoted in L. Gershoy, *The Era of the French Revolution, 1789–1799* (New York: Van Nostrand, 1957), p. 150.
4. Quoted in Wim Klooster, *Revolutions in the Atlantic World: A Comprehensive History* (New York: New York University Press, 2009), p. 74.
5. T. Blanning, *The French Revolutionary Wars, 1787–1802* (London: Arnold, 1996), pp. 116–128.
6. D. Sutherland, *France, 1789–1815: Revolution and Counterrevolution* (New York: Oxford University Press, 1986), p. 420.
7. John K. Thornton, "'I Am the Subject of the King of Congo': African Political Ideology and the Haitian Revolution," *Journal of World History* 4, no. 2 (Fall 1993): 181–214.
8. Laurent Dubois, *Avengers of the New World: The Story of the Haitian Revolution* (Cambridge, Mass.: Belknap Press, 2004), pp. 43–45, 99–100.
9. Quoted ibid., p. 97.

LOOKING BACK LOOKING AHEAD

A great revolutionary wave swept both sides of the Atlantic Ocean in the late eighteenth century. The revolutions in British North America, France, and Haiti were individual and unique, but they had common origins and consequences for Western and, indeed, world history. Despite the French monarchy's ongoing claims to the absolutist rule imposed by Louis XIV, the eighteenth century had inaugurated monumental changes, as population grew, urbanization spread, and literacy increased. Enlightenment ideals, especially those of John Locke and the baron de Montesquieu, influenced all orders of society, and reformers increasingly championed limiting monarchical authority in the name of popular sovereignty.

The Atlantic world was the essential context for this age of revolutions. The movement of peoples, commodities, and ideas across the Atlantic Ocean in the eighteenth century created a world of common debates, conflicts, and aspirations. Moreover, the high stakes of colonial empire heightened competition among European states, leading to a series of wars that generated crushing costs for overburdened treasuries. For both the British in their North American colonies and the French at home, the desperate need for new taxes weakened government authority and opened the door to revolution. In turn, the ideals of the French Revolution inspired slaves and free people of color in Saint-Domingue, thus opening the promise of liberty, equality, and fraternity to people of all races.

The chain reaction did not end with the birth of an independent Haiti in 1804. On the European continent throughout the nineteenth and early twentieth centuries, periodic convulsions occurred as successive generations struggled over political rights first proclaimed by the generation of 1789. Meanwhile, as dramatic political events unfolded, a parallel economic revolution was gathering steam. This was the Industrial Revolution, originating around 1780 and accelerating through the end of the eighteenth century (see Chapter 20). After 1815 the twin forces of industrialization and democratization would combine to transform Europe and the world.

MAKE CONNECTIONS

Think about the larger developments and continuities within and across chapters.

1. What were major differences and similarities among the American, French, and Haitian Revolutions?

2. How did the increased circulation of goods, people, and ideas across the Atlantic in the eighteenth century (Chapter 17) contribute to the outbreak of revolution on both sides of the ocean?

3. To what extent would you characterize the revolutions discussed in this chapter as Enlightenment movements (Chapter 16)?

Chapter Review

IDENTIFY KEY TERMS

Identify and explain the significance of each item below.

Estates General (p. 596)

estates (p. 597)

National Assembly (p. 598)

Great Fear (p. 599)

Jacobin Club (p. 602)

second revolution (p. 603)

Girondists (p. 603)

the Mountain (p. 603)

sans-culottes (p. 603)

Reign of Terror (p. 604)

Thermidorian reaction (p. 606)

Napoleonic Code (p. 608)

Grand Empire (p. 609)

Continental System (p. 609)

REVIEW THE MAIN IDEAS

Answer the focus questions from each section of the chapter.

1. What were the factors leading to the revolutions of the late eighteenth century? (p. 586)

2. Why and how did American colonists forge a new, independent nation? (p. 589)

3. How did the events of 1789 result in a constitutional monarchy in France, and what were the consequences? (p. 595)

4. Why and how did the French Revolution take a radical turn entailing terror at home and war with European powers? (p. 601)

5. How did Napoleon Bonaparte assume control of France and much of Europe, and what factors led to his downfall? (p. 607)

6. How did slave revolt on colonial Saint-Domingue lead to the creation of the independent nation of Haiti in 1804? (p. 613)

wages were low and investment capital was scarce, there was little point in adopting mechanized production until significant increases in the machines' productivity, and a drop in the cost of manufacturing them, occurred in the first decades of the nineteenth century.[2]

Families using cotton in cottage industry were freed from their constant search for adequate yarn from scattered part-time spinners, since all the thread needed could be spun in the cottage on the jenny or obtained from a nearby factory. The income of weavers, now hard-pressed to keep up with the spinners, rose markedly until about 1792. They were among the highest-earning workers in England. As a result, large numbers of agricultural laborers became handloom weavers, while mechanics and capitalists sought to invent a power loom to save on labor costs. This Edmund Cartwright achieved in 1785. But the power looms of the factories worked poorly at first and did not replace handlooms until the 1820s.

Working conditions in the early cotton factories were so poor that adult weavers and spinners were reluctant to work in them. Factory owners often turned to young orphans and children instead. By placing them in "apprenticeship" with factory owners, parish officers charged with caring for such children saved money. At the same time, the factory owners gained workers over whom they exercised almost the authority of slave owners. Apprenticed as young as five or six years of age, boy and girl workers were forced by law to labor for their masters for as many as fourteen years. Housed, fed, and locked up nightly in factory dormitories, the young workers labored thirteen or fourteen hours a day for little or no pay. Harsh physical punishment maintained brutal discipline. To be sure, poor children typically worked long hours in many types of demanding jobs, but this wholesale coercion of orphans as factory apprentices constituted exploitation on a truly unprecedented scale.

The creation of the world's first machine-powered factories in the British cotton textile industry in the 1770s and 1780s, which grew out of the putting-out system of cottage production, was a major historical development. Both symbolically and substantially, the big new cotton mills marked the beginning of the Industrial Revolution in Britain. By 1831 the largely mechanized cotton textile industry accounted for fully 22 percent of the country's entire industrial production.

The Steam Engine Breakthrough

Human beings have long used their toolmaking abilities to construct machines that convert one form of energy into another for their own benefit. In the medieval period, Europeans began to adopt water mills to grind their grain and windmills to pump water and drain swamps. More efficient use of water and wind in the sixteenth and seventeenth centuries enabled them to accomplish more. Nevertheless, even into the eighteenth century Europe, like other areas of the world, continued to rely mainly on wood for energy, and human beings and animals continued to perform most work. This dependence meant that Europe and the rest of the world remained poor in energy and power.

By the eighteenth century wood was in ever-shorter supply in Britain. Processed wood (charcoal) was the fuel that was mixed with iron ore in the blast furnace to

James Nasmyth's Mighty Steam Hammer   Nasmyth's invention was the forerunner of the modern pile driver, and its successful introduction in 1832 epitomized the rapid development of steam-power technology in Britain. In this painting by the inventor himself, workers manipulate a massive iron shaft being hammered into shape at Nasmyth's foundry near Manchester. (Ann Ronan Pictures/Print Collector/Getty Images)

produce pig iron, crude iron molded into ingots called "pigs" that could be processed into steel, cast iron, or wrought iron. The iron industry's appetite for wood was enormous, and by 1740 the British iron industry was stagnating. Vast forests enabled Russia in the eighteenth century to become the world's leading producer of iron, much of which was exported to Britain. As wood became ever more scarce, the British looked to coal (combustible rock composed of fossilized organic matter) as an alternative. They had first used coal in the late Middle Ages as a source of heat. By 1640 most homes in London were heated with coal, and it was also used in industry to provide heat for making beer, glass, soap, and other products. The breakthrough came when industrialists began to use coal to produce mechanical energy and to power machinery.

To produce more coal, mines had to be dug deeper and deeper and, as a result, were constantly filling with water. Mechanical pumps, usually powered by animals walking in circles at the surface, had to be installed. Animal power was expensive and bothersome. In an attempt to overcome these disadvantages, Thomas Savery in 1698 and Thomas Newcomen in 1705 invented the first primitive **steam engines**. Both engines burned coal to produce steam, which was then used to operate a pump. Although both models were extremely inefficient, by the early 1770s many of the Savery engines and hundreds of the Newcomen engines were operating successfully in English and Scottish mines.

In 1763 a gifted young Scot named James Watt (1736–1819) was drawn to a critical study of the steam engine. Watt was employed at the time by the University of Glasgow as a skilled craftsman making scientific instruments. Scotland's Enlightenment emphasis on practicality and social progress had caused its universities to become pioneers in technical education. In 1763 Watt was called on to repair a Newcomen engine being used in a physics course. After a series of observations, Watt saw that the Newcomen engine's waste of energy could be reduced by adding a separate condenser. This splendid invention, patented in 1769, greatly increased the efficiency of the steam engine.

To invent something is one thing; to make it a practical success is quite another. Watt needed skilled workers, precision parts, and capital, and the relatively advanced nature of the British economy proved essential. A partnership in 1775 with Matthew Boulton, a wealthy English industrialist, provided Watt with adequate capital and exceptional skills in salesmanship. Among Britain's highly skilled locksmiths, tinsmiths, and millwrights, Watt found mechanics who could install, regulate, and repair his sophisticated engines. From ingenious manufacturers such as the cannonmaker John Wilkinson, Watt was gradually able to purchase precision parts. This support allowed him to create an effective vacuum in the condenser and regulate a complex engine. In more than twenty years of constant effort, Watt made many further improvements. By the late 1780s the firm of Boulton and Watt had made the steam engine a practical and commercial success in Britain.

The coal-burning steam engine of Watt and his followers was the Industrial Revolution's most fundamental advance in technology. For the first time in history, humanity had, at least for a few generations, almost unlimited power at its disposal. For the first time, inventors and engineers could devise and implement all kinds of power equipment to aid people in their work. The steam-power plant began to replace waterpower in cotton-spinning factories during the 1780s, contributing greatly to that industry's phenomenal rise. Steam also took the place of waterpower in flour mills, in the malt mills used in breweries, in the flint mills supplying the pottery industry, and in the mills exported by Britain to the West Indies to crush sugarcane.

The British iron industry was radically transformed. Originally, the smoke and fumes resulting from coal burning meant that coal could not be substituted for charcoal in smelting iron. Starting around 1710, ironmakers began to use coke—a smokeless and hot-burning fuel produced by heating coal to rid it of water and other impurities—to smelt pig iron. After 1770 the adoption of steam-driven bellows in blast furnaces allowed for great increases in the quantity of pig iron produced by

British ironmakers. In the 1780s Henry Cort developed the puddling furnace, which allowed pig iron to be refined in turn with coke.

Strong, skilled ironworkers — the puddlers — "cooked" molten pig iron in a great vat, raking off globs of refined iron for further processing. Cort also developed steam-powered rolling mills, which were capable of turning out finished iron in every shape and form. The economic consequence of these technical innovations was a great boom in the British iron industry. In 1740 annual British iron production was only 17,000 tons. With the spread of coke smelting and the impact of Cort's inventions, production had reached 260,000 tons by 1806. In 1844 Britain produced 3 million tons of iron. Once expensive, iron became the cheap, basic, indispensable building block of the British economy.

Steam-Powered Transportation

The coal industry had long used plank roads and rails to move coal wagons within mines and at the surface. Rails reduced friction and allowed a horse or a human being to pull a much heavier load. Thus, once a rail capable of supporting a heavy locomotive was developed in 1816, all sorts of experiments with steam engines on rails went forward.

The first steam locomotive was built by Richard Trevithick after much experimentation. George Stephenson acquired glory for his locomotive named **Rocket**, which sped down the track of the just-completed Liverpool and Manchester Railway at a maximum speed of 35 miles per hour, without a load, in 1829. The line from Liverpool to Manchester was a financial as well as a technical success, and many private companies quickly began to build more rail lines. Within twenty years they had completed the main trunk lines of Great Britain (Map 20.1). Other countries were quick to follow, with the first steam-powered trains operating in the United States in the 1830s and in Brazil, Chile, Argentina, and the British colonies of Canada, Australia, and India in the 1850s.

The arrival of the railroad had many significant consequences. It dramatically reduced the cost and uncertainty of shipping freight over land. Previously, markets had tended to be small and local; as the barrier of high transportation costs was lowered, markets became larger and even nationwide. Larger markets encouraged larger factories with more sophisticated machinery in a growing number of industries. Such factories could make goods more cheaply and gradually subjected most cottage workers and many urban artisans to severe competitive pressures. In all countries, the construction of railroads created a strong demand for unskilled labor and contributed to the growth of a class of urban workers.

The steam engine also transformed water travel. French engineers completed the first steamships in the 1770s, and the first commercial steamships came into use in North America several decades later. The *Clermont* began to travel the waters of the Hudson River in New York State in 1807, shortly followed by ships belonging to brewer John Molson on the St. Lawrence River. The steamship brought the advantages of the railroad — speed, reliability, efficiency — to water travel.

MAP 20.1 The Industrial Revolution in Great Britain, ca. 1850
Industry concentrated in the rapidly growing cities of the north and the center of England, where rich coal and iron deposits were close to one another.

Industry and Population

In 1851 London hosted an industrial fair called the Great Exhibition in the newly built **Crystal Palace**. More than 6 million visitors from all over Europe marveled at the gigantic new exhibition hall set in the middle of a large, centrally located park. The building was made entirely of glass and iron, both of which were now cheap and abundant. Sponsored by the British royal family, the exhibition celebrated the new era of industrial technology and the kingdom's role as world economic leader.

Britain's claim to be the "workshop of the world" was no idle boast, for it produced two-thirds of the world's coal and more than half of all iron and cotton cloth. More generally, in 1860 Britain produced a remarkable 20 percent of the entire world's output of industrial goods, whereas it had produced only about 2 percent of the total in 1750.[3] As the British economy significantly increased its production of manufactured goods, the gross national product (GNP) rose roughly fourfold at constant prices between 1780 and 1851. At the same time, the population of Britain boomed, growing from about 9 million in 1780 to almost 21 million in 1851. Thus growing numbers consumed much of the increase in total production.

Rapid population growth in Britain was key to industrial development. More people meant a more mobile labor force, with many young workers in need of employment and ready to go where the jobs were. Sustaining the dramatic increase in population, in turn, was only possible through advances in production in agriculture and industry. Based on the lessons of history, many contemporaries feared that the rapid growth in population would inevitably lead to disaster. In his *Essay on the*

Principle of Population (1798), Thomas Malthus (1766–1834) examined the dynamics of human populations. He argued:

> There are few states in which there is not a constant effort in the population to increase beyond the means of subsistence. This constant effort as constantly tends to subject the lower classes of society to distress, and to prevent any great permanent melioration of these conditions.[4]

Given the limited resources available, Malthus concluded that the only hope of warding off such "positive checks" to population growth as famine and disease was "prudential restraint." That is, young men and women had to limit the growth of population by marrying late in life. But Malthus was not optimistic about this possibility. The powerful attraction of the sexes, he feared, would cause most people to marry early and have many children.

Economist David Ricardo (1772–1823) spelled out the pessimistic implications of Malthus's thought. Ricardo's depressing **iron law of wages** posited that over an extended period of time, because of the pressure of population growth, wages would always sink to subsistence level. That is, wages would be just high enough to keep workers from starving.

Malthus, Ricardo, and their followers were proved wrong in the long run, largely because industrialization improved productivity beyond what they could imagine. However, until the 1820s, or even the 1840s, contemporary observers might reasonably have concluded that the economy and the total population were racing neck and neck, with the outcome very much in doubt. There was another problem as well. Perhaps workers, farmers, and ordinary people did not get their rightful share of the new wealth. Perhaps only the rich got richer, while the poor got poorer or made no progress. We will turn to this great issue after situating the process of industrialization in its European and global context.

Industrialization in Europe and the World

Focus Question	How did countries in Europe and around the world respond to the challenge of industrialization?

As new technologies and a new organization of labor began to revolutionize production in Britain, other countries took notice and began to emulate its example. With the end of the Napoleonic Wars, the nations of the European continent quickly adopted British inventions and achieved their own pattern of technological innovation and economic growth. By the last decades of the nineteenth century, western European countries as well as the United States and Japan had industrialized their economies to a considerable, albeit variable, degree.

Industrialization in other parts of the world proceeded more gradually, with uneven jerks and national and regional variations. Scholars are still struggling to explain these variations as well as the dramatic gap that emerged for the first time in history between Western and non-Western levels of economic production. These questions are especially important because they may offer valuable lessons for poor countries that today are seeking to improve their material condition through industrialization and economic development. The latest findings on the nineteenth-century experience are encouraging. They suggest that there were alternative paths to the industrial world and that there was and is no need to follow a rigid, predetermined British model.

National and International Variations

Comparative data on industrial production in different countries over time help give us an overview of what happened. One set of data, the work of a Swiss scholar, compares the level of industrialization on a per capita basis in several countries from 1750 to 1913. These data are far from perfect, but they reflect basic trends and are presented in Table 20.1 for closer study.

Table 20.1 presents a comparison of how much industrial product was produced, on average, for each person in a given country in a given year. All the numbers are expressed in terms of a single index number of 100, which equals the per capita level of industrial goods in Great Britain in 1900. Every number in the table is thus a percentage of the 1900 level in Britain and is directly comparable with other numbers. The countries are listed in roughly the order that they began to use large-scale, power-driven technology.

What does this overview tell us? First, one sees in the first column that in 1750 all countries were fairly close together, including non-Western nations such as China and India. Both China and India had been extremely important players in early modern world trade; both were sophisticated, technologically advanced, and economically powerful up to 1800 (see Chapter 14). However, the column headed 1800 shows that Britain had opened up a noticeable lead over all countries by 1800, and that gap

TABLE 20.1 Per Capita Levels of Industrialization, 1750–1913

	1750	1800	1830	1860	1880	1900	1913
Great Britain	10	16	25	64	87	100	115
Belgium	9	10	14	28	43	56	88
United States	4	9	14	21	38	69	126
France	9	9	12	20	28	39	59
Germany	8	8	9	15	25	52	85
Austria-Hungary	7	7	8	11	15	23	32
Italy	8	8	8	10	12	17	26
Russia	6	6	7	8	10	15	20
China	8	6	6	4	4	3	3
India	7	6	6	3	2	1	2

Note: All entries are based on an index value of 100, equal to the per capita level of industrialization in Great Britain in 1900. Data for Great Britain includes Ireland, England, Wales, and Scotland.

Source: P. Bairoch, "International Industrialization Levels from 1750 to 1980," *Journal of European Economic History* 11 (Spring 1982): 294, U.S. Journals at Cambridge University Press.

progressively widened as the Industrial Revolution accelerated through 1830 and reached full maturity by 1860.

Second, the table shows that Western countries began to emulate the British model successfully over the course of the nineteenth century, with significant variations in the timing and in the extent of industrialization. Belgium, achieving independence from the Netherlands in 1831 and rich in iron and coal, led in adopting Britain's new technology, and it experienced a great surge between 1830 and 1860. France developed factory production more gradually and did not experience "revolutionary" growth in overall industrial output.

Slow but steady growth in France was overshadowed by the spectacular rise of the German lands and the United States after 1860 in what has been termed the "second industrial revolution." In general, eastern and southern Europe began the process of modern industrialization later than northwestern and central Europe. Nevertheless, these regions made real progress in the late nineteenth century, as growth after 1880 in Austria-Hungary, Italy, and Russia suggests. This meant that all European states as well as the United States managed to raise per capita industrial levels in the nineteenth century.

These increases stood in stark contrast to the decreases that occurred at the same time in many non-Western countries, most notably in China and India, as Table 20.1 shows. European countries industrialized to a greater or lesser extent even as most of the non-Western world stagnated. Japan, which is not included in this table, stands out as an exceptional area of non-Western industrial growth in the second half of the nineteenth century. After the forced opening of the country to the West in the 1850s, Japanese entrepreneurs began to adopt Western technology and manufacturing methods, resulting in a production boom by the late nineteenth century. Different rates of wealth- and power-creating industrial development, which heightened disparities within Europe, also greatly magnified existing inequalities between Europe and the rest of the world.

Industrialization in Continental Europe

Throughout Europe the eighteenth century was an era of agricultural improvement, population increase, expanding foreign trade, and growing cottage industry. Thus, when the pace of British industry began to accelerate in the 1780s, continental businesses began to emulate the new methods. British industry enjoyed clear superiority, but the European continent was close behind. During the period of the revolutionary and Napoleonic wars, from 1793 to 1815, however, western Europe experienced tremendous political and social upheaval that temporarily halted economic development. With the return of peace in 1815, western European countries again began to play catch-up.

They faced significant challenges. In the newly mechanized industries, British goods were being produced very economically, and these goods had come to dominate world markets. In addition, British technology had become so advanced that few engineers or skilled technicians outside England understood it. Moreover, the technology of steam power had grown much more expensive. It involved large investments in the iron and coal industries and, after 1830, in railroads. Continental business people had difficulty amassing the large sums of money the new methods demanded, and laborers bitterly resisted the move to working in factories. All these factors slowed the spread of machine-powered industry (Map 20.2).

Nevertheless, western European nations possessed a number of advantages that helped them respond to these challenges. First, most had rich traditions of putting-out enterprise, merchant capitalists, and skilled urban artisans. These assets gave their firms the ability to adapt and survive in the face of new market conditions. Second, continental capitalists did not need to develop their own advanced technology. Instead, they could simply "borrow" the new methods developed in Great Britain. European countries also had a third asset that many non-Western areas lacked in the nineteenth century: they had strong, independent governments that did not fall under foreign political control. These governments would use the power of the state to promote industry and catch up with Britain.

MAP 20.2 Continental Industrialization, ca. 1850
Although continental countries were beginning to make progress by 1850, they still lagged far behind Great Britain. For example, continental railroad building was still in an early stage, whereas the British rail system was essentially complete (see Map 20.1). Coal played a critical role in nineteenth-century industrialization both as a power source for steam engines and as a raw material for making iron and steel.

Most continental businesses adopted factory technology slowly, and handicraft methods lived on. Indeed, continental industrialization usually brought substantial but uneven expansion of handicraft industry in both rural and urban areas for a time. Artisan production of luxury items grew in France as the rising income of the international middle class created increased foreign demand for silk scarves, embroidered needlework, perfumes, and fine wines. Focusing on artisanal luxury production made sense for French entrepreneurs given their long history of dominance in that sector. Rather than being a "backward" refusal to modernize, it represented a sound strategic choice that allowed the French to capitalize on their know-how and international reputation for high-quality goods.

Agents of Industrialization

Western European success in adopting British methods took place despite the best efforts of the British to prevent it. The British realized the great value of their technical discoveries and tried to keep their secrets to themselves. Until 1825 it was illegal for artisans and skilled mechanics to leave Britain; until 1843 the export of textile machinery and other equipment was forbidden. Many talented, ambitious workers, however, slipped out of the country illegally and introduced the new methods abroad.

One such man was William Cockerill, a Lancashire carpenter. He and his sons began building cotton-spinning equipment in French-occupied Belgium in 1799. In 1817 the most famous son, John Cockerill, built a large industrial enterprise in Liège in southern Belgium, which produced machinery, steam engines, and then railway locomotives. He also established modern ironworks and coal mines. Cockerill's plants in the Liège area became a center for the gathering and transmitting of industrial information across Europe. Many skilled British workers came to work for Cockerill, and some went on to found their own companies throughout Europe.

Thus British technicians and skilled workers were a powerful force in the spread of early industrialization. A second agent of industrialization consisted of talented entrepreneurs such as Fritz Harkort (1793–1880), a pioneer in the German machinery industry. Serving in England as a Prussian army officer during the Napoleonic Wars, Harkort was impressed with what he saw. Harkort set up shop building steam engines in the Ruhr Valley, on the western border with France. In spite of problems obtaining skilled workers and machinery, Harkort succeeded in building and selling engines. However, his ambitious efforts also resulted in large financial losses for himself and his partners. His career illustrates both the great efforts of a few important business leaders to duplicate the British achievement and the difficulty of the task.

National governments played an even more important role in supporting industrialization in continental Europe than in Britain. **Tariff protection** was one such support, and it proved to be important. The French, for example, responded to a flood of cheap British goods in 1815 after the Napoleonic Wars by laying high taxes on imported goods. Customs agreements emerged among some German states starting in 1818, and in 1834 a number of states signed a treaty creating a customs union, or *Zollverein*. The treaty allowed goods to move between member states without tariffs, while erecting a single uniform tariff against other nations.

The Circle of the Rue Royale, Paris, 1868 The Circle of the Rue Royale was an exclusive club of aristocrats, bankers, railway owners, and other members of Parisian high society. This group portrait projects the wealth and elegance of the club's members, who are gathered on the balcony of a hotel. (*The Circle of the Rue Royale, Paris, 1868*, by James Jacques Joseph Tissot [1836–1902], [oil on canvas]/Fine Art Images/Heritage Images/Getty Images)

After 1815 continental governments also bore the cost of building roads, canals, and railroads to improve transportation. Belgium led the way in the 1830s and 1840s. Built rapidly as a unified network, Belgium's state-owned railroads stimulated the development of heavy industry and made the country an early industrial leader. In France, the state shouldered all the expense of acquiring and laying roadbed, including bridges and tunnels. In short, governments helped pay for railroads, the all-important leading sector in continental industrialization.

Finally, banks also played a larger and more creative role on the continent than in Britain. Previously, almost all banks in Europe had been private. Because of the possibility of unlimited financial loss, the partners of private banks tended to be conservative and were content to deal with a few rich clients and a few big merchants. They generally avoided industrial investment as being too risky.

In the 1830s two important Belgian banks pioneered in a new direction. They received permission from the growth-oriented government to establish themselves as corporations enjoying limited liability. That is, if the bank went bankrupt, stockholders could now lose only their original investments in the bank's common stock, and they could not be forced by the courts to pay for any additional losses out of other property they owned. Limited liability helped these Belgian banks attract investors.

They mobilized impressive resources for investment in big companies, became industrial banks, and successfully promoted industrial development.

Similar corporate banks became important in France and the German lands in the 1850s and 1860s. Usually working in collaboration with governments, corporate banks established and developed many railroads and many companies working in heavy industry, which were also increasingly organized as limited liability corporations.

The combined efforts of governments, skilled workers, entrepreneurs, and industrial banks meshed successfully after 1850 and the financial crash of 1873. In Belgium, France, and the German states, key indicators of modern industrial development — such as railway mileage, iron and coal production, and steam engine capacity — increased at average annual rates of 5 to 10 percent. As a result, rail networks were completed in western and much of central Europe, and the leading continental countries mastered the industrial technologies that had first been developed by the British. In the early 1870s Britain was still Europe's most industrial nation, but a select handful of nations had closed the gap.

The Global Picture

The Industrial Revolution did not have a transformative impact beyond Europe prior to the 1860s, with the exception of the United States and Japan, both early adopters of British practices. In many countries, national governments and pioneering entrepreneurs did make efforts to adopt the technologies and methods of production that had proved so successful in Britain, but they fell short of transitioning to an industrial economy. For example, in Russia the imperial government brought steamships to the Volga River and a railroad to the capital, St. Petersburg, in the first decades of the nineteenth century. By midcentury ambitious entrepreneurs had established steam-powered cotton factories using imported British machines. However, these advances did not lead to overall industrialization of the country, most of whose people remained mired in rural servitude. Instead, Russia confirmed its role as provider of raw materials, especially timber and grain, to the hungry West.

Egypt, a territory of the Ottoman Empire, similarly began an ambitious program of modernization after a reform-minded viceroy took power in 1805. This program included the use of imported British technology and experts in textile manufacture and other industries. These industries, however, could not compete with lower-priced European imports. Like Russia, Egypt fell back on agricultural exports to European markets, like sugar and cotton.

Such examples of faltering efforts at industrialization could be found in many other regions of the Middle East, Asia, and Latin America. Where European governments maintained direct or indirect political control, they acted to monopolize colonial markets as both sources of raw materials and consumers for their own products, rather than encouraging the spread of industrialization. Such regions could not respond to low-cost imports by raising tariffs, as the United States and western European nations had done, because they were controlled by imperial powers that did not allow them to do so. In India, millions of poor textile workers lost their livelihood because they could not compete with industrially produced British cottons. The British charged stiff import duties on Indian cottons entering the kingdom, but prohibited the Indians from doing the same to British imports. As a British trade encyclopedia boasted in 1844:

> The British manufacturer brings the cotton of India from a distance of 12,000 miles, commits it to his spinning jennies and power-looms, carries back their products to the East, making them again to travel 12,000 miles; and in spite of the loss of time, and of the enormous expense incurred by this voyage of 24,000 miles, the cotton manufactured by his machinery becomes less costly than the cotton of India spun and woven by the hand near the field that produced it.[5]

Latin American economies were disrupted by the early-nineteenth-century wars of independence. As these countries' economies recovered in the mid-nineteenth century, they increasingly adopted steam power for sugar and coffee processing and for transportation. Like elsewhere, this technology first supported increased agricultural production for export and only later drove domestic industrial production. As in India, the arrival of cheap British cottons destroyed the pre-existing textile industry that had employed many people.

The rise of industrialization in Britain, western Europe, and the United States thus caused other regions of the world to become increasingly economically dependent. Instead of industrializing, many territories underwent a process of deindustrialization due to imperialism and economic competition. In turn, relative economic weakness made them vulnerable to the new wave of imperialism undertaken by industrialized nations in the second half of the nineteenth century (see Chapter 24).

As for China, it did not adopt mechanized production until the end of the nineteenth century, but continued as a market-based, commercial society with a massive rural sector and industrial production based on traditional methods. Some regions of China experienced slow economic growth, while others were stagnant. In the 1860s and 1870s, when Japan was successfully adopting industrial methods, the Chinese government showed similar interest in Western technology and science. However, China faced widespread uprisings in the mid-nineteenth century, which drained attention and resources to the military. With China poised to surpass the United States in economic production by 2020, scholars now wonder whether the ascension of Europe and the West from 1800 was merely a brief interruption in a much longer pattern of Asian dominance.

New Patterns of Working and Living

Focus Question	How did work evolve during the Industrial Revolution, and how did daily life change for working people?

Having first emerged in the British countryside in the late eighteenth century, factories and industrial labor began migrating to cities by the early nineteenth century. As factories moved from rural to urban areas, their workforce evolved as well, from pauper children to families to men and women uprooted from their traditional rural communities. Many women, especially young single women and poor women, continued to work, but married women began to limit their participation in the workforce when possible. For some people, the Industrial Revolution brought improvements, but living and working conditions for the poor stagnated or even deteriorated until around 1850, especially in overcrowded industrial cities.

Work in Early Factories

The first factories of the Industrial Revolution were cotton mills, which began functioning in the 1770s along fast-running rivers and streams and were often located in sparsely populated areas. Cottage workers, accustomed to the putting-out system, were reluctant to work in the new factories even when they received relatively good wages. In a factory, workers had to keep up with the machine and follow its relentless tempo. Moreover, they had to show up every day, on time, and work long, monotonous hours under the constant supervision of demanding overseers, and they were punished systematically if they broke the work rules. For example, if a worker was late to work, or accidentally spoiled material, the employer deducted fines from the weekly pay. Employers frequently beat children and adolescents for their infractions.

Cottage workers were not used to that way of life. All members of the family worked hard and long, but in spurts, setting their own pace. They could interrupt their work when they wished. Women and children could break up their long hours of spinning with other tasks. On Saturday afternoon the head of the family delivered the week's work to the merchant manufacturer and got paid. Saturday night was a time of relaxation and drinking, especially for the men.

Also, early factories resembled English poorhouses, where destitute people went to live at public expense. Some poorhouses were industrial prisons, where the inmates had to work in order to receive food and lodging. The similarity between large brick factories and large stone poorhouses increased the cottage workers' fear of factories and their hatred of factory discipline. It was cottage workers' reluctance to work in factories that prompted early cotton mill owners to turn to pauper children. Mill owners contracted with local officials to employ large numbers of such children, who had no say in the matter. Attitudes began to change in the last decade of the eighteenth century, as middle-class reformers publicized the brutal toil imposed on society's most vulnerable members.

Working Families and Children

By the 1790s the early pattern had begun to change. The use of pauper apprentices was in decline, and in 1802 it was forbidden by Parliament. Many more textile factories were being built, mainly in urban areas, where they could use steam power rather than waterpower and attract a workforce more easily than in the countryside. People came from near and far to work in the cities, as factory workers and as porters, builders, and domestic servants. Collectively, these wage laborers came to be known as the "working class," a term first used in the late 1830s.

In some cases, workers accommodated to the system by carrying over familiar working traditions. Some came to the mills and the mines in the family units in which they had labored on farms and in the putting-out system. The mill or mine owner bargained with the head of the family and paid him or her for the efforts of the whole family. In the cotton mills, children worked for their mothers or fathers, collecting scraps and "piecing" broken threads together. In the mines, children sorted coal and worked the ventilation equipment. Their mothers hauled coal in the tunnels below the surface, while their fathers hewed with pick and shovel at the face of the seam.

Ties of kinship were particularly important for newcomers, who often traveled great distances to find work. Many urban workers in Great Britain were from Ireland. They were forced out of rural Ireland by population growth and deteriorating economic conditions from 1817 on, and their numbers increased dramatically in the desperate years of the potato famine, from 1845 to 1851 (see Chapter 21). As early as 1824 most of the workers in the Glasgow cotton mills were Irish; in 1851 one-sixth of the population of Liverpool was Irish. Like many other immigrant groups held together by ethnic and religious ties, however, the Irish worked together, formed their own neighborhoods, and preserved their cultural traditions.

In the early decades of the nineteenth century, however, technical changes made it less and less likely that workers could continue to labor in family groups. As control and discipline passed into the hands of impersonal managers and overseers, adult workers began to protest against inhuman conditions on behalf of their children. Some enlightened employers and social reformers in Parliament argued that more humane standards were necessary, and they used widely circulated parliamentary reports to influence public opinion. For example, Robert Owen (1771–1858), a successful manufacturer in Scotland, testified in 1816 before an investigating committee on the basis of his experience. He argued that employing children under ten years of age as factory workers was "injurious to the children, and not beneficial to the proprietors."[6] Workers also provided graphic testimony at such hearings as reformers pressed Parliament to pass corrective laws. These efforts resulted in a series of British **Factory Acts** from 1802 to 1833 that progressively limited the workday of child laborers and set minimum hygiene and safety requirements. The Factory Act of 1833 installed a system of full-time professional inspectors to enforce the provisions of previous acts. Children between ages nine and thirteen could work a maximum of eight hours per day, not including two hours for education. Teenagers aged fourteen to eighteen could work up to twelve hours, while those under nine were banned from employment. The Factory Acts constituted significant progress in preventing the exploitation of children. One unintended drawback of restrictions on child labor, however, was that they broke the pattern of whole families working together in the factory because efficiency required standardized shifts for all workers. After 1833 the number of children employed in industry declined rapidly.

The New Sexual Division of Labor

With the restriction of child labor and the collapse of the family work pattern in the 1830s came a new sexual division of labor. By 1850 the man was emerging as the family's primary wage earner, while the married woman found only limited job opportunities. Generally denied good jobs at high wages in the growing urban economy, wives were expected to concentrate on their duties at home.

This new pattern of **separate spheres** had several aspects. First, all studies agree that married women from the working classes were much less likely to work full-time for wages outside the house after the first child arrived, although they often earned small amounts doing putting-out handicrafts at home and taking in boarders. Second, when married women did work for wages outside the house, they usually came from the poorest families, where the husbands were poorly paid, sick, unemployed, or missing. Third, these poor married or widowed women were joined by legions of young unmarried women, who worked full-time but only in certain jobs, of which textile factory work, laundering, and domestic service were particularly important. Fourth, all women were generally confined to low-paying, dead-end jobs. Evolving gradually, but largely in place by 1850, the new sexual division of labor constituted a major development in the history of women and of the family.

Several factors combined to create this new sexual division of labor. First, the new and unfamiliar discipline of the clock and the machine was especially hard on married women of the laboring classes. Relentless factory discipline conflicted with child care in a way that labor on the farm or in the cottage had not. A woman operating earsplitting spinning machinery could mind a child of seven or eight working beside her (until such work was outlawed), but she could no longer pace herself through pregnancy or breast-feed her baby on the job. Thus a working-class woman had strong incentives to stay home, if she could afford it. Caring for babies was a less important factor in areas of continental Europe, such as northern France and Scandinavia, where women relied on paid wet nurses instead of breast-feeding their babies (see Chapter 18).

Second, running a household in conditions of primitive urban poverty was an extremely demanding job in its own right. There were no supermarkets or public transportation. Shopping, washing clothes, and feeding the family constituted a never-ending challenge. Taking on a brutal job outside the house—a "second shift"—had limited appeal for the average married woman from the working class. Thus many women might well have accepted the emerging division of labor as the best available strategy for family survival in the industrializing society.[7]

Third, to a large degree the young, generally unmarried women who did work for wages outside the home were segregated from men and confined to certain "women's jobs" because the new sexual division of labor replicated long-standing patterns of gender segregation and inequality. In the preindustrial economy, a small sector of the labor market had always been defined as "women's work," especially tasks involving needlework, spinning, food preparation, child care, and nursing. This traditional sexual division of labor took on new overtones, however, in response to the factory system. Previously, at least in theory, young people worked under a watchful parental eye. The growth of factories and mines brought unheard-of opportunities for girls and boys to mix on the job, free of familial supervision. Such opportunities led to more unplanned pregnancies and fueled the illegitimacy explosion that had begun in the late eighteenth century and that gathered force until at least 1850. Thus segregation of jobs by gender was partly an effort by older people to control the sexuality of working-class youths.

Investigations into the British coal industry before 1842 provide a graphic example of this concern. The middle-class men leading the inquiry professed horror at the sight of girls and women working without shirts, which was a common practice because of the heat, and they quickly assumed the prevalence of licentious sex with the male miners, who also wore very little clothing. In fact, many girls and married women worked for related males in a family unit that provided considerable protection and restraint. Yet many witnesses from the working class also believed that the mines were inappropriate and dangerous places for women and girls. Some miners stressed particularly the danger of sexual aggression for girls working past puberty. As one explained, "I consider it a scandal for girls to work in the pits. Till they are 12 or 14 they may work very well but after that it's an abomination. . . . The work of the pit does not hurt them, it is the effect on their morals that I complain of."[8] The **Mines Act of 1842** prohibited underground work for all women and girls as well as for boys under ten.

Child Labor in Coal Mines Public sentiment against child labor in coal mines was provoked by the publication of dramatic images of the harsh working conditions children endured. The Mines Act of 1842 prohibited the employment underground of women and girls and boys under the age of ten. (*Child Labour in an English Coal Mine*, 1844, colored lithograph/akg-images)

Some women who had to support themselves protested against being excluded from coal mining, which paid higher wages than most other jobs open to working-class women. But provided they were part of families that could manage economically, the girls and the women who had worked underground were generally pleased with the law. In explaining her satisfaction in 1844, one mother of four provided real insight into why many married working women accepted the emerging sexual division of labor:

> While working in the pit I was worth to my [miner] husband seven shillings a week, out of which we had to pay 2½ shillings to a woman for looking after the younger children. I used to take them to her house at 4 o'clock in the morning, out of their own beds, to put them into hers. Then there was one shilling a week for washing; besides, there was mending to pay for, and other things. The house was not guided. The other children broke things; they did not go to school when they were sent; they would be playing about, and get ill-used by other children, and their clothes torn. Then when I came home in the evening, everything was to do after the day's labor, and I was so tired I had no heart for it; no fire lit, nothing cooked, no water fetched, the house dirty, and nothing comfortable for my husband. It is all far better now, and I wouldn't go down again.[9]

A final factor encouraging working-class women to withdraw from paid labor was the domestic ideals emanating from middle-class women, who had largely embraced the "separate spheres" ideology. Middle-class reformers published tracts and formed societies to urge poor women to devote more care and attention to their homes and families.

Living Standards for the Working Class

Despite the best efforts of hard-working men and women, living conditions for the industrialized poor were often abysmal. Although the evidence is complex and sometimes contradictory, most historians of the Industrial Revolution now agree that overall living standards for the working class did not rise substantially until the 1840s at the earliest. British wages were always high compared to those in the rest of Europe, but the stresses of war with France from 1792 to 1815 led to a decline in the average British worker's real wages and standard of living. These difficult war years, with high unemployment and inflation, lent a grim color to the new industrial system. Factory wages began to rise after 1815, but these gains were modest and were offset by a decline in the labor of children and married women, meaning that many households had less total income than before. Moreover, many people still worked outside the factories as cottage workers or rural laborers, and in those sectors wages declined. Thus the increase in the productivity of industry did not lead to an increase in the purchasing power of the British working classes. Only after 1830, and especially after 1840, did real wages rise substantially, so that the average worker earned roughly 30 percent more in real terms in 1850 than in 1770.[10]

Up to that point, the demands of labor in the new industries probably outweighed their benefits as far as working people were concerned. Many landless poor people in the late eighteenth century were self-employed cottage workers living in close-knit rural communities; with industrialization they worked longer and harder at jobs that were often more grueling and more dangerous. In England nonagricultural workers labored about 250 days per year in 1760 as compared to 300 days per year in 1830, while the normal workday remained an exhausting eleven hours throughout the entire period. In 1760 nonagricultural workers still observed many religious and public holidays by not working, and many workers took Monday off. These days of leisure and relaxation declined rapidly after 1760, and by 1830 nonagricultural workers had joined landless agricultural laborers in toiling six rather than five days a week.[11]

As the factories moved to urban areas, workers followed them in large numbers, leading to an explosion in the size of cities, especially in the north of England. Life in the new industrial cities, such as Manchester and Glasgow, was grim. Migrants to the booming cities found expensive, hastily constructed, overcrowded apartments and inadequate sanitary systems. Infant mortality, disease, malnutrition, and accidents took such a high toll in human life that life expectancy was only around twenty-five to twenty-seven years, some fifteen years less than the national average.[12] Perhaps the most shocking evidence of the impact of the Industrial Revolution on living standards is the finding that child mortality levels rose after 1825, especially in industrial areas.

Another way to consider the workers' standard of living is to look at the goods they purchased. Such evidence is somewhat contradictory, but generally suggestive of stagnant or declining living standards until the middle of the nineteenth century. One important area of improvement was in the consumption of cotton goods, which became much cheaper and could be enjoyed by all classes. Now millions of poor people could afford to wear cotton slips and underpants as well as cotton dresses and shirts. However, in other areas, food in particular, the modest growth in factory wages was not enough to compensate for rising prices.

From the 1840s onward, matters improved considerably as wages made substantial gains and the prices of many goods dropped. A greater variety of foods became available, including the first canned goods. Some of the most important advances were in medicine. Smallpox vaccination became routine, and surgeons began to use anesthesia in the late 1840s. By 1850 trains had revolutionized transportation for the masses, while the telegraph made instant communication possible for the first time in human history. In addition, gaslights greatly expanded the possibilities of nighttime activity. Gas lighting is one of the most important examples of a direct relationship between the scientific advances of the eighteenth century—in this case, chemistry—and the development of new technologies of the Industrial Revolution.

More difficult to measure than real wages or life expectancy was the impact of the Industrial Revolution on community and social values. As young men and women migrated away from their villages to seek employment in urban factories, many close-knit rural communities were destroyed. Village social and cultural traditions disappeared without new generations to carry them on. Although many young people formed new friendships and appreciated the freedoms of urban life, they also suffered from the loneliness of life in the anonymous city. The loss of skills and work autonomy, along with the loss of community, must be included in the assessment of the Industrial Revolution's effect on the living conditions of workers.

Relations Between Capital and Labor

Focus Question	How did the changes brought about by the Industrial Revolution lead to new social classes, and how did people respond to the new structure?

In Great Britain, industrial development led to the creation of new social groups and intensified long-standing conflicts between capital and labor. A new class of factory owners and industrial capitalists arose. These men and women and their families strengthened the wealth and size of the middle class, which had previously been made up mainly of merchants and professional people. The demands of modern industry regularly brought the interests of the middle-class industrialists into conflict with those of the people who worked for them—the working class. As observers took notice of these changes, they raised new questions about how industrialization affected social relationships. Meanwhile, enslaved labor in European colonies contributed to the industrialization process in multiple ways.

The New Class of Factory Owners

Early industrialists operated in a highly competitive economic system. As the careers of James Watt and Fritz Harkort illustrate, there were countless production problems, and success and large profits were by no means certain. Manufacturers therefore waged a constant battle to cut their production costs and stay afloat. Much of the profit had to go back into the business for new and better machinery.

Most early industrialists drew upon their families and friends for labor and capital, but they came from a variety of backgrounds. Many, such as Harkort, were from well-established families with rich networks of contacts and support. Others, such as Watt and Cockerill, were of modest means, especially in the early days. Artisans and skilled workers of exceptional ability had unparalleled opportunities. Members of ethnic and religious groups who had been discriminated against jumped at the new chances and often helped each other. Scots, Quakers, and other Protestant dissenters were tremendously important in Britain; Protestants and Jews dominated banking in Catholic France. Many of the industrialists were newly rich, and, not surprisingly, they were very proud and self-satisfied.

As factories and firms grew larger, opportunities declined, at least in well-developed industries. It became considerably harder for a gifted but poor young mechanic to start a small enterprise and end up as a wealthy manufacturer. Formal education became more important for young men as a means of success and advancement, but studies at the advanced level were expensive. In Britain by 1830 and in France and Germany by 1860, leading industrialists were more likely to have inherited their well-established enterprises, and they were financially much more secure than their struggling parents had been. They also had a greater sense of class-consciousness; they were fully aware that ongoing industrial development had widened the gap between themselves and their workers.

Just like working-class women, the wives and daughters of successful business-men found fewer opportunities for active participation in Europe's increasingly complex business world. Rather than contributing as vital partners in a family-owned enterprise, as so many middle-class women had done, these women were increasingly valued for their ladylike gentility. By 1850 some influential women writers and most businessmen assumed that middle-class wives and daughters should avoid work in offices and factories. Rather, a middle-class lady was expected to concentrate on her proper role as wife and mother, preferably in an elegant residential area far removed from ruthless commerce and the volatile working class.

Responses to Industrialization

From the beginning, the British Industrial Revolution had its critics. Among the first were the Romantic poets. William Blake (1757–1827) called the early factories "satanic mills" and protested against the hard life of the London poor. William Wordsworth (1770–1850) lamented the destruction of the rural way of life and the pollution of the land and water. Some handicraft workers — notably the **Luddites**, who attacked factories in northern England in 1811 and later — smashed the new machines, which they believed were putting them out of work. Doctors and reformers wrote of problems in the factories and new towns, while Malthus and Ricardo concluded that workers would earn only enough to stay alive.

This pessimistic view was accepted and reinforced by Friedrich Engels (1820–1895), the future revolutionary and colleague of Karl Marx (see Chapter 21). After studying conditions in northern England, this young son of a wealthy Prussian cotton manufacturer published in 1844 *The Condition of the Working Class in England*, a blistering indictment of the capitalist classes. "At the bar of world opinion," he wrote, "I charge the English middle classes with mass murder, wholesale robbery, and all the other crimes in the calendar." The new poverty of industrial workers was worse than

Luddite Rioters
Named after a mythic leader, "General Ludd," the Luddite riots began in 1811 in Nottinghamshire and quickly spread to manufacturing districts throughout England. Their target was the mechanized looms that led to lower wages, and unemployment among hand-weavers. Machine breaking was quickly declared a capital crime, and a number of Luddites were executed. (*Luddite Rioters*, 19th century English engraving/ Private Collection/Bridgeman Images)

the old poverty of cottage workers and agricultural laborers, according to Engels. The culprit was industrial capitalism, with its relentless competition and constant technical change. Engels's extremely influential charge of capitalist exploitation and increasing worker poverty was embellished by Marx and later socialists (see Chapter 21).

Analysis of industrial capitalism, often combined with reflections on the French Revolution, led to the development of a new overarching interpretation—a new paradigm—regarding social relationships. Briefly, this paradigm argued that individuals were members of separate classes based on their relationship to the means of production, that is, the machines and factories that dominated the new economy. As owners of expensive industrial machinery and as dependent laborers in their factories, the two main groups of society had separate and conflicting interests. Accordingly, the comfortable, well-educated "public" of the eighteenth century came increasingly to be defined as the middle class ("middle" because they were beneath the small group of aristocracy at the top of society who claimed to be above industrial activity), and the "people" gradually began to perceive themselves as composing a modern working class. And if the new class interpretation was more of a simplification than a fundamental truth for some critics, it appealed to many because it seemed to explain what was happening. Therefore, conflicting classes existed, in part, because many individuals came to believe they existed and developed an awareness that they belonged to a particular social class—what Karl Marx called **class-consciousness**.

Meanwhile, other observers believed that conditions were improving for the working people. In his 1835 study of the cotton industry, Andrew Ure (yoo-RAY) wrote that conditions in most factories were not harsh and were even quite good. Edwin Chadwick, a government official well acquainted with the problems of the working population, concluded that the "whole mass of the laboring community" was increasingly able "to buy more of the necessities and minor luxuries of life."[13] Nevertheless, those who thought—correctly—that conditions were getting worse for working people were probably in the majority.

The Early British Labor Movement

Not everyone worked in large factories and coal mines during the Industrial Revolution. In 1850 more British people still worked on farms than in any other single occupation, although rural communities were suffering from outward migration. The second-largest occupation was domestic service, with more than 1 million household servants, 90 percent of whom were women. Thus many old, familiar jobs outside industry lived on and provided alternatives to industrial labor.

Within industry itself, the pattern of artisans working with hand tools in small shops remained unchanged in many trades, even as others were revolutionized by technological change. For example, the British iron industry was completely dominated by large-scale capitalist firms by 1850. Many large ironworks had more than one thousand people on their payrolls. Yet the firms that fashioned iron into small metal goods, such as tools, tableware, and toys, employed on average fewer than ten wage workers who used handicraft skills. The survival of small workshops gave many workers an alternative to factory employment.

Working-class solidarity and class-consciousness developed both in small workshops and in large factories. In the northern factory districts, anticapitalist sentiments were frequent by the 1820s. Commenting in 1825 on a strike in the woolen center of Bradford and the support it had gathered from other regions, one newspaper claimed with pride that "it is all the workers of England against a few masters of Bradford."[14] Even in trades that did not undergo mechanization, unemployment and stagnant wages contributed to class awareness.

Such sentiments ran contrary to the liberal tenets of economic freedom championed by eighteenth-century thinkers like Adam Smith. Liberal economic principles were embraced by statesmen and middle-class business owners in the late eighteenth century and continued to gather strength in the early nineteenth century. In 1799 Parliament passed the **Combination Acts**, which outlawed unions and strikes. In 1813 and 1814 Parliament repealed an old law regulating the wages of artisans and the conditions of apprenticeship. As a result of these and other measures, certain skilled artisan workers, such as bootmakers and high-quality tailors, found aggressive capitalists ignoring traditional work rules and trying to flood their trades with unorganized women workers and children to beat down wages.

The capitalist attack on artisan guilds and work rules was bitterly resented by many craftworkers, who subsequently played an important part in Great Britain and in other countries in gradually building a modern labor movement. The Combination Acts were widely disregarded by workers. Printers, papermakers, carpenters, tailors, and other such craftsmen continued to take collective action, and societies of skilled factory workers also organized unions in defiance of the law. Unions sought to control the number of skilled workers, to limit apprenticeship to members' own children, and to bargain with owners over wages.

They were not afraid to strike; there was, for example, a general strike of adult cotton spinners in Manchester in 1810. In the face of widespread union activity, Parliament repealed the Combination Acts in 1824, and unions were tolerated, though not fully accepted, after 1825.

The next stage in the development of the British trade-union movement was the attempt to create a single large national union. This effort was led not so much by working people as by social reformers such as Robert Owen. Owen, a self-made cotton manufacturer, had pioneered in industrial relations by combining firm discipline with concern for the health, safety, and hours of his workers. After 1815 he experimented with cooperative and socialist communities, including one at New Harmony, Indiana. Then in 1834 Owen was involved in the organization of one of the largest and most visionary of the early national unions, the Grand National Consolidated Trades Union.

When Owen's and other ambitious schemes collapsed, the British labor movement moved once again after 1851 in the direction of craft unions. The most famous of these was the Amalgamated Society of Engineers, which represented skilled machinists. These unions won real benefits for members by fairly conservative means and thus became an accepted part of the industrial scene.

British workers also engaged in direct political activity in defense of their interests. After the collapse of Owen's national trade union, many working people went into the Chartist movement, which sought political democracy. The key Chartist demand — that all men be given the right to vote — became the great hope of millions of common people. Workers were also active in campaigns to limit the workday in factories to ten hours and to permit duty-free importation of wheat into Great Britain to secure cheap bread. Thus working people developed a sense of their own identity and played an active role in shaping the new industrial system. They were neither helpless victims nor passive beneficiaries.

The Impact of Slavery

Another mass labor force of the Industrial Revolution was composed of the millions of enslaved men, women, and children who toiled in European colonies in the Caribbean and in North and South America. Historians have long debated the extent to which revenue from slavery contributed to Britain's achievements in the Industrial Revolution.

Most now agree that profits from colonial plantations and slave trading were a small portion of British national income in the eighteenth century and were probably more often invested in land than in industry. Nevertheless, the impact of slavery on Britain's economy was much broader than its direct profits alone. In the mid-eighteenth century the need for items to exchange for colonial cotton, sugar, tobacco, and slaves stimulated demand for British manufactured goods in the Caribbean, North America, and West Africa. Britain's dominance in the slave trade also led to the development of finance and credit institutions that helped early industrialists obtain capital for their businesses. Investments in canals, roads, and railroads made possible by profits from colonial trade provided the necessary infrastructure to move raw materials and products of the factory system.

The British Parliament abolished the slave trade in 1807 and freed all slaves in British territories in 1833, but by 1850 most of the cotton processed by British mills was supplied by the labor of enslaved people in the southern United States. Thus the Industrial Revolution was deeply entangled with the Atlantic world and the misery of slavery.

NOTES

1. N. F. R. Crafts, *British Economic Growth During the Industrial Revolution* (Oxford: Oxford University Press, 1985), p. 32.
2. Robert C. Allen, *The British Industrial Revolution in Global Perspective* (Cambridge: Cambridge University Press, 2009), pp. 1–2.
3. P. Bairoch, "International Industrialization Levels from 1750 to 1980," *Journal of European Economic History* 11 (Spring 1982): 269–333.
4. Quoted in J. Bowditch and C. Ramsland, eds., *Voices of the Industrial Revolution* (Ann Arbor: University of Michigan Press, 1961), p. 55, from the fourth edition of Thomas Malthus, *Essay on the Principle of Population* (1807).
5. Quoted in Emma Griffin, *A Short History of the British Industrial Revolution* (Basingstoke, U.K.: Palgrave Macmillan, 2010), p. 126.
6. Quoted in E. R. Pike, *"Hard Times": Human Documents of the Industrial Revolution* (New York: Praeger, 1966), p. 109.

7. See especially J. Brenner and M. Rama, "Rethinking Women's Oppression," *New Left Review* 144 (March–April 1984): 33–71, and sources cited there.

8. J. Humphries, ". . . 'The Most Free from Objection' . . . The Sexual Division of Labor and Women's Work in Nineteenth-Century England," *Journal of Economic History* 47 (December 1987): 941; Pike, "*Hard Times*," p. 266.

9. Quoted in Pike, "*Hard Times*," p. 208.

10. Joel Mokyr, *The Enlightened Economy: An Economic History of Britain, 1700–1850* (New Haven, Conn.: Yale University Press, 2009), pp. 460–461.

11. Hans-Joachim Voth, *Time and Work in England, 1750–1830* (Oxford: Oxford University Press, 2000), pp. 118–133, 268–270.

12. Mokyr, *The Enlightened Economy*, p. 455.

13. Quoted in W. A. Hayek, ed., *Capitalism and the Historians* (Chicago: University of Chicago Press, 1954), p. 126.

14. Quoted in D. Geary, ed., *Labour and Socialist Movements in Europe Before 1914* (Oxford: Berg, 1989), p. 29.

LOOKING BACK LOOKING AHEAD

The Industrial Revolution was a long process of economic innovation and growth occurring first in Britain around 1780 and spreading to the European continent after 1815. The development of machines powered first by water and then by steam allowed for a tremendous growth in productivity, which enabled Britain to assume the lead in the world's production of industrial goods. Industrialization fundamentally changed the social landscape of European countries, creating a new elite of wealthy manufacturers and a vast working class of urban wage laborers whose living conditions remained grim until the mid-nineteenth century.

One popular idea in the 1830s, first developed by a French economist, was that Britain's late-eighteenth-century "industrial revolution" paralleled the political events in France during the French Revolution. One revolution was economic, while the other was political; one was ongoing and successful, while the other had failed and come to a definite end in 1815, when Europe's conservative monarchs defeated Napoleon and restored the French kings of the Old Regime.

In fact, in 1815 the French Revolution, like the Industrial Revolution, was an unfinished revolution. Just as Britain was in the midst of its economic transformation and the states of northwestern Europe had only begun industrialization, so too after 1815 were the political conflicts and ideologies of revolutionary France still very much alive. The French Revolution had opened the era of modern political life not just in France but across Europe. It had brought into existence many of the political ideologies that would interact with the social and economic forces of industrialization to refashion Europe and create a new urban society. Moreover, in 1815 the unfinished French Revolution carried the very real possibility of renewed political upheaval. This possibility, which conservatives feared and radicals longed for, would become dramatic reality in 1848, when political revolutions swept across Europe like a whirlwind.

MAKE CONNECTIONS

Think about the larger developments and continuities within and across chapters.

1. Why did Great Britain take the lead in industrialization, and when did other countries begin to adopt the new techniques and organization of production?
2. How did the achievements in agriculture and rural industry of the late seventeenth and eighteenth centuries (Chapter 17) pave the way for the Industrial Revolution of the late eighteenth century?
3. How would you compare the legacy of the political revolutions of the late eighteenth century (Chapter 19) with that of the Industrial Revolution? Which seems to you to have created the most important changes, and why?

Chapter Review

IDENTIFY KEY TERMS

Identify and explain the significance of each item below.

Industrial Revolution (p. 623)

spinning jenny (p. 625)

water frame (p. 625)

steam engines (p. 628)

Rocket (p. 629)

Crystal Palace (p. 630)

iron law of wages (p. 631)

tariff protection (p. 635)

Factory Acts (p. 640)

separate spheres (p. 641)

Mines Act of 1842 (p. 642)

Luddites (p. 646)

class-consciousness (p. 647)

Combination Acts (p. 648)

REVIEW THE MAIN IDEAS

Answer the focus questions from each section of the chapter.

1. Why did the Industrial Revolution begin in Britain, and how did it develop between 1780 and 1850? (p. 622)
2. How did countries in Europe and around the world respond to the challenge of industrialization? (p. 631)
3. How did work evolve during the Industrial Revolution, and how did daily life change for working people? (p. 638)
4. How did the changes brought about by the Industrial Revolution lead to new social classes, and how did people respond to the new structure? (p. 645)

CHRONOLOGY

ca. 1765	Hargreaves invents spinning jenny; Arkwright creates water frame
1769	Watt patents modern steam engine
ca. 1780–1850	Industrial Revolution; population boom in Britain
1799	Combination Acts passed in England
1802–1833	Series of Factory Acts passed by British government to limit the workday of child laborers and set minimum hygiene and safety requirements
1805	Egypt begins process of modernization
1810	Strike of Manchester cotton spinners
ca. 1815	Western European countries seek to adopt British industrial methods
1824	Combination Acts repealed
1829	Stephenson's *Rocket*, an early locomotive
1830s	Industrial banks in Belgium
1834	*Zollverein* erected among most German states
1842	Mines Act passed in Britain
1844	Engels, *The Condition of the Working Class in England*
1850s	Japan begins to adopt Western technologies; industrial gap widens between the West and the rest of the world
1851	Great Exhibition held at Crystal Palace in London
1860s	Germany and the United States begin to rapidly industrialize

21

Ideologies and Upheavals

1815–1850

THE MOMENTOUS ECONOMIC AND POLITICAL TRANSFORMATION of modern times that began in the late eighteenth century with the "unfinished" revolutions—the Industrial Revolution in England and the political revolution in France—would play out with unpredictable consequences in the first half of the nineteenth century. Attempts to halt the spread of the progressive forces associated with the French Revolution led first to a reassertion of conservative political control in continental Europe. Following the leadership of Austrian foreign minister Klemens von Metternich, the aristocratic leaders of the Great Powers sought to stamp out the spread of liberal and democratic reforms.

The political and cultural innovations made possible by the unfinished revolutions, however, proved difficult to contain. In politics, powerful new ideologies— liberalism, nationalism, and socialism—emerged to oppose Metternich's revitalized conservatism. In literature, art, and music, Romanticism—an intellectual and artistic movement that challenged the certainties of the Enlightenment and fed the growth of popular nationalism—captured the intensity of the era. A successful revolution in Greece, liberal reform in Great Britain, and popular unrest in France gave voice to ordinary people's desire for political and social change. All these movements helped launch the great wave of revolutions that swept across Europe in 1848, and the dramatic results would have a lasting impact on the shape of Western civilization.

The Aftermath of the Napoleonic Wars

Focus Question	How was peace restored and maintained after 1815?

The eventual eruption of revolutionary political forces in 1848 was by no means predictable as the Napoleonic era ended. Quite the contrary. After finally defeating Napoleon, the conservative, aristocratic monarchies of Russia, Prussia, Austria, and Great Britain—known as the Quadruple Alliance—reaffirmed their determination to hold France in line. Even before Napoleon's final defeat, the allies had agreed to meet to fashion a general peace accord in 1814 at the Congress of Vienna, where they faced a great challenge: how could they construct a lasting settlement that would not sow the seeds of another war? By carefully managing the balance of power, redrawing the boundaries of formerly French-held territories, and embracing conservative restoration, they brokered an agreement that contributed to fifty years of peace in Europe (Map 21.1).

The European Balance of Power

Elite representatives of the Quadruple Alliance (plus a representative of the restored Bourbon monarch of France)—including Tsar Alexander I of Russia, King Friedrich Wilhelm III of Prussia, Emperor Franz II of Austria, and their foreign ministers—met to fashion the peace at the **Congress of Vienna** from September 1814 to June 1815. A host of delegates from the smaller European states also attended the conference and offered minor assistance.

Such a face-to-face meeting of kings and emperors was very rare at the time. Professional ambassadors and court representatives had typically conducted state-to-state negotiations; now national leaders engaged in what we would today call "summit diplomacy." Participants at the congress enjoyed any number of festivities associated with aristocratic court culture, including formal receptions, military parades and reviews, sumptuous dinner parties, fancy ballroom dances, fireworks displays, and operatic and theatrical productions. Participation in Vienna's vibrant salon culture offered further opportunities to socialize, discuss current issues, and make informal deals that could be confirmed at the conference table. All the while, newspapers, pamphlets, periodicals, and satiric cartoons kept readers across Europe up-to-date on social events as well as the latest political developments and agreements. The conference thus marked an important transitional moment in Western history. The salon society and public sphere of the seventeenth-century Enlightenment (see Chapter 16) gradually shifted toward nineteenth-century cultures of publicity and public opinion informed by more modern mass-media campaigns.[1]

The allied powers were concerned first and foremost with the defeated enemy, France. Self-interest and traditional ideas about the balance of power motivated allied moderation toward the former foe. To Klemens von Metternich (MEH-tuhr-nihk) and Robert Castlereagh (KA-suhl-ray), the foreign ministers of Austria and Great Britain, the balance of power meant an international equilibrium of political and

MAP 21.1 Europe in 1815

In 1815 Europe contained many different states, but after the defeat of Napoleon international politics was dominated by the five Great Powers: Russia, Prussia, Austria, Great Britain, and France. (The number rises to six if one includes the Ottoman Empire.) At the Congress of Vienna, the Great Powers redrew the map of Europe.

military forces that would discourage aggression by any combination of states or, worse, the domination of Europe by any single state. Their French negotiating partner, the skillful and cynical diplomat Charles Talleyrand, concurred.

The allies offered France lenient terms after Napoleon's abdication. They agreed to restore the Bourbon king to the French throne. The first Treaty of Paris, signed before the conference (and before Napoleon escaped from Elba and attacked the Bourbon regime), gave France the boundaries it had possessed in 1792, which were larger than those of 1789. In addition, France did not have to pay war reparations. Thus the victorious powers avoided provoking a spirit of victimization and desire for revenge in the defeated country.

Congress of Vienna   The Congress of Vienna was renowned for its intense diplomatic deal making, resulting in the Treaty of Vienna, the last page of which was signed and sealed in 1815 by the representatives of the various European states attending the conference. The congress won additional notoriety for its ostentatious parades, parties, and dance balls. The painting here portrays a mounted group of European royalty, led by the Prussian emperor and the Russian tsar, in a flamboyant parade designed to celebrate Napoleon's defeat the year before. Onlookers toast the victorious monarchs. The display of flags, weapons, and heraldic emblems symbolizes the unity of Europe's Great Powers, while the long tables in the background suggest the extent of the festivities. Such images were widely distributed to engender popular support for the conservative program. (*The Celebration of the Prater in the Presence of the Reigning Monarchs*, 1815/Collection of the Palaces Artstetten and Luberegg/akg-image)

The Quadruple Alliance combined leniency with strong defensive measures designed to raise barriers against the possibility of renewed French aggression. Belgium and Holland—incorporated into the French empire under Napoleon—were united under an enlarged and independent "Kingdom of the Netherlands" capable of opposing French expansion to the north. The German-speaking lands on France's eastern border, also taken by Napoleon (see Chapter 19), were returned to Prussia. As a famous German anthem put it, the expanded Prussia would now stand as the "watch on the Rhine" against French attack. In addition, the allies reorganized the German-speaking territories of central Europe. A new German Confederation, a loose association of German-speaking states based on Napoleon's reorganization of the territory dominated by Prussia and Austria, replaced the roughly three hundred principalities, free cities, and dynastic states of the Holy Roman Empire with just thirty-eight German states (see Map 21.1).

Austria, Britain, Prussia, and Russia furthermore used the balance of power to settle their own potentially dangerous disputes. The victors generally agreed that each of them should receive compensation in the form of territory for their victory over the French. Great Britain had already won colonies and strategic outposts during the long wars. Austria gave up territories in Belgium and southern Germany but expanded greatly elsewhere, taking the rich provinces of Venetia and Lombardy in northern Italy as well as former Polish possessions and new lands on the eastern coast of the Adriatic.

Russian and Prussian claims for territorial expansion were more contentious. When Russia had pushed Napoleon out of central Europe, its armies had expanded its control over Polish territories. Tsar Alexander I wished to make Russian rule permanent. But when France, Austria, and Great Britain all argued for limits on Russian gains, the tsar ceded territories back to Prussia and accepted a smaller Polish kingdom. Prussian claims on the state of Saxony, a wealthy kingdom in the German Confederation, were particularly contentious. The Saxon king had supported Napoleon to the bitter end; now Wilhelm III wanted to incorporate Saxony into Prussia. Under pressure, he agreed to partition the state, leaving an independent Saxony in place, a change that posed no real threat to its Great Power neighbors but soothed their fears of Prussian expansionism. These territorial changes and compromises fell very much within the framework of balance-of-power ideology.

Unfortunately for France, in February 1815 Napoleon suddenly escaped from his "comic kingdom" on the island of Elba and re-ignited his wars of expansion for a brief time (see Chapter 19). Yet the second Treaty of Paris, concluded in November 1815 after Napoleon's final defeat at Waterloo, was still relatively moderate toward France. The elderly Louis XVIII was restored to his throne for a second time. France lost only a little territory, had to pay an indemnity of 700 million francs, and was required to support a large army of occupation for five years. The rest of the settlement concluded at the Congress of Vienna was left intact. The members of the Quadruple Alliance, however, did agree to meet periodically to discuss their common interests and to consider appropriate measures for the maintenance of peace in Europe. This agreement marked the beginning of the European "Congress System," which lasted long into the nineteenth century and settled many international crises peacefully, through international conferences or "congresses" and balance-of-power diplomacy.

Metternich and Conservatism

The political ideals of conservatism, often associated with Austrian foreign minister Prince Klemens von Metternich (1773–1859), dominated Great Power discussions at the Congress of Vienna. Metternich's determined defense of the monarchical status quo made him a villain in the eyes of most progressive, liberal thinkers of the nineteenth century. Yet rather than denounce his politics, we can try to understand the general conservatism he represented. Born into the landed nobility of the Rhineland, Metternich was an internationally oriented aristocrat who made a brilliant diplomatic career. Austrian foreign minister from 1809 to 1848, the cosmopolitan and conservative Metternich had a pessimistic view of human nature, which he believed was ever prone to error, excess, and self-serving behavior. The disruptive events of the French Revolution and the Napoleonic Wars confirmed these views, and Metternich's conservatism would emerge as a powerful new political ideological force in response to the revolutionary age.

Metternich firmly believed that liberalism, as embodied in revolutionary America and France, bore the responsibility for the untold bloodshed and suffering caused by twenty-five years of war. Like Edmund Burke (see Chapter 19) and other conservatives, Metternich blamed liberal middle-class revolutionaries for stirring up the lower classes. Authoritarian, aristocratic government, he concluded, was necessary to protect society from the baser elements of human behavior, which were easily released in a democratic system. Organized religion was another pillar of strong government. Metternich despised the anticlericalism of the Enlightenment and the French Revolution and maintained that Christian morality was a vital bulwark against radical change.

Metternich defended his elite class and its rights and privileges with a clear conscience. The church and nobility were among Europe's most ancient and valuable institutions, and conservatives regarded tradition as the basic foundation of human society.

The threat of liberalism appeared doubly dangerous to Metternich because it generally went with aspirations for national independence. Liberals believed that each people, each national group, had a right to establish its own independent government and fulfill its own destiny. Though Metternich and other conservatives might accept some form of constitutional monarchy, the idea of national self-determination under liberal constitutional government was repellent because it threatened to revolutionize central Europe and destroy the Austrian Empire.

After centuries of war, royal intermarriage, and territorial expansion, the vast Austrian Empire of the Habsburgs included many regions and peoples within its borders (Map 21.2). The numerous kingdoms, duchies, and principalities under Habsburg rule included the lands of the Austrian crown, the Kingdom of Hungary, the Kingdom of Bohemia, and the Kingdom of Lombardy-Venetia, to name just the largest. Noble houses in these territories maintained some control, but ultimate authority rested with the Habsburg emperor. The peoples of the Austrian Empire spoke at least eleven different languages and observed vastly different customs; an astonishing variety of different ethnic groups mingled in the same provinces and the same villages. They included about 8 million Germans, about one-fourth of the population. Some 5.5 million Magyars (Hungarians), 5 million Italians, 4 million Czechs, and 2 million Poles lived alongside each other in the imperial state, as did smaller groups of Slovenes, Croats, Serbs, Romanians, Jews, and Armenians.[2] The various Slavic groups, together with the Italians and the Romanians, lived in widely scattered regions, yet they outnumbered the politically dominant Germans and Hungarians (see Map 21.2).

The multiethnic empire Metternich served had strengths and weaknesses. A large population and vast territories gave the empire economic and military clout, but its potentially dissatisfied ethnicities and nationalities undermined political unity. In these circumstances, Metternich and the Habsburg dynasty virtually had to oppose

MAP 21.2 Peoples of the Habsburg Monarchy, 1815
The old dynastic state ruled by the Habsburg monarchy was a patchwork of nationalities and ethnic groups, in which territorial borders barely reflected the diversity of where different peoples actually lived. Note especially the widely scattered pockets of Germans and Hungarians. How do you think this ethnic diversity might have led to the rise of national independence movements in the Austrian Empire?

liberalism and nationalism—if Austria was to remain intact and powerful, it could hardly accommodate ideologies that demanded national independence.

On the Austrian Empire's borders, the Russian Empire and, to a lesser extent, the Ottoman Empire supported and echoed Metternich's efforts to hold back liberalism and nationalism. Bitter enemies, the far-flung Russian and Ottoman Empires were both absolutist states with powerful armies and long traditions of expansion and conquest. Because of those conquests, both were also multinational empires with many peoples, languages, and religions, but in each case most of the ruling elite came from the dominant ethnic group—the Orthodox Christian Russians of central and northern Russia and the Muslim Ottoman Turks of Anatolia (much of modern Turkey). After 1815 both of these multinational absolutist states worked to preserve their respective traditional conservative orders. Only after 1840 did each in turn experience a profound crisis and embark on a program of fundamental reform and modernization, as we shall see in Chapter 23.

Repressing the Revolutionary Spirit

Conservative political ideologies had important practical consequences. Under Metternich's leadership, Austria, Prussia, and Russia embarked on a decades-long crusade against the liberties and civil rights associated with the French and American Revolutions. The first step was the formation in September 1815 of the **Holy Alliance** by Austria, Prussia, and Russia. First proposed by Russia's Alexander I, the alliance worked to repress reformist and revolutionary movements and stifle desires for national independence across Europe.

The conservative restoration first brought its collective power to bear on southern Europe. In 1820 revolutionaries successfully forced the kings of Spain and the southern Italian Kingdom of the Two Sicilies to establish constitutional monarchies, with press freedoms, universal male suffrage, and other liberal reforms. Metternich was horrified; revolution was rising once again. Calling a conference at Troppau in Austria, he and Alexander I proclaimed the principle of active intervention to maintain all autocratic regimes whenever they were threatened. Austrian forces then marched into Naples in 1821 and restored the autocratic power of Ferdinand I in the Two Sicilies. A French invasion of Spain in 1823 likewise returned power to the king there.

The conservative policies of Metternich and the Holy Alliance limited reform not only in Austria and the Italian peninsula but also in the entire German Confederation. The states in the German Confederation retained independence, and though ambassadors from each met in a Confederation Diet, or assembly, it had little real political power. When liberal reformers and university students began to protest for the national unification of the German states, the Austrian and Prussian leadership used the diet to issue and enforce the infamous **Karlsbad Decrees** in 1819. These decrees required the German states to outlaw liberal political organizations, police their universities and newspapers, and establish a permanent committee with spies and informers to clamp down on liberal or radical reformers.

The forces of reaction squelched reform in Russia as well. In St. Petersburg in December 1825, a group of about three thousand army officers inspired by liberal ideals staged a protest against the new tsar, Nicholas I. Troops loyal to Nicholas I surrounded and assaulted the group with gunfire, cavalry, and cannon, leaving some sixty men dead; the surviving leaders were publicly hanged, and the rest sent to exile in Siberia. Through censorship, military might, secret police, imprisonment, and execution, conservative regimes in central Europe used the powers of the state to repress liberal reform wherever possible.

Limits to Conservative Power and Revolution in South America

Metternich liked to call himself "the chief Minister of Police in Europe," and the members of the Holy Alliance continually battled liberal political change.[3] Metternich's system proved quite effective in central Europe, at least until 1848, but the monarchists failed to stop dynastic change in France in 1830 or prevent Belgium from winning independence from the Netherlands in 1831.

The most dramatic challenge to conservative power occurred not in Europe, but overseas in South America. In the 1820s South American elites rose up and broke away from the Spanish crown and established a number of new republics based at first on liberal Enlightenment ideals. The leaders of the revolutions were primarily wealthy Creoles, direct descendants of Spanish parents born in the Americas. The well-established and powerful Creoles — only about 5 percent of the population — resented the political and economic control of an even smaller elite minority of *peninsulares*, people born in Spain who lived in and ruled the colonies. The vast majority of the population, composed of "mestizos" and "mulattos" (people of ethnically mixed heritage), enslaved and freed Africans, and native indigenous peoples, languished at the bottom of the social pyramid.

By the late 1700s the Creoles had begun to question Spanish policy and even the necessity of further colonial rule. The spark for revolt came during the Napoleonic Wars, when the French occupation of Spain in 1808 weakened the power of the auto-cratic Spanish crown and the Napoleonic rhetoric of rights inspired revolutionaries. Yet the Creoles hesitated, worried that open revolt might upend the social pyramid or even lead to a slave revolution as in Haiti (see Chapter 19).

The South American revolutions thus began from below, with spontaneous upris-ings by subordinated peoples of color. Creole leaders quickly took control of a struggle that would prove to be more prolonged and violent than the American Revolution, with outcomes less clear. In the north, the competent general Simón Bolívar — the Latin American equivalent of George Washington — defeated Spanish forces and established a short-lived "Gran Colombia," which lasted from 1819 to 1830. Bolívar, the "people's liberator," dreamed of establishing a federation of South American states, modeled on the United States. To the south, José de San Martín, a liberal-minded military commander, successfully threw off Spanish control by 1825.

Dreams of South American federation and unity proved difficult to realize. By 1830 the large northern state established by Bolívar had fractured, and by 1840 the borders of the new nations looked much like the map of Latin America today. Most of the new states initially received liberal constitutions, but these were difficult to imple-ment in lands where the vast majority of people had no experience with constitutional rule and women and the great underclass of non-Creoles were not allowed to vote. Experiments with liberal constitutions soon gave way to a new political system con-trolled by *caudillos* (cow-DEE-yohs), or strong men, sometimes labeled warlords. Often former Creoles, the caudillos ruled limited territories on the basis of military strength, family patronage, and populist politics. The South American revolutions had failed to establish lasting constitutional republics, but they did demonstrate the revo-lutionary potential of liberal ideals and the limits on conservative control.

The Spread of Radical Ideas

Focus Question	What new ideologies emerged to challenge conservatism?

In the years following the peace settlement of 1815, intellectuals and social observers sought to harness the radical ideas of the revolutionary age to new political movements. Many rejected conservatism, with its stress on tradition, a hereditary monarchy, a privileged landowning aristocracy, and an official state church. Often inspired by liberties championed during the French Revolution, radical thinkers developed and refined alternative ideologies — or political philosophies — and tried to convince people to follow them. In so doing, they helped articulate the basic political ideals that continue to shape Western society today.

Liberalism and the Middle Class

The principal ideas of **liberalism** — liberty and equality — were by no means defeated in 1815. First realized successfully in the American Revolution and then achieved in part in the French Revolution, liberalism demanded representative government as opposed to autocratic monarchy, and equality before the law for all as opposed to separate classes with separate legal rights. Liberty also meant specific individual freedoms: freedom of the press, freedom of speech, freedom of assembly, freedom of worship, and freedom from arbitrary arrest. Such ideas are still the guiding beliefs in modern democratic states, but in Europe in 1815 only France with Louis XVIII's Constitutional Charter and Great Britain with its Parliament had realized any of the liberal program. Even in those countries, liberalism had only begun to succeed.

Although conservatives still saw liberalism as a profound threat, it had gained a group of powerful adherents: the new upper classes made wealthy through growing industrialization and global commerce. This group promoted the liberal economic doctrine of **laissez faire** (lay-say FEHR), which called for free trade (including relaxation of import/export duties), unrestricted private enterprise, and no government interference in the economy.

As we saw in Chapter 17, Adam Smith posited the idea of economic liberalism and free-market capitalism in 1776 in opposition to mercantilism and its attempt to regulate trade. Smith argued that freely competitive private enterprise would give all citizens a fair and equal opportunity to do what they did best and would result in greater income for everyone, not just the rich. (Smith's form of liberalism is often called "classical liberalism" in the United States, in order to distinguish it sharply from modern American liberalism, which generally favors more government programs to meet social needs and regulate the economy.)

In the first half of the nineteenth century, liberal political ideals became closely associated with narrow class interests. Starting in the 1820s in Britain, business elites enthusiastically embraced laissez-faire policies because they proved immensely profitable, and used liberal ideas to defend their right to do as they wished in their factories. Labor unions were outlawed because, these elites argued, unions restricted free competition and the individual's "right to work." Early-nineteenth-century liberals favored representative government, but they generally wanted property qualifications attached to the right to vote. In practice, this meant limiting the vote to very small numbers of the well-to-do. Workers, peasants, and women, as well as middle-class shopkeepers, clerks, and artisans, did not own the necessary property and thus could not vote.

As liberalism became increasingly identified with upper-class business interests, some opponents of conservatism felt that liberalism did not go nearly far enough. Inspired by memories of the French Revolution and the example of Jacksonian democracy in the young American republic, this group embraced republicanism: an expanded liberal ideology that endorsed universal democratic voting rights, at least for males, and radical equality for all. Republicans were more willing than most liberals to endorse violent upheaval to achieve goals. In addition, republicans might advocate government action to create jobs, redistribute income, and level social differences. As the results of the revolutions of 1830 and 1848 suggest, liberals and radical republicans could join forces against conservatives only up to a point.

The Growing Appeal of Nationalism

Nationalism — destined to have an enormous influence in the modern world — was another radical idea that gained popularity in the years after 1815. The nascent power of nationalism was revealed in the success of the French armies in the revolutionary and Napoleonic wars, when soldiers inspired by patriotic loyalty to the French nation achieved victory after victory (see Chapter 19). Early nationalists found inspiration in the vision of a people united by a common language, a common history and culture, and a common territory. In German-speaking central Europe, defeat by Napoleon's armies had made the vision of a national people united in defense of their "fatherland" particularly attractive.

In the early nineteenth century such national unity was more a dream than a reality as far as most ethnic groups or nationalities were concerned. Local dialects abounded, even in relatively cohesive countries like France, where peasants from nearby villages often failed to understand each other. Moreover, a variety of ethnic groups shared the territory of most states, not just the Austrian, Russian, and Ottoman Empires discussed earlier. Over the course of the nineteenth century, nationalism nonetheless gathered force as a political philosophy. Advancing literacy rates, the establishment of a mass press, the growth of large state bureaucracies, compulsory education, and conscription armies all created a common culture that encouraged ordinary people to take pride in their national heritage.

In multiethnic states, however, nationalism could promote disintegration. Recognizing the power of the "national idea," European nationalists — generally educated, middle-class liberals and intellectuals — sought to turn the cultural unity that they desired into political reality. They believed that every nation, like every citizen, had the right to exist in freedom and to develop its unique character and spirit, and they hoped to make the territory of each people coincide with well-defined borders in an independent nation-state.

This political goal made nationalism explosive, particularly in central and eastern Europe, where different peoples overlapped and intermingled. As discussed, the Austrian, Russian, and Ottoman central states refused to allow national minorities independence. This suppression fomented widespread discontent among nationalists who wanted freedom from oppressive imperial rule. In the many different principalities of the Italian peninsula and the German Confederation, to the contrary, nationalists yearned for national unification across what they saw as divisive and obsolete state borders. Whether they sought independence or unification, before 1850 nationalist movements were fresh, idealistic, and progressive, if not revolutionary.

In recent years historians have tried to understand why the nationalist vision, which typically fit poorly with existing conditions and promised much upheaval, was so successful in the long run. Of fundamental importance in the rise of nationalism was the development of a complex industrial and urban society, which required more sophisticated forms of communication between individuals and groups.[4] The need for improved communication promoted the use of a standardized national language in many areas, creating at least a superficial cultural unity as a standard tongue spread through mass education and the emergence of the popular press. When a minority population was large and concentrated, the nationalist campaign for a standardized language often led the minority group to push for a separate nation-state.

Scholars generally argue that nations are recent creations, the product of a new, self-conscious nationalist ideology. Thus nation-states emerged in the nineteenth century as "imagined communities" that sought to bind millions of strangers together around the abstract concept of an all-embracing national identity. This meant bringing citizens together with emotionally charged symbols and ceremonies, such as independence holidays and patriotic parades. On these occasions the imagined nation of equals might celebrate its most hallowed traditions, which were often recent inventions.[5]

Between 1815 and 1850 most people who believed in nationalism also believed in either liberalism or radical republicanism. They typically shared a deep belief in the creativity and nobility of the people. Liberals and especially republicans, for example, saw the people as the ultimate source of all government. Yet nationally minded liberals and republicans agreed that the benefits of self-government would be possible only if individuals were bonded together by common traditions that transcended local interests and even class differences. Thus in the early nineteenth century the liberty of the individual and the love of a free nation overlapped greatly.

Despite some confidence that a world system based on independent nation-states would promote global harmony, early nationalists eagerly emphasized the differences between peoples and developed a strong sense of "us" versus "them." To this "us-them" outlook, nationalists could all too easily add two highly volatile ingredients: a sense of national mission and a sense of national superiority. As Europe entered an age of increased global interaction, these powerful ideas would lead to aggression and conflict, as powerful nation-states backed by patriotic citizens competed with each other on the international stage.

The Foundations of Modern Socialism

More radical than liberalism or nationalism was **socialism**. Early socialist thinkers were a diverse group with wide-ranging ideas. Yet they shared a sense that the political revolution in France, the growth of industrialization in Britain, and the rise of laissez faire had created a profound spiritual and moral crisis. Modern capitalism, they believed, fomented a selfish individualism that encouraged inequality and split the community into isolated fragments. Society urgently required fundamental change to re-establish cooperation and a new sense of community.

Early socialists felt an intense desire to help the poor, and they preached that the rich and the poor should be more nearly equal economically. To this end, they believed that private property should be strictly regulated by the government, or abolished outright and replaced by state or community ownership. Economic planning, greater social equality, and state regulation of property were the key ideas of early socialism — and have remained central to all socialism since.

One influential group of early socialist advocates became known as the "utopian socialists" because their grand schemes for social improvement ultimately proved unworkable. The Frenchmen Count Henri de Saint-Simon (awn-REE duh san-see-MOHN) (1760–1825) and Charles Fourier (sharl FAWR-ee-ay) (1772–1837), as well as the British industrialist Robert Owen, all founded movements intended to establish model communities that would usher in a new age of happiness and equality.

Saint-Simon's "positivism" optimistically proclaimed the tremendous possibilities of industrial development: "The golden age of the human species . . . is before us!"[6] The key to progress was proper social organization that required the "parasites" — the court, the aristocracy, lawyers, and churchmen — to give way, once and for all, to the "doers" — the leading scientists, engineers, and industrialists. The doers would carefully plan the economy and guide it forward by undertaking vast public works projects and establishing investment banks. Saint-Simon also stressed in highly moralistic terms that every social institution ought to have as its main goal improved conditions for the poor.

After 1830 the utopian critique of capitalism became sharper. Charles Fourier called for the construction of mathematically precise, self-sufficient communities called "phalanxes," each made up of 1,620 people. In the phalanx, all property was owned by the community and used for the common good. Fourier was an early proponent of the total emancipation of women. According to Fourier, under capitalism young single women were shamelessly "sold" to their future husbands for dowries and other financial considerations. Therefore, he called for the abolition of marriage and for sexual freedom and free unions based only on love. The great British utopian Robert Owen, an early promoter of labor unions, likewise envisaged a society organized into socialistic industrial-agricultural communities. Saint-Simon, Fourier, and Owen all had followers who tried to put their ideas into practice. Though these attempts had mostly collapsed by the 1850s, utopian socialist ideas remained an inspiration for future reformers and revolutionaries.

Some socialist thinkers embraced the even more radical ideas of anarchism. In his 1840 pamphlet *What Is Property?* Pierre-Joseph Proudhon (1809–1865), a self-educated printer, famously argued "property is theft!" Property, he claimed, was profit that was stolen from the worker, the source of all wealth. Distrustful of all authority and political systems, Proudhon believed that states should be abolished and that society should be organized in loose associations of working people.

Other early socialists, like Louis Blanc (1811–1882), a sharp-eyed, intelligent journalist, focused on more practical reforms. In his *Organization of Work* (1839), he urged workers to agitate for universal voting rights and take control of the state peacefully. Blanc believed that the government should set up publicly funded workshops and factories to guarantee full employment. The right to work had to become as sacred as any other right.

As industrialization advanced in European cities, working people began to embrace the socialist message. This happened first in France, where workers cherished the memory of the radical phase of the French Revolution and became violently opposed to laissez-faire laws that denied their right to organize in guilds and unions. Developing a sense of class in the process of their protests, workers favored collective action and government intervention in economic life. Thus the aspirations of workers and radical theorists reinforced each other, and a genuine socialist movement emerged in Paris in the 1830s and 1840s.

The Birth of Marxist Socialism

In the 1840s France was the center of socialism, but in the following decades the German intellectual Karl Marx (1818–1883) would weave the diffuse strands of socialist thought into a distinctly modern ideology. Marxist socialism — or **Marxism** — would have a lasting impact on political thought and practice.

The son of a Jewish lawyer who had converted to Lutheranism, the young Marx was a brilliant student. After earning a Ph.D. in philosophy at Humboldt University in Berlin in 1841, he turned to journalism, and his critical articles about the laboring poor caught the attention of the Prussian police. Forced to flee Prussia in 1843, Marx traveled around Europe, promoting socialism and avoiding the authorities. He lived a modest, middle-class life with his wife, Jenny, and their children, often relying on his friend and colleague Friedrich Engels (see Chapter 20) for financial support. After the revolutions of 1848, Marx settled in London, where he spent the rest of his life as an advocate of working-class revolution. *Capital*, his magnum opus, appeared in 1867.

Karl Marx and His Family Active in the revolutions of 1848, Marx fled Germany and eventually settled in London, where he wrote *Capital*, the weighty exposition of his socialist theories. Despite his advocacy of radical revolution, Marx and his wife, Jenny, pictured here with two of their daughters, lived a respectable though modest middle-class life. Standing on the left is Friedrich Engels, an accomplished writer and political theorist who was Marx's long-time friend, financial supporter, and intellectual collaborator. (© Mary Evans Picture Library/Marx Memorial Library/The Image Works)

Marx was a dedicated scholar, and his work united sociology, economics, philosophy, and history in an impressive synthesis. From Scottish and English political economists like Adam Smith and David Ricardo, Marx learned to apply social-scientific analysis to economic problems, though he pushed these liberal ideas in radical directions. Deeply influenced by the utopian socialists, Marx championed ideals of social equality and community. He criticized his socialist predecessors, however, for their fanciful utopian schemes, claiming that his version of "scientific" socialism was rooted in historic law, and therefore realistic. Following German philosophies of idealism associated with Georg Hegel (1770–1831), Marx came to believe that history had patterns and purpose and moved forward in stages toward an ultimate goal.

Bringing these ideas together, Marx argued that class struggle over economic wealth was the great engine of human history. In his view, one class had always exploited the other, and with the advent of modern industry, society was split more clearly than ever before: between the upper class—the **bourgeoisie** (boor-ZHWAH-zee)—and the working class—the **proletariat**. The bourgeoisie, a tiny minority, owned the means of production and grew rich by exploiting the labor of workers. Over time, Marx argued, the proletariat would grow ever larger and ever poorer, and their increasing alienation would lead them to develop a sense of revolutionary class-consciousness. Then, just as the bourgeoisie had triumphed over the feudal aristocracy in the French Revolution, the proletariat would overthrow the bourgeoisie in a violent revolutionary cataclysm. The result would be the end of class struggle and the arrival of communism, a system of radical equality.

Fascinated by the rapid expansion of modern capitalism, Marx based his revolutionary program on an insightful yet critical analysis of economic history. Under feudalism, he wrote, labor had been organized according to long-term contracts of rights and privileges. Under capitalism, to the contrary, labor was a commodity like any other, bought and sold for wages in the free market. The goods workers produced were always worth more than what those workers were paid, and the difference—"surplus value," in Marx's terms—was pocketed by the bourgeoisie in the form of profit.

According to Marx, capitalism was immensely productive but highly exploitative. In a never-ending search for profit, the bourgeoisie would squeeze workers dry and then expand across the globe, until all parts of the world were trapped in capitalist relations of production. Contemporary ideals, such as free trade, private property, and even marriage and Christian morality, were myths that masked and legitimized class exploitation. To many people, Marx's argument that the contradictions inherent in this unequal system would eventually be overcome in a working-class revolution appeared to be the irrefutable capstone of a brilliant interpretation of historical trends.

When Marx and Engels published *The Communist Manifesto* on the eve of the revolutions of 1848, their opening claim that "a spectre is haunting Europe—the spectre of Communism" was highly exaggerated. The Communist movement was in its infancy. Scattered groups of socialists, anarchists, and labor leaders were hardly united around Marxist ideas. But by the time Marx died in 1883, Marxist socialism had profoundly reshaped left-wing radicalism in ways that would inspire revolutionaries around the world for the next one hundred years.

The Romantic Movement

Focus Question	What were the characteristics of the Romantic movement?

The early nineteenth century brought changes to literature and the other arts as well as political ideas. Followers of the new Romantic movement, or Romanticism, revolted against the emphasis on rationality, order, and restraint that characterized the Enlightenment and the controlled style of classicism. Forerunners appeared from about 1750 on, but the movement crystallized fully in the 1790s, primarily in England and Germany. Romanticism gained strength and swept across Europe until the 1840s, when it gradually gave way to Realism.

The Tenets of Romanticism

Like other cultural movements, **Romanticism** was characterized by intellectual diversity. Nonetheless, common parameters stand out. Artists inspired by Romanticism repudiated the emphasis on reason associated with well-known Enlightenment philosophes like Voltaire or Montesquieu (see Chapter 16). Romantics championed instead emotional exuberance, unrestrained imagination, and spontaneity in both art and personal life. Preoccupied with emotional excess, Romantic works explored the awesome power of love and desire and of hatred, guilt, and despair.

Where Enlightenment thinkers applied the scientific method to social issues and cast rosy predictions for future progress, Romantics valued intuition and nostalgia for the past. Where Enlightenment thinkers embraced secularization, Romantics sought the inspiration of religious ecstasy. Where Enlightenment thinkers valued public life and civic affairs, Romantics delved into the supernatural and turned inward, to the hidden recesses of the self. As the Austrian composer Franz Schubert exclaimed in 1824:

> Oh imagination, thou supreme jewel of mankind, thou inexhaustible source from which artists and scholars drink! Oh, rest with us — despite the fact that thou art recognized only by a few — so as to preserve us from that so-called Enlightenment, that ugly skeleton without flesh or blood![7]

Nowhere was the break with Enlightenment classicism more apparent than in Romanticism's general conception of nature. Classicists were not particularly interested in nature. The Romantics, in contrast, were enchanted by stormy seas, untouched forests, and icy arctic wastelands. Nature could be awesome and tempestuous, a source of beauty or spiritual inspiration. Most Romantics saw the growth of modern industry as an ugly, brutal attack on their beloved nature and on venerable traditions. They sought escape — in the unspoiled Lake District of northern England, in exotic North Africa, in an imaginary and idealized Middle Ages.

The study of history became a Romantic obsession. History held the key to a universe now perceived to be organic and dynamic, not mechanical and static, as Enlightenment thinkers had believed. Historical novels like Sir Walter Scott's *Ivanhoe* (1820), a passionate romance set in twelfth-century England, found eager readers among the literate middle classes. Professional historians influenced by Romanticism, such as Jules Michelet, went beyond the standard accounts of great men or famous battles. Michelet's many books on the history of France consciously promoted the growth of national aspirations; by fanning the embers of memory, Michelet encouraged the French people to search the past for their special national destiny.

Romanticism was a lifestyle as well as an intellectual movement. Many early-nineteenth-century Romantics lived lives of tremendous emotional intensity. Obsessive love affairs, duels to the death, madness, strange illnesses, and suicide were not uncommon. Romantic artists typically led bohemian lives, wearing their hair long and uncombed in preference to donning powdered wigs, and rejecting the manners and morals of refined society. Great individualists, the Romantics believed that the full development of one's unique human potential was the supreme purpose in life.

Romantic Literature

Romanticism found its distinctive voice in poetry, as the Enlightenment had in prose. Though Romantic poetry had important forerunners in the German "Storm and Stress" movement of the 1770s and 1780s, its first great poets were English: William Blake, William Wordsworth, Samuel Taylor Coleridge, and Sir Walter Scott were all active by 1800, followed shortly by Lord Byron, Percy Bysshe Shelley, and John Keats.

A towering leader of English Romanticism, William Wordsworth was deeply influenced by Rousseau and the spirit of the early French Revolution. Wordsworth settled in the rural Lake District of England with his sister, Dorothy, and Samuel Taylor Coleridge (1772–1834). In 1798 Wordsworth and Coleridge published their *Lyrical Ballads*, which abandoned flowery classical conventions for the language of ordinary speech and endowed simple subjects with the loftiest majesty. Wordsworth believed that all natural things were sacred, and his poetry often expressed a mystical appreciation of nature:

> To every natural form, rock, fruit or flower
> Even the loose stones that cover the high-way
> I gave a moral life, I saw them feel,
> Or link'd them to some feeling: the great mass
> Lay bedded in a quickening soul, and all
> That I beheld, respired with inward meaning.[8]

Here Wordsworth expressed his love of nature in commonplace forms that a variety of readers could appreciate. The short stanza well illustrates his famous conception of poetry as the "spontaneous overflow of powerful feeling [which] takes its origin from emotion recollected in tranquility."[9]

In France under Napoleon, classicism remained strong and at first inhibited the growth of Romanticism. An early French champion of the new movement, Germaine de Staël (duh STAHL) (1766–1817) urged the French to throw away their worn-out classical models. Her study *On Germany* (1810) extolled the spontaneity and enthusiasm of German writers and thinkers, and it had a powerful impact on the post-1815 generation in France. Between 1820 and 1850 the Romantic impulse broke through in the poetry and prose of Alphonse de Lamartine, Victor Hugo, and George Sand (pseudonym of the woman writer Amandine-Aurore-Lucile Dudevant). Of these, Victor Hugo (1802–1885) became the most well known.

Son of a Napoleonic general, Hugo achieved an amazing range of rhythm, language, and image in his lyric poetry. His powerful novels exemplified the Romantic fascination with fantastic characters, exotic historical settings, and extreme emotions. The hero of Hugo's famous *The Hunchback of Notre Dame* (1831) is the great cathedral's deformed bell-ringer, a "human gargoyle" overlooking the teeming life of fifteenth-century Paris. Renouncing his early conservatism, Hugo equated freedom in literature with liberty in politics and society. His political evolution was thus exactly the opposite of Wordsworth's, in whom youthful radicalism gave way to middle-aged caution. As the contrast between the two artists suggests, Romanticism was compatible with many political beliefs.

In central and eastern Europe, literary Romanticism and early nationalism often reinforced one another. Well-educated Romantics championed their own people's histories, cultures, and unique greatness. Like modern anthropologists, they studied peasant life and transcribed the folk songs, tales, and proverbs that the cosmopolitan Enlightenment had disdained. The brothers Jacob and Wilhelm Grimm were particularly successful at rescuing German fairy tales from oblivion. In the Slavic lands, Romantics played a decisive role in converting spoken peasant languages into modern written languages. In the vast Austrian, Russian, and Ottoman Empires, with their many ethnic minorities, the combination of Romanticism and nationalism was particularly potent. Ethnic groups dreaming of independence could find revolutionary inspiration in Romantic visions of a historic national destiny.

Romanticism in Art and Music

Romantic concerns with nature, history, and the imagination extended well beyond literature, into the realms of art and music. France's Eugène Delacroix (oo-ZHEHN deh-luh-KWAH) (1798–1863), one of Romanticism's greatest artists, painted dramatic, colorful scenes that stirred the emotions. Delacroix was fascinated with remote and exotic subjects, whether lion hunts in Morocco or dreams of languishing, sensuous women in a sultan's harem. The famous German painter Casper David Friedrich (1774–1840) preferred somber landscapes of ruined churches or remote arctic shipwrecks, which captured the divine presence in natural forces.

In England the Romantic painters Joseph M. W. Turner (1775–1851) and John Constable (1776–1837) were fascinated by nature, but their interpretations of it contrasted sharply, aptly symbolizing the tremendous emotional range of the Romantic movement. Turner depicted nature's power and terror; wild storms and sinking ships were favorite subjects. Constable painted gentle Wordsworthian landscapes in which human beings lived peacefully with their environment, the comforting countryside of unspoiled rural England.

Musicians and composers likewise explored the Romantic sensibility. Abandoning well-defined musical structures, the great Romantic composers used a wide range of forms to create profound musical landscapes that evoked powerful emotions. They transformed the small classical orchestra, tripling its size by adding wind instruments,

Delacroix, *Massacre at Chios*, 1824 This moving masterpiece by Romantic artist Eugène Delacroix portrays an Ottoman massacre of ethnic Greeks on the island of Chios during the struggle for national independence in Greece. The Greek revolt won the enthusiastic support of European liberals, nationalists, and Romantics, and this massive oil painting (ca. 13 feet by 11 feet) portrays the Ottomans as cruel and violent oppressors holding back the course of history. (Musée du Louvre, Paris, France/ Bridgeman Images)

percussion, and more brass and strings. The crashing chords evoking the surge of the masses in Chopin's "Revolutionary Etude" and the bottomless despair of the funeral march in Beethoven's Third Symphony—such were the modern orchestra's musical paintings that plumbed the depths of human feeling.

This range and intensity gave music and musicians much greater prestige and publicity than in the past. Music no longer simply complemented a church service or helped a nobleman digest his dinner. It became a sublime end in itself, most perfectly realizing the endless yearning of the soul. The unbelievable one-in-a-million performer—the great virtuoso who could transport the listener to ecstasy and hysteria—became a cultural hero. People swooned, for example, for Franz Liszt (1811–1886), the greatest pianist of his age, as they scream for rock stars today.

The first great Romantic composer is also the most famous today. Ludwig van Beethoven (1770–1827) used contrasting themes and tones to produce dramatic conflict and inspiring resolutions. As one contemporary admirer wrote, "Beethoven's music sets in motion the lever of fear, of awe, of horror, of suffering, and awakens just that infinite longing which is the essence of Romanticism."[10] Beethoven's range and output were tremendous. At the peak of his fame, he began to lose his hearing. He considered suicide but eventually overcame despair: "I will take fate by the throat; it will not bend me completely to its will."[11] Beethoven continued to pour out immortal music, although his last years were silent, spent in total deafness.

Reforms and Revolutions Before 1848

Focus Question	How and where was conservatism challenged after 1815?

While the Romantics enacted a revolution in the arts, liberal, national, and socialist forces battered against the conservative restoration of 1815. Political change could result from gradual and peaceful reform or from violent insurrection, but everywhere it took the determination of ordinary people standing up to the prerogatives of the powerful. Between 1815 and 1848 three important countries—Greece, Great Britain, and France—experienced variations on this basic theme.

National Liberation in Greece

Though conservative statesmen had maintained the autocratic status quo despite revolts in Spain and the Two Sicilies, a national revolution succeeded in Greece in the 1820s. Since the fifteenth century the Greeks had lived under the domination of the Ottoman Turks. In spite of centuries of foreign rule, the Greeks had survived as a people, united by their language and the Greek Orthodox religion. In the early nineteenth century the general growth of national aspirations inspired a desire for independence. This rising national movement led to the formation of secret societies and then to open revolt in 1821, led by Alexander Ypsilanti (ihp-suh-LAN-tee), a Greek patriot and a general in the Russian army.

At first, the Great Powers, particularly Metternich, opposed the revolution and refused to back Ypsilanti, primarily because they sought a stable Ottoman Empire as a bulwark against Russian interests in southeast Europe. Yet the Greek cause had powerful defenders. Educated Europeans and Americans cherished the culture of classical Greece; Russians admired the piety of their Orthodox brethren. Writers and artists, moved by the Romantic impulse, responded enthusiastically to the Greek national struggle. The famous English Romantic poet Lord Byron even joined the Greek revolutionaries to fight (as he wrote in a famous poem) "that Greece might yet be free."

The Greeks, though often quarreling among themselves, battled the Ottomans while hoping for the support of European governments. In 1827 Britain, France, and Russia yielded to popular demands at home and directed Ottoman leaders to accept an armistice. When they refused, the navies of these three powers trapped the Ottoman fleet at Navarino. Russia then declared another of its periodic wars of expansion against the Ottomans. This led to the establishment of a Russian protectorate over much of present-day Romania, which had also been under Ottoman rule. Great Britain, France, and Russia finally declared Greece independent in 1830 and installed a German prince as king of the new country in 1832. Despite this imposed regime, which left the Greek people restive, they had won their independence in a heroic war of liberation against a foreign empire.

Liberal Reform in Great Britain

Pressure from below also reshaped politics in Great Britain, but through a process of gradual reform rather than revolution. Eighteenth-century Britain had been remarkably stable. The landowning aristocracy dominated society, but that class was neither closed nor rigidly defined. Successful business and professional people could buy land and become gentlefolk, while the common people enjoyed limited civil rights. Yet the constitutional monarchy was hardly democratic. With only about 8 percent of the population allowed to vote, the British Parliament, easily manipulated by the king, remained in the hands of the upper classes. Government policies supported the aristocracy and the new industrial capitalists at the expense of the laboring classes.

Anti–Corn Law League   This line drawing, printed on silk fabric, graced the interior crown of a top hat sold as the "Corn Law Repeal Hat." The Anti–Corn Law League, a forerunner of today's political pressure groups, successfully used a number of propaganda techniques to mobilize a broad urban coalition dedicated to free trade and the end of tariffs on imported grain. For example, each league supporter was encouraged to join the national organization and receive a membership card. How do the various texts and scenes on the hat lining evoke arguments against the Corn Laws? Why would these arguments win popular support? (Universal History Archive/UIG/Bridgeman Images)

By the 1780s there was growing interest in some kind of political reform, and organized union activity began to emerge in force during the Napoleonic Wars (see Chapter 19). Yet the radical aspects of the French Revolution threw the British aristocracy into a panic for a generation, making it extremely hostile to any attempts to change the status quo.

In 1815 open conflict between the ruling class and laborers emerged when the aristocracy rammed far-reaching changes in the **Corn Laws** through Parliament. Britain had been unable to import cheap grain from eastern Europe during the war years, leading to high prices and large profits for the landed aristocracy. With the war over, grain (which the British generically called "corn") could be imported again, allowing the price of wheat and bread to go down and benefiting almost everyone—except aristocratic landlords. The new Corn Laws placed high tariffs (or fees) on imported grain. Its cost rose to improbable levels, ensuring artificially high bread prices for working people and handsome revenues for aristocrats. Seldom has a class legislated more selfishly for its own narrow economic advantage or done more to promote a class-based view of political action.

The change in the Corn Laws, coming as it did at a time of widespread unemployment and postwar economic distress, triggered protests and demonstrations by urban laborers, who enjoyed the support of radical intellectuals. In 1817 the Tory government, controlled completely by the landed aristocracy, responded by temporarily suspending the traditional rights of peaceable assembly and habeas corpus, which gives a person under arrest the right to a trial. Two years later, Parliament passed the infamous Six Acts, which, among other things, placed controls on a heavily taxed press and practically eliminated all mass meetings. These acts followed an enormous but orderly protest, at Saint Peter's Fields in Manchester, which was savagely broken up by armed cavalry. Nicknamed the **Battle of Peterloo**, in scornful reference to the British victory at Waterloo, this incident demonstrated the government's determination to repress dissenters.

Strengthened by ongoing industrial development, emerging manufacturing and commercial groups insisted on a place for their new wealth alongside the landed wealth of the aristocracy in the framework of political power and social prestige. They called for many kinds of liberal reform: changes in town government, organization of a new police force, more rights for Catholics and dissenters, and reform of the Poor Laws to provide aid to some low-paid workers. In the 1820s a less frightened Tory government moved in the direction of better urban administration, greater economic liberalism, civil equality for Catholics, and limited imports of foreign grain. These actions encouraged the middle classes to press on for reform of Parliament so they could have a larger say in government.

The Whig Party, though led like the Tories by elite aristocrats, had by tradition been more responsive to middle-class commercial and manufacturing interests. In 1830 a Whig ministry introduced "an act to amend the representation of the people of England and Wales." After a series of setbacks, the Whigs' **Reform Bill of 1832** was propelled into law by a mighty surge of popular support. Significantly, the bill moved British politics in a democratic direction and allowed the House of Commons to emerge as the all-important legislative body, at the expense of the aristocrat-dominated House of Lords. The new industrial areas of the country gained representation in the

Commons, and many old "rotten boroughs"—electoral districts that had very few voters and that the landed aristocracy had bought and sold—were eliminated. The number of voters increased by about 50 percent, to include about 12 percent of adult men in Britain and Ireland. Comfortable middle-class groups in the urban population, as well as some substantial farmers who leased their land, received the vote. Thus the conflicts building in Great Britain were successfully—though only temporarily—resolved. Continued peaceful reform within the system appeared difficult but not impossible.

The "People's Charter" of 1838 and the Chartist movement it inspired pressed British elites for yet more radical reform (see Chapter 20). Inspired by the economic distress of the working class in the 1830s and 1840s, the Chartists demanded universal male (but not female) suffrage. They saw complete political democracy and rule by the common people—the great majority of the population—as the means to a good and just society. Hundreds of thousands of people signed gigantic petitions calling on Parliament to grant all men the right to vote, first in 1839, again in 1842, and yet again in 1848. Parliament rejected all three petitions. In the short run, the working poor failed with their Chartist demands, but they learned a valuable lesson in mass politics.

While calling for universal male suffrage, many working-class people joined with middle-class manufacturers in the Anti–Corn Law League, founded in Manchester in 1839. Mass participation made possible a popular crusade led by fighting liberals, who argued that lower food prices and more jobs in industry depended on repeal of the Corn Laws. Much of the working class agreed. When Ireland's potato crop failed in 1845 and famine prices for food seemed likely in England, Tory prime minister Robert Peel joined with the Whigs and a minority of his own party to repeal the Corn Laws in 1846 and allow free imports of grain. England escaped famine. Thereafter the liberal doctrine of free trade became almost sacred dogma in Great Britain.

The following year, the Tories passed a bill designed to help the working classes, but in a different way. The Ten Hours Act of 1847 limited the workday for women and young people in factories to ten hours. In competition with the middle class for the support of the working class, Tory legislators continued to support legislation regulating factory conditions. This competition between a still-powerful aristocracy and a strong middle class was a crucial factor in Great Britain's peaceful political evolution. The working classes could make temporary alliances with either competitor to better their own conditions.

Ireland and the Great Famine

The people of Ireland did not benefit from the political competition in England. In the mid-nineteenth century, Ireland was an agricultural nation, and the great majority of the rural population (outside of the northern counties of Ulster, which were partly Presbyterian) were Irish Catholics. They typically rented their land from a tiny minority of Church of England Protestant landowners, who often resided in England. Using a middleman system, these absentee landlords leased land for short periods only, set rents at will, and easily evicted their tenants. In short, landlords used their power to grab as much profit as possible.

Trapped in an exploitative tenant system driven by a pernicious combination of religion and class, Irish peasants lived in abominable conditions. Wretched one-room mud cabins dotted the Irish countryside; the typical tenant farmer could afford neither shoes nor stockings. Hundreds of shocking accounts described hopeless poverty. The novelist Sir Walter Scott wrote:

> The poverty of the Irish peasantry is on the extreme verge of human misery; their cottages would scarce serve for pig styes even in Scotland; and their rags seem the very refuse of a sheep, and are spread over their bodies with such an ingenious variety of wretchedness that you would think nothing but some sort of perverted taste could have assembled so many shreds together.[12]

A compassionate French traveler agreed, writing that Ireland was "pure misery, naked and hungry. . . . I saw the American Indian in his forests and the black slave in his chains, and I believed that I was seeing the most extreme form of human misery; but that was before I knew the lot of poor Ireland."[13]

Despite the terrible conditions, population growth sped upward, part of Europe's general growth trend begun in the early eighteenth century (see Chapter 17). Between 1780 and 1840 the Irish population doubled from 4 million to 8 million. Extensive cultivation of the humble potato was largely responsible for this rapid growth. A single acre of land planted with the nutritious potato could feed a family of six for a year, and the hardy tuber thrived on Ireland's boggy wastelands. About one-half of the Irish population subsisted on potatoes and little else. Needing only a big potato patch to survive, the rural poor married early. To be sure, a young couple faced a life of extreme poverty. They would literally live on potatoes, supplemented perhaps with a bit of grain or milk. Yet the decision to marry and have large families made sense. A couple could manage rural poverty better than someone living alone, and children meant extra hands in the fields.

As population and potato dependency grew, however, conditions became more precarious. From 1820 onward, deficiencies and diseases in the potato crop occurred with disturbing frequency. Then in 1845 and 1846, and again in 1848 and 1851, the potato crop failed in Ireland. Blight attacked the young plants, and leaves and tubers rotted. Unmitigated disaster—the **Great Famine**—followed, as already impoverished peasants experienced widespread sickness and starvation.

The British government, committed to rigid free-trade ideology, reacted slowly. Relief efforts were tragically inadequate. Moreover, the government continued to collect taxes, landlords demanded their rents, and tenants who could not pay were evicted and their homes destroyed. Famine or no, Ireland remained the conquered jewel of foreign landowners.

The Great Famine shattered the pattern of Irish population growth. Fully 1 million emigrants fled the famine between 1845 and 1851, mostly to the United States and Canada, and up to 1.5 million people died. The elderly and the very young were hardest hit. Alone among the countries of Europe, Ireland experienced a declining population in the second half of the nineteenth century, as it became a land of continuous out-migration, early death, late marriage, and widespread celibacy.

The Great Famine intensified anti-British feeling and promoted Irish nationalism, for the bitter memory of starvation, exile, and British inaction burned deeply into the popular consciousness. Patriots of the later nineteenth and early twentieth centuries could call on powerful collective emotions in their campaigns for land reform, home rule, and, eventually, Irish independence.

The Revolution of 1830 in France

Like Greece and the British Isles, France experienced dramatic political change in the first half of the nineteenth century, and the French experience especially illustrates the disruptive potential of popular liberal politics. The Constitutional Charter granted by Louis XVIII in the Bourbon restoration of 1814 was a limited liberal constitution (see Chapter 19). The charter protected economic and social gains made by sections of the middle class and the peasantry in the French Revolution, permitted some intellectual and artistic freedom, and created a parliament with upper and lower houses. Immediately after Napoleon's abortive Hundred Days, the moderate, worldly king refused to bow to the wishes of die-hard aristocrats who wanted to sweep away all the revolutionary changes. Instead, Louis appointed as his ministers moderate royalists, who sought and obtained the support of a majority of the representatives elected to the lower Chamber of Deputies between 1816 and Louis's death in 1824.

Louis XVIII's charter was liberal but hardly democratic. Only about 100,000 of the wealthiest males out of a total population of 30 million had the right to vote for the deputies who, with the king and his ministers, made the laws of the nation. Nonetheless, the "notable people" who did vote came from very different backgrounds. There were wealthy businessmen, war profiteers, successful professionals, ex-revolutionaries, large landowners from the old aristocracy and the middle class, Bourbons, and Bonapartists. The old aristocracy, with its pre-1789 mentality, was a minority within the voting population.

Louis's conservative successor, Charles X (r. 1824–1830), a true reactionary, wanted to re-establish the old order in France. Increasingly blocked by the opposition of the deputies, Charles's government turned in 1830 to military adventure in an effort to rally French nationalism and gain popular support. A long-standing economic and diplomatic dispute with Muslim Algeria, a vassal state of the Ottoman Empire, provided the opportunity.

In June 1830 a French force of thirty-seven thousand crossed the Mediterranean, landed to the west of Algiers, and took the capital city in three short weeks. Victory seemed complete, but in 1831 Algerians in the interior revolted and waged a fearsome war that lasted until 1847, when French armies finally subdued the country. The conquest of Algeria marked the rebirth of French imperial expansion, and the colonial government encouraged French, Spanish, and Italian immigrants to move to Algeria and settle on large tracts of land expropriated from the region's Muslim inhabitants.

Emboldened by the initial good news from Algeria, Charles repudiated the Constitutional Charter in an attempted coup in July 1830. He censored the press and issued decrees stripping much of the wealthy middle class of its voting rights. The immediate reaction, encouraged by liberal lawyers, journalists, and middle-class businessmen, was an insurrection in the capital. Printers, other artisans, and small traders fired up by popular republicanism rioted in the streets of Paris, and three days of vicious street fighting brought down the government. Charles fled. Then the upper middle class, which had fomented the revolt, abandoned the more radical workers and skillfully seated Charles's cousin, Louis Philippe, duke of Orléans, on the vacant throne.

Events in Paris reverberated across Europe. In the Netherlands, Belgian Catholics revolted against the Dutch king and established the independent kingdom of Belgium. In Switzerland, regional liberal assemblies forced cantonal governments to amend their constitutions, leading to two decades of political conflict. And in partitioned Poland, an armed nationalist rebellion against the tsarist government was crushed by the Russian Imperial Army.

Despite the abdication of Charles X, in France the political situation remained fundamentally unchanged. The new king, Louis Philippe (r. 1830–1848), accepted the Constitutional Charter of 1814 and adopted the red, white, and blue flag of the French Revolution. Beyond these symbolic actions, however, popular demands for more thorough reform went unanswered. The upper middle class had effected a change in dynasty that maintained the status quo and the narrowly liberal institutions of 1815. Republicans, democrats, social reformers, and the poor of Paris were bitterly disappointed. They had made a revolution, but it seemed for naught.

The Revolutions of 1848

Focus Question	**What were the main causes and results of the revolutions of 1848?**

In the late 1840s Europe entered a period of tense economic and political crisis. Bad harvests across the continent caused widespread distress. Uneven industrial development failed to provide jobs or raise incomes, and boosted the popularity of radical ideologies. As a result, limited revolts broke out across Europe: a rebellion in the northern part of Austria in 1846, a civil war in Switzerland in 1847, and an uprising in Naples, Italy, in January 1848.

Full-scale revolution broke out in France in February 1848, and its shock waves rippled across the continent. Only the most developed countries—Great Britain, Belgium, and the Netherlands—and the least developed—the Ottoman and Russian Empires—escaped untouched. Elsewhere governments toppled, as monarchs and ministers bowed or fled. National independence, liberal democratic constitutions, and social reform: the lofty aspirations of a generation seemed at hand. Yet in the end, the revolutions failed.

A Democratic Republic in France

By the late 1840s revolution in Europe was almost universally expected, but it took events in Paris—once again—to turn expectations into realities. For eighteen years Louis Philippe's reign, labeled the "bourgeois monarchy" because it served the selfish interests of France's wealthy elites, had been characterized by stubborn inaction and complacency. Corrupt politicians refused to approve social legislation or consider electoral reform. Frustrated desires for change, high-level financial scandals, and a general sense of stagnation dovetailed with a severe depression that began with crop failures in 1846 to 1847. The government did little to prevent the agrarian crisis from dragging down the entire economy.

The government's failures united a diverse group of opponents against the king. Bourgeois merchants, opposition deputies, and liberal intellectuals shared a sense of outrage with middle-class shopkeepers, skilled artisans, and unskilled working people. Widespread discontent eventually touched off a popular revolt in Paris. On the night of February 22, 1848, workers joined by some students began tearing up cobblestones and building barricades. Armed with guns and dug in behind their makeshift fortresses, the workers and students demanded a new government. On February 24 the National Guard broke ranks and joined the revolutionaries. Louis Philippe refused to call in the army and abdicated in favor of his grandson. But the common people in arms would tolerate no more monarchy. This refusal led to the proclamation of a provisional republic, headed by a ten-man executive committee and certified by cries of approval from the revolutionary crowd.

The revolutionaries immediately set about drafting a democratic, republican constitution for France's Second Republic. Building such a republic meant giving the right to vote to every adult male, and this was quickly done. Bold decrees issued by the provisional republican government expressed sympathy for revolutionary freedoms by calling for liberty, fraternity, and equality. The revolutionary government guaranteed workplace reforms, freed all slaves in French colonies, and abolished the death penalty. Yet there were profound differences within the revolutionary coalition. On the one hand, the moderate liberal republicans of the middle class viewed universal male suffrage as the ultimate concession to dangerous popular forces, and they strongly opposed any further radical social measures. On the other hand, radical republicans, influenced by a generation of utopian socialists and appalled by the poverty and misery of the urban poor, were committed to some kind of socialism. Hard-pressed urban artisans, who hated the unrestrained competition of cutthroat capitalism, advocated a combination of strong craft unions and worker-owned businesses.

Worsening depression and rising unemployment brought these conflicting goals to the fore in 1848. Louis Blanc (see page 665), who along with a worker named Albert represented the republican socialists in the provisional government, pressed for recognition of a socialist right to work. Blanc urged the creation of the permanent government-sponsored cooperative workshops he had advocated in *The Organization of Work*. Such workshops would be an alternative to capitalist employment and a decisive step toward a new, noncompetitive social order.

The moderate republicans, willing to provide only temporary relief, wanted no such thing. The resulting compromise set up national workshops—soon to become little more than a vast program of pick-and-shovel public works—and established a special commission under Blanc to "study the question." This satisfied no one. The national workshops were, however, better than nothing. An army of desperate poor from the French provinces and even from foreign countries streamed into Paris to sign up for the workshops. As the economic crisis worsened, the number enrolled in the workshops soared from 10,000 in March to 120,000 by June, and another 80,000 tried unsuccessfully to join.

MAP 21.3 The Revolutions of 1848
In February and March 1848 revolutions broke out in the European heartlands: France, the Austrian Empire, and the German Confederation. In contrast, relative stability reigned in Great Britain, Belgium, the Netherlands, and the Russian and Ottoman Empires. Why did some regions descend into revolution, and not others? Can a study of geography help explain the difference?

Yet the revolutionary coalition lacked stability. When the monarchy abolished serfdom, with its degrading forced labor and feudal services, the newly free peasants lost interest in the political and social questions agitating the cities. Meanwhile, the coalition of urban revolutionaries broke down along class lines over the issue of socialist workshops and universal voting rights for men.

Conflicting national aspirations further weakened and ultimately destroyed the revolutionary coalition. In March the Hungarian revolutionary leaders pushed through an extremely liberal, almost democratic, constitution for the Kingdom of Hungary. But the Hungarian revolutionaries also sought to transform the mosaic of provinces and peoples in their territories into a unified, centralized Hungarian nation. The minority groups that formed half of the population—the Croats, Serbs, and Romanians—rejected such unification (see Map 21.2). Each group felt entitled to political autonomy and cultural independence. In a similar way, Czech nationalists based in Prague and other parts of Bohemia came into conflict with German nationalists living in the same region. Thus desires for national autonomy within the Austrian Empire enabled the monarchy to play off one ethnic group against the other.

Finally, conservative aristocratic forces rallied under the leadership of the archduchess Sophia, a Bavarian princess married to the Habsburg emperor's brother. Deeply ashamed of the emperor's collapse before a "mess of students," she insisted that Ferdinand I, who had no heir, abdicate in favor of her son, Franz Joseph.[15] Powerful nobles organized around Sophia in a secret conspiracy to reverse and crush the revolution.

The first conservative breakthrough came when the army bombarded Prague and savagely crushed a working-class revolt there on June 17, 1848. By August the Austrians had crushed the Italian insurrection. At the end of October, the well-equipped, predominantly peasant troops of the regular Austrian army bombarded the student and working-class radicals dug in behind barricades in Vienna with heavy artillery. They retook the city at the cost of more than four thousand casualties. The determination of the Austrian aristocracy and the loyalty of its army sealed the triumph of reaction and the defeat of revolution.

When Franz Joseph (r. 1848–1916) was crowned emperor of Austria immediately after his eighteenth birthday in December 1848, only the Hungarians had yet to be brought under control. Another determined conservative, Nicholas I of Russia (r. 1825–1855), obligingly lent his iron hand. On June 6, 1849, 130,000 Russian troops poured into Hungary and subdued the country after bitter fighting. For a number of years, the Habsburgs ruled the Kingdom of Hungary as a conquered territory.

Prussia, the German Confederation, and the Frankfurt National Parliament

After Austria, Prussia was the largest and most influential kingdom in the German Confederation. Since the Napoleonic Wars, liberal German reformers had sought to transform absolutist Prussia into a constitutional monarchy, hoping it would then lead the thirty-eight states of the German Confederation into a unified nation-state. The agitation that followed the fall of Louis Philippe, on top of several years of crop failure and economic crises, encouraged liberals to press their demands. In March 1848 excited crowds in urban centers across the German Confederation called for liberal reforms and a national parliament, and many regional rulers quickly gave in to their demands.

When artisans and factory workers rioted in Berlin, the capital of Prussia, and joined temporarily with the middle-class liberals in the struggle against the monarchy, the autocratic yet compassionate Prussian king, Friedrich Wilhelm IV (r. 1840–1861), vacillated and then caved in. On March 21 he promised to grant Prussia a liberal constitution and to merge Prussia into a new national German state.

But urban workers wanted much more—and the Prussian aristocracy wanted much less—than the moderate constitutional liberalism conceded by the king. The ended in failure. Conservative monarchies revived, nationalist movements collapsed, and hopes for German unification withered. Yet protest on the barricades and debate in liberal parliaments had given a generation a wealth of experience with new forms of participatory politics, and the ideologies associated with the French Revolution would continue to invigorate reformers and revolutionaries after 1850. Nationalism, with its commitment to the imagined community of a great national family and the nation-state, would become a dominant political force, particularly as European empires extended their reach after 1875. At the same time, as agriculture and rural life gradually declined in economic importance, the consolidation of industrialization would raise living standards, sustain a growing urban society, and reshape family and class relationships. Diverse, complicated, and fascinating, pockets of this new urban society already existed in 1850. By 1900 it dominated northwestern Europe and was making steady inroads to the east and south.

MAKE CONNECTIONS

Think about the larger developments and continuities within and across chapters.

1. Why did the ideas of the Romantic movement so easily support reformist and radical political ideas, including liberalism, republicanism, and nationalism? What does this reveal about the general connections between art and politics?

2. How did the spread of radical ideas and the movements for reform and revolution explored in this chapter draw on the "unfinished" political and industrial revolutions (Chapters 19 and 20) of the late eighteenth century?

3. The years between 1815 and 1850 witnessed the invention of a number of new political ideologies and the application of these ideologies in a variety of struggles for political power. What impact would these ideologies and struggles have later in the nineteenth and twentieth centuries? Do they still have an impact today?

Chapter Review

IDENTIFY KEY TERMS

Identify and explain the significance of each item below.

Congress of Vienna (p. 654)

Holy Alliance (p. 660)

Karlsbad Decrees (p. 660)

liberalism (p. 662)

laissez faire (p. 662)

nationalism (p. 663)

socialism (p. 664)

Marxism (p. 666)

bourgeoisie (p. 667)

proletariat (p. 667)

Romanticism (p. 668)

Corn Laws (p. 674)

Battle of Peterloo (p. 674)

Reform Bill of 1832 (p. 674)

Great Famine (p. 676)

Greater Germany (p. 684)

REVIEW THE MAIN IDEAS

Answer the focus questions from each section of the chapter.

1. How was peace restored and maintained after 1815? (p. 654)
2. What new ideologies emerged to challenge conservatism? (p. 661)
3. What were the characteristics of the Romantic movement? (p. 668)
4. How and where was conservatism challenged after 1815? (p. 672)
5. What were the main causes and results of the revolutions of 1848? (p. 678)

CHRONOLOGY

1790s–1840s	Romantic movement in literature and the arts
1809–1848	Metternich serves as Austrian foreign minister
1810	Germaine de Staël publishes *On Germany*
1814–1815	Congress of Vienna
1815	Revision of Corn Laws in Great Britain; Holy Alliance formed
June 18, 1815	Napoleon defeated at the Battle of Waterloo
1819	Karlsbad Decrees issued by German Confederation
1820	Congress of Troppau proclaims the principle of intervention to maintain autocratic regimes
1821	Austria crushes a liberal revolution in Naples and restores the Sicilian autocracy
1823	French armies restore the Spanish crown
1830	Greece wins independence from Ottomans
	France invades Algeria
	Charles X repudiates the Constitutional Charter; insurrection and collapse of the government follow
	Louis Philippe succeeds to the throne and maintains a narrowly liberal regime
1832	Reform Bill in Britain
1839	Socialist Louis Blanc publishes *The Organization of Work*
1840	Anarchist Pierre-Joseph Proudhon publishes *What Is Property?*
1845–1851	Great Famine in Ireland
1847	Ten Hours Act in Britain
1848	Revolutions in France, Austria, and Prussia; Marx and Engels publish *The Communist Manifesto*

The People and Occupations of the Middle Classes

By the beginning of the twentieth century, the diversity and range within the urban middle class were striking. Indeed, it makes sense to replace the idea of a single "middle class" with a group of "middle classes" whose members engaged in occupations requiring mental, rather than physical, skill.

Below the wealthy top tier, the much larger, much less wealthy, and increasingly diversified middle class included moderately successful industrialists and merchants as well as professionals in law, business, and medicine. As industry and technology expanded in the nineteenth century, a growing demand developed for experts with specialized knowledge, and advanced education soared in importance among the middle classes. Engineering, for example, emerged from the world of skilled labor as a full-fledged profession with considerable prestige. Architects, chemists, accountants, and surveyors, to name only a few, first achieved professional standing in this period. They established criteria for advanced training and certification and banded together in organizations to promote and defend their interests. As governments grew and provided more services, and very large corporations (such as railroads or arms manufacturers) controlled ever-larger numbers of human and physical resources, middle-class professionals also found jobs as managers in large public and private institutions. Government officials and private executives had specialized knowledge and the capacity to earn a good living.

Industrialization expanded and diversified the lower middle class as well. The number of independent, property-owning shopkeepers and small business people grew, and so did the number of white-collar employees—a mixed group of traveling salesmen, bookkeepers, store managers, and clerks who staffed the offices and branch stores of large corporations. White-collar employees owned little property and often earned no more than better-paid skilled or semiskilled workers. Yet white-collar workers were fiercely committed to the middle-class ideal of upward social mobility. The suit, the tie, the soft, clean hands that accompanied low-level retail and managerial work became important status symbols that set this group above those who earned a living through manual labor.

Relatively well educated but without complex technical skills, many white-collar occupational groups strove to achieve professional standing and higher social status. Elementary school teachers largely succeeded in this effort. Miserably paid part-time workers in the early nineteenth century, teachers rode the wave of mass education to respectable middle-class status and income. Nurses also rose from the lower ranks of unskilled labor to precarious middle-class standing. Dentistry was taken out of the hands of working-class barbers and placed in the hands of highly trained (and middle-class) professionals.

Middle-Class Culture and Values

Despite growing occupational diversity and conflicting interests, lifestyle preferences loosely united the European middle classes. Food, housing, clothes, and behavior all expressed middle-class values and testified to the superior social standing of this group over the working classes.

Unlike the working classes, the middle classes had the money to eat well, and spent a substantial portion of their household budget on food and entertainment. They consumed meat in abundance: a well-off family might spend 10 percent of its annual income on meat and fully 25 percent on food and drink. The dinner party—a favored social occasion—boosted spending. A wealthy middle-class family might give a lavish party for eight to twelve almost every week, and such parties were especially common on holidays.

The middle-class wife could cope with this endless procession of meals, courses, and dishes because she had servants as well as money at her disposal. Indeed, the employment of at least one full-time maid to cook and clean was the clearest sign that a family had crossed the cultural divide separating the working classes from what some contemporary observers called the "servant-keeping classes." The greater a family's income, the greater the number of servants it employed. Servants absorbed about another 25 percent of income at all levels of the middle class.

Well fed and well served, the middle classes were also well housed by 1900. Many prosperous families rented, rather than owned, their homes, complete with tiny rooms for servants in the basement or under the eaves of the top floor. And, just as the aristocracy had long divided the year between palatial country estates and lavish town-houses during "the season," so the upper middle class purchased country places or built beach houses for weekend and summer use.

The middle classes paid great attention to outward appearances, especially their clothes. The factory, the sewing machine, and the department store had all helped reduce the cost and expand the variety of clothing. Middle-class women were particularly attentive to the dictates of fashion, though men also wore the now-appropriate business suit. Ownership of private coaches and carriages, expensive items in the city, further testified to rising social status.

Rich Europeans could devote more time to "culture" and leisure pursuits than less wealthy or well-established families could. The keystones of culture and leisure were books, music, and travel. The long Realist novel, the heroic operas of composers Wagner and Verdi, the diligent striving of the dutiful daughter at the piano, and the packaged tour to a foreign country were all sources of middle-class pleasure.

In addition to their material tastes, the middle classes generally agreed upon a strict code of behavior, manners, and morality. They stressed hard work, self-discipline, and personal achievement. Middle-class social reformers denounced drunkenness and gambling as vices and celebrated sexual purity and fidelity as virtues, especially for women. Men and women who fell into vice, crime, or poverty were held responsible for their own circumstances. A stern sense of Christian morals, preached tirelessly by religious leaders, educators, and politicians, reaffirmed these values. The middle-class individual was supposed to know right from wrong and act accordingly.

The People and Occupations of the Working Classes

At the beginning of the twentieth century, about four out of five people belonged to the working classes—that is, people whose livelihoods depended primarily on physical labor and who did not employ domestic servants. Many of them were still small land-owning peasants and hired farm hands, and this was especially the case in eastern

One of the largest components of the unskilled group was domestic servants, whose numbers grew steadily in the nineteenth century. In Great Britain, for example, one out of every seven employed persons in 1911 was a domestic servant. The great majority were women; indeed, one out of every three girls in Britain between the ages of fifteen and twenty worked as a domestic servant. Throughout Europe, many female domestics in the cities were recent migrants from rural areas. As in earlier times, domestic service meant hard work at low pay with limited personal independence and the danger of sexual exploitation. For the full-time general maid in a lower-middle-class family, an unending routine of babysitting, shopping, cooking, and cleaning defined a lengthy working day. In the wealthiest households, the serving girl was at the bottom of a rigid hierarchy of status-conscious butlers and housekeepers.

Nonetheless, domestic service had real attractions for young women from rural areas who had few specialized skills. Marriage prospects were better, or at least more varied, in the city than back home. And though wages were low, they were higher and more regular than in hard agricultural work—which was being replaced by mechanization, at any rate. Finally, as one London observer noted, young girls and other migrants from the countryside were drawn to the city by "the contagion of numbers, the sense of something going on, the theaters and the music halls, the brightly lighted streets and busy crowds—all, in short, that makes the difference between the Mile End fair on a Saturday night, and a dark and muddy country lane, with no glimmer of gas and with nothing to do."[5]

Many young domestics made the successful transition to working-class wife and mother. Yet with an unskilled or unemployed husband, a growing family, and limited household income, many working-class wives had to join the broad ranks of working women in the **sweated industries**. These industries expanded rapidly after 1850 and resembled the old putting-out and cottage industries of earlier times (see Chapter 17). The women normally worked at home and were paid by the piece, not by the hour. They and their young children who helped them earned pitiful wages and lacked any job security. Women decorated dishes or embroidered linens, took in laundry for washing and ironing, or made clothing, especially after the advent of the sewing machine. An army of poor women, usually working at home, accounted for many of the inexpensive ready-made clothes displayed on department store racks and in tiny shops.

Working-Class Leisure and Religion

Notwithstanding hard physical labor and lack of wealth, the urban working classes sought fun and recreation, and they found both. Across Europe, drinking remained unquestionably the favorite leisure-time activity of working people. For many middle-class moralists, as well as moralizing historians since, love of drink was the curse of the modern age—a sign of social dislocation and popular suffering. Certainly, drinking was deadly serious business. One English slum dweller recalled that "drunkenness was by far the commonest cause of dispute and misery in working class homes. On account of it one saw many a decent family drift down through poverty into total want."[6]

Generally, however, heavy problem drinking declined in the late nineteenth century as it became less socially acceptable. This decline reflected in part the moral leadership of the labor aristocracy. At the same time, drinking became more publicly acceptable. Cafés and pubs became increasingly bright, friendly places. Working-class

Moulin Rouge   A group of barmaids perform the French cancan in 1895 at the Moulin Rouge, a famous Parisian cabaret/nightclub, while a live orchestra plays in the balcony above. The cancan was a fast and provocative dance that involved rapid dips and turns, and high kicks that revealed the performers' legs and frilly underwear. The new industrial society made leisure time available to more and more people of all classes, and mixed-couple entertainment including dance balls, theater performance, and dining out became increasingly popular. (Photo © Dazy René/Bridgeman Images)

political activities, both moderate and radical, were also concentrated in taverns and pubs. Moreover, social drinking in public places by married couples and sweethearts became an accepted and widespread practice for the first time. This greater participation by women undoubtedly helped civilize the world of drink and hard liquor.

The two other leisure-time passions of working-class culture were sports and music halls. "Cruel sports," such as bullbaiting and cockfighting, still popular in the middle of the century, had greatly declined throughout Europe by the 1880s. Commercialized spectator sports filled their place; horse racing and soccer were the most popular. Working people gambled on sports events, and for many a working person a desire to decipher racing forms provided a powerful incentive toward literacy. Music halls and vaudeville theaters, the working-class counterparts of middle-class opera and classical theater, were enormously popular throughout Europe. In 1900 London had more than fifty such halls and theaters. Music hall audiences included men and women, which may account for the fact that drunkenness, premarital sex, marital difficulties, and mothers-in-law were all favorite themes of broad jokes and bittersweet songs.

In more serious moments, religion continued to provide working people with solace and meaning. The eighteenth-century vitality of popular religion in Catholic countries and the Protestant rejuvenation exemplified by German Pietism and English Methodism (see Chapter 18) carried over into the nineteenth century. Indeed, many historians see the early nineteenth century as an age of religious revival. Yet historians recognize that by the last few decades of the nineteenth century, a considerable decline in both church attendance and church donations had occurred in most European countries. And it seems clear that this decline was greater for the urban working classes than for their rural counterparts or for the middle classes.

Why did working-class church attendance decline? On one hand, the construction of churches failed to keep up with the rapid growth of urban population, especially in new working-class neighborhoods. On the other, throughout the nineteenth century workers saw Catholic and Protestant churches as conservative institutions that defended status quo politics, hierarchical social order, and middle-class morality. Socialist political parties, in particular, attacked organized religion as a pillar of bourgeois society; and as the working classes became more politically conscious, they tended to see established churches as allied with their political opponents. In addition, religion underwent a process historians call "feminization": in the working and middle classes alike, women were more pious and attended service more regularly than men. Urban workingmen in particular developed vaguely antichurch attitudes, even though they might remain neutral or positive toward religion itself.

The pattern was different in the United States, where most nineteenth-century churches also preached social conservatism. But because church and state had always been separate and because a host of denominations and even different religions competed for members, working people identified churches much less with the political and social status quo. Instead, individual churches in the United States were often closely identified with an ethnic group rather than a social class, and churches thrived, in part, as a means of asserting ethnic identity. This same process occurred in Europe if the church or synagogue had never been linked to the state and served as a focus for ethnic cohesion. Irish Catholic churches in Protestant Britain, Catholic churches in partitioned Polish lands, and Jewish synagogues in Russia were outstanding examples.

Changing Family Lifestyles

Focus Question | **How did urbanization affect family life and gender roles?**

By the 1850s the family had stabilized considerably after the disruption of the late eighteenth and early nineteenth centuries. With the consolidation caused by industrialization and urbanization, the growing middle classes created a distinctive middle-class lifestyle, which set them off from peasants, workers, and the aristocracy. New ideas about courtship and marriage, family and gender roles, and homemaking and child rearing expressed middle-class norms and values in ways that would have a profound impact on family life in the century to come. Changes in family life affected both men and women and all social classes, but to varying degrees. Leading a middle-class lifestyle was prohibitively expensive for workers and peasants, and middle-class family values at first had little relevance for their lives. Yet as the nineteenth century drew to a close, the middle-class lifestyle increasingly became the norm for all classes.

Middle-Class Marriage and Courtship Rituals

Rather than marry for convenience, or for economic or social reasons—as was still common among workers, peasants, and aristocrats—by the 1850s the middle-class couple was supposed to follow an idealized model: they met, courted, fell deeply in love, and joined for life because of a shared emotional bond. Of course, economic considerations in marriage by no means disappeared. But an entire culture of romantic love—popularized in advice manuals, popular fiction, and art, and practiced in court-ship rituals, weddings, and married life—now surrounded the middle-class couple with a tender emotional charge. The growing popularity among all classes toward the end of the nineteenth century of what historians call **companionate marriage** under-scores the impact of historical change on human emotions and behaviors.

Strict rules for courtship and engagement enshrined in the concept of falling in love ensured that middle-class individuals would make an appropriate match. Parents, chaperones, and the general public closely guarded the boundary between courtship and sex, between the proper and the improper. Young couples were seldom alone before they became engaged, and individuals rarely paired off with someone from an inap-propriate class background. Premarital sex was taboo for women, though men might experiment, a double standard that revealed the value the middle classes placed on sexual morality and especially women's virginity before marriage.

Engagement also followed a complicated set of rules and rituals. Secret engage-ments led to public announcements, and then the couple could appear together, though only escorted by chaperones in potentially delicate situations. Couples might walk arm in arm, but custom placed strict limits on physical intimacy. A couple might find ways to experiment with sexual behaviors, but only in secret—secrecy that confirmed the special feelings of "true love" between the couple.

Marriage had its own set of rules. Usually a middle-class man could marry only if he could support a wife, children, and a servant, which meant he had to be well established in his career and fairly prosperous. As a result, some middle-class men never married, because they could not afford it. These customs created special dif-ficulties for young middle-class women, who could rarely pursue an independent career or acquire a home without a husband. The system encouraged mixed-age marriages. A new husband was typically much older than his young wife, who usu-ally had no career and entered marriage directly out of her parents' home or perhaps a girl's finishing school. She would have had little experience with the realities of adult life.

Love meant something different to men and women. Trained to fall passionately in love with "Mr. Right," young women equated marriage with emotional intensity. Men, on the other hand, were supposed to "find a wife": they took a more active but dispassionate role in courtship. Since women generally were quite young, the man was encouraged to see himself as the protector of a young and fragile creature. In short, the typical middle-class marriage was more similar to a child-parent relation-ship than a partnership of equals, a situation finely portrayed in Henrik Ibsen's famous play *A Doll's House* (1879). The inequality of marriage was codified in European legal systems that, with rare exceptions, placed property ownership in the hands of the husband.

Middle- and Working-Class Sexuality

A double standard in sexual relations paralleled the gender inequalities built into middle-class standards of love and marriage. Middle-class moralists of all stripes cast men as aggressively sexual creatures, while women — the "angel in the house" — were supposed to be pure and chaste and act as a brake on male desire. Contemporary science legitimized this double standard. According to late-nineteenth-century physicians, men, easily aroused by the sight of a wrist or ankle, fell prey to their raging biological drives, while respectable women were supposedly uninterested in sex by nature.

Middle-class moralists assumed that men would enter marriage with some sexual experience, though this was unthinkable for a middle-class woman. When middle-class men did seek premarital sex, middle-class women were off limits. Instead, bourgeois men took advantage of their class status and sought lower-class women, domestic servants, or prostitutes. If a young middle-class woman had experimented with or even was suspected of having had premarital sex, her chances for an acceptable marriage fell dramatically.

The sexual standards of the working classes stood in marked contrast to these norms in the early nineteenth century, but that changed over time. Premarital sex for both men and women was common and more acceptable among workers. In the first half of the nineteenth century, among the lower classes, about one-third of the births in many large European cities occurred outside of wedlock. The second half of the century saw the reversal of this high rate of illegitimacy: in western, northern, and central Europe, more babies were born to married mothers. Young, unmarried workers were probably engaging in just as much sexual activity as their parents and grandparents who had created the illegitimacy explosion of 1750 to 1850 (see Chapter 18). But in the later part of the nineteenth century, pregnancy for a young single woman, which a couple might see as the natural consequence of a serious relationship, led increasingly to marriage and the establishment of a two-parent household. Indeed, one in three working-class women was pregnant when she married. This important development reflected the spread of middle-class ideals of family respectability among the working classes, as well as their gradual economic improvement. Romantic love held working-class families together, and marriage was less of an economic challenge. The urban working-class couple of the late nineteenth century thus became more stable, and that stability strengthened the family as an institution.

Prostitution

In the late nineteenth century prostitution was legal in much of Europe. In Italy, France, Great Britain, and much of Germany, the state licensed brothels and registered individual prostitutes. In Paris, 155,000 women were registered as prostitutes between 1871 and 1903, and 750,000 others were suspected of prostitution in the same years. In Berlin, in 1909 alone, the authorities registered over 40,000 prostitutes. The totals are probably low, since most women in the sex trade tried to avoid government registration.

In streets, dance halls, and pubs across Europe, young working-class women used prostitution as a source of second income or as a way to weather a period of unemployment. Their clients were generally lower-class men, soldiers, and sailors, though middle- and upper-class men looking to "sow wild oats" also paid for sexual encounters. Streetwalking offered women some measure of financial independence, but the work was dangerous. Violence and rape, police harassment, and venereal disease were commonplace hazards.

Prostitutes clearly violated middle-class ideals of feminine respectability, but among the working classes prostitution was tolerated as more-or-less acceptable work of a temporary nature. Like domestic service, prostitution was a stage of life, not permanent employment. After working as prostitutes in their youth, many women went on to marry (or live with) men of their own class and establish homes and families.

As middle-class family values became increasingly prominent after the 1860s, prostitution generated great concern among social reformers. The prostitute — immoral, lascivious, and unhealthy in middle-class eyes — served as the dark mirror image of the respectable middle-class woman. Authorities blamed prostitutes for spreading crime and disease, particularly syphilis. Before the discovery of penicillin, syphilis was indeed a terrifying and widespread affliction. Its painful symptoms led to physical and mental decline and often death; medical treatment was embarrassing and for the most part ineffective.

As general concerns with public health gained recognition, state and city authorities across Europe subjected prostitutes — in their eyes the vector of contagious disease — to increased surveillance. The British Contagious Diseases Acts, in force between 1864 and 1886, exemplified the trend. Under these acts, special plainclothes policemen required women identified as "common prostitutes" to undergo biweekly medical exams. If they showed signs of venereal disease, they were interned in a "lock hospital" and forced to undergo treatment; when the outward signs of disease went away, they were released.

The Contagious Diseases Acts were controversial from the start. A determined middle-class feminist campaign against the policy, led by feminist Josephine Butler and the Ladies National Association, loudly proclaimed that the acts physically abused poor women, violated their constitutional rights, and legitimized male vice. Under pressure, Parliament repealed the laws in 1886. Yet heavy-handed government regulation had devastated the informality of working-class prostitution. Now branded as "registered girls," prostitutes experienced new forms of public humiliation, and the trade was increasingly controlled by male pimps rather than by the women themselves. Prostitution had never been safe, but it had been accepted, at least among the working classes. Prostitutes were now stigmatized as social and sexual outsiders.

Separate Spheres and the Importance of Homemaking

After 1850 the work of wives became increasingly distinct and separate from that of their husbands in all classes. The preindustrial pattern among both peasants and cottage workers, in which husbands and wives both worked and shared basic household duties, became less common. In wealthier homes, this change was particularly dramatic. The good middle-class family man earned the wages to support the household; the public world of work, education, and politics was male space. Respectable middle-class women did not work outside the home and rarely even traveled alone in public.

Working-class women, including servants and prostitutes, were more visible in public places, but if a middle-class woman went out without a male escort, she might be accused of low morals or character. Thus many historians have stressed that the societal ideal in nineteenth-century Europe became a strict division of labor by gender within rigidly constructed **separate spheres**: the "private sphere," where the woman acted as wife, mother, and homemaker, and the "public sphere," where the husband acted as wage earner and family provider.

For the middle classes, the private single-family home, a symbol of middle-class status and a sanctuary from the callous outside world of competitive capitalism, was central to the notion of separate spheres. At the heart of the middle-class home stood the woman: notions of femininity, motherhood, and family life came together in the ideal of domestic space. Middle-class floor plans grew to include separate sleeping rooms for parents and each family member—unheard of among the lower classes—as well as a special drawing room (or parlor), used to entertain guests. Plump sofas, bric-a-brac, and souvenirs graced domestic interiors; curtains of heavy red velvet and colorful silks draped doors and windows. Such ostentatious displays were far too expensive for the working classes, who made up 80 percent of the population.

Middle-class women were spared the masculine burdens of the outside working world, and lower-class servants ensured that they had free time to turn the private sphere into a domestic refuge of love and privacy. Numerous middle-class housekeeping manuals made the wife's responsibilities quite clear, as this Swedish handbook from 1889 suggests: "A man who spends most of his day away from the family, who has to work outside the home, counts on finding a restful and refreshing atmosphere when he returns home, and sometimes even a little merriment or a surprise. . . . It is his wife's duty to ensure that he is not disappointed in his expectation. She must do her utmost to make his stay at home as pleasant as possible; she can thus continue to keep her influence over him and retain his affection undiminished."[7]

By 1900 working-class families had adopted many middle-class values, but they did not have the means to fully realize the ideal of separate spheres. Women were the primary homemakers, and, as in the upper classes, men did little or no domestic labor. But many working-class women also made a monetary contribution to family income by taking in a boarder, doing piecework at home in the sweated industries (see page 702), or getting an outside job. While middle-class family life centered on an ample daily meal, working-class women struggled to put sufficient food on the table. Working women worked to create a homelike environment that at least resembled that of the middle class—cleaning house, collecting trinkets, and decorating domestic interiors—but working men often preferred to spend time in the local pub with workmates, rather than come home. Indeed, alcoholism and domestic violence afflicted many working-class families, even as they worked to build a relationship based on romantic love.

Feminist historians have often criticized the middle-class ideal of separate spheres because it restricted women's educational and employment opportunities, and the women's rights movement that emerged in the late nineteenth century certainly challenged the limitations of the model. In recent years, however, some scholars have been rethinking gender roles within the long-term development of consumer behavior and household economies. In the era of industrialization, these scholars suggest, the "breadwinner-homemaker" household that developed from about 1850 onward was rational consumer behavior that improved the lives of all family members, especially in the working classes.[8]

According to this view, when husbands specialized in earning an adequate cash income — the "family wage" that labor unions demanded — and wives specialized in managing the home, the working-class wife could produce desirable benefits that could not be bought in a market, such as improved health, better eating habits, and better behavior. For example, higher wages from the breadwinner could buy more raw food, but only the homemaker's careful selection, processing, and cooking would allow the family to benefit from increased spending on food. Running an urban household was a complicated, demanding, and valuable task. Twice-a-day food shopping, careful economizing, and fighting the growing crusade against dirt — not to mention child rearing — constituted a full-time occupation. Working yet another job for wages outside the home had limited appeal for most married women unless the earnings were essential for family survival. The homemaker's managerial skills, however, enabled the working-class couple to maximize their personal well-being.

The woman's guidance of the household went hand in hand with the increased pride in the home and family and the emotional importance attached to them in working- and middle-class families alike. According to one historian, by 1900 the English song "Home, Sweet Home" had become "almost a second national anthem."[9] Domesticity and family ties were now central to the lives of millions of people of all classes.

Child Rearing

Another striking sign of deepening emotional ties within the family was a growing emphasis on the love and concern that mothers gave their infants. Early emotional bonding and a willingness to make real sacrifices for the welfare of the infant became increasingly important among the comfortable classes by the end of the eighteenth century, though the ordinary mother of modest means adopted new attitudes only as the nineteenth century progressed. The baby became more important, and women became better mothers.

The surge of maternal feeling was shaped by and reflected in a wave of specialized books on child rearing and infant hygiene, such as French family reformer Gustav Droz's phenomenally successful book *Papa, Mama, and Baby*, which went through 121 editions between 1866 and 1884. Droz urged fathers to become affectionate toward their children and pitied those "who do not know how to roll around on the carpet, play at being a horse and a great wolf, and undress their baby."[10] Following expert advice, mothers increasingly breast-fed their infants, rather than paying wet nurses to do so. Breast-feeding involved sacrifice — a temporary loss of freedom, if nothing else. Yet when there was no good alternative to mother's milk, it saved lives. Another sign, from France, of increased parental affection is that fewer illegitimate babies were abandoned as foundlings after about 1850. Moreover, the practice of swaddling disappeared completely. Instead, ordinary mothers allowed their babies freedom of movement and delighted in their spontaneity.

The loving care lavished on infants was matched by greater concern for older children and adolescents. They, too, were bound in the strong emotional ties of a more intimate and protective family. For one thing, European women began to limit the number of children they bore in order to care adequately for those they had (Figure 22.2). By the end of the nineteenth century, the birthrate was declining across Europe, and it continued to do so until after World War II. The Englishwoman who married in the 1860s, for example, had an average of about six children; her daughter marrying in the 1890s had only four; and her granddaughter marrying in the 1920s had only two or possibly three.

The most important reason for this revolutionary reduction in family size, in which the comfortable and well-educated classes took the lead, was parents' desire to improve their economic and social position and that of their children. Children were no longer an economic asset in the late nineteenth century. By having fewer youngsters, parents could give those they had valuable advantages, from music lessons and summer vacations to long, expensive university educations and suitable dowries. A young German skilled worker with only one child spoke for many in his class when he said, "We want to get ahead, and our daughter should have things better than my wife and sisters did."[11] Thus the growing tendency of couples in the late nineteenth century to use a variety of contraceptive methods — the rhythm method, the withdrawal method, and mechanical devices, including after the 1840s condoms and diaphragms made of vulcanized rubber — reflected increased concern for children.

In middle-class households, parents expended considerable effort to ensure that they raised their children according to prevailing family values. Indeed, many parents, especially in the middle classes, probably became too concerned about their children, unwittingly subjecting them to an emotional pressure cooker of almost unbearable intensity. Professional family experts, including teachers, doctors, and reformers like Droz, produced a vast popular literature on child rearing that encouraged parents to focus on developing their children's self-control, self-fulfillment, and sense of Christian morality. Family specialists recommended against corporal punishment — still common in worker and peasant households — but even though

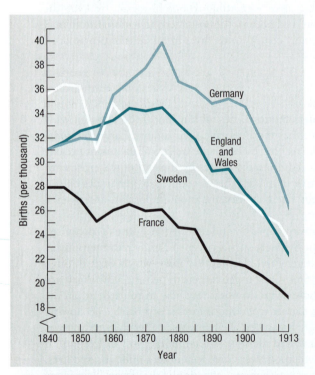

FIGURE 22.2 The Decline of Birthrates in England and Wales, France, Germany, and Sweden, 1840–1913
Women had fewer babies for a variety of reasons, including the fact that their children were increasingly less likely to die before reaching adulthood. How do these numbers compare with those in Figure 22.1?

they typically escaped beatings, the children of the wealthy grew up under constant observation and discipline, a style of parenting designed to teach the self-control necessary for adult success. Parents carefully monitored their children's sexual behavior, and masturbation—according to one expert "the most shameful and terrible of all vices"—was of particular concern.[12]

Attempts to repress the child's sexuality generated unhealthy tension, often made worse by the rigid division of gender roles within the family. While family experts lauded parental love, and especially love between mother and child, they believed that relations between father and child were troubled by a lack of emotional bonding. At work all day, the father came home a stranger to his offspring; his world of business was far removed from the maternal world of spontaneous affection. Moreover, the father set demanding rules, often expecting the child to succeed where he himself had failed and making his approval conditional on achievement. This kind of distance was especially the case in the wealthiest families, in which domestic servants, nannies, and tutors did much of the work of child rearing. Wealthy parents saw their children only over dinner, or on special occasions like birthdays or holidays.

The children of the working classes probably had more avenues of escape from such tensions than did those of the middle classes. Unlike their middle-class counterparts, who remained economically dependent on their families until a long education was finished or a proper marriage secured, working-class boys and girls went to work when they reached adolescence. Earning wages on their own, they could bargain with their parents by the time they were sixteen or seventeen for greater independence within the household. If they were unsuccessful in these negotiations, they could and did leave home to live cheaply as paying lodgers in other working-class homes. Not until the twentieth century would middle-class youths be equally free to break away from the family when emotional ties became oppressive.

The Feminist Movement

The ideal of separate spheres and the rigid gender division of labor meant that middle-class women faced great obstacles when they needed—or wanted—to move into the man's world of paid employment outside the home. Married women were subordinated to their husbands by law and lacked many basic legal rights. In England, a wife had no legal identity and hence no right to own property in her own name. Even the wages she might earn belonged to her husband. In France, the Napoleonic Code (see Chapter 19) enshrined the principle of female subordination and gave the wife few legal rights regarding property, divorce, and custody of the children.

Facing discrimination in education and employment and suffering from a lack of legal rights, some women rebelled and began the long-continuing fight for equality of the sexes and the rights of women. Their struggle proceeded on two main paths. First, following in the steps of women such as Mary Wollstonecraft (see Chapter 19), organizations founded by middle-class feminists campaigned for equal legal rights for women as well as access to higher education, professional employment, and the vote. Middle-class feminists argued that unmarried women and middle-class widows with inadequate incomes simply had to have more opportunities to support themselves. Second, feminists argued that paid (as opposed to unpaid) work could relieve the

First-Wave Feminists in Action   In May 1914 suffragette leader Emily Pankhurst was arrested by a police superintendent when she tried to present a petition to the king at Buckingham Palace. The British suffragettes often engaged in provocative public acts of civic disobedience in their campaign for women's right to vote. How do you account for the reaction of the male onlookers? (© Museum of London, UK/Bridgeman Images)

monotony that some women found in their sheltered middle-class existence and add greater meaning to their lives. In the late nineteenth century women's organizations scored some significant victories, such as the 1882 law giving English married women full property rights. More women gradually found professional and white-collar employment, especially after 1880, in fields such as teaching, nursing, and social work.

Progress toward women's rights was slow and hard-won. In Britain, the women's **suffrage movement** mounted a militant struggle for the right to vote, particularly in the decade before World War I. Inspired by the slogan "Deeds Not Words," women "suffragettes" marched in public demonstrations, heckled members of Parliament, and slashed paintings in London's National Gallery. Jailed for political activities, they went on highly publicized hunger strikes. Yet conservatives dismissed what they called "the shrieking sisterhood," and British women received the vote only in 1919.

In Germany before 1900, women were not admitted as fully registered students at a single university. Determined pioneers had to fight with tremendous fortitude to break through sexist barriers to advanced education and subsequent professional employment. By 1913 the Federation of German Women's Association, an umbrella organization for regional feminist groups, had some 470,000 members. Their protests had a direct impact on the revised German Civil Code of 1906, which granted women substantial gains in family law and property rights.

Women inspired by utopian and especially Marxist socialism (see Chapter 21) blazed an alternative path. Often scorning the reform programs of middle-class feminists, socialist women leaders argued that the liberation of working-class women would come only with the liberation of the entire working class through revolution. In the meantime, they championed the cause of working women and won some practical improvements, especially in Germany, where the socialist movement was most effectively organized. In a general way, these different approaches to women's issues reflected the diversity of classes in urban society.

Science and Thought

Focus Question	How and why did intellectual life change in this period?

Major changes in Western science and thought accompanied the emergence of urban society. Two aspects of these complex intellectual developments stand out as especially significant. First, scientific knowledge in many areas expanded rapidly. Breakthroughs in chemistry, physics, and electricity profoundly influenced the Western worldview and spurred the creation of new products and whole industries. The natural and social sciences were also established as highly respected fields of study. Second, between about the 1840s and the 1890s Western arts and literature underwent a shift from soaring Romanticism to tough-minded Realism.

The Triumph of Science in Industry

The quickening pace of scientific advancements in the last third of the nineteenth century resulted in many practical benefits. The intellectual achievements of the Scientific Revolution (see Chapter 16) had resulted in few such benefits, and theoretical knowledge had also played a relatively small role in the Industrial Revolution in England (see Chapter 20). But breakthroughs in industrial technology in the late eighteenth century enormously stimulated basic scientific inquiry as researchers sought to explain theoretically how such things as steam engines and blast furnaces actually worked. The result was an explosive growth of fundamental scientific discoveries from the 1830s onward. In contrast to earlier periods, these theoretical discoveries were increasingly transformed into material improvements for the general population.

A perfect example of the translation of better scientific knowledge into practical human benefits was the work of Louis Pasteur and his followers in biology and the medical sciences (see page 693). Another was the development of the branch of physics known as **thermodynamics**. Building on Isaac Newton's laws of mechanics and on studies of steam engines, thermodynamics investigated the relationship between heat and mechanical energy. The law of conservation of energy held that different forms of energy—such as heat, electricity, and magnetism—could be converted but neither created nor destroyed. By midcentury, physicists had formulated the fundamental laws of thermodynamics, which were then applied to mechanical engineering, chemical processes, and many other fields.

Chemistry and electricity were two other fields characterized by extremely rapid scientific progress. And in both fields, "science was put in the service of industry," as the influential economist Alfred Marshall (1842–1924) argued at the time. Chemists devised ways of measuring the atomic weight of different elements, and in 1869 the Russian chemist Dmitri Mendeleev (mehn-duh-LAY-uhf) (1834–1907) codified the rules of chemistry in the periodic law and the periodic table. Chemistry was subdivided into many specialized branches, including organic chemistry — the study of the compounds of carbon. Applying theoretical insights gleaned from this new field, researchers in large German chemical companies discovered ways of transforming the dirty, useless coal tar that accumulated in coke ovens into beautiful, expensive synthetic dyes for the world of fashion. German production of synthetic dyes soared, and by 1900 German chemical companies controlled 90 percent of world production.

Electricity, a scientific curiosity in 1800, was totally transformed by a century of tremendous technological advancement. It became a commercial form of energy, first used in communications (the telegraph, which spurred quick international communication with the laying of underwater cables), then in electrochemistry (refining aluminum, for example), and finally in central power generation (for lighting, transportation, and industrial motors). And by 1890 the internal combustion engine fueled by petroleum was an emerging competitor to steam and electricity alike.

The successful application of scientific research in the fast-growing electrical and organic chemical industries between 1880 and 1913 provided a model for other industries. Systematic "R&D" — research and development — was born in the late nineteenth century. Above all, the burst of industrial creativity and technological innovation, often called the **Second Industrial Revolution**, promoted the strong economic growth in the last third of the nineteenth century that drove the urban reforms and the rising standard of living considered in this chapter.

The triumph of science and technology had three other significant consequences. First, though ordinary citizens continued to lack detailed scientific knowledge, everyday experience and innumerable articles in newspapers and magazines impressed the importance of science on the popular mind. Second, as science became more prominent in popular thinking, the philosophical implications of science formulated in the Enlightenment spread to broad sections of the population. Natural processes appeared to be determined by rigid laws, leaving little room for either divine intervention or human will. Yet scientific and technical advances had also fed the Enlightenment's optimistic faith in human progress, which now appeared endless and automatic to growing numbers of people. Third, the methods of science acquired unrivaled prestige after 1850. For many, the union of careful experiment and abstract theory was the only reliable route to truth and objective reality. The "unscientific" intuitions of poets and the revelations of saints seemed hopelessly inferior.

Darwin and Natural Selection

Scientific research also progressed rapidly outside of the world of industry and technology, sometimes putting forth direct challenges to traditional beliefs. In geology, for example, Charles Lyell (1797–1875) effectively discredited the long-standing view that the earth's surface had been formed by short-lived cataclysms, such as biblical floods and earthquakes. Instead, according to Lyell's principle of uniformitarianism, the same geological processes that are at work today slowly formed the earth's surface over an immensely long time. The vast timescale required for the processes that Lyell described to have these effects undermined traditional beliefs about the age of the earth based on religious teachings. Similarly, the evolutionary view of biological development, first proposed by the Greek Anaximander in the sixth century B.C.E., re-emerged in a more modern form in the work of French naturalist Jean-Baptiste Lamarck (1744–1829). Lamarck asserted that all forms of life had arisen through a long process of continuous adjustment to the environment, a dramatic challenge to the belief in divine creation of species.

Lamarck's work was flawed — he believed that the characteristics parents acquired in the course of their lives could be inherited by their children — and was not accepted, but it helped prepare the way for Charles Darwin (1809–1882), the most influential of all nineteenth-century evolutionary thinkers. As the official naturalist on a five-year scientific cruise to Latin America and the South Pacific beginning in 1831, Darwin carefully collected specimens of the different animal species he encountered on the voyage. Back in England, convinced by fossil evidence and by his friend Lyell that the earth and life on it were immensely ancient, Darwin came to doubt the general belief in a special divine creation of each species of animal. Instead, he concluded, all life had gradually evolved from a common ancestral origin in an unending "struggle for survival." After long hesitation, Darwin published his research, which immediately attracted wide attention.

Darwin's great originality lay in suggesting precisely how biological evolution might have occurred. His theory of **evolution** is summarized in the title of his work *On the Origin of Species by the Means of Natural Selection* (1859). Decisively influenced by the gloomy assertions of Thomas Malthus (MAL-thuhs) that populations naturally grow faster than their food supplies (see Chapter 20), Darwin argued that chance differences among the individual members of a given species help some survive while others die. Thus the variations that prove useful in the struggle for survival are selected naturally, and they gradually spread to the entire species through reproduction.

Darwin's controversial theory had a powerful and many-sided influence on European thought and the European middle classes. Because his ideas seemed to suggest that evolution moved along without God's intervention, and that humans were simply one species among many others, some conservatives accused Darwin of anti-Christian beliefs and mocked him for suggesting that humans descended from apes. Others hailed Darwin as the great scientist par excellence, the "Newton of biology," who had revealed once again the powers of objective science.

Some thinkers went a step further and applied Darwin's theory of biological evolution to human affairs. English philosopher Herbert Spencer (1820–1903) saw the human race as driven forward to ever-greater specialization and progress by a brutal economic struggle that determined the "survival of the fittest." The poor were the ill-fated weak; the prosperous were the chosen strong. Spencer's **Social Darwinism** gained adherents among nationalists, who viewed global competition between countries as a grand struggle for survival, as well as among imperialists, who used Social Darwinist ideas to justify the "natural" rule of the supposedly more civilized West over their colonial subjects and territories.

The Modern University and the Social Sciences

By the 1880s major universities across Europe had been modernized and professionalized. Education now emphasized controlled research projects in newly established clinics and laboratories; advanced students conducted independent research in seminar settings. An increasingly diversified professoriate established many of the academic departments still found in today's universities, from anthropology to zoology. In a striking development, faculty devoted to the newly instituted human or social sciences took their place alongside the hard sciences. Using critical methods often borrowed from natural science, social scientists studied massive sets of numerical data that governments had begun to collect on everything from birthrates to crime and from population to prostitution. Like Karl Marx, they were fascinated by the rise of capitalism and modernity; unlike Marx, they preferred to understand rather than revolutionize society.

Sociology, the critical analysis of contemporary or historical social groups, emerged as a leading social science. Perhaps the most prominent and influential late-nineteenth-century sociologist was the German Max Weber (1864–1920). In his most famous book, *The Protestant Ethic and the Spirit of Capitalism* (1890), Weber argued that the rise of capitalism was directly linked to Protestantism in northern Europe. Pointing to the early and successful modernization of countries like the Netherlands and England, he concluded that Protestantism gave religious approval to hard work, saving, and investing—the foundations for capitalist development—because worldly success was a sign of God's approval. This famous argument seriously challenged the basic ideas of Marxism: ideas, for Weber, were just as important as economics or class struggle in the rise of capitalism. Yet like Marx, Weber held a critical view of the rationalization of the human spirit, trapped in what he called the "iron cage" of capitalist relations. Modern industrial society, according to Weber, had turned people into "specialists without spirit, hedonists without heart." An ambitious scholar, Weber wrote extensively on capitalist rationalization, modern bureaucracy, industrialization and agriculture, and the forms of political leadership.

In France, the prolific sociologist Émile Durkheim (1858–1917) earned an international reputation for his wide-ranging work. His study of the psychic and social basis of religion, *The Elementary Forms of Religious Life* (1912), remains a classic of social-scientific thought. In his pioneering work of quantitative sociology, *Suicide* (1897), Durkheim concluded that ever-higher suicide rates were caused by widespread feelings of "anomie," or rootlessness. Because modern society had stripped life of all sense of tradition, purpose, and belonging, Durkheim believed, anomie was inescapable; only an entirely new moral order might offer some relief.

Other sociologists contributed to the critique of modern society. The German Ferdinand Tönnies (1855–1936) argued that with industrialization Western civilization had undergone a fundamental transformation from "community" to "society." Rationalized self-interest had replaced traditional values, leading to intensified alienation and a cold bureaucratic age. In *The Crowd* (1895), French sociologist Gustav Le Bon (1841–1931) wrote that the alienated masses were prone to gathering in mass crowds, in which individuals lost control over their emotions and actions. According to the deeply conservative Le Bon, a strong, charismatic leader could easily manipulate the crowd's collective psyche and turn the servile mass into a violent and dangerous revolutionary mob.

The new sociologists cast a bleak light on urban industrial society. While they acknowledged some benefits of rationalization and modernization, they bemoaned the accompanying loss of community and tradition. In some ways, their diagnosis of the modern individual as an isolated atom suffering from anomie and desperately seeking human connection was chillingly prescient: the powerful Communist and Fascist movements that swept through Europe after World War I seemed to win popular support precisely by offering ordinary people a renewed sense of social belonging.

Realism in Art and Literature

In art and literature, the key themes of **Realism** emerged in the 1840s and continued to dominate Western culture until the 1890s. Realist artists and writers believed that artistic works should depict life exactly as it was. Forsaking the personal, emotional viewpoint of

Realism in the Arts   Realist depictions of gritty everyday life challenged the Romantic emphasis on nature and the emotions, as well as the Neoclassical focus on famous men and grand events. French painter Honoré Daumier's *The Third-Class Carriage*, completed in 1864, is a famous example of Realism in the arts that portrays the effects of industrialization in the mid-nineteenth century. In muted colors, Daumier's painting captures the grinding poverty and weariness of the poor but also lends a sense of dignity to their humble lives. (Metropolitan Museum of Art, New York, USA/Bridgeman Images)

the Romantics for strict, supposedly factual objectivity, the Realists observed and recorded the world around them—often to expose the sordid reality of modern life.

Emphatically rejecting the Romantic search for the exotic and the sublime, Realism (or "Naturalism," as it was often called) energetically pursued the typical and the commonplace. Beginning with a dissection of the middle classes, from which most of them sprang, many Realists eventually focused on the working classes, especially the urban working classes, which had been neglected in imaginative literature before this time. The Realists put a microscope to many unexplored and taboo subjects, including sex, labor strikes, violence, and alcoholism, and hastened to report that slums and factories teemed with savage behavior. Shocked middle-class critics denounced Realism as ugly sensationalism wrapped provocatively in pseudoscientific declarations and crude language—even as the movement attracted a growing middle-class audience, fascinated by the sensationalist view "from below."

The Realist movement began in France, where Romanticism had never been completely dominant. Artists like Gustave Courbet, Jean-François Millet, and Honoré Daumier painted scenes of laboring workers and peasants in somber colors and simple compositions, exemplified in Daumier's 1864 painting *The Third-Class Carriage* (see page 717). Daumier's art championed the simple virtues of the working class and lampooned the greed and ill will of the rich bourgeoisie; a caricature of King Louis Philippe earned him six months in prison.

Literary Realism also began in France, where Honoré de Balzac, Gustave Flaubert, and Émile Zola became internationally famous novelists. Balzac (1799–1850) spent thirty years writing a vastly ambitious panorama of postrevolutionary French life. Known collectively as *The Human Comedy*, this series of nearly one hundred stories, novels, and essays vividly portrays more than two thousand characters from virtually all sectors of French society. Balzac pictured urban society as grasping, amoral, and brutal. In his novel *Father Goriot* (1835), the hero, a poor student from the provinces, eventually surrenders his idealistic integrity to feverish ambition and society's pervasive greed.

Madame Bovary (1857), the masterpiece of Flaubert (floh-BEHR) (1821–1880), is far narrower in scope than Balzac's work but is still famous for its depth of psychological insight and critique of middle-class values. Unsuccessfully prosecuted as an outrage against public morality and religion, Flaubert's carefully crafted novel tells the ordinary, even banal, story of a frustrated middle-class housewife who has an adulterous love affair and is betrayed by her lover. Without moralizing, Flaubert portrays the provincial middle class as petty, smug, and hypocritical.

Émile Zola (1840–1902) was most famous for his seamy, animalistic view of working-class life. But he also wrote gripping, carefully researched stories featuring the stock exchange, the big department store, and the army, as well as urban slums and bloody battles between police and sturdy coal strikers. Like many later Realists, Zola sympathized with socialism, a view evident in his overpowering novel *Germinal* (1885).

Realism quickly spread beyond France. In England, Mary Ann Evans (1819–1880), who wrote under the pen name George Eliot, brilliantly achieved a more deeply felt, less sensational kind of Realism in her great novel *Middlemarch: A Study of Provincial Life* (1871–1872). The novels of Thomas Hardy (1840–1928), such as *Tess of the D'Urbervilles* (1891) and *The Return of the Native* (1878), depict ordinary men and women frustrated and crushed by social prejudice, sexual puritanism, and bad luck. The greatest Russian Realist, Count Leo Tolstoy (1828–1910), combined Realism in description and character development with an atypical moralizing, especially in his later work. In *War and Peace* (1864–1869), a monumental novel set against the background of Napoleon's invasion of Russia in 1812, Tolstoy developed his fatalistic theory of human history, which regards free will as an illusion and the achievements of even the greatest leaders as only the channeling of historical necessity. Yet Tolstoy's central message is one that most of the people discussed in this chapter would have readily accepted: human love, trust, and everyday family ties are life's enduring values.

NOTES

1. S. Marcus, "Reading the Illegible," in *The Victorian City: Images and Realities*, ed. H. J. Dyos and Michael Wolff, vol. 1 (London: Routledge & Kegan Paul, 1973), p. 266.
2. Quoted in E. Chadwick, *Report on the Sanitary Condition of the Labouring Population of Great Britain*, ed. M. W. Flinn (Edinburgh: University of Edinburgh Press, 1965; original publication, 1842), pp. 315–316.
3. J. McKay, *Tramways and Trolleys: The Rise of Urban Mass Transport in Europe* (Princeton, N.J.: Princeton University Press, 1976), p. 81.
4. Quoted in R. P. Neuman, "The Sexual Question and Social Democracy in Imperial Germany," *Journal of Social History* 7 (Winter 1974): 276.
5. Quoted in J. A. Banks, "The Contagion of Numbers," in *The Victorian City: Images and Realities*, ed. H. J. Dyos and Michael Wolff, vol. 1 (London: Routledge & Kegan Paul, 1973), p. 112.
6. Quoted in R. Roberts, *The Classic Slum: Salford Life in the First Quarter of the Century* (Manchester, U.K.: University of Manchester Press, 1971), p. 95.
7. J. Frykman and O. Löfgren, *Culture Builders: A Historical Anthropology of Middle-Class Life* (New Brunswick, N.J.: Rutgers University Press, 1987), p. 134.
8. See the pioneering work of J. de Vries, *The Industrious Revolution: Consumer Behavior and the Household Economy* (Cambridge: Cambridge University Press, 2008), especially pp. 186–237.
9. Roberts, *The Classic Slum*, p. 35.
10. Quoted in T. Zeldin, *France, 1848–1945*, vol. 1 (Oxford: Clarendon Press, 1973), p. 328.
11. Quoted in Neuman, "The Sexual Question," p. 281.
12. Frykman and Löfgren, *Culture Builders*, p. 114.

LOOKING BACK LOOKING AHEAD

When the peoples of northwestern Europe looked out at the economic and social landscape in the early twentieth century, they had good reason to feel that the promise of the Industrial Revolution was being realized. The dark days of urban squalor and brutal working hours had given way after 1850 to a gradual rise in the standard of living for all classes. Scientific discoveries were combining with the applied technology of public health and industrial production to save lives and drive continued economic growth.

Moreover, social and economic advances seemed to be matched by progress in the political sphere. The years following the dramatic failure of the revolutions of 1848 saw the creation of unified nation-states in Italy and Germany, and after 1870, as we shall see in the following chapters, nationalism and the nation-state reigned in Europe. Although the rise of nationalism created tensions among the European countries, these tensions would not explode until 1914 and the outbreak of the First World War. Instead, the most aggressive and destructive aspects of European nationalism found their initial outlet in the final and most powerful surge of Western overseas expansion. Thus Europe, transformed by industrialization and nationalism, rushed after 1875 to seize territory and build new or greatly expanded authoritarian empires in Asia and Africa.

MAKE CONNECTIONS

Think about the larger developments and continuities within and across chapters.

1. What were the most important changes in everyday life from the eighteenth century (Chapter 18) to the nineteenth century? What main causes or agents drove these changes?

2. Did the life of ordinary people improve, stay the same, or even deteriorate over the nineteenth century when compared to the previous century? What role did developments in science, medicine, and urban planning play in this process?

3. How did the emergence of a society divided into working and middle classes affect the workplace, homemaking, and family values and gender roles?

Chapter Review

IDENTIFY KEY TERMS

Identify and explain the significance of each item below.

utilitarianism (p. 691)

germ theory (p. 693)

labor aristocracy (p. 701)

sweated industries (p. 702)

companionate marriage (p. 705)

separate spheres (p. 708)

suffrage movement (p. 712)

thermodynamics (p. 713)

Second Industrial Revolution (p. 714)

evolution (p. 715)

Social Darwinism (p. 715)

Realism (p. 717)

REVIEW THE MAIN IDEAS

Answer the focus questions from each section of the chapter.

1. How did urban life change in the nineteenth century? (p. 689)

2. What did the emergence of urban industrial society mean for rich and poor and those in between? (p. 696)

3. How did urbanization affect family life and gender roles? (p. 704)

4. How and why did intellectual life change in this period? (p. 713)

CHRONOLOGY	
ca. 1840s–1890s	Realism dominant in Western arts and literature
1848	Cholera epidemic and first public health law in Britain
ca. 1850–1870	Modernization of Paris
1850–1914	Condition of working classes improves
1854	Pasteur begins studying fermentation and in 1863 develops pasteurization
1854–1870	Development of germ theory
1859	Darwin publishes *On the Origin of Species by the Means of Natural Selection*
1865	Completion of London sewer system
1869	Mendeleev creates periodic table
1880–1913	Second Industrial Revolution; birthrate steadily declines in Europe
1890	Max Weber publishes *The Protestant Ethic and the Spirit of Capitalism*
1890s	Electric streetcars introduced in Europe

23

The Age of Nationalism

1850–1914

IN THE YEARS THAT FOLLOWED THE REVOLUTIONS OF 1848, Western society progressively developed, for better or worse, an effective organizing principle capable of coping with the many-sided challenges of the unfinished industrial and political revolutions and the emerging urban society. That principle was nationalism—mass identification with the nation-state. Just as industrialization and urbanization had brought vast changes to class relations, family lifestyles, and science and culture, the triumph of nationalism remade territorial boundaries and forged new relations between the nation-state and its citizens.

The rise of nationalism and the nation-state, enormously significant historical developments, was by no means completely predictable. Nationalism had been a powerful force since at least 1789, but the goal of creating independent nation-states, inhabited by people sharing a common ethnicity, language, history, and territory, had repeatedly failed, most spectacularly in the revolutions of 1848. By 1914, however, most Europeans lived in nation-states, and the ideology of nationalism had become an almost universal faith in the Western world. The governments of the new nation-states took various forms, from conservative authoritarianism to parliamentary monarchy to liberal republicanism. Whatever the political system, in most cases the nation-state became increasingly responsive to the needs of its people, opening the political franchise and offering citizens at least rudimentary social and economic benefits. At the same time, the nation-state demanded more from its citizens, most obviously in the form of rising income taxes and universal military service. Nationalism, which before 1848 appealed primarily to liberals seeking political reform or national independence, became an ever more conservative ideology. At its worst, populists and fanatics eagerly manipulated and sometimes abused the growing patriotism of ordinary people to justify exclusionary policies against Jews and other ethnic minorities, and to promote expansionary projects in overseas colonies.

Napoleon III in France

Focus Question	How did Napoleon III seek to reconcile popular and conservative forces in an authoritarian nation-state?

Early nationalism was generally liberal and idealistic and could be democratic and radical (see Chapter 21). Yet nationalism also flourished in authoritarian states, which imposed social and economic changes from above. Napoleon Bonaparte's France had already combined national feeling with authoritarian rule. Napoleon's nephew, Louis Napoleon, revived and extended this combination.

France's Second Republic

Although Louis Napoleon Bonaparte had played no part in French politics before 1848, universal male suffrage and widespread popular support gave him three times as many votes as the four other presidential candidates combined in the French presidential election of December 1848. This outcome occurred for several reasons. First, he had the great name of his uncle, whom romantics had transformed into a demigod after 1820. Second, as Karl Marx stressed at the time, middle-class and peasant property owners feared the socialist challenge of urban workers and the chaos of the revolution of 1848, and they wanted a tough ruler to protect their property and provide stability. Third, Louis Napoleon enunciated a positive program for France in pamphlets widely circulated before the election.

Above all, Louis Napoleon promoted a vision of national unity and social progress. He believed that the government should represent the people and help them economically. But how could these tasks be accomplished? Corrupt parliaments and political parties were not the answer, according to Louis Napoleon. French politicians represented special-interest groups, particularly middle-class ones. The answer was a strong, even authoritarian, national leader, like the first Napoleon, whose efforts to provide jobs and stimulate the economy would serve all people, rich and poor. This leader would be linked to each citizen by direct democracy, his sovereignty uncorrupted by politicians and legislative bodies. To the many common people who voted for him, Louis Napoleon appeared to be a strong leader and a forward-looking champion of popular interests.

Elected to a four-year term by an overwhelming majority, Louis Napoleon was required by the constitution to share power with the National Assembly, which was overwhelmingly conservative. With some misgivings, he signed conservative-sponsored bills that increased greatly the role of the Catholic Church in primary and secondary education and deprived many poor people of the right to vote. He took these steps in hopes that the Assembly would vote funds to pay his personal debts and change the constitution so he could run for a second term.

But in 1851, after the Assembly failed to cooperate with that last aim, Louis Napoleon began to conspire with key army officers. On December 2, 1851, he illegally dismissed the legislature and seized power in a coup d'état. There was some armed resistance in Paris and widespread insurrection in the countryside in southern France, but the army crushed these popular protests. Restoring universal male suffrage and claiming to stand above political bickering, Louis Napoleon called on the conservative national state that promised economic growth, social benefits, and national unity, as in France? This was one of the great political questions in the 1850s and 1860s. In Europe, the national unification of Italy and Germany offered a resounding answer. In the United States, nation building marked by sectional differences over slavery offered another.

Italy to 1850

Before 1850 Italy had never been united. The Italian peninsula was divided in the Middle Ages into competing city-states. A battleground for the Great Powers after 1494, Italy was reorganized in 1815 at the Congress of Vienna into a hodgepodge of different states. Austrian foreign minister Prince Klemens von Metternich captured the essence of the situation when he dismissed Italy as only "a geographical expression" (Map 23.1).

MAP 23.1 The Unification of Italy, 1859–1870
The leadership of Sardinia-Piedmont, nationalist fervor, and Garibaldi's attack on the Kingdom of the Two Sicilies were decisive factors in the unification of Italy.

Between 1815 and 1848 the goal of a unified Italian nation captured the imaginations of many Italians. There were three basic approaches. First, the radical and idealistic patriot Giuseppe Mazzini called for a centralized democratic republic based on universal male suffrage and the will of the people. Second, Vincenzo Gioberti, a Catholic priest, sought a federation of existing states under the presidency of a progressive pope. The third approach centered on Victor Emmanuel II, the autocratic king of Sardinia-Piedmont. Many Italians sought a federation under this prominent king, much as Germans looked to Prussia for national leadership. It helped that Piedmont was one of the most industrialized, modern territories in the Italian peninsula.

The third alternative was strengthened by the failures of 1848, when Austria smashed Mazzini's republicanism. Victor Emmanuel II, crowned in 1849, retained the liberal constitution granted by his father under duress the previous year. This constitution combined a strong monarchy with a fair degree of civil liberties and parliamentary government, though deputies were elected by a limited franchise based on income. To some of the Italian middle classes, the Kingdom of Sardinia-Piedmont appeared to be a liberal, progressive state ideally suited to drive Austria out of northern Italy and lead a united Italy. By contrast, Mazzini's brand of democratic republicanism seemed quixotic and too radical.

As for the papacy, the initial cautious support for unification under Pope Pius IX (pontificate 1846–1878) had given way to hostility after he was temporarily driven from Rome during the upheavals of 1848. For a long generation, the papacy opposed not only national unification but also most modern trends. In 1864 in the *Syllabus of Errors*, Pius IX denounced rationalism, socialism, separation of church and state, and religious liberty. The Catholic Church would be a bulwark against liberalism and progressive reform for the next two decades.

Cavour and Garibaldi in Italy

The struggle for Italian unification under Emmanuel II was supported by a brilliant statesman, Count Camillo Benso di Cavour (kuh-VOOR), who served as prime minister of Sardinia-Piedmont from 1852 until his death in 1861. A nobleman who made a substantial fortune in business before entering politics, Cavour had limited and realistic national goals. Until 1859 he sought unity only with the states of northern and perhaps central Italy, which would nonetheless greatly expand the existing kingdom.

In the 1850s Cavour worked to consolidate Sardinia-Piedmont as a liberal constitutional state capable of leading northern Italy. His program of building highways and railroads, expanding civil liberties, and opposing clerical privilege increased support for his efforts throughout northern Italy. Yet Cavour realized that Sardinia-Piedmont could not drive Austria out of the north without the help of a powerful ally. Accordingly, he established a secret alliance with Napoleon III against Austria in July 1858.

Cavour then goaded Austria into attacking Piedmont in 1859, and Louis Napoleon came to Italy's defense. After defeating the Austrians at the Battles of Magenta and Solferino, however, Napoleon did a sudden about-face. Worried by criticism from French Catholics for supporting the pope's declared enemy, he abandoned Cavour and made a compromise peace with the Austrians in July 1859. The Kingdom of Sardinia-Piedmont received only Lombardy, the area around Milan, from Austria. The rest of Italy remained essentially unchanged.

government's most enthusiastic supporters. Alexander II consolidated imperial control by suppressing nationalist movements among Poles, Ukrainians, and Baltic peoples in the western lands of the Russian Empire. By 1900 the Russian Empire commanded a vast and diverse array of peoples and places.

Alexander II's political reforms outraged reactionaries but never went far enough for liberals and radicals. In 1881 a member of the "People's Will," a small anarchist group, assassinated the tsar, and the era of reform came to an abrupt end. The new tsar, Alexander III (r. 1881–1894), was a determined reactionary. Nevertheless, from 1890 to 1900 economic modernization and industrialization surged ahead for the second time, led by Sergei Witte (suhr-GAY VIH-tuh), finance minister from 1892 to 1903. The tough, competent Witte believed that industrial backwardness threatened Russia's greatness. Under his leadership, the government doubled the network of state-owned railways to thirty-five thousand miles. Witte established high protective tariffs to support Russian industry, and he put the country on the gold standard to strengthen Russian finances.

Witte's greatest innovation was to use Westerners to catch up with the West. He encouraged foreigners to build factories in Russia, believing that "the inflow of foreign capital is . . . the only way by which our industry will be able to supply our country quickly with abundant and cheap products."[1] His efforts to entice western Europeans to locate their factories in Russia were especially successful in southern Russia. There, in eastern Ukraine, foreign entrepreneurs and engineers built an enormous and very modern steel and coal industry. In 1900 peasants still constituted the great majority of the population, but Russia was catching up with the more industrialized West.

The Russian Revolution of 1905

Catching up partly meant further territorial expansion, for this was the age of Western imperialism. By 1903 Russia had established a sphere of influence in Chinese Manchuria and was eyeing northern Korea, which put Russia in conflict with the goals of an equally imperialistic Japan. Tsar Nicholas II (r. 1894–1917), who replaced his father in 1894, ignored their diplomatic protests. In response, the Japanese launched a surprise attack on Port Arthur, a Russian naval base in northern China, in February 1904. The resulting Russo-Japanese war lasted less than a year. After Japan scored repeated victories, which included annihilating a Russian fleet, the humiliated Russians surrendered in September 1905.

Once again, military disaster abroad brought political upheaval at home. The business and professional classes had long wanted a liberal, representative government. Urban factory workers were organized in a radical and still-illegal labor movement. Peasants had gained little from the era of reforms and suffered from poverty and overpopulation. At the same time, the empire's minorities and subject nationalities, such as the Poles, the Ukrainians, and the Latvians, continued to call for self-rule. With the army pinned down in Manchuria, all these currents of discontent converged in the revolution of 1905.

On a Sunday in January 1905, a massive crowd of workers and their families converged peacefully on the Winter Palace in St. Petersburg to present a petition to Nicholas II. Suddenly troops opened fire, killing and wounding hundreds. The

Bloody Sunday massacre produced a wave of general indignation that turned many Russians against the tsar.

By the summer of 1905 strikes and political rallies, peasant uprisings, revolts among minority nationalities, and mutinies by troops were sweeping the country. The revolutionary surge culminated in October 1905 in a paralyzing general strike that forced the government to capitulate. The tsar then issued the October Manifesto, which granted full civil rights and promised a popularly elected **Duma** (or parliament) with real legislative power. The manifesto split the opposition. Frightened middle-class leaders embraced it, which helped the government repress the popular uprising and survive as a constitutional monarchy.

On the eve of the opening of the first Duma in May 1906, the government issued the new constitution, the Fundamental Laws. The tsar retained great powers. The Duma, elected indirectly by universal male suffrage with a largely appointive upper house, could debate and pass laws, but the tsar had an absolute veto. As in Bismarck's Germany, the tsar appointed his ministers, who did not need to command a majority in the Duma.

The predominantly middle-class liberals, the largest group in the newly elected Duma, saw the Fundamental Laws as a step backward. Cooperation with Nicholas II's ministers soon broke down, and after months of deadlock the tsar dismissed the Duma. Thereupon he and his advisers, including the talented Pyotr Stolypin, who served as prime minister, unilaterally rewrote the electoral law. These revisions greatly increased the electoral weight of the conservative propertied classes. When new elections were held, the tsar could count on a legislative majority loyal to the monarchy. His government then pushed through important agrarian reforms designed to break down collective village ownership of land and encourage the more enterprising peasants—Stolypin's "wager on the strong and sober," meant to encourage economic growth. The government reformed the education and banking systems, but these acts were accompanied by harsh repression of dissidents and radicals. About three thousand suspected revolutionaries were executed by the state, and the hangman's noose became known as "Stolypin's necktie." In 1914, on the eve of the First World War, Russia was partially modernized, a conservative constitutional monarchy with a peasant-based but industrializing economy and significant pockets of discontent.

Reform and Readjustment in the Ottoman Empire

By the early nineteenth century the economic and political changes reshaping Europe were also at play in the Ottoman Empire, which stretched around the northeastern, eastern, and southern shores of the Mediterranean Sea. The borderlands of this vast empire experienced constant flux and conflict. Russia had occupied Ottoman provinces on the Danube River in the last decades of the eighteenth century and grabbed more during the Napoleonic Wars. In 1816 the Ottomans were forced to grant Serbia local autonomy. In 1830 the Greeks won independence, and French armies began their long and bloody takeover of Ottoman Algeria. Yet the Ottomans achieved important victories during the same decades. Egyptian forces under the leadership of Muhammad Ali, the Ottoman governor in Egypt, restored order in the Islamic holy lands and conquered significant portions of Sudan, south of Egypt.

Pasha Hilim Receiving Archduke Maximilian of Austria   As this painting suggests, Ottoman leaders became well versed in European languages and culture. They also mastered the game of power politics, playing one European state against another to secure the Ottoman Empire's survival. (By Peter Johann Nepomuk Geiger [1805–1880]/Miramare Palace, Trieste, Italy/ Alfredo Dagli Orti/The Art Archive at Art Resource, NY)

Muhammad Ali, a ruthless and intelligent soldier-politician, ruled Egypt in the name of the Ottoman sultan from 1805 to 1848. His modernizing reforms of agriculture, industry, and the military (see Chapter 24) helped turn Egypt into the most powerful state in the eastern Mediterranean. In time, his growing strength directly challenged the Ottoman sultan and Istanbul's ruling elite. From 1831 to 1840 Egyptian troops under the leadership of Muhammad Ali's son Ibrahim occupied and governed the Ottoman province of Syria and Palestine, and threatened to depose the Ottoman sultan Mahmud II (r. 1808–1839).

This conflict forced the Ottomans to seek European support. Mahmud II's dynasty survived, but only because the European powers, led by Britain, allied with the Ottomans to discipline Muhammad Ali. The European powers preferred a weak and dependent Ottoman Empire to a strong, economically independent state under a dynamic leader such as Muhammad Ali.

Faced with growing European military and economic competition, liberal Ottoman statesmen in 1839 launched an era of radical reforms known as the **Tanzimat**, or "Reorganization." The Tanzimat reforms, borrowed from western European models, were designed to modernize the empire. The high point of reform came when the new liberal-minded sultan, Abdul Mejid (r. 1839–1861), issued the Imperial Rescript of 1856, just after the Crimean War. Articles in the decree called for equality before the law regardless of religious faith, a modernized administration and army, and private ownership of land. As part of the reform policy, and under economic pressure from the European powers that had paid for the empire's war against Russia in Crimea, Ottoman leaders adopted free-trade policies. New commercial laws removed tariffs on foreign imports and permitted foreign merchants to operate freely throughout the empire.

The turn to nineteenth-century liberal capitalism had mixed effects. On one hand, with the growth of Western-style banking and insurance systems, elite Christian and Jewish businessmen in the empire prospered. Yet the bulk of the profits went to foreign investors rather than Ottoman subjects. More important, the elimination of traditional state-controlled monopolies sharply cut imperial revenues. In 1851 Sultan Mejid was forced to borrow 55 million francs from British and French bankers to cover state deficits. Other loans followed, and intractable indebtedness led to the bankruptcy of the Ottoman state two decades later.

Intended to bring revolutionary modernization, the Tanzimat permitted partial recovery but fell short of its goals. The Ottoman initiatives did not curtail the appetite of Western imperialists, who secured a stranglehold on the imperial economy via issuing loans. The reforms also failed to halt the growth of nationalism among some Christian subjects in the Balkans, which resulted in crises and increased pressure from neighboring Austria and Russia, eager to gain access to the Balkans and the eastern Mediterranean.

Finally, equality before the law for all citizens, regardless of religious affiliation, actually increased religious disputes, which were often encouraged and manipulated by the European powers eager to seize any pretext for intervention. This development embittered relations between religious conservatives and social liberals, a struggle that ultimately distracted the government from its reform mission. Religious conservatives in both the Muslim and Greek Orthodox communities detested the religious reforms, which they viewed as an impious departure from tradition. These conservatives became dependable supporters of Sultan Abdülhamid II (ahb-dool-hah-MEED) (r. 1876–1909), who in 1876 halted the reform movement and turned away from European liberalism in his long and repressive reign.

Abdülhamid II's government failed to halt foreign efforts to fragment and ultimately take control over key Ottoman territories. Defeat in the Russo-Turkish War (1877–1878) meant the loss to Russia of Ottoman districts in the Caucasus; formal declarations of independence for Romania, Montenegro, and Serbia, all former Ottoman territories in the Balkans; and the establishment of an autonomous Bulgaria, still nominally under the Ottoman sultan's control. By the 1890s the government's failures had encouraged a powerful resurgence of the modernizing impulse under the banner of the Committee of Union and Progress (CUP), an umbrella organization that united multiethnic reformist groups from across the empire. These fervent patriots, unofficially called the **Young Turks**, seized power in a 1908 coup and forced the sultan to implement new reforms. Although they failed to stop the rising tide of anti-Ottoman nationalism in the Balkans, the Young Turks helped prepare the way for the rise of modern secular Turkey after the defeat and collapse of the Ottoman Empire in World War I.

The Responsive National State, 1871–1914

Focus Question	What general domestic political trends emerged after 1871?

The decades after 1870 brought rapid change to the structures and ideas of European politics. Despite some major differences between countries, European domestic politics had a new common framework, the nation-state. The common themes within that framework were the emergence of mass politics and growing popular loyalty toward the nation. Traditional elites hardly disappeared, but they were forced into new arrangements in order to exercise power, and a group of new, pragmatic politicians took leading roles. The major states of western Europe adopted constitutions of some sort, and universal male suffrage was granted in Britain, France, and Germany and elsewhere, at least in voting for the lower houses of parliament. New political parties representing a broad spectrum of interests and groups, from workers and liberals to Catholics and conservatives, engaged in hard-fought election campaigns to provide benefits to their constituencies.

Powerful bureaucracies emerged to govern growing populations and manage modern economies, and the growth of the state spurred a growth in the social responsibilities of government. The new responsive national state offered its citizens free education and some welfare and public health benefits, and for good reason many ordinary people felt increasing loyalty to their governments and their nations.

Building popular support for strong nation-states had a less positive side. Conservative and moderate leaders both found that workers who voted socialist—whose potential revolutionary power they feared—would rally around the flag in a diplomatic crisis or cheer when colonial interests seized a distant territory of doubtful value. Therefore, after 1871 governing elites frequently used antiliberal militarist and imperialist policies in attempts to unite national populations and overcome or mask intractable domestic conflicts. In the end, the manipulation of foreign policy to manage domestic issues inflamed the international tensions that erupted in the cataclysms of World War I and the Russian Revolution.

The German Empire

The history of Germany after 1871 exemplified many of these general political developments. Like the United States, the new German Empire adopted a federal system: a union of Prussia and twenty-four smaller states, each with separate legislatures. Much of the everyday business of government was conducted by the individual states, but there was a strong national government with a chancellor—until 1890, Bismarck—and a popularly elected national parliament called the **Reichstag** (RIKES-tahg). Although Bismarck repeatedly ignored the wishes of the parliamentary majority, he nonetheless preferred to win the support of the Reichstag to lend legitimacy to his policy goals. This situation gave the political parties opportunities to influence national policy. Until 1878 Bismarck relied mainly on the National Liberals, who had rallied to him after 1866. They supported legislation useful for economic growth and unification of the country.

Less wisely, the National Liberals backed Bismarck's attack on the Catholic Church, the so-called **Kulturkampf** (kool-TOOR-kahmpf), or "culture struggle." Like Bismarck, the middle-class National Liberals were alarmed by Pius IX's declaration of papal infallibility in 1870. That dogma seemed to ask German Catholics to put loyalty to their church, a foreign power, above their loyalty to their newly unified nation. Kulturkampf initiatives aimed at making the Catholic Church subject to government control. However, only in Protestant Prussia did the Kulturkampf have even limited success, because elsewhere Catholics generally voted for the Center Party, which blocked passage of laws hostile to the church.

In 1878 Bismarck abandoned his attack on the church and instead courted the Catholic Center Party, whose supporters included many Catholic small farmers in western and southern Germany. By revoking free-trade policy and enacting high tariffs on cheap grain from the United States, Canada, and Russia, he won over both the Catholic Center and the conservative Protestant Junkers, nobles with large landholdings in East Prussia.

Other governments followed Bismarck's lead, and the 1880s and 1890s saw a widespread return to protectionism in Europe. France, in particular, established very high tariffs to protect agriculture and industry. By raising tariffs, European governments offered an effective response to a major domestic economic problem — foreign competition — in a way that won greater popular loyalty. At the same time, the rise of protectionism exemplified the dangers of self-centered nationalism: new tariffs led to international name-calling and nasty trade wars.

After the failure of the Kulturkampf, Bismarck's government tried to stop the growth of the **German Social Democratic Party (SPD)**, Germany's Marxist, working-class political party, which was established in the 1870s. Both conservative elites and middle-class liberals genuinely feared the SPD's revolutionary language and allegiance to a Marxist movement that transcended the nation-state. In 1878 Bismarck pushed through the Reichstag the Anti-Socialist Laws, which banned Social Democratic associations, meetings, and publications. The Social Democratic Party was driven underground, but it maintained substantial influence, and Bismarck decided to try another tack.

In an attempt to win working-class support, Bismarck urged the Reichstag to enact a variety of state-supported social welfare measures. Big business and some conservatives accused him of creating "state socialism," but Bismarck ably pressed his program in many lively speeches, as the following excerpt suggests:

> Give the working-man the right to work as long as he is healthy; assure him care when he is sick; assure him maintenance when he is old. If you do that, and do not fear the [financial] sacrifice, or cry out at State Socialism as soon as the words "provision for old age" are uttered, — if the state would show a little more Christian solicitude for the working-man, then I believe the gentlemen of the Wyden [Social Democratic] program will sound their bird-call in vain, and that the thronging toward them will cease as soon as working-men see that the Government and legislative bodies are earnestly concerned with their welfare.[2]

> In all advanced countries we see the privileges of the capitalist bourgeoisie yielding step by step to democratic organizations. Under the influence of this, and driven by the movement of the working classes which is daily becoming stronger, a social reaction has set in against the exploiting tendencies of capital.[5]

Socialists, according to thinkers like Bernstein, should reform their doctrines and tactics to meet these changed conditions. They should combine with other progressive forces to win continued evolutionary gains for workers through legislation, unions, and further economic development. These views were denounced as heresy by the SPD and later by the Second International. Yet the revisionist, gradualist approach continued to gain the tacit acceptance of many German socialists, particularly in the trade unions.

Moderation found followers elsewhere. In France, the great socialist leader Jean Jaurès (1859–1914) formally repudiated revisionism in order to establish a unified socialist party, but he remained at heart a gradualist and optimistic secular humanist. Questions of revolution or revisionism also divided Russian Marxists.

By the early twentieth century socialist parties had clear-cut national characteristics. Russians and socialists in the Austro-Hungarian Empire tended to be the most radical. The German party talked revolution and practiced reformism, greatly influenced by its enormous trade-union movement. The French party talked revolution and tried to practice it, unrestrained by a trade-union movement that was both very weak and very radical. In Britain, the socialist but non-Marxist Labour Party, reflecting the well-established union movement, was formally committed to gradual reform. In Spain and Italy, Marxist socialism was very weak. There anarchism, seeking to smash the state rather than the bourgeoisie, dominated radical thought and action.

In short, socialist policies and doctrines varied from country to country. Socialism itself was to a large extent "nationalized" behind the façade of international unity. This helps explain why when war came in 1914, almost all socialist leaders and most workers supported their national governments and turned away from international solidarity.

NOTES

1. Quoted by J. McKay in *Pioneers for Profit: Foreign Entrepreneurship and Russian Industrialization, 1885–1913* (Chicago: University of Chicago Press, 1970), p. 11.
2. W. Dawson, *Bismarck and State Socialism* (London: Swan Sonnenschein & Co., 1890), pp. 63–64.
3. E. Weber, *Peasants into Frenchmen: The Modernization of Rural France, 1870–1914* (Stanford: Stanford University Press, 1976).
4. See E. Hobsbawm, "Mass Producing Traditions: Europe, 1870–1914," in *The Invention of Tradition*, ed. E. Hobsbawm and T. Ranger (New York: Cambridge University Press, 1992), pp. 263–307.
5. E. Bernstein, *Evolutionary Socialism: A Criticism and Affirmation*, trans. E. Harvey (New York: B. W. Huebsch, 1909), pp. x–xvi, quoted in J. H. Hexter et al., *The Traditions of the Western World* (Chicago: Rand McNally, 1967), pp. 797–798.

LOOKING BACK LOOKING AHEAD

In 1900 the triumph of the national state in Europe seemed almost complete. In the aging Austro-Hungarian, Russian, and Ottoman Empires, ethnic minorities continued to fight for national independence, and class, region, religion, and ethnicity still generated social and political differences across Europe. Nonetheless, the politically unified nation-state, resting solidly upon ongoing industrialization and the emerging urban society, governed with the consent and even the devotion of many of its citizens. Ordinary people developed a sense of patriotic allegiance to the nation and saw themselves as members of a national group — for instance, Swedes, Germans, Italians, or Americans. This newfound sense of national identity often eroded or leveled out other social differences.

Responsive and capable of tackling many practical problems, the European nation-state of 1900 was in part the realization of ideologues and patriots like Mazzini and the middle-class liberals active in the unsuccessful revolutions of 1848. Yet whereas early nationalists had envisioned a Europe of free peoples and international peace, the nationalists of 1900 had been nurtured in an atmosphere of competition between European states and the wars of unification in the 1850s and 1860s. This new generation of nationalists reveled in the strength of their unity, and the nation-state became the foundation stone of a new system of global power.

Thus after 1870, even as the responsive nation-state improved city life and brought social benefits to ordinary people, Europe's leading countries extended their imperial control around the globe. In Asia and Africa, the European powers seized territory, fought brutal colonial wars, and built authoritarian empires. Moreover, in Europe itself the universal faith in nationalism, which usually reduced social tensions within states, promoted a bitter, almost Darwinian, competition between states. Thus European nationalism threatened the very progress and unity it had helped to build. In 1914 the power of unified nation-states would turn on itself, unleashing the First World War and doling out self-inflicted wounds of enormous proportions to all of Europe's peoples.

MAKE CONNECTIONS

Think about the larger developments and continuities within and across chapters.

1. By 1900 most countries in Europe and North America had established modern nation-states, but the road to nation building varied dramatically from place to place. Which countries were most successful in building viable nation-states? What accounts for the variation?

2. How and why did the relationship between the state and its citizens change in the last decades of the nineteenth century?

3. Liberalism, socialism, and nationalism first emerged as coherent ideologies in the decades around 1800 (Chapter 21). How had they changed by 1900?

Chapter Review

IDENTIFY KEY TERMS

Identify and explain the significance of each item below.

Red Shirts (p. 728)

Homestead Act (p. 735)

Crimean War (p. 736)

Bloody Sunday (p. 739)

Duma (p. 739)

Tanzimat (p. 741)

Young Turks (p. 741)

Reichstag (p. 742)

Kulturkampf (p. 743)

German Social Democratic Party (SPD) (p. 743)

Dreyfus affair (p. 745)

People's Budget (p. 746)

Zionism (p. 752)

revisionism (p. 755)

REVIEW THE MAIN IDEAS

Answer the focus questions from each section of the chapter.

1. How did Napoleon III seek to reconcile popular and conservative forces in an authoritarian nation-state? (p. 723)
2. How did conflict and war lead to the construction of strong nation-states in Italy, Germany, and the United States? (p. 725)
3. What steps did Russia and the Ottoman Turks take toward modernization, and how successful were they? (p. 735)
4. What general domestic political trends emerged after 1871? (p. 742)
5. How did popular nationalism evolve in the last decades of the nineteenth century? (p. 749)
6. Why did the socialist movement grow, and how revolutionary was it? (p. 753)

CHRONOLOGY

1839–1876	Western-style Tanzimat reforms in Ottoman Empire
1852–1870	Reign of Napoleon III in France
1859–1870	Unification of Italy
1861	Freeing of Russian serfs
1861–1865	U.S. Civil War
1866	Austro-Prussian War
1870–1871	Franco-Prussian War; unification of Germany
1870–1878	Kulturkampf, Bismarck's attack on Catholic Church
1873	Stock market crash spurs renewed anti-Semitism, beginning in central and eastern Europe
1880s	Educational reforms in France create a secular public school system
1880s–1890s	Widespread return to protectionism among European states
1883	First social security laws to help workers in Germany
1890–1900	Witte initiates second surge of Russian industrialization
1905	Revolution in Russia
1906–1914	Social reform in Great Britain
1908	Young Turks seize power in Ottoman Empire

24

The West and the World

1815–1914

WHILE INDUSTRIALIZATION AND NATIONALISM were transforming urban and rural life throughout Europe, western Europeans were reshaping the world. At the peak of its power and pride, the West entered the third and most dynamic phase of the aggressive expansion that had begun with the Crusades and continued with the rise of seaborne colonial empires. At the same time, millions of Europeans picked up stakes and emigrated abroad, primarily to North and South America but also to Australia, North and South Africa, and Asiatic Russia. An ever-growing stream of people, products, and ideas flowed into and out of Europe in the nineteenth century. Hardly any corner of the globe was left untouched.

The most spectacular manifestations of Western expansion came in the late nineteenth century when the leading European nations established or enlarged their far-flung colonial empires. This political annexation of territory in the 1880s—the "New Imperialism," as it is often called by historians—was the capstone of Europe's underlying economic and technological transformation. More directly, Europe's New Imperialism rested on a formidable combination of superior military might and strong authoritarian rule, and it posed a brutal challenge to African and Asian peoples. Different societies met this Western challenge in different ways. By 1914 non-Western elites in many lands were rallying their peoples and leading an anti-imperialist struggle for dignity and genuine independence that would eventually triumph after 1945.

Industrialization and the World Economy

Focus Question	What were some of the global consequences of European industrialization between 1815 and 1914?

The Industrial Revolution created, first in Great Britain and then in continental Europe and North America, a tremendously dynamic economic system. In the course of the nineteenth century, that system expanded across the face of the earth. Some of this extension into non-Western areas was peaceful and beneficial, for the West had many products and techniques the rest of the world desired. If peaceful methods failed, however, Europeans used their superior military power to force non-Western nations to open their doors to Western economic interests. In general, Europeans fashioned the global economic system so that the largest share of the ever-increasing gains from trade, technology, and migration flowed to the West and its propertied classes.

The Rise of Global Inequality

The Industrial Revolution in Europe marked a momentous turning point in human history. Those regions of the world that industrialized in the nineteenth century (mainly Europe and North America) increased their wealth and power enormously in comparison to those that did not. A gap between the core industrializing regions and the soon-to-be colonized or semi-colonized regions outside the European–North American core (mainly in Africa, Asia, the Middle East, and Latin America) emerged and widened throughout the nineteenth century.

Moreover, this pattern of uneven global development became institutionalized, or built into the structure of the world economy. Thus a "lopsided world" evolved, a world with a rich north and a poor south (albeit with regional variations).

In recent years economic historians have charted the long-term evolution of this gap, and Figure 24.1 summarizes the findings of one important study. Three main points stand out. First, in 1750 the average standard of living was no higher in Europe as a whole than in the rest of the world. Second, it was industrialization that opened the gaps in average wealth and well-being among countries and regions. Third, income per person stagnated in the colonized world before 1913, in striking contrast

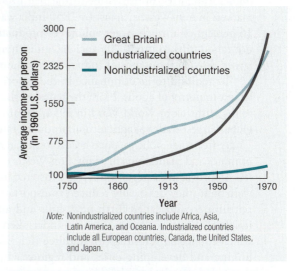

Note: Nonindustrialized countries include Africa, Asia, Latin America, and Oceania. Industrialized countries include all European countries, Canada, the United States, and Japan.

FIGURE 24.1 The Growth of Average Income per Person in Industrialized Countries, Nonindustrialized Countries, and Great Britain, 1750–1970
Growth is given in 1960 U.S. dollars and prices.

to the industrializing regions. Only after 1945, in the era of decolonization and political independence, did former colonies make real economic progress, beginning in their turn the critical process of industrialization.

The rise of these enormous income disparities, which indicate similar and striking disparities in food and clothing, health and education, and life expectancy and general material well-being, has generated a great deal of debate. One school of interpretation stresses that the West used science, technology, capitalist organization, and even its rational worldview to create massive wealth, and then used that wealth and power to its advantage. Another school argues that the West used its political and economic power to steal much of the world's riches, continuing in the nineteenth and twentieth centuries the rapacious colonialism born of the era of expansion. Because these issues are complex and there are few simple answers, it is helpful to consider them in the context of world trade in the nineteenth century.

The World Market

Commerce between nations has always stimulated economic development. In the nineteenth century Europe directed an enormous increase in international commerce. Great Britain took the lead in cultivating export markets for its booming industrial output, as British manufacturers looked first to Europe and then around the world, seeking consumers for Britain's growing numbers of mass-produced goods.

Take the case of cotton textiles. By 1820 Britain was exporting 50 percent of its production. Europe bought 50 percent of these cotton textile exports, while India bought only 6 percent and had its own well-established textile industry. Then as European nations and the United States erected protective tariff barriers to promote domestic industry, British cotton textile manufacturers aggressively sought other foreign markets in non-Western areas. By 1850 India was buying 25 percent and Europe only 16 percent of a much larger volume of production. As a British colony, India could not raise tariffs to protect its ancient, indigenous cotton textile industry, which collapsed, leaving thousands of Indian weavers unemployed.

In addition to its dominance in the export market, Britain was also the world's largest importer of goods. From the repeal of the Corn Laws in 1846 (see Chapter 21) to the outbreak of World War I in 1914, Britain remained the world's emporium, the globe's largest trader of agricultural products, raw materials, and manufactured goods. Under free-trade policies, open access to Britain's market stimulated the development of mines and plantations in many non-Western areas.

Improved transportation systems fostered international trade. Wherever railroads were built, they drastically reduced transportation costs, opened new economic opportunities, and called forth new skills and attitudes. European investors funded much of the railroad construction undertaken in Latin America, Asia, and Africa, which connected seaports with resource-rich inland cities and regions, as opposed to linking and developing cities and regions within a given country. Thus railroads dovetailed effectively with Western economic interests, facilitating the inflow and sale of Western manufactured goods and the export and the development of local raw materials.

The power of steam revolutionized transportation by sea as well as by land. Steam power began to supplant sails on the oceans of the world in the late 1860s. Passenger and freight rates tumbled as ship design became more sophisticated, and the intercontinental shipment of low-priced raw materials became feasible. The time needed to cross the Atlantic dropped from three weeks in 1870 to about ten days in 1900, and the opening of the Suez and Panama Canals (in 1869 and 1914, respectively) shortened transport time to other areas of the globe considerably. In addition, improved port facilities made loading and unloading cargo less expensive, faster, and more dependable.

The revolution in land and sea transportation encouraged European entrepreneurs to open up and exploit vast new territories around the world. Improved transportation enabled Asia, Africa, and Latin America to ship not only familiar agricultural products — spices, tea, sugar, coffee — but also new raw materials for industry, such as jute, rubber, cotton, and coconut oil. The export of raw materials supplied by these "primary producers" to Western manufacturers boosted economic growth in core countries but did little to establish independent industry in the nonindustrialized periphery.

New communications systems were used to direct the flow of goods across global networks. Transoceanic telegraph cables, firmly in place by the 1880s, enabled rapid communications among the financial centers of the world. While a British tramp freighter steamed from Calcutta to New York, a broker in London could arrange by telegram for it to carry American cargo to Australia. The same communications network conveyed world commodity prices instantaneously.

As their economies grew, Europeans began to make massive foreign investments beginning about 1840. By the outbreak of World War I in 1914, Europeans had invested more than $40 billion abroad. Great Britain, France, and Germany were the principal investing countries (Map 24.1). The great gap between rich and poor within Europe meant that the wealthy and moderately well-to-do could and did send great sums abroad in search of interest and dividends.

Most of the capital exported did not go to European colonies or protectorates in Asia and Africa. About three-quarters of total European investment went to other European countries, or to settler colonies — so-called **neo-Europes**, a term coined by historian Alfred Crosby to describe regions where the climate and topography resembled the European homeland, including the United States, Canada, Australia, New Zealand, Latin America, and parts of Siberia. In these relatively advanced regions, which had already attracted significant settler populations of ethnic Europeans, Europe found its most profitable opportunities for investment in construction of railroads, ports, and utilities. By lending money to construct foreign railroads, Europeans enabled white settlers to buy European rails and locomotives and develop sources of cheap food and raw materials.

Much of this investment was peaceful and mutually beneficial for lenders and borrowers. The extension of Western economic power and the construction of neo-Europes, however, were disastrous for indigenous peoples. Native Americans and Australian Aborigines especially were decimated by the diseases, liquor, and weapons of an aggressively expanding Western society.

MAP 24.1 European Investment to 1914
Foreign investment grew rapidly after 1850, and Britain, France, and Germany were the major investing nations. As this map suggests, most European investment was not directed to the African and Asian areas seized in the New Imperialism after 1880.

The Opening of China

Europe's development of robust offshoots in sparsely populated North America, Australia, and much of Latin America absorbed huge quantities of goods, investments, and migrants. Yet Europe's economic and cultural penetration of old, densely populated civilizations was also profoundly significant. Interaction with such civilizations increased the Europeans' trade and profit, and they were prepared to use force, if necessary, to attain their desires. This was what happened in China, a striking example of the pattern of European intrusion into non-Western lands.

For centuries China had sent more goods and inventions to Europe than it had received, and such was still the case in the early nineteenth century. Trade with Europe was carefully regulated by the Chinese imperial government, ruled by the Qing (ching), or Manchu, Dynasty in the nineteenth century. Qing officials required all foreign merchants to live in the southern port of Guangzhou (Canton) and to buy and sell only to licensed Chinese merchants. Practices considered harmful to Chinese interests were strictly forbidden.

For years the little community of foreign merchants in Guangzhou had to accept this Chinese system. By the 1820s, however, the dominant group of these merchants,

Commissioner Lin Zexu Overseeing the Destruction of Opium at Guangzhou, 1839 A formidable Chinese bureaucrat known for his competence and high moral standards, Lin Zexu was sent to Guangzhou (Canton) as imperial commissioner in late 1838 to halt the illegal importation of opium by the British. He made a huge impact on the opium trade within a matter of months. As a result, British troops invaded China, and the ultimate British victory in the Opium Wars forced China to grant European merchants one-sided trade agreements. (Pictures from History/Bridgeman Images)

the British, were flexing their muscles. Moreover, in opium—that "destructive and ensnaring vice" denounced by Chinese decrees—the British found a means to break China's self-imposed isolation. British merchants smuggled opium grown legally in British-occupied India into China, where its use and sale were illegal. Huge profits and growing addiction led to a rapid increase in sales. By 1836 the British merchants in Guangzhou aggressively demanded the creation of an independent British colony in China and "safe and unrestricted liberty" in their Chinese trade. Spurred on by economic motives, they pressured the British government to take decisive action and enlisted the support of British manufacturers with visions of vast Chinese markets to be opened to their goods as well.

At the same time, the Qing government decided that the opium trade had to be stamped out. It was ruining the people and stripping the empire of its silver, which went to British merchants to pay for the drug. The government began to vigorously prosecute Chinese drug dealers. In 1839 it sent special envoy Lin Zexu to Guangzhou to deal with the crisis. Lin Zexu punished Chinese who purchased opium and seized the opium supplies of the British merchants, who then withdrew to the barren island of Hong Kong. He sent a famous letter justifying his policy to Queen Victoria in London.

The wealthy, well-connected British merchants appealed to their allies in London for support, and the British government responded. It also wanted free, unregulated trade with China, as well as the establishment of diplomatic relations on the European model, complete with ambassadors, embassies, and published treaties. Using troops from India and taking advantage of its control of the seas, Britain occupied several coastal cities and in the first of two **Opium Wars** forced China to give in to British demands. In the Treaty of Nanking in 1842, the imperial government was required to cede the island of Hong Kong to Britain forever, pay an indemnity of $100 million, and open up four large cities to unlimited foreign trade with low tariffs.

With Britain's new power over Chinese commerce, the opium trade flourished, and Hong Kong developed rapidly as an Anglo-Chinese enclave. But disputes over trade between China and the Western powers continued. Finally, the second Opium War (1856–1860) culminated in the occupation of Beijing by seventeen thousand British and French troops, who intentionally burned down the emperor's summer palace. Another round of one-sided treaties gave European merchants and missionaries greater privileges and protection and forced the Chinese to accept trade and investment on unfavorable terms in several more cities. Thus did Europeans use opium addiction and military aggression to blow a hole in the wall of Chinese seclusion and open the country to foreign trade and foreign ideas.

Japan and the United States

China's neighbor Japan had its own highly distinctive civilization and even less use for Westerners. European traders and missionaries first arrived in Japan, an archipelago nation slightly smaller than California, in the sixteenth century. By 1640 Japanese leaders had reacted quite negatively to their presence. The government decided to expel all foreigners and seal off the country from all European influences in order to preserve traditional Japanese culture and society. When American and British whaling ships began to appear off Japanese coasts almost two hundred years later, the policy of exclusion was still in effect. An order of 1825 commanded Japanese officials to "drive away foreign vessels without second thought."[1]

Japan's unbending isolation seemed hostile and barbaric to the West, particularly to the United States. It complicated the practical problems of ensuring the safety of shipwrecked American sailors and the provisioning of whaling ships and China traders sailing in the eastern Pacific. It also thwarted American business leaders' hope of trade and profit. Moreover, Americans shared the self-confidence and dynamism of expanding Western society, and they felt destined to play a great role in the Pacific. To Americans it seemed the duty of the United States to force the Japanese to open their ports and behave as a "civilized" nation.

After several unsuccessful American attempts to establish commercial relations with Japan, Commodore Matthew Perry steamed into Edo (now Tokyo) Bay in 1853. Relying on **gunboat diplomacy** by threatening to attack, Perry demanded diplomatic negotiations with the emperor. Japan entered a grave crisis. Some Japanese military leaders urged resistance, but senior officials realized how defenseless their cities were against naval bombardment. Shocked and humiliated, they reluctantly signed a treaty with the United States that opened two ports and permitted trade. Over the next five years, more treaties spelled out the rights and privileges of the Western nations and their merchants in Japan. Japan was "opened." What the British had done in China with two wars, the Americans had achieved in Japan with the threat of one.

Western Penetration of Egypt

Egypt's experience illustrates not only the explosive power of the expanding European economy and society but also their seductive appeal. European involvement in Egypt also led to a new model of formal political control, which European powers applied widely in Africa and Asia after 1882.

Of great importance in African and Middle Eastern history, the ancient land of the pharaohs had since 525 B.C.E. been ruled by a succession of foreigners, most recently by the Ottoman sultans. In 1798 French armies under young General Napoleon Bonaparte invaded the Egyptian part of the Ottoman Empire and occupied the territory for three years. Into the power vacuum left by the French withdrawal stepped an extraordinary Albanian-born, Turkish-speaking general, Muhammad Ali (1769–1849).

First appointed governor of Egypt in 1805 by the Ottoman sultan, Muhammad Ali set out to build his own state on the strength of a large, powerful army organized along European lines. He drafted for the first time the illiterate peasant masses of Egypt, and he hired French and Italian army officers to train both these raw recruits and their Turkish officers in modern military methods. He reformed the government bureaucracy, cultivated new lands, and improved communication networks. By the end of his reign in 1848, Muhammad Ali had established a strong and virtually independent Egyptian state, to be ruled by his family on a hereditary basis within the Ottoman Empire (see Chapter 23).

Muhammad Ali's modernization program attracted large numbers of Europeans to the banks of the Nile. The port city of Alexandria had more than fifty thousand Europeans by 1864. Europeans served not only as army officers but also as engineers, doctors, government officials, and police officers. Others turned to trade, finance, and shipping.

To pay for his ambitious plans, Muhammad Ali encouraged the development of commercial agriculture. This move had profound implications. Egyptian peasants were poor but largely self-sufficient, growing food for their own consumption on state-owned lands allotted to them by tradition. Faced with the possibility of export agriculture, high-ranking officials and members of Muhammad Ali's family began carving large private landholdings out of the state domain. These new landlords made the peasants their tenants and forced them to grow cash crops such as cotton and rice geared to European markets. Egyptian landowners "modernized" agriculture, but to the detriment of peasant living standards.

These trends continued under Muhammad Ali's grandson Ismail (ihs-MAH-eel), who in 1863 began his sixteen-year rule as Egypt's khedive (kuh-DEEV), or prince. Educated at France's leading military academy, Ismail was a westernizing autocrat. The large irrigation networks he promoted boosted cotton production and exports to Europe, and with his support a French company completed the Suez Canal in 1869. The Arabic of the Egyptian masses replaced the Turkish spoken by Ottoman rulers as the official language. Young Egyptians educated in Europe spread new skills, and Cairo acquired modern boulevards and Western hotels. As Ismail proudly declared, "My country is no longer in Africa, we now form part of Europe."[2]

Yet Ismail was too impatient and reckless. His projects were enormously expensive, and by 1876 Egypt owed foreign bondholders a colossal debt that it could not pay. France and Great Britain intervened and forced Ismail to appoint French and British commissioners to oversee Egyptian finances and ensure payment of the Egyptian debt in full. This momentous decision marked a sharp break with the past. Throughout most of the nineteenth century, Europeans had used military might and political force primarily to make sure that non-Western lands would accept European trade and investment. Now Europeans were going to effectively rule Egypt.

Foreign financial control evoked a violent nationalistic reaction among Egyptian religious leaders, young intellectuals, and army officers. In 1879, under the leadership of Colonel Ahmed Arabi, they formed the Egyptian Nationalist Party. Continuing diplomatic pressure on the government, which forced Ismail to abdicate in favor of his ineffectual son, Tewfiq (r. 1879–1892), resulted in bloody anti-European riots in Alexandria in 1882. A number of Europeans were killed, and Tewfiq and his court had to flee to British ships for safety. When the British fleet bombarded Alexandria, more riots swept the country, and Colonel Arabi led a revolt. But a British expeditionary force put down the rebellion and occupied all of Egypt that year.

The British said their occupation was temporary, but British armies remained in Egypt until 1956. Before the First World War (1914–1918), they maintained the façade of Egypt as an autonomous province of the Ottoman Empire, but the khedive was a mere puppet. British rule did result in tax reforms and somewhat better conditions for peasants, while foreign bondholders received their interest and Egyptian nationalists nursed their injured pride.

The British takeover in Egypt provided a new model for European expansion in densely populated lands. Such expansion was based on military force, political domination, and a self-justifying ideology of beneficial reform. This model predominated until 1914. Thus did Europe's Industrial Revolution lead to tremendous political as well as economic expansion throughout the world after 1880.

Global Migration Around 1900

Focus Question	How was massive migration an integral part of Western expansion?

A poignant human drama accompanied economic expansion: millions of people pulled up stakes and left their ancestral lands in the course of history's greatest migration. To millions of ordinary people for whom the opening of China and the interest on the Egyptian debt had not the slightest significance, this great movement was the central experience in the saga of Western expansion. It was, in part, because of this **global mass migration** that the West's impact on the world in the nineteenth century was so powerful and many-sided.

A note on vocabulary may be in order here: *migration* refers to general human movement; *emigrants* (or *emigration*) refers to people leaving one country for another; *immigrants* (or *immigration*) refers to people entering one country from another. When people migrate, they emigrate from and immigrate to.

The Pressure of Population

In the early eighteenth century European population growth entered its third and decisive stage, which continued unabated until the early twentieth century. Birthrates eventually declined in the nineteenth century, but so did death rates, mainly because of the rising standard of living and the revolution in public health (see Chapter 22). During the hundred years before 1900 the population of Europe (including Asiatic Russia) more than doubled, from approximately 188 million to roughly 432 million.

These figures actually understate Europe's population explosion, for between 1815 and 1932 more than 60 million Europeans left the subcontinent. These emigrants went primarily to the rapidly growing neo-Europes — North and South America, Australia, New Zealand, and Siberia. Since the population of native Africans, Asians, and Americans grew more slowly than that of Europeans, the number of Europeans and people of predominantly European origin jumped from about 24 percent of the world's total in 1800 to about 38 percent on the eve of World War I.

The growth of the European population provided further impetus for Western expansion, and it drove more and more people to emigrate. As in the eighteenth century, the rapid increase in numbers in Europe proper led to land hunger and relative overpopulation in area after area. In most countries, emigration increased twenty years after a rapid growth in population, as children grew up, saw little available land and few opportunities, and departed. This pattern was especially prevalent when rapid population increase predated extensive industrial development, which offered the best long-term hope of creating jobs and reducing poverty. Thus millions of country folk in industrialized parts of Europe moved to cities in search of work, while those in more slowly industrializing regions went abroad.

Before looking more closely at the people who emigrated, consider these three facts. First, the number of men and women who left Europe increased rapidly at the end of the nineteenth century and leading up to World War I. As Figure 24.2 shows, more than 11 million left in the first decade of the twentieth century, over five times the number departing in the 1850s. Thus large-scale emigration was a defining characteristic of European society at the turn of the century.

Second, different countries had very different patterns of migration. People left Britain and Ireland in large numbers from the 1840s on. This outflow reflected not only rural poverty but also the movement of skilled industrial technicians and the preferences shown to British migrants in the overseas British Empire. Ultimately, about one-third of all European emigrants between 1840 and 1920 came from the British Isles. German emigration was quite different. It grew irregularly after about 1830, reaching a first peak in the early 1850s and another peak in the early 1880s. Thereafter it declined rapidly, for at that point Germany's rapid industrialization provided adequate jobs at home. This pattern contrasted sharply with that of Italy. More and more Italians left the country right up to 1914, forced out by relatively slow industrial growth and poor living standards in Italian villages. In short, migration patterns mirrored social and economic conditions in the various European countries and provinces.

Third, although the United States did absorb the largest overall number of European emigrants, fewer than half of all these emigrants went to the United States. Asiatic

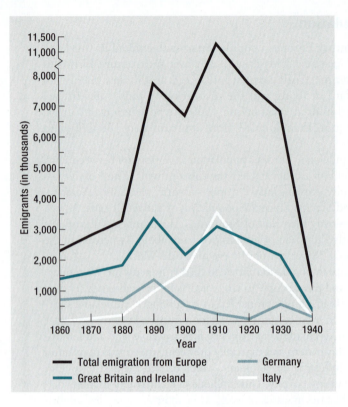

FIGURE 24.2

Emigration from Europe by Decade, 1860–1940

Emigration from Europe followed regional economic trends, as the comparison in this chart suggests. Overall, emigration from Europe grew quickly until the outbreak of World War I in 1914, after which it declined rapidly.

Russia, Canada, Argentina, Brazil, Australia, and New Zealand also attracted large numbers, as Figure 24.3 shows. Moreover, immigrants accounted for a larger proportion of the total population in Argentina, Brazil, and Canada than in the United States. The common American assumption that European emigration meant immigration to the United States is quite inaccurate.

European Emigration

What kind of people left Europe, and what were their reasons for doing so? The European emigrant was generally an energetic small farmer or skilled artisan trying hard to stay ahead of poverty, not a desperately impoverished landless peasant or urban proletarian. Small peasant landowners and village craftsmen typically left Europe because of the lack of available land and the growing availability of inexpensive factory-made goods, which threatened their traditional livelihoods.

Determined to maintain or improve their status, immigrants brought great benefits to the countries that received them, in large part because the vast majority were young, typically unmarried, and ready to work hard in the new land, at least for a time. Many Europeans moved but remained within Europe, settling temporarily or permanently in another European country. Jews from central Europe and peasants from Ireland moved to Great Britain; Russians and Poles sought work in Germany; and Spaniards, Portuguese, and Italians went to France. A substantial number of

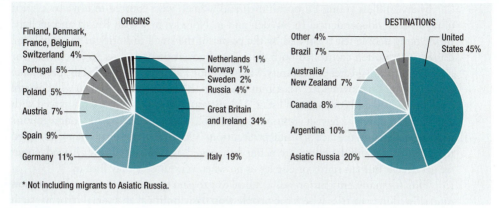

FIGURE 24.3 Origins and Destinations of European Emigrants, 1851–1960
European emigrants came from many countries; almost half of them went to the United States.

Europeans were actually migrants as opposed to immigrants who settled in new lands — that is, they returned home after some time abroad. One in two immigrants to Argentina and probably one in three to the United States eventually returned to their native lands.

The likelihood of repatriation varied greatly by nationality. People who emigrated from the Balkans, for instance, were much more likely to return to their countries than people from Ireland or eastern European Jews. For those who returned, the possibility of buying land in the old country was of central importance. In Ireland (as well as in England and Scotland), large, often-absentee landowners owned most land; little was up for sale. In Russia, most Jews faced discrimination and were forced to live in the Pale of Settlement (see Chapter 16), and non-Jews owned most property. Therefore, when Irish farmers and Russian Jewish artisans emigrated in search of opportunity, or, for Jews, to escape pogroms (see Chapter 23), it was basically a once-and-for-all departure.

The mass movement of Italians illustrates many of the characteristics of European emigration. As late as the 1880s, three of every four Italians worked in agriculture. With the influx of cheap North American wheat, many small landowning peasants whose standard of living was falling began to leave their country. Numerous Italians went to the United States, but before 1900 even greater numbers went to Argentina and Brazil.

Many Italians had no intention of permanently settling abroad. Some called themselves "swallows." After harvesting their own wheat and flax in Italy, they "flew" to Argentina to harvest wheat between December and April. Returning to Italy for the spring planting, they repeated this exhausting process. This was a very hard life, but a frugal worker could save $250 to $300 in the course of a season, at a time when an Italian agricultural worker earned less than $1 a day in Italy.

Ties of family and friendship played a crucial role in the emigration process. Many people from a given province or village settled together in rural enclaves or tightly knit urban neighborhoods thousands of miles away. Very often a prominent individual — a businessman, a religious leader, an ambitious family member — would blaze the way, and others would follow, forming a "migration chain."

Many landless young European men and women were spurred to leave by a spirit of revolt and independence. In Sweden and in Norway, in Jewish Russia and in Italy, these young people felt frustrated by the power of the small minority in the privileged classes, which often controlled both church and government and resisted demands for liberal reform and greater opportunity. Many a young Norwegian seconded the passionate cry of Norway's national poet, Martinius Bjørnson (BYURN-sawn): "Forth will I! Forth! I will be crushed and consumed if I stay."[3] Many young Jews wholeheartedly agreed with a spokesman of Kiev's Jewish community in 1882, who summed up his congregation's growing defiance in the face of brutal persecution: "Our human dignity is being trampled upon, our wives and daughters are being dishonored, we are looted and pillaged; either we get decent human rights or else let us go wherever our eyes may lead us."[4]

Thus for many, emigration was a radical way to gain basic human rights. Emigration rates slowed in countries where the people won basic political and social reforms, such as the right to vote, equality before the law, and social security.

Asian Emigration

Not all emigration was from Europe. A substantial number of Chinese, Japanese, Indians, and Filipinos — to name only four key groups — also responded to rural hardship with temporary or permanent emigration. At least 3 million Asians moved abroad before 1920. Most went as indentured laborers to work under incredibly difficult conditions on the plantations or in the gold mines of Latin America, southern

Vaccinating Migrants Bound for Hawaii, 1904 First Chinese, then Japanese, and finally Koreans and Filipinos went across the Pacific in large numbers to labor in Hawaii on American-owned sugar plantations in the late nineteenth century. The native Hawaiians had been decimated by disease, creating a severe labor shortage for Hawaii's plantation economy. U.S. plantation owners filled the shortage with East Asian immigrant workers. (© Corbis)

Asia, Africa, California, Hawaii, and Australia. This marked the rise of a new global trend: white estate owners very often used Asian immigrants to replace or supplement black workers after the suppression of the slave trade.

In the 1840s, for example, the Spanish government actively recruited Chinese laborers to meet the strong demand for field hands in Cuba. Between 1853 and 1873, when such immigration was stopped, more than 130,000 Chinese laborers went to Cuba. The majority spent their lives as virtual slaves. The great landlords of Peru also brought in more than 100,000 workers from China in the nineteenth century, and there were similar movements of Asians elsewhere.

Emigration from Asia would undoubtedly have grown to much greater proportions if planters and mine owners in search of cheap labor had been able to hire as many Asian workers as they wished. But they could not. Many Asians fled the plantations and gold mines as soon as possible, seeking greater opportunities in trade and towns. There they came into conflict with local populations, whether in Malaya, southern Africa, or areas settled by Europeans. When that took place in neo-Europes, European settlers demanded a halt to Asian immigration. By the 1880s the American and Australian governments had instituted exclusionary acts—discriminatory laws designed to keep Asians from entering the country.

In fact, the explosion of mass mobility in the late nineteenth century, combined with the growing appeal of nationalism and scientific racism (see Chapter 23), encouraged a variety of attempts to control immigration flows and seal off national borders. National governments established strict rules for granting citizenship and asylum to foreigners. Passports and customs posts monitored movement across increasingly tight national boundaries. Such attempts were often inspired by **nativism**, beliefs that led to policies giving preferential treatment to established inhabitants above immigrants. Thus French nativists tried to limit the influx of Italian migrant workers, German nativists stopped Poles from crossing eastern borders, and American nativists (in the 1920s) restricted immigration from southern and eastern Europe and banned it outright from much of Asia.

A crucial factor in migration patterns before 1914 was, therefore, immigration policies that offered preferred status to "acceptable" racial and ethnic groups in the open lands of possible permanent settlement. This, too, was part of Western dominance in the increasingly lopsided world. Largely successful in monopolizing the best overseas opportunities, Europeans and people of European ancestry reaped the main benefits from the mass migration. By 1913 people in Australia, Canada, and the United States had joined the British in having the highest average incomes in the world, while incomes in Asia and Africa lagged far behind.

Western Imperialism, 1880–1914

Focus Question	How did Western imperialism change after 1880?

The expansion of Western society reached its apex between about 1880 and 1914. In those years, the leading European nations not only continued to send massive streams of migrants, money, and manufactured goods around the world, but also rushed to create or enlarge vast empires. This political empire building, under direct European rule, contrasted sharply with the economic penetration of non-Western territories between 1816 and 1880, which had left a China or a Japan "opened" but politically independent. By contrast, the empires of the late nineteenth century recalled the old European colonial empires of the sixteenth to eighteenth centuries. Because this renewed imperial push came after a long pause in European expansionism, contemporaries termed it the **New Imperialism**.

Characterized by a frantic rush to plant the flag over as many people and as much territory as possible, the New Imperialism had momentous consequences. By the early twentieth century almost 84 percent of the globe was dominated by European nations, and Britain alone controlled one-quarter of the earth's territory and one-third of its population. The New Imperialism created tensions among competing European states and led to wars and threats of war with non-European powers. Aimed primarily at Africa and Asia, the New Imperialism put millions of non-Western peoples directly under European rule.

The European Presence in Africa Before 1880

Prior to 1880, European nations controlled only about 10 percent of Africa. The French had begun conquering Algeria in 1830, and by 1880 substantial numbers of French, Italian, and Spanish colonists had settled among the overwhelming Arab majority there. Yet the overall effect on Africa was minor.

At the southern tip of the continent, Britain had taken possession of the Dutch settlements in and around Cape Town during the wars with Napoleon I. This takeover of the Cape Colony had led disgruntled Dutch cattle ranchers and farmers in 1835 to make their so-called Great Trek into the interior, where they fought the Zulu and Xhosa (KO-sah) peoples for land. After 1853 the Boers, or **Afrikaners** (a-frih-KAH-nuhrz), as the descendants of the Dutch in the Cape Colony were beginning to call themselves, proclaimed their independence and defended it against British armies. By 1880 Afrikaner and British settlers, who detested each other and lived in separate areas, had wrested control of much of South Africa from the Zulu, Xhosa, and other African peoples.

In addition to the French in the north and the British and Afrikaners in the south, European trading posts and forts dating back to the Age of Discovery and the slave trade dotted the coast of West Africa, and the Portuguese maintained a loose hold on their old possessions in Angola and Mozambique. Elsewhere, over the great mass of the continent, Europeans did not rule.

After 1880 the situation changed drastically. In a spectacular manifestation of the New Imperialism, European countries jockeyed for territory in Africa, breaking sharply with previous patterns of colonization and diplomacy.

The Scramble for Africa After 1880

Between 1880 and 1900 Britain, France, Belgium, Germany, and Italy scrambled for African possessions as if their national livelihoods depended on it (Map 24.2). By 1900 nearly the whole continent had been carved up and placed under European rule: only

MAP 24.2 The Partition of Africa

The European powers carved up Africa after 1880 and built vast political empires. European states also seized territory in Asia in the nineteenth century, although some Asian states and peoples managed to maintain their political independence (see Map 24.3, page 778). Compare the patterns of European imperialism in Africa and Asia, using this map and Map 24.3.

Ethiopia, which fought off Italian invaders, and Liberia, which had been settled by freed slaves from the United States, remained independent. In all other African territories, European powers tightened their control and established colonial governments in the years before 1914.

In the complex story of the European seizure of Africa, certain events and individuals stand out. Of enormous importance was the British occupation of Egypt in 1882, which established the new model of formal political control (see page 768). King Leopold II of Belgium (r. 1865–1909), an energetic, strong-willed monarch of a tiny country with a lust for distant territory, also played a crucial role. As early as 1861, he had laid out his vision of expansion: "The sea bathes our coast, the world lies before us. Steam and electricity have annihilated distance, and all the nonappropriated lands on the surface of the globe can become the field of our operations and of our success."[5]

By 1876 Leopold's expansionism focused on central Africa. He formed a financial syndicate under his personal control to send Henry M. Stanley, a sensation-seeking journalist and part-time explorer, to the Congo basin. Stanley established trading stations, signed unfair treaties with African chiefs, and planted the Belgian flag. Leopold's actions alarmed the French, who quickly sent out an expedition under Pierre de Brazza. In 1880 de Brazza signed a treaty of protection with the chief of the large Teke tribe and began to establish a French protectorate on the north bank of the Congo River.

Leopold's intrusion into the Congo area called attention to the possibilities of African colonization, and by 1882 Europe had caught "African fever." A gold-rush mentality led to a determined race for territory, and rampant greed threatened the balance of power in Europe. To lay down some basic rules for this new and dangerous global competition, Jules Ferry of France and Otto von Bismarck of Germany arranged an international conference on Africa in Berlin in 1884 and 1885. The **Berlin Conference**, attended by over ten Western powers including the United States, established the principle that European claims to African territory had to rest on "effective occupation" (a strong presence on the ground) to be recognized by other states. This meant that Europeans would push relentlessly into interior regions from all sides and that no single European power would be able to claim the entire continent. The conference recognized Leopold's personal rule over a neutral Congo Free State and agreed to work to stop slavery and the slave trade in Africa.

The Berlin Conference coincided with Germany's sudden emergence as an imperial power. Prior to about 1880, Bismarck, like many other European leaders at the time, had seen little value in colonies. In 1884 and 1885, as political agitation for expansion increased, Bismarck did an abrupt about-face, and Germany established protectorates over a number of small African kingdoms and tribes in Togo, the Cameroons region, southwest Africa, and, later, East Africa. In acquiring colonies, Bismarck cooperated against the British with France's Jules Ferry, an ardent republican who also embraced imperialism. With Bismarck's tacit approval, the French pressed southward from Algeria, eastward from their old forts on the Senegal coast, and northward from their protectorate on the Congo River to take control of parts of West and Central Africa.

Meanwhile, the British began to enlarge their own African colonies, beginning at the southern tip of the African continent. Led by Cecil Rhodes (1853–1902), prime minister of Britain's Cape Colony, British colonists leapfrogged over the two Afrikaner states — the Orange Free State and the Transvaal (see Map 24.2) — in the early 1890s and established protectorates over Bechuanaland (bech-WAH-nuh-land; now Botswana) and Rhodesia (now Zimbabwe and Zambia), named in honor of its founder.

English-speaking capitalists like Rhodes developed fabulously rich gold mines in the Transvaal, and this unilateral territorial and economic expansion heightened tensions between the British and Afrikaner (Dutch Boer) settlers. In 1899 the conflict erupted in the bloody South African War, or Boer War (1899–1902). After a series of defeats at the hands of the determined Boers, the British shipped some 180,000 troops to southern Africa. Overwhelming British forces put the Boers on the defensive, and they responded with an intensive guerrilla war that took two years to put down. During the fighting, both sides enlisted the support of indigenous African troops. The British forces resorted to "scorched earth" policies, burning crops and villages in Boer regions, and, most notoriously, placed Boers and native Africans in rudimentary concentration camps in an attempt to halt the guerrilla campaign. News of these tactics provoked liberal outrage at home in Britain.

The war ended with a British victory in 1902, and in 1910 the Afrikaner territories were united with the old Cape Colony and the eastern province of Natal in a new Union of South Africa, established as a largely "self-governing" colony but still under British control. Gradually, however, the defeated Afrikaners used their numerical superiority over the British settlers to take political power, as even the most educated nonwhites lost the right to vote, except in the Cape Colony.

The British also fought to enlarge their colonies in West Africa, impatiently pushing northward from the Cape Colony, westward from Zanzibar, and southward from Egypt. In 1885 British troops stationed in the Sudanese city of Khartoum, an outpost on the Nile that protected imperial interests in Egypt, were massacred by fiercely independent Muslim Sudanese. A decade later the British sought to establish permanent rule in the disputed territory. Under the command of General Sir Herbert Kitchener (who would serve Britain as secretary of state for war during World War I), a well-armed force moved cautiously and more successfully up the Nile River, building a railroad to supply arms and reinforcements as it went. Finally, in 1898 these British troops confronted the poorly armed Sudanese army at the Battle of Omdurman (ahm-duhr-MAHN) (see Map 24.2). Sudanese soldiers charged the British lines time and time again, only to be cut down by the recently invented Maxim machine gun. In the solemn words of one English observer, "It was not a battle but an execution. The bodies were . . . spread evenly over acres and acres." In the end, about 10,000 Sudanese soldiers lay dead, while 28 Britons had been killed and 145 wounded.[6]

Continuing up the Nile after the battle, Kitchener's armies found that a small French force had already occupied the village of Fashoda (fuh-SHOH-duh). Locked in imperial competition with Britain ever since the British occupation of Egypt, France had tried to be first to reach one of Africa's last unclaimed areas — the upper reaches of the Nile. The result was a serious diplomatic crisis and the threat of war between two major European powers. Wracked by the Dreyfus affair (see Chapter 23) and unwilling to fight, France eventually backed down and withdrew its forces, allowing the British to take over.

Territories held by Western Powers

- Great Britain
- France
- Netherlands
- United States
- Russian Empire
- Japan and its territories
- Independent states
- 1842 Date of colonization or occupation
- ···· Major railroad

Tools for Empire Building   Western technological advances aided Western political ambitions in Africa and Asia. The Maxim machine gun was highly mobile and could lay down a continuous barrage that would decimate charging enemies, as in the slaughter of Muslim soldiers at the Battle of Omdurman in the Sudan. (© Lordprice Collection/Alamy Stock Photo)

The British conquest of Sudan exemplifies the general process of empire building in Africa. The fate of the Muslim-Sudanese force at Omdurman was inflicted on native peoples who openly resisted European control: they were blown away by vastly superior military force. The violent German suppression of armed rebellions in the colonies of German East Africa and German Southwest Africa, where revolt led to full-scale warfare and the deaths of some one hundred thousand Herero and Nama Africans, confirmed the rule. But as the Fashoda incident showed, however much the European powers squabbled for territory around the world, they had the sense to stop short of actually fighting each other. Imperial ambitions were not worth a great European war.

Imperialism in Asia

Although their sudden division of Africa was more spectacular, Europeans also exerted political control over much of Asia. Here the Dutch were a major player. In 1815 the Dutch ruled little more than the island of Java in the East Indies. Thereafter they gradually brought almost all of the three-thousand-mile Malay Archipelago under their political authority, though — in good imperialist fashion — they had to share some of the spoils with Britain and Germany. In the critical decade of the 1880s, the French under the leadership of Ferry took Indochina. India, Japan, and China also experienced a profound imperialist impact (Map 24.3).

Two other great imperialist powers, Russia and the United States, also acquired territories in Asia. Russia moved steadily forward on two fronts throughout the

< MAP 24.3 Asia in 1914
India remained under British rule, while China preserved a precarious political independence. The Dutch Empire in modern-day Indonesia was old, but French control of Indochina was a product of the New Imperialism. Russia continued to expand to the south and to the east as well.

nineteenth century. Russians conquered Muslim areas to the south in the Caucasus and in Central Asia, reaching the border of Afghanistan in 1885. Russia also proceeded to nibble greedily on China's outlying provinces, especially in the 1890s.

The great conquest by the United States was the Philippines, taken from Spain in 1898 through the Spanish-American War. When it quickly became clear that the United States had no intention of granting the independence it had promised, Philippine patriots rose in revolt and were suppressed only after long, bitter fighting. Some Americans protested the taking of the Philippines, but to no avail. Thus another great Western power joined the imperialist ranks in Asia.

Causes of the New Imperialism

Many factors contributed to the late-nineteenth-century rush for empire, which was in turn one aspect of Western society's overall expansion in the age of industry and nationalism. It is little wonder that controversies have raged over interpretation of the New Imperialism, especially since authors of every persuasion have often exaggerated particular aspects in an attempt to prove their own theories. Yet despite complexity and controversy, basic causes are clearly identifiable.

Economic motives played an important role in the extension of political empires, especially in the British Empire. By the late 1870s France, Germany, and the United States were industrializing rapidly behind rising tariff barriers. Great Britain was losing its early economic lead and facing increasingly tough competition in foreign markets. In this changing economic climate, the seizure of Asian and African territory by continental powers in the 1880s raised alarms in Britain. Fearing that France and Germany would seal off their empires with high tariffs, resulting in the permanent loss of future economic opportunities, the British followed suit and began their own push to expand empire.

Actually, the overall economic gains of the New Imperialism proved quite limited before 1914. The new colonies were simply too poor to buy much, and they offered few immediately profitable investments. Nonetheless, even the poorest, most barren desert was jealously prized, and no territory was ever abandoned. This was because colonies became important for political and diplomatic reasons. Each leading country saw colonies as crucial to national security and military power. For instance, safeguarding the Suez Canal played a key role in the British occupation of Egypt, and protecting Egypt in turn led to the bloody conquest of Sudan. Far-flung possessions guaranteed ever-growing navies the safe havens and the dependable coaling stations they needed in time of crisis or war.

Along with economic motives, many people were convinced that colonies were essential to great nations. "There has never been a great power without great colonies," wrote one French publicist. The influential nationalist historian of Germany, Heinrich von Treitschke, spoke for many when he wrote: "Every virile people has established colonial power. . . . All great nations in the fullness of their strength have desired to set their mark upon barbarian lands and those who fail to participate in this great rivalry will play a pitiable role in time to come."[7]

Treitschke's harsh statement reflects not only the increasing aggressiveness of European nationalism after Bismarck's wars of German unification, but also Social

Darwinian theories of brutal competition among races (see Chapter 23). As one prominent English economist argued, the "strongest nation has always been conquering the weaker . . . and the strongest tend to be best." Thus European nations, which saw themselves as racially distinct parts of the dominant white race, had to seize colonies to show they were strong and powerful. Moreover, since victory of the fittest in the struggle for survival was nature's inescapable law, the conquest of "inferior" peoples was just. "The path of progress is strewn with the wreck . . . of inferior races," wrote one professor in 1900. "Yet these dead peoples are, in very truth, the stepping stones on which mankind has risen to the higher intellectual and deeper emotional life of today."[8] Social Darwinism and pseudoscientific racial doctrines fostered imperialist expansion.

So did the industrial world's unprecedented technological and military superiority. Three aspects were particularly important. First, the rapidly firing Maxim machine gun, so lethal at Omdurman, was an ultimate weapon in many another unequal battle. Second, newly discovered quinine proved no less effective in controlling malaria, which had previously decimated whites in the tropics whenever they left breezy coastal enclaves and dared to venture into mosquito-infested interiors. Third, the combination of the steamship and the international telegraph permitted Western powers to quickly concentrate their firepower in a given area when it was needed. Never before—and never again after 1914—would the technological gap between the West and non-Western regions of the world be so great.

Social tensions and domestic political conflicts also contributed mightily to overseas expansion. In Germany and Russia, and in other countries to a lesser extent, conservative political leaders manipulated colonial issues to divert popular attention from the class struggle at home and to create a false sense of national unity. Thus imperial propagandists relentlessly stressed that colonies benefited workers as well as capitalists, providing jobs and cheap raw materials that raised workers' standard of living. Government leaders and their allies in the tabloid press successfully encouraged the masses to savor foreign triumphs and to glory in the supposed increase in national prestige. In short, conservative leaders defined imperialism as a national necessity, which they used to justify the status quo and their hold on power.

Finally, certain special-interest groups in each country were powerful agents of expansion. White settlers in the colonial areas demanded more land and greater state protection. Missionaries and humanitarians wanted to spread religion and stop the slave trade within Africa. Shipping companies wanted lucrative subsidies to protect rapidly growing global trade. Military men and colonial officials foresaw rapid advancement and highly paid positions in growing empires. The actions of such groups pushed the course of empire forward.

A "Civilizing Mission"

Western society did not rest the case for empire solely on naked conquest and a Darwinian racial struggle or on power politics and the need for naval bases on every ocean. Imperialists developed additional arguments for imperialism to satisfy their consciences and answer their critics.

A favorite idea was that Westerners could and should civilize more primitive nonwhite peoples. According to this view, Westerners shouldered the responsibility for governing and converting the supposed savages under their charge and strove to remake them on superior European models. Africans and Asians would eventually receive the benefits of industrialization and urbanization, Western education, Christianity, advanced medicine, and finally higher standards of living. In time, they might be ready for self-government and Western democracy. Thus the French repeatedly spoke of their imperial endeavors as a sacred "civilizing mission." Other imperialists agreed; as one German missionary put it, a combination of prayer and hard work under German direction would lead "the work-shy native to work of his own free will" and thus lead him to "an existence fit for human beings."[9] Another argument was that imperial government protected natives from tribal warfare as well as from cruder forms of exploitation by white settlers and business people. In 1899 Rudyard Kipling (1865–1936), who wrote masterfully of Anglo-Indian life and was perhaps the most influential British writer of the 1890s, summarized such ideas in his poem "The White Man's Burden."

Many Americans accepted the ideology of the **white man's burden**. It was an important factor in the decision to rule, rather than liberate, the Philippines after the

A Missionary School   A Swahili schoolboy leads his classmates in a reading lesson in Dar es Salaam in German East Africa in 1903; portraits of Emperor Wilhelm II and his wife look down on the classroom, a reminder of imperial control. Europeans argued that they were spreading the benefits of a superior civilization with schools like this one, which is unusually well built and furnished because of its strategic location in the capital city. Schoolrooms were typically segregated by sex, and lessons for young men and women adhered to Western notions of gender difference. (ullstein bild/Granger, NYC—All rights reserved)

Spanish-American War. Like their European counterparts, these Americans believed that their civilization had reached unprecedented heights and that they had unique benefits to bestow on supposedly less advanced peoples.

Though the colonial administrators and military generals in charge of imperial endeavors were men, European women played a central role in the "civilizing mission." Proponents of imperial expansion actively encouraged women to "serve" in the colonies, and many answered the call. Some women worked as colonial missionaries, teachers, and nurses; others accompanied their husbands overseas. Europeans who embraced the "white man's burden" believed that the presence of white women in the colonies might help stop the spread of what they called "race mixing": the tendency of European men to establish cross-race marriages or relationships with indigenous women. If they stayed in the colonies long enough to establish a semipermanent household, European women might oversee native servants. Colonial encounters thus established complicated social hierarchies that entangled race, class, and gender.

Peace and stability under European control also facilitated the spread of Christianity. Catholic and Protestant missionaries — both men and women — competed with Islam south of the Sahara, seeking converts and building schools to spread the Gospel. Many Africans' first real contact with whites was in mission schools. Some peoples, such as the Ibo in Nigeria, became highly Christianized.

Such occasional successes in sub-Saharan Africa contrasted with the general failure of missionary efforts in India, China, and the Islamic world. There Christians often preached in vain to peoples with ancient, complex religious beliefs. Yet the number of Christian believers around the world did increase substantially in the nineteenth century, and missionary groups kept trying.

Orientalism

Even though many Westerners shared a sense of superiority over non-Western peoples, they were often fascinated by foreign cultures and societies. In the late 1970s the influential literary scholar Edward Said (sigh-EED) (1935–2003) coined the term Orientalism to describe this fascination and the stereotypical and often racist Western understandings of non-Westerners that dominated nineteenth-century Western thought. Said originally used "Orientalism" to refer to the way Europeans viewed "the Orient," or Arab societies in North Africa and the Middle East. The term caught on, however, and is often used more broadly to refer to Western views of non-Western peoples across the globe.

Said believed that it was almost impossible for people in the West to look at or understand non-Westerners without falling into some sort of Orientalist stereotype. Politicians, scholarly experts, writers and artists, and ordinary people readily adopted "us versus them" views of foreign peoples. The West, they believed, was modern, while the non-West was primitive. The West was white, the non-West colored; the West was rational, the non-West emotional; the West was Christian, the non-West pagan or Islamic. As part of this view of the non-West as radically "other," Westerners imagined the Orient as a place of mystery and romance, populated with exotic, dark-skinned peoples, where Westerners might have remarkable experiences of foreign societies and cultures.

Such views swept through North American and European scholarship, arts, and literature in the late nineteenth century. The emergence of ethnography and anthropology as academic disciplines in the 1880s was part of the process. Inspired by a new culture of collecting, scholars and adventurers went into the field, where they studied supposedly primitive cultures and traded for, bought, or stole artifacts from non-Western peoples. The results of their work were reported in scientific studies, articles, and books, and intriguing objects filled the display cases of new public museums of ethnography and natural history. In a slew of novels published around 1900, authors portrayed romance and high adventure in the colonies and so contributed to the Orientalist worldview. Artists followed suit, and dramatic paintings of ferocious Arab warriors, Eastern slave markets, and the sultan's harem adorned museum walls and wealthy middle-class parlors. Scholars, authors, and artists were not necessarily racists or imperialists, but they found it difficult to escape Orientalist stereotypes. In the end they helped spread the notions of Western superiority and justified colonial expansion.

Critics of Imperialism

The expansion of empire aroused sharp, even bitter, critics. The forceful attack made by radical English economist J. A. Hobson (1858–1940) in *Imperialism* (1902), a work that influenced Lenin and others, was exemplary. Deeply angered by British tactics during the unpopular South African (Boer) War, Hobson contended that the rush to acquire colonies was due to the economic needs of unregulated capitalism, particularly the need of the rich to find outlets for their surplus capital. Yet, Hobson argued, imperial possessions did not pay off economically for the entire country. Only unscrupulous special-interest groups profited from them, at the expense of both European taxpayers and the natives. Moreover, Hobson argued that the quest for empire diverted popular attention away from domestic reform and the need to reduce the great gap between rich and poor.

Like Hobson, Marxist critics offered a thorough analysis and critique of Western imperialism. Rosa Luxemburg, a radical member of the German Social Democratic Party, argued that capitalism needed to expand into noncapitalist Asia and Africa to maintain high profits. The Russian Marxist and future revolutionary leader Vladimir Lenin concluded that imperialism represented the "highest stage" of advanced monopoly capitalism and predicted that its onset signaled the coming decay and collapse of capitalist society. These and similar arguments were not very persuasive, however. Most people then (and now) were sold on the idea that imperialism was profitable for the homeland and beneficial to the colonized, and the masses developed a broad and genuine enthusiasm for empire.

Hobson and many other critics struck home, however, with their moral condemnation of whites' imperiously ruling nonwhites. They rebelled against crude Social Darwinian thought. "O Evolution, what crimes are committed in thy name!" cried one foe. Another sardonically coined a new beatitude: "Blessed are the strong, for they shall prey on the weak."[10] Kipling and his kind were lampooned as racist bullies whose rule rested on brutality, racial contempt, and the Maxim gun. Similarly, in 1902 in the novel *Heart of Darkness*—a demolishing critique of the Belgian exploitation of the Congo—Polish-born novelist Joseph Conrad (1857–1924) castigated the "pure selfishness" of Europeans in supposedly civilizing Africa. The main character, once a liberal scholar, turns into a savage brute.

Critics charged Europeans with applying a degrading double standard and failing to live up to their own noble ideals. At home, Europeans had won or were winning representative government, individual liberties, and a certain equality of opportunity. In their empires, Europeans imposed military dictatorships. Colonial administrators forced Africans and Asians to work involuntarily, almost like slaves, and subjected them to shameless discrimination. Only by renouncing imperialism, its critics insisted, and giving captive peoples the freedoms Western society had struggled for since the French Revolution would Europeans be worthy of their traditions. These critics provided colonial peoples with a Western ideology of liberation.

Responding to Western Imperialism

Focus Question	What was the general pattern of non-Western responses to Western expansion?

To Africans and Asians, Western expansion represented a profoundly disruptive assault. Everywhere it threatened existing ruling classes, local economies, and long-standing ways of life. Christian missionaries and European secular ideologies challenged established beliefs and values. Non-Western peoples experienced imperialism as an invasion, one made all the more painful by the power and arrogance of the European intruders.

The Pattern of Response

Generally, the initial response of African and Asian rulers to aggressive Western expansion was to try to drive the unwelcome foreigners away. This was the case in China, Japan, and Sudan, as we have seen. Violent antiforeign reactions exploded elsewhere again and again, as in the lengthy U.S.-Indian wars, but the superior military technology of the industrialized West almost invariably prevailed. Beaten in battle, many Africans and Asians concentrated on preserving their cultural traditions at all costs. Others found themselves forced to reconsider their initial hostility. Some (such as Ismail of Egypt) concluded that the West was indeed superior in some ways and that it was therefore necessary to copy some European achievements, especially if they wished to escape full-blown Western political rule.

Thus it is possible to think of responses to the Western impact as a spectrum, with "traditionalists" at one end, "westernizers" or "modernizers" at the other, and many shades of opinion in between. Both before and after European domination, the struggle among these groups was often intense. With time, however, the modernizers tended to gain the upper hand.

When the power of both the traditionalists and the modernizers was thoroughly shattered by superior force, some Asians and Africans accepted imperial rule. Political participation in non-Western lands was historically limited to small elites, and ordinary people often did what their rulers told them to do. In these circumstances Europeans, clothed in power and convinced of their righteousness, tried to govern smoothly and effectively. At times they received considerable support from both traditionalists (local chiefs, landowners, religious leaders) and modernizers (Western-educated professional classes and civil servants).

Nevertheless, imperial rule was in many ways an imposing edifice built on sand. Support for European rule among subjugated peoples was shallow and weak. Colonized lands were primarily peasant societies, and much of the burden of colonization fell on small farmers who tenaciously fought for some measure of autonomy. When colonists demanded extra taxes or crops, peasants played dumb and hid the extent of their harvest; when colonists asked for increased labor, peasants dragged their feet. These "weapons of the weak" stopped short of open defiance but nonetheless presented a real challenge to Western rule.[11] Moreover, native people followed with greater or lesser enthusiasm the few determined personalities who came to openly oppose the Europeans. Such leaders always arose, both when Europeans ruled directly and when they manipulated native governments, for at least two basic reasons.

First, the nonconformists—the eventual anti-imperialist leaders—developed a burning desire for human dignity, economic emancipation, and political independence, all incompatible with foreign rule. Second, and somewhat ironically, potential leaders found in the Western world the ideologies underlying and justifying their protest. They discovered liberalism, with its credos of civil liberties and political self-determination. They echoed the demands of anti-imperialists in Europe and America that the West live up to its own ideals. Above all, they found themselves attracted to nationalism, which asserted that every people had the right to control its own destiny. After 1917 anti-imperialist revolt would find another European-made weapon in Lenin's version of Marxist socialism. Thus the anti-imperialist search for dignity drew strength from Western thought and culture, as is particularly apparent in the development of three major Asian countries—India, Japan, and China.

Empire in India

India was the jewel of the British Empire, and no colonial area experienced a more profound British impact. Unlike Japan and China, which maintained a real if precarious independence, and unlike African territories, which Europeans annexed only at the end of the nineteenth century, India was ruled more or less absolutely by Britain for a very long time.

Arriving in India on the heels of the Portuguese in the seventeenth century, the British East India Company had conquered the last independent native state by 1848. The last "traditional" response to European rule—an attempt by the existing ruling classes to drive the invaders out by military force—was broken in India in 1857 and 1858. Those were the years of the **Great Rebellion** (which the British called a "mutiny"), an insurrection by Muslim and Hindu mercenaries in the British army that spread throughout northern and central India before it was finally crushed, primarily by loyal indigenous troops from southern India. Britain then established direct control until Indian independence was gained in 1947.

India was ruled by the British Parliament in London and administered by a tiny, all-white civil service in India. In 1900 this elite consisted of fewer than 3,500 top officials, who controlled a population of 300 million. The white elite, backed by white officers and indigenous troops, was competent and generally well disposed toward the welfare of the Indian peasant masses. Yet it practiced strict job discrimination and social segregation, and most of its members quite frankly considered what they saw as the jumble of Indian peoples and castes to be racially inferior. As Lord Kitchener, one of the most distinguished top military commanders in India, stated:

> It is this consciousness of the inherent superiority of the European which has won for us India. However well educated and clever a native may be, and however brave he may prove himself, I believe that no rank we can bestow on him would cause him to be considered an equal of the British officer.[12]

British women played an important part in the imperial enterprise, especially after the opening of the Suez Canal in 1869 made it much easier for civil servants and business-men to bring their wives and children with them to India. These British families tended to live in their own separate communities, where they occupied large houses with well-shaded porches, handsome lawns, and a multitude of servants. It was the wife's responsibility to manage this complex household. Many officials' wives learned to relish their duties, and they directed their households and servants with the same self-confident authoritarianism that characterized their husbands' political rule.

A small minority of British women—many of them feminists, social reformers, or missionaries, both married and single—sought to go further and shoulder what one historian has called the "white women's burden" in India.[13] These women tried especially to improve the lives of Indian women, both Hindu and Muslim, promoting education and legislation to move them closer to the better conditions they believed Western women had attained. Their greatest success was educating some elite Hindu women who took up the cause of reform.

Inspired by the "civilizing mission"—as well as strong feelings of racial and cultural superiority—British imperialists worked energetically to westernize Indian society. Realizing that they needed well-educated Indians to serve as skilled subordinates in both the government and the army, the British established a modern system of secondary education, with all instruction in English. Thus some Indians gained excellent oppor-tunities for economic and social advancement. High-caste Hindus, particularly quick to respond, emerged as skillful intermediaries between the British rulers and the Indian people, and soon they formed a new elite profoundly influenced by Western thought and culture.

This new Indian elite joined British officials and businessmen to promote modern economic development, a second result of British rule. Examples included constructing irrigation projects for agriculture, building the world's third-largest railroad network for good communications, and forming large tea and jute plantations geared to the world economy. Unfortunately, the lot of the Indian masses improved little, for the profits from the increase in production went to indigenous and British elites.

Finally, with a well-educated, English-speaking Indian bureaucracy and steps toward economic development, the British created a unified, powerful state. They placed under the same system of law and administration the different Hindu and Muslim peoples and the vanquished kingdoms of the entire subcontinent—groups that had fought each other for centuries and had been repeatedly conquered by Muslim and Mongol invaders. It was as if Europe, with its many states and varieties of Christianity, had been conquered and united in a single great empire.

Despite these achievements, the decisive reaction to European rule was the rise of nationalism among the Indian elite. No matter how anglicized and necessary a member of the indigenous educated classes became, he or she could never become the white ruler's equal. The top jobs, the best clubs, the modern hotels, and even certain railroad compartments were off limits to darker-skinned Indians. The peasant masses might accept such inequality as the latest version of age-old oppression, but the well-educated, English-speaking elite eventually could not. For them, racial discrimination meant injured pride and bitter injustice. It flagrantly contradicted the cherished Western concepts of human rights and equality that they had learned about in Western schools. Moreover, it was based on dictatorship, no matter how benign.

By 1885, when educated Indians came together to found the predominantly Hindu Indian National Congress, demands were increasing for the equality and self-government that Britain had already granted white-settler colonies, such as Canada and Australia. By 1907, emboldened in part by Japan's success (see the next section), a radical faction in the Indian National Congress called for Indian independence. Although there were sharp divisions between Hindus and Muslims on what shape the Indian future should take, among other issues, Indians were finding an answer to the foreign challenge. The common heritage of British rule and Western ideals, along with the reform and revitalization of the Hindu religion, had created a genuine movement for national independence.

The Example of Japan

When Commodore Matthew Perry arrived in Tokyo in 1853 with his crude but effective gunboat diplomacy, Japan was a complex feudal society. At the top stood a figurehead emperor, but real power was in the hands of a hereditary military governor, the shogun. With the help of a warrior nobility known as samurai, the shogun governed a country of hard-working, productive peasants and city dwellers. The intensely proud samurai were humiliated by the sudden American intrusion and the unequal treaties with Western countries that followed.

When foreign diplomats and merchants began to settle in Yokohama, radical samurai reacted with a wave of antiforeign terrorism and antigovernment assassinations that lasted from 1858 to 1863. In response, an allied fleet of American, British, Dutch, and French warships demolished key forts, further weakening the power and prestige of the shogun's government. Then in 1867 a coalition led by patriotic samurai seized control of the government with hardly any bloodshed and restored the political power of the emperor in the **Meiji Restoration**, a great turning point in Japanese history.

The battle cry of the Meiji (MAY-jee) reformers was "Enrich the state and strengthen the armed forces," and the immediate goal of the new government was to meet the foreign threat. Yet how were these tasks to be accomplished? In a remarkable about-face, the leaders of Meiji Japan dropped their antiforeign attacks. Convinced that

Western civilization was indeed superior in its military and industrial aspects, they initiated a series of measures to reform Japan along modern lines. In the broadest sense, the Meiji leaders tried to harness Western industrialization and political reform to protect their country and catch up with Europe.

In 1871 the new leaders abolished the old feudal structure of aristocratic, decentralized government and formed a strong unified state. Following the example of the French Revolution, they dismantled the four-class legal system and declared social equality. They decreed freedom of movement in a country where traveling abroad had been a serious crime. They created a free, competitive, government-stimulated economy. Japan began to build railroads and modern factories. The new generation adopted many principles of a free, liberal society, and, as in Europe, the resulting freedom resulted in a tremendously creative release of human energy.

Yet the overriding concern of Japan's political leadership was always to maintain a powerful state and a strong military. State leaders created a powerful modern navy and completely reorganized the army along European lines, forming a professional officer corps and requiring three years of military service of all males. This army of draftees effectively put down disturbances in the countryside, and in 1877 it crushed

The Russo-Japanese War, 1904–1905   This 1904 Japanese print portrays the surprise Japanese naval attack on the Russian fleet at Port Arthur as a glorious victory. Though the opening battle was in fact inconclusive, with few losses on either side, the Japanese won the war. Defeat by a supposedly "primitive" Asian nation encouraged reform movements in the Russian Empire and became a factor in the outbreak of the Russian Revolution of 1905 (see Chapter 23). (Universal History Archive/Getty Images)

a major rebellion by feudal elements protesting the loss of their privileges. In addition, Japan skillfully adapted the West's science and technology, particularly in industry, medicine, and education, and many Japanese studied abroad. The government paid large salaries to attract foreign experts, who were replaced by trained Japanese as soon as possible.

By 1890, when the new state was firmly established, the wholesale borrowing of the early restoration had given way to a more selective emphasis on those things foreign that were in keeping with Japanese tradition. Following the model of the German Empire, Japan established an authoritarian constitution and rejected democracy. The power of the emperor and his ministers was vast, that of the legislature limited.

Japan also successfully copied the imperialism of Western society. Expansion proved that Japan was strong and cemented the nation together in a great mission. Having "opened" Korea with its own gunboat diplomacy in 1876, Japan decisively defeated China in a war over Korea in 1894 and 1895 and took Formosa (modern-day Taiwan). In the next years, Japan competed aggressively with European powers for influence and territory in China, particularly in Manchuria, where Japanese and Russian imperialism collided. In 1904 Japan launched the Russo-Japanese War (1904–1905) by attacking Russia without a formal declaration of war. After a series of bloody battles, victorious Japan took over Russia's former protectorate in Port Arthur and emerged with a valuable foothold in China (see Map 24.3). By 1910, with the annexation of Korea, Japan had become a major imperialist power.

Japan became the first non-Western country to use an ancient love of country to transform itself and thereby meet the many-sided challenge of Western expansion. Moreover, Japan demonstrated convincingly that a modern Asian nation could defeat and humble a great Western power. Japan's achievement fascinated many Chinese and Vietnamese nationalists and provided patriots throughout Asia and Africa with an inspiring example of national recovery and liberation.

Toward Revolution in China

In 1860 the two-hundred-year-old Qing Dynasty in China appeared on the verge of collapse. Efforts to repel foreigners had failed, and rebellion and chaos wracked the country. Yet the government drew on its traditional strengths and made a surprising comeback that lasted more than thirty years.

Two factors were crucial in this reversal. First, the traditional ruling groups temporarily produced new and effective leadership. Loyal scholar-statesmen and generals quelled disturbances such as the great Tai Ping rebellion. The remarkable empress dowager Tzu Hsi (tsoo shee) governed in the name of her young son, combining shrewd insight with vigorous action to revitalize the bureaucracy.

Second, destructive foreign aggression lessened, for the Europeans had obtained their primary goal of establishing commercial and diplomatic relations. Indeed, some Europeans contributed to the dynasty's recovery. A talented Irishman effectively reorganized China's customs office, increasing government tax receipts, and a sympathetic American diplomat represented China in foreign lands, helping to strengthen the Chinese government. Such efforts dovetailed with the dynasty's efforts to adopt some aspects of Western government and technology while maintaining traditional Chinese values and beliefs.

The parallel movement toward domestic reform and limited cooperation with the West collapsed under the blows of Japanese imperialism. Defeat in the Sino-Japanese War (1894–1895) and the subsequent harsh peace treaty revealed China's helplessness in the face of aggression, triggering a rush by foreign powers for concessions and protectorates. At the high point of this rush in 1898, it appeared that the European powers might actually divide China among themselves, as they had recently divided Africa. Probably only the jealousy each nation felt toward its imperialist competitors saved China from partition. In any event, the tempo of foreign encroachment greatly accelerated after 1894.

China's precarious position after the war with Japan led to a renewed drive for fundamental reforms. Like the leaders of the Meiji Restoration, some modernizers saw salvation in Western institutions. In 1898 they convinced the young emperor to launch a desperate **hundred days of reform** in an attempt to meet the foreign challenge. More radical reformers, such as the revolutionary Sun Yatsen (1866–1925), who came from the peasantry and was educated in Hawaii by Christian missionaries, sought to overthrow the dynasty altogether and establish a republic.

The efforts at radical reform by the young emperor and his allies threatened the Qing establishment and the empress dowager Tzu Hsi, who had dominated the court for a quarter of a century. In a palace coup, she and her supporters imprisoned the emperor, rejected the reform movement, and put reactionary officials in charge. Hope for reform from above was crushed.

A violent antiforeign reaction swept the country, encouraged by the Qing court and led by a secret society that foreigners called the Boxers. The conservative, patriotic Boxers blamed China's ills on foreigners, charging foreign missionaries with undermining Chinese reverence for their ancestors and thereby threatening the Chinese family and the society as a whole. In the agony of defeat and unwanted reforms, the Boxers and other secret societies struck out at their enemies. In northeastern China, more than two hundred foreign missionaries and several thousand Chinese Christians were killed, prompting threats and demands from Western governments. The empress dowager answered by declaring war on the foreign powers, hoping that the Boxers might relieve the foreign pressure on the government.

The imperialist response was swift and harsh. After the Boxers besieged the embassy quarter in Beijing, foreign governments (including Japan, Britain, France, Germany, and the United States) organized an international force of twenty thousand soldiers to rescue their diplomats and punish China. These troops defeated the Boxers and occupied and plundered Beijing. In 1901 China was forced to accept a long list of penalties, including a heavy financial indemnity payable over forty years.

The years after this heavy defeat were ever more troubled. Anarchy and foreign influence spread as the power and prestige of the Qing Dynasty declined still further. Antiforeign, antigovernment revolutionary groups agitated and plotted. Finally, in 1912 a spontaneous uprising toppled the Qing Dynasty. After thousands of years of emperors, a loose coalition of revolutionaries proclaimed a Western-style republic and called for an elected parliament. The transformation of China under the impact of expanding Western society entered a new phase, and the end was not in sight.

NOTES

1. Quoted in J. W. Hall, *Japan: From Prehistory to Modern Times* (New York: Delacorte Press, 1970), p. 250.
2. Quoted in Earl of Cromer, *Modern Egypt* (London, 1911), p. 48.
3. Quoted in T. Blegen, *Norwegian Migration to America*, vol. 2 (Northfield, Minn.: Norwegian-American Historical Association, 1940), p. 468.
4. Quoted in I. Howe, *World of Our Fathers* (New York: Harcourt Brace Jovanovich, 1975), p. 290.
5. Quoted in W. L. Langer, *European Alliances and Alignments, 1871–1890* (New York: Vintage Books, 1931), p. 290.
6. Quoted in J. Ellis, *The Social History of the Machine Gun* (New York: Pantheon Books, 1975), pp. 86, 101. The numbers given for British casualties at the Battle of Omdurman vary; the total casualties quoted here come from an original British army report. See Lieutenant General H. M. L. Rundle, M.G., Chief of Staff, "Herewith Returns of Killed and Wounded of the Expeditionary Force at the Battle of Khartum, on September 2, 1898," Khartum, September 9, 1898, at North East Medals, http://www.britishmedals.us/kevin/other/lgomdurman.html.
7. Quoted in G. H. Nadel and P. Curtis, eds., *Imperialism and Colonialism* (New York: Macmillan, 1964), p. 94.
8. Quoted in W. L. Langer, *The Diplomacy of Imperialism*, 2d ed. (New York: Alfred A. Knopf, 1951), pp. 86, 88.
9. Quoted in S. Conrad, *Globalisation and the Nation in Imperial Germany* (New York: Cambridge University Press, 2010), p. 78.
10. Quoted in Langer, *The Diplomacy of Imperialism*, p. 88.
11. J. C. Scott, *Weapons of the Weak: Everyday Forms of Peasant Resistance* (New Haven: Yale University Press, 1985), p. xvi.
12. Quoted in K. M. Panikkar, *Asia and Western Dominance: A Survey of the Vasco da Gama Epoch of Asian History* (London: George Allen & Unwin, 1959), p. 116.
13. A. Burton, "The White Women's Burden: British Feminists and 'The Indian Women,' 1865–1915," in *Western Women and Imperialism: Complicity and Resistance*, ed. N. Chauduri and M. Strobel (Bloomington: Indiana University Press, 1992), pp. 137–157.

LOOKING BACK LOOKING AHEAD

In the early twentieth century educated Europeans had good reason to believe that they were living in an age of progress. The ongoing triumphs of industry and science and the steady improvements in the standard of living beginning about 1850 were undeniable, and it was generally assumed that these favorable trends would continue. There had also been progress in the political realm. The bitter class conflicts that culminated in the bloody civil strife of 1848 had given way in most European countries to stable nation-states with elected legislative bodies that reflected the general population, responded to real problems, and enjoyed popular support. Moreover, there had been no general European war since Napoleon's defeat in 1815. Only the brief, limited wars connected with German and Italian unification at midcentury had broken the peace in the European heartland.

In the global arena, peace was much more elusive. In the name of imperialism, Europeans (and North Americans) used war and the threat of war to open markets and punish foreign governments around the world. Although criticized by some intellectuals and leftists such as J. A. Hobson, these foreign campaigns resonated with European citizens and stimulated popular nationalism. Like fans in a sports bar, the peoples of Europe followed their colonial teams and cheered them on to victories that were almost certain. Thus imperialism and nationalism reinforced and strengthened each other in Europe, especially after 1875.

This was a dangerous development. Easy imperialist victories over weak states and poorly armed non-Western peoples encouraged excessive pride and led Europeans to underestimate the fragility of their accomplishments as well as the murderous power of their weaponry. Imperialism also made nationalism more aggressive and militaristic. At the same time that European imperialism was dividing the world, the leading European states were also dividing themselves into two opposing military alliances. Thus when the two armed camps stumbled into war in 1914, there would be a super-abundance of nationalistic fervor, patriotic sacrifice, and cataclysmic destruction.

MAKE CONNECTIONS

Think about the larger developments and continuities within and across chapters.

1. How did the expansion of European empires transform everyday life around the world?

2. Historians often use the term *New Imperialism* to describe the globalization of empire that began in the last decades of the nineteenth century. Was the New Imperialism really that different from earlier waves of European expansion (Chapters 14 and 17)?

3. How did events and trends in European colonies connect to or reflect events and trends in the European homeland?

Chapter Review

IDENTIFY KEY TERMS

Identify and explain the significance of each item below.

neo-Europes (p. 763)

Opium Wars (p. 766)

gunboat diplomacy (p. 766)

global mass migration (p. 768)

nativism (p. 773)

New Imperialism (p. 774)

Afrikaners (p. 774)

Berlin Conference (p. 776)

white man's burden (p. 782)

Orientalism (p. 783)

Great Rebellion (p. 786)

Meiji Restoration (p. 788)

hundred days of reform (p. 791)

REVIEW THE MAIN IDEAS

Answer the focus questions from each section of the chapter.

1. What were some of the global consequences of European industrialization between 1815 and 1914? (p. 761)

2. How was massive migration an integral part of Western expansion? (p. 768)

3. How did Western imperialism change after 1880? (p. 773)
4. What was the general pattern of non-Western responses to Western expansion? (p. 785)

CHRONOLOGY	
1805–1848	Muhammad Ali modernizes Egypt
1839–1842	First Opium War; Treaty of Nanking
1853	Perry "opens" Japan for trade
1856–1860	Second Opium War
1857–1858	Britain crushes Great Rebellion in India
1863–1879	Reign of Ismail in Egypt
1867	Meiji Restoration in Japan
1869	Suez Canal opens
1880–1900	Most of Africa falls under European rule
1884–1885	Berlin Conference
1885	Russian expansion reaches borders of Afghanistan
1898	United States takes over Philippines; hundred days of reform in China; Battle of Omdurman
1899	Kipling writes "The White Man's Burden"
1899–1902	South African War
1902	Conrad publishes *Heart of Darkness*; Hobson publishes *Imperialism*
1912	Western-style republic replaces China's Qing Dynasty
1914	Panama Canal opens

25

War and Revolution

1914–1919

IN THE SUMMER OF 1914 the nations of Europe went willingly to war. They believed they had no other choice. Both peoples and governments confidently expected a short war leading to a decisive victory and thought that European society would be able to go on as before. These expectations were totally mistaken. The First World War was long, indecisive, and tremendously destructive. To the shell-shocked generation of survivors, it was known simply as the Great War because of its unprecedented scope and intensity.

From today's perspective, it is clear that the First World War was closely connected to the ideals and developments of the previous century. Industrialization, which promised a rising standard of living, now produced horrendous weapons that killed and maimed millions. Imperialism, which promised to civilize those the Europeans considered savages, now led to intractable international conflicts. Nationalism, which promised to bring compatriots together in a harmonious nation-state, now encouraged hateful prejudice and chauvinism. The extraordinary violence of world war shook confidence in such nineteenth-century certainties to their core.

The war would have an enormous impact on the century that followed. The need to provide extensive supplies and countless soldiers for the war effort created mass suffering, encouraged the rise of the bureaucratic state, and brought women in increasing numbers into the workplace. Millions were killed or wounded at the front, and millions more grieved these losses. Grand states collapsed: the Russian, Austro-Hungarian, and Ottoman Empires passed into history. The trauma of war contributed to the rise of extremist politics—in the Russian Revolution of 1917 the Bolsheviks established a radical Communist regime, and totalitarian Fascist movements gained popularity across Europe in the postwar decades. Explaining the war's causes and consequences remains one of the great challenges for historians of modern Europe.

The Road to War

Focus Question	What caused the outbreak of the First World War?

Historians have long debated why Europeans so readily pursued a war that was long and costly and failed to resolve the problems faced by the combatant nations. There was no single most important cause. Growing competition over colonies and world markets, a belligerent arms race, and a series of diplomatic crises sharpened international tensions. On the home front, new forms of populist nationalism strengthened people's unquestioning belief in "my country right or wrong" while ongoing domestic conflicts encouraged governments to pursue aggressive foreign policies in attempts to bolster national unity. All helped pave the road to war.

Growing International Conflict

The First World War began, in part, because European statesmen failed to resolve the diplomatic problems created by Germany's rise to Great Power status. The Franco-Prussian War and the unification of Germany opened a new era in international relations. By the war's end in 1871, France was defeated, and Bismarck had made Prussia-Germany the most powerful nation in Europe (see Chapter 23). After 1871 Bismarck declared that Germany was a "satisfied" power. Within Europe, he stated, Germany had no territorial ambitions and wanted only peace.

But how was peace to be preserved? Bismarck's first concern was to keep France—bitter over its defeat and the loss of Alsace and Lorraine—diplomatically isolated and without allies. His second concern was the threat to peace posed by the enormous multinational empires of Austria-Hungary and Russia, particularly in southeastern Europe, where the waning strength of the Ottoman Empire had created a threatening power vacuum in the disputed border territories of the Balkans.

Bismarck's accomplishments in foreign policy were effective, but only temporary. From 1871 to the late 1880s, he maintained German leadership in international affairs, and he signed a series of defensive alliances with Austria-Hungary and Russia designed to isolate France. Yet in 1890 the new emperor Wilhelm II incautiously dismissed Bismarck, in part because he disagreed with the chancellor's friendly policy toward Russia. Under Wilhelm II, Bismarck's carefully planned alliance system began to unravel. Germany refused to renew a nonaggression pact with Russia, the centerpiece of Bismarck's system, in spite of Russian willingness to do so. This fateful move prompted long-isolated republican France to court absolutist Russia, offering loans, arms, and diplomatic support. In early 1894 France and Russia became military allies. As a result, continental Europe was divided into two rival blocs. The **Triple Alliance** of Austria, Germany, and Italy faced an increasingly hostile Dual Alliance of Russia and France, and the German general staff began secret preparations for a war on two fronts (Map 25.1).

As rivalries deepened on the continent, Great Britain's foreign policy became increasingly crucial. After 1891 Britain was the only uncommitted Great Power. Many Germans and some Britons felt that the advanced, racially related Germanic

MAP 25.1 European Alliances at the Outbreak of World War I, 1914
At the start of World War I, Europe was divided into two hostile alliances: the Triple Entente of Britain, France, and Russia, and the Triple Alliance of Germany, Austria-Hungary, and Italy. Italy never fought with the Triple Alliance but instead joined the Entente in 1915.

and Anglo-Saxon peoples were natural allies. However, the good relations that had prevailed between Prussia and Great Britain since the mid-eighteenth century gave way to a bitter Anglo-German rivalry.

There were several reasons for this ill-fated development. Commercial rivalry in world markets between Germany and Great Britain increased sharply in the 1890s, as Germany became a great industrial power. Germany's ambitious pursuit of colonies further threatened British interests. Above all, Germany's decision in 1900 to expand significantly its battle fleet posed a challenge to Britain's long-standing naval supremacy. In response to German expansion, British leaders prudently shored up their exposed global position with alliances and agreements. Britain improved its often-strained relations with the United States, concluded an alliance with Japan in

1902, and allied with France in the Anglo-French Entente of 1904, which settled all outstanding colonial disputes between Britain and France.

Alarmed by Britain's closer ties to France, Germany's leaders decided to test the strength of their alliance. In 1905 Wilhelm II declared that Morocco—where France had colonial interests—was an independent, sovereign state and demanded that Germany receive the same trading rights as France. Wilhelm II insisted on an international conference in hopes that his saber rattling would settle the Moroccan question to Germany's benefit. But his crude bullying only brought France and Britain closer together, and Germany left the conference empty-handed.

The result of the First Moroccan Crisis in 1905 was something of a diplomatic revolution. Britain, France, Russia, and even the United States began to see Germany as a potential threat. At the same time, German leaders began to see sinister plots to encircle Germany and block its development as a world power. In 1907 Russia, battered by its disastrous war with Japan and the revolution of 1905, agreed to settle its quarrels with Great Britain in Persia and Central Asia and signed the Anglo-Russian Agreement. This agreement laid the foundation of the **Triple Entente** (ahn-TAHNT), an alliance between Britain, Russia, and France.

Germany's decision to expand its navy with a large, enormously expensive fleet of big-gun battleships, known as "dreadnoughts" because of their great size and power, heightened international tensions. German patriots saw a large navy as the legitimate right of a great world power and as a source of national pride. But British leaders saw the German buildup as a military challenge that forced them to spend the "People's Budget" (see Chapter 23) on battleships rather than social welfare. In 1909 the London *Daily Mail* hysterically informed its readers that "Germany is deliberately preparing to destroy the British Empire."[1] By then Britain had sided psychologically, if not officially, with France and Russia.

The leading nations of Europe were divided into two hostile camps, both ill-prepared to deal with the worsening situation in the Balkans. Britain, France, and Russia—the Triple Entente—were in direct opposition to the German-led Triple Alliance (see Map 25.1). This unfortunate treaty system only confirmed the failure of all European leaders to incorporate Bismarck's mighty empire permanently and peacefully into the international system. By 1914 many believed that war was inevitable.

The Mood of 1914

Diplomatic rivalries and international crises played key roles in the rush to war, but a complete understanding of the war's origins requires an account of the "mood of 1914"—the attitudes and convictions of Europeans around 1914.[2] Widespread militarism (the popular approval of military institutions and their values) and nationalism encouraged leaders and citizens alike to see international relations as an arena for the testing of national power, with war if necessary.

Germany was especially famous for its powerful and aggressive army, but military institutions played a prominent role in affairs of state and in the lives of ordinary people across Europe. In a period marked by diplomatic tensions, politicians relied on generals and military experts to help shape public policy. All the Great Powers built up their armed forces and designed mobilization plans to rush men and weapons to the field of battle. Universal conscription in Germany, France, Italy, Austria-Hungary, and Russia—only Britain still relied on a volunteer army—exposed hundreds of thousands of young men each year to military culture and discipline.

The continent had not experienced a major conflict since the Franco-Prussian War (1870–1871), so Europeans vastly underestimated the destructive potential of modern weapons. Encouraged by the patriotic national press, many believed that war was glorious, manly, and heroic. If they expected another conflict, they thought it would be over quickly. Leading politicians and intellectuals likewise portrayed war as a test of strength that would lead to national unity and renewal. Such ideas permeated European society. As one German volunteer wrote in his diary as he left for the front in 1914, "I believe that this war is a challenge for our time and for each individual, a test by fire, that we may ripen into manhood, become men able to cope with the coming stupendous years and events."[3]

Support for military values was closely linked to a growing sense of popular nationalism, the notion that one's country was superior to all others (see Chapters 21 and 23). Since the 1850s the spread of the idea that members of an ethnic group should live together in a homogeneous, united nation-state had provoked all kinds of international conflicts over borders and citizenship rights. Nationalism drove the spiraling arms race and the struggle over colonies. Broad popular commitment to national interests above all else weakened groups that thought in terms of international communities and consequences. Expressions of antiwar sentiment by socialists, pacifists, and women's groups were seen as a betrayal of country in time of need. Inspired by nationalist beliefs, much of the population was ready for war.

Leading statesmen had practical reasons for promoting militarism and nationalism. Political leaders had long used foreign adventurism and diplomatic posturing to distract the people from domestic conflicts. In Great Britain, leaders faced civil war in Northern Ireland and a vocal and increasingly radical women's movement. In Russia, defeat in the Russo-Japanese War (1904–1905) and the revolution of 1905 had greatly weakened support for the tsarist regime. In Germany, the victory of the Marxist Social Democratic Party in the parliamentary elections of 1912 led government authorities to worry that the country was falling apart. The French likewise faced difficult labor and budget problems.

Determined to hold on to power and frightened by rising popular movements, ruling classes across Europe were willing to gamble on diplomatic brinksmanship and even war to postpone dealing with intractable social and political conflicts. Victory promised to preserve the privileged positions of elites and rally the masses behind the national cause. The patriotic nationalism bolstered by the outbreak of war did bring unity in the short run, but the wealthy governing classes underestimated the risk of war to themselves. They had forgotten that great wars and great social revolutions very often go hand in hand.

The Outbreak of War

On June 28, 1914, Archduke Franz Ferdinand, heir to the Austro-Hungarian throne, was assassinated by Serbian revolutionaries during a state visit to the Bosnian capital of Sarajevo (sar-uh-YAY-voh). After a series of failed attempts to bomb the archduke's

German Militarism   The German emperor Wilhelm II reviews his troops with the Italian king Victor Emmanuel in front of the royal palace in Potsdam in 1902. Aggressive militarism and popular nationalism helped pave the road to war. (© Scherl/SZ Photo/The Image Works)

neutral Belgium — the quickest way to reach Paris — before turning on Russia. On August 3 German armies invaded Belgium. Great Britain, infuriated by the German violation of Belgian neutrality, declared war on Germany the following day.

The speed of the so-called July Crisis created shock, panic, and excitement, and a bellicose public helped propel Europe into war. In the final days of July and the first few days of August, massive crowds thronged the streets of Paris, London, St. Petersburg, Berlin, and Vienna. Shouting prowar slogans, the enthusiastic crowds pushed politicians and military leaders toward the increasingly inevitable confrontation. Events proceeded rapidly, and those who opposed the war could do little to prevent its arrival. In a little over a month, a limited Austrian-Serbian war had become a European-wide conflict, and the First World War had begun.

Waging Total War

Focus Question	**How did the First World War differ from previous wars?**

When the Germans invaded Belgium in August 1914, they and many others thought that the war would be short and relatively painless. Many sincerely believed that "the boys will be home by Christmas." They were wrong. On the western front in France and the eastern front in Russia, and on the borders of the Ottoman Empire, the belligerent armies bogged down in a new and extremely costly kind of war, later labeled **total war** by German general Erich Ludendorff. Total war meant new roles for soldiers and civilians alike. At the front, total war meant lengthy, deadly battles fought with all the destructive weapons a highly industrialized society could produce. At home, national economies were geared toward the war effort. Governments revoked civil liberties, and many civilians lost lives or livelihoods as occupying armies moved through their towns and cities. The struggle expanded outside Europe, and the Middle East, Africa, East Asia, and the United States were all brought into the maelstrom of total war.

Stalemate and Slaughter on the Western Front

In the face of the German invasion, the Belgian army heroically defended its homeland and fell back in good order to join a rapidly landed British army corps near the Franco-Belgian border. At the same time, Russian armies attacked eastern Germany, forcing the Germans to transfer much-needed troops to the east. Instead of quickly capturing Paris as per the Schlieffen Plan, by the end of August dead-tired German soldiers were advancing slowly along an enormous front in the scorching summer heat. Afraid that armed Belgian partisans (called *francs-tireurs*) were attacking German troops behind the lines, the German occupiers dealt harshly with local resistance. German soldiers executed civilians suspected of joining the partisans and, in an out-of-control tragedy, burned the medieval core of the Belgian city of Louvain. Entente propaganda made the most of the German "Rape of Belgium" and the atrocities committed by German troops.

On September 6 the French attacked a gap in the German line at the Battle of the Marne. For three days, France threw everything into the attack. At one point, the French government desperately requisitioned all the taxis of Paris to rush reserves to the front. Finally, the Germans fell back. France had been miraculously saved (Map 25.3).

With the armies stalled, both sides began to dig trenches to protect themselves from machine-gun fire. By November 1914 an unbroken line of four hundred miles of defensive positions extended from the Belgian coast through northern France and on to the Swiss frontier. Armies on both sides dug in behind rows of trenches, mines, and barbed wire, and slaughter on the western front began in earnest. The cost in lives of **trench warfare** was staggering, the gains in territory minuscule. For ordinary soldiers, conditions in the trenches were atrocious. Recently invented weapons, the products of an industrial age, made battle impersonal, traumatic, and extremely deadly. The machine gun, hand grenades, poison gas, flamethrowers, long-range artillery, the airplane, and the tank were all used to murderous effect. All favored the defense, increased casualty rates, and revolutionized the practice of war.

The leading generals of the combatant nations, who had learned military tactics and strategy in the nineteenth century, struggled to understand trench warfare. For four years they repeated the same mistakes, mounting massive offensives designed to achieve decisive breakthroughs. Brutal frontal assaults against highly fortified trenches might overrun the enemy's frontline, but attacking soldiers rarely captured any

Legend:
- Triple Entente and allies
- Central Powers and allies
- Greatest extent of territory gained by Germany-Austria
- German submarine war zone
- Neutral nations
- Farthest advance by Central Powers on date marked
- Farthest advance by Entente Powers on date marked
- British naval blockade
- Major battle
- Treaty of Brest-Litovsk, March 1918

"Greetings from the trenches." This German postcard shows three soldiers writing letters to their loved ones at home; the card was probably produced on a small, frontline printing press, for quick use by soldiers in the field. The post was typically the only connection between soldiers and their relatives, and over 28 billion pieces of mail passed between home and front on all sides during the war. (© Sammlung Sauer/dpa/Corbis)

Ein Gruss aus dem Schützengraben.

substantial territory. The French and British offensives of 1915 never gained more than three miles of territory. In 1916 the unsuccessful German campaign against Verdun left over 700,000 soldiers killed or wounded, and ended with the combatants in their original positions. The results in 1917 were little better. In hard-fought battles on all fronts, millions of young men were wounded or died for no real gain.

The Battle of the Somme, a great British offensive undertaken in the summer of 1916 in northern France, exemplified the horrors of trench warfare. The battle began with a weeklong heavy artillery bombardment on the German lines, intended to cut the barbed wire fortifications, decimate the enemy trenches, and prevent the Germans from making an effective defense. For seven days and nights, the British artillery fired nonstop on the German lines, delivering about 1.5 million shells. On July 1 the British went "over the top," climbing out of the trenches and moving into no-man's land toward the German lines, dug into a series of ridges about half a mile away.

During the bombardment, the Germans had fled to their dugouts—underground shelters dug deep into the trenches—where they suffered from lack of water, food, and sleep. But they survived. As the British soldiers neared the German lines and the

< **MAP 25.3** World War I in Europe and the Middle East, 1914–1918
Trench warfare on the western front was concentrated in Belgium and northern France, while the war in the east and the Ottoman Empire encompassed an enormous territory.

shelling stopped, the Germans emerged from their bunkers, set up their machine guns, and mowed down the approaching troops. In many places, the wire had not been cut by the bombardment, so the attackers, held in place by the wire, made easy targets. About 20,000 British men were killed and 40,000 more were wounded on just the first day, a crushing loss that shook troop morale and public opinion at home. The battle lasted until November, and in the end the British did push the Germans back—a whole seven miles. Some 420,000 British, 200,000 French, and 600,000 Germans were killed or wounded fighting over an insignificant scrap of land.

As the war ground on, exhausted soldiers found it difficult to comprehend or describe the bloody reality of their experiences at the front. As one French soldier wrote:

> I went over the top, I ran, I shouted, I hit, I can't remember where or who. I crossed the wire, jumped over holes, crawled through shell craters still stinking of explosives, men were falling, shot in two as they ran; shouts and gasps were half muffled by the sweeping surge of gunfire. But it was like a nightmare mist all around me. . . . Now my part in it is over for a few minutes. . . . Something is red over there; something is burning. Something is red at my feet: blood.[5]

The anonymous, almost unreal qualities of high-tech warfare made their way into the art and literature of the time. In each combatant nation, artists and writers sought to portray the nightmarish quality of total war. Works by artists like Paul Nash or the poems of the famous British "trench poets" may do more to capture the experience of the war than contemporary photos or the dry accounts of historians.

The Widening War

On the eastern front, the slaughter did not immediately degenerate into trench warfare, and the fighting was dominated by Germany. Repulsing the initial Russian attacks, the Germans won major victories at the Battles of Tannenberg and the Masurian Lakes in August and September 1914. Russia put real pressure on the relatively weak Austro-Hungarian army, but by 1915 the eastern front had stabilized in Germany's favor. A staggering 2.5 million Russian soldiers had been killed, wounded, or captured. German armies occupied huge swaths of the Russian Empire in central Europe, including ethnic Polish, Belorussian, and Baltic territories. Yet Russia continued to fight, marking another failure of the Schlieffen Plan.

To govern these occupied territories, the Germans installed a vast military bureaucracy, with some 15,000 army administrators and professional specialists. Anti-Slavic prejudice dominated the mind-set of the occupiers, who viewed the local Slavs as savages and ethnic "mongrels." German military administrators used prisoners of war and refugees as forced labor. They stole animals and crops from local farmers to supply the occupying army or send home to Germany. About one-third of the civilian population died or became refugees under this brutal occupation. In the long run, the German state hoped to turn these territories into German possessions, a chilling forerunner of Nazi policies in World War II.[6]

The changing tides of victory and hopes for territorial gains brought neutral countries into the war (see Map 25.3). Italy, a member of the Triple Alliance since 1882, had declared its neutrality in 1914 on the grounds that Austria had launched a war of aggression. Then in May 1915 Italy switched sides to join the Triple Entente in return for promises of Austrian territory. The war along the Italian-Austrian front was bitter and deadly and cost some 600,000 Italian lives.

In October 1914 the Ottoman Empire joined Austria and Germany, by then known as the Central Powers. The following September Bulgaria followed the Ottoman Empire's lead in order to settle old scores with Serbia. The Balkans, with the exception of Greece, were occupied by the Central Powers.

The entry of the Ottomans carried the war into the Middle East. Heavy fighting between the Ottomans and the Russians in the Caucasus enveloped the Armenians, who lived on both sides of the border and had experienced brutal repression by the Ottomans in 1909. When in 1915 some Armenians welcomed Russian armies as liberators, the Ottoman government, with German support, ordered a mass deportation of its Armenian citizens from their homeland. In this early example of modern ethnic cleansing, often labeled genocide, about 1 million Armenians died from murder, starvation, and disease.

In 1915, at the Battle of Gallipoli, British forces tried and failed to take the Dardanelles and Constantinople from the Ottoman Turks. The invasion force was pinned down on the beaches, and the ten-month-long battle cost the Ottomans 300,000 and the British 265,000 men killed, wounded, or missing.

The British were more successful at inciting the Arabs to revolt against their Ottoman rulers. They bargained with the foremost Arab leader, Hussein ibn-Ali (1856–1931), the chief magistrate (*sharif*) of Mecca, the holiest city in the Muslim world, and ruler for the Ottoman sultan of much of the Ottoman Empire's territory along the Red Sea, an area known as the Hejaz. In a famous exchange of diplomatic notes with Sir Henry McMahon, the British high commissioner in Cairo, Hussein managed in 1915 to win vague British commitments for an independent Arab kingdom. In 1916 Hussein rebelled against the Turks, proclaiming himself king of the Arabs. Hussein was aided by the British liaison officer T. E. Lawrence, who in 1917 helped lead Arab soldiers in a successful guerrilla war against the Turks on the Arabian peninsula.

The British enjoyed similar victories in the Ottoman province of Mesopotamia (today's Iraq). British troops quickly occupied the southern Iraqi city of Basra in 1914, securing their access to the region's oil fields. After a series of setbacks at the hands of Ottoman troops, the British captured Baghdad in 1917. In September 1918 British armies and their Arab allies rolled into Syria, a large and diverse Ottoman territory that included the holy lands of Palestine and the present-day countries of Syria, Lebanon, Jordan, and Israel. This offensive culminated in the triumphal entry of Hussein's son Faisal into Damascus. Arab patriots in Syria and Iraq now expected a large, unified Arab nation-state to rise from the dust of the Ottoman collapse — though they would later be disappointed by the Western powers (see page 824).

The war spread to East Asia and colonial Africa as well. Japan declared war on Germany in 1914, seized Germany's Pacific and East Asian colonies, and used the opportunity to expand its influence in China. In Africa, instead of rebelling as the Germans hoped, colonial subjects of the British and French generally supported the Allied powers and helped local British and French commanders take over German colonies.

while the Espionage and Sedition Acts weakened civil liberties. The war may have been deadly for citizen armies, but it was certainly good for the growth of the bureaucratic nation-state.

The Social Impact

The social changes wrought by total war were no less profound than the economic impact, though again there were important national variations. National conscription sent millions of men to the front, exposing many to foreign lands for the first time in their lives. The insatiable needs of the military created a tremendous demand for workers, making jobs readily available. This situation — seldom, if ever, seen before 1914, when unemployment and poverty had been facts of urban life — brought momentous changes.

The need for workers meant greater power and prestige for labor unions. Unions cooperated with war governments on workplace rules, wages, and production schedules in return for real participation in important decisions. The entry of labor leaders and unions into policymaking councils paralleled the entry of socialist leaders into war governments. Both reflected a new government openness to the needs of those at the bottom of society.

The role of women changed dramatically. The production of vast amounts of arms and ammunition required huge numbers of laborers, and women moved into skilled industrial jobs long considered men's work. Women became highly visible in public — as munitions workers, bank tellers, and mail carriers, and even as police officers, firefighters, and farm laborers. Women also served as auxiliaries and nurses at the front.

The war expanded the range of women's activities and helped change attitudes about proper gender roles, but the long-term results were mixed. Women gained experience in jobs previously reserved for men, but at war's end millions of demobilized soldiers demanded their jobs back, and governments forced women out of the workplace. Thus women's employment gains were mostly temporary, except in nursing and social work, already considered "women's work." The great dislocations of war loosened sexual morality, and some women bobbed their hair, shortened their skirts, and smoked in public. Yet supposedly "loose" women were often criticized for betraying their soldier-husbands away at the front. As a result of women's many-sided war effort, the United States, Britain, Germany, Poland, and other countries granted women the right to vote immediately after the war. Yet women's rights movements faded in the 1920s and 1930s, in large part because feminist leaders found it difficult to regain momentum after the crisis of war.

To some extent, the war promoted greater social equality, blurring class distinctions and lessening the gap between rich and poor. This blurring was most apparent in Great Britain, where the bottom third of the population generally lived better than they ever had, for the poorest gained most from the severe shortage of labor. Elsewhere, greater equality was reflected in full employment, distribution of scarce rations according to physical needs, and a sharing of hardships. In general, despite some war profiteering, European society became more uniform and egalitarian.

Women Workers Building a Truck in a London Workshop, 1917   Millions of men on all sides were drafted to fight in the war, creating a serious labor shortage on the home front. When women began to fill jobs formerly reserved for men, they challenged middle-class gender roles. (© Hulton-Deutsch Collection/Corbis)

Death itself had no respect for traditional social distinctions. It savagely decimated the young aristocratic officers who led the charge, and it fell heavily on the mass of drafted peasants and unskilled workers who followed, leading commentators to speak of a "lost generation." Yet death often spared highly skilled workers and foremen. Their lives were too valuable to squander at the front, for they were needed to train the newly recruited women and older unskilled men laboring valiantly in war plants at home.

Growing Political Tensions

During the first two years of war, many soldiers and civilians supported their governments. Patriotic nationalism and belief in a just cause united peoples behind their national leaders. Each government used rigorous censorship and crude propaganda to bolster popular support. German propaganda pictured black soldiers from France's African empire abusing German women, while the French and British ceaselessly recounted and exaggerated German atrocities in Belgium and elsewhere. Patriotic posters and slogans, slanted news, and biased editorials inflamed national hatreds, helped control public opinion, and encouraged soldiers to keep fighting.

Political and social tensions re-emerged, however, and by the spring of 1916 ordinary people were beginning to crack under the strain of total war. Strikes and protest marches over war-related burdens and shortages flared up on every home front. On May 1, 1916, several thousand demonstrators in Berlin heard the radical socialist leader Karl Liebknecht (1871–1919) attack the costs of the war effort. Liebknecht was arrested and imprisoned, but his daring action electrified Europe's far left. In France, Georges Clemenceau (zhorzh kleh-muhn-SOH) (1841–1929) established a virtual dictatorship, arrested strikers, and jailed without trial journalists and politicians who dared to suggest a compromise peace with Germany.

In April 1916 Irish republican nationalists took advantage of the tense wartime conditions to step up their rebellion against British rule. During the great Easter Rising, armed republican militias took over parts of Dublin and proclaimed an independent Irish Republic. After a week of bitter fighting, British troops crushed the rebels and executed their leaders. Though the republicans were defeated, the punitive aftermath fueled anti-British sentiment in Ireland. The Rising set the stage for the success of the nationalist Sinn Fein Party and a full-scale civil war for Irish independence in the early 1920s.

On all sides, soldiers' morale began to decline. Numerous French units mutinied and refused to fight after the disastrous French offensive of May 1917. Only tough military justice, including executions for mutiny leaders, and a tacit agreement with the troops that there would be no more grand offensives, enabled the new general-in-chief, Henri-Philippe Pétain (pay-TAN), to restore order. Facing defeat, wretched conditions at the front, and growing hopelessness, Russian soldiers deserted in droves, providing fuel for the Russian Revolution of 1917. After the murderous Battle of Caporetto in northern Italy, which lasted from October to November in 1917, the Italian army collapsed in despair. In the massive battles of 1916 and 1917, the British armies had been "bled dry." Only the promised arrival of fresh troops from the United States stiffened the resolve of the Allies.

The strains were even worse for the Central Powers. In October 1916 a young socialist assassinated the chief minister of Austria-Hungary. The following month, when the aging emperor Franz Joseph died, a symbol of unity disappeared. In spite of absolute censorship, political dissatisfaction and conflicts among nationalities grew. Both Czech and Balkan leaders demanded independent states for their peoples. By April 1917 the Austro-Hungarian people and army were exhausted. Another winter of war would bring revolution and disintegration.

Germans likewise suffered immensely. The British naval blockade greatly limited food imports, and the scarcity of basic necessities had horrific results: some 750,000 German civilians starved to death. For the rest, heavy rationing of everyday goods such as matches, bread, cooking oil, and meat undermined morale. A growing minority of moderate socialists in the Reichstag gave voice to popular discontent when they called for a compromise "peace without annexations or reparations."

Such a peace was unthinkable for the Fatherland Party. Yet Germany's rulers faced growing unrest. When the bread ration was further reduced in April 1917, more than 200,000 workers and women struck and demonstrated for a week in Berlin, returning to work only under the threat of prison and military discipline. That same month, radicals left the Social Democratic Party to form the Independent Social Democratic Party; in 1918 they would found the German Communist Party. Thus Germany, like its ally Austria-Hungary (and its enemy France), was beginning to crack in 1917. Yet it was Russia that collapsed first and saved the Central Powers—for a time.

The Russian Revolution

Focus Question	Why did world war lead to revolution in Russia, and what was its outcome?

Growing out of the crisis of the First World War, the Russian Revolution of 1917 was one of modern history's most momentous events. For some, the revolution was Marx's socialist vision come true; for others, it was the triumph of a despised Communist dictatorship. To all, it presented a radically new prototype of state and society.

The Fall of Imperial Russia

Like their allies and enemies, many Russians had embraced war with patriotic enthusiasm in 1914. At the Winter Palace, throngs of people knelt and sang "God Save the Tsar!" while Tsar Nicholas II (r. 1894–1917) repeated the oath Alexander I had sworn in 1812 during Napoleon's invasion of Russia (see Chapter 19), vowing never to make peace as long as the enemy stood on Russian soil. Russia's lower house of parliament, the Duma, voted to support the war. Conservatives anticipated expansion in the Balkans, while liberals and most socialists believed that alliance with Britain and France would bring democratic reforms. For a moment, Russia was united.

Enthusiasm for the war soon waned as better-equipped German armies inflicted terrible losses. By 1915 substantial numbers of Russian soldiers were being sent to the front without rifles; they were told to find their arms among the dead. Russia's battered peasant army nonetheless continued to fight, and Russia moved toward full mobilization on the home front. The government set up special committees to coordinate defense, industry, transportation, and agriculture. These efforts improved the military situation, but overall Russia mobilized less effectively than the other combatants.

One problem was weak leadership. Under the constitution resulting from the revolution of 1905 (see Chapter 23), the tsar had retained complete control over the bureaucracy and the army. A kindly but narrow-minded aristocrat, Nicholas II distrusted the publicly elected Duma and resisted popular involvement in government, relying instead on the old bureaucracy. Excluded from power, the Duma, the educated middle classes, and the masses became increasingly critical of the tsar's leadership. In September 1915 parties ranging from conservative to moderate socialist formed the Progressive bloc, which called for a completely new government responsible to the Duma instead of the tsar. In answer, Nicholas temporarily adjourned the Duma. The tsar then announced that he was traveling to the front in order to lead and rally Russia's armies, leaving the government in the hands of his wife, the strong-willed and autocratic Tsarina Alexandra.

His departure was a fatal turning point. In his absence, Tsarina Alexandra arbitrarily dismissed loyal political advisers. She turned to her court favorite, the disreputable and unpopular Rasputin, an uneducated Siberian preacher whose influence with the tsarina rested on his purported ability to heal Alexis—Alexandra's only son and heir to the throne—from his hemophilia. In a desperate attempt to right the situation, three members of the high aristocracy murdered Rasputin in December 1916. The ensuing scandal further undermined support for the tsarist government.

Imperial Russia had entered a terminal crisis. Tens of thousands of soldiers deserted, swelling the number of the disaffected at home. By early 1917 the cities were wracked by food shortages, heating fuel was in short supply, and the economy was breaking down. In March violent street demonstrations broke out in Petrograd (now named St. Petersburg), spread to the factories, and then engulfed the city. From the front, the tsar ordered the army to open fire on the protesters, but the soldiers refused to shoot and joined the revolutionary crowd instead. The Duma declared a provisional government on March 12, 1917. Three days later, Nicholas abdicated.

The Provisional Government

The **February Revolution**, then, was the result of an unplanned uprising of hungry, angry people in the capital, but it was eagerly accepted throughout the country. (The name of the revolution matches the traditional Russian calendar, which used a different dating system.) The patriotic upper and middle classes embraced the prospect of a more determined war effort, while workers anticipated better wages and more food. After generations of autocracy, the provisional government established equality before the law, granting freedoms of religion, speech, and assembly, as well as the right of unions to organize and strike.

Yet the provisional government made a crucial mistake: though the Russian people were sick of fighting, the new leaders failed to take Russia out of the war. A government formed in May 1917 included the fiery agrarian socialist Alexander Kerensky, who became prime minister in July. For the patriotic Kerensky, as for other moderate socialists, the continuation of war was still a national duty. Turning his back on needed reforms, Kerensky refused to confiscate large landholdings and give them to peasants, fearing that such drastic action would complete the disintegration of Russia's peasant army. Human suffering and war-weariness grew, testing the limited strength of the provisional government.

From its first day, the provisional government had to share power with a formidable rival—the **Petrograd Soviet** (or council) of Workers' and Soldiers' Deputies. Modeled on the revolutionary soviets of 1905, the Petrograd Soviet comprised two to three thousand workers, soldiers, and socialist intellectuals. Seeing itself as a true grassroots product of revolutionary democracy, the Soviet acted as a parallel government. It issued its own radical orders, weakening the authority of the provisional government.

The most famous edict of the Petrograd Soviet was Army Order No. 1, issued in May 1917, which stripped officers of their authority and placed power in the hands of elected committees of common soldiers. Designed to protect the revolution from resistance by the aristocratic officer corps, the order led to a collapse of army discipline.

In July 1917 the provisional government mounted a poorly considered summer offensive against the Germans. The campaign was a miserable failure, and desertions mounted as peasant soldiers returned home to help their families get a share of the land, which peasants were seizing in a grassroots agrarian revolt. By the summer of 1917 Russia was descending into anarchy. It was an unparalleled opportunity for the most radical and talented of Russia's many revolutionary leaders, Vladimir Ilyich Lenin (1870–1924).

Lenin and the Bolshevik Revolution

Born into the middle class, Lenin became an enemy of imperial Russia when his older brother was executed for plotting to kill archconservative Tsar Alexander III in 1887. As a law student, Lenin eagerly studied Marxist socialism, which began to win converts among radical intellectuals during Russia's industrialization in the 1890s. A pragmatic and flexible thinker, Lenin updated Marx's revolutionary philosophy to address existing conditions in Russia.

Three interrelated concepts were central for Lenin. First, he stressed that only violent revolution could destroy capitalism. He tirelessly denounced all "revisionist" theories of a peaceful evolution to socialism (see Chapter 23) as a betrayal of Marx's message of violent class conflict. Second, Lenin argued that under certain conditions a Communist revolution was possible even in a predominantly agrarian country like Russia. Peasants, who were numerous, poor, and exploited, could take the place of Marx's traditional working class in the coming revolutionary conflict.

Third, Lenin believed that the possibility of revolution was determined more by human leadership than by historical laws. He called for a highly disciplined workers' party strictly controlled by a small, dedicated elite of intellectuals and professional revolutionaries. This elite would not stop until revolution brought it to power. Lenin's version of Marxism had a major impact on events in Russia and ultimately changed the way future revolutionaries engaged in radical revolt around the world.

Other Russian Marxists challenged Lenin's ideas. At meetings of the Russian Social Democratic Labor Party in London in 1903, matters came to a head. Lenin demanded a small, disciplined, elitist party dedicated to Communist revolution, while his opponents wanted a more democratic, reformist party with mass membership (like the German SPD). The Russian Marxists split into two rival factions. Lenin called his camp the **Bolsheviks**, or "majority group"; his opponents were Mensheviks, or "minority group." The Bolsheviks had only a tenuous majority of a single vote, but Lenin kept the name for propaganda reasons and they became the revolutionary party he wanted: tough, disciplined, and led from above.

Unlike other socialists, Lenin had not rallied around the national flag in 1914. Observing events from neutral Switzerland, where he lived in exile to avoid persecution by the tsar's police, Lenin viewed the war as a product of imperialist rivalries and an opportunity for socialist revolution. After the February Revolution of 1917, the German government provided Lenin with safe passage across Germany and back into Russia. The Germans hoped Lenin would undermine the sagging war effort of the provisional government. They were not disappointed.

Arriving triumphantly at Petrograd's Finland Station on April 3, Lenin attacked at once. He rejected all cooperation with what he called the "bourgeois" provisional government. His slogans were radical in the extreme: "All power to the soviets"; "All land to the peasants"; "Stop the war now." Lenin was a superb tactician. His promises of "Peace, Land, and Bread" spoke to the expectations of suffering soldiers, peasants, and workers and earned the Bolsheviks substantial popular support. The moment for revolution was at hand.

Yet Lenin and the Bolsheviks almost lost the struggle for Russia. A premature attempt to seize power in July collapsed, and Lenin went into hiding. However, this temporary setback made little difference in the long run. The army's commander in

At first, Lenin's fellow Bolsheviks refused to accept such great territorial losses. But when German armies resumed their unopposed march into Russia in February 1918, Lenin had his way in a very close vote. A third of old Russia's population was sliced away by the **Treaty of Brest-Litovsk**, signed with Germany in March 1918. With peace, Lenin escaped the disaster of continued war and could pursue his goal of absolute power for the Bolsheviks—now also called Communists—within Russia.

The peace treaty and the abolition of the Constituent Assembly inspired armed opposition to the Bolshevik regime. People who had supported self-rule in November saw that once again they were getting dictatorship. The officers of the old army organized the so-called White opposition to the Bolsheviks in southern Russia, Ukraine, Siberia, and the area west of Petrograd. The Whites came from many social groups and were united only by their hatred of communism and the Bolsheviks—the Reds.

By the summer of 1918 Russia was in a full-fledged civil war. Eighteen self-proclaimed regional governments—several of which represented minority nationalities—challenged Lenin's government in Moscow. By the end of the year White armies were on the attack. In October 1919 they closed in on central Russia from three sides, and it appeared they might triumph. They did not.

Lenin and the Red Army beat back the counter-revolutionary White armies for several reasons. Most important, the Bolsheviks had quickly developed a better army. Once again, Trotsky's leadership was decisive. At first, the Bolsheviks had preached democracy in the military and had even elected officers in 1917. But beginning in March 1918, Trotsky became war commissar of the newly formed Red Army. He re-established strict discipline and the draft. Soldiers deserting or disobeying an order were summarily shot. Moreover, Trotsky made effective use of former tsarist army officers, who were actively recruited and given unprecedented powers over their troops. Trotsky's disciplined and effective fighting force repeatedly defeated the Whites in the field.

Ironically, foreign military intervention helped the Bolsheviks. For a variety of reasons, but primarily to stop the spread of communism, the Western Allies (including the United States, Britain, France, and Japan) sent troops to support the White armies. Yet their efforts were limited and halfhearted. By 1919, with the Great War over, Westerners were sick of war, and few politicians wanted to get involved in a new military crusade. Allied intervention failed to offer effective aid, though it did permit the Bolsheviks to appeal to the patriotic nationalism of ethnic Russians, in particular former tsarist army officers who objected to foreign involvement in Russian affairs.

Other conditions favored a Bolshevik victory as well. Strategically, the Reds controlled central Russia and the crucial cities of Moscow and Petrograd. The Whites attacked from the fringes and lacked coordination. Moreover, the poorly defined political program of the Whites was a mishmash of liberal republicanism and monarchism incapable of uniting the Bolsheviks' enemies. And while the Bolsheviks promised ethnic minorities in Russian-controlled territories substantial autonomy, the nationalist Whites sought to preserve the tsarist empire.

The Bolsheviks mobilized the home front for the war by establishing a system of centralized controls called **War Communism**. The leadership nationalized banks and industries and outlawed private enterprise. Bolshevik commissars introduced rationing, seized grain from peasants to feed the cities, and maintained strict workplace discipline. Although normal economic activity broke down, these measures maintained labor discipline and kept the Red Army supplied with men and material.

Revolutionary terror also contributed to the Communist victory. Lenin and the Bolsheviks set up a fearsome secret police known as the Cheka, dedicated to suppressing counter-revolutionaries. During the civil war, the Cheka imprisoned and executed without trial tens of thousands of supposed "class enemies." Victims included clergymen, aristocrats, the wealthy Russian bourgeoisie, deserters from the Red Army, and political opponents of all kinds. The tsar and his family were callously executed in July 1918. The "Red Terror" of 1918 to 1920 helped establish the secret police as a central tool of the emerging Communist government.

By the spring of 1920 the White armies were almost completely defeated, and the Bolsheviks had retaken much of the territory ceded to Germany under the Treaty of Brest-Litovsk. The Red Army reconquered Belarus and Ukraine, both of which had briefly gained independence. Building on this success, the Bolsheviks moved westward into Polish territory, but they were halted on the outskirts of Warsaw in August 1920 by troops under the leadership of the Polish field marshal and chief of state Jozef Pilsudski. This defeat halted Bolshevik attempts to spread communism farther into Europe, though in 1921 the Red Army overran the independent national governments of the Caucasus. The Russian civil war was over, and the Bolsheviks had won an impressive victory.

The Peace Settlement

| Focus Question | **In what ways was the Allied peace settlement flawed?** |

Even as civil war raged in Russia and chaos engulfed much of central and eastern Europe, the war in the west came to an end in November 1918. Early in 1919 the victorious Western Allies came together in Paris, where they worked out terms for peace with Germany and created the peacekeeping League of Nations. Expectations were high; optimism was almost unlimited. Nevertheless, the peace settlement of 1919 turned out to be a disappointment for peoples and politicians alike. Rather than lasting peace, the immediate postwar years brought economic crisis and violent political conflict.

The End of the War

In early 1918 the German leadership decided that the time was ripe for a last-ditch, all-out attack on France. The defeat of Russia had released men and materials for the western front. The looming arrival of the first U.S. troops and the growth of dissent at home quickened German leaders' resolve. In the great Spring Offensive of 1918, Ludendorff launched an extensive attack on the French lines. German armies came within thirty-five miles of Paris, but Ludendorff's exhausted, overextended forces never broke through. They were stopped in July at the second Battle of the Marne, where 140,000 American soldiers saw action. The late but massive American intervention tipped the scales in favor of Allied victory.

blamed the Social Democrats for the murders of Liebknecht and Luxemburg and the repression in Bavaria. Right-wing nationalists, including the new Nazi Party, despised the government from the start. They spread the myth that the German army had never actually lost the war — instead, the nation was "stabbed in the back" by social-ists and pacifists at home. In Germany, the end of the war brought only a fragile sense of political stability.

The Treaty of Versailles

In January 1919 over seventy delegates from twenty-seven nations met in Paris to hammer out a peace accord. The conference produced several treaties, including the **Treaty of Versailles**, which laid out the terms of the postwar settlement with Germany. The peace negotiations inspired great expectations. A young British diplomat later wrote that the victors "were journeying to Paris . . . to found a new order in Europe. We were preparing not Peace only, but Eternal Peace."[9]

This idealism was greatly strengthened by U.S. president Wilson's January 1918 peace proposal, the **Fourteen Points**. The plan called for open diplomacy, a reduction in armaments, freedom of commerce and trade, and the establishment of a **League of Nations**, an international body designed to provide a place for peaceful resolution of international problems. Perhaps most important, Wilson demanded that peace be based on the principle of **national self-determination**, meaning that peoples should be able to choose their own national governments through democratic majority-rule elections and live free from outside interference in territories with clearly defined, permanent borders. Despite the general optimism inspired by these ideas, the conference and the treaty itself quickly generated disagreement.

The "Big Three" — the United States, Great Britain, and France — controlled the conference. Germany, Austria-Hungary, and Russia were excluded, though their lands were placed on the negotiating table. Italy took part, but its role was quite limited. Representatives from the Middle East, Africa, and East Asia attended as well, but their concerns were largely ignored.

Almost immediately, the Big Three began to quarrel. Wilson, who was wildly cheered by European crowds as the champion of democratic international coopera-tion, was almost obsessed with creating the League of Nations. He insisted that this question come first, for he passionately believed that only a permanent international organization could avert future wars. Wilson had his way — the delegates agreed to create the League, though the details would be worked out later and the final struc-ture was too weak to achieve its grand purpose. Prime Ministers Lloyd George of Great Britain and Georges Clemenceau of France were unenthusiastic about the League. They were primarily concerned with punishing Germany.

The question of what to do with Germany dominated discussions among the Big Three. Clemenceau wanted Germany to pay for its aggression. The war in the west had been fought largely on French soil, and like most French people, Clemenceau wanted revenge, economic retribution, and lasting security for France. This, he believed, required the creation of a buffer state between France and Germany, the permanent demilitarization of Germany, and vast reparation payments. Lloyd George supported Clemenceau, but was less harsh. Wilson disagreed. Clemenceau's demands seemed vindictive, and they violated Wilson's sense of Christian morality and the principle of national self-determination. By April the conference was deadlocked, and Wilson packed his bags to go home.

In the end, Clemenceau, fearful of future German aggression, agreed to a compromise. Clemenceau gave up the French demand for a Rhineland buffer state in return for French military occupation of the region for fifteen years and a formal defensive alliance with the United States and Great Britain. Both Wilson and Lloyd George promised that their countries would come to France's aid in the event of a German attack. The Allies moved quickly to finish the settlement, believing that further adjustments would be possible within the dual framework of a strong Western alliance and the League of Nations.

The various agreements signed at Versailles redrew the map of Europe, and the war's losers paid the price. The new independent nations carved out of the Austro-Hungarian and Russian Empires included Poland, Czechoslovakia, Finland, the Baltic States, and Yugoslavia. The Ottoman Empire was also split apart, or "partitioned," its territories placed under the control of the victors.

The Treaty of Versailles, signed by the Allies and Germany, was key to the settlement. Germany's African and Asian colonies were given to France, Britain, and Japan as League of Nations mandates or administered territories, though Germany's losses within Europe were relatively minor, thanks to Wilson. Alsace-Lorraine was returned to France. Ethnic Polish territories seized by Prussia during the eighteenth-century partition of Poland (see Chapter 16) were returned to a new independent Polish state. Predominantly German Danzig was also placed within the Polish border but as a self-governing city under League of Nations protection. Germany had to limit its army to one hundred thousand men, agree to build no military fortifications in the Rhineland, and accept temporary French occupation of that region.

More harshly, in Article 231, the famous **war guilt clause**, the Allies declared that Germany (with Austria) was entirely responsible for the war and thus had to pay reparations equal to all civilian damages caused by the fighting. This much-criticized clause expressed French and to some extent British demands for revenge. For the Germans, reparations were a crippling financial burden. Moreover, the clause was a cutting insult to German national pride. Many Germans believed wartime propaganda that had repeatedly claimed that Germany was an innocent victim, forced into war by a circle of barbaric enemies. When presented with these terms, the new German government protested vigorously but to no avail. On June 28, 1919, representatives of the German Social Democrats signed the treaty in Louis XIV's Hall of Mirrors at Versailles, where Bismarck's empire had been joyously proclaimed almost fifty years before (see Chapter 23).

The rapidly concluded Versailles treaties were far from perfect, but within the context of war-shattered Europe they were a beginning. Germany had been punished but not dismembered. A new world organization complemented a traditional defensive alliance of satisfied powers: Britain, France, and the United States. The remaining serious problems, the Allies hoped, could be worked out in the future. Allied leaders had seen speed as essential because they feared that the Bolshevik Revolution might spread. The best answer to Lenin's unending calls for worldwide upheaval, they believed, was peace and tranquillity.

MAKE CONNECTIONS

Think about the larger developments and continuities within and across chapters.

1. While the war was being fought, peoples on all sides of the fighting often referred to the First World War as "the Great War." Why would they find this label appropriate?

2. How did the First World War draw on long-standing political rivalries and tensions among the European powers (Chapters 19, 23, and 24)?

3. To what extent was the First World War actually a "world" war?

Chapter Review

IDENTIFY KEY TERMS

Identify and explain the significance of each item below.

Triple Alliance (p. 796)

Triple Entente (p. 798)

Schlieffen Plan (p. 801)

total war (p. 803)

trench warfare (p. 803)

February Revolution (p. 814)

Petrograd Soviet (p. 814)

Bolsheviks (p. 815)

Treaty of Brest-Litovsk (p. 818)

War Communism (p. 818)

Treaty of Versailles (p. 822)

Fourteen Points (p. 822)

League of Nations (p. 822)

national self-determination (p. 822)

war guilt clause (p. 823)

mandate system (p. 824)

Balfour Declaration (p. 825)

REVIEW THE MAIN IDEAS

Answer the focus questions from each section of the chapter.

1. What caused the outbreak of the First World War? (p. 796)

2. How did the First World War differ from previous wars? (p. 802)

3. In what ways did the war transform life on the home front? (p. 808)

4. Why did world war lead to revolution in Russia, and what was its outcome? (p. 813)

5. In what ways was the Allied peace settlement flawed? (p. 819)

CHRONOLOGY	
1914–1918	World War I
June 28, 1914	Serbian nationalist assassinates Archduke Franz Ferdinand
August 1914	War begins
September 1914	Battle of the Marne; German victories on the eastern front
October 1914	Ottoman Empire joins the Central Powers
1915	Italy joins the Triple Entente; German submarine sinks the *Lusitania*; Germany halts unrestricted submarine warfare; Battle of Gallipoli
1915–1918	Armenian genocide; German armies occupy large parts of east-central Europe
1916	Battles of Verdun and the Somme
1916–1918	Antiwar movement spreads throughout Europe; Arab rebellion against Ottoman Empire
1917	Germany resumes unrestricted submarine warfare
March 1917	February Revolution in Russia
April 1917	United States enters the war
October–November 1917	Battle of Caporetto
November 1917	Bolshevik Revolution in Russia; Balfour Declaration on Jewish homeland in Palestine
1918	Treaty of Brest-Litovsk; revolution in Germany
1918–1920	Civil war in Russia
1919	Treaty of Versailles; Allies invade Turkey
1923	Treaty of Lausanne recognizes Turkish independence

of the century supporters of these philosophies had some cause for optimism. Women and workers were gradually gaining support in their struggles for political and social recognition, and the rising standard of living, the taming of the city, and the growth of state-supported social programs suggested that life was indeed improving. Such developments encouraged faith in the ability of a rational human mind to discover the laws of society and then wisely act on them.

Nevertheless, in the late nineteenth century a small group of serious thinkers mounted a determined attack on these optimistic beliefs. These critics rejected the general faith in progress and the rational human mind. The German philosopher Friedrich Nietzsche (NEE-chuh) (1844–1900) was particularly influential, though not until after his death. Never a systematic philosopher, he wrote more as a prophet in a provocative and poetic style. In the first of his *Untimely Meditations* (1873), he argued that ever since classical Athens, the West had overemphasized rationality and stifled the authentic passions and animal instincts that drive human activity and true creativity.

Nietzsche questioned the conventional values of Western society. He believed that reason, progress, and respectability were outworn social and psychological constructs that suffocated self-realization and excellence. Though he was the son of a Lutheran minister, Nietzsche famously rejected religion. In his 1887 book, *On the Genealogy of Morals*, he claimed that Christianity embodied a "slave morality" that glorified weakness, envy, and mediocrity. In one of his most famous lines, an apparent madman proclaims that "God is dead," metaphorically murdered by lackadaisical modern Christians who no longer really believed in him.

Nietzsche painted a dark world, perhaps foreshadowing his own loss of sanity in 1889. He warned that Western society was entering a period of nihilism—the philosophical idea that human life is entirely without meaning, truth, or purpose. Nietzsche asserted that all moral systems were invented lies and that liberalism, democracy, and socialism were corrupt systems designed to promote the weak at the expense of the strong. The West was in decline; false values had triumphed; the death of God left people disoriented and depressed. According to Nietzsche, the only hope for the individual was to accept the meaninglessness of human existence and then make that very meaninglessness a source of self-defined personal integrity and hence liberation. In this way, at least a few superior individuals could free themselves from the humdrum thinking of the masses and become true heroes.

Little read during his active years, Nietzsche's works attracted growing attention in the early twentieth century. Artists and writers experimented with his ideas, which were fundamental to the rise of the philosophy of existentialism in the 1920s. Subsequent generations remade Nietzsche to suit their own needs, and his influence remains enormous to this day.

The growing dissatisfaction with established ideas before 1914 was apparent in other important thinkers as well. In the 1890s French philosophy professor Henri Bergson (1859–1941), for one, argued that immediate experience and intuition were as important as rational and scientific thinking for understanding reality. According to Bergson, a religious experience or mystical poem was often more accessible to human comprehension than a scientific law or a mathematical equation.

The First World War accelerated the revolt against established certainties in philosophy, but that revolt went in two very different directions. In English-speaking countries, the main development was the acceptance of logical positivism in university circles. In the continental countries, the primary development in philosophy was existentialism.

Logical positivism was truly revolutionary. Adherents of this worldview argued that what we know about human life must be based on rational facts and direct observation. They concluded that theology and most traditional philosophy were meaningless because even the most cherished ideas about God, eternal truth, and ethics were impossible to prove using logic. This outlook is often associated with the Austrian philosopher Ludwig Wittgenstein (VIHT-guhn-shtine) (1889–1951), who later immigrated to England, where he trained numerous disciples.

In his pugnacious *Tractatus Logico-Philosophicus* (Essay on Logical Philosophy), published in 1922, Wittgenstein argued that philosophy is only the logical clarification of thoughts and that therefore it should concentrate on the study of language, which expresses thoughts. In his view, the great philosophical issues of the ages — God, freedom, morality, and so on — were quite literally senseless, a great waste of time, for neither scientific experiments nor mathematical logic could demonstrate their validity. Statements about such matters reflected only the personal preferences of a given individual. As Wittgenstein put it in the famous last sentence of this work, "Of what one cannot speak, of that one must keep silent." Logical positivism, which has remained dominant in England and the United States to this day, drastically reduced the scope of philosophical inquiry and offered little solace to ordinary people.

On the continent, others looked for answers in **existentialism**. This new philosophy loosely united highly diverse and even contradictory thinkers in a search for usable moral values in a world of anxiety and uncertainty. Modern existentialism had many nineteenth-century forerunners, including Nietzsche, the Danish religious philosopher Søren Kierkegaard (1813–1855), and the Russian novelist Fyodor Dostoyevsky (1821–1881). The philosophy gained recognition in Germany in the 1920s when philosophers Martin Heidegger (1889–1976) and Karl Jaspers (1883–1969) found a sympathetic audience among disillusioned postwar university students. These writers placed great emphasis on the loneliness and meaninglessness of human existence and the need to come to terms with the fear caused by this situation.

Most existential thinkers in the twentieth century were atheists. Often inspired by Nietzsche, they did not believe that a supreme being had established humanity's fundamental nature and given life its meaning. In the words of French existentialist Jean-Paul Sartre (ZHAWN-pawl SAHR-truh) (1905–1980), "existence precedes essence." By that, Sartre meant that there are no God-given, timeless truths outside or independent of individual existence. Only after they are born do people struggle to define their essence, entirely on their own. According to thinkers like Sartre and his lifelong intellectual partner Simone de Beauvoir (1908–1986), existence itself is absurd. Human beings are terribly alone, for there is no God to help them. They are left to confront the inevitable arrival of death and so are hounded by despair. The crisis of the existential thinker epitomized the modern intellectual crisis — the shattering of beliefs in God, reason, and progress.

At the same time, existentialists recognized that human beings must act in the world. Indeed, in the words of Sartre, "man is condemned to be free." Because life is meaningless, existentialists believe that individuals are forced to create their own meaning and define themselves through their actions. Such radical freedom is frightening, and Sartre concluded that most people try to escape it by structuring their lives around conventional social norms. According to Sartre, to escape is to live in "bad faith," to hide from the hard truths of existence. To live authentically, individuals must become "engaged" and choose their own actions in full awareness of their responsibility for their own behavior. Existentialism thus had a powerful ethical component. It placed great stress on individual responsibility and choice, on "being in the world" in the right way.

Existentialism had important precedents in the late nineteenth and early twentieth centuries, but the philosophy really came of age in France during and immediately after World War II. The terrible conditions of that war, discussed in the next chapter, reinforced the existential view of and approach to life. After World War II, French existentialists such as Sartre and Albert Camus (1913–1960) became enormously influential. They offered powerful but unsettling answers to the profound moral issues and the crises of the first half of the twentieth century.

The Revival of Christianity

Though philosophers such as Nietzsche, Wittgenstein, and Sartre all argued that religion had little to teach people in the modern age, the decades after the First World War witnessed a tenacious revival of Christian thought. Christianity—and religion in general—had been on the defensive in intellectual circles since the Enlightenment. In the years before 1914 some theologians, especially Protestant ones, had felt the need to interpret Christian doctrine and the Bible so that they did not seem to contradict science, evolution, and common sense. They saw Christ primarily as a great moral teacher and downplayed the mysterious, spiritual aspects of his divinity. Indeed, some modern theologians were embarrassed by the miraculous, unscientific aspects of Christianity and rejected them.

Especially after World War I, a number of thinkers and theologians began to revitalize the fundamental beliefs of Christianity. Sometimes called Christian existentialists because they shared the loneliness and despair of atheistic existentialists, they stressed human beings' sinful nature, their need for faith, and the mystery of God's forgiveness. The revival of Christian belief after World War I was fed by the rediscovery of the work of the nineteenth-century Danish theologian Søren Kierkegaard (KIHR-kuh-gahrd), whose ideas became extremely influential. Kierkegaard believed it was impossible for ordinary individuals to prove the existence of God, but he rejected the notion that Christianity was an empty practice. In his classic *Sickness unto Death* (1849), Kierkegaard mastered his religious doubts by suggesting that people must take a "leap of faith" and accept the existence of an objectively unknowable but nonetheless awesome and majestic God.

In the 1920s the Swiss Protestant theologian Karl Barth (1886–1968) propounded similar ideas. In brilliant and influential writings, Barth argued that human beings were imperfect, sinful creatures whose reason and will are hopelessly flawed. Religious truth is therefore made known to human beings only through God's grace, not through reason. People have to accept God's word and the supernatural revelation of Jesus Christ with awe, trust, and obedience, not reason or logic.

Among Catholics, the leading existential Christian was Gabriel Marcel (1889–1973). Born into a cultivated French family, Marcel found in the Catholic Church an answer to what he called the postwar "broken world." Catholicism and religious belief provided the hope, humanity, honesty, and piety for which he hungered. Marcel and his countryman Jacques Maritain (1882–1973) denounced anti-Semitism and supported closer ties with non-Catholics.

After 1914 religion became much more meaningful to intellectuals than it had been before the war. Between about 1920 and 1950, in addition to Marcel and Maritain, poets T. S. Eliot and W. H. Auden, novelists Evelyn Waugh and Aldous Huxley, historian Arnold Toynbee, writer C. S. Lewis, psychoanalyst Karl Stern, and physicist Max Planck all either converted to a faith or became attracted to religion for the first time. Religion, often of a despairing, existential variety, was one meaningful answer to uncertainty and anxiety and the horrific costs of the First and Second World Wars. In the words of English novelist Graham Greene, a Roman Catholic convert, "One began to believe in heaven because one believed in hell."[2]

The New Physics

Ever since the Scientific Revolution of the seventeenth century, scientific advances and their implications had greatly influenced the beliefs of thinking people. By the late nineteenth century science was one of the main pillars supporting Western society's optimistic and rationalistic worldview. Progressive minds believed that science, unlike religion or philosophical speculation, was based on hard facts and controlled experiments. Unchanging natural laws seemed to determine physical processes and permit useful solutions to more and more problems. All this was comforting, especially to people no longer committed to traditional religious beliefs. And all this was challenged by the new physics.

An important first step came at the end of the nineteenth century with the discovery that atoms were not like hard, permanent little billiard balls. They were actually composed of many far-smaller, fast-moving particles, such as electrons and protons. Polish-born physicist Marie Curie (1867–1934) and her French husband, Pierre, discovered that radium constantly emits subatomic particles and thus does not have a constant atomic weight. Building on this and other work in radiation, German physicist Max Planck (1858–1947) showed in 1900 that subatomic energy is emitted in uneven little spurts, which Planck called "quanta," and not in a steady stream, as previously believed. Planck's discovery called into question the old sharp distinction between matter and energy: the implication was that matter and energy might be different forms of the same thing. The view of atoms as the stable basic building blocks of nature, with a different kind of unbreakable atom for each of the ninety-two chemical elements, was badly shaken.

In 1905 the German-Jewish genius Albert Einstein (1879–1955) went further than the Curies and Planck in undermining Newtonian physics. His **theory of special relativity** postulated that time and space are relative to the viewpoint of the observer and that only the speed of light is constant for all frames of reference in the universe. In order to make his revolutionary and paradoxical idea somewhat comprehensible to the nonmathematical layperson, Einstein used analogies involving moving trains. For example, if a woman in the middle of a moving car got up and walked forward to the door, she had gone, relative to the train, a half car length. But relative to an observer on the embankment, she had gone farther. To Einstein, this meant that time and distance were not natural universals but depended on the position and motion of the observer.

In addition, Einstein's theory stated that matter and energy are interchangeable and that even a particle of matter contains enormous levels of potential energy. These ideas unified an apparently infinite universe with the incredibly small, fast-moving subatomic world. In comparison, the closed framework of the Newtonian physics developed during the Scientific Revolution, exemplified by Newton's supposedly immutable laws of motion and mechanics, was quite limited (see Chapter 16).

The 1920s opened the "heroic age of physics," in the apt words of Ernest Rutherford (1871–1937), one of its leading pioneers. Breakthrough followed breakthrough. In 1919 Rutherford showed that the atom could be split. By 1944 seven subatomic particles had been identified, the most important of which was the neutron. Physicists realized that the neutron's capacity to shatter the nucleus of another atom could lead to chain reactions of shattered atoms that would release unbelievable force. This discovery was fundamental to the subsequent development of the nuclear bomb.

Although few nonscientists truly understood the revolution in physics, its implications, as presented by newspapers and popular science fiction writers, were disturbing to millions of men and women in the 1920s and 1930s. As unsettling as Einstein's ideas was a notion popularized by German physicist Werner Heisenberg (VER-nuhr HIGH-zuhn-buhrg) (1901–1976). In 1927 Heisenberg formulated the "uncertainty principle," which postulates that nature itself is ultimately unknowable and unpredictable. He suggested that the universe lacked any absolute objective reality. Everything was "relative," that is, dependent on the observer's frame of reference. Such ideas caught on among ordinary people, who found the unstable, relativistic world described by the new physicists strange and troubling. Instead of Newton's dependable, rational laws, there seemed to be only tendencies and probabilities in an extraordinarily complex and uncertain universe. Like modern philosophy, physics no longer provided comforting truths about natural laws or optimistic answers about humanity's place in an understandable world.

Freudian Psychology

With physics presenting an uncertain universe so unrelated to ordinary human experience, questions regarding the power and potential of the rational human mind assumed special significance. The findings and speculations of Sigmund Freud were particularly influential, yet also deeply disturbing.

Before Freud, poets and mystics had probed the unconscious and irrational aspects of human behavior. But most scientists assumed that the conscious mind processed sense experiences in a rational and logical way. Human behavior in turn was the result of rational calculation — of "thinking." Beginning in the late 1880s Freud developed a very different view of the human psyche. Basing his insights on the analysis of dreams and of "hysteria," a sort of nervous breakdown, Freud concluded that human behavior was basically irrational, governed by the unconscious, a mental reservoir that contained vital instinctual drives and powerful memories. Though the unconscious profoundly influenced people's behavior, it was unknowable to the conscious mind, leaving people unaware of the source or meaning of their actions.

Freud explained these ideas in his magisterial book *The Interpretation of Dreams*, first published in 1900.

Freud eventually described three structures of the self—the **id**, the **ego**, and the **superego**—that were basically at war with one another. The primitive, irrational id was entirely unconscious. The source of sexual, aggressive, and pleasure-seeking instincts, the id sought immediate fulfillment of all desires and was totally amoral. Keeping the id in check was the superego, the conscience or internalized voice of parental or social control. For Freud, the superego was also irrational. Overly strict and puritanical, it was constantly in conflict with the pleasure-seeking id. The third component was the ego, the rational self that was mostly conscious and worked to negotiate between the demands of the id and the superego.

For Freud, the healthy individual possessed a strong ego that effectively balanced the id and superego. Neurosis, or mental illness, resulted when the three structures were out of balance. Since the id's instinctual drives were extremely powerful, the danger for individuals and indeed whole societies was that unacknowledged drives might overwhelm the control mechanisms of the ego in a violent, distorted way. Freud's "talking cure"—in which neurotic patients lay back on a couch and shared their innermost thoughts with the psychoanalyst—was an attempt to resolve such unconscious tensions and restore the rational ego to its predominant role.

Yet Freud, like Nietzsche, believed that the mechanisms of rational thinking and traditional moral values could be too strong. In his book *Civilization and Its Discontents* (1930), Freud argued that civilization was possible only when individuals renounced their irrational instincts in order to live peaceably in groups. Such renunciation made communal life possible, but it left basic instincts unfulfilled and so led to widespread unhappiness. Freud gloomily concluded that Western civilization was itself inescapably neurotic.

Freudian psychology and clinical psychiatry had become an international medical movement by 1910, but only after 1919 did they receive more public attention, especially in northern Europe. In the United States, Freud's ideas attained immense popularity after the Second World War. Many opponents and even some enthusiasts interpreted Freud as saying that the first requirement for mental health was an uninhibited sex life—popular understandings of Freud thus reflected and encouraged growing sexual experimentation, particularly among middle-class women. For more serious students, the psychology of Freud and his followers contributed to the weakening of the old easy optimism about the rational and progressive nature of the human mind.

Modernism in Architecture, Art, Literature, and Music

Focus Question	How did modernism revolutionize Western culture?

Like the scientists and intellectuals who were part of this increasingly unsettled modern culture, creative artists rejected old forms and old values. **Modernism** in architecture, art, literature, and music meant constant experimentation and a search for new kinds confidence in the economy. The franc was stabilized at about one-fifth of its prewar value, and the economy remained fairly stable until 1930.

Britain, too, faced challenges after 1920. The great problem was unemployment. In June 1921 almost 2.2 million people — or 23 percent of the labor force — were out of work, and throughout the 1920s unemployment hovered around 12 percent, leading to a massive general strike in 1926. Yet the state provided unemployment benefits and supplemented the payments with subsidized housing, medical aid, and increased old-age pensions. These and other measures kept living standards from seriously declining, helped moderate class tensions, and pointed the way toward the welfare state Britain would establish after World War II.

Relative social harmony was accompanied by the rise of the Labour Party as a determined champion of the working class and of greater social equality. Committed to the kind of moderate revisionist socialism that had emerged before World War I (see Chapter 23), the Labour Party replaced the Liberal Party as the main opposition to the Conservatives. This shift reflected the decline of old liberal ideals of competitive capitalism, limited government control, and individual responsibility. In 1924 and from 1929 to 1931, the Labour Party under Ramsay MacDonald (1866–1937) governed the country with the support of the smaller Liberal Party. Yet Labour moved toward socialism gradually and democratically, so as not to antagonize the middle classes.

The British Conservatives showed the same compromising spirit on social issues. In 1922 Britain granted southern, Catholic, Ireland full autonomy after a bitter guerrilla war, thereby removing a key source of prewar friction. Despite conflicts such as the 1926 strike by hard-pressed coal miners, which led to an unsuccessful general strike, social unrest in Britain was limited in the 1920s and 1930s. Developments in both international relations and the domestic politics of the leading democracies across western Europe gave cause for optimism in the late 1920s.

The Great Depression, 1929–1939

Focus Question	What were the causes and consequences of the Great Depression?

This fragile optimism was short-lived. Beginning in 1929, a massive economic downturn struck the entire world with ever-greater intensity. Recovery was slow and uneven, and contemporaries labeled the economic crisis the **Great Depression**, to emphasize its severity and duration. Only with the Second World War did the depression disappear in much of the world.

The social and political consequences of the Great Depression were enormous. Mass unemployment and failing farms made insecurity and unemployment a reality for millions of people (Map 26.1). In Europe and the United States, governments instituted a variety of social welfare programs intended to manage the crisis. Yet the prolonged economic collapse shattered the fragile political stability of the mid-1920s and encouraged the growth of extremists on both ends of the political spectrum. Democratic government faltered, and authoritarian and Fascist parties gained power across Europe.

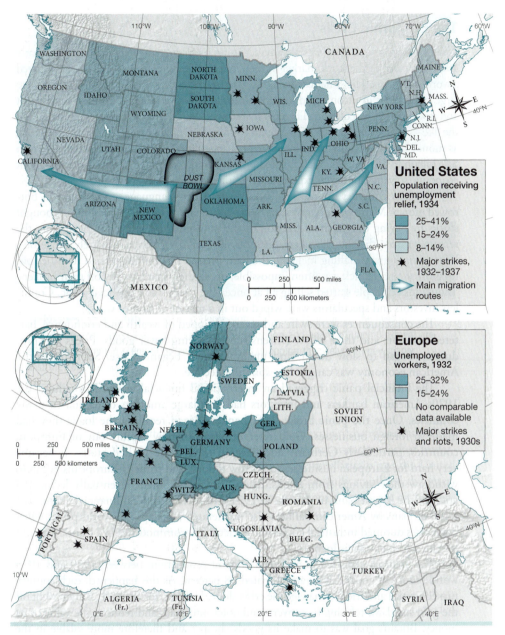

MAP 26.1 The Great Depression in the United States and Europe, 1929–1939
These maps show that unemployment was high almost everywhere, but that national and regional differences were also substantial.

nineteenth century and were exacerbated by the searing events of the war. The situation was worsened by ongoing political and economic turmoil. The Treaty of Versailles had failed to create a lasting peace or resolve the question of Germany's role in Europe. The Great Depression revealed the fragility of the world economic system and cast millions out of work. In the end, perhaps, the era's intellectual achievements and the overall sense of crisis were closely related.

Sigmund Freud captured the general mood of gloom and foreboding in 1930. "Men have gained control over the forces of nature to such an extent that . . . they would have no difficulty in exterminating one another to the last man," he wrote. "They know this, and hence comes a large part of their current unrest, their unhappiness and their mood of anxiety."[9] Freud's dark words reflected the extraordinary human costs of World War I and the horrific power of modern weaponry. They also expressed his despair over the growing popularity of repressive dictatorial regimes. During the interwar years, many European nations — including Italy, Germany, Spain, Poland, Portugal, Austria, and Hungary — would fall one by one to authoritarian or Fascist dictatorships, succumbing to the temptations of totalitarianism. Liberal democracy was severely weakened. European stability was threatened by the radical programs of Soviet Communists on the left and Fascists on the right, and Freud uncannily predicted the great conflict to come.

MAKE CONNECTIONS

Think about the larger developments and continuities within and across chapters.

1. How did trends in politics, economics, culture, and the arts and sciences come together to create a general sense of crisis in the 1920s and 1930s?
2. To what extent did the problems of the 1920s and 1930s have roots in the First World War (Chapter 25)?
3. What made modern art and intellectual thought "modern"?

Chapter Review

IDENTIFY KEY TERMS

Identify and explain the significance of each item below.

logical positivism (p. 835)

existentialism (p. 835)

theory of special relativity (p. 837)

id, ego, and superego (p. 839)

modernism (p. 839)

functionalism (p. 840)

Bauhaus (p. 840)

Dadaism (p. 842)

stream-of-consciousness technique (p. 843)

"modern girl" (p. 846)

Dawes Plan (p. 852)

Great Depression (p. 854)

Popular Front (p. 860)

REVIEW THE MAIN IDEAS

Answer the focus questions from each section of the chapter.

1. How did intellectual developments reflect the general crisis in Western thought? (p. 833)

2. How did modernism revolutionize Western culture? (p. 839)

3. How did consumer society change everyday life? (p. 845)

4. What obstacles to lasting peace did European leaders face? (p. 849)

5. What were the causes and consequences of the Great Depression? (p. 854)

CHRONOLOGY	
1887	Nietzsche publishes *On the Genealogy of Morals*
1900	Freud publishes *The Interpretation of Dreams*
1913	Stravinsky's *The Rite of Spring* premieres in Paris
1919	Treaty of Versailles; Freudian psychology gains popularity; Keynes publishes *The Economic Consequences of the Peace*; Rutherford splits the atom; Bauhaus school founded
1920s	Existentialism, Dadaism, and Surrealism gain prominence
1922	Eliot publishes *The Waste Land*; Joyce publishes *Ulysses*; Woolf publishes *Jacob's Room*; Wittgenstein writes on logical positivism
1922	First radio broadcast by British Broadcasting Company (BBC)
1923	French and Belgian armies occupy the Ruhr; Corbusier publishes *Towards a New Architecture*
1924	Dawes Plan
1925	Berg's opera *Wozzeck* first performed; Kafka publishes *The Trial*
1926	Germany joins the League of Nations
1927	Heisenberg formulates the "uncertainty principle"
1928	Kellogg-Briand Pact
1929	Faulkner publishes *The Sound and the Fury*
1929–1939	Great Depression
1932	Franklin Roosevelt announces "New Deal for the forgotten man"
1933	The National Socialist Party takes power in Germany
1935	Release of Riefenstahl's documentary film *Triumph of the Will*
1936	Formation of Popular Front in France

A charismatic leader typically dominated the totalitarian state—Stalin in the Soviet Union, Mussolini in Italy, Hitler in Germany. All three created political parties of a new kind, dedicated to promoting idealized visions of collective harmony. They used force and terror to intimidate and destroy political opponents and pursued policies of imperial expansion to exploit other lands. They censored the mass media and instituted propaganda campaigns to advance their goals. Finally, and perhaps most important, totalitarian governments engaged in massive projects of state-controlled social engineering dedicated to replacing individualism with a unified "people" capable of exercising the collective will.

Communism and Fascism

Communism and fascism clearly shared a desire to revolutionize state and society. Yet some scholars—arguing that the differences between the two systems are more important than the similarities—have moved beyond the totalitarian model. What were the main differences between these two systems? To answer this question, it is important to consider the way ideology, or a guiding political philosophy, was linked to the use of state-sponsored repression and violence.

Following Marx, Soviet Communists strove to create an international brotherhood of workers. In the Communist utopia ruled by the revolutionary working class, economic exploitation would supposedly disappear and society would be based on radical social equality (see Chapter 21). Under Stalinism—the name given to the Communist system during Stalin's rule—the state aggressively intervened in all walks of life to pursue this social leveling. Using brute force to destroy the upper and middle classes, the Stalinist state nationalized private property, pushed rapid industrialization, and collectivized agriculture (see pages 868–876).

The Fascist vision of a new society was quite different. Leaders who embraced **fascism**, such as Mussolini and Hitler, claimed that they were striving to build a new community on a national—not an international—level. Extreme nationalists, and often racists, Fascists glorified war and the military. For them, the nation was the highest embodiment of the people, and the powerful leader was the materialization of the people's collective will.

Like Communists, Fascists promised to improve the lives of ordinary workers. Fascist governments intervened in the economy, but unlike Communist regimes they did not try to level class differences and nationalize private property. Instead, they presented a vision of a community bound together by nationalism. In the ideal Fascist state, all social strata and classes would work together to build a harmonious national community.

Communists and Fascists differed in another crucial respect: the question of race. Where Communists sought to build a new world around the destruction of class differences, Fascists typically sought to build a new national community grounded in racial homogeneity. Fascists embraced the doctrine of **eugenics**, a pseudoscience that maintained that the selective breeding of human beings could improve the general characteristics of a national population. Eugenics was popular throughout the Western world in the 1920s and 1930s and was viewed by many as a legitimate social policy. But Fascists, especially the German National Socialists, or Nazis, pushed these ideas to the extreme.

Adopting a radicalized view of eugenics, the Nazis maintained that the German nation had to be "purified" of groups of people deemed "unfit" by the regime. Following state policies intended to support what they called "racial hygiene," Nazi authorities attempted to control, segregate, or eliminate those of "lesser value," including Jews, Sinti and Roma (often called Gypsies, a term that can have pejorative connotations) and other ethnic minorities, homosexuals, and people suffering from chronic mental or physical disabilities. The pursuit of "racial hygiene" ultimately led to the Holocaust, the attempt to purge Germany and Europe of all Jews and other undesirable groups by mass killing during World War II (see page 891). Though the Soviets readily persecuted specific ethnic groups they believed were disloyal to the Communist state, in general they justified these attacks using ideologies of class rather than race or biology.

Perhaps because both championed the overthrow of existing society, Communists and Fascists were sworn enemies. The result was a clash of ideologies, which was in large part responsible for the horrific destruction and loss of life in the middle of the twentieth century. Explaining the nature of totalitarian dictatorships thus remains a crucial project for historians, even as they look more closely at the ideological differences between communism and fascism.

One important set of questions explores the way dictatorial regimes generated popular consensus. Neither Hitler nor Stalin ever achieved the total control each sought. Nor did they rule alone; modern dictators need the help of large state bureaucracies and the cooperation of large numbers of ordinary people. Which was more important for generating popular support: terror and coercion or material rewards? Under what circumstances did people resist or perpetrate totalitarian tyranny? These questions lead us toward what Holocaust survivor Primo Levi called the "gray zone" of moral compromise, which defined everyday life in totalitarian societies.

Eugenics in Nazi Germany Nazi "race scientists" believed they could use the eugenic methods of social engineering to build a powerful Aryan race. In this photograph, published in a popular magazine in 1933, a clinician measures a man's nose. Such pseudoscientific methods were used to determine an individual's supposed "racial value." (© Hulton-Deutsch Collection/Corbis)

Stalin's Soviet Union

Focus Question	How did Stalin and the Communist Party build a totalitarian state in the Soviet Union?

Lenin's harshest critics claim that he established the basic outlines of a modern totalitarian dictatorship after the Bolshevik Revolution and during the Russian civil war. If so, Joseph Stalin (1879–1953) certainly finished the job. A master of political infighting, Stalin cautiously consolidated his power and eliminated his enemies in the mid-1920s. Then in 1928, as undisputed leader of the ruling Communist Party, Stalin launched the first **five-year plan** — the "revolution from above," as he aptly termed it — the beginning of a radical attempt to transform Soviet society into a Communist state. The ultimate goal of this immensely ambitious effort was to generate new attitudes, new loyalties, and a new socialist humanity. The means were constant propaganda, enormous sacrifice by the people, harsh repression that included purges and executions, and rewards for those who followed the party line. Thus the Soviet Union in the 1930s became a dynamic totalitarian state.

From Lenin to Stalin

By spring 1921 Lenin and the Bolsheviks had won the civil war, but they ruled a shattered and devastated land. Many farms were in ruins, and food supplies were exhausted. In southern Russia, drought combined with the ravages of war to produce the worst famine in generations. Industrial production had broken down completely. In the face of economic disintegration, riots by peasants and workers, and an open rebellion by previously pro-Bolshevik sailors at Kronstadt, Lenin was tough but, as ever, flexible. He repressed the Kronstadt rebels, and in March 1921 he replaced War Communism with the **New Economic Policy (NEP)**, which re-established limited economic freedom in an attempt to rebuild agriculture and industry. During the civil war, the Bolsheviks had simply seized grain without payment. Now peasant producers were permitted to sell their surpluses in free markets, and private traders and small handicraft manufacturers were allowed to reappear. Heavy industry, railroads, and banks, however, remained wholly nationalized.

The NEP was a political and economic success. Politically, it was a necessary but temporary compromise with the Soviet Union's overwhelming peasant majority. Realizing that his government was not strong enough to take land from the peasants and turn them into state workers, Lenin made a deal with the only force capable of overturning his government. The NEP brought rapid economic recovery, and by 1926 industrial output surpassed, and agricultural production almost equaled, prewar levels.

In 1924, as the economy recovered and the government partially relaxed its censorship and repression, Lenin died without a chosen successor, creating an intense struggle for power in the inner circles of the Communist Party. The principal contenders were Stalin and Trotsky. Joseph Dzhugashvili (joo-guhsh-VEEL-yih) — later known as Stalin (from the Russian for "steel") — was a good organizer but a poor speaker and writer, and he had no experience outside of Russia. Trotsky, a great and inspiring leader who had planned the 1917 Bolshevik takeover and then created the victorious Red Army, appeared to have all the advantages in the power struggle. Yet Stalin won because he was more effective at gaining the all-important support of the party. Having risen to general secretary of the party's Central Committee in 1922, he used his office to win friends and allies with jobs and promises.

Stalin also won because he was better able to relate Marxist teaching to Soviet realities in the 1920s. Stalin developed a theory of "socialism in one country" that was more appealing to the majority of party members than Trotsky's doctrine of "permanent revolution." Stalin argued that the Russian-dominated Soviet Union had the ability to build socialism on its own. Trotsky maintained that socialism in the Soviet Union could succeed only if a socialist revolution swept throughout Europe. To many Russian Communists, this view sold their country short and promised risky conflicts with capitalist countries. Stalin's willingness to revoke NEP reforms furthermore appealed to young party militants, who detested the NEP's reliance on capitalist free markets.

Stalin's ascendancy had a momentous impact on the policy of the new Soviet state toward non-Russians. The Communists had inherited the vast multiethnic territories of the former Russian Empire. Lenin initially argued that these ethnic groups should have the right to self-determination even if they claimed independence from the Soviet state. In 1922, reflecting such ideas, the Union of Soviet Socialist Republics (or U.S.S.R.) was organized as a federation of four Soviet republics: the Russian Soviet Federative Socialist Republic, Ukraine, Belorussia, and a Transcaucasian republic. The last was later split into Armenia, Azerbaijan, and Georgia, and five Central Asian republics were established in the 1920s and 1930s (Map 27.1).

Ethnic Minorities in the U.S.S.R.   The Soviet Union inherited the vast and diverse territories of the former Russian Empire. In this propaganda poster, titled "The Great Stalin Is the Banner of Friendship Between the Peoples of the U.S.S.R.!" the Soviet dictator receives flowers from a diverse group of Soviet citizens, including ethnic Russians and East and Central Asians. This idealized testament to peaceful coexistence within the Soviet empire masked the tensions aroused by Russian domination. How does this poster represent the relationship between Stalin and the Soviet people?

In contrast to Lenin, Stalin argued for more centralized Russian control of these ethnic regions. His view would dominate state policy until the breakup of the Soviet Union in the early 1990s. The Soviet republics were granted some cultural independence but no true political autonomy. Party leaders allowed the use of non-Russian languages in regional schools and government institutions, but the right to secede was a fiction, and real authority remained in Moscow, in the hands of the Russian Communist Party. The Stalinists thus established a far-flung Communist empire on the imperial holdings of the former tsars.

With cunning skill, Stalin achieved supreme power between 1922 and 1927. First he allied with Trotsky's personal enemies to crush his rival, and then he moved against all who might challenge his ascendancy, including former allies. Stalin's final triumph came at the party congress of December 1927, which condemned all "deviation from the general party line" that he had formulated. The dictator and his followers were ready to launch the revolution from above, radically changing the lives of millions of people.

The Five-Year Plans

The party congress of 1927, which ratified Stalin's consolidation of power, marked the end of the NEP. The following year marked the beginning of the era of socialist five-year plans. The first of these plans had staggering economic objectives. In just five years, total industrial output was to increase by 250 percent, with heavy industry, the preferred sector, growing even faster. Agricultural production was slated to increase by 150 percent, and one-fifth of the peasants in the Soviet Union were to give up their private plots and join collective farms.

Stalin unleashed his "second revolution" for a variety of interrelated reasons. There were, first of all, ideological considerations. Stalin and his militant supporters were deeply committed to socialism as they understood it. They feared a gradual restoration of capitalism and wished to promote the working classes. Moreover, Communist leaders were eager to abolish the NEP's private traders, independent artisans, and property-owning peasants. Economic motivations were also important. A fragile economic recovery stalled in 1927 and 1928, and a new offensive seemed necessary to ensure industrial and agricultural growth. Such economic development would allow the U.S.S.R. to catch up with the West and so overcome traditional Russian "backwardness."

The independent peasantry remained a major problem as well. For centuries the peasants had wanted to own the land, and finally they had it. Sooner or later, Stalinists reasoned, landowning peasants would embrace conservative capitalism and pose a threat

< MAP 27.1 The Formation of the U.S.S.R.
When the Bolsheviks successfully overthrew the tsarist government and won the civil war that followed, they inherited the vast territories of the former Russian Empire. Following policies instituted by Stalin, they established a Union of Soviet Socialist Republics (U.S.S.R.) that gave limited cultural autonomy but no real political independence to the Soviet republics now under Communist control.

to the regime. At the same time, the Communists—mainly urban dwellers—believed that the feared and despised "class enemy" in the villages could be squeezed to provide the enormous sums needed for all-out industrialization.

To resolve these issues, in 1929 Stalin ordered the **collectivization of agriculture**—the forced consolidation of individual peasant farms into large, state-controlled enterprises that served as agricultural factories. Peasants across the Soviet Union were compelled to move off their small plots onto large state-run farms, where their tools, livestock, and produce would be held in common and central planners could control all work.

The increasingly repressive measures instituted by the state first focused on the **kulaks**, the class of well-off peasants who had benefited the most from the NEP. The kulaks were small in number, but propagandists cast them as the great enemy of progress. Stalin called for their "liquidation" and seizure of their property. Stripped of land and livestock, many starved or were deported to forced-labor camps for "re-education."

Forced collectivization led to disaster. Large numbers of peasants opposed to the change slaughtered their animals and burned their crops rather than turn them over to state commissars. Between 1929 and 1933 the number of horses, cattle, sheep, and goats in the Soviet Union fell by at least half. Nor were the state-controlled collective farms more productive. The output of grain barely increased over the first five-year plan, and collectivized agriculture was unable to make any substantial financial contribution to Soviet industrial development in the first five-year plan.

Collectivization in the fertile farmlands of the Ukraine was more rapid and violent than in other Soviet territories. The drive against peasants snowballed into an assault on Ukrainians in general, who had sought independence from Soviet rule after the First World War. Stalin and his associates viewed this peasant resistance as an expression of unacceptable anti-Soviet nationalism. In 1932, as collectivization and deportations continued, party leaders set levels of grain deliveries for the Ukrainian collectives at excessively high levels and refused to relax those quotas or allow food relief when Ukrainian Communist leaders reported that starvation was occurring. The result was a terrible man-made famine in Ukraine in 1932 and 1933, which claimed 3 to 3.5 million lives.

Collectivization was a cruel but real victory for Stalinist ideologues. Though millions died, by the end of 1938 government representatives had moved 93 percent of peasant households onto collective farms, neutralizing them as a political threat. Nonetheless, peasant resistance had forced the supposedly all-powerful state to make modest concessions. Peasants secured the right to limit a family's labor on the state-run farms and to cultivate tiny family plots, which provided them with much of their food. In 1938 these family plots produced 22 percent of all Soviet agricultural produce on only 4 percent of all cultivated land.

The rapid industrialization mandated by the five-year plans was more successful—indeed, quite spectacular. A huge State Planning Commission, the "Gosplan," was created to set production goals and control deliveries of raw and finished materials. This was a complex and difficult task, and production bottlenecks and slowdowns often resulted. In addition, Stalinist planning favored heavy industry over the production of consumer goods, which led to shortages of basic necessities.

Despite such problems, Soviet industry produced about four times as much in 1937 as it had in 1928. No other major country had ever achieved such rapid industrial growth.

Steel was the idol of the Stalinist age. The Soviet state needed heavy machinery for rapid development, and an industrial labor force was created almost overnight as peasant men and women began working in the huge steel mills built across the country. Independent trade unions lost most of their power. The government could assign workers to any job anywhere in the U.S.S.R., and an internal passport system ensured that individuals could move only with permission. When factory managers needed more hands, they called on their counterparts on the collective farms, who sent them millions of "unneeded" peasants over the years. Rapid industrial growth led to urban development: more than 25 million people, mostly peasants, migrated to cities during the 1930s.

The new workers often lived in deplorable conditions in hastily built industrial cities such as Magnitogorsk (Magnetic Mountain City) in the Ural Mountains. Yet they also experienced some benefits of upward mobility. In a letter published in the Magnitogorsk newspaper, an ordinary electrician described the opportunities created by rapid industrialization:

> In old tsarist Russia, we weren't even considered people. We couldn't dream about education, or getting a job in a state enterprise. And now I'm a citizen of the U.S.S.R. Like all citizens I have the right to a job, to education, to leisure. . . . In 1931, I came to Magnitogorsk. From a common laborer I have turned into a skilled worker. . . . I live in a country where one feels like living and learning. And if the enemy should attack this country, I will sacrifice my life in order to destroy the enemy and save my country.[1]

We should read such words with care, since they appeared in a state-censored publication. Yet the enthusiasm was at least partly authentic. The great industrialization drive of 1928 to 1937 was an awe-inspiring achievement, purchased at enormous sacrifice on the part of ordinary Soviet citizens.

Life and Culture in Soviet Society

Daily life was difficult in Stalin's Soviet Union. The lack of housing was a particularly serious problem. Millions were moving into the cities, but the government built few new apartments. A relatively lucky family received one room for all its members and shared both a kitchen and a toilet with others living on the same floor.

There were constant shortages of goods as well. Because consumption was reduced to pay for investment, there was little improvement in the average standard of living in the years before World War II. The average nonfarm wage purchased only about half as many goods in 1932 as it had in 1928. After 1932 real wages rose slowly, but by 1937 workers could still buy only about 60 percent of what they had bought in 1928 and less than they could purchase in 1913. Collectivized peasants experienced greater hardships.

Life was by no means hopeless, however. Idealism and ideology had real appeal for many Communists and ordinary citizens, who saw themselves heroically building the world's first socialist society while capitalism crumbled in a worldwide depression and degenerated into fascism in the West. This optimistic belief in the future of the Soviet Union attracted many disillusioned Westerners to communism in the 1930s. On a more practical level, Soviet workers received important social benefits, such as old-age pensions, free medical services, free education, and day-care centers for children. Unemployment was almost unknown.

Communism also opened possibilities for personal advancement. Rapid industrialization required massive numbers of skilled workers, engineers, and plant managers. In the 1930s the Stalinist state broke with the egalitarian policies of the 1920s and offered tremendous incentives to those who could serve its needs. It paid the mass of unskilled workers and collective farmers very low wages, but provided high salaries and special privileges to its growing technical and managerial elite. This group joined with the political and artistic elites in a new upper class, whose members grew rich and powerful.

The radical transformation of Soviet society had a profound impact on women's lives. Marxists had traditionally believed that both capitalism and middle-class husbands exploited women, and the Russian Revolution of 1917 immediately proclaimed complete equality for women. In the 1920s divorce and abortion were made easily available, and women were urged to work outside the home. After Stalin came to power, he reversed this trend. The government revoked many laws supporting women's emancipation in order to strengthen the traditional family and build up the state's population.

At the same time, women saw lasting changes in education. The Soviets opened higher education to women, who could now enter the ranks of the better-paid specialists in industry and science. Medicine practically became a woman's profession. By 1950, 75 percent of all doctors in the Soviet Union were female.

Alongside such advances, however, Soviet society demanded great sacrifices from women. The vast majority of women had to work outside the home. Wages were so low that it was almost impossible for a family or couple to live only on the husband's earnings. Peasant women continued to work on farms, and millions of women toiled in factories and in heavy construction, building dams, roads, and steel mills in summer heat and winter frost. Men continued to dominate the very best jobs. Finally, rapid change and economic hardship led to many broken families, creating further physical and emotional strains for women. In any event, the massive mobilization of women was a striking characteristic of the Soviet state.

Culture was thoroughly politicized for propaganda and indoctrination purposes. Party activists lectured workers in factories and peasants on collective farms, while newspapers, films, and radio broadcasts endlessly revealed capitalist plots and recounted socialist achievements. Whereas the 1920s had seen considerable modernist experimentation in art and theater, in the 1930s intellectuals were ordered by Stalin to become "engineers of human minds." Following the dictates of "Socialist Realism," they were instructed to exalt the lives of ordinary workers and glorify Russian nationalism. Russian history was rewritten so that early tsars such as Ivan the Terrible and Peter the Great became worthy forerunners of the greatest Russian leader of all—Stalin. Writers and artists who could effectively combine genuine creativity and political propaganda became the darlings of the regime.

Stalin seldom appeared in public, but his presence was everywhere—in portraits, statues, books, and quotations from his writings. Although the government persecuted those who practiced religion and turned churches into "museums of atheism," the state had both an earthly religion and a high priest—Marxism-Leninism and Joseph Stalin.

Stalinist Terror and the Great Purges

In the mid-1930s the great offensive to build socialism and a new society culminated in ruthless police terror and a massive purging of the Communist Party. First used by the Bolsheviks in the civil war to maintain their power, terror as state policy was revived in the collectivization drive against the peasants. Top members of the party and government publicly supported Stalin's initiatives, but there was some grumbling. At a small gathering in November 1932, even Stalin's wife complained bitterly about the misery of the people and the horrible famine in Ukraine. Stalin showered her with insults, and she committed suicide that night. In late 1934 Stalin's number-two man, Sergei Kirov, was mysteriously killed. Stalin—who probably ordered Kirov's murder— blamed the assassination on "Fascist agents" within the party. He used the incident to launch a reign of terror that purged the Communist Party of supposed traitors and solidified his own control.

Murderous repression picked up steam over the next two years. It culminated in the "great purge" of 1936 to 1938, a series of spectacular public show trials in which false evidence, often gathered using torture, was used to incriminate party administrators and Red Army leaders. In August 1936 sixteen "Old Bolsheviks"—prominent leaders who had been in the party since the Russian Revolution—confessed to all manner of contrived plots against Stalin. All were executed. In 1937 the secret police arrested a mass of lesser party officials and newer members, using torture to extract confessions and precipitating more show trials. In addition to the party faithful, union officials, managers, intellectuals, army officers, and countless ordinary citizens were accused of counterrevolutionary activities. At least 6 million people were arrested, and probably 1 to 2 million of these were executed or never returned from prisons and forced-labor camps.

Stalin's mass purges remain baffling, for most historians believe that the victims posed no threat and were innocent of their supposed crimes. Some scholars have argued that the terror was a defining characteristic of the totalitarian state, which must always fight real or imaginary enemies. Certainly the highly publicized purges sent a warning: no one was secure; everyone had to serve the party and its leader with redoubled devotion.

The long-standing interpretation that puts most of the blame for the purges on Stalin has been confirmed by recent research in newly opened Soviet archives. Apparently fearful of active resistance, Stalin and his allies used the harshest measures against their political enemies, real or imagined. Moreover, many in the general population shared such fears. Bombarded with ideology and political slogans, numerous people responded energetically to Stalin's directives. Investigations and trials snowballed into mass hysteria, resulting in a modern witch-hunt that claimed millions of victims. In this view of the 1930s, a deluded Stalin found large numbers of willing collaborators for crime as well as for achievement.[2]

The purges seriously weakened the Soviet Union in economic, intellectual, and military terms. But they left Stalin in command of a vast new state apparatus, staffed by the 1.5 million new party members enlisted to replace the purge victims. Thus more than half of all Communist Party members in 1941 had joined since the purges, and they experienced rapid social advance. Often the children of workers, they had usually studied in the new technical schools, and they soon proved capable of managing the government and large-scale production. Despite their human costs, the great purges thus brought substantial practical rewards to this new generation of committed Communists. They would serve Stalin effectively until his death in 1953, and they would govern the Soviet Union until the early 1980s.

Mussolini and Fascism in Italy

| Focus Question | What kind of government did Mussolini establish in Italy? |

Mussolini's Fascist movement and his seizure of power in 1922 were important steps in the rise of dictatorships in Europe between the two world wars. Mussolini and his supporters were the first to call themselves "Fascists" — revolutionaries determined to create a new totalitarian state based on extreme nationalism and militarism.

The Seizure of Power

In the early twentieth century, Italy was a liberal constitutional monarchy that recognized the civil rights of Italians. On the eve of World War I, the parliament granted universal male suffrage, and Italy appeared to be moving toward democracy. But there were serious problems. Much of the Italian population was still poor, and many peasants were more attached to their villages and local interests than to the national state. Moreover, the papacy, many devout Catholics, conservatives, and landowners remained strongly opposed to liberal institutions, and relations between church and state were often tense. Class differences were also extreme, leading to the development of a powerful revolutionary socialist movement.

World War I worsened the political situation. To win support for the war effort, the Italian government had promised territorial expansion as well as social and land reform, which it could not deliver. Instead, the Versailles treaty denied Italy any territorial gains, and soaring unemployment and inflation after the war created mass hardship. In response, the Italian Socialist Party followed the Bolshevik example, and radical workers and peasants began occupying factories and seizing land in 1920. These actions mobilized the property-owning classes. Moreover, after the war the pope lifted his ban on participation by Catholics in Italian politics, and a strong Catholic party quickly emerged. Thus by 1921 revolutionary socialists, conservatives, Catholics, and property owners were all opposed — though for different reasons — to the liberal government.

Into these crosscurrents of unrest and fear stepped bullying, blustering Benito Mussolini (1883–1945). Mussolini began his political career before World War I as a

Mussolini and Hitler Italian dictator Benito Mussolini and Nazi leader Adolf Hitler, in front of the Shrine of Fallen Nazis, review a military parade passing by in their honor. In September 1937 Mussolini visited Hitler in Germany to cement the Rome-Berlin Axis alliance. (Istituto Nazionale Luce/Alinari via Getty Images)

Socialist Party leader and radical newspaper editor. In 1914 he had urged that Italy join the Allies, a stand for which he was expelled from the Socialist Party. Returning home after being wounded at the front in 1917, Mussolini began organizing bitter war veterans like himself into a band of Fascists—from the Italian word for "a union of forces."

At first Mussolini's program was a radical combination of nationalist and socialist demands. As such, it competed directly with the well-organized Socialist Party and failed to get off the ground. When Mussolini saw that his violent verbal assaults on rival Socialists won him growing support from conservatives and the frightened middle classes, he shifted gears in 1920 and became a sworn enemy of socialism. Mussolini and his private militia of **Black Shirts** grew increasingly violent. Few people were killed, but Socialist Party newspapers, union halls, and local headquarters were destroyed, and the Black Shirts managed to push Socialists out of city governments in northern Italy.

Fascism soon became a mass movement, one which Mussolini claimed would help the little people against the established interests. In 1922, in the midst of chaos largely created by his Black Shirt militias, Mussolini stepped forward as the savior of order and property. Striking a conservative, anticommunist note in his speeches and gaining the support of army leaders, Mussolini demanded the resignation of the existing government. In October 1922 a band of armed Fascists marched on Rome to threaten the king and force him to appoint Mussolini prime minister of Italy. The threat worked. Victor Emmanuel III (r. 1900–1946)—who himself had no love for the liberal regime—asked Mussolini to take over the government and form a new cabinet. Thus, after widespread violence and a threat of armed uprising, Mussolini seized power using the legal framework of the Italian constitution.

The Regime in Action

Mussolini became prime minister in 1922, but moved cautiously in his first two years in office to establish control of the government. At first, he promised a "return to order" and consolidated his support among Italian elites. Fooled by Mussolini's apparent moderation, the Italian parliament passed a new electoral law that gave two-thirds of the representatives in the parliament to the party that won the most votes. This change allowed the Fascist Party and its allies to win an overwhelming majority in April 1924. Shortly thereafter, a group of Fascist extremists kidnapped and murdered the leading Socialist politician Giacomo Matteotti (JAHK-oh-moh mat-tee-OH-tee). Alarmed, a group of prominent parliamentary leaders demanded that Mussolini's armed squads be dissolved and all violence be banned.

Mussolini may not have ordered Matteotti's murder, but he took advantage of the resulting political crisis. Declaring his desire to "make the nation Fascist," he imposed a series of repressive measures. The government ruled by decree, abolished freedom of the press, and organized fixed elections. Mussolini arrested his political opponents, disbanded all independent labor unions, and put dedicated Fascists in control of Italy's schools. Mussolini trumpeted his goal in a famous slogan: "Everything in the state, nothing outside the state, nothing against the state." By the end of 1926 Italy was a one-party dictatorship under Mussolini's unquestioned leadership.

Mussolini's Fascist Party drew support from broad sectors of the population, in large part because he was willing to compromise with the traditional elites that controlled the army, the economy, and the state. He left big business to regulate itself, and there was no land reform. Mussolini also drew increasing support from the Catholic Church. In the **Lateran Agreement** of 1929, he recognized the Vatican as an independent state, and he agreed to give the church significant financial support in return for the pope's support. Because he was forced to compromise with these conservative elites, Mussolini never established complete totalitarian control.

Mussolini's government nonetheless proceeded with attempts to bring fascism to Italy. The state engineered popular consent by staging massive rallies and sporting events, creating Fascist youth and women's movements, and providing new welfare benefits. Newspapers, radio, and film promoted a "cult of the Duce" (leader), portraying Mussolini as a powerful strongman who embodied the best qualities of the Italian people. Like other Fascist regimes, his government was vehemently opposed to liberal feminism and promoted traditional gender roles. Mussolini also gained support by manipulating popular pride in the grand history of the ancient Roman Empire — as one propagandist put it, "Fascism, in its entirety, is the resurrection of Roman-ness."[3]

Mussolini matched his aggressive rhetoric with military action: Italian armies invaded the African nation of Ethiopia in October 1935. After surprising setbacks at the hands of the poorly armed Ethiopian army, the Italians won in 1936, and Mussolini could proudly declare that Italy again had its empire. Though it shocked international opinion, the war resulted in close ties between Italy and Nazi Germany. After a visit to Berlin in the fall of 1937, the Italian dictator pledged support for Hitler and promised that Italy and Germany would "march together right to the end."[4]

Deeply influenced by Hitler's example (see below), Mussolini's government passed a series of anti-Jewish racial laws in 1938. Though the laws were unpopular,

Jews were forced out of public schools and dismissed from professional careers. Nevertheless, extreme anti-Semitic persecution did not occur in Italy until late in World War II, when Italy was under Nazi control. Though Mussolini's repressive tactics were never as ruthless as those in Nazi Germany, his government did much to turn Italy into a totalitarian police state.

Hitler and Nazism in Germany

Focus Question	What policies did Nazi Germany pursue, and how did they lead to World War II?

The most frightening dictatorship developed in Nazi Germany. National Socialism (or Nazism) shared some characteristics with Italian fascism, but Nazism was far more interventionist. Under Hitler, the Nazi dictatorship smashed or took over most independent organizations, established firm control over the German state and society, and violently persecuted the Jewish population and non-German peoples. Truly totalitarian in aspiration, Nazi Germany acted with a dynamism, based on racial aggression and territorial expansion, that led to history's most destructive war.

The Roots of National Socialism

National Socialism grew out of many complex developments, of which the most influential were nationalism and racism. These two ideas captured the mind of the young Adolf Hitler (1889–1945), and he dominated Nazism until the end of World War II.

The son of an Austrian customs official, Hitler spent his childhood in small towns in Austria. A mediocre student, Hitler dropped out of high school at age fourteen. He then moved to Vienna, where he was exposed to extreme Austro-German nationalists who believed Germans to be a superior people and the natural rulers of central Europe. They advocated the union of Austria with Germany and the violent expulsion of "inferior" peoples as the means of maintaining German domination of the Austro-Hungarian Empire.

In Vienna, Hitler developed an unshakable belief in the crudest distortions of Social Darwinism (see Chapter 24), the superiority of Germanic races, and the inevitability of racial conflict. Exposure to poor eastern European Jews contributed to his anti-Semitic prejudice. Jews, Hitler now claimed, directed an international conspiracy of finance capitalism and Marxist socialism against German culture, German unity, and the German people.

Hitler was not alone. Racist anti-Semitism became wildly popular on the far-right wing of European politics in the decades surrounding the First World War. Such irrational beliefs, rooted in centuries of Christian anti-Semitism, were given pseudo-scientific legitimacy by nineteenth-century developments in biology and eugenics. These ideas came to define Hitler's worldview and would play an immense role in the ideology and actions of National Socialism.

Hitler greeted the outbreak of the First World War as a salvation. The struggle and discipline of war gave life meaning, and Hitler served bravely as a dispatch carrier on the western front. Germany's defeat shattered his world. Convinced that Jews and Marxists had "stabbed Germany in the back," he vowed to fight on.

In late 1919 Hitler joined a tiny extremist group in Munich called the German Workers' Party. In addition to denouncing Jews, Marxists, and democrats, the party promised a uniquely German National Socialism that would abolish the injustices of capitalism and create a mighty "people's community." By 1921 Hitler had gained control of this small but growing party, which had been renamed the National Socialist German Workers' Party, or Nazis for short. Hitler became a master of mass propaganda and political showmanship. In wild, histrionic speeches, he worked his audience into a frenzy with demagogic attacks on the Versailles treaty, Jews, war profiteers, and the Weimar Republic.

In late 1923 that republic seemed on the verge of collapse, and Hitler, inspired by Mussolini's recent victory, organized an armed uprising in Munich—the so-called Beer Hall Putsch. Despite the failure of the poorly planned coup and Hitler's arrest, National Socialism had been born.

Hitler's Road to Power

At his trial, Hitler gained enormous publicity by denouncing the Weimar Republic. He used his brief prison term to dictate his book *Mein Kampf* (My Struggle), where he laid out his basic ideas on "racial purification" and territorial expansion that would define National Socialism.

In *Mein Kampf*, Hitler claimed that Germans were a "master race" that needed to defend its "pure blood" from groups he labeled "racial degenerates," including Jews, Slavs, and others. The German race was destined to triumph and grow, and, according to Hitler, it needed *Lebensraum* (living space). This space could be found to Germany's east, which Hitler claimed was inhabited by the "subhuman" Slavs and Jews. The future dictator outlined a sweeping vision of war and conquest in which the German master race would colonize east and central Europe and ultimately replace the "sub-humans" living there. He championed the idea of the leader-dictator, or *Führer* (FYOUR-uhr), whose unlimited power would embody the people's will and lead the German nation to victory. These ideas would ultimately propel the world into the Second World War.

In the years of relative prosperity and stability between 1924 and 1929, Hitler built up the Nazi Party. From the failed beer hall revolt, he had concluded that he had to come to power through electoral competition rather than armed rebellion. To appeal to middle-class voters, Hitler de-emphasized the anticapitalist elements of National Socialism and vowed to fight communism. The Nazis still remained a small splinter group in 1928, when they received only 2.6 percent of the vote in the general elections and only twelve seats in the Reichstag, the German parliament. There the Nazi deputies pursued the legal strategy of using democracy to destroy democracy.

The Great Depression of 1929 brought the ascent of National Socialism. Now Hitler promised German voters economic as well as political salvation. His appeals for "national rebirth" appealed to a broad spectrum of voters, including middle- and lower-class groups—small business owners, officeworkers, artisans, peasants, and skilled workers. Seized by panic as bankruptcies increased, unemployment soared, and the Communists made dramatic election gains, voters deserted conservative and moderate parties for the Nazis. In the election of 1930 the Nazis won 6.5 million votes and 107 seats, and in July 1932 they gained 14.5 million votes—38 percent of the total. They were now the largest party in the Reichstag.

The breakdown of democratic government helped the Nazis seize power. Chancellor Heinrich Brüning (BROU-nihng) tried to overcome the economic crisis by cutting back government spending and ruthlessly forcing down prices and wages. His conservative policies intensified Germany's economic collapse and convinced many voters that the country's republican leaders were stupid and corrupt, adding to Hitler's appeal.

Division on the left also contributed to Nazi success. Even though the two left-wing parties together outnumbered the Nazis in the Reichstag, the Communists refused to cooperate with the Social Democrats. Failing to resolve their differences, these parties could not mount an effective opposition to the Nazi takeover.

Finally, Hitler excelled in the dirty backroom politics of the decaying Weimar Republic. In 1932 Hitler cleverly gained the support of the conservative politicians in power, who thought they could use Hitler for their own advantage, to resolve the political crisis, but also to clamp down on leftists. They accepted Hitler's demand to be appointed chancellor in a coalition government, reasoning that he could be used and controlled. On January 30, 1933, Adolf Hitler, leader of the most popular political party in Germany, was appointed chancellor by President Hindenburg.

State and Society in Nazi Germany

Hitler moved rapidly and skillfully to establish an unshakable dictatorship that would pursue the Nazi program of racial segregation and spatial expansion. First, Hitler and the Nazi Party worked to consolidate their power. To maintain appearances, Hitler called for new elections. In February 1933, in the midst of an electoral campaign plagued by violence—much of it caused by Nazi toughs—the Reichstag building was partly destroyed by fire. Hitler blamed the Communists and convinced Hindenburg to sign emergency acts that abolished freedom of speech and assembly as well as most personal liberties.

The façade of democratic government was soon torn asunder. When the Nazis won only 44 percent of the vote in the elections, Hitler outlawed the Communist Party and arrested its parliamentary representatives. Then on March 23, 1933, the Nazis pushed through the Reichstag the **Enabling Act**, which gave Hitler dictatorial power for four years. The Nazis' deceitful stress on legality, coupled with divide-and-conquer techniques, disarmed the opposition until it was too late for effective resistance.

Germany became a one-party Nazi state. Elections were farces. The new regime took over the government bureaucracy intact, installing Nazis in top positions. At the same time, it created a series of overlapping Nazi Party organizations responsible solely to Hitler. As recent research has shown, the resulting system of dual government was riddled with rivalries, contradictions, and inefficiencies. The Nazi state was often disorganized and lacked the all-encompassing unity that its propagandists claimed. Yet this fractured system suited Hitler and his purposes. The lack of unity encouraged competition among state personnel, who worked to outdo each other to fulfill Hitler's vaguely expressed goals. The Führer thus played the established bureaucracy against his personal party government and maintained dictatorial control.

Once the Nazis were firmly in command, Hitler and the party turned their attention to constructing a National Socialist society defined by national unity and racial exclusion. First they eliminated political enemies. Communists, Social Democrats, and trade-union leaders were forced out of their jobs or arrested and taken to hastily built concentration camps. The Nazis outlawed strikes and abolished independent labor unions, which were replaced by the Nazi-controlled German Labor Front.

Hitler then purged the Nazi Party itself of its more extremist elements. The Nazi storm troopers (the SA), the quasi-military band of 3 million toughs in brown shirts who had fought Communists and beaten up Jews before the Nazis took power, now expected top positions in the army. Some SA radicals even talked of a "second revolution" that would create equality among all Germans by sweeping away capitalism. Now that he was in power, however, Hitler was eager to win the support of the traditional military and maintain social order. He decided that the leadership of the SA had to be eliminated. On the night of June 30, 1934, Hitler's elite personal guard— the SS—arrested and executed about one hundred SA leaders and other political enemies. Afterward, the SS grew rapidly. Under its methodical, ruthless leader Heinrich Himmler (1900–1945), the SS took over the political police and the concentration camp system.

The Nazis instituted a policy called "coordination," which forced existing institutions to conform to National Socialist ideology. Professionals—doctors and lawyers, teachers and engineers—saw their previously independent organizations swallowed up by Nazi associations. Charity and civic organizations were also put under Nazi control, and universities, publishers, and writers were quickly brought into line. Democratic, socialist, and Jewish literature was put on ever-growing blacklists. Passionate students and radicalized professors burned forbidden books in public squares. Modern art and architecture—which the Nazis considered "degenerate"—were prohibited. Life became violently anti-intellectual. By 1934 a brutal dictatorship characterized by frightening dynamism and obedience to Hitler was largely in place.

Acting on its vision of racial eugenics, the party began a many-faceted campaign against those deemed incapable of making positive biological contributions to the "master race." The Nazis persecuted a number of groups. Jews headed the list, but Slavic peoples, Sinti and Roma, homosexuals, and Jehovah's Witnesses were also considered social "deviants." Nazi bureaucrats furthermore invented two categories targeted for "racial hygiene": the "hereditarily ill" and "asocials." The "hereditarily ill" included people with chronic mental or physical disabilities, such as schizophrenics, manic depressives, epileptics, and people suffering from what Nazi physicians called "congenital feeblemindedness." The catchall category of "asocials" included common criminals, alcoholics, prostitutes, the "work shy" (or chronically unemployed), beggars and vagrants, and others on the margins of German society.

Nazi leaders used a variety of measures to convince Germans that "racial hygiene" was justified and necessary. In what some historians term the Nazi "racial state," barbarism and race hatred were institutionalized with the force of science and law.[5] New university academies, such as the German Society for Racial Research, wrote studies that measured and defined racial differences; prejudice was thus presented in the guise of enlightened medical science, a means for creating a strong national race. Schoolroom lessons, articles in the popular press, feature films, traveling exhibitions, and even children's board games touted the benefits of racist eugenic practice.

The results were monstrous, a barbaric violation of the ethical norms most of us take for granted. Thousands of innocent people faced social ostracism and then brutal repression, simply because the Nazis deemed them racial outsiders. Convinced by their own racial ideology, Nazi authorities denied outsiders welfare benefits and put them out of work, forced people with disabilities into special hospitals where they could be segregated from "healthy" Germans, and imprisoned homosexuals and "asocials" in concentration camps for "re-education." A series of sterilization laws exemplified the ethical breakdown. Nazi medical workers forcibly sterilized some four hundred thousand German citizens, mainly "asocials" or the "hereditarily ill," so their "degenerate blood" would not pollute the "Aryan race." The eugenics campaign reached a crescendo in 1938, when the authorities initiated a coldhearted euthanasia program—dubbed "mercy killing" by Nazi physicians and administrators—and systematically murdered about seventy thousand Germans with chronic disabilities (see page 891).

From the beginning, German Jews were a special target of Nazi racial persecution. Anti-Jewish propaganda was ever present in Nazi Germany. Ugly posters of stereotypical Jews; feature films and documentaries about the Jewish "menace"; signs in shop windows, banks, and parks forbidding Jewish entry—all and more were used to stigmatize German Jews. Such means were backed up with harsh legal oppression. Shortly after they took power, Nazi authorities issued the Professional Civil Service Restoration Act, which banned Jews from working in government jobs; by 1934 many Jewish lawyers, doctors, professors, civil servants, and musicians had been summarily dismissed from their jobs. In 1935 the infamous Nuremberg Laws classified as Jewish anyone having three or more Jewish grandparents, outlawed marriage and sexual relations between Jews and those defined as German, and deprived Jews of all rights of citizenship. Conversion to Christianity and abandonment of the Jewish faith made no difference. For the vast majority of German citizens not targeted by such laws, the creation of a demonized outsider group may well have contributed to feelings of national unity and support for the Hitler regime.

In late 1938 the assault on the Jews accelerated. During a well-organized wave of violence known as Kristallnacht (or the Night of Broken Glass pogrom), Nazi gangs smashed windows and looted over 7,000 Jewish-owned shops, destroyed many homes, burned down over 200 synagogues, and killed dozens of Jews. German Jews were then rounded up and made to pay for the damage. By 1939 some 300,000 of Germany's 500,000 Jews had emigrated, sacrificing almost all their property in order to escape persecution. Some Germans privately opposed these outrages, but most went along or looked the other way. Historians still debate the degree to which this lack of opposition expressed popular anti-Semitism. In any case, it revealed widespread support for Hitler's government.

Popular Support for National Socialism

Why did millions of ordinary Germans back a brutally repressive, racist regime? A combination of coercion and reward enlisted popular support for the racial state. Using the secret police and the growing concentration camp system in a reign of ruthless terror, the regime persecuted its political and "racial" enemies. Yet for the large majority of ordinary German citizens who were not Jews, Communists, or members of other targeted groups, Hitler's government brought new opportunities. The German "master race" clearly benefited from Nazi policies and programs.

Hitler had promised the masses economic recovery, and he delivered. The Nazi state launched a large public works program to help pull Germany out of the depression. Work began on superhighways, offices, gigantic sports stadiums, and public housing, which created jobs and instilled pride in national recovery. By 1938 unemployment had fallen to 2 percent, and there was a shortage of workers. Between 1932 and 1938 the standard of living for the average worker increased moderately. Business profits rose sharply.

The persecution of Jews brought substantial benefits to ordinary Germans as well. As Jews were forced out of their jobs and compelled to sell their homes and businesses, Germans stepped in to take their place in a process known as Aryanization (named after the "Aryan master race" prized by the Nazis for their supposedly pure German blood). For millions of so-called Aryans, a rising standard of living—at whatever ethical price—was tangible evidence that Nazi promises were more than show and propaganda.

Economic recovery was accompanied by a wave of social and cultural innovation intended to construct what Nazi propagandists called the *Volksgemeinschaft*—a "people's community" for racially pure Germans. The party set up mass organizations to spread Nazi ideology and enlist volunteers for the Nazi cause. Millions of Germans joined the Hitler Youth, the League of German Women, and the German Labor Front. Mass rallies, such as annual May Day celebrations and Nazi Party conventions in Nuremberg, brought together thousands of participants. Glowing reports on such events in the Nazi-controlled press brought the message home to millions more.

As the economy recovered, the government proudly touted a glittering array of inexpensive and enticing people's products. Items such as the Volkswagen (the "People's Car") were intended to link individuals' desire for consumer goods to the collective ideology of the "people's community." Though such programs faltered as the state increasingly focused on rearmament for the approaching war, they suggested to all that the regime was working hard to improve German living standards.

Women played a special role in the Nazi state. Promising to "liberate women from women's liberation," Nazi ideologues championed a return to traditional family values. They outlawed abortion, discouraged women from holding jobs or obtaining higher education, and glorified domesticity and motherhood. Women were cast as protectors of the hearth and home and were instructed to raise young boys and girls in accordance with Nazi ideals. In the later 1930s, facing labor shortages, the Nazis had to reluctantly reverse course and encourage women to enter the labor force. Whatever the employment situation, the millions of women enrolled in Nazi mass organizations, which organized charity drives and other social programs, experienced a sense of freedom and community in these public activities.

Few historians today believe that Hitler and the Nazis brought about a real social revolution, as an earlier generation of scholars thought. Yet Hitler's rule promoted economic growth, and Nazi propagandists continually played up the supposed accomplishments of the regime. The vision of a "people's community," national pride in recovery, and feelings of belonging created by acts of racial exclusion led many Germans to support the regime. Hitler himself remained popular with broad sections of the population well into the war.

Not all Germans supported Hitler, however, and a number of groups actively resisted him after 1933. But opponents of the Nazis were never unified, which helps explain their lack of success. Furthermore, the regime harshly clamped down on dissidents: tens of thousands of political enemies were imprisoned, and thousands were executed. After Communists and socialists were smashed by the SS system, a second group of opponents arose in the Catholic and Protestant churches. Their efforts, however, were directed primarily at preserving religious life, not at overthrowing Hitler. In 1938 and again during the war, a few high-ranking army officers, who feared the consequences of Hitler's reckless aggression, plotted against him, but their plans were unsuccessful.

Aggression and Appeasement

The nazification of German society fulfilled only part of the Nazi agenda. While building the "people's community," the regime aggressively pursued policies meant to achieve territorial expansion for the supposedly superior German race. At first, Hitler carefully camouflaged his expansionist goals. Germany was still militarily weak, and the Nazi leader proclaimed his peaceful intentions. Germany's withdrawal from the League of Nations in October 1933 nonetheless indicated that Gustav Stresemann's policy of peaceful cooperation was dead (see Chapter 26). Then in March 1935 Hitler declared that Germany would no longer abide by the disarmament clauses of the Treaty of Versailles. He established a military draft and began to build up the German army. France and Great Britain protested strongly and warned against future aggressive actions.

Any hope of a united front against Hitler quickly collapsed. Britain adopted a policy of **appeasement**, granting Hitler what he demanded to avoid war. British appeasement, which practically dictated French policy, was motivated in large part by the pacifism of a population still horrified by the memory of the First World War. As in Germany, many powerful conservatives in Britain underestimated Hitler. They believed that Soviet communism was the real danger and that Hitler could be used to stop it. Such strong anticommunist feelings made an alliance between the Western powers and Stalin against Hitler highly unlikely.

When Hitler suddenly marched his armies into the demilitarized Rhineland in March 1936, brazenly violating the treaties of Versailles and Locarno (Map 27.2), Britain refused to act. France could do little without British support. Emboldened, Hitler moved ever more aggressively, enlisting powerful allies in international affairs. Italy and Germany established the so-called Rome-Berlin Axis in 1936.

MAP 27.2 The Growth of Nazi Germany, 1933–1939
Until March 1939 Hitler's conquests brought ethnic Germans into the Nazi state; then he turned on the Slavic and Jewish peoples he had always hated. He stripped Czechoslovakia of its independence and prepared to attack Poland in September 1939.

Japan, also under the rule of a Fascist dictatorship, joined the Axis alliance that same year.

At the same time, Germany and Italy intervened in the Spanish Civil War (1936–1939), where their military aid helped General Francisco Franco's revolutionary Fascist movement defeat the democratically elected republican government. Republican Spain's only official aid in the fight against Franco came from the Soviet Union, for public opinion in Britain and especially in France was hopelessly divided on whether to intervene.

In late 1937 Hitler moved forward with plans to seize Austria and Czechoslovakia as the first step in his long-contemplated drive for living space in the east. By threatening Austria with invasion, Hitler forced the Austrian chancellor to put local Nazis in control of the government in March 1938. The next day, in the Anschluss (annexation), German armies moved in unopposed, and Austria became part of Greater Germany (see Map 27.2).

Simultaneously, Hitler demanded that territories inhabited mostly by ethnic Germans in western Czechoslovakia—the Sudetenland—be ceded to Nazi Germany. Though democratic Czechoslovakia was allied with France and the Soviet Union and prepared to defend itself, appeasement triumphed again. In negotiations British prime minister Arthur Neville Chamberlain and the French agreed with Hitler that Germany should immediately take over the Sudetenland. Returning to London from the Munich Conference in September 1938, Chamberlain told cheering crowds that he had secured "peace with honor . . . peace for our time." Sold out by the Western powers, Czechoslovakia gave in.

Chamberlain's peace was short-lived. In March 1939 Hitler's armies invaded and occupied the rest of Czechoslovakia. The effect on Western public opinion was electrifying. This time, there was no possible rationale of self-determination for Nazi aggression, since Hitler was seizing ethnic Czechs and Slovaks—not Germans—as captive peoples. When Hitler next used the question of German minorities in Danzig as a pretext to confront Poland, a suddenly militant Chamberlain declared that Britain and France would fight if Hitler attacked his eastern neighbor. Hitler did not take these warnings seriously.

In August 1939, in an about-face that stunned the world, sworn enemies Hitler and Stalin signed a nonaggression pact that paved the road to war. Each dictator promised to remain neutral if the other became involved in open hostilities. An attached secret protocol ruthlessly divided Poland, the Baltic nations, Finland, and a part of Romania into German and Soviet spheres of influence. Stalin agreed to the pact because he remained distrustful of Western intentions and because Hitler offered immediate territorial gain.

For Hitler, everything was now set. On September 1, 1939, German armies and warplanes smashed into Poland from three sides. Two days later, Britain and France, finally true to their word, declared war on Germany. The Second World War had begun.

The Second World War

| Focus Question | How did Germany and Japan conquer enormous empires during World War II, and how did the Allies defeat them? |

Nazi Germany's unlimited ambition unleashed an apocalyptic cataclysm. Hitler's armies quickly conquered much of western and eastern Europe, establishing a vast empire of expropriation, destruction, and death. At the same time, Japanese armies overran much of Southeast Asia and created their own racial empire. This reckless aggression brought together a coalition of unlikely but powerful allies determined to halt the advance of

Europe Under Nazi Occupation

Hitler's New Order was based firmly on the guiding principle of National Socialism: racial imperialism. Occupied peoples were treated according to their place in the Nazi racial hierarchy. All were subject to harsh policies dedicated to ethnic cleansing and the plunder of resources for the Nazi war effort.

Within this **New Order**, the so-called Nordic peoples—the Dutch, Danes, and Norwegians—received preferential treatment, for the Germans believed them related to the Aryan master race. In Holland, Denmark, and Norway, the Nazis established puppet governments of various kinds. Though many people hated the conquerors, the Nazis found willing collaborators who ruled in accord with German needs. France was divided into two parts. The German army occupied the north, including Paris. The southeast remained nominally independent. There the aging First World War general Marshal Henri-Philippe Pétain formed a new French government—the Vichy (VIH-shee) regime—that adopted many aspects of National Socialist ideology and willingly placed French Jews in the hands of the Nazis.

In all conquered territories, the Nazis used a variety of techniques to enrich Germany and support the war effort. Occupied nations were forced to pay for the costs of the war and for the occupation itself, and the price was high. Nazi administrators stole goods and money from local Jews, set currency exchanges at favorable rates, and forced occupied peoples to accept worthless wartime scrip. Soldiers were encouraged not only to steal but also to purchase goods at cheap exchange rates and send them home. A flood of plunder thus reached Germany, helping maintain high living standards and preserving home-front morale well into the war. Nazi victory, furthermore, placed national Jewish populations across Europe under German control, allowing the mass murder of Europe's Jews.

In central and eastern Europe, the war and German rule were far more ruthless and deadly than in the west. From the start, the Nazi leadership had cast the war in the east as one of annihilation. The Nazis now set out to build a vast colonial empire where Jews would be exterminated and Poles, Ukrainians, and Russians would be enslaved and forced to die out. According to the plans, ethnic German peasants would resettle the resulting abandoned lands, a "mass settlement space." In pursuit of such goals, large parts of western Poland were incorporated into Germany. Another part of Poland was placed under the rule of a merciless civilian administration.

With the support of military commanders, German policemen, and bureaucrats in the occupied territories, Nazi administrators and Himmler's elite SS corps now implemented a program of destruction and annihilation to create a "mass settlement space" for racially pure Germans. Across the east, the Nazi armies destroyed cities and factories, stole crops and farm animals, and subjected conquered peoples to forced starvation and mass murder. Nazi occupation in the east destroyed the lives of millions.[6]

In response to such atrocities, small but determined underground resistance groups fought back. They were hardly unified. Communists and socialists often disagreed with more centrist or nationalist groups on long-term goals and short-term tactics. In Yugoslavia, for example, Communist and royalist military resistance groups attacked the Germans, but also each other. The resistance nonetheless presented a real challenge to the Nazi New Order. Poland, under German occupation longer than any other nation, had the most determined and well-organized resistance. The Nazis had closed all Polish universities and outlawed national newspapers, but the Poles organized secret classes and maintained a thriving underground press. Underground members of the Polish Home Army, led by the government in exile in London, passed intelligence about German operations to the Allies and committed sabotage. The famous French resistance undertook similar actions, as did groups in Italy, Greece, Russia, and the Netherlands.

The German response was swift and deadly. The Nazi army and the SS tortured captured resistance members and executed hostages in reprisal for attacks. Responding to actions undertaken by resistance groups, the German army murdered the male populations of Lidice (Czechoslovakia) and Oradour (France) and leveled the entire towns, brutal examples of Nazi barbarism in pursuit of a racial New Order. Despite reprisals, Nazi occupiers were never able to eradicate popular resistance to their rule.

The Holocaust

The ultimate abomination of Nazi racism was the condemnation of all European Jews and other peoples considered racially inferior to extreme racial persecution and then annihilation in the **Holocaust**, a great spasm of racially inspired mass murder.

As already described, the Nazis began to use social, legal, and economic means to persecute Jews and other "undesirable" groups immediately after taking power. Between 1938 and 1940 persecution turned deadly in the Nazi euthanasia (mercy killing) campaign, an important step toward genocide. Just as Germany began the war, some 70,000 people with physical and mental disabilities were forced into special hospitals, barracks, and camps. Deemed by Nazi administrators to be "unworthy lives" who might "pollute" the German race, they were murdered in cold blood. The victims were mostly ethnic Germans, and the euthanasia campaign was stopped after church leaders and ordinary families spoke out. The staff involved took what they learned in implementing this program with them to the extermination camps the Nazis would soon build in the east (Map 27.4).

The German victory over Poland in 1939 brought some 3 million Jews under Nazi control. Jews in German-occupied territories were soon forced to move into urban districts termed "ghettos." In walled-off ghettos in cities large and small — two of the most important were in Warsaw and Lodz — hundreds of thousands of Polish Jews lived in crowded and unsanitary conditions, without real work or adequate sustenance. Over 500,000 people died under these conditions.

The racial violence reached new extremes when Germany invaded the Soviet Union in 1941. Three military death squads known as Special Task Forces (*Einsatzgruppen*) and other military units followed the advancing German armies. They moved systematically from town to town, shooting Jews and other target populations. The victims of these mobile killing units were often forced to dig their own graves in local woods or fields before they were shot. In this way the German armed forces murdered some 2 million civilians.

In late 1941 Hitler and the Nazi leadership, in some still-debated combination, ordered the SS to implement the mass murder of all Jews in Europe. What the Nazi to the ground. In Auschwitz itself, in October 1944, a group of Jewish prisoners revolted and burned down one of the camp's crematoriums before all were captured and summarily executed.

The murderous attack on European Jews was the ultimate monstrosity of Nazi "racial hygiene" and racial imperialism. By 1945 the Nazis had killed about 6 million Jews and some 5 million other Europeans, including millions of ethnic Poles and Russian POWs. Who was responsible for this terrible crime? Historians continue to debate this critical question. Some lay the guilt on Hitler and the Nazi leadership, arguing that ordinary Germans had little knowledge of the extermination camps or were forced to participate by Nazi terror and totalitarian control. Other scholars conclude that far more Germans knew about and were at best indifferent to the fate of "racial inferiors."

The question remains: what inspired those who actually worked in the killing machine — the "desk murderers" in Berlin who sent trains to the east, the soldiers who shot Jews in the Polish forests, the guards at Auschwitz? Some historians believe that widely shared anti-Semitism led "ordinary Germans" to become Hitler's "willing executioners." Others argue that heightened peer pressure, the desire to advance in the ranks, and the need to prove one's strength under the most brutalizing wartime violence turned average Germans into reluctant killers. The conditioning of racist Nazi propaganda clearly played a role. Whatever the motivation, numerous Germans were somehow prepared to join the SS ideologues and perpetrate ever-greater crimes, from mistreatment to arrest to mass murder.[7]

Japanese Empire and the War in the Pacific

The racist war of annihilation in Europe was matched by racially inspired warfare in East Asia. In response to political divisions and economic crisis, a Fascist government had taken control of Japan in the 1930s. As in Germany and Italy, the Japanese government was highly nationalistic and militaristic, and it was deeply committed to imperial expansion. According to Japanese race theory, the Asian races were far superior to Western ones. In speeches, schools, and newspapers, ultranationalists eagerly voiced the extreme anti-Western views that had risen in the 1920s and 1930s. They glorified the warrior virtues of honor and sacrifice and proclaimed that Japan would liberate East Asia from Western colonialists.

Japan soon acted on its racial-imperial ambitions. In 1931 Japanese armies invaded and occupied Manchuria, a vast territory bordering northeastern China. In 1937 Japan brutally invaded China itself. Seeking to cement ties with the Fascist regimes of Europe, in 1940 the Japanese entered into a formal alliance with Italy and Germany, and in summer 1941 Japanese armies occupied southern portions of the French colony of Indochina (now Vietnam and Cambodia).

The goal was to establish what the Japanese called the Greater East Asia Co-Prosperity Sphere. Under the slogan "Asia for Asians," Japanese propagandists maintained that this expansion would free Asians from hated Western imperialists. By promising to create a mutually advantageous union for long-term development, the Japanese tapped currents of nationalist sentiment, and most local populations were glad to see the Westerners go.

But the Co-Prosperity Sphere was a sham. Real power remained in the hands of the Japanese. They exhibited great cruelty toward civilian populations and prisoners of war, and exploited local peoples for Japan's wartime needs, arousing local populations against them. Nonetheless, the ability of the Japanese to defeat the Western colonial powers set a powerful example for national liberation groups in Asia, which would become important in the decolonization movement that followed World War II.

Japanese expansion from 1937 to 1941 evoked a sharp response from U.S. president Franklin Roosevelt, and Japan's leaders came to believe that war with the United States was inevitable. After much debate, they decided to launch a surprise attack on the U.S. fleet based at Pearl Harbor in the Hawaiian Islands. On December 7, 1941, the Japanese sank or crippled every American battleship, but by chance all the American aircraft carriers were at sea and escaped unharmed. Pearl Harbor brought the Americans into the war in a spirit of anger and revenge.

As the Americans mobilized for war, Japanese armies overran more European and American colonies in Southeast Asia. By May 1942 Japan controlled a vast empire (Map 27.5) and was threatening Australia. The Americans pushed back and engaged the Japanese in a series of hard-fought naval battles. In July 1943 the Americans and their Australian allies opened a successful island-hopping campaign that slowly forced Japan out of its conquered territories. The war in the Pacific was extremely brutal—a "war without mercy," in the words of a leading American scholar—and soldiers on both sides committed atrocities. A product of spiraling violence, mutual hatred, and dehumanizing racial stereotypes, the fighting intensified as the United States moved toward Japan.[8]

The "Hinge of Fate"

While the Nazis and the Japanese built their savage empires, Great Britain, the United States, and the Soviet Union joined together in a military pact Churchill termed the Grand Alliance. This was a matter of circumstance more than of choice. It had taken the Japanese surprise attack to bring the isolationist United States into the war. Moreover, the British and Americans were determined opponents of Soviet communism, and disagreements between the Soviets and the capitalist powers during the course of the war sowed mutual distrust. Stalin repeatedly urged Britain and the United States to open a second front in France to relieve pressure on Soviet forces, but Churchill and Roosevelt refused until the summer of 1944. Despite such tensions, the overriding goal of defeating the Axis powers brought together these reluctant allies.

In one area of agreement, the Grand Alliance concurred on a policy of "Europe first." Only after Hitler was defeated would the Allies mount an all-out attack on Japan, the lesser threat. The Allies also agreed to concentrate on immediate military needs, postponing tough political questions about the eventual peace settlement that might have divided them. To further encourage mutual trust, the Allies adopted the principle of the unconditional surrender of Germany and Japan. This policy cemented the Grand Alliance because it denied Hitler any hope of dividing his foes. It also meant that Soviet and Anglo-American armies would almost certainly be forced to invade and occupy all of Germany, and that Japan would fight to the bitter end.

Great Britain and the United States had made critical advances in the western theater, but the worst German defeats came at the hands of the Red Army on the eastern front. Although the Germans had almost captured the major cities of Moscow and Leningrad in early winter 1941, they were forced back by determined Soviet counterattacks. The Germans mounted a second and initially successful invasion of the Soviet Union in the summer of 1942, but the campaign turned into a disaster. The downfall came at the Battle of Stalingrad, when in November 1942 the Soviets surrounded and systematically destroyed the entire German Sixth Army of 300,000 men. In January 1943 only 123,000 soldiers were left to surrender. Hitler, who had refused to allow a retreat, suffered a catastrophic defeat. For the first time, German public opinion turned decisively against the war. In summer 1943 the larger, better-equipped Soviet armies took the offensive and began to push the Germans back along the entire eastern front (see Map 27.3).

Allied Victory

The balance of power was now clearly in Allied hands, yet bitter fighting continued in Europe for almost two years. Germany, less fully mobilized for war in 1941 than Britain, stepped up its efforts. The German war industry, under the Nazi minister of armaments Albert Speer, put to work millions of prisoners of war and slave laborers from across occupied Europe. Between early 1942 and July 1944, German war production tripled despite heavy Anglo-American bombing.

German resistance against Hitler also failed to halt the fighting. An unsuccessful attempt by conservative army leaders to assassinate Hitler in July 1944 only brought increased repression by the fanatic Nazis who had taken over the government. Closely disciplined by the regime, frightened by the prospect of unconditional surrender, and terrorized by Nazi propaganda that portrayed the advancing Russian armies as rapacious Slavic beasts, the Germans fought on with suicidal resolve.

On June 6, 1944, American and British forces under General Dwight Eisenhower landed on the beaches of Normandy, France, in history's greatest naval invasion. In a hundred dramatic days, more than 2 million men and almost half a million vehicles broke through the German lines and pushed inland. Rejecting proposals to strike straight at Berlin in a massive attack, Eisenhower moved forward cautiously on a broad front. Not until March 1945 did American troops cross the Rhine and enter Germany. By spring of 1945 the Allies had finally forced the Germans out of the Italian peninsula. That April, Mussolini was captured in northern Italy by Communist partisans and executed, along with his mistress and other Fascist leaders.

The Soviets, who had been advancing steadily since July 1943, reached the outskirts of Warsaw by August 1944. Anticipating German defeat, the Polish underground Home Army ordered an uprising, so that the Poles might take the city on their own and establish independence from the Soviets. The Warsaw Uprising was a tragic miscalculation. Citing military pressure, the Red Army refused to enter the city. Stalin and Soviet leaders thus allowed the Germans to destroy the Polish insurgents, a cynical move that paved the way for the establishment of a postwar Communist regime. Only after the decimated Home Army surrendered did the Red Army continue its advance. Warsaw lay in ruins, and between 150,000 and 200,000 Poles—mostly civilians—had lost their lives.

Over the next six months, the Soviets moved southward into Romania, Hungary, and Yugoslavia. In January 1945 the Red Army crossed Poland into Germany, and on April 26 met American forces on the Elbe River. The Allies had overrun Europe and closed their vise on Nazi Germany. As Soviet forces fought their way into Berlin, Hitler committed suicide, and on May 8 the remaining German commanders capitulated.

The war in the Pacific also drew to a close. Despite repeated U.S. victories through the summer of 1945, Japanese troops had continued to fight with enormous courage and determination. American commanders believed the invasion and conquest of Japan itself might cost 1 million American casualties and claim 10 to 20 million Japanese lives. In fact, Japan was almost helpless, its industry and dense, fragile wooden cities largely destroyed by intense American bombing. Yet the Japanese seemed determined to fight on, ready to die for a hopeless cause.

Nuclear Wasteland at Hiroshima   Only a handful of buildings remain standing in the ruins of Hiroshima in September 1945. Fearing the costs of a prolonged ground and naval campaign against the Japanese mainland, the United States dropped atomic bombs on Hiroshima and Nagasaki in August 1945. The bombings ended the war and opened the nuclear age. (AP Photo/AP Images)

3. What kind of government did Mussolini establish in Italy? (p. 876)

4. What policies did Nazi Germany pursue, and how did they lead to World War II? (p. 879)

5. How did Germany and Japan conquer enormous empires during World War II, and how did the Allies defeat them? (p. 887)

CHRONOLOGY

1921	New Economic Policy (NEP) in U.S.S.R.
1922	Mussolini gains power in Italy
1924	Mussolini seizes dictatorial powers
1924–1929	Buildup of Nazi Party in Germany
1927	Stalin comes to power in U.S.S.R.
1928	Stalin's first five-year plan
1929	Lateran Agreement; start of collectivization in Soviet Union
1929–1939	Great Depression
1931	Japan invades Manchuria
1932–1933	Famine in Ukraine
1933	Hitler appointed chancellor in Germany; Reichstag passes the Enabling Act, granting Hitler absolute dictatorial power
1935	Nuremberg Laws deprive Jews of citizenship rights
1936	Start of great purges under Stalin; Spanish Civil War begins
1937	Japanese army invades China
1938	Kristallnacht marks beginning of more aggressive anti-Jewish policy in Germany
1939	Germany occupies Czech lands and invades western Poland; Britain and France declare war on Germany, starting World War II; Soviet Union occupies eastern Poland
1940	Germany defeats and occupies France; Battle of Britain begins
1941	Germany invades U.S.S.R.; Japan attacks Pearl Harbor; United States enters war
1941–1945	The Holocaust
1942–1943	Battle of Stalingrad
1944	Allied invasion at Normandy
1945	Soviet and U.S. forces enter Germany; United States drops atomic bombs on Japan; World War II ends

28

Cold War Conflict and Consensus

1945–1965

THE DEFEAT OF THE NAZIS AND THEIR ALLIES in 1945 left Europe in ruins. In the immediate postwar years, as Europeans struggled to overcome the effects of rampant death and destruction, the victorious Allies worked to shape an effective peace accord. Disagreements between the Soviet Union and the Western allies emerged during this process and quickly led to an apparently endless Cold War between the two new superpowers—the United States and the Soviet Union. This conflict split much of Europe into a Soviet-aligned Communist bloc and a U.S.-aligned capitalist bloc and spurred military, economic, and technological competition.

Amid these tensions, battered western European countries fashioned a remarkable recovery, building strong democratic institutions and vibrant economies. In the Soviet Union and the "East Bloc" (the label applied to central and eastern European countries governed by Soviet-backed Communist regimes), Communist leaders repressed challenges to one-party rule but also offered limited reforms, leading to stability there as well. Yet the postwar period was by no means peaceful. Anti-Soviet uprisings in East Bloc countries led to military intervention and death and imprisonment for thousands. Colonial independence movements in the developing world sometimes erupted in violence, even after liberation was achieved. Cold War hostilities had an immense impact on the decolonization process, often to the detriment of formerly colonized peoples.

Cold War conflicts notwithstanding, the postwar decades witnessed the construction of a relatively stable social and political consensus in both Communist and capitalist Europe. At the same time, changing class structures, new migration patterns,

official courts to sanction collaborators or send them to prison. A small number received the death sentence.

In Germany and Austria, occupation authorities set up "denazification" procedures meant to identify and punish former Nazi Party members responsible for the worst crimes and eradicate National Socialist ideology from social and political institutions. At the Nuremberg trials (1945–1946), an international military tribunal organized by the four Allied powers tried the highest-ranking Nazi military and civilian leaders who had survived the war, charging them with war crimes and crimes against humanity. After chilling testimony from victims of the regime, which revealed the full systematic horror of Nazi atrocities, twelve were sentenced to death and ten more to lengthy prison terms.

The Nuremberg trials marked the last time the four Allies worked closely together to punish former Nazis. As the Cold War developed and the Soviets and the Western Allies drew increasingly apart, each carried out separate denazification programs in their own zones of occupation. In the Western zones, military courts at first actively prosecuted leading Nazis. But the huge numbers implicated in Nazi crimes, German opposition to the proceedings, and the need for stability in the looming Cold War made thorough denazification impractical. Except for the worst offenders, the Western authorities had quietly shelved denazification by 1948. The process was similar in the Soviet zone. At first, punishment was swift and harsh. About 45,000 former party officials, upper-class industrialists, and large landowners identified as Nazis were sentenced to prison or death. As in the West, however, former Nazis who cooperated with the Soviet authorities could avoid prosecution. Thus many former Nazis found leading positions in government and industry in both the Soviet and Western zones.

The Peace Settlement and Cold War Origins

In the years immediately after the war, as ordinary people across Europe struggled to come to terms with the war and recover from the ruin, the victorious Allies—the U.S.S.R., the United States, and Great Britain—tried to shape a reasonable and lasting peace. Yet the Allies began to quarrel almost as soon as the unifying threat of Nazi Germany disappeared, and the interests of the Communist Soviet Union and the capitalist Britain and United States increasingly diverged. The hostility between the Eastern and Western superpowers was the sad but logical outgrowth of military developments, wartime agreements, and long-standing political and ideological differences that stretched back to the Russian Revolution.

Once the United States entered the war in late 1941, the Americans and the British had made military victory their highest priority. They did not try to take

< **MAP 28.1 The Aftermath of World War II in Europe, ca. 1945–1950**
By 1945 millions of people displaced by war and territorial changes were on the move. The Soviet Union and Poland took land from Germany, which the Allies partitioned into occupation zones. Those zones subsequently formed the basis of the East and West German states. Austria was detached from Germany and similarly divided, but the Soviets subsequently permitted Austria to reunify as a neutral state.

The Place de la Concorde in Paris, 1956   The consumer revolution of the late 1950s brought a rapid increase in the number of privately owned automobiles across western Europe. Major European cities began to experience one of the more unfortunate but increasingly common aspects of postwar life: the traffic jam. (Peter Cornelius/akg-images)

by war and eager to rebuild their homes and families, western Europeans embraced the new products of consumer society. Like North Americans, they filled their houses and apartments with modern appliances such as washing machines, and they eagerly purchased the latest entertainment devices of the day: radios, record players, and televisions.

The purchase of consumer goods was greatly facilitated by the increased use of installment purchasing, which allowed people to buy on credit. With the expansion of social security safeguards reducing the need to accumulate savings for hard times and old age, ordinary people were increasingly willing to take on debt, and new banks and credit unions offered loans for consumer purchases on easy terms. The consumer market became an increasingly important engine for general economic growth. For example, the European automobile industry expanded phenomenally after lagging far behind that of the United States since the 1920s. In 1948 there were only 5 million cars in western Europe; by 1965 there were 44 million. Car ownership was democratized and became possible for better-paid workers — the consumer revolution brought a vast array of new items into everyday activities, changing both lifestyles and attitudes.

Visions of consumer abundance became a powerful weapon in an era of Cold War competition. Politicians in both East and West claimed that their respective systems could best provide citizens with ample consumer goods. In the competition over consumption, Western capitalism clearly surpassed Eastern planned economies in the production and distribution of inexpensive products. Western leaders boasted about the abundance of goods on store shelves and promised new forms of social equality in which all citizens would have equal access to consumer items — rather than relying on class leveling mandated by the state, as in the despised East Bloc. The race to provide ordinary people with higher living standards would be a central aspect of the Cold War, as the Communist East Bloc struggled to catch up to Western standards of prosperity.

Developments in the Soviet Union and the East Bloc

Focus Question	**What was the pattern of postwar development in the Soviet bloc?**

While western Europe surged ahead economically and increased its independent political power as American influence gradually waned, East Bloc countries followed a different path. The Soviet Union first tightened its grip on peoples it had "liberated" during the Second World War and then refused to let go. Though limited reforms after Stalin's death in 1953 led to some economic improvement and limited gains in freedoms, postwar recovery in Communist central and eastern Europe proceeded along Soviet lines, and political and social developments there were strongly influenced by developments in the U.S.S.R.

Postwar Life in the East Bloc

The "Great Patriotic War of the Fatherland" had fostered Russian nationalism and a relaxation of dictatorial terror. It also had produced a rare but real unity between Soviet rulers and most citizens. Having made a heroic war effort, the vast majority of the Soviet people hoped in 1945 that a grateful party and government would grant greater freedom and democracy. Such hopes were soon disappointed.

Even before the war ended, Stalin was moving the U.S.S.R. back toward rigid dictatorship. By early 1946 Stalin was arguing that another war was inevitable as long as capitalism existed. Working to extend Communist influence across the globe, the Soviets established the Cominform, or Communist Information Bureau, an international organization dedicated to maintaining Russian control over Communist parties abroad, in western Europe and the East Bloc. Stalin's new superpower foe, the United States, served as an excuse for re-establishing a harsh dictatorship in the U.S.S.R. itself. Stalin reasserted the Communist Party's control of the government and his absolute mastery of the party. Rigid ideological indoctrination, attacks on religion, and the absence of civil liberties were soon facts of life for citizens of the Soviet empire. Millions of supposed political enemies were sent to prison, exile, or forced-labor camps.

To some degree, the Great Powers regarded their empires very differently after 1945 than before 1914, or even before 1939. Empire had rested on self-confidence and self-righteousness; Europeans had believed their superiority to be not only technical and military but also spiritual, racial, and moral. The horrors of the First and Second World Wars undermined such complacent arrogance and gave opponents of imperialism much greater influence in Europe. Increasing pressure from the United States, which had long presented itself as an enemy of empire despite its own imperialist actions in the Philippines and the Americas, encouraged Europeans to let go of their former colonies. Indeed, Americans were eager to extend their own influence in Europe's former colonies. Economically weakened, and with their political power and moral authority in tatters, the imperial powers preferred to avoid bloody colonial wars and generally turned to rebuilding at home.

Furthermore, the imperial powers faced dedicated anticolonial resistance. Popular politicians, including China's Mao Zedong, India's Mohandas Gandhi, Egypt's Gamal Abdel Nasser, and many others, provided determined leadership in the struggle against European imperialism. A new generation of intellectuals, such as Jomo Kenyatta of Kenya and Aimé Césaire and Frantz Fanon, both from Martinique, wrote trenchant critiques of imperial power, often rooted in Marxist ideas. Anticolonial politicians and intellectuals alike helped inspire colonized peoples to resist and overturn imperial rule.

Around the globe, the Cold War had an inescapable impact on decolonization. Liberation from colonial rule had long been a central goal for proponents of Communist world revolution. The Soviets and, after 1949, the Communist Chinese advocated rebellion in the developing world and promised to help end colonial exploitation and bring freedom and equality in a socialist state. They supported Communist independence movements with economic and military aid, and the guerrilla insurgent armed with a Soviet-made AK-47 machine gun became the new symbol of Marxist revolution.

Western Europe and particularly the United States offered a competing vision of independence, based on free-market economics and, ostensibly, liberal democracy—though the United States was often willing to support authoritarian regimes that voiced staunch anticommunism. Like the U.S.S.R., the United States extended economic aid and weaponry to decolonizing nations. The Americans promoted cautious moves toward self-determination in the context of containment, attempting to limit the influence of communism in newly liberated states.

After they had won independence, the leaders of the new nations often found themselves trapped between the superpowers, compelled to voice support for one bloc or the other. Many new leaders followed a third way, adopting a policy of **nonalignment**, remaining neutral in the Cold War and playing both sides for what they could get.

< **MAP 28.3 Decolonization in Africa and Asia, 1947 to the Present**
Divided primarily along religious lines into two states, British India led the way to political independence in 1947. Most African territories achieved statehood by the mid-1960s as European empires passed away, unlamented.

Where Indian nationalism drew on Western parliamentary liberalism, Chinese nationalism developed and triumphed in the framework of Marxist-Leninist ideology. After the withdrawal of the occupying Japanese army in 1945, China erupted again in open civil war. The authoritarian Guomindang (Kuomintang, National People's Party), led by Jiang Jieshi (traditionally called Chiang Kai-shek; 1887–1975), fought to repress the Chinese Communists, led by Mao Zedong (MA-OW zuh-DOUNG) and supported by a popular grassroots uprising. The Soviets gave Mao aid, and the Americans gave Jiang much more. Winning the support of the peasantry by promising to expropriate the holdings of the big landowners, the tougher, better-organized Communists forced the Guomindang to withdraw to the island of Taiwan in 1949. Mao and the Communists united China's 550 million inhabitants in a strong centralized state. Once in power, the "Red Chinese" began building a new society that adapted Marxism to Chinese conditions. The new government promoted land reform, extended education and health-care programs to the peasantry, and introduced Soviet-style five-year plans that boosted industrial production. It also brought Stalinist-style repression—mass arrests, forced-labor camps, and ceaseless propaganda campaigns—to the Chinese people.

Independence and Conflict in the Middle East

In some areas of the Middle East, the movement toward political independence went relatively smoothly. The French League of Nations mandates in Syria and Lebanon had collapsed during the Second World War, and Saudi Arabia and Transjordan had already achieved independence from Britain. But events in the British mandate of Palestine and in Egypt showed that decolonization in the Middle East could follow a dangerous and difficult path.

As part of the peace accords that followed the First World War, the British government had advocated a Jewish homeland alongside the Arab population (see Chapter 25). This tenuous compromise unraveled after World War II. Neither Jews nor Arabs were happy with British rule, and violence and terrorism mounted on both sides. In 1947 the frustrated British decided to leave Palestine, and the United Nations voted in a nonbinding resolution to divide the territory into two states—one Arab and one Jewish. The Jews accepted the plan and founded the state of Israel in 1948.

The Palestinians and the surrounding Arab nations viewed Jewish independence as a betrayal of their own interests, and they attacked the Jewish state as soon as it was proclaimed. The Israelis drove off the invaders and conquered more territory. Roughly nine hundred thousand Arab Palestinians fled or were expelled from their homes, creating a persistent refugee problem. Holocaust survivors from Europe streamed into Israel, as Theodor Herzl's Zionist dream came true (see Chapter 23). The next fifty years saw four more wars between the Israelis and the Arab states and innumerable clashes between Israelis and Palestinians.

The Arab defeat in 1948 triggered a powerful nationalist revolution in Egypt in 1952, led by the young army officer Gamal Abdel Nasser (1918–1970). The revolutionaries drove out the pro-Western king, and in 1954 Nasser became president of an Egyptian republic. A crafty politician, Nasser advocated nonalignment and expertly played the superpowers against each other, securing loans from the United States and purchasing Soviet arms.

In July 1956 Nasser abruptly nationalized the foreign-owned Suez Canal Company, the last symbol and substance of Western power in the Middle East. Infuriated, the British and the French, along with the Israelis, planned a secret military operation. The Israeli army invaded the Sinai Peninsula bordering the canal, and British and French bombers attacked Egyptian airfields. World opinion was outraged, and the United States feared that such a blatant show of imperialism would propel the Arab states into the Soviet bloc. The Americans joined with the Soviets to force the British, French, and Israelis to back down. Egyptian nationalism triumphed: Nasser got his canal, and Israel left the Sinai. The Suez crisis, a watershed in the history of European imperialism, showed that the European powers could no longer maintain their global empires and demonstrated the power and appeal of nonalignment.

Decolonization in Africa

In less than a decade, most of Africa won independence from European imperialism, a remarkable movement of world historical importance. In much of the continent south of the Sahara, decolonization proceeded relatively smoothly. Yet the new African states were quickly caught up in the struggles between the Cold War superpowers, and decolonization all too often left a lasting legacy of violence, economic decline, and political conflict (see Map 28.3).

Starting in 1957 most of Britain's African colonies achieved independence with little or no bloodshed and then entered a very loose association with Britain as members of the British Commonwealth. Ghana, Nigeria, Tanzania, and other countries gained independence in this way, but there were exceptions to this relatively smooth transfer of power. In Kenya, British forces brutally crushed the nationalist Mau Mau rebellion in the early 1950s, but nonetheless recognized Kenyan independence in 1963. In South Africa, the white-dominated government left the Commonwealth in 1961 and declared an independent republic in order to preserve apartheid—an exploitative system of racial segregation enforced by law.

The decolonization of the Belgian Congo was one of the great tragedies of the Cold War. Belgian leaders, profiting from the colony's wealth of natural resources and proud of their small nation's imperial status, maintained a system of apartheid there and dragged their feet in granting independence. These conditions sparked an anticolonial movement that grew increasingly aggressive in the late 1950s under the able leadership of the charismatic Patrice Lumumba. In January 1960 the Belgians gave in and hastily announced that the Congo would be independent six months later, a schedule that was irresponsibly fast. Lumumba was chosen prime minister in democratic elections, but when the Belgians pulled out on schedule, the new government was entirely unprepared. Chaos broke out when the Congolese army attacked Belgian military officers who remained in the country.

With substantial financial investments in the Congo, the United States and western Europe worried that the new nation might fall into Soviet hands. U.S. leaders cast Lumumba as a Soviet proxy, an oversimplification of his nonalignment policies, and migration, and new roles for women and youths had dramatic impacts on everyday life, albeit with different effects in the East Bloc and western Europe. Yet such large-scale changes had transformative effects on both sides of the iron curtain: social and cultural trends joined political and economic recovery to build stability in the postwar decades.

Changing Class Structures

The combination of rapid economic growth, growing prosperity and mass consumption, and the implementation of generous welfare policies went a long way toward creating a new society in Europe after the Second World War. Old class barriers relaxed, and class distinctions became fuzzier.

Changes in the structure of the middle class were particularly influential in this result. In the nineteenth and early twentieth centuries, the model for the middle class had been the independent, self-employed individual who owned a business or practiced a liberal profession such as law or medicine. Ownership of property—frequently inherited property—and strong family ties had often been the keys to wealth and standing within the middle class. After 1945 this pattern changed drastically in western Europe. A new breed of managers and experts—so-called white-collar workers—replaced property owners as the leaders of the middle class. The ability to serve the needs of a big organization largely replaced inherited property and family connections in determining an individual's social position in the middle and upper-middle classes. At the same time, the middle class grew massively and became harder to define.

There were several reasons for these developments. Rapid industrial and technological expansion and the consolidation of businesses created a powerful demand for technologists and managers in large corporations and government agencies. Moreover, the old propertied middle class lost control of many family-owned businesses. Numerous small businesses (including family farms) could no longer turn a profit, so their former owners regretfully joined the ranks of salaried employees.

Similar processes were at work in the Communist states of the East Bloc, where class leveling was an avowed goal of the authoritarian socialist state. The nationalization of industry, expropriation of property, and aggressive attempts to open employment opportunities to workers and equalize wage structures effectively reduced class differences. Communist Party members typically received better jobs and more pay than nonmembers, but by the 1960s the income differential between the top and bottom strata of East Bloc societies was far smaller than in the West.

In both East and West, managers and civil servants represented the model for a new middle class. Well paid and highly trained, often with backgrounds in engineering or accounting, these pragmatic experts were primarily concerned with efficiency and with practical solutions to concrete problems.

The structure of the lower classes also became more flexible and open. Continuing trends that began in the nineteenth century, large numbers of people left the countryside for the city. The population of one of the most traditional and least mobile groups in European society—farmers—drastically declined. Meanwhile, the number of industrial workers in western Europe also began to fall, as new jobs for white-collar and service employees grew rapidly. This change marked a significant transition in the world of labor. The welfare benefits extended by postwar governments also helped promote greater social equality because they raised lower-class living standards and were paid for in part by higher taxes on the wealthy. In general, European workers were better educated and more specialized than before, and the new workforce bore a greater resemblance to the growing middle class of salaried specialists than to traditional industrial workers.

Patterns of Postwar Migration

The 1850s to the 1930s had been an age of global migration, as countless Europeans moved around the continent and the world seeking economic opportunity or freedom from political or religious persecution (see Chapter 24). The 1950s and 1960s witnessed new waves of migration that had a significant impact on European society.

Some postwar migration took place within countries. Declining job prospects in Europe's rural areas encouraged many peasants and small farmers to seek better prospects in cities. In the poorer countries of Spain, Portugal, and Italy, millions moved to more developed regions of their own countries. The process was similar in the East Bloc, where the forced collectivization of agriculture and state subsidies for heavy industry opened opportunities in urban areas. And before the erection of the Berlin Wall in 1961, some 3.5 million East Germans moved to the Federal Republic of Germany, seeking higher pay and a better life.

Many other Europeans moved across national borders seeking work. The general pattern was from south to north. Workers from less developed countries like Italy, Spain, and socialist Yugoslavia moved to the industrialized north, particularly to West Germany, which—having lost 5 million people during the war—was in desperate need of able-bodied workers. In the 1950s and 1960s West Germany and other prosperous countries implemented **guest worker programs** designed to recruit much-needed labor for the booming economy. West Germany signed labor agreements with Italy, Greece, Spain, Portugal, Yugoslavia, Turkey, and the North African countries of Tunisia and Morocco. By the early 1970s there were 2.8 million foreign workers in Germany and another 2.3 million in France, where they made up 11 percent of the workforce.

Most guest workers were young, unskilled single men who labored for low wages in entry-level jobs and sent much of their pay to their families at home. According to government plans, these guest workers were supposed to return to their home countries after a specified period. Many built new lives, however, and, to the dismay of the authorities, chose to live permanently in their adoptive countries.

Europe was also changed by **postcolonial migration**, the movement of people from the former colonies and the developing world into prosperous Europe. In contrast to guest workers, who joined formal recruitment programs, postcolonial migrants could often claim citizenship rights from their former colonizers and moved spontaneously. Immigrants from the Caribbean, India, Africa, and Asia moved to Britain; people from North Africa, especially Algeria, and from sub-Saharan countries such as Cameroon and the Ivory Coast moved to France; Indonesians migrated to the Netherlands. Postcolonial immigrants also moved to eastern Europe, though in far fewer numbers.

Challenging the Postwar Order

1960–1991

AS EUROPE ENTERED THE 1960S, the political and social systems forged in the postwar era appeared sound. Centrist politicians in western Europe agreed that managed economic expansion, abundant jobs, and state-sponsored welfare benefits would continue to improve living standards and create social consensus. In the Soviet Union and the East Bloc, although conditions varied by country, modest economic growth and limited reforms amid continued political repression likewise contributed to a sense of stability. Cold War tensions diminished, and it seemed that a remarkable age of affluence would ease political differences and lead to social harmony.

By the late 1960s, however, this hard-won sense of stability had begun to disappear as popular protest movements in East and West arose to challenge dominant certainties. In the early 1970s the astonishing postwar economic advance ground to a halt, with serious consequences. In western Europe, a new generation of conservative political leaders advanced new policies to deal with economic decline and the growth of global competition. New political groups across the political spectrum, from feminists and environmentalists to national separatists and right-wing populists, added to the atmosphere of crisis and conflict.

In the East Bloc, leaders vacillated between central economic control and liberalization and left in place tight controls on social freedom, leading to stagnation and frustration. In the 1980s popular dissident movements emerged in Poland and other satellite states, and efforts to reform the Communist system in the Soviet Union from the top down snowballed out of control. In 1989, as revolutions swept away Communist rule throughout the entire Soviet bloc, the Cold War reached a dramatic conclusion.

Reform and Protest in the 1960s

| Focus Question | Why did the postwar consensus of the 1950s break down? |

In the early 1960s politics and society in prosperous western Europe remained relatively stable. East Bloc governments, bolstered by modest economic growth and state-enforced political conformity, and committed to generous welfare benefits for their citizens, maintained control. As the 1960s progressed, politics in the West shifted noticeably to the left, and Social Democratic governments worked to normalize East-West relations. Amid this more liberalized society, a youthful counterculture emerged among the children of affluence to critique the status quo. In the East Bloc, Khrushchev's limited reforms also inspired rebellions. Thus activists around the world rose in protest against the perceived inequalities of both capitalism and communism, leading to dramatic events in 1968, exemplified in Paris and Prague.

Cold War Tensions Thaw

In western Europe, the first two decades of postwar reconstruction had been overseen for the most part by center-right Christian Democrats, who successfully maintained postwar stability around Cold War politics, free-market economics with limited state intervention, and welfare provisions (see Chapter 28). In the mid- to late 1960s, buoyed by the rapidly expanding economy, much of western Europe moved politically to the left. Socialists entered the Italian government in 1963. In Britain, the Labour Party returned to power in 1964, after thirteen years in opposition. In West Germany, the aging postwar chancellor Konrad Adenauer (1876–1967) retired in 1963, and in 1969 Willy Brandt (1913–1992) became the first Social Democratic West German chancellor; his party would govern Germany until 1982. There were important exceptions to this general trend. Though the tough-minded, independent French president Charles de Gaulle resigned in 1969, the centrist Gaullists remained in power in France until 1981. And in Spain, Portugal, and Greece, authoritarian regimes remained in power until the mid-1970s.

Despite these exceptions, the general leftward drift eased Cold War tensions. Though the Cold War continued to rage outside Europe and generally defined relations between the Soviet Union and the United States, western European leaders took major steps to normalize relations with the East Bloc. Willy Brandt took the lead. In December 1970 he flew to Poland for the signing of a historic treaty of reconciliation. In a dramatic moment rich in symbolism, Brandt laid a wreath at the tomb of the Polish unknown soldier and another at the monument commemorating the armed uprising of Warsaw's Jewish ghetto against occupying Nazi armies. Standing before the ghetto memorial, a somber Brandt fell to his knees as if in prayer. "I wanted," Brandt said later, "to ask pardon in the name of our people for a million-fold crime which was committed in the misused name of the Germans."[1]

Brandt's gesture at the Warsaw Ghetto memorial and the treaty with Poland were part of his broader, conciliatory foreign policy termed **Ostpolitik** (German for "Eastern policy"). Brandt aimed at nothing less than a comprehensive peace settlement for of domestic entertainment while vacuum cleaners, refrigerators, and washing machines transformed women's housework. Studies later showed that these new "laborsaving devices" caused women to spend even more time cleaning and cooking to new exacting standards, but at the time electric appliances were considered indispensable to what contemporaries called a "modern lifestyle." The establishment of U.S.-style self-service supermarkets across western Europe changed the way food was produced, purchased, and prepared, and threatened to force independent bakers, butchers, and neighborhood grocers out of business.

Intellectuals and cultural critics greeted the age of affluence with a chorus of criticism. Some worried that rampant consumerism created a bland conformity that wiped out regional and national traditions. The great majority of ordinary people, they argued, now ate the same foods, wore the same clothes, and watched the same programs on television, sapping creativity and individualism. Others complained bitterly that these changes threatened to Americanize Europe. Neither group could do much to stop the spread of consumer culture.

Worries about the Americanization of Europe were overstated. European nations preserved distinctive national cultures even during the consumer revolution, but social change nonetheless occurred. The moral authority of religious doctrine lost ground before the growing materialism of consumer society. In predominantly Protestant lands—Great Britain, Scandinavia, and parts of West Germany—church membership and regular attendance both declined significantly. Even in traditionally Catholic countries, such as Italy, Ireland, and France, outward signs of popular belief seemed to falter. At the **Second Vatican Council**, convened from 1962 to 1965, Catholic leaders agreed on a number of reforms meant to democratize and renew the church and broaden its appeal. They called for new openness in Catholic theology and declared that masses would henceforth be said in local languages rather than in Latin, which few could understand. These resolutions, however, did little to halt the slide toward secularization.

Family ties also weakened in the age of affluence. The number of adults living alone grew remarkably, men and women married later, the nuclear family became smaller and more mobile, and divorce rates rose rapidly. By the 1970s the baby boom of the postwar decades was over, and population growth leveled out across Europe and even began to decline in prosperous northwestern Europe.

The Counterculture Movement

The dramatic emergence of a youthful counterculture, which came of age in the mid-1960s, accompanied growing economic prosperity. The "sixties generation" angrily criticized the comforts of the affluent society and challenged the social and political status quo.

What accounts for the emergence of the counterculture? Simple demographics played an important role. Young soldiers returning home after World War II in 1945 eagerly established families, and the next two decades brought a dramatic increase in the number of births per year in Europe and North America. The children born during the postwar baby boom grew up in an era of political liberalism and unprecedented material abundance. They remembered the horrors of totalitarian government that caused World War II and watched as colonial peoples forged new paths to freedom during the decades of decolonization. The counterculture challenged the growing conformity that seemed to be an inherent part of consumer society and the unequal distribution of wealth that arose from market economics. In short, when the baby boomers came of age in the 1960s, they had the education to see problems like inequality and the lack of social justice, as well as the freedom from want to act on their concerns.

Counterculture movements in both Europe and the United States drew much inspiration from the American civil rights movement. In the late 1950s and early 1960s African Americans effectively challenged institutionalized inequality using the courts, public demonstrations, sit-ins, and boycotts, and thereby threw off a deeply entrenched system of segregation and repression. The landmark Civil Rights Act of 1964, which prohibited discrimination in public services and on the job, and the Voting Rights Act of 1965, which guaranteed all African Americans the right to vote, were the crowning achievements of the long struggle against racism.

If dedicated African Americans and their white supporters could successfully reform entrenched power structures, student leaders reasoned, so could they. In 1964 and 1965, at the University of California–Berkeley, students consciously adapted the tactics of the civil rights movement, including demonstrations and sit-ins, to challenge limits on free speech and academic freedom at the university. Their efforts were contagious. Soon students across the United States and western Europe, where rigid rules controlled student activities at overcrowded universities, were engaged in active protests. The youth movement had come of age, and it mounted a determined challenge to the Western consensus.

Dreaming of economic justice and freer, more tolerant societies, student activists in western Europe and the United States embraced new forms of Marxism, creating a multidimensional and heterogeneous movement that came to be known as the **New Left**. In general, adherents of the various strands of the New Left felt that Marxism in the Soviet Union had been perverted to serve the needs of a repressive totalitarian state but that Western capitalism, with its cold disregard for social equality, was little better. What was needed was a more humanitarian style of socialism that could avoid the worst excesses of both capitalism and Soviet-style communism. New Left critics further attacked what they saw as the conformity of consumer society. The "culture industry," which controlled mass culture, fulfilled only false needs and so contributed to the dehumanization they saw at the core of Western society.

Such rarefied ideas fascinated student intellectuals, but much counterculture activity revolved around a lifestyle rebellion that seemed to have broad appeal. Politics and daily life merged, a process captured in the popular 1960s slogan "the personal is political." Nowhere was this more obvious than in the so-called sexual revolution. The 1960s brought frank discussion about sexuality, a new willingness to engage in premarital sex, and a growing acceptance of homosexuality. Sexual experimentation was facilitated by the development of the birth control pill, which helped eliminate the risk of unwanted pregnancy for millions of women after it went on the market in most western European countries in the 1960s. Much of the new openness about sex crossed generational lines, but for the young the idea of sexual emancipation was closely linked to radical politics. Sexual openness and "free love," the sixties clashed with police in the West and East Blocs as well. Berlin and London witnessed massive, sometimes-violent demonstrations, students in Warsaw protested government censorship, and youths in Prague were in the forefront of the attempt to radically reform communism from within (see page 952).

One of the most famous and perhaps most far-reaching of these revolts occurred in France in May 1968, when massive student protests coincided with a general strike that brought the French economy to a standstill. The "May Events" began when a group of students dismayed by conservative university policies and inspired by New Left ideals occupied buildings at the University of Paris. Violent clashes with police followed. When police tried to clear the area around the university on the night of May 10, a pitched street battle took place. At the end of the night, 460 arrests had been made by police, 367 people were wounded, and about 200 cars had been burned by protesters. The slogans that appeared as graffiti scrawled on walls in Paris captured the New Left spirit: "Power to the Imagination"; "Be Realistic, Demand the Impossible"; "Forget Everything You've Been Taught. Start by Dreaming."

The "May Events" might have been a typically short-lived student protest against overcrowded universities, U.S. involvement in Vietnam, and the abuses of capitalism, but the demonstrations triggered a national revolt. By May 18 some 10 million workers were out on strike, and protesters occupied factories across France. For a brief moment, it seemed as if counterculture dreams of a revolution from below would come to pass. The French Fifth Republic was on the verge of collapse, and a shaken President de Gaulle surrounded Paris with troops.

In the end, however, the New Left goals of the radical students contradicted the bread-and-butter demands of the striking workers. When the government promised workplace reforms, including immediate pay raises, the strikers returned to work. President de Gaulle dissolved the French parliament and called for new elections. His conservative party won almost 75 percent of the seats, showing that the majority of the French people supported neither general strikes nor student-led revolutions. The universities shut down for the summer, administrators enacted educational reforms, and the protests had dissipated by the time the fall semester began. The May Events marked the high point of counterculture activism in Europe; in the early 1970s the movement declined.

As the political enthusiasm of the counterculture waned, committed activists disagreed about the best way to continue to fight for social change. Some followed what West German student leader Rudi Dutschke called "the long march through the institutions" and began to work for change from within the system. They ran for office and joined the emerging feminist, antinuclear, and environmental groups that would gain increasing prominence in the following decades (see pages 958–961).

Others followed a more radical path. Across Europe, but particularly in Italy and West Germany, fringe New Left groups tried to bring radical change by turning to violence and terrorism. Like the American Weather Underground, the Italian Red Brigades and the West German Red Army Faction robbed banks, bombed public buildings, and kidnapped and killed business leaders and conservative politicians. After spasms of violence in the late 1970s — in Italy, for example, the Red Brigades murdered former prime minister Aldo Moro in 1978 — security forces succeeded in incarcerating most of the terrorist leaders, and the movement fizzled out.

Counterculture protests generated a great deal of excitement and trained a generation of activists. In the end, however, the protests of the sixties generation resulted in short-term and mostly limited political change. Lifestyle rebellions involving sex, drugs, and rock music certainly expanded the boundaries of acceptable personal behavior, but they hardly overturned the existing system.

The 1960s in the East Bloc

The building of the Berlin Wall in 1961 suggested that communism was there to stay, and NATO's refusal to intervene showed that the United States and western Europe basically accepted the premise. In the West, the wall became a potent symbol of the repressive nature of communism in the East Bloc, where halting experiments with economic and cultural liberalization brought only limited reform.

East Bloc economies clearly lagged behind those of the West, exposing the weaknesses of central planning. To address these problems, in the 1960s Communist governments implemented cautious forms of decentralization and limited market policies. The results were mixed. Hungary's so-called New Economic Mechanism, which broke up state monopolies, allowed some private retail stores, and encouraged private agriculture, was perhaps most successful. East Germany's New Economic System, inaugurated in 1963, also brought moderate success, though it was reversed when the government returned to centralization in the late 1960s. In other East Bloc countries, however, economic growth flagged.

Recognizing that the overwhelming emphasis on heavy industry was generating popular discontent, Communist planning commissions began to redirect resources to the consumer sector. Again, the results varied. By 1970, for example, ownership of televisions in the more developed nations of East Germany, Czechoslovakia, and Hungary approached that of the affluent nations of western Europe, and other consumer goods were also more available. In Poland, by contrast, the economy stagnated in the 1960s. In the more conservative Albania and Romania, where leaders held fast to Stalinist practices, provision of consumer goods faltered. In general, ordinary people in the East Bloc grew increasingly tired of the shortages of basic consumer goods that seemed an endemic problem in Communist society.

In the 1960s Communist regimes cautiously granted cultural freedoms. In the Soviet Union, the cultural thaw allowed dissidents like Aleksandr Solzhenitsyn to publish critical works of fiction (see Chapter 28), and this relative tolerance spread to other East Bloc countries as well. In East Germany, for example, during the Bitterfeld Movement—named after a conference of writers, officials, and workers held at Bitterfeld, an industrial city south of Berlin—the regime encouraged intellectuals to take a more critical view of life in the East Bloc, as long as they did not directly oppose communism. Author Christa Wolf's novel *Divided Heaven* (1963) is a classic example of the genre. Though the protagonist's boyfriend emigrates to West Germany in search of better work conditions and she sees very real problems in her small-town factory, she remains committed to building socialism.

Cultural openness only went so far, however. The most outspoken dissidents were harassed and often forced to emigrate to the West; other critics contributed to the rise of an underground *samizdat* (SAH-meez-daht) literature that emerged in the Soviet at $35 an ounce. In the postwar decades the United States spent billions of dollars on foreign aid and foreign wars, weakening the value of American currency. In 1971 President Nixon attempted to reverse this trend by abruptly stopping the exchange of U.S. currency for gold. The value of the dollar fell sharply, and inflation accelerated worldwide. Countries abandoned fixed rates of currency exchange, and great uncertainty replaced postwar predictability in international trade and finance.

Even more damaging to the global economy was the dramatic reversal in the price and availability of energy. The great postwar boom had been fueled in large part by cheap oil from the Middle East. The fate of the developed world was thus increasingly linked to this turbulent region, where strains began to show in the late 1960s. In 1967, in the Six-Day War, Israel quickly defeated Egypt, Jordan, and Syria and occupied more of the former territories of Palestine, angering Arab leaders and exacerbating anti-Western feeling in the Arab states. Economics fed tension between Arab states and the West. Over the years **OPEC**, the Organization of Petroleum Exporting Countries, had watched the price of crude oil decline consistently compared with the rising price of Western manufactured goods. OPEC decided to reverse that trend by presenting a united front against Western oil companies.

The stage was thus already set for a revolution in energy prices when Egypt and Syria launched a surprise attack on Israel in October 1973, setting off the fourth Arab-Israeli war. With the help of U.S. weapons, Israel again achieved a quick victory. In response, the Arab members of OPEC declared an embargo on oil shipments to the United States and other industrialized nations that supported Israel in the war, and they simultaneously raised oil prices. Within a year, crude oil prices quadrupled. Western nations realized that the rapid price increase was economically destructive, but together they did nothing. Thus governments, industry, and individuals dealt piecemeal with the so-called oil shock—a "shock" that turned out to be an earthquake.

Coming on the heels of the upheaval in the international monetary system, the revolution in energy prices plunged the world into its worst economic decline since the 1930s. Energy-intensive industries that had driven the economy up in the 1950s and 1960s now dragged it down. Unemployment rose, productivity and living standards declined, and inflation soared. Economists coined a new term—**stagflation**—to describe the combination of low growth and high inflation that drove the worldwide recession. By 1976 a modest recovery was in progress, but in 1979 a fundamentalist Islamic revolution overthrew the shah of Iran. When oil production in that country collapsed, the price of crude oil doubled again, and the world economy succumbed to its second oil shock. Unemployment and inflation rose dramatically before another uneven recovery began in 1982.

Anxious observers, recalling the disastrous consequences of the Great Depression, worried that the European Common Market would disintegrate in the face of severe economic dislocation and that economic nationalism would halt steps toward European unity. Yet the Common Market continued to attract new members. In 1973 Britain finally joined, as did Denmark and Ireland. After replacing authoritarian regimes with democratic governments in the 1970s, Greece joined in 1981, and Portugal and Spain entered in 1986. The nations of the Common Market cooperated more closely in international undertakings, and the movement toward western European unity stayed alive.

The developing world was hit hard by slow growth, and the global economic downturn widened the gap between rich and poor countries. Governments across South America, sub-Saharan Africa, and South Asia borrowed heavily from the United States and western Europe in attempts to restructure their economies, setting the stage for a serious international debt crisis. At the same time, the East Asian countries of Japan and then Singapore, South Korea, and Taiwan started exporting high-tech consumer goods to the West. Competition from these East Asian "tiger economies," whose labor costs were comparatively low, shifted manufacturing jobs away from the highly industrialized countries of northern Europe and North America.

Even though the world economy slowly began to recover in the 1980s, western Europe could no longer create enough jobs to replace those that were lost. By the end of the 1970s, the foundations of economic growth in the industrialized West had begun shifting to high-tech information industries, such as computing and biotechnology, and to services, including medicine, banking, and finance. Scholars spoke of the shift as the arrival of "the information age" or **postindustrial society**. Technological advances streamlined the production of many goods, making many industrial jobs superfluous. In western Europe, heavy industry, such as steel, mining, automobile manufacture, and shipbuilding, lost ground. Factory closings led to the emergence of "rust belts"—formerly prosperous industrialized areas that were now ghost lands, with vacant lots, idle machinery, and empty inner cities. The highly industrialized Ruhr district in northwest West Germany and the once-extensive factory regions around Birmingham (Great Britain) and Detroit, Michigan, were classic examples. By 1985 the unemployment rate in western Europe had risen to its highest level since the Great Depression. Nineteen million people were jobless.

The crisis struck countless ordinary people, and there were heartbreaking human tragedies—bankruptcies, homelessness, and mental breakdowns. The punk rock songs of the late 1970s captured the mood of hostility and cynicism among young people. Yet on the whole, the welfare system fashioned in the postwar era prevented mass suffering and degradation. The responsive, socially concerned national state undoubtedly contributed to the preservation of political stability and democracy in the face of economic difficulties that might have brought revolution and dictatorship in earlier times.

With the commitment of governments to supporting social needs, government spending in most European countries continued to rise sharply during the 1970s and early 1980s. In 1982 western European governments spent an average of more than 50 percent of all national income on social programs, as compared to only 37 percent fifteen years earlier. Across western Europe, people were willing to see their governments increase spending, but they resisted higher taxes. This imbalance contributed to the rapid growth of budget deficits, national debts, and inflation. While this increased spending was generally popular, a powerful reaction against government's ever-increasing role had set in by the late 1970s that would transform governance in the 1980s.

The New Conservatism

The transition to a postindustrial society was led to a great extent by a new generation of conservative political leaders, who believed they had viable solutions for restructuring the relations between the state and the economy. During the thirty years following

Challenges and Victories for Women

The 1970s marked the arrival of a diverse and widespread feminist movement devoted to securing genuine gender equality and promoting the general interests of women. Three basic reasons accounted for this dramatic development. First, ongoing changes in underlying patterns of motherhood and paid work created novel conditions and new demands (see Chapter 28). Second, a vanguard of feminist intellectuals articulated a powerful critique of gender relations, which stimulated many women to rethink their assumptions and challenge the status quo. Third, taking a lesson from the civil rights movement in the United States and protests against the Vietnam War, dissatisfied women recognized that they had to band together if they were to influence politics and secure fundamental reforms.

Feminists could draw on a long heritage of protest, stretching back to the French Revolution and the women's movements of the late nineteenth century (see Chapters 19 and 22). They were also inspired by recent writings, such as the foundational book *The Second Sex* (1949) by the French writer and philosopher Simone de Beauvoir (1908–1986). Beauvoir, who worked closely with the existentialist philosopher Jean-Paul Sartre, analyzed the position of women within the framework of existential thought. Drawing on history, philosophy, psychology, biology, and literature, Beauvoir argued

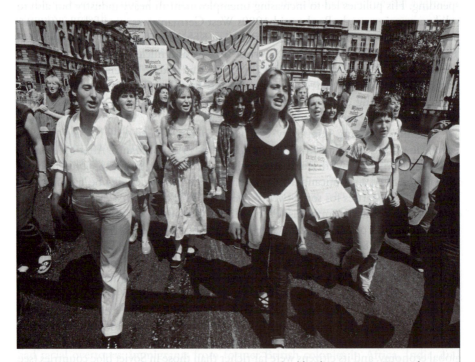

Feminist Protest in London, 1982   In a protest organized by the grassroots Women's Fightback Network, women march for equal pay and employment opportunity. (Roberto Koch/ Contrasto/Redux)

that women had almost always been trapped by particularly inflexible and limiting conditions. Only through courageous action and self-assertive creativity could a woman become a completely free person and escape the role of the inferior "other" that men had constructed for her gender.

The Second Sex inspired a generation of women intellectuals, and by the late 1960s and the 1970s "second-wave feminism" had spread through North America and Europe. In the United States, writer and organizer Betty Friedan's (1921–2006) pathbreaking study *The Feminine Mystique* (1963) pointed the way. Friedan called attention to the stifling aspects of women's domestic life, devoted to the service of husbands and children. Housewives lived in a "gilded cage," she concluded, because they were usually not allowed to hold professional jobs or become mature adults and genuine human beings. In 1966 Friedan helped found the National Organization for Women (NOW) to press for women's rights. NOW flourished, growing from seven hundred members in 1967 to forty thousand in 1974.

Many other women's organizations rose in Europe and North America. The diverse groups drew inspiration from Marx, Freud, or political liberalism, but in general feminists attacked patriarchy (the domination of society by men) and sexism (the inequalities faced by women simply because they were female). Throughout the 1970s a proliferation of publications, conferences, and institutions devoted to women's issues reinforced the emerging international movement. Advocates of women's rights pushed for new statutes governing the workplace: laws against discrimination, acts requiring equal pay for equal work, and measures such as maternal leave and affordable day care designed to help women combine careers and family responsibilities.

The movement also addressed gender and family questions, including the right to divorce (in some Catholic countries), legalized abortion, the needs of single mothers, and protection from rape and physical violence. In almost every country, the effort to decriminalize abortion served as a catalyst in mobilizing an effective, self-conscious women's movement—and, as in the United States, in creating opposition to it.

In countries that had long placed women in a subordinate position, the legal changes were little less than revolutionary. In Italy, for example, new laws abolished restrictions on divorce and abortion that had been strengthened by Mussolini and defended energetically by the Catholic Church in the postwar era. By 1988 divorce and abortion were common in Italy, which had the lowest birthrate in Europe. While the women's movement of the 1970s won new rights for women, subsequently it became more diffuse, a victim of both its successes and the resurgence of an antifeminist opposition.

The Rise of the Environmental Movement

Like feminism, environmentalism had roots in the 1960s counterculture. Early environmentalists drew inspiration from writers like U.S. biologist Rachel Carson, whose book *Silent Spring*, published in 1962, was quickly translated into twelve European languages. Carson's chilling title referred to a future spring, when people in developed society would wake up and hear no birds singing, because they had all been killed by the rampant use of pesticides. The book had a striking impact on the growth of environmental movements in Europe and North America.

and 1980s. Populist leaders like Jean-Marie Le Pen, the founder of the French National Front, opposed European integration and called for a return to traditional national customs, often at the expense of the non-European immigrants who were a growing proportion of western Europe's working-class population (see Chapter 28). New right-wing politicians promoted themselves as the champions of ordinary (white) workers, complaining that immigrants swelled welfare rolls and stole jobs from native-born Europeans. Though their programs at times veered close to open racism, in the 1980s they began to win seats in national parliaments.

The Decline of "Developed Socialism"

Focus Question	What led to the decline of Soviet power in the East Bloc?

In the postwar decades the Communist states of the East Bloc had achieved a shaky social consensus based on a rising standard of living, an extensive welfare system, and political repression. When the Marxist utopia still had not arrived in the 1970s, Communist leaders told citizens that an egalitarian society would be realized sometime in the future; until then, they would have to accept the system as it was. In the long run, leaders promised, "developed socialism" would prove better than capitalism. Such claims were an attempt to paper over serious tensions in socialist society. Everyday life could be difficult. Limits on personal and political freedoms encouraged the growth of determined reform movements, and a revival of Cold War tensions accompanied the turn to the right in the United States and western Europe in the 1980s.

When Mikhail Gorbachev burst on the scene in 1985, the new Soviet leader opened an era of reform that was as sweeping as it was unexpected. Although many believed that Gorbachev would soon fall from power, his reforms rapidly transformed Soviet culture and politics and drastically reduced Cold War tensions. But communism, which Gorbachev wanted so desperately to revitalize, continued to stagnate and decline.

State and Society in the East Bloc

By the 1970s many of the professed goals of communism had been achieved. Communist leaders in central and eastern Europe and the Soviet Union adopted the term **developed socialism** (sometimes called "real existing socialism") to describe the accomplishments of their societies. Agriculture had been thoroughly collectivized, and though Poland was an exception, 80 to 90 percent of Soviet and East Bloc farmers worked on huge collective farms. Industry and business had been nationalized, and only a small portion of the economy remained in private hands in most East Bloc countries. The state had also done much to level class differences. Though some people—particularly party members—clearly had greater access to opportunities and resources, the gap between rich and poor was far smaller than in the West. An extensive system of government-supported welfare benefits included free medical care, guaranteed employment, inexpensive public transportation, and large subsidies for rent and food.

Everyday life under developed socialism was defined by an uneasy mixture of outward conformity and private disengagement—or apathy. The Communist Party dominated public life. Party-led mass organizations for youth, women, workers, and sports groups staged huge rallies, colorful festivals, and new holidays that exposed citizens to the values of the socialist state. East Bloc citizens might grudgingly participate in party-sponsored public events, but at home, and in private, they often grumbled about and sidestepped the Communist authorities.

East Bloc living standards were well above those in the developing world, but below those in the West. Centralized economic planning continued to lead to shortages, and people complained about the poor quality and lack of choice of the most basic goods. Under these conditions, informal networks of family and friends helped people find hard-to-get goods and offered support beyond party organizations. Though the secret police persecuted those who openly challenged the system and generated mountains of files on ordinary people, they generally left alone those who demonstrated the required conformity.

Women in particular experienced the contradictions of the socialist system. Official state policy guaranteed equal rights for women and encouraged them to join the workforce in positions formerly reserved for men, and an extensive system of state-supported child care freed women to accept these employment opportunities and eased the work of parenting. Yet women rarely made it into the upper ranks of business or politics, and they faced the same double burden as those in the West (see Chapter 28). In addition, government control of the public sphere meant that the independent groups dedicated to feminist reform that emerged in the West in the 1970s developed more slowly in the East Bloc and the Soviet Union. Women could complain to the Communist authorities about unequal or sexist conditions at work or at home, but until the 1980s they could not build private, nongovernmental organizations to lobby for change.

Though everyday life was fairly comfortable in the East Bloc, a number of deeply rooted structural problems undermined popular support for Soviet-style communism. These fundamental problems would contribute to the re-emergence of civic dissent and ultimately to the revolutions of 1989. East Bloc countries—like those in the West—were hard hit by the energy crisis and stagflation of the 1970s. For a time, access to inexpensive oil from the Soviet Union, which had huge resources, helped prop up faltering economies, but this cushion began to fall apart in the 1980s. For a number of reasons, East Bloc leaders refused to make the economic reforms that might have made developed socialism more effective.

First, a move toward Western-style postindustrial society would have required fundamental changes to the Communist system. As in the West, it would have hurt the already-tenuous living standard of industrial workers. But Communist East Bloc states were publicly committed to supporting the working classes, including coal miners, shipbuilders, and factory and construction workers. To pursue the neoliberal reforms undertaken in the West would have undermined popular support for the government among these basic constituencies, which was already tenuous at best.

Second, East Bloc regimes refused to cut spending on the welfare state because that was, after all, one of the proudest achievements of socialism. Third, the state continued to provide subsidies to heavy industries such as steel and mining. High-tech industries failed to take off in Communist Europe, in part because the West maintained embargoes on technology exports. The industrial goods produced in the East Bloc became increasingly uncompetitive in the new global system. To stave off total collapse, governments borrowed massive amounts of hard currency from Western banks and governments, helping to convince ordinary people that communism was bankrupt, and setting up a cycle of indebtedness that helped bring down the entire system in 1989.

Economic decline was not the only reason people increasingly questioned one-party Communist rule. The best career and educational opportunities were reserved for party members or handed out as political favors, leaving many talented people underemployed and resentful. Tight controls on travel continually called attention to the burdens of daily life in a repressive society. The one-party state had repeatedly quashed popular reform movements, retreated from economic liberalization, and jailed or exiled dissidents, even those who wished to reform communism from within. Though many East Bloc citizens still found the promise of Marxist egalitarian socialism appealing, they increasingly doubted the legitimacy of Soviet-style communism: the dream of distributing goods "from each according to his means, to each according to his needs" (as Marx had once put it) hardly made up for the great structural weaknesses of developed socialism.

Dissent in Czechoslovakia and Poland

Stagnation in the East Bloc encouraged small numbers of dedicated people to try to change society from below. Developments in Czechoslovakia and Poland were the most striking and significant, and determined protest movements re-emerged in both countries in the mid-1970s. Remembering a history of violent repression and Soviet invasion, dissenters carefully avoided direct challenges to government leaders. Nor did they try to reform the Communist Party from within, as Dubček and his followers had attempted in Prague in 1968. Instead, they worked to build a civil society from below — to create a realm of freedom beyond formal politics, where civil liberties and human rights could be exercised independent of the Communist system.

In Czechoslovakia in 1977 a small group of citizens, including future Czechoslovak president Václav Havel (VAH-slahf HAH-vuhl) (1936–2011), signed a manifesto that came to be known as Charter 77. The group criticized the government for ignoring the human rights provision of the Helsinki Accords and called on Communist leaders to respect civil and political liberties. They also criticized censorship and argued for improved environmental policies. Despite immediate state repression, the group challenged passive acceptance of Communist authority and voiced public dissatisfaction with developed socialism.

In Poland, an unruly satellite from the beginning, the Communists had failed to dominate society to the extent seen elsewhere in the East Bloc. Most agricultural land remained in private hands, and the Catholic Church thrived. The Communists also failed to manage the economy effectively. The 1960s brought stagnation, and in 1970 Poland's working class rose again in angry protest. A new Communist leader came to power, and he wagered that massive inflows of Western capital and technology, especially from rich and now-friendly West Germany, could produce a Polish economic miracle. Instead, bureaucratic incompetence and the first oil shock in 1973 sent the economy into a nosedive. Workers, intellectuals, and the church became increasingly restive. Then the real Polish miracle occurred: Cardinal Karol Wojtyla (KAH-rohl voy-TIH-wah), archbishop of Kraków, was elected pope in 1978 as John Paul II. In June 1979 he returned to Poland from Rome, preaching love of Christ and country and the "inalienable rights of man." The pope drew enormous crowds and electrified the Polish nation.

In August 1980 strikes broke out across Poland; at the gigantic Lenin Shipyards in Gdansk (formerly known as Danzig) sixteen thousand workers laid down their tools and occupied the plant. As other workers joined "in solidarity," the strikers advanced the ideals of civil society, including the right to form trade unions free from state control, freedom of speech, release of political prisoners, and economic reforms. After the strikers occupied the shipyard for eighteen days, the government gave in and accepted the workers' demands in the Gdansk Agreement. In a state in which the Communist Party claimed to rule on behalf of the proletariat, a working-class revolt had won an unprecedented, even revolutionary, victory.

Led by feisty Lenin Shipyards electrician and devout Catholic Lech Wałęsa (lehk vah-WEHN-suh) (b. 1943), the workers proceeded to organize a free and democratic trade union called **Solidarity**. As had been the case in Czechoslovakia, Solidarity worked cautiously to shape an active civil society. Joined by intellectuals and supported by the Catholic Church, it became a national union with a full-time staff of 40,000 and 9.5 million members. Cultural and intellectual freedom blossomed in Poland, and Solidarity enjoyed tremendous public support. But Solidarity's leaders pursued a self-limiting revolution, meant only to defend the concessions won in the Gdansk Agreement. Solidarity thus practiced moderation, refusing to challenge directly the Communist monopoly on political power. At the same time, the ever-present threat of calling a nationwide strike gave them real leverage in ongoing negotiations with the Communist bosses.

Solidarity's combination of strength and moderation postponed a showdown, as the Soviet Union played a waiting game of threats and pressure. After a confrontation in March 1981, Wałęsa settled for minor government concessions, and Solidarity dropped plans for a massive general strike. Criticism of Wałęsa's moderate leadership gradually grew, and Solidarity lost its cohesiveness. The worsening economic crisis also encouraged radical actions among disgruntled Solidarity members, and the Polish Communist leadership shrewdly denounced the union for promoting economic collapse and provoking a possible Soviet invasion. In December 1981 Wojciech Jaruzelski (VOY-chehk yahr-oo-ZEHL-skee), the general who headed Poland's Communist government, suddenly proclaimed martial law and arrested Solidarity's leaders.

Outlawed and driven underground, Solidarity survived in part because of the government's unwillingness (and probably its inability) to impose full-scale terror. Moreover, millions of Poles decided to continue acting as if they were free — the hallmark of civil society — even though they were not. Cultural and intellectual life remained extremely vigorous as the Polish economy continued to deteriorate. Thus popular support for outlawed Solidarity remained strong under martial law in the 1980s, preparing the way for the union's political rebirth toward the end of the decade.

The rise and survival of Solidarity showed that ordinary Poles would stubbornly struggle for greater political and religious liberty, cultural freedom, trade-union rights, patriotic nationalism, and a more humane socialism. Not least, Solidarity's challenge encouraged fresh thinking in the Soviet Union, ever the key to lasting change in the East Bloc.

From Détente Back to Cold War

The Soviets and the leaders of the Soviet satellite states faced challenges from abroad as optimistic hopes for détente in international relations gradually faded in the late 1970s. Brezhnev's Soviet Union ignored the human rights provisions of the Helsinki agreement, and East-West political competition remained very much alive outside Europe. Many Americans became convinced that the Soviet Union was taking advantage of détente, steadily building up its military might and pushing for political gains and revolutions in Africa, Asia, and Latin America. The Soviet invasion of Afghanistan in December 1979, designed to save an increasingly unpopular Marxist regime, alarmed the West. Many Americans feared that the oil-rich states of the Persian Gulf would be next, and once again they looked to the NATO alliance and military might to thwart Communist expansion.

President Jimmy Carter (U.S. pres. 1977–1981) tried to lead NATO beyond verbal condemnation of the Soviet Union and urged economic sanctions against it, but only Great Britain among the European allies supported the American initiative. The alliance showed the same lack of concerted action when the Solidarity movement rose in Poland. Some observers concluded that NATO had lost the will to act decisively in dealing with the Soviet bloc.

The Atlantic alliance endured, however, and the U.S. military buildup launched by Carter in his last years in office was greatly accelerated by President Reagan, who was swept into office in 1980 by a wave of patriotism and economic discontent. The new American leadership acted as if the military balance had tipped in favor of the Soviet Union, which Reagan anathematized as the "evil empire." Increasing defense spending enormously, the Reagan administration deployed short-range nuclear missiles in western Europe and built up the navy to preserve American power in the post-Vietnam age. The broad shift toward greater conservatism in the 1980s gave Reagan invaluable allies in western Europe. Margaret Thatcher worked well with Reagan and was a forceful advocate for a revitalized Atlantic alliance, and under Helmut Kohl West Germany likewise worked with the United States to coordinate military and political policy toward the Soviet bloc.

Gorbachev's Reforms in the Soviet Union

Cold War tensions aside, the Soviet Union's Communist elite seemed safe from any challenge from below in the early 1980s. A well-established system of administrative controls stretched downward from the central ministries and state committees to provincial cities and from there to factories, neighborhoods, and villages. At each level of this massive state bureaucracy, the overlapping hierarchy of the 17.5-million-member Communist Party maintained tight state control. Organized opposition was impossible, and average people left politics to the bosses.

Although the massive state and party bureaucracy safeguarded the elite, it promoted widespread apathy and stagnation. When the ailing Brezhnev finally died in 1982, his successor, the long-time chief of the secret police, Yuri Andropov (1914–1984), tried to invigorate the system. Relatively little came of his efforts, but they combined with a sharply worsening economic situation to set the stage for the emergence in 1985 of Mikhail Gorbachev (b. 1931), the most vigorous Soviet leader in a generation.

A lawyer and experienced Communist Party official, Gorbachev was smart, charming, and tough. He believed in communism, but realized that the Soviet Union was failing to keep up with the West and was losing its superpower status. Thus Gorbachev tried to revitalize the Soviet system with fundamental reforms. An idealist who wanted to improve conditions for ordinary citizens, Gorbachev understood that the enormous expense of the Cold War arms race had had a disastrous impact on living conditions in the Soviet Union; improvement at home, he realized, required better relations with the West.

In his first year in office, Gorbachev attacked corruption and incompetence in the bureaucracy and consolidated his power. He condemned alcoholism and drunkenness, which were deadly scourges of Soviet society, and worked out an ambitious reform program designed to transform and restructure the economy in order to provide for the real needs of the Soviet population. To accomplish this economic restructuring, or **perestroika** (pehr-uh-STROY-kuh), Gorbachev and his supporters permitted an easing of government price controls on some goods, more independence for state enterprises, and the creation of profit-seeking private cooperatives to provide

Mikhail Gorbachev
Soviet president Mikhail Gorbachev (center, with red tie) walks with a crowd of delegates to the twenty-eighth and last congress of the Soviet Communist Party in July 1990. Gorbachev took office in 1985 with the goal of reforming communism from within. His plans spiraled out of control. By 1991 the Soviet Union and the East Bloc had disintegrated into independent, noncommunist states. (© Pascal Le Segretain/Sygma/Corbis)

personal services. These timid reforms initially produced a few improvements, but shortages grew as the economy stalled at an intermediate point between central planning and free-market mechanisms. By late 1988 widespread consumer dissatisfaction posed a serious threat to Gorbachev's leadership and the entire reform program.

Gorbachev's bold and far-reaching campaign for greater freedom of expression was much more successful. Very popular in a country where censorship, dull uniformity, and outright lies had long characterized public discourse, the newfound openness, or **glasnost** (GLAZ-nohst), of the government and the media marked an astonishing break with the past. Long-banned émigré writers sold millions of copies of their works in new editions, while denunciations of Stalin and his terror became standard fare in plays and movies. In another example of glasnost in action, after several days of hesitation the usually secretive Soviet government issued daily reports on the 1986 nuclear plant accident at Chernobyl, one of the worst environmental disasters in history. Indeed the initial openness in government pronouncements quickly went much further than Gorbachev intended and led to something approaching free speech, a veritable cultural revolution.

Democratization was another element of reform. Beginning as an attack on corruption in the Communist Party, it led to the first free elections in the Soviet Union since 1917. Gorbachev and the party remained in control, but a minority of critical independents was elected in April 1989 to a revitalized Congress of People's Deputies. Millions of Soviets then watched the new congress for hours on television as Gorbachev and his ministers saw their proposals debated and even rejected. Thus millions of Soviet citizens took practical lessons in open discussion, critical thinking, and representative government. An active civil society was emerging—a new political culture at odds with the Communist Party's monopoly of power and control.

Democratization also ignited demands for greater political and cultural autonomy and even national independence among non-Russian minorities living in the fifteen Soviet republics. The Soviet population numbered about 145 million ethnic Russians and 140.6 million non-Russians, including 55 million Muslims in the Central Asian republics and over 44 million Ukrainians. Once Gorbachev opened the doors to greater public expression, tensions flared between central Soviet control and national separatist movements. Independence groups were particularly active in the Baltic Soviet socialist republics of Lithuania, Latvia, and Estonia; in western Ukraine; and in the Transcaucasian republics of Armenia, Azerbaijan, and Georgia.

Finally, Gorbachev brought reforms to the field of foreign affairs. He withdrew Soviet troops from Afghanistan in February 1989 and sought to reduce East-West tensions. Of enormous importance, the Soviet leader sought to halt the arms race with the United States and convinced President Reagan of his sincerity. In a Washington summit in December 1987, the two leaders agreed to eliminate all land-based intermediate-range missiles in Europe, setting the stage for more arms reductions. Gorbachev pledged to respect the political choices of the peoples of East Bloc countries, repudiating the Brezhnev Doctrine and giving encouragement to reform movements in Poland, Czechoslovakia, and Hungary. By early 1989 it seemed that if Gorbachev held to his word, the tragic Soviet occupation of eastern Europe might wither away, taking the long Cold War with it once and for all.

The Revolutions of 1989

Focus Question	Why did revolution sweep through the East Bloc in 1989, and what were the immediate consequences?

In 1989 Gorbachev's plan to reform communism from within snowballed out of control. A series of largely peaceful revolutions swept across eastern Europe, overturning existing Communist regimes (Map 29.2). The revolutions of 1989 had momentous consequences. First, the peoples of the East Bloc gained political freedom after about forty years of dictatorial Communist rule. Second, West Germany absorbed its East German rival, and a reunified Germany emerged as the most influential country in Europe. Third, as Gorbachev's reforms boomeranged, a complicated anticommunist revolution swept through the Soviet Union, and the multinational empire broke into a large Russia and fourteen other independent states. The Cold War came to an end, and the United States suddenly stood as the world's only superpower.

The Collapse of Communism in the East Bloc

The collapse of Communist rule in the Soviet satellite states surprised many Western commentators, who had expected Cold War divisions to persist for many years. Yet while the revolutions of 1989 appeared to erupt quite suddenly, long-standing, structural weaknesses in the Communist system had in some ways made revolt inevitable. East Bloc economies never really recovered from the economic catastrophe of the 1970s. State spending on outdated industries and extensive welfare systems led to massive indebtedness to Western banks and undermined economic growth, while limits on personal and political freedoms fueled a growing sense of injustice (see page 963).

In this general climate of economic stagnation and popular anger, Solidarity and the Polish people led the way to revolution. In 1988 widespread strikes, raging inflation, and the outlawed Solidarity's refusal to cooperate with the military government had brought Poland to the brink of economic collapse. Poland's frustrated Communist leaders offered to negotiate with Solidarity if the outlawed union's leaders could get the strikers back to work and resolve the political stalemate and the economic crisis. The subsequent agreement in April 1989 legalized Solidarity and declared that a large minority of representatives to the Polish parliament would be chosen by free elections that June. Still guaranteed a parliamentary majority and expecting to win many of the contested seats, the Communists believed that their rule was guaranteed for four years and that Solidarity would keep the workers in line.

Lacking access to the state-run media, Solidarity succeeded nonetheless in mobilizing the country and winning all but one of the contested seats in an overwhelming victory. Moreover, many angry voters crossed off the names of unopposed party candidates, so that the Communist Party failed to win the majority its leaders had anticipated. Solidarity members jubilantly entered the Polish parliament, and a dangerous stalemate quickly developed. But Lech Wałęsa, a gifted politician who always repudiated violence, adroitly obtained a majority by securing the allegiance of two minor procommunist parties that had been part of the coalition government after

MAP 29.2 Democratic Movements in Eastern Europe, 1989
Countries that had been satellites in the orbit of the Soviet Union began to set themselves free in 1989.

World War II. In August 1989 Tadeusz Mazowiecki (Ta-DAY-ush MAH-zoe-vee-ETS-key) (1927–2013), the editor of one of Solidarity's weekly newspapers, was sworn in as Poland's new noncommunist prime minister.

In its first year and a half, the new Solidarity government cautiously introduced revolutionary political changes. It eliminated the hated secret police, the Communist ministers in the government, and finally Communist Party leader Jaruzelski himself, but it did so step-by-step in order to avoid confrontation with the army or the Soviet Union. In economics, however, the Solidarity government was radical from the beginning. It applied economic shock therapy, an intense dose of neoliberal policy designed to make a clean break with state planning and move quickly to market mechanisms and private property (see Chapter 30). Thus the government abolished controls on many prices on January 1, 1990, and reformed the monetary system with a big bang.

Hungary followed Poland. Hungary's moderate Communist Party leader János Kádár (KAH-dahr) had permitted liberalization of the rigid planned economy after the 1956 uprising in exchange for political loyalty and continued Communist control. In May 1988, in an effort to retain power by granting modest political concessions, the party replaced the ill and aging Kádár with a reform-minded Communist. But liberal opposition groups rejected piecemeal progress, and in the summer of 1989 the Hungarian Communist Party agreed to hold free elections the following March. Welcoming Western investment and moving rapidly toward multiparty democracy, Hungary's Communists now enjoyed considerable popular support, and they believed, quite mistakenly, that they could defeat the opposition in the upcoming elections.

In an effort to strengthen their support at home, the Hungarians opened their border to East Germans and tore down the barbed wire curtain separating Hungary from Austria. Tens of thousands of dissatisfied East German "vacationers" then poured into Hungary, crossed into Austria as refugees, and continued on to immediate re-settlement in thriving West Germany.

The flight of East Germans fed the rapid growth of a homegrown, spontaneous protest movement in East Germany. Workers joined intellectuals, environmentalists, and Protestant ministers in huge candlelight demonstrations, arguing that a democratic but still socialist East Germany was both possible and desirable. These "stayers" failed to convince the "leavers," however, who continued to depart en masse. In a desperate attempt to stabilize the situation, the East German government opened the Berlin Wall in November 1989, and people danced for joy atop that grim symbol of the prison state. A new, reformist government took power and scheduled free elections.

In Czechoslovakia, Communist rule began to dissolve peacefully in November to December 1989. This so-called **Velvet Revolution** grew out of popular demonstrations led by students and joined by intellectuals and a dissident playwright-turned-moral-revolutionary named Václav Havel (1936–2011). When the protesters took control of the streets, the Communist government resigned, leading to a power-sharing arrangement termed the "Government of National Understanding." As 1989 ended, the Czechoslovakian assembly elected Havel president.

In Romania, popular revolution turned violent and bloody. There the dictator Nicolae Ceaușescu (chow-SHESS-koo) (1918–1989) had long combined tight party control with stubborn independence from Moscow. Faced with mass protests in December 1989, Ceaușescu ordered his ruthless security forces to quell unrest, sparking an armed uprising. Perhaps 750 people were killed in the fighting; the numbers were often exaggerated. After the dictator and his wife were captured and executed by a military court, Ceaușescu's forces were defeated. A coalition government emerged, although the legacy of Ceaușescu's long and oppressive rule left a troubled country.

German Unification and the End of the Cold War

The dissolution of communism in East Germany that began in 1989 reopened the "German question" and raised the threat of renewed Cold War conflict over Germany. Taking power in October 1989, East German reform Communists, enthusiastically

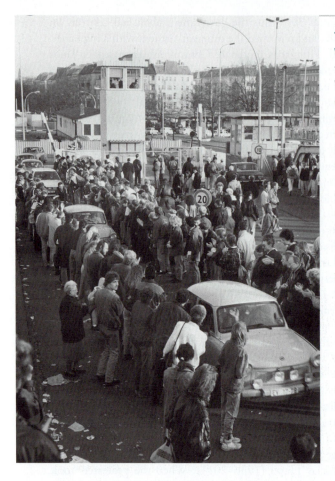

The Opening of the Berlin Wall The sudden and unanticipated opening of the Berlin Wall on November 10, 1989, dramatized the spectacular fall of communism throughout east-central Europe. West Berliners welcomed the East Germans who piled into their "Trabi" automobiles to cross the border. Millions of East German citizens traveled into West Berlin and the Federal Republic of Germany in the first few days after the surprise relaxation of inter-German travel controls. (© DPA/Courtesy Everett Collection)

supported by leading intellectuals and former dissidents, wanted to preserve socialism by making it genuinely democratic and responsive to the needs of the people. They argued for a "third way" that would go beyond the failed Stalinism they had experienced and the ruthless capitalism they saw in the West. These reformers supported closer ties with West Germany but feared unification, hoping to preserve a distinct East German identity with a socialist system.

Over the next year, however, East Germany was absorbed into an enlarged West Germany, much as a faltering company is swallowed by a stronger rival and ceases to exist. Three factors were particularly important in this outcome. First, in the first week after the Berlin Wall was opened, almost 9 million East Germans—roughly half of the total population—poured across the border into West Germany. Almost all returned to their homes in the east, but the joy of warm welcomes from long-lost friends and relatives and the exhilaration of crossing a long-closed border aroused long-dormant hopes of unity among ordinary citizens.

Second, West German chancellor Helmut Kohl and his closest advisers skillfully exploited the historic opportunity handed them. Sure of support from the United States, whose leadership he had steadfastly followed, in November 1989 Kohl presented a ten-point plan for step-by-step unification in cooperation with both

East Germany and the international community. Kohl then promised the struggling citizens of East Germany an immediate economic bonanza—a generous though limited exchange of East German marks in savings accounts and pensions into much more valuable West German marks. This offer helped popularize the conservative-liberal Alliance for Germany, a well-financed political party established in East Germany with the support of Kohl's West German Christian Democrats. In March 1990 the Alliance won almost 50 percent of the votes in an East German parliamentary election, outdistancing the Party of Democratic Socialism (the renamed East German Communist Party) (16 percent) and the revived Social Democratic Party (22 percent). The Alliance for Germany quickly negotiated an economic and political union on favorable terms with Kohl. The rapid pace of reunification quickly overwhelmed those who argued for the preservation of an independent socialist society in East Germany.

Third, in the summer of 1990 the crucial international aspect of German unification was successfully resolved. Unification would once again make Germany the strongest state in central Europe and would directly affect the security of the Soviet Union. But Gorbachev swallowed hard—Western cartoonists showed Stalin turning over in his grave—and negotiated the best deal he could. In a historic agreement signed by Gorbachev and Kohl in July 1990, Kohl solemnly affirmed Germany's peaceful intentions and pledged never to develop nuclear, biological, or chemical weapons. The Germans sweetened the deal by promising enormous loans to the hard-pressed Soviet Union. In October 1990 East Germany merged into West Germany, forming a single nation under the West German laws and constitution.

The peaceful reunification of Germany accelerated the pace of agreements to liquidate the Cold War. In November 1990 delegates from twenty-two European countries joined those from the United States and the Soviet Union in Paris and agreed to a scaling down of all their armed forces. The delegates also solemnly affirmed that all existing borders in Europe, including those of unified Germany and the emerging Baltic States, were legal and valid. The Paris Accord was for all practical purposes a general peace treaty bringing an end to both World War II and the Cold War.

Peace in Europe encouraged the United States and the Soviet Union to scrap a significant portion of their nuclear weapons in a series of agreements. In September 1991 a confident President George H. W. Bush canceled the around-the-clock alert status for American bombers outfitted with atomic bombs, and a floundering Gorbachev quickly followed suit with his own forces. For the first time in four decades, Soviet and American nuclear weapons were not standing ready for mutual destruction.

The Disintegration of the Soviet Union

As 1990 began, the tough work of dismantling some forty-five years of Communist rule had begun in all but two East Bloc states—tiny Albania and the vast Soviet Union. The great question now became whether the Soviet Union would follow its former satellites.

In February 1990, as competing Russian politicians noisily presented their programs and nationalists in the non-Russian republics demanded autonomy or independence from the Soviet Union, the Communist Party suffered a stunning defeat in local elections throughout the country. As in East Bloc countries, democrats and anticommunists won clear majorities in the leading cities of the Russian Soviet Federative Socialist Republic (S.F.S.R.), by far the largest republic in the Soviet Union. Moreover, in Lithuania the people elected an uncompromising nationalist as president, and the newly chosen parliament declared Lithuania an independent state.

Gorbachev responded by placing an economic embargo on Lithuania, but he refused to use the army to crush the separatist government. The result was a tense political stalemate that undermined popular support for Gorbachev. Separating himself further from Communist hardliners, Gorbachev asked Soviet citizens to ratify a new constitution that formally abolished the Communist Party's monopoly of political power and expanded the power of the Congress of People's Deputies. While retaining his post as party secretary, Gorbachev then convinced a majority of deputies to elect him president of the Soviet Union.

Despite his victory, Gorbachev's power continued to erode, and his unwillingness to risk a universal suffrage election for the presidency strengthened his great rival, Boris Yeltsin (1931–2007). A radical reform Communist, Yeltsin embraced the democratic movement, and in May 1990 he was elected parliamentary leader of the Russian Soviet Republic. He boldly announced that Russia would put its interests first and declare its independence from the Soviet Union, broadening the base of the anticommunist movement by joining the patriotism of ordinary Russians with the democratic aspirations of big-city intellectuals. Gorbachev tried to save the Soviet Union with a new treaty that would link the member republics in a looser, freely accepted confederation, but six of the fifteen Soviet republics rejected his plan.

Opposed by democrats and nationalists, Gorbachev was also challenged by the Communist old guard. In August 1991 a gang of hardliners kidnapped him and his family in the Caucasus and tried to seize the Soviet government. The attempted coup collapsed in the face of massive popular resistance that rallied around Yeltsin. As the spellbound world watched on television, Yeltsin defiantly denounced the rebels from atop a stalled tank in central Moscow and declared the "rebirth of Russia." The army supported Yeltsin, and Gorbachev was rescued and returned to power as head of the Soviet Union.

The leaders of the coup had wanted to preserve Communist power, state ownership, and the multinational Soviet Union; they succeeded in destroying all three. An anticommunist revolution swept Russia as Yeltsin and his supporters outlawed the Communist Party and confiscated its property. Locked in a personal and political duel with Gorbachev, Yeltsin and his democratic allies declared Russia independent, withdrew from the Soviet Union, and changed the country's name from the Russian Soviet Republic to the Russian Federation. All the other Soviet republics also withdrew. Gorbachev resigned on December 25, 1991, and the next day the Supreme Soviet dissolved itself, marking the end of the Soviet Union. The independent republics of the old Soviet Union then established a loose confederation, the Commonwealth of Independent States, which played only a minor role in the 1990s.

NOTES

1. Quoted in Kessing's Research Report, *Germany and East Europe Since 1945: From the Potsdam Agreement to Chancellor Brandt's "Ostpolitik"* (New York: Charles Scribner's Sons, 1973), pp. 284–285.
2. M. Mitterauer, *The History of Youth* (Oxford: Basil Blackwell, 1992), p. 40.
3. See R. Guha, *Environmentalism: A Global History* (New York: Longman, 2000), p. 79.

LOOKING BACK LOOKING AHEAD

The unexpected collapse of Communist Europe capped three decades of turbulent change. In the 1960s the counterculture challenged the status quo and steered western Europe to the left as reformists attempted (but failed) to liberalize East Bloc communism. In the 1970s a global recession had devastating effects in the West and East Blocs alike. In the 1980s conservative Western leaders pushed neoliberal plans to revive growth and meet growing global competition. In the East Bloc, structural problems and spontaneous revolt brought down communism, dissolved the Soviet Union, and ended the Cold War.

With the world economy on the road to recovery and new free-market systems in place across the former East Bloc, all of Europe would now have the opportunity to enter the information age. After forty years of Cold War division, the continent regained an underlying unity as faith in democratic government and market economics became the common European creed. In 1991 hopes for peaceful democratic progress were almost universal. According to philosopher Francis Fukuyama, the world had reached "the end of history" — the end of the Cold War, he argued, would lead to peaceful development based on growing tolerance, free-market economics, and liberal democracy.

The post–Cold War years saw the realization of some of these hopes, but the new era brought its own problems and tragedies. New ethnic and nationalist tensions flared, leading to a disastrous civil war in the former Yugoslavia. The struggle to rebuild the shattered societies of the former East Bloc countries was far more difficult than the people living in them had hoped. Poor economic growth continued to complicate attempts to deal with the wide-open global economy. New conflicts with Islamic nations in the Middle East involved some European nations in war. The European Union expanded, but political disagreements, environmental issues, increased anxiety about non-Western immigrants, and a host of other problems undermined moves toward true European unity. History was far from over — the realities of a post–Cold War world continued to produce difficult challenges as Europe entered the twenty-first century.

MAKE CONNECTIONS

Think about the larger developments and continuities within and across chapters.

1. How did the revolts that shook western European countries and the East Bloc develop out of issues left unresolved in the 1950s era of postwar reconstruction (Chapter 28)?

2. Both East and West Blocs faced similar economic problems in the 1970s, yet communism collapsed in the East and capitalism recovered. How do you account for the difference? Were economic problems the main basis for popular opposition to communism?

3. What were some of the basic ideas behind the neoliberal economic policies that emerged in the West in the 1970s and 1980s? Why are they still popular today?

Chapter Review

IDENTIFY KEY TERMS

Identify and explain the significance of each item below.

Ostpolitik (p. 943)

détente (p. 944)

Second Vatican Council (p. 946)

New Left (p. 947)

Brezhnev Doctrine (p. 953)

OPEC (p. 954)

stagflation (p. 954)

postindustrial society (p. 955)

neoliberalism (p. 956)

privatization (p. 956)

developed socialism (p. 962)

Solidarity (p. 965)

perestroika (p. 967)

glasnost (p. 968)

Velvet Revolution (p. 971)

REVIEW THE MAIN IDEAS

Answer the focus questions from each section of the chapter.

1. Why did the postwar consensus of the 1950s break down? (p. 943)

2. What were the consequences of economic decline in the 1970s? (p. 953)

3. What led to the decline of Soviet power in the East Bloc? (p. 962)

4. Why did revolution sweep through the East Bloc in 1989, and what were the immediate consequences? (p. 969)

CHRONOLOGY

1961	Building of Berlin Wall suggests permanence of the East Bloc
1962–1965	Second Vatican Council
1963	Wolf publishes *Divided Heaven;* Friedan publishes *The Feminine Mystique*
1964	Civil Rights Act in the United States
1964–1973	Peak of U.S. involvement in Vietnam War
1966	Formation of National Organization for Women (NOW)
1968	Soviet invasion of Czechoslovakia; "May Events" protests in France
1971	Founding of Greenpeace
1973	OPEC oil embargo
1975	Helsinki Accords
1979	Margaret Thatcher becomes British prime minister; founding of West German Green Party; Soviet invasion of Afghanistan
1985	Mikhail Gorbachev named Soviet premier
1987	United States and Soviet Union sign arms reduction treaty
1989	Soviet withdrawal from Afghanistan
1989–1991	Fall of communism in eastern Europe
December 1991	Dissolution of the Soviet Union

30

Life in an Age of Globalization

1990 TO THE PRESENT

ON NOVEMBER 9, 2009, THE TWENTIETH ANNIVERSARY of the opening of the Berlin Wall, jubilant crowds filled the streets around the Brandenburg Gate at the former border between East and West Berlin. World leaders and tens of thousands of onlookers applauded as former Polish president Lech Wałęsa pushed over a line of one thousand eight-foot-tall foam dominos, symbolizing the collapse of communism.

The crowd had reason to celebrate. The revolutions of 1989 had opened a new chapter in European and world history. Capitalism spread across the former East Bloc and Soviet Union (now the Russian Federation and fourteen other republics), along with the potential for political reform. Some of these hopes were realized, but the new era also brought problems and tragedies. The process of remaking formerly Communist societies was more difficult than expected. At the same time, across the West and around the world, globalization, the digital revolution, and the ongoing flow of immigrants into western Europe had impacts both positive and negative.

As Europeans faced serious tensions and complex changes in the twenty-first century, they also came together to form a strong new European Union that would prove a formidable economic competitor to the United States. Ties between western Europe and the United States began to loosen, but Europe and North America—as well as the rest of the world—confronted common challenges. Finding solutions to problems in the Middle East and addressing challenges regarding economic growth, energy needs, the environment, and human rights would require not only innovation but also creative cooperation.

Reshaping the Soviet Union and the Former East Bloc

| Focus Question | How did life change in Russia and the former East Bloc countries after 1989? |

Establishing stable democratic governments in the former East Bloc countries and the diverse territories of the Soviet Union, now divided into fifteen republics with Russia at its core, was not easy. While Russia initially moved toward economic reform and political openness, by 2010 it had returned to its authoritarian traditions. Stability proved elusive in many of the former Soviet Socialist Republics, and conflict undermined Russia's relations with some of these new nation-states.

The transformation of the Communist East Bloc was also difficult. After a period of tense reform, some countries, such as Poland, the Czech Republic, and Hungary, established relatively prosperous democracies and joined NATO and then the European Union. Others, such as Romania and Bulgaria, lagged behind. In multiethnic Yugoslavia, the collapse of communism and the onset of a disastrous civil war broke the country apart. All these changes produced mixed results for ordinary folk.

Economic Shock Therapy in Russia

Politics and economics were closely intertwined in Russia after the dissolution of the Soviet Union (see Chapter 29). President Boris Yeltsin (pres. 1991–1999), his democratic supporters, and his economic ministers wanted to create conditions that would prevent a return to communism and right the faltering economy. Following the example of Poland (see Chapter 29), and agreeing with neoliberal Western advisers who argued that a quick turn to free markets would speed economic growth, Russian reformers opted in January 1992 for liberalization at breakneck speed.

To implement the plan, the Russians abolished price controls on most consumer goods, with the exception of bread, vodka, oil, and public transportation. The government launched a rapid privatization program, selling formerly state-owned industries and agricultural concerns to private investors. As a result, thousands of factories and mines were turned over to new private companies. In an attempt to share the wealth privatization was expected to generate, each citizen received a voucher worth 10,000 rubles (about $22) to buy stock in these private companies. Ownership of these formerly public assets, however, usually remained in the hands of the old bosses—the managers and government officials from the Communist era—undermining the reformers' goal of worker participation.

President Yeltsin and his economic advisers believed that shock therapy would revive production and bring widespread prosperity. The results were quite different. Prices increased 250 percent on the very first day and kept on soaring, increasing by a factor of twenty-six in the course of 1992. At the same time, production fell a staggering 20 percent. Nor did the situation stabilize quickly. After 1995 inflation still raged, though at slower rates, and output continued to fall. According to most estimates, Russia produced from one-third to one-half less in 1996 than it had in 1991. The Russian economy crashed again in 1998 in the wake of Asia's financial crisis.

Rich and Poor in Postcommunist Russia   A woman sells knitted scarves in front of a department store window in Moscow in September 2005. The collapse of the Soviet Union and the use of shock therapy to reform the Russian economy created new poverty as well as new wealth. (Sovfoto/UIG via Getty Images)

Rapid economic liberalization worked poorly in Russia for several reasons. Soviet industry had been highly monopolized and strongly tilted toward military goods. Production of many items had been concentrated in one or two gigantic factories or in interconnected combines. With privatization, these powerful state monopolies became powerful private monopolies that cut production and raised prices in order to maximize profits. Moreover, Yeltsin's government handed out enormous subsidies to corporate managers and bureaucrats, ostensibly to reinforce faltering firms and avoid bankruptcies, but also to buy political allegiance. New corporate leaders included criminals who intimidated would-be rivals in attempts to prevent the formation of competing businesses.

Runaway inflation and poorly executed privatization brought a profound social revolution to Russia. The new capitalist elite — the so-called Oligarchs — acquired great wealth and power, while large numbers of people fell into abject poverty and the majority struggled to make ends meet. Managers, former Communist officials, and financiers who came out of the privatization process with large shares of the old state monopolies stood at the top. The Oligarchs, Yeltsin's main supporters, maintained control with corrupt business practices and rampant cronyism. The new elite held more wealth than ever before.

At the other extreme, the vast majority of people saw their savings become practically worthless. Pensions lost much of their value, living standards drastically declined, and many people sold their personal goods to survive. Under these conditions, effective representative government failed to develop, and many Russians came to equate democracy with the corruption, poverty, and national decline they experienced throughout the 1990s. Yeltsin became increasingly unpopular; only the backing of the Oligarchs kept him in power.

Russian Revival Under Vladimir Putin

This widespread disillusionment set the stage for the rise of Vladimir Putin (POO-tihn) (b. 1952), who was elected president as Yeltsin's chosen successor in 2000 and re-elected in a landslide in March 2004. A colonel in the secret police during the Communist era, Putin maintained relatively liberal economic policies but re-established semi-authoritarian political rule. Critics labeled Putin's system an "imitation democracy," and indeed a façade of democratic institutions masked authoritarian rule from above in postcommunist Russia.[1] Putin's government maintained control with rigged elections, weak parliamentary rule, the intimidation of political opponents, and the distribution of state-owned public assets to win support of the new elite. Yet Putin's argument that the transition to free markets required strong political rule to control corruption and prevent a collapse into complete chaos resonated with ordinary Russians worried about the disintegration of the Communist state. The president enjoyed strong popular support, at least in the first years of his rule.

Putin's government combined authoritarian politics with economic reform. The regime clamped down on the excesses of the Oligarchs, lowered corporate and business taxes, and re-established some government control over key industries. Such reforms—aided greatly by high world prices for oil and natural gas, Russia's most important exports—led to a decade of economic expansion, encouraging the growth of a new middle class. In 2008, however, the global financial crisis and a rapid drop in the price of oil caused a downturn, and the Russian stock market collapsed. The government initiated a $200 billion rescue plan, and the economy stabilized and returned to modest growth in 2010.

During his first two terms as president, Putin's domestic and foreign policies proved immensely popular with a majority of Russians. His housing, education, and health-care reforms significantly improved living standards. Putin repeatedly evoked the glories of Russian history, expressed pride in the accomplishments of the Soviet Union, and downplayed the abuses of the Stalinist system; he thus capitalized on popular feelings of Russian patriotism. In addition, the Russian president centralized power in the Kremlin, increased military spending, and expanded the secret police. Putin's carefully crafted manly image and his forceful international diplomacy soothed the country's injured pride and symbolized its national revival.

In foreign relations, the president generally championed assertive anti-Western policies in an attempt to bolster Russia's status as a great Eurasian power and world player. Putin forcefully opposed the expansion of NATO into the former East Bloc and regularly challenged U.S. and NATO foreign policy goals. In the Syrian civil war that broke out in 2011, for example, Russian backing of Syrian president

Conflicts in the Caucasus

RUSSIAN FEDERATION

CHECHNYA, Grozny — Declared independence 1991; ongoing war with Russia

SOUTH OSSETIA — Breakaway republic established 2008

■ Ongoing conflict

DAGESTAN

AZER.

ARMENIA

GEORGIA · Tbilisi

ABKHAZIA

AJARIA

TURKEY

Black Sea

MONGOLIA

CHINA

200 miles

200 kilometers

KAZAKHSTAN

Astana (since 1998)

Almaty (to 1997)

Bishkek

KYRGYZSTAN

Lake Balkhash

Tashkent

UZBEKISTAN

Dushanbe

TAJIKISTAN

Aral Sea

TURKMENISTAN

Ashgabat

AFGHANISTAN

IRAN

Caspian Sea

Baku

AZERBAIJAN

GEORGIA

Tbilisi

Yerevan

ARMENIA

See inset map

IRAQ

SYRIA

LEBANON

CYPRUS

TURKEY

Crimea

Black Sea

MOLDOVA

Chisinau

ROMANIA

UKRAINE

Kiev

Chernobyl

Minsk

BELARUS

POLAND

LITHUANIA

Vilnius

LATVIA

Riga

ESTONIA

Tallinn

(RUS. FED.)

SWEDEN

FINLAND

Baltic Sea

St. Petersburg

Moscow

RUSSIAN FEDERATION

Volga R.

Volga R.

Ural R.

Kama R.

Ob R.

Irtysh R.

ARCTIC OCEAN

— Boundary of the Soviet Union, 1991

BELARUS Member of the CIS, 1991

N E S W

Bashar al-Assad flew in the face of U.S. attempts to depose him. Putin's support in summer 2015 for a deal to limit Iran's nuclear capabilities marked a rare moment of Russian cooperation with the United States, the EU, and the United Nations.

Putin's Russia has taken an aggressive and at times interventionist stance toward the Commonwealth of Independent States, a loose confederation of most of the former Soviet republics (Map 30.1). The annexation of the Crimea in 2014 and support for insurrectionist pro-Russian rebels in eastern Ukraine are only the latest examples.

Putin's government moved decisively to limit political opposition at home. The 2003 arrest and imprisonment for tax evasion and fraud of the corrupt oil billionaire Mikhail Khodorkovsky, an Oligarch who had openly supported opposition parties, showed early on that Putin and his United Russia Party would use state powers to stifle dissent. Though the Russian constitution guarantees freedom of the press, the government cracked down on the independent media. Using a variety of tactics, officials and pro-government businessmen influenced news reports and intimidated critical journalists. The suspicious murder in 2006 of journalist Anna Politkovskaya, a prominent critic of the government's human rights abuses and its war in Chechnya, reinforced Western worries that the country was returning to Soviet-style press censorship.

Putin stepped down when his term limits expired in 2008. His handpicked successor, Dmitry Medvedev (mehd-VEHD-yehf) (b. 1965), easily won election that year and then appointed Putin prime minister, leading observers to believe that the former president was still the dominant figure. This suspicion was confirmed when Putin won the presidential election of March 2012 with over 60 percent of the vote. International observers agreed that the election itself was democratic, but reported irregularities during the vote-counting process. Some fifteen thousand protesters marched through downtown Moscow to protest election fraud and the authoritarian aspects of Putin's rule, and demonstrations accompanied the president's inauguration that May.

Tensions between political centralization and openness continue to define Russia's difficult road away from communism. On one hand, Putin's return to the presidency seemed to reinforce Russia's system of authoritarian central control. On the other, the fact that mass assemblies and marches against the president took place with relatively little repression attests to some degree of political openness and new limits on Russian state power in the twenty-first century.

< **MAP 30.1 Russia and the Successor States, 1991–2015**
After the failure of an attempt in August 1991 to depose Gorbachev, an anticommunist revolution swept the Soviet Union. The republics that formed the Soviet Union each declared their sovereignty and independence, with Russia, under President Boris Yeltsin, being the largest. Eleven of the fourteen republics then joined with Russia to form a loose confederation called the Commonwealth of Independent States, but the integrated economy of the Soviet Union dissolved into separate national economies, each with its own goals and policies. Conflict continued to simmer over these goals and policies, as evidenced by the ongoing civil war in Chechnya, the struggle between Russia and Georgia over South Ossetia, the Russian annexation of the Crimea, and the Ukrainian separatist movement.

Coping with Change in the Former East Bloc

Developments in the former East Bloc paralleled those in Russia in important ways. The former satellites worked to replace state planning and socialism with market mechanisms and private property. Western-style electoral politics also took hold.

New leaders across the former East Bloc faced similar economic problems: how to restructure Communist economic systems and move state-owned businesses and property into private hands. Under Soviet-style communism, central planners determined production and distribution goals and often set wage and price controls; now former East Bloc countries would adopt market-based economic systems. In addition, industries, businesses, and farms, considered the "people's property" and managed by the state in the name of the entire population, would now be privatized.

The methods of restructuring and privatization varied from country to country. Poland's new leaders turned to "shock therapy," the most rapid and comprehensive form of economic transformation, advocated by neoliberal Western institutions, including the International Monetary Fund and the World Bank. Starting in 1990, the Poles liberalized prices and trade policies, raised taxes, cut spending to reduce budget deficits, and quickly sold state-owned industries to private investors. As they would in Russia a few years later, these radical moves at first brought high inflation and a rapid decline in living standards, which generated public protests and strikes. But because the plan had the West's approval, Poland received Western financial support that eased the pain of transition. By the end of the decade, the country had one of the strongest economies in the former East Bloc.

Other countries followed alternate paths. Czechoslovakia took a more gradual approach. As in Russia, the Czechoslovak state issued vouchers to its citizens, which they could use to bid for shares in privatized companies. In Slovenia, one of the countries carved out of the former Yugoslavia, privatization included the transfer of up to 60 percent of company ownership to employees. In Estonia, reformers experimented with employee ownership, vouchers, and worker cooperatives. Compared to Poland's approach, privatization in all three countries was slower, continued more practices from the Communist past, and caused less social disruption.

Economic growth in the former Communist countries was varied, but most observers agreed that Poland, the Czech Republic, and Hungary were the most successful. Each met the critical challenge of economic reconstruction more successfully than did Russia, and each could claim to be the economic leader in the former East Bloc, depending on the criteria selected. The reasons for these successes included considerable experience with limited market reforms before 1989, flexibility and lack of dogmatism in government policy, and an enthusiastic embrace of capitalism by a new entrepreneurial class. In its first five years of reform, Poland created twice as many new businesses as did Russia in a comparable period, despite having only a quarter of Russia's population.

Poland, the Czech Republic, and Hungary also did far better than Russia in creating new civic institutions, legal systems, and independent media outlets that reinforced political freedom and national revival. Lech Wałęsa in Poland and Václav Havel in Czechoslovakia were elected presidents of their countries and proved as remarkable in power as in opposition (see Chapter 29). After Czechoslovakia's Velvet Revolution in 1989, the Czechoslovak parliament accepted a "velvet divorce" in 1993, when Slovakian nationalists wanted to break off and form their own state, creating the separate Czech and Slovak Republics. Above all, and in sharp contrast to Russia, the popular goal of adopting the liberal democratic values of western Europe reinforced political moderation and compromise. In 1999 Poland, Hungary, and the Czech Republic were accepted into NATO, and in 2004 they and Slovakia gained admission to the European Union (EU) (see page 991).

Romania and Bulgaria lagged behind in the postcommunist transition. Western traditions were weaker there, and both countries were poorer than their more successful neighbors. Romania and Bulgaria did make progress after 2000, however, and joined NATO in 2004 and the EU in 2007.

The social consequences of rebuilding the former East Bloc were similar to those in Russia, though people were generally spared the widespread shortages and misery that characterized Russia in the 1990s. Ordinary citizens and the elderly were once again the big losers, while the young and former Communist Party members were the big winners. Inequalities between richer and poorer regions also increased. Capital cities such as Warsaw, Prague, and Budapest concentrated wealth, power, and opportunity as never before, while provincial centers stagnated and old industrial areas declined. Crime, corruption, and gangsterism increased in both the streets and the executive suites.

Though few former East Bloc residents wanted to return to communism, some expressed longings for the stability of the old system. They missed the guaranteed jobs and generous social benefits provided by the Communist state, and they found the individualism and competitiveness of capitalism cold and difficult. One Russian woman living on a pension of $448 a month in 2003 summed up the dilemma: "What we want is for our life to be as easy as it was in the Soviet Union, with the guarantee of a good, stable future and low prices—and at the same time this freedom that did not exist before."[2]

The question of whether or how to punish former Communist leaders who had committed political crimes or abused human rights emerged as a pressing issue in the former East Bloc. Germany tried major offenders and opened the records of the East German secret police (the Stasi) to the public, and by 1996 more than a million former residents had asked to see their files.[3] Other countries designed various means to deal with former Communist elites who might have committed crimes, with right-wing leaders generally taking a more punitive stand. The search for fair solutions proceeded slowly and with much controversy, a reminder of the troubling legacies of communism and the Cold War.

Tragedy in Yugoslavia

The great postcommunist tragedy occurred in Yugoslavia, which under Josip Broz Tito had been a federation of republics under centralized Communist rule (see Chapter 28). After Tito's death in 1980, power passed increasingly to the sister republics, which encouraged a revival of centuries-old regional and ethnic conflicts that were exacerbated by charges of ethnically inspired massacres during World War II and a dramatic economic decline in the mid-1980s.

rebels took over the regional capital Donetsk and other cities in eastern Ukraine and declared the establishment of the separatist, pro-Russian Donetsk and Luhansk "People's Republics" (see Map 30.1).

A full-scale military assault by Ukrainian government troops failed to push back or defeat the separatist forces. According to Ukrainian and U.S. sources, only direct Russian intervention, including substantial supplies of weaponry and troops, prevented the defeat of the insurrection. In response, the United States and the European Union placed economic sanctions on Russia, and since February 2015 a shaky cease-fire has dampened hostilities in eastern Ukraine. Yet the outcome of the conflict remains uncertain, a telling example of the way great power interests continue to create instability in the former Soviet republics.

The New Global System

| Focus Question | How did globalization affect European life and society? |

Contemporary observers often assert that the world has entered a new era of **globalization**. Such assertions do not mean that there were never international connections before. Europe has long had close—sometimes productive, sometimes destructive—ties to other parts of the world. Yet new global relationships and increasing interdependence did emerge in the last decades of the twentieth century.

First, the growth of multinational corporations restructured national economies on a global scale. Second, an array of international governing bodies, such as the European Union, the United Nations, the World Trade Organization, and a number of nongovernmental organizations (or NGOs), increasingly set policies that challenged the autonomy of traditional nation-states. Finally, the expansion and ready availability of highly efficient computer and media technologies led to ever-faster exchanges of information and entertainment around the world. Taken together, these global transformations had a remarkable impact, both positive and negative, on many aspects of Western society.

The Global Economy

Though large business interests had long profited from international trade and investment, multinational corporations grew and flourished in a world economy increasingly organized around policies of free-market neoliberalism, which relaxed barriers to international trade (see Chapter 29). Multinational corporations built global systems of production and distribution that generated unprecedented wealth and generally escaped the control of regulators and politicians acting on the national level.

Conglomerates such as Siemens and Vivendi exemplified this business model. Siemens, with international headquarters in Berlin and Munich and offices around the globe, is one of the world's largest engineering companies, with vast holdings in energy, construction, health care, financial services, and industrial production. Vivendi, an extensive media and telecommunications company headquartered in Paris, controls a vast international network of producers and products, including music and film, publishing, television broadcasting, pay-TV, Internet services, and video games.

The development of sophisticated personal computer technologies and the Internet at the end of the twentieth century, coupled with the deregulation of national and international financial systems, further encouraged the growth of international trade. The ability to rapidly exchange information and capital meant that economic activity was no longer centered on national banks or stock exchanges, but rather flowed quickly across international borders. Large cities like London, Moscow, New York, and Hong Kong became global centers of banking, trade, and financial services. The influence of financial and insurance companies, communications conglomerates, and energy and legal firms headquartered in these global cities extended far beyond the borders of the traditional nation-state.

At the same time, the close connections between national economies also made the entire world vulnerable to economic panics and downturns. In 1997 a banking crisis in Thailand spread to Indonesia, South Korea, and Japan and then echoed around the world. The resulting slump in oil and gas prices hit Russia especially hard, leading to high inflation, bank failures, and the collapse of the Russian stock market. The crisis then spread to Latin America, plunging most countries there into a severe economic downturn. A decade later, a global recession triggered by a crisis in the U.S. housing market and financial system created the worst worldwide economic crisis since the Great Depression of the 1930s (see page 1011).

The New European Union

Global economic pressures encouraged the expansion and consolidation of the European Common Market, which in 1993 proudly rechristened itself the **European Union (EU)** (Map 30.3). The EU added the free movement of capital and services and eventually individuals across national borders to the existing free trade in goods. In addition, member states sought to create a monetary union in which all EU countries would share a single currency. Membership in the monetary union required states to meet strict financial criteria defined in the 1991 **Maastricht Treaty**, which also set legal standards and anticipated the development of common policies on defense and foreign affairs.

Western European elites and opinion makers generally supported the economic integration embodied in the Maastricht Treaty. They felt that membership requirements, which imposed financial discipline on national governments, would combat Europe's ongoing economic problems and viewed the establishment of a single European currency as an irreversible historic step toward basic political unity. This unity would allow Europe as a whole to regain its place in world politics and to deal with the United States as an equal.

Support for the Maastricht Treaty was hardly universal. Ordinary people, leftist political parties, and right-wing nationalists expressed considerable opposition to the new rules. Many people resented the EU's ever-growing bureaucracy in Brussels, which imposed common standards on everything from cheese production to day care, supposedly undermining national customs and local traditions. Moreover, increased unity meant yielding still more power to distant "Eurocrats" and political insiders, which limited national sovereignty and democratic control.

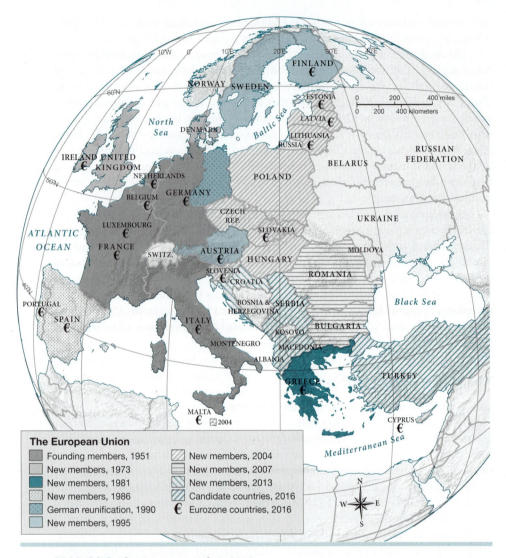

MAP 30.3 The European Union, 2016
No longer divided by ideological competition and the Cold War, much of today's Europe has banded together in a European Union that facilitates the open movement of people, jobs, and currency across national borders.

Above all, many citizens feared that the European Union would operate at their expense. Joining the monetary union required national governments to meet stringent fiscal standards, impose budget cuts, and contribute to the EU operating budget. The resulting reductions in health care and social benefits hit ordinary citizens and did little to reduce high unemployment. When put to the public for a vote, ratification of the Maastricht Treaty was usually very close. In France, for example, the treaty passed with just 50.1 percent of the vote. Even after the treaty was ratified, battles over budgets, benefits, and high unemployment continued throughout the EU in the 1990s.

Then in 2002, brand-new euros finally replaced the national currencies of all Eurozone countries. The establishment of the European monetary union built confidence in member nations and increased their willingness to accept new members. On May 1, 2004, the European Union began admitting its former East Bloc neighbors. By 2016, with the recent admission of Croatia, the EU was home to about 500 million citizens in twenty-eight countries. It included most of the former East Bloc and, with the Baltic nations, three republics of the former Soviet Union.

This rapid expansion underscored the need to reform the EU's unwieldy governing structure. In June 2004 a special commission presented a new EU constitution that created a president, a foreign minister, and a voting system weighted to reflect the populations of the different states. The proposed constitution moved toward a more centralized federal system, though each state retained veto power over taxation, social policy, foreign affairs, and other sensitive areas. After many contentious referendum campaigns across the continent, the constitution failed to win the unanimous support required to take effect. Ultimately, nationalist fears about losing sovereignty and cultural identity outweighed the perceived benefits of a more unified Europe. Fears that an unwieldy European Union would grow to include Ukraine, Georgia, and Muslim Turkey—countries with cultures and histories that were very different from those of western Europe—were particularly telling.

Though the constitution did not go into effect, the long postwar march toward greater European unity did not stop. In 2007 the rejected constitution was replaced with the Treaty of Lisbon. The new treaty kept many sections of the constitution, but further streamlined the EU bureaucracy and reformed its political structure. When the Treaty of Lisbon went into effect on December 1, 2009, after ratification by all EU states, it capped a remarkable fifty-year effort to unify what had been a deeply divided and war-torn continent.

Yet profound questions about the meaning of European unity and identity remained. Would the European Union expand as promised to include the postcommunist nations of the former Soviet Union, and if so, how could Muslim Turkey's long-standing application be ignored? Could a union of twenty-eight diverse countries have any real cohesion and common identity? Would the EU remain closely linked with the United States in NATO, or would it develop an independent defense policy? Could member states agree on an economic policy to master the stubborn recession that emerged in 2008 and the Greek debt crisis of 2015 and keep the nineteen-state Eurozone intact (see page 1012)? Would they be able to manage the refugee crisis that emerged in 2015? The EU struggled to shape institutions and policies to address these complicated issues.

Supranational Organizations

Beyond the European Union, the trend toward globalization empowered a variety of other supranational organizations that had tremendous reach. National governments still played the leading role in defining and implementing policy, but they increasingly had to take the policies of institutions such as the United Nations and the World Trade Organization into consideration.

The United Nations (UN), established in 1945 after World War II, remains an important player on the world stage. Representatives from all independent countries meet in the UN General Assembly in New York City to try to forge international agreements. UN agencies deal with issues such as world hunger and poverty, and the International Court of Justice in The Hague, Netherlands, hears cases that violate international law. The UN also sends troops in attempts to preserve peace between warring parties — as in Yugoslavia in the 1990s. While the smaller UN Security Council has broad powers, including the ability to impose sanctions to punish uncooperative states and even to endorse military action, its five permanent members — the United States, Russia, France, Great Britain, and China — can each veto resolutions introduced in that body. The predominance of the United States and western European powers on the Security Council has led some critics to accuse the UN of implementing Western neocolonial policies (see Chapter 28). Others argue that UN policies should never take precedence over national needs, and UN resolutions are at times ignored or downplayed.

A trio of nonprofit international financial institutions have also gained power in a globalizing world. Like the United Nations, the World Bank and the International Monetary Fund (IMF) were established in the years following World War II. Initially founded to help rebuild war-torn Europe, these organizations now provide loans to the developing world. Their funding comes primarily from donations from the United States and western Europe, and they typically extend loans on the condition that recipient countries adopt neoliberal economic reforms, including budget reduction, deregulation, and privatization. In the 1990s the World Bank and the IMF played especially active roles in shaping economic and social policy in the former East Bloc.

The third economic supranational, the **World Trade Organization (WTO)**, is one of the most powerful supranational financial institutions. It sets trade and tariff agreements for over 150 member countries, thus helping manage a large percentage of the world's import-export policies. Like the IMF and the World Bank, the WTO generally promotes neoliberal policies.

The rise of these institutions, which typically represent the shared interests of national governments, was paralleled by the emergence of a variety of **nongovernmental organizations (NGOs)**. Some NGOs act as lobbyists on specific issues; others conduct international programs and activities. Exemplary NGOs include Doctors Without Borders, a charitable organization of physicians headquartered in France; Greenpeace, an international environmental group; and Oxfam, a British-based group dedicated to alleviating famine, disease, and poverty in the developing world. Though financed by donations from governments and private citizens, NGOs' annual budgets can total hundreds of millions of dollars and their work can be quite extensive.

The Human Side of Globalization

Globalization transformed the lives of millions of people, as the technological changes associated with postindustrial society (see Chapter 29) remade workplaces and lifestyles around the world. Low labor costs in the industrializing world — including the former East Bloc, Latin America, and East Asia — encouraged corporations to outsource labor-intensive manufacturing jobs to these regions. Widespread adoption of neoliberal free-trade policies and low labor costs in developing countries made it less expensive to manufacture steel, automotive parts, computer components, and all manner of consumer goods in developing countries and then import them for sale in the West. In the 1990s China, with its low wages and rapidly growing industrial infrastructure, emerged as an economic powerhouse that supplied goods across the world—even as the West's industrial heartlands continued to decline. Under these conditions, a car made by Volkswagen could still be sold as a product of high-quality German engineering despite being assembled in Chattanooga, Tennessee, using steel imported from South Korea and computer chips made in Taiwan.

The outsourcing of manufacturing jobs dramatically changed the nature of work in western Europe and North America. In France in 1973, for example, some 40 percent of the employed population worked in industry—in mining, construction, manufacturing, and utilities. About 49 percent worked in services, including retail, hotels and restaurants, transportation, communications, financial and business services, and social and personal services. In 2004 only 24 percent of the French worked in industry, and a whopping 72 percent worked in services. The numbers varied country by country, yet across Europe the trend was clear: by 2005 only about one in three workers was still employed in the once-booming manufacturing sector.[4]

The deindustrialization of Europe established a multitiered society with winners and losers. At the top was a small, affluent group of experts, executives, and professionals—about one-quarter of the total population—who managed the new global enterprises. In the second, larger tier, the middle class struggled with stagnating incomes and a declining standard of living as once-well-paid industrial workers faced stubborn unemployment and cuts in both welfare and workplace benefits. Many were forced to take low-paying jobs in the retail service sector.

In the bottom tier—in some areas as much as a quarter of the population—a poorly paid underclass performed the unskilled jobs of a postindustrial economy or were chronically unemployed. In western Europe and North America, inclusion in this lowest segment of society was often linked to race, ethnicity, and a lack of educational opportunity. Recently arrived immigrants had trouble finding jobs and often lived in unpleasant, hastily built housing, teetering on the edge of poverty. In London, unemployment rates among youths and particularly young black men soared above those of their white compatriots. Frustration over these conditions, coupled with anger at a police shooting, boiled over in immigrant neighborhoods across the city in August 2011, when angry youths rioted in the streets, burning buildings and looting stores.

Geographic contrasts further revealed the unequal aspects of globalization. Regions in Europe that had successfully shifted to a postindustrial economy, such as northern Italy and southern Germany and Austria, enjoyed prosperity. Lagging behind were regions historically dependent on heavy industry, such as the former East Bloc countries and the factory districts north of London, or underdeveloped areas, such as rural sections of southern Italy, Spain, and Greece. In addition, a global north-south divide increasingly separated Europe and North America—both still affluent despite their economic problems—from the industrializing nations of Africa and Latin America. Though India, China, and other East Asian nations experienced solid growth, other industrializing nations struggled to overcome decades of underdevelopment.

The human costs of globalization resulted in new forms of global protest. Critics accused global corporations and financial groups of doing little to address problems caused by their activities, such as social inequality, pollution, and unfair labor practices. The Slow Food movement that began in Italy, for example, criticized American-style fast-food chains that proliferated in Europe and the world in the 1990s. Cooking with local products and traditional methods, followers argued, was healthier and kept jobs and profits in local neighborhoods. The fast-food giant McDonald's was often targeted as an example of the ills of corporate globalization. José Bové, a French farmer and antiglobalization activist, made world headlines by driving his truck through the windows of a McDonald's in a small French village to protest the use of hormone-fed beef and genetically modified foods as well as the reach of corporate capital.

The general tone of the antiglobalization movement was captured at the 1999 meeting of the WTO in Seattle, Washington. Tens of thousands of protesters from around the world, including environmentalists, consumer and antipoverty activists, and labor rights groups, marched in the streets and disrupted the meeting. Comparable demonstrations took place at later meetings of the WTO, the World Bank, and other supranational groups.

Similar feelings inspired the Occupy movement, which began in the United States in 2011 and quickly spread to over eighty countries. Under the slogan "We are the 99 percent," thousands of people camped out in (or "occupied") public places to protest the rapidly growing social inequality that divided a tiny wealthy elite (the "1 percent") from the vast majority of ordinary people. Though the diverse groups in the Occupy movement failed to mount a sustained and successful challenge to the public officials and business leaders who profited from globalization, their calls for greater social equality and democracy showed that the struggle for reform continued.

Life in the Digital Age

The growing sophistication of information technologies — a hallmark of the globalizing age — has had a profound and rapidly evolving effect on patterns of communications, commerce, and politics. As tiny digital microchips replaced bulky transistors and the Internet grew in scope and popularity, more and more people organized their everyday lives around the use of ever-smaller and more powerful high-tech devices.

Leisure-time pursuits were a case in point. The arrival of cable television, followed swiftly by DVDs and then online video streaming, enabled individuals to watch full-length movies or popular television shows on their personal computers or smartphones at any time and greatly diversified the options for home entertainment. Europe's once-powerful public broadcasting systems, such as the BBC, were forced to compete with a variety of private enterprises, including Netflix, a U.S. online video provider that entered the European media market in 2014. Music downloads and streaming audio files replaced compact discs, which themselves had replaced vinyl records and cassettes; digital cameras eliminated the need for expensive film; e-book readers, including Kindles and iPads, offered a handheld portable library; smartphone apps provided an apparently endless variety of conveniences and distractions.

Digitalization transformed familiar forms of communication in a few short decades. Many of these changes centered on the Internet, which began its rapid expansion around the globe in the late 1980s. In the first decade of the twenty-first century, the evolution of the cell phone into the smartphone, with its multimedia telecommunications features and more functions and power than the desktop computers of the previous decade, hastened the change. The growing popularity of Internet-based communication tools such as e-mail, text messaging, Facebook, Twitter, and other social media changed the way friends, families, and businesses kept in touch. Letter writing with pen and paper became a quaint relic of the past. Skype, first introduced in 2003, offered personal computer and smartphone users video telecommunications around the world. The old-fashioned "landline," connected to a stationary telephone, seemed ready to join the vinyl LP and the handwritten letter in the junk bin of history.

Entire industries were dramatically changed by the emergence of the Internet. With faster speeds and better online security came online shopping. People increasingly relied on the Internet to purchase goods from clothes to computers to groceries. Online file sharing of books and popular music transformed the publishing and music industries, while massive online retailers such as Amazon and eBay, which sell millions of goods across the globe without physical storefronts, transformed familiar retail systems.

The rapid growth of the Internet and social media raised complex questions related to personal privacy and politics. Governments and businesses used online tracking systems to amass an extraordinary amount of information on individuals and then monitor their political activities or target them with advertising. Privacy advocates worked with government regulators to shape laws that might preserve key elements of online privacy, and in general, rules were more stringent in Europe than in the United States.

The vast amount of information circulating on the Internet could also lead to the exposure of government and business secrets. The numerous materials posted online by the nonprofit organization WikiLeaks, dedicated to the publication of secret information and news leaks, documented numerous examples of government and corporate misconduct. The classified U.S. National Security Agency information leaked in 2013 by former CIA contractor Edward Snowden embarrassed U.S. diplomats and fueled further debates about Internet surveillance, national security, and privacy protection. In addition, individuals could use smartphones and social media sites to organize protest campaigns. Facebook and Twitter, for example, helped mobilize demonstrators in Egypt during the Arab Spring (see page 1010) and allowed members of the Occupy movement to share news and shape strategy. A number of authoritarian states from North Korea to Iran to Cuba, recognizing the disruptive powers of the Internet, strictly limited online access.

Ethnic Diversity in Contemporary Europe

Focus Question	What are the main causes and effects of growing ethnic diversity in contemporary Europe?

As the twenty-first century opened and ongoing globalization transformed European society and politics, Europeans witnessed the remaking of their ethnic communities. First, Europe experienced a remarkable decline in birthrates that seemed to predict a shrinking and aging population in the future. Second, the peaceful, wealthy European Union attracted rapidly growing numbers of refugees and immigrants from the former Soviet Union and East Bloc, North Africa, and the Middle East. The unexpected arrival of so many newcomers raised perplexing questions about ethnic diversity and the costs and benefits of multiculturalism.

The Prospect of Population Decline

In 2016 population rates were still growing rapidly in many poor countries but not in the world's industrialized nations. In 2000 families in developed countries had only 1.6 children on average; only in the United States did families have, almost exactly, the 2.1 children necessary to maintain a stable population. In Europe, where birthrates had been falling since the 1950s, national fertility rates ranged from 1.2 to 1.8 children per woman of childbearing age. By 2013 Italy and Ireland, once known for large Catholic families, had each achieved one of Europe's lowest birthrates—a mere 1.3 babies per woman. None of the twenty-eight countries in the EU had birthrates above 2.0; the average fertility rate was about 1.55 children per woman.[5]

If the current baby bust continues, the long-term consequences could be dramatic, though hardly predictable. At the least, Europe's population would decline and age. Projections for Germany are illustrative. Total German population, barring much greater immigration, would gradually decline from about 81 million in 2015 to just under 72 million around 2050. The number of people of working age would fall, and due to longer life spans, nearly a third of the population would be over sixty. Social security taxes paid by the shrinking labor force would need to soar to meet the skyrocketing costs of pensions and health care for seniors—a recipe for generational conflict. As the premier of Bavaria, Germany's biggest state, has warned, the prospect of demographic decline is a "ticking time bomb under our social welfare system and entire economy."[6]

Why, in times of peace, did Europeans fail to reproduce? Studies showed that European women and men in their twenties, thirties, and early forties still wanted two or even three children—like their parents. But unlike their parents, young couples did not realize their ideal family size. Many women postponed the birth of their first child into their thirties in order to finish their education and establish careers. Then, finding that balancing a child and a career was more difficult than anticipated, new mothers tended to postpone and eventually forgo having a second child. The better educated and the more economically successful a woman was, the more likely she was to have just one child or no children at all. In addition, the uneven, uninspiring European economic conditions since the mid-1970s played a role. High unemployment fell heavily on young people, especially after the recession of 2008, convincing youths to delay settling down and having children.

In 2013 some population experts concluded that European birthrates had stablized, though women continued to postpone having children. Moreover, the frightening implications of dramatic population decline emerged as a major public issue. Opinion leaders, politicians, and the media started to advocate for larger families and propose policies to provide more support for families with children. Europeans may yet respond with enough vigor to reverse their population decline and avoid societal crisis.

Changing Immigration Flows

As European demographic vitality waned in the 1990s, a surge of migrants from the former Soviet Bloc, Africa, and most recently the Middle East headed for western Europe. Some migrants entered the European Union legally, with proper documentation, but increasing numbers were smuggled in past beefed-up border patrols. Large-scale immigration, both documented and undocumented, emerged as a critical and controversial issue.

Historically a source rather than a destination of immigrants, western Europe saw rising numbers of immigrants in postcolonial population movements beginning in the 1950s, augmented by the influx of manual laborers in its boom years from about 1960 until about 1973 (see Chapter 28). A new and different surge of migration into western Europe began in the 1990s. The collapse of communism in the East Bloc and savage civil wars in Yugoslavia drove hundreds of thousands of refugees westward. Equally brutal conflicts in Somalia and Rwanda, the U.S.-led invasions of Afghanistan and Iraq, and then the turmoil in North Africa and the Middle East unleashed by the "Arab Spring," brought hundreds of thousands more. In 2013 immigration to the EU from nonmember countries topped 1.7 million people.

Undocumented or irregular immigration into the European Union also exploded. The number of irregular migrants is difficult to quantify, but in 2014 approximately 260,000 non-European nationals were turned back at Europe's borders, while almost 550,000 irregular migrants already lived in the EU. That same year, about 275,000 migrants entered Europe irregularly, an increase of almost 140 percent from 2013.[7]

Why was Europe such an attractive destination for non-European migrants, regular and irregular? First, even with all the economic problems of western Europe, economic opportunity undoubtedly was a major attraction for immigrants. Germans, for example, earned on average three and a half times more than neighboring Poles, who in turn earned much more than people farther east and in North Africa. In 1998 most European Union states abolished all border controls; entrance into one country allowed for unimpeded travel almost anywhere (though Ireland and the United Kingdom opted out of this agreement). This meant that irregular migrants could enter across the relatively lax borders of Greece and south-central Europe, and then move north across the continent in search of refuge and jobs.

Second, EU immigration policy offered migrants the possibility of acquiring asylum status, if they could demonstrate that they faced severe persecution, based on race, nationality, religion, political belief, or membership in a specific social group in their home countries. Many migrants turned to Europe as they fled civil wars in Syria and Iraq, violence in Libya, and poverty and harsh social and political repression in parts of Africa. The rules for attaining asylum status varied by nation, though Germany and Sweden offered relatively liberal policies, housing for applicants, and high benefit payments (still only about $425 per month, per adult). The regulations were nonetheless restrictive: though numerous migrants applied for asylum, after an average fifteen-month wait many were rejected, classified as illegal job seekers, and expelled.

Irregular immigration was aided by powerful criminal gangs that smuggled people for profit. In the 1990s these gangs contributed to the large number of young

Europe's Refugee Crisis   A volunteer helps Middle Eastern refugees ashore at the Greek island of Lesbos on November 29, 2015. Exhausted and emotional, they traveled by boat from Turkey. Under Europe's system of open internal borders, the island's thinly patrolled, easily accessible coastline, within sight of the Turkish coast, offered a tempting entry into the European Union for migrants ultimately seeking residence in Germany or Sweden. In fall and early winter of 2015–2016, about five thousand refugees reached Europe each day along the so-called Balkan migrant route. Their unprecedented numbers stoked anti-immigrant tensions across Europe and called into question the internal open-border system. (Oage Elif Kizil/Anadolu Agency/Getty Images)

female illegal immigrants from eastern Europe, especially Russia and Ukraine. Often lured by criminals promising jobs as maids or waitresses, these women were often trafficked into the most prosperous parts of Europe and forced into prostitution.

More recently, immigration flows have shifted to reflect the dislocation that emerged in North Africa and the Middle East in the wake of the failed "Arab Spring" and the war against the Islamic State (see page 1010). Smugglers with a callous disregard for the well-being of their charges can demand thousands of euros to bring undocumented migrants from North Africa and the Middle East across the Mediterranean into Spain and Italy; the safer and less expensive route across Turkey and Greece and the north into more prosperous European countries is particularly well traveled (Map 30.4).

In the summer of 2015 the migration issue reached crisis proportions. Tens of thousands of migrants, most displaced by war in Syria and Iraq, entered Hungary through Serbia and struggled to travel into more hospitable Austria, Germany, and northern Europe. Others continued to enter the EU through the relatively accessible

Greek islands. As Germany promised homes for eight hundred thousand migrants and encouraged other EU nations to take their share, thousands of migrants choked train and bus stations on the Hungarian-Austrian border. Others languished in quickly established refugee camps built in northern Greece and the Hungarian countryside, and Hungary's anti-immigrant government quickly built a 108-mile razor-wire fence along the border with Serbia to squelch further movement.

The discovery of seventy-one dead migrants locked in an abandoned truck on an Austrian highway—and the deaths of thousands more who in the last several years attempted to cross the Mediterranen in rudimentary rubber rafts and leaky boats—underscored the venality of the smugglers and the human costs of uncontrolled immigration. As this text was being written, European leaders were still struggling to contain the humanitarian crisis caused by the largest movement of peoples across Europe since the end of World War II, with little end in sight.

Toward a Multicultural Continent

By 2015 immigration to Europe had profoundly changed the ethnic makeup of the continent, though the effects were unevenly distributed. One way to measure the effect of these new immigrants is to consider the rapid rise of their numbers. Since the 1960s the foreign population of western European nations has grown by two to ten times. In the Netherlands in 1960, only 1 percent of the population was foreign-born. In 2006 the foreign born made up 10 percent. Over the same years the proportion of immigrants grew from 1.2 percent to 12.3 percent in Germany and from 4.7 percent to almost 11 percent in France.[8] In 2005 immigrants constituted about 10 percent of most western European nations (though a far smaller share of the former East Bloc nations). For centuries the number of foreigners living in Europe had been relatively small. Now, permanently displaced ethnic groups, or **diasporas**, brought ethnic diversity to the continent.

The new immigrants were divided into two main groups. A small percentage were highly trained specialists who could find work in the upper ranks of education, business, and high-tech industries. Engineers from English-speaking India, for example, could find positions in international computer companies. Most immigrants, however, did not have access to high-quality education or language training, which limited their employment opportunities and made integration more difficult. They often lived in separate city districts marked by poor housing and crowded conditions, which set them apart from more established residents. Districts of London were home to tens of thousands of immigrants from the former colonies, and in Paris North Africans dominated some working-class *banlieues* (suburbs).

A variety of new cultural forms, ranging from sports and cuisine to music, the fine arts, and film, brought together native and foreign traditions and transformed European lifestyles. Food was a case in point. Recipes and cooks from former colonies in North Africa enlivened French cooking, while the döner kebab—the Turkish version of a gyro sandwich—became Germany's "native" fast food. Indian restaurants proliferated across Britain, and controversy raged when the British foreign minister announced in 2001 that chicken tikka masala—a spicy Indian stew—was Great Britain's new national dish.[9]

The **multiculturalism** and ethnic diversity associated with globalization have inspired numerous works in literature, film, and the fine arts. From rap to reggae to rai, multiculturalism has also had a profound effect on popular music, a medium with a huge audience. Rai, which originated in the Bedouin culture of North Africa, exemplified the new pop music forms that emerged from cultural mixing. In the 1920s rai traveled with Algerian immigrants to France. In its current form, it blends Arab and North African folk music, U.S. rap, and French and Spanish pop styles. Lyrics range from sentimental love stories to blunt and sometimes critical descriptions of daily life in immigrant communities.

The growth of immigration and ethnic diversity created rich social and cultural interactions but also generated controversy and conflict in western Europe. In most EU nations, immigrants can become full citizens if they meet certain legal qualifications; adopting the culture of the host country is not a requirement. This legal process has raised questions about who, exactly, could or should be European, and about the way these new citizens might change European society. The idea that cultural and ethnic diversity could be a force for vitality and creativity has run counter to deep-seated beliefs about national homogeneity. Some commentators have accused the newcomers of taking jobs from unemployed native Europeans and undermining national unity. Government welfare programs intended to support struggling immigrants have been criticized by some as a misuse of money, especially in times of economic downturn.

Europe and Its Muslim Population

General concerns with migration often fused with fears of Muslim migrants and Muslim residents who have grown up in Europe. Islam is now the largest minority religion in Europe. The EU's 15 to 20 million Muslims outnumber Catholics in Europe's mainly Protestant north, and they outnumber Protestants in Europe's Catholic south. Major cities have substantial Muslim minorities. Muslim residents make up about 25 percent of the population in Marseilles and Rotterdam, 15 percent in Brussels, and about 10 percent in Paris, Copenhagen, and London.[10]

Worries increased after the September 11, 2001, al-Qaeda attack on New York's World Trade Center (see page 1007) and the subsequent war in Iraq. Terrorist attacks in Europe organized by Islamist extremists heightened anxieties. On a morning in March 2004, radical Moroccan Muslims living in Spain exploded bombs planted on trains bound for Madrid, killing 191 commuters and wounding 1,800 more. A year

< MAP 30.4 Major Migration Routes into Contemporary Europe
In the wake of wars and the collapse of the Arab Spring, in-migration from northern Africa and the Middle East into Europe reached crisis proportions. Aided by smugglers, thousands of migrants traveled two main routes: through Libya and across the Mediterranean Sea into southern Italy, and across Turkey to close-by Greek islands and then north through the Balkans. Countries with relatively lenient refugee regulations, such as Sweden and Germany, were favorite destinations. Under the so-called Schengen Agreement, the EU's open-border policy made travel through Europe fairly easy. As the number of migrants increased in fall 2015 and spring 2016, however, European politicians began to close national borders, and many migrants were stranded in quickly built refugee camps.

Terrorist Attacks in Paris, November 2015   At a makeshift memorial made of flowers, candles, and messages left by mourners and passersby, onlookers observe a moment of silence for the victims of the November 13, 2015, terrorist attacks in central Paris. Islamic State jihadists claimed responsibility for the series of coordinated assaults, which killed 130 people and wounded hundreds more at a concert hall (Le Bataclan), restaurants, and the national stadium. (Jacques Demarthon/AFP/Getty Images)

later, an attack on the London transit system carried out by British citizens of Pakistani descent killed over 50 people. Since then, a number of attacks have kept Islamist terrorism in the public eye—including the murderous January 2015 assault on the staff of the satiric French magazine *Charlie Hebdo*, which had published cartoons critical of the Prophet Muhammad, and the even more deadly attacks in Paris in November 2015, when extremists motivated by the ideologies of the Islamic State killed 130 people.

The vast majority of Europe's Muslims clearly supported democracy and rejected violent extremism, but these spectacular attacks and other assaults by Islamist militants nonetheless sharpened the debate on immigration. Security was not the only focus of concern. Critics across the political spectrum warned that Europe's rapidly growing Muslim population posed a dire threat to the West's liberal tradition, which embraced freedom of thought, representative government, toleration, separation of church and state, and, more recently, equal rights for women and gays. Islamist extremists and radical clerics living in Europe, critics proclaimed, rejected these fundamental Western values and preached the supremacy of Islamic laws for Europe's Muslims.

Secular Europeans at times had a hard time understanding the depths of Muslim spirituality. French attempts to enforce a ban on wearing the hijab (the headscarf worn by many faithful Muslim women) in public schools expressed the tension between Western secularism and Islamic religiosity on a most personal level and evoked outrage and protests in the Muslim community. As busy mosques came to outnumber dying churches in European cities, nationalist politicians exploited widespread doubts that immigrant populations from Muslim countries would ever assimilate into Western culture. A Danish-Muslim imam (spiritual leader) captured the dilemma: "The Danish shelves for faith and spirituality are empty," he reported. "They fill them instead with fear of the 'strong foreigner.'"[11] Time was on the side of Euro-Islam, critics warned. Europe's Muslim population, estimated at 20 million in 2010, appeared likely to grow to 30 million by 2025 and to increase rapidly thereafter—even though that total would only be 4 percent of Europe's then-projected 750 million people.

By the 1990s in France, some 70 percent of the population believed that there were "too many Arabs," and 30 percent supported right-wing politician Jean-Marie Le Pen's calls to rid France of its immigrants altogether.[12] In the last decade, Le Pen's National Front and other anti-immigration, far-right political parties, such as the Danish People's Party and Austria's Freedom Party, have made impressive gains in national elections. Their success has been aided by bigotry and popular misconceptions. According to one 2013 poll, about 50 percent of respondents in Spain, Germany, France, Switzerland, Britain, and Sweden believe that "Islam is not compatible with the West." Other polls show that Europeans routinely overestimate the number of Muslims in Europe. In France, for example, the public believes that 31 percent of the population is Muslim, when the actual number is about 8 percent; the British believe that 21 percent of the population is Muslim, when the actual number is only 5 percent.[13]

In Germany, tens of thousands of people have joined the anti-immigrant movement called Pegida (Patriotic Europeans Against the Islamization of the West), and in the first six months of 2015 the German authorities recorded over two hundred attacks against migrant housing or against the migrants themselves. Immigration and the supposed "Islamization" of Europe, along with fundamentalist terrorism, have become highly charged political issues, and conservative and far-right pundits and politicians across Europe offer a variety of diagnoses and solutions to these perceived problems.

Admitting that Islamist extremism could pose a serious challenge, some observers focused instead on the issue of integration. Whereas the first generation of Muslim migrants—predominantly Turks in Germany, Algerians in France, Pakistanis in Britain, and Moroccans in the Netherlands—had found jobs as unskilled workers in Europe's great postwar boom, they and their children had been hard hit after 1973 by the general economic downturn and the decline of manufacturing. Immigrants also suffered from a lack of educational opportunities. Provided with modest welfare benefits and housed minimally in dilapidated housing projects, many second- and third-generation Muslim immigrants were outcasts in their adopted countries. To these observers, economics, inadequate job training, and discrimination had more influence on immigrant attitudes about their host communities than did religion and extremist teachings.

This argument was strengthened by widespread rioting by Muslim youths in France in 2005 and again in 2007 and 2009. Almost always French by birth, language, and education, marauding groups labeled "Arabs" in press reports torched hundreds of automobiles night after night in Paris suburbs and other large cities. The rioters complained bitterly of high unemployment, systematic discrimination, and exclusion, and studies sparked by the rioting showed that religious ideology had almost no influence on their thinking.

A minority used such arguments to challenge anti-immigrant, anti-Muslim discrimination and its racist overtones. They argued that Europe badly needed newcomers—preferably talented newcomers—to limit the impending population decline and provide valuable technical skills. Some asserted that Europe should recognize that Islam has for centuries been a European religion and a vital part of European life. This recognition might open the way to political and cultural acceptance of European Muslims and head off the resentment that can drive a tiny minority to separatism and acts of terror.

Confronting Long-Term Challenges

Focus Question	What challenges will Europeans face in the coming decades?

Russian irredentism, uncontrolled immigration, and radical Islamic terrorism posed major problems for Europeans in the second decade of the twenty-first century. Yet with goodwill, one could believe that these might be temporary crises, resolvable with determined government action. At the same time, European societies faced a number of interconnected challenges that seemed to pose longer-term challenges. The growing distance in international affairs between the United States and Europe revealed differences in social values and political goals, though both struggled to deal with turmoil in the Muslim world. A persistent economic recession had a devastating impact on the lives of millions and called into question the unity of the Eurozone. Climate change and environmental degradation exposed the dangers of industrial development and the heavy dependence on fossil fuels for energy. At the same time, the relative wealth of European societies in the global context provoked serious thinking about European identity and Europe's humanitarian mission in the community of nations.

Growing Strains in U.S.-European Relations

In the fifty years after World War II, the United States and western Europe generally maintained close diplomatic relations. Though they were never in total agreement, they usually worked together to promote international consensus under U.S. guidance, as represented by the NATO alliance. For example, a U.S.-led coalition that included thousands of troops from France and the United Kingdom and smaller contributions from other NATO allies attacked Iraqi forces in Kuwait in the 1990–1991 Persian Gulf War, freeing the small nation from attempted annexation by Iraqi dictator Saddam Hussein. Over time, however, the growing power of the European Union and the new unilateral thrust of Washington's foreign policy created strains in traditional transatlantic relations.

The growing gap between the United States and Europe had several causes. For one, the European Union was now the world's largest trading block, challenging the predominance of the United States. Prosperous European businesses invested heavily in the United States, reversing a decades-long economic relationship in which investment dollars had flowed the other way. For another, under Presidents George W. Bush (U.S. pres. 2001–2009) and Barack Obama (U.S. pres. 2009–), the United States often ignored international opinion in pursuit of its own interests. Citing the economic impact, Washington refused to ratify the Kyoto Protocol of 1997, which was intended to limit global warming and which had been agreed to by nearly two hundred countries. Nor did the United States join the International Criminal Court, a global tribunal meant to prosecute individuals accused of crimes against humanity, which nearly 140 states agreed to join. These positions troubled EU leaders, as did unflagging U.S. support for Israel in the ongoing Palestinian-Israeli crisis.

A values gap between the United States and Europe contributed to cooler relations. Ever more secular Europeans had a hard time understanding the religiosity of many Americans. Relatively lax gun control laws and use of capital punishment in the United States were viewed with dismay in Europe, where most countries had outlawed private handgun ownership and abolished the death penalty. Despite President Obama's health-care reforms—which evoked controversy among Americans—U.S. reluctance to establish a single-payer, state-funded program surprised Europeans, who saw their own such programs as highly advantageous.

Hardball geopolitical issues relating to NATO further widened the gap. The dissolution of the Communist Warsaw Pact left NATO without its Cold War adversaries. Yet NATO continued to expand, primarily in the territories in the former East Bloc—the defensive belt the Soviet Union had established after World War II. NATO's expansion angered Russia's leaders, particularly when President Bush moved to deploy missile defense systems in Poland and the Czech Republic in 2008. Even within the alliance there were tensions. By 2009, with twenty-eight member states, it was difficult to shape unanimous support for NATO actions. France, for example, did not support NATO's engagement in Bosnia in 1995 because the alliance failed to get UN approval for the action, and in 2011 Germany and Poland refused to back NATO air strikes against the Libyan regime. As the EU expanded, some argued that Europe should determine its own military and defense policy without U.S. or NATO guidance.

American-led wars in Afghanistan and Iraq, undertaken in response to the September 11 terrorist attacks against the United States, further strained U.S.-European relations. On the morning of September 11, 2001, passenger planes hijacked by terrorists destroyed the World Trade Center towers in New York City and crashed into the Pentagon. Perpetrated by the radical Islamist group al-Qaeda, the attacks took the lives of more than three thousand people from many countries and put the personal safety of ordinary citizens at the top of the West's agenda.

Immediately after the September 11 attacks, the peoples and governments of Europe and the world joined Americans in heartfelt solidarity. Over time, however, tensions between Europe and the United States re-emerged and deepened markedly, particularly after President Bush declared a unilateral U.S. **war on terror**—a determined effort to fight terrorism in all its forms, around the world. The main acts in

Bush's war on terror were a U.S.-led war in Afghanistan, which started in 2001, and another in Iraq, which lasted from 2003 to 2011. Both succeeded in quickly bringing down dictatorial regimes. At the same time, they fomented anti-Western sentiment in the Muslim world and failed to stop regional violence driven by ethnic and religious differences.

The U.S. invasion of Iraq and subsequent events caused some European leaders, notably in France and Germany, to question the rationale for and indeed the very effectiveness of a "war" on terror. Military victory, even over rogue states, would hardly end terrorism, since terrorist groups easily moved across national borders. Terrorism, they concluded, was better fought through police and intelligence measures. Europeans certainly shared U.S. worries about stability in the Middle East, and they faced their own problems with Islamist terrorism, especially after the Madrid and London train bombings of 2004 and 2005, and the attacks in Paris in 2015. But European leaders worried that the tactics used in the Iraq War, exemplified by Washington's readiness to use its military without international agreements or UN backing, violated international law.

American conduct of the war on terror also raised serious human rights concerns. The revelation of the harsh interrogation techniques used on prisoners held by American forces and abuse of prisoners in Iraq shocked many Europeans. U.S. willingness to engage in "extraordinary rendition"—secretly moving terrorism suspects to countries that allow coercive interrogation techniques—caused further concern.

The election of Barack Obama, America's first African American president, in 2008, and his re-election in 2012, brought improvement to U.S.-European foreign relations. Upon election, Obama announced that he would halt deployment of missiles in central Europe and reduce nuclear arms, easing tensions with Russia. He took U.S. troops out of Iraq in 2011 and Afghanistan in 2014, and quietly shelved the language of the "war on terror." Despite these changes, many Europeans continued to find U.S. willingness to undertake unilateral military action disturbing—American drone attacks on suspected terrorists along the Afghanistan-Pakistan border were particularly unpopular.[14] In the long run, though ties with the United States remained firm, European states increasingly responded independently to global affairs.

Turmoil in the Muslim World

Over the past decade, civil wars, terrorist sectarian attacks, civilian dislocation and misery, and a loss of social, political, and economic stability have shaken much of the Muslim world in North Africa and the Middle East. In many ways, these problems were the results of recent historical events. Yet the turmoil in North Africa and the Middle East, along with Islamic challenges to Western interests and policies, had a much deeper history, which included the legacies of European colonialism and the mandate system established after World War I, Cold War power plays, and the Palestinian-Israeli conflict.

Radical political Islam, a mixture of traditional religious beliefs and innovative social and political reform ideas, was at first a reaction against the foreign control and secularization represented by the mandate system established in the Middle East after

World War I (see Chapter 25). Groups like the **Muslim Brotherhood**, founded in Egypt in 1928, called for national liberation from European control and a return to shari'a law (based on Muslim legal codes), and demanded land reform, extensive social welfare programs, and economic independence. The appeal of such ideas crossed class lines and national borders. By the 1960s the Brotherhood had established chapters across the Middle East and North Africa, and a variety of other groups and leaders advocated similar ideas about the need for Islamic revival and national autonomy. The broad spectrum of Islamist ideas is difficult to summarize, but adherents tended to fall into two main groups: a moderate or centrist group that worked peacefully to reform society within existing institutions, and a much smaller, more militant minority willing to use violence to achieve its goals.

Decolonization and the Cold War sharpened anti-Western and particularly anti-U.S. sentiments among radical Islamists. As the western European powers loosened their ties to the Middle East, the Americans stepped in. Applying containment policy to limit the spread of communism, and eager to preserve steady supplies of oil, the United States supported secular, authoritarian regimes friendly to U.S. interests in Egypt, Saudi Arabia, Iran, and elsewhere. Such regimes often played on U.S. concerns about communism or the threat of radical Islam to bolster American support.

U.S. policies in the Middle East at times produced "blowback," or unforeseen and unintended consequences. One example was the Iranian revolution of 1979, when Islamist radicals antagonized by Western intervention, state corruption, and secularization overthrew the U.S.-supported shah and established an Islamic republic. The successful revolution encouraged militant Islamists elsewhere. So did the example of the mujahideen, the Muslim guerrilla fighters in Afghanistan who successfully fought off the Soviet army from 1979 to 1989 (see Chapter 29). U.S. military aid and arms, funneled to the mujahideen during the war, also generated blowback. Many of the U.S.-armed mujahideen would go on to support the Taliban, a militant Islamist faction that came to rule Afghanistan in 1996. The Taliban established a strict Islamist state based on shari'a law that denied women's right to education and banned Western movies and music. The Taliban also provided a safe haven for the Saudi-born millionaire Osama bin Laden and the al-Qaeda terrorist network.

As a result of these policies, the United States, along with western Europe, became the main target for Islamist militants. During the 1990s bin Laden and al-Qaeda mounted several terrorist attacks on U.S. installations, leading up to the horrific September 11 assault. After that attack, President Bush declared with some justification that the terrorists "hate our freedoms: our freedom of religion, our freedom of speech, our freedom to vote."[15] In public calls for jihad (or struggle) against the United States and the West, however, bin Laden gave a more pragmatic list of grievances, including U.S. support for Israel in the Israeli-Palestinian crisis, the sanctions on Iraq that followed the Persian Gulf War, and the presence of U.S. military bases in Saudi Arabia—seen as an insult to the Muslim holy sites in Mecca and Medina.[16]

The Bush administration hoped that the invasions of Afghanistan—a direct response to the September 11 attacks—and Iraq would end the terrorist attacks and bring peace and democracy to the Middle East, but both brought chaos instead. The military campaign in Afghanistan quickly achieved one of its goals, bringing down the Taliban, and the United States installed a friendly government. But U.S. troops failed to find bin Laden or disable al-Qaeda, and Taliban insurgents mounted a determined and lasting guerrilla war.

With heavy fighting still under way in Afghanistan in late 2001, the Bush administration turned its attention to Saddam Hussein's Iraq, arguing that it was necessary to expand the war on terror to other hostile regimes in the Middle East. U.S. leaders effectively played on American fears of renewed terrorism and charged that Saddam Hussein was still developing weapons of mass destruction in flagrant disregard of his 1991 promise to end all such programs. Some Americans shared the widespread doubts held by Europeans about the legality—and wisdom—of an American attack on Iraq, especially after UN inspectors found no weapons of mass destruction in the country. Though they failed to win UN approval, in March 2003 the United States and Britain, with token support from a handful of other European states, invaded Iraq.

The U.S.-led invasion quickly overwhelmed the Iraqi army, and Saddam's dictatorship collapsed in April, but America's subsequent efforts to establish a stable pro-American Iraq proved difficult. Poor postwar planning and management by administration officials was one factor, but there were others. Iraq, a creation of Western imperialism after the First World War (see Chapter 25), was a fragile state with three distinct groups: non-Arab Kurds, Arab Sunni Muslims, and Arab Shi'ite Muslims. By 2006 deadly sectarian conflicts among these groups and against the United States and its Iraqi supporters had taken hold. Casualties in Iraq began to decline after President Bush sent additional troops to the country in 2007, and when President Obama took office in 2009 his administration moved forward with agreements to withdraw all U.S. forces in 2011. The shaky Iraqi government continued to struggle with ethnic divisions and terrorist violence, however.

Although U.S. commandos finally killed Osama bin Laden in Pakistan in May 2011, the apparently unwinnable guerrilla war in Afghanistan became increasingly unpopular in the United States and among NATO allies in Europe. Though the conflict continued, President Obama withdrew U.S. combat troops from the country in 2014.

In early 2011 an unexpected chain of events that came to be called the **Arab Spring** further destabilized the Middle East and North Africa. In a provincial town in Tunisia, a poor fruit vendor set himself on fire to protest official harassment. His death eighteen days later unleashed a series of spontaneous mass protests that brought violence, chaos, and regime change; six weeks later, Tunisia's authoritarian president fled the country, opening the way for reform. Massive popular demonstrations calling for more open democractic government and social tolerance broke out across the Middle East. In Egypt, demonstrators forced the resignation of President Hosni Mubarak, a U.S.-friendly leader who had ruled for thirty years. An armed uprising in Libya, supported by NATO air strikes, brought down the dictatorial government of Muammar Gaddafi that October. A civil war broke out in Syria in July 2011, but dragged on into 2016 as Bashar al-Assad, with Russian support, hurled his army at the rebels and Western powers disagreed about what to do. Protests arose in other countries in the region as well, evoking a mixed response of repression and piecemeal reform.

As the popular movements inspired by the Arab Spring faltered, the emergence of the **Islamic State** (sometimes called ISIS or ISIL) suggested that events in the

Middle East had spiraled out of control. The Islamic State, an extremist Islamist militia dedicated to the establishment of a new caliphate to unify Muslims around the world, grew out of al-Qaeda and the various other insurgent groups fighting in Iraq and the Syrian civil war. By summer 2015 Islamic State soldiers had taken control of substantial parts of central Syria and Iraq—including Mosul, Ramadi, and Fallujah, cities central to U.S. combat missions in the Iraq war. Over 4 million Syrians and Iraqis lost their homes during the fighting, and hundreds of thousands streamed north in attempts to find asylum in Europe (see page 1000).

In the territories under their control, Islamic State militants set up a terroristic government based on an extremist reading of shari'a law. Islamic State terror tactics included the violent persecution of sectarian religious groups; use of sexual assault and rape as tools of conquest; mass executions and beheadings of military, political, or sectarian enemies; and the "cultural cleansing" (destruction and looting) of ancient cultural monuments and shrines that failed to meet its stringent religious ideals, most recently in the classical city of Palmyra in Syria. All these actions were well documented in widespread Internet propaganda campaigns; videos recorded by militants, intended to demonstrate their power and entice recruits, were regularly posted on the Internet.

In summer 2016, as this was being written, the outcome of the turmoil in the Middle East was difficult to predict. The Arab Spring seemed, for the most part, a dismal failure. The young activists who sought greater political and social liberties from authoritarian regimes quickly lost control of the changes they unleashed. Multiple players now vied for power: military leaders and old elites, local chieftains representing ethnic or sectarian interests, and moderate and radical Islamists. In Egypt, the first open elections in decades brought to power representatives of the moderate wing of the Muslim Brotherhood; a year later, military leaders overthrew this elected government. In Libya, Yemen, and especially Syria, persistent civil wars undermined the search for stability. The hold of the Islamic State was likewise difficult to shake. In Iraq, air strikes by a U.S.-NATO coalition and assaults by Iraqi ground troops only slowly repulsed the extremists.

In the period leading up to 2016, Western policymakers grappled in vain for clear and effective ways to help defeat the Islamic State and bring order to the region. Their efforts were especially freighted, since the turmoil in the Muslim world was at the center of many of Europe's problems. These included the immigration emergency of 2015–2016, the persistent extremist Islamist terrorist attacks, the destabilization of Europe's energy supplies, and the disastrous human rights crisis faced by millions of Middle East residents.

The Global Recession and the Viability of the Eurozone

While chaos and change roiled the Muslim world, economic crisis sapped growth and political unity in Europe and North America. In 2008 the United States entered a deep recession, caused by the burst of the housing boom, bank failures, and an overheated financial securities market. The U.S. government spent massive sums to recharge the economy. Banks, insurance agencies, auto companies, and financial services conglomerates received billions of dollars in federal aid. By 2016 the economy had improved

Anti-Austerity Protests in Greece   With protest marches and a rally in front of the Greek parliament, thousands of anti-austerity voters celebrated the results of the July 2015 Greek referendum in the streets of Athens. The popular vote soundly rejected a bailout deal proposed by the IMF, the European Common Bank, and the European Union, which would have required the Greek government to implement harsh austerity measures. Just days after the vote, Greek leaders backed down and accepted the plan anyway. (© Bjorn Kietzmann/Demotix/Corbis)

and much of the housing market had recovered, though some critics claimed that income inequality was higher than ever.

The 2008 recession swept across Europe, where a housing bubble, high national deficits, and a weak bond market made the crisis particularly acute. One of the first countries affected, and one of the hardest hit, was Iceland, where the currency and banking system collapsed outright. Other countries followed—Ireland and Latvia made deep and painful cuts in government spending to balance national budgets. By 2010 Britain was deeply in debt, and Spain, Portugal, and especially Greece were close to bankruptcy.

This sudden "euro crisis" put the very existence of the Eurozone in question. The common currency grouped together countries with vastly divergent economies. Germany and France, the zone's two strongest economies, felt pressure to provide financial support to ensure the stability of far weaker countries, including Greece and Portugal. They did so with strings attached: recipients of EU support were required to reduce deficits through austerity measures. Even so, the transfer of monies within the Eurozone angered the citizens of wealthier countries, who felt they were being asked to subsidize countries in financial difficulties of their own making. Such feelings were particularly powerful in Germany, forcing Chancellor Angela Merkel (r. 2005–), the nation's first woman chancellor, to move cautiously in providing financial stimulus to troubled Eurozone economies.

The difficulty dealing with the stubborn Greek debt crisis prompted debates about the viability of a single currency for nations with vastly different economies as well as widespread speculation that the Eurozone might fall apart. In 2010 and 2012 Greece received substantial bailouts from the IMF, the European Common Bank, and the European Union (the so-called Troika). In return for loans and some debt relief, Greek leaders were required to implement a painful austerity plan—which meant raising taxes, privatizing state-owned businesses, reforming labor markets, and drastically reducing government spending on employee wages, pensions, and other popular social benefits. Greek unemployment hit a record 25 percent in 2012, and more than half of young adults lacked jobs. Rampant joblessness meant declining tax revenues, and the Greek economy continued to weaken. As the government cut popular social programs, demonstrators took to the streets to protest declining living standards and the lack of work; in Athens, protests large and small were almost a daily occurrence.

The 2015 Greek elections brought the left-wing Syriza Party and the charismatic prime minister Alexis Tsipras to power. In the Thessaloniki Programme, Tsipras and his party promised voters a tough stand against the Troika's fiscal demands and an end to austerity. Yet Troika negotiators, led by Germany, maintained an uncompromising line: if Tsipras and Syriza failed to meet Greek debt payments, they would be forced into a "Grexit" (a Greek exit from the Eurozone). After a dramatic series of events, which included a resounding "no" vote in a Greek referendum on the deal proposed by the Troika, Tsipras backtracked and accepted further austerity measures in return for yet another bailout loan. Among other conditions, Greek leaders promised to sell off about 50 billion euros' worth of government-owned property, including airports, power plants and energy assets, roads and railroads, and the national post office.

Even as the Greek crisis shook European unity, in June 2016 Great Britain voted to leave the EU all together. The campaign for the "Brexit" (British exit from the EU) was intense. The narrow victory of those wanting "out" showed that many Brits did not want "Eurocrats" in Brussels intruding on national policy and did not appreciate the EU's relatively open immigration policies. Prime Minister David Cameron (r. 2010–2016) resigned immediately. Though Britain had two years to negotiate the terms of the exit, global financial markets fell, far-right populist parties on the continent rejoiced, and EU supporters expressed deep concern about the future of the union.

Dependence on Fossil Fuels

One of the most significant long-term challenges facing Europe and the world in the early twenty-first century was the need for adequate energy resources. Maintaining standards of living in industrialized countries and modernizing the developing world required extremely high levels of energy use, and supplies were heavily dependent on fossil fuels: oil, coal, and natural gas. In 2011 Europe and Russia combined had about 12 percent of the world's population but annually consumed about 34 percent of the world's natural gas production, 22 percent of oil production, and 13 percent of coal output. Scientists warned that such high levels of usage were unsustainable over the long run and predicted that fossil fuel supplies will eventually run out, especially as the countries of the developing world — including giants such as India and China — increased their own rates of consumption.[17]

Struggles to control and profit from these shrinking resources often resulted in tense geopolitical conflicts. The need to preserve access to oil, for example, has led to a transformation in military power in the post–Cold War world. Between 1945 and 1990 the largest areas of military buildup were along the iron curtain in Europe and in East Asia, as U.S. forces formed a bulwark against the spread of communism. Today military power is increasingly concentrated in oil-producing areas such as the Middle East, which holds about 65 percent of the world's oil reserves. One scholar labeled conflicts in the Persian Gulf and Central Asia "resource wars" because they are fought, in large part, to preserve the West's access to the region's energy supplies.[18]

The global struggle for ample energy has placed Russia, which in 2011 became the world's number-one oil producer (surpassing Saudi Arabia) and the number-two natural gas producer, in a powerful but strained position. The Russian invasions of Chechnya and Georgia, and intervention in Ukraine, were attempts to maintain political influence in these territories, but also to preserve Russian control of the region's rich energy resources.

Beyond military action, Russian leaders readily use their control over energy to assert political influence. The Russian corporation Gazprom, one of the world's largest producers of natural gas, sells Europe about 30 percent of its natural gas, and the EU treads softly with Russia to maintain this supply. Russia is willing to play hardball: it has engaged in over fifty politically motivated disruptions of natural gas supply in the former Soviet republics, including one in January 2009 when Russia shut off supplies to Ukraine for three weeks, resulting in closed factories and no heat for hundreds of thousands of people. "Yesterday tanks, today oil," a Polish politician remarked about Russia's willingness to use energy to exert influence in central Europe.[19]

Climate Change and Environmental Degradation

Even setting aside the question of the supply of fossil fuels, their use has led to serious environmental problems. Burning oil and coal releases massive amounts of carbon dioxide (CO_2) into the atmosphere, the leading cause of **climate change**, or global warming. While the future effects of climate change are difficult to predict, the vast majority of climatologists agree that global warming is proceeding far more quickly than previously predicted and that some climatic disruption is now unavoidable. Rising average temperatures already play havoc with familiar weather patterns, melting glaciers and polar ice packs, and drying up freshwater resources. Moreover, in the next fifty years rising sea levels may well flood low-lying coastal areas around the world.

Since the 1990s the EU has spearheaded efforts to control energy consumption and contain climate change. EU leaders have imposed tight restrictions on CO_2 emissions, and Germany, the Netherlands, and Denmark have become world leaders in harnessing alternative energy sources such as solar and wind power. Some countries, hoping to combat the future effects of global warming, have also taken pre-emptive measures. The Dutch government, for example, has spent billions of dollars constructing new dikes, levees, and floodgates. These efforts provided models for U.S. urban planners after floodwaters churned up by Hurricane Sandy swamped low-lying swaths of New York City in October 2012.

Environmental degradation encompasses a number of problems beyond climate change. Overfishing and toxic waste threaten the world's oceans and freshwater lakes, which once seemed to be inexhaustible sources of food and drinking water. The disaster that resulted when an offshore oil rig exploded in the Gulf of Mexico in April 2010, spewing millions of gallons of oil into the gulf waters, underscored the close connections between energy consumption and water pollution. Deforestation, land degradation, soil erosion, and overfertilization; species extinction related to habitat loss; the accumulation of toxins in the air, land, and water; the disposal of poisonous nuclear waste — all will continue to pose serious problems in the twenty-first century.

Though North American and European governments, NGOs, and citizens have taken a number of steps to limit environmental degradation and regulate energy use, the overall effort to control energy consumption has been an especially difficult endeavor, underscoring the interconnectedness of the contemporary world. Rapidly industrializing countries such as India and China — the latter surpassed the United States in 2008 as the largest emitter of CO_2 — have had a difficult time balancing environmental concerns and the energy use necessary for economic growth. Because of growing demand for electricity, for example, China currently accounts for about 47 percent of the world's coal consumption, causing hazardous air pollution in Chinese cities and contributing to climate change.[20]

Can international agreements and good intentions make a difference? In December 2015 representatives of almost two hundred nations met at the annual United Nations Climate Change Conference in Paris, France. They extended the Kyoto Protocol on climate change, set ambitious goals for the reduction of CO_2 emissions by 2020, and promised to help developing countries manage the effects of climate change. Such changes would require substantial modifications in the planet's consumption of energy derived from fossil fuels, however, and the ultimate success of ambitious plans to limit the human impact on the environment remains uncertain.

Promoting Human Rights

Though regional differences persisted in the twenty-eight EU member states, Europeans entering the twenty-first century enjoyed some of the highest living standards in the world, the sweet fruit of more than fifty years of peace, security, and overall economic growth. The recent agonies of barbarism and war in the former Yugoslavia as well as the memories of the horrors of World War II and the Holocaust cast in bold relief the ever-present reality of collective violence. For some Europeans, the realization that they had so much and so many others had so little kindled a desire to help. As a result, European intellectuals and opinion makers began to envision a new historic mission for Europe: the promotion of domestic peace and human rights in lands plagued by instability, violence, and oppression.

European leaders and humanitarians believed that more global agreements and new international institutions were needed to set moral standards and to regulate countries, leaders, armies, corporations, and individuals. In practice, this meant more current situation and helps save us from exaggerated self-pity in the face of our own predicaments. Perhaps our Western heritage may rightly inspire us with measured pride and self-confidence. We stand, momentarily, at the head of the long procession of Western civilization. Sometimes the procession has wandered, or backtracked, or done terrible things. But it has also carried the efforts and sacrifices of generations of toiling, struggling ancestors. Through no effort of our own, we are the beneficiaries of those sacrifices and achievements. Now that it is our turn to carry the torch onward, we may remember these ties with our forebears.

To change the metaphor, we in the West are like card players who have been dealt many good cards. Some of them are obvious, such as our technical and scientific heritage, our environmental resources, and our commitment to human rights and individual freedoms. Others are not so obvious, sometimes half-forgotten or even hidden up the sleeve. Think, for example, of the almost-miraculous victory of peaceful revolution in the East Bloc in 1989 — an expression of what Czech playwright-turned-president Václav Havel called "the power of the powerless." Here we again see the regenerative strength of the Western ideals of individual rights and democratic government. We hold a good hand.

Our study of history, of mighty struggles and fearsome challenges, of shining achievements and tragic failures, gives a sense of the essence of life itself: the process of change over time. Again and again we have seen how peoples and societies evolve, influenced by ideas, human passions, and material conditions. This process of change will continue as the future becomes the present and then the past. Students of history are better prepared to make sense of this unfolding process because they have closely observed it. They understand that change is rooted in existing historical forces, and they have tools to explore the intricate web of activity that propels life forward. Students of history are prepared for the new and unexpected in human development, for they have already seen great breakthroughs and revolutions. They have an understanding of how things really happen.

MAKE CONNECTIONS

Think about the larger developments and continuities within and across chapters.

1. Did people's lives really change dramatically during the wave of globalization that emerged in the late twentieth century? How have they stayed the same?

2. The globalization of today's world seems inseparable from advances in digital technology. How are the two connected? Were there other times in the history of Western society during which technological developments drove social, political, or cultural change?

3. How are the challenges that confront Europeans in the twenty-first century rooted in events and trends that came before?

Chapter Review

IDENTIFY KEY TERMS

Identify and explain the significance of each item below.

ethnic cleansing (p. 987)

Color Revolutions (p. 989)

globalization (p. 990)

European Union (EU) (p. 991)

Maastricht Treaty (p. 991)

World Trade Organization
  (WTO) (p. 994)

nongovernmental organizations
  (NGOs) (p. 994)

diasporas (p. 1001)

multiculturalism (p. 1003)

war on terror (p. 1007)

Muslim Brotherhood (p. 1009)

Arab Spring (p. 1010)

Islamic State (p. 1010)

climate change (p. 1014)

REVIEW THE MAIN IDEAS

Answer the focus questions from each section of the chapter.

1. How did life change in Russia and the former East Bloc countries after 1989? (p. 979)

2. How did globalization affect European life and society? (p. 990)

3. What are the main causes and effects of growing ethnic diversity in contemporary Europe? (p. 997)

4. What challenges will Europeans face in the coming decades? (p. 1006)

CHRONOLOGY

1980s–1990s	Emergence of globalization
1990s–2010s	New waves of legal and illegal immigration to Europe
1991	Maastricht Treaty
1991–2001	Civil war in Yugoslavia
1992–1997	Decline of Russian economy
1993	Creation of the European Union
1999	Protests against WTO in Seattle
2000–2008	Resurgence of Russian economy under Putin
2001	September 11 terrorist attack on the United States; war in Afghanistan begins
2002	Euro replaces national currencies in Eurozone
2003–2011	Iraq War
2004	Train bombings in Madrid by Islamic extremists
2005	Young Muslims riot in France; subway bombing in London by Islamic extremists
2008	Worldwide financial crisis begins
2009	Ratification of Treaty of Lisbon; young Muslims riot in France
2011	Start of Arab Spring
2012–2013	Mass protests against government austerity plans in Greece and Spain
2013	France legalizes same-sex marriage
2014	Russian Federation annexes Crimea; pro-Russian insurrection in eastern Ukraine
2014–2015	Rise of the Islamic State
2015–2016	Greek debt crisis; EU immigration emergency

Glossary

Afrikaners Descendants of the Dutch settlers in the Cape Colony in southern Africa. (p. 774)

appeasement The British policy toward Germany prior to World War II that aimed at granting Hitler's territorial demands, including western Czechoslovakia, in order to avoid war. (p. 885)

Arab Spring A series of popular revolts in several countries in the Middle East and North Africa that sought an end to authoritarian, often Western-supported regimes. (p. 1010)

Atlantic slave trade The forced migration of Africans across the Atlantic for slave labor on plantations and in other industries; the trade reached its peak in the eighteenth century and ultimately involved more than 12 million Africans. (p. 543)

Aztec Empire A large and complex Native American civilization in modern Mexico and Central America that possessed advanced mathematical, astronomical, and engineering technology. (p. 425)

Balfour Declaration A 1917 British statement that declared British support of a National Home for the Jewish People in Palestine. (p. 825)

Battle of Peterloo The army's violent suppression of a protest that took place at Saint Peter's Fields in Manchester in reaction to the revision of the Corn Laws. (p. 674)

Bauhaus A German interdisciplinary school of fine and applied arts that brought together many leading modern architects, designers, and theatrical innovators. (p. 840)

Berlin Conference A meeting of European leaders held in 1884 and 1885 in order to lay down some basic rules for imperialist competition in sub-Saharan Africa. (p. 776)

"Black Legend" The notion that the Spanish were particularly ruthless and cruel in their conquest and domination of the Americas, an idea often propagated by Spain's rivals. (p. 441)

Black Shirts Mussolini's private militia that destroyed socialist newspapers, union halls, and Socialist Party headquarters, eventually pushing Socialists out of the city governments of northern Italy. (p. 877)

blood sports Events such as bullbaiting and cockfighting that involved inflicting violence and bloodshed on animals and that were popular with the eighteenth-century European masses. (p. 567)

Bloody Sunday A massacre of peaceful protesters at the Winter Palace in St. Petersburg in 1905, triggering a revolution that overturned absolute tsarist rule and made Russia into a conservative constitutional monarchy. (p. 739)

Bolsheviks Lenin's radical, revolutionary arm of the Russian party of Marxist socialism, which successfully installed a dictatorial socialist regime in Russia. (p. 815)

bourgeoisie The middle-class minority who owned the means of production and, according to Marx, exploited the working-class proletariat. (p. 667)

boyars The highest-ranking members of the Russian nobility. (p. 470)

Brezhnev Doctrine Doctrine created by Leonid Brezhnev that held that the Soviet Union had the right to intervene in any East Bloc country when necessary to preserve Communist rule. (p. 953)

cameralism View that monarchy was the best form of government, that all elements of society should serve the monarch, and that, in turn, the state should use its resources and authority to increase the public good. (p. 513)

caravel A small, maneuverable, three-mast sailing ship developed by the Portuguese in the fifteenth century that gave the Portuguese a distinct advantage in exploration and trade. (p. 418)

carnival The few days of revelry in Catholic countries that preceded Lent and that included drinking, masquerading, dancing, and rowdy spectacles that upset the established order. (p. 568)

Cartesian dualism Descartes's view that all of reality could ultimately be reduced to mind and matter. (p. 497)

charivari Degrading public rituals used by village communities to police personal behavior and maintain moral standards. (p. 557)

Christian Democrats Center-right political parties that rose to power in western Europe after the Second World War. (p. 915)

class-consciousness Awareness of belonging to a distinct social and economic class whose interests might conflict with those of other classes. (p. 647)

climate change Changes in long-standing weather patterns caused primarily by carbon dioxide emissions from the burning of fossil fuels. (p. 1014)

Cold War The rivalry between the Soviet Union and the United States that divided much of Europe into a Soviet-aligned Communist bloc and a U.S.-aligned capitalist bloc between 1945 and 1989. (p. 904)

collectivization of agriculture The forcible consolidation of individual peasant farms into large state-controlled enterprises in the Soviet Union under Stalin. (p. 872)

Color Revolutions A series of popular revolts and insurrections that challenged regional politicians and Russian interests in the former Soviet republics during the first decade of the twenty-first century. (p. 989)

Columbian exchange The exchange of animals, plants, and diseases between the Old and the New Worlds. (p. 433)

Combination Acts British laws passed in 1799 that outlawed unions and strikes, favoring capitalist business people over skilled artisans. Bitterly resented and widely disregarded by many craft guilds, the acts were repealed by Parliament in 1824. (p. 648)

Common Market The European Economic Community, created by six western and central European countries in the West Bloc in 1957 as part of a larger search for European unity. (p. 917)

community controls A pattern of cooperation and common action in a traditional village that sought to uphold the economic, social, and moral stability of the closely knit community. (p. 557)

companionate marriage Marriage based on romantic love and middle-class family values that became increasingly dominant in the second half of the nineteenth century. (p. 705)

Congress of Vienna A meeting of the Quadruple Alliance (Russia, Prussia, Austria, and Great Britain), restoration France, and smaller European states to fashion a general peace settlement that began after the defeat of Napoleon's France in 1814. (p. 654)

conquistador Spanish for "conqueror"; Spanish soldier-explorers, such as Hernán Cortés and Francisco Pizarro, who sought to conquer the New World for the Spanish crown. (p. 417)

constitutionalism A form of government in which power is limited by law and balanced between the authority and power of the government, on the one hand, and the rights and liberties of the subjects or citizens on the other hand; could include constitutional monarchies or republics. (p. 477)

consumer revolution The wide-ranging growth in consumption and new attitudes toward consumer goods that emerged in the cities of northwestern Europe in the second half of the eighteenth century. (p. 570)

Continental System A blockade imposed by Napoleon to halt all trade between continental Europe and Britain, thereby weakening the British economy and military. (p. 609)

Copernican hypothesis The idea that the sun, not the earth, was the center of the universe. (p. 492)

Corn Laws British laws governing the import and export of grain, which were revised in 1815 to prohibit the importation of foreign grain unless the price at home rose to improbable levels, thus benefiting the aristocracy but making food prices high for working people. (p. 674)

Cossacks Free groups and outlaw armies originally comprising runaway peasants living on the borders of Russian territory from the fourteenth century onward. By the end of the sixteenth century they had formed an alliance with the Russian state. (p. 471)

cottage industry A stage of industrial development in which rural workers used hand tools in their homes to manufacture goods on a large scale for sale in a market. (p. 531)

Council for Mutual Economic Assistance (COMECON) An economic organization of Communist states meant to help rebuild East Bloc countries under Soviet auspices. (p. 911)

Crimean War A conflict fought between 1853 and 1856 over Russian desires to expand into Ottoman territory; Russia was defeated by France, Britain, and the Ottomans, underscoring the need for reform in the Russian Empire. (p. 736)

Crystal Palace The location of the Great Exhibition in 1851 in London; an architectural masterpiece made entirely of glass and iron. (p. 630)

Dadaism An artistic movement of the 1920s and 1930s that attacked all accepted standards of art and behavior and delighted in outrageous conduct. (p. 842)

Dawes Plan War reparations agreement that reduced Germany's yearly payments, made payment dependent on economic prosperity, and granted large U.S. loans to promote recovery. (p. 852)

debt peonage A form of serfdom that allowed a planter or rancher to keep his workers or slaves in perpetual debt bondage by periodically advancing food, shelter, and a little money. (p. 543)

decolonization The postwar reversal of Europe's overseas expansion caused by the rising demand of the colonized peoples themselves, the declining power of European nations, and the freedoms promised by U.S. and Soviet ideals. (p. 925)

deism Belief in a distant, noninterventionist deity; common among Enlightenment thinkers. (p. 504)

de-Stalinization The liberalization of the post-Stalin Soviet Union led by reformer Nikita Khrushchev. (p. 922)

détente The progressive relaxation of Cold War tensions that emerged in the early 1970s. (p. 944)

developed socialism A term used by Communist leaders to describe the socialist accomplishments of their societies, such as nationalized industry, collective agriculture, and extensive social welfare programs. (p. 962)

diasporas Enclaves of ethnic groups settled outside their homelands. (p. 1001)

displaced persons Postwar refugees, including 13 million Germans, former Nazi prisoners and forced laborers, and orphaned children. (p. 905)

Dreyfus affair A divisive case in which Alfred Dreyfus, a Jewish captain in the French army, was falsely accused and convicted of treason. The Catholic Church sided with the anti-Semites against Dreyfus; after Dreyfus was declared innocent, the French government severed all ties between the state and the church. (p. 745)

Duma The Russian parliament that opened in 1906, elected indirectly by universal male suffrage but controlled after 1907 by the tsar and the conservative classes. (p. 739)

economic liberalism A belief in free trade and competition based on Adam Smith's argument that the invisible hand of free competition would benefit all individuals, rich and poor. (p. 537)

economic miracle Term contemporaries used to describe rapid economic growth, often based on the consumer sector, in post–World War II western Europe. (p. 914)

empiricism A theory of inductive reasoning that calls for acquiring evidence through observation and experimentation rather than deductive reason and speculation. (p. 496)

Enabling Act An act pushed through the Reichstag by the Nazis that gave Hitler absolute dictatorial power for four years. (p. 881)

enclosure The movement to fence in fields in order to farm more effectively, at the expense of poor peasants who relied on common fields for farming and pasture. (p. 525)

encomienda system A system whereby the Spanish crown granted the conquerors the right to forcibly employ groups of Indians in exchange for providing food, shelter, and Christian teaching. (p. 431)

enlightened absolutism Term coined by historians to describe the rule of eighteenth-century monarchs who, without renouncing their own absolute authority, adopted Enlightenment ideals of rationalism, progress, and tolerance. (p. 512)

Enlightenment The influential intellectual and cultural movement of the late seventeenth and eighteenth centuries that introduced a new worldview based on the use of reason, the scientific method, and progress. (p. 500)

estates The three legal categories, or orders, of France's inhabitants: the clergy, the nobility, and everyone else. (p. 597)

Estates General A legislative body in prerevolutionary France made up of representatives of each of the three classes, or estates. It was called into session in 1789 for the first time since 1614. (p. 596)

ethnic cleansing The attempt to establish ethnically homogeneous territories by intimidation, forced deportation, and killing. (p. 987)

eugenics A pseudoscientific doctrine that maintains that the selective breeding of human beings can improve the general characteristics of a national population, which helped inspire Nazi ideas about "race and space" and ultimately contributed to the Holocaust. (p. 866)

European Union (EU) The economic, cultural, and political alliance of twenty-eight European nations. (p. 991)

evolution The idea, applied by thinkers in many fields, that stresses gradual change and continuous adjustment. (p. 715)

existentialism A philosophy that stresses the meaninglessness of existence and the importance of the individual in searching for moral values in an uncertain world. (p. 835)

Factory Acts English laws passed from 1802 to 1833 that limited the workday of child laborers and set minimum hygiene and safety requirements. (p. 640)

fascism A movement characterized by extreme, often expansionist nationalism; anti-socialism; a dynamic and violent leader; and glorification of war and the military. (p. 866)

February Revolution Unplanned uprisings accompanied by violent street demonstrations begun in March 1917 (old calendar February) in Petrograd, Russia, that led to the abdication of the tsar and the establishment of a provisional government. (p. 814)

five-year plan A plan launched by Stalin in 1928 and termed the "revolution from above," aimed at modernizing the Soviet Union and creating a new Communist society with new attitudes, new loyalties, and a new socialist humanity. (p. 868)

Fourteen Points Wilson's 1918 peace proposal calling for open diplomacy, a reduction in armaments, freedom of commerce and trade, the establishment of the League of Nations, and national self-determination. (p. 822)

Fronde A series of violent uprisings during the early reign of Louis XIV triggered by growing royal control and increased taxation. (p. 457)

functionalism The principle that buildings, like industrial products, should serve as well as possible the purpose for which they were made, without excessive ornamentation. (p. 840)

German Social Democratic Party (SPD) A German working-class political party founded in the 1870s, the SPD championed Marxism but in practice turned away from Marxist revolution and worked instead in the German parliament for social and workplace reform. (p. 743)

germ theory The idea that disease was caused by the spread of living organisms that could be controlled. (p. 693)

Girondists A moderate group that fought for control of the French National Convention in 1793. (p. 603)

glasnost Soviet premier Mikhail Gorbachev's popular campaign for openness in government and the media. (p. 968)

globalization The emergence of a freer, more technologically connected global economy, accompanied by a worldwide exchange of cultural, political, and religious ideas. (p. 990)

global mass migration The mass movement of people from Europe in the nineteenth century; one reason that the West's impact on the world was so powerful and many-sided. (p. 768)

Grand Empire The empire over which Napoleon and his allies ruled, encompassing virtually all of Europe except Great Britain and Russia. (p. 609)

Great Depression A worldwide economic depression from 1929 through 1939, unique in its severity and duration and with slow and uneven recovery. (p. 854)

Greater Germany A liberal plan for German national unification that included the German-speaking parts of the Austrian Empire, put forth at the national parliament in 1848 but rejected by Austrian rulers. (p. 684)

Great Famine (Ireland) The result of four years of potato crop failure in the late 1840s in Ireland, a country that had grown dependent on potatoes as a dietary staple. (p. 676)

Great Fear The fear of noble reprisals against peasant uprisings that seized the French countryside and led to further revolt. (p. 599)

Great Rebellion The 1857 and 1858 insurrection by Muslim and Hindu mercenaries in the British army that spread throughout northern and central India before finally being crushed. (p. 786)

guest worker programs Government-run programs in western Europe designed to recruit labor for the booming postwar economy. (p. 935)

guild system The organization of artisanal production into trade-based associations, or guilds, each of which received a monopoly over its trade and the right to train apprentices and hire workers. (p. 536)

gunboat diplomacy The use or threat of military force to coerce a government into economic or political agreements. (p. 766)

Haskalah The Jewish Enlightenment of the second half of the eighteenth century, led by the Prussian philosopher Moses Mendelssohn. (p. 517)

Holocaust The systematic effort of the Nazi state to exterminate all European Jews and other groups deemed racially inferior during the Second World War. (p. 891)

Holy Alliance An alliance formed by the conservative rulers of Austria, Prussia, and Russia in September 1815 that became a symbol of the repression of liberal and revolutionary movements all over Europe. (p. 660)

Homestead Act An American law enacted during the Civil War that gave western land to settlers, reinforcing the concept of free labor in a market economy. (p. 735)

hundred days of reform A series of Western-style reforms launched in 1898 by the Chinese government in an attempt to meet the foreign challenge. (p. 791)

id, ego, and superego Freudian terms to describe the three parts of the self and the basis of human behavior, which Freud saw as basically irrational. (p. 839)

illegitimacy explosion The sharp increase in out-of-wedlock births that occurred in Europe between 1750 and 1850, caused by low wages and the breakdown of community controls. (p. 558)

Inca Empire The vast and sophisticated Peruvian empire centered at the capital city of Cuzco that was at its peak from 1438 until 1532. (p. 425)

Industrial Revolution A term first coined in 1799 to describe the burst of major inventions and economic expansion that began in Britain in the late eighteenth century. (p. 623)

industrious revolution The shift that occurred as families in northwestern Europe focused on earning wages instead of producing goods for household consumption; this reduced their economic self-sufficiency but increased their ability to purchase consumer goods. (p. 535)

iron law of wages Theory proposed by English economist David Ricardo suggesting that the pressure of population growth prevents wages from rising above the subsistence level. (p. 631)

Islamic State A radical Islamist militia in control of substantial parts of central Syria and Iraq, where it applies an extremist version of shari'a law. (p. 1010)

Jacobin Club A political club in revolutionary France whose members were well-educated radical republicans. (p. 602)

janissary corps The core of the sultan's army, composed of slave conscripts from non-Muslim parts of the empire; after 1683 it became a volunteer force. (p. 476)

Jansenism A sect of Catholicism originating with Cornelius Jansen that emphasized the heavy weight of original sin and accepted the doctrine of predestination; it was outlawed as heresy by the pope. (p. 577)

Junkers The nobility of Brandenburg and Prussia, they were reluctant allies of Frederick William in his consolidation of the Prussian state. (p. 467)

just price The idea that prices should be fair, protecting both consumers and producers, and that they should be imposed by government decree if necessary. (p. 568)

Karlsbad Decrees Issued in 1819, these repressive regulations were designed to uphold Metternich's conservatism, requiring the German states to root out subversive ideas and squelch any liberal organizations. (p. 660)

kulaks The better-off peasants who were stripped of land and livestock under Stalin and were generally not permitted to join collective farms; many of them starved or were deported to forced-labor camps for "re-education." (p. 872)

Kulturkampf Bismarck's attack on the Catholic Church within Germany from 1870 to 1878, resulting from Pius IX's declaration of papal infallibility. (p. 743)

labor aristocracy The highly skilled workers, such as factory foremen and construction bosses, who made up about 15 percent of the working classes from about 1850 to 1914. (p. 701)

laissez faire A doctrine of economic liberalism that calls for unrestricted private enterprise and no government interference in the economy. (p. 662)

Lateran Agreement A 1929 agreement that recognized the Vatican as an independent state, with Mussolini agreeing to give the church heavy financial support in return for public support from the pope. (p. 878)

law of inertia A law formulated by Galileo that states that motion, not rest, is the natural state of an object, and that an object continues in motion forever unless stopped by some external force. (p. 493)

law of universal gravitation Newton's law that all objects are attracted to one another and that the force of attraction is proportional to the objects' quantity of matter and inversely proportional to the square of the distance between them. (p. 494)

League of Nations A permanent international organization, established during the 1919 Paris Peace Conference, designed to protect member states from aggression and avert future wars. (p. 822)

liberalism The principal ideas of this movement were equality and liberty; liberals demanded representative government and equality before the law as well as individual freedoms such as freedom of the press, freedom of speech, freedom of assembly, freedom of worship, and freedom from arbitrary arrest. (p. 662)

logical positivism A philosophy that sees meaning in only those beliefs that can be empirically proven, and that therefore rejects most of the concerns of traditional philosophy, from the existence of God to the meaning of happiness, as nonsense. (p. 835)

Luddites Group of handicraft workers who attacked factories in northern England in 1811 and later, smashing the new machines that they believed were putting them out of work. (p. 646)

Maastricht Treaty The basis for the formation of the European Union, which set financial and cultural standards for potential member states and defined criteria for membership in the monetary union. (p. 991)

mandate system The plan to allow Britain and France to administer former Ottoman territories, put into place after the end of the First World War. (p. 824)

Marshall Plan American plan for providing economic aid to western Europe to help it rebuild. (p. 911)

Marxism An influential political program based on the socialist ideas of German radical Karl Marx, which called for a working-class revolution to overthrow capitalist society and establish a Communist state. (p. 666)

Meiji Restoration The restoration of the Japanese emperor to power in 1867, leading to the subsequent modernization of Japan. (p. 788)

mercantilism A system of economic regulations aimed at increasing the power of the state based on the belief that a nation's international power was based on its wealth, specifically its supply of gold and silver. (p. 460)

Methodists Members of a Protestant revival movement started by John Wesley, so called because they were so methodical in their devotion. (p. 575)

millet system A system used by the Ottomans whereby subjects were divided into religious communities, with each millet (nation) enjoying autonomous self-government under its religious leaders. (p. 476)

Mines Act of 1842 English law prohibiting underground work for all women and girls as well as for boys under ten. (p. 642)

"modern girl" Somewhat stereotypical image of the modern and independent working woman popular in the 1920s. (p. 846)

modernism A label given to the artistic and cultural movements of the late nineteenth and early twentieth centuries, which were typified by radical experimentation that challenged traditional forms of artistic expression. (p. 839)

Mountain, the Led by Robespierre, the French National Convention's radical faction, which seized legislative power in 1793. (p. 603)

multiculturalism The mixing of ethnic styles in daily life and in cultural works such as film, music, art, and literature. (p. 1003)

Muslim Brotherhood Islamic social and political reform group founded in Egypt in 1928 that called for national liberation from European control and a return to shari'a law (based on Muslim legal codes), and demanded land reform, extensive social welfare programs, and economic independence. (p. 1009)

Napoleonic Code French civil code promulgated in 1804 that reasserted the 1789 principles of the equality of all male citizens before the law and the absolute security of wealth and private property, as well as restricting rights accorded to women by previous revolutionary laws. (p. 608)

National Assembly The first French revolutionary legislature, made up primarily of representatives of the third estate and a few from the nobility and clergy, in session from 1789 to 1791. (p. 598)

nationalism The idea that each people had its own genius and specific identity that manifested itself especially in a common language and history, and often led to the desire for an independent political state. (p. 663)

national self-determination The notion that peoples should be able to choose their own national governments through democratic majority-rule elections and live free from outside interference in nation-states with clearly defined borders. (p. 822)

National Socialism A movement and political party driven by extreme nationalism and racism, led by Adolf Hitler; its adherents ruled Germany from 1933 to 1945 and forced Europe into World War II. (p. 879)

nativism Policies and beliefs, often influenced by nationalism, scientific racism, and mass migration, that give preferential treatment to established inhabitants over immigrants. (p. 773)

NATO The North Atlantic Treaty Organization, an anti-Soviet military alliance of Western governments. (p. 912)

natural philosophy An early modern term for the study of the nature of the universe, its purpose, and how it functioned; it encompassed what we would call "science" today. (p. 490)

Navigation Acts A series of English laws that controlled the import of goods to Britain and British colonies. (p. 539)

neocolonialism A postcolonial system that perpetuates Western economic exploitation in former colonial territories. (p. 933)

neo-Europes Settler colonies with established populations of Europeans, such as North America, Australia, New Zealand, and Latin America, where Europe found outlets for population growth and its most profitable investment opportunities in the nineteenth century. (p. 763)

neoliberalism Philosophy of 1980s conservatives who argued for privatization of state-run industries and decreased government spending on social services. (p. 956)

New Economic Policy (NEP) Lenin's 1921 policy to re-establish limited economic freedom in an attempt to rebuild agriculture and industry in the face of economic disintegration. (p. 868)

New Imperialism The late-nineteenth-century drive by European countries to create vast political empires abroad. (p. 774)

New Left A 1960s counterculture movement that embraced updated forms of Marxism to challenge both Western capitalism and Soviet-style communism. (p. 947)

New Order Hitler's program based on racial imperialism, which gave preferential treatment to the "Nordic" peoples; the French, an "inferior" Latin people, occupied a middle position; and Slavs and Jews were treated harshly as "subhumans." (p. 890)

nonalignment Policy of postcolonial governments to remain neutral in the Cold War and play both the United States and the Soviet Union for what they could get. (p. 929)

nongovernmental organizations (NGOs) Independent organizations with specific agendas, such as humanitarian aid or environmental protection, that conduct international programs and activities. (p. 994)

OPEC The Organization of Petroleum Exporting Countries. (p. 954)

Opium Wars Two mid-nineteenth-century conflicts between China and Great Britain over the British trade in opium, which were designed to "open" China to European free trade. In defeat, China gave European traders and missionaries increased protection and concessions. (p. 766)

Orientalism A term coined by literary scholar Edward Said to describe the way Westerners misunderstood and described colonial subjects and cultures. (p. 783)

Ostpolitik German for Chancellor Willy Brandt's new "Eastern policy"; West Germany's attempt in the 1970s to ease diplomatic tensions with East Germany, exemplifying the policies of détente. (p. 943)

Peace of Utrecht A series of treaties, from 1713 to 1715, that ended the War of the Spanish Succession, ended French expansion in Europe, and marked the rise of the British Empire. (p. 463)

Peace of Westphalia The name of a series of treaties that concluded the Thirty Years' War in 1648 and marked the end of large-scale religious violence in Europe. (p. 453)

People's Budget A bill proposed after the Liberal Party came to power in Britain in 1906, it was designed to increase spending on social welfare services but was initially vetoed in the House of Lords. (p. 746)

perestroika Economic restructuring and reform implemented by Premier Mikhail Gorbachev in the Soviet Union in 1985. (p. 967)

Petrograd Soviet A huge, fluctuating mass meeting of two to three thousand workers, soldiers, and socialist intellectuals modeled on the revolutionary soviets of 1905. (p. 814)

philosophes A group of French intellectuals who proclaimed that they were bringing the light of knowledge to their fellow humans in the Age of Enlightenment. (p. 502)

Pietism A Protestant revival movement in early-eighteenth-century Germany and Scandinavia that emphasized a warm and emotional religion, the priesthood of all believers, and the power of Christian rebirth in everyday affairs. (p. 574)

Popular Front A short-lived New Deal–inspired alliance in France led by Léon Blum that encouraged the union movement and launched a far-reaching program of social reform. (p. 860)

postcolonial migration The postwar movement of people from former colonies and the developing world into Europe. (p. 935)

postindustrial society A society that relies on high-tech and service-oriented jobs for economic growth rather than heavy industry and manufacturing jobs. (p. 955)

privatization The sale of state-managed industries such as transportation and communication networks to private owners; a key aspect of broader neoliberal economic reforms meant to control government spending, increase private profits, and foster economic growth, which were implemented in western Europe in response to the economic crisis of the 1970s. (p. 956)

proletarianization The transformation of large numbers of small peasant farmers into landless rural wage earners. (p. 527)

proletariat The industrial working class who, according to Marx, were unfairly exploited by the profit-seeking bourgeoisie. (p. 667)

Protectorate The English military dictatorship (1653–1658) established by Oliver Cromwell following the execution of Charles I. (p. 480)

Ptolemy's *Geography* A second-century-c.e. work that synthesized the classical knowledge of geography and introduced the concepts of longitude and latitude. Reintroduced to Europeans about 1410 by Arab scholars, its ideas allowed cartographers to create more accurate maps. (p. 418)

public sphere An idealized intellectual space that emerged in Europe during the Enlightenment, where the public came together to discuss important issues relating to society, economics, and politics. (p. 511)

Puritans Members of a sixteenth- and seventeenth-century reform movement within the Church of England that advocated purifying it of Roman Catholic elements, like bishops, elaborate ceremonials, and wedding rings. (p. 478)

putting-out system The eighteenth-century system of rural industry in which a merchant loaned raw materials to cottage workers, who processed them and returned the finished products to the merchant. (p. 533)

rationalism A secular, critical way of thinking in which nothing was to be accepted on faith, and everything was to be submitted to reason. (p. 501)

Realism A literary movement that, in contrast to Romanticism, stressed the depiction of life as it actually was. (p. 717)

Red Shirts The guerrilla army of Giuseppe Garibaldi, who invaded Sicily in 1860 in an attempt to liberate it, winning the hearts of the Sicilian peasantry. (p. 728)

Reform Bill of 1832 A major British political reform that increased the number of male voters by about 50 percent and gave political representation to new industrial areas. (p. 674)

Reichstag The popularly elected lower house of government of the new German Empire after 1871. (p. 742)

Reign of Terror The period from 1793 to 1794 during which Robespierre's Committee of Public Safety tried and executed thousands suspected of treason and a new revolutionary culture was imposed. (p. 604)

republicanism A form of government in which there is no monarch and power rests in the hands of the people as exercised through elected representatives. (p. 477)

revisionism An effort by moderate socialists to update Marxist doctrines to reflect the realities of the late nineteenth century. (p. 755)

Rocket The name given to George Stephenson's effective locomotive that was first tested in 1829 on the Liverpool and Manchester Railway at 35 miles per hour. (p. 629)

rococo A popular style in Europe in the eighteenth century, known for its soft pastels, ornate interiors, sentimental portraits, and starry-eyed lovers protected by hovering cupids. (p. 510)

Romanticism An artistic movement at its height from about 1790 to the 1840s that was in part a revolt against classicism and the Enlightenment, characterized by a belief in emotional exuberance, unrestrained imagination, and spontaneity in both art and personal life. (p. 668)

salons Regular social gatherings held by talented and rich Parisians in their homes, where philosophes and their followers met to discuss literature, science, and philosophy. (p. 510)

sans-culottes The laboring poor of Paris, so called because the men wore trousers instead of the knee breeches of the aristocracy and middle class; the word came to refer to the militant radicals of the city. (p. 603)

Schlieffen Plan Failed German plan calling for a lightning attack through neutral Belgium and a quick defeat of France before turning on Russia. (p. 801)

Second Industrial Revolution The burst of industrial creativity and technological innovation that promoted strong economic growth in the last third of the nineteenth century. (p. 714)

second revolution From 1792 to 1795, the second phase of the French Revolution, during which the fall of the French monarchy introduced a rapid radicalization of politics. (p. 603)

Second Vatican Council A meeting of Catholic leaders convened from 1962 to 1965 that initiated a number of reforms, including the replacement of Latin with local languages in church services, designed to democratize the church and renew its appeal. (p. 946)

sensationalism The idea that all human ideas and thoughts are produced as a result of sensory impressions. (p. 502)

separate spheres A gender division of labor with the wife at home as mother and homemaker and the husband as wage earner. (pp. 641, 708)

Social Darwinism A body of thought drawn from the ideas of Charles Darwin that applied the theory of biological evolution to human affairs and saw the human race as driven by an unending economic struggle that would determine the survival of the fittest. (p. 715)

socialism A backlash against the emergence of individualism and the fragmentation of industrial society, and a move toward cooperation and a sense of community; the key ideas were economic planning, greater social equality, and state regulation of property. (p. 664)

Socialist Realism Artistic movement that followed the dictates of Communist ideals, enforced by state control in the Soviet Union and East Bloc countries in the 1950s and 1960s. (p. 921)

Solidarity Independent Polish trade union that worked for workers' rights and political reform throughout the 1980s. (p. 965)

spinning jenny A simple, inexpensive, hand-powered spinning machine created by James Hargreaves in 1765. (p. 625)

stadholder The executive officer in each of the United Provinces of the Netherlands, a position often held by the princes of Orange. (p. 482)

stagflation Term coined in the early 1980s to describe the combination of low growth and high inflation that led to a worldwide recession. (p. 954)

steam engines A breakthrough invention by Thomas Savery in 1698 and Thomas Newcomen in 1705 that burned coal to produce steam, which was then used to operate a pump; the early models were superseded by James Watt's more efficient steam engine, patented in 1769. (p. 628)

stream-of-consciousness technique A literary technique, found in works by Virginia Woolf, James Joyce, and others, that uses interior monologue—a character's thoughts and feelings as they occur—to explore the human psyche. (p. 843)

suffrage movement A militant movement for women's right to vote led by middle-class British women around 1900. (p. 712)

sultan The ruler of the Ottoman Empire; he owned all the agricultural land of the empire and was served by an army and bureaucracy composed of highly trained slaves. (p. 475)

sweated industries Poorly paid handicraft production, often carried out by married women paid by the piece and working at home. (p. 702)

Tanzimat A set of reforms designed to remake the Ottoman Empire on a western European model. (p. 741)

tariff protection A government's way of supporting and aiding its own economy by laying high taxes on imported goods from other countries, as when the French responded to cheaper British goods flooding their country by imposing high tariffs on some imported products. (p. 635) war on terror Abroad response under President George W. Bush to fight global terrorism in all but first phase in Afghanistan; beginning in late 2001, it spread to Iraq. (p. 000)

Warsaw Pact Soviet-backed military alliance of East Bloc Communist countries in Europe. (p. 000)

water frame A spinning machine created by Richard Arkwright that, like Thomas Highs's "water frame," harnessed water and used a waterpower to drive a belt; used more specialized roller bearing spindles and used waterpower. (p. 000)

wet-nursing A widespread and flourishing business of the eighteenth century in which women were paid to breast-feed other women's babies. (p. 000)

white man's burden The idea that Europeans could and should civilize more "primitive" nonwhite peoples and that in return they would eventually provide markets with modern advancements for higher standards of living. (p. 000)

World Trade Organization (WTO) A powerful supranational and financial institution that sets trade and tariff agreements for over 150 member countries, and oversees many large economic networks' trade policies. Like the IMF and the World Bank, the WTO promotes neoliberal policies around the world. (p. 000)

Young Turks Reform-minded persons who seized power in a 1908 coup in the Ottoman Empire; the term is now used to refer to implement reform. (p. 000)

Zionism A movement dedicated to building a Jewish national homeland in Palestine; it established the state of Israel. (p. 000)

Index

About the Authors

John P. McKay (Ph.D., University of California, Berkeley) is professor emeritus at the University of Illinois. He has written or edited numerous works, including the Herbert Baxter Adams Prize–winning book *Pioneers for Profit: Foreign Entrepreneurship and Russian Industrialization, 1885–1913*.

Bennett D. Hill (Ph.D., Princeton University), late of Georgetown University, published *Church and State in the Middle Ages* and numerous articles and reviews, and he was one of the contributing editors to *The Encyclopedia of World History*. He taught for many years at the University of Illinois and was a Benedictine monk of St. Anselm's Abbey in Washington, D.C.

John Buckler (Ph.D., Harvard University), late of the University of Illinois, published numerous works, including *Theban Hegemony, 371–362 B.C.*; *Philip II and the Sacred War*; and *Aegean Greece in the Fourth Century B.C.* With Hans Beck, he published *Central Greece and the Politics of Power in the Fourth Century*.

Clare Haru Crowston (Ph.D., Cornell University) teaches at the University of Illinois, where she is currently professor of history and department chair. She is the author of *Credit, Fashion, Sex: Economies of Regard in Old Regime France* and *Fabricating Women: The Seamstresses of Old Regime France, 1675–1791*, which won the Berkshire and Hagley Prizes. She edited two special issues of the *Journal of Women's History*, has published numerous journal articles and reviews, and is one of the editors of the *Journal of Social History* and past president of the Society for French Historical Studies.

Merry E. Wiesner-Hanks (Ph.D., University of Wisconsin–Madison) taught first at Augustana College in Illinois, and since 1985 at the University of Wisconsin–Milwaukee, where she is currently UWM Distinguished Professor in the department of history. She is the senior editor of the *Sixteenth Century Journal*, one of the editors of the *Journal of Global History*, and the author or editor of more than twenty books, including *A Concise History of the World* (2015). She is the former Chief Reader for Advanced Placement World History.

Joe Perry (Ph.D., University of Illinois at Urbana-Champaign) is associate professor of modern German and European history at Georgia State University. He has published numerous articles and is author of *Christmas in Germany: A Cultural History*. His current research interests focus on issues of consumption, gender, and popular culture in West Germany and Western Europe after World War II.

(Continued from the inside front cover)

Avoiding Plagiarism and Managing Sources

Most students are aware that plagiarism can be committed on purpose, but unintentional or accidental plagiarism is also problematic. Keeping track of source material has always been tough, and technology has made it easy to cut text from an online source and copy it into your paper. You may have intended to modify or acknowledge it later but then forgot where it came from. Omitting a citation of a source by accident is still a breach of academic ethics. Here are four steps that you can use to help avoid plagiarism.

Step 1: *Manage Sources Efficiently*

Many academic professionals and students take notes and keep track of sources using index cards. Write one piece of evidence — a quote, a fact, an idea — on each card along with the original source of that data. This can also be done electronically, by creating a single file for each source that you consult and housing all of these files in a folder called "Sources."

Step 2: *Use Sources Properly*

Using sources properly as you take notes and incorporate them into your writing is another crucial component of the research and writing process. You will not be able to cite your sources properly if you don't know which note is a quote, which note is a partial paraphrase of another author's point, and which one is paraphrased fully.

Step 3: *Acknowledge Sources Appropriately*

There are some general rules about what types of information require citation or acknowledgment and what types do not. Widely accepted facts or common knowledge do not need to be cited, but another person's words or ideas (even if not quoted verbatim) require a citation.

Step 4: *Cite Sources Completely and Consistently*

Historians and others writing about history have adopted the citation guidelines from the *Chicago Manual of Style* (CMS). The citations are indicated by superscript numbers within the text that refer to a note with a corresponding number either at the bottom of the page (footnote) or at the end of the paper (endnote). Here are just a few brief examples of CMS-style notes:

Book: David Brion Davis, *Inhuman Bondage: The Rise and Fall of Slavery in the New World* (New York: Oxford University Press, 2006), 73.

Journal Article: Alden T. Vaughan and Virginia Mason Vaughan, "Before Othello: Elizabethan Representations of Sub-Saharan Africans," *William and Mary Quarterly*, 3rd ser., 54 (January 1997): 19–44.

Internet Source: Official Report on the Trials of Sundry Negroes charged with an Attempt to Raise an Insurrection in the State of South Carolina in 1822. *Slaves and the Courts, 1740–1860*, Library of Congress, Document ID rbcmisc lst0101 urn: hdl:loc.rbc/rbcmisc.lst0101, http://hdl.loc.gov/loc.rbc/rbcmisc.lst0101.

Instructors: For more information on the **Bedford Custom Tutorials for History**, contact your Bedford representative, or visit **macmillanlearning.com/historytutorials**.

LaunchPad with LearningCurve

Works simply. Simply works.

 LearningCurve
macmillan learning

learningcurveworks.com

Put "testing to learn" into action. Based on research, **LearningCurve** adaptive quizzing really works.

Each chapter-based **LearningCurve** activity gives students multiple chances to understand key concepts, return to the narrative textbook if they need to reread, and answer questions correctly.

Over 90% of students report satisfaction with LearningCurve's fun and accessible game-like interface.

"What I like best about *LearningCurve* is that it helps me prepare for the quizzes and exams. I feel like I wouldn't do as well in the class without *LearningCurve*."

"I like how *LearningCurve* will tell you where in the book to find the correct answers to questions so you can go back and read about what you have missed."

LearningCurve is available in **LaunchPad**, our interactive course space. There you'll find an interactive e-Book for *A History of Western Society* plus many other resources to help you succeed in your course.

In a survey of almost 6,000 students, 81.3% said LaunchPad helped them improve their knowledge of the course material.

See what LaunchPad can do for you.

launchpadworks.com

macmillanlearning.com

 bedford
st.martin's
Macmillan Learning

ISBN 978-1-319-03106-0
NBZI
90000

9 781319 031060